WHERE ARCHITECTS
SLEEP

WHERE ARCHITECTS SLEEP

—

SARAH MILLER

THE MOST STYLISH
HOTELS IN THE WORLD

CONTENTS

KEY

All-time favorite
These are the properties that the architects wouldn't hesitate to return to.

Beach
These properties front gorgeous beaches, have a spectacular situation on a coastline, or clifftop view of the sea.

Best-kept secret
These are the properties that the architects really didn't want the world to know about…luckily for you, we're quite persuasive.

Budget
Architects know good value and low-key charm when they see it—these properties are friendly on the wallet but don't scrimp on quality.

Countryside
This is where the architects go to experience rolling countryside, rural idylls, or peaceful villages.

Desert
These properties are an oasis amid unspoiled stretches of sand, scrub, and little else.

Eco-conscious
Staying in a hotel needn't cost the earth. These properties are ecologically minded—from organic farms to futuristic building technologies.

Family friendly
These properties are suitable for children—from having a pool to providing a babysitting service.

Island
Stay here to be cut off from the mainland or have a castaway experience on a small island in an archipelago. These properties range from private resorts to simple over-water huts.

Luxury
The idea of what luxury is can differ depending on the person. For some, it means escaping the crowds; for others, it's exceptional service or a lavish jungle spa. Ultimately, these properties invite you to indulge all your senses.

Mountains
This is where the architects go to commune with nature—from skiing the pistes, swimming in a lake, or basking in the desert sun.

Spa
These properties are designed to enhance wellbeing— and wellness—from medical spas to traditional thermal baths.

Urban
From small alleyways to big plazas and piazzas, there's nothing better than staying in a city to explore it.

Where I live
These are the properties in the architect's hometown.

Wish I'd designed
Professional respect and admiration make this the hotel that the architect wishes they'd designed themselves.

Worth the travel
Across the country or on the other side of the world, there's no distance the architect wouldn't travel to stay at this hotel.

INTRODUCTION

I discovered hotels very early on in life, spending hours after school in the property owned by my grandparents in London. The wonder of being in reception and looking at room reservations—carefully charted in pencil, rubbed out and then re-marked—and the joy of seeing room numbers drop down like blinking eyelids as cords criss-crossed the telephone switchboard. The excitement of being back of house where you could play hide-and-seek in the laundry baskets. Feeling grown-up when sitting in the dining room on leather banquettes, admiring the tables laid with starched linen tablecloths and the heaviest of silver cutlery. Doing homework at the roll-top desk in my grandfather's study—Room No. 6. But, best of all, if we were very lucky, staying the night in high single beds with the smoothest, coolest, cotton sheets.

Several years later, having wanted to be an architect but becoming an editor instead, hotels arrived again on my horizon—but what a different vista. Leaving the distinctly other-worldly environs of broadsheet newspapers to join the glossy world of Condé Nast Publications in 1997, I launched the British edition of *Condé Nast Traveller*, handpicking a crack editorial team, none of whom had worked in the travel sector before—just like me.

As Editor-in-Chief, I got to discover "Planet Hotel" in every detail, not just by sending an army of contributors and photographers to bring back stunning reports of their adventures, but also through meeting every hotel general manager, every resort company CEO, every marketing executive; in short, everyone from top chefs to bellhops the world over.

I became an expert in the details that made some-where exceptional. Resorts where staff squeezed the oranges in front of your eyes were a cut above those serving buffet jugs of juice; I knew which hotel lobby teams really went the extra welcoming mile; and I antici-pated which hotels were going to be hot and which were not. But above all, I felt privileged to experience exceptional architecture and design, from chic-shack surf lodges to lavishly updated monasteries.

My world has always been a mix of journalism and architecture—my parents ran an architectural practice together—and the pleasure of producing *Condé Nast Traveller* every month for sixteen years, which entailed receiving reader feedback and daily enquiries about where to stay, synthesized all my interests, passions, curiosity, and wanderlust.

Where Architects Sleep is a further amalgamation of all the things I love. It is an insider's guide to the best places to stay in the world—the result of having spoken to some 270 architects around the world, who have provided us with more than 1,200 recommendations of the best places to stay, in more than 100 countries, across eight regions. We were overwhelmed by the number of excellent responses we received; there were so many that we were unable to include all of them in the following pages. But, what this demonstrates is that no one appreciates a building quite like an architect. And, while their budgets might vary, none of the contributors to this book, we believe, would sleep in a room without style or character. When creating the ultimate global accommodation list, architects are the ones who know exactly what to look for: not just excellent location and design, but also things like fantastic service.

None of the star-rating systems beloved by the hospitality industry apply here. The result is an eclectic travel companion—whether you are looking for a ger in Mongolia or a palapa in Mexico. It is an essential tool for anyone who loves to discover the world's best treat —a great home away from home.

SARAH MILLER

THE ARCHITECTS

MICHEL ABBOUD
SOMA
New York City, NY, USA and Beirut, Lebanon
SOMA was founded in 2004 by Michel Abboud. With its focus on incorporating craft, digital technologies, and environmental responsibility, the firm works across residential, hospitality, and mixed-use developments.

OLAJUMOKE ADENOWO
AD CONSULTING
Lagos, Nigeria
AD Consulting was established in 1994 by Olajumoke Adenowo. Projects span architecture, master planning, and brand environment, with clients including L'Oreal, Coca-Cola, and the National Arts Theater, Lagos.

MANUEL AIRES MATEUS
AIRES MATEUS E ASSOCIADOS
Lisbon, Portugal
Aires Mateus is led by Manuel and Francisco Aires Mateus. The studio is renowned for its hospitality, cultural, and residential projects, which often embody a cool minimalism.

FLAVIO ALBANESE
ASA STUDIO
Venice, Italy
Founded in Venice in 1987 by Flavio and Franco Albanese, ASA Studio is a multi-disciplinary firm working at a variety of scales, from urban strategies to interior design.

WILL ALSOP
ALL DESIGN
Multiple offices including London, UK
Architcture and design studio aLL Design was co-founded by the late Will Alsop and Marcos Rosello. Notable projects include Le Grand Bleu (1994) in Marseille, and the Ontario College of Art and Design University (2004). *During the making of this book, Alsop sadly passed away. Phaidon has retained his recommendations as a mark of respect for his contribution to the industry.*

ENE CORDT ANDERSEN
ANDERSEN & SIGURDSSON ARCHITECTS
Frederiksberg, Denmark
Andersen & Sigurdsson Architects was established in 1997 by Ene Cordt Andersen and Thorhallur Sigurdsson. The studio's expertise spans cultural, educational, residential, and public projects.

STEFAN ANTONI
SAOTA
Cape Town, South Africa

SAOTA is led by Stefan Antoni, Philip Olmesdahl, Greg Truen, Phillippe Fouché, and Mark Bullivant. The firm's projects range from residential to hospitality, commercial, public, mixed-use, and master planning.

RAÚL DE ARMAS
MDEAS ARCHITECTS
New York City, NY, USA

Raúl de Armas is a founding principal of MdeAS. Founded in 1991, it focuses on large-scale urban projects, including numerous high-profile lobby renovations throughout New York City.

EMRE AROLAT
EMRE AROLAT ARCHITECTURE (EAA)
Multiple offices including Istanbul, Turkey

Emre Arolat Architecture (EAA) was established in 2004 by Emre Arolat and Gonca Paşolar. Notable projects include the Ipekyol Textile Factory (2006) and the Sancaklar Mosque (2013), both in Turkey.

DIEGO ARRAIGADA
DIEGO ARRAIGADA ARQUITECTOS
Rosario, Argentina

Diego Arraigada established his practice in 2005. The studio's work has been displayed in several international exhibitions.

FELIPE ASSADI
FELIPE ASSADI ARCHITECTS
Santiago, Chile

Architect Felipe Assadi has lectured at several Chilean and international universities and, since 2011, has served as Dean of the Faculty of Architecture and Design of the Finis Terrae University.

GASTON ATELMAN
AFT ARQUITECTOS
Buenos Aires and Córdoba, Argentina

AFT Arquitectos is an architecture, planning, and design practice formed in 1995 by Gastón Atelman, Martín Fourcade, and Alfredo Tapia.

FORTH BAGLEY
KOHN PEDERSEN FOX
Multiple offices including New York City, NY, USA

Forth Bagley joined Kohn Pedersen Fox Associates (KPF) in 2005, leading the design and management of a variety of commercial projects across the world, including the Guangzhou CTF Finance Center (2016).

KELLY BAIR
CENTRAL STANDARD OFFICE OF DESIGN
Chicago, IL, USA

Central Standard Office of Design Principal Kelly Bair has had her work exhibited in Los Angeles, Toronto, Ann Arbor/Detroit, and in the 2015 Chicago Architecture Biennial.

HANS BALDAUF
BCV ARCHITECTURE + INTERIORS
San Francisco, CA, USA and New York, NY, USA

BCV Architecture + Interiors is an architecture, interior design, and planning firm founded by principals Hans Baldauf and Chris von Eckartsberg in 1997.

SHIGERU BAN
SHIGERU BAN ARCHITECTS
Multiple offices including Tokyo, Japan

Internationally acclaimed architect Shigeru Ban likes to explore the use of various unusual materials in construction, particularly bamboo and cardboard. In 2014, Ban received the Pritzker Architecture Prize.

STEPHEN BARRETT
ROGERS STIRK HARBOUR + PARTNERS
London, UK and Shanghai, China

Rogers Stirk Harbour + Partners has been recognized with numerous awards, including two RIBA Stirling Prizes. One of these was for Terminal 4, Barajas Airport (2006) in Madrid, for which Stephen Barrett was project architect.

THOMAS BARTLETT
WALDO WORKS
London, UK

Led by Thomas Bartlett, Waldo Works' projects span architecture, interior design, and custom products and furniture. In 2016 the firm was listed among *House & Garden*'s Top 100 Interior Designers.

JODI BATAY-CSORBA
BATAY-CSORBA ARCHITECTS
Toronto, Canada

Batay-Csorba Architects was established in 2010 by Andrew and Jodi Batay-Csorba. The studio's work encompasses a range of projects, from small-scale installations to urban planning.

CARLO BAUMSCHLAGER
BAUMSCHLAGER HUTTER PARTNERS
Multiple offices including Dornbirn, Austria

Baumschlager Hutter Partners was established in 2010 by Carlo Baumschlager and Jesco Hutter. The firm has won a number of awards for its range of institutional, educational, commercial, and residential projects.

AHMED BELKHODJA
FALA ATELIER
Porto, Portugal

Fala Atelier was founded in 2013 by Ahmed Belkodhja, Filipe Magalhães, and Ana Luisa Soares. The studio works on residential conversions that utilize a minimal palette. Between them, the trio has previously worked with SANAA, Toyo Ito, and Atelier Bow-Wow.

DEBORAH BERKE
DEBORAH BERKE PARTNERS
New York City, NY, USA

Deborah Berke Partners has received numerous accolades, including a National Design Award from the Cooper-Hewitt, Smithsonian Design Museum in 2017. In 2016 she was appointed Dean at the Yale School of Architecture.

BEN VAN BERKEL
UNSTUDIO
**Multiple offices including Amsterdam,
The Netherlands**

UNStudio was founded in 1988 by Ben van Berkel and Caroline Bos. With offices around the world, the studio has created a range of high-profile projects, including Arnhem Centraal railway station (2015).

BORIS BERNASKONI
BERNASKONI
Moscow, Russia

Boris Bernaskoni, founder of BERNASKONI, works across architecture, communication, and industrial design. Projects include Matrex (2017) and Hypercube (2010) for the Skolkovo Innovation Center in Moscow.

PAUL BERNIER
PAUL BERNIER ARCHITECTE
Montreal, Canada

Paul Bernier Architecte was established in 1999. The firm has been honored with numerous awards, including the 2009 Marcel Parizeau Prize, Prix d'excellence de l'Ordre des architectes du Québec for the Bernier-Thibault House (2007) in Montreal.

ERIN AND IAN BESLER
BESLER & SONS
Multiple offices including New York City, NY, USA

Erin and Ian Besler are co-founders of Besler & Sons, a multi-disciplinary office that designs buildings, objects, videos, software, and exhibitions. Erin is also an Assistant Professor of Architecture at Princeton University School of Architecture, and Ian teaches at the Pratt Institute and Santa Monica College.

THOMAS BIRKKJÆR
ARKITEMA ARCHITECTS
Multiple offices including Aarhus, Denmark

Arkitema Architects was founded in 1969, and is today one of Scandinavia's largest architectural companies. The firm's work spans residential, corporate, healthcare, educational, cultural, and urban projects. Thomas Birkkjær is a Senior Partner at the practice.

SHANE DE BLACAM
DE BLACAM AND MEAGHER
Dublin, Ireland

De Blacam & Meagher was established in 1976 by Shane de Blacam and John Meagher. The firm is known for its use of natural materials, especially wood, in its residential, commercial, public, and conservation projects. De Blacam and Meagher represented Ireland at the 2010 Venice Biennale.

TIM BLACK
BKK ARCHITECTS
Melbourne, Australia

BKK Architects was established in 2000 and is led by architects Tim Black, George Huon, and Simon Knott. Their projects include residential, commercial, and institutional buildings, as well as infrastructure and urban design projects.

7132 Hotel **227**..Spa
CitizenM New York Times Square Hotel **422**.........Urban
Fairmont Chateau Lake Louise **368**.................Mountains
Freycinet Lodge **61**.......................................Beach
Jackalope Hotel **63**.....................................Luxury
Mungo Shearers' Quarters **58**......................Desert
QT Melbourne **63**.............................Where I live

MARIO BOTTA
MARIO BOTTA ARCHITETTI
Mendrisio, Switzerland

The work of Mario Botta Architetti encompasses many typologies, including houses, schools, banks, libraries, museums, and sacred buildings. Notable projects include the original building for SFMoMA (1995) in San Francisco.

Hotel Schweizerhof Bern & The Spa **223**.................Urban

PAOLO BRAMBILLA
CALVI BRAMBILLA
Milan, Italy

Founded by Paolo Brambilla and Fabio Calvi and in Milan in 2006, Calvi Brambilla is a multidisciplinary firm that combines architecture, and interior and product design. Clients include Bialetti, FontanaArte, and Flos.

Capofaro **284**..Island
Eden Hotel **280**......................................Mountains
Hotel Aire de Bardenas **251**.......................Desert
Hotel Briol **286**....................Best-kept secret
Hotel Fazenda Calà & Divino **489**.........Worth the travel
Hotel Praktik Rambla **254–255**.........................Urban
Hotel Terminal Neige Totem **202**.........Wish I'd designed
Hotel Whitepod **229**.............................Eco-conscious
Juvet Landscape Hotel **161**..................All-time favorite
The Pearl Hotel **388**.......................Family friendly
Room Mate Giulia **280**.........................Where I live
Sextantio Le Grotte Della Civita **274**.....................Luxury

NUNO BRANDÃO COSTA
BRANDÃO COSTA ARQUITECTOS
Porto, Portugal

Nuno Brandão Costa established his own studio in 1998, having previously worked at Herzog & de Meuron and José Fernando Gonçalves & Paulo Providência.

7 Cidades Lake Lodge **263**.................Best-kept secret
7132 Hotel **227**..Spa
Beau-Rivage Palace **230**.............................Luxury

Duas Portas **267**...............................Family friendly
Four Seasons Hotel Ritz.........................Wish I'd designed
 Lisbon **270**
Hôtel Odéon Saint Germain **216**.....................Urban
Hotel Santa Maria de Bouro **266**.................Mountains
Radisson Collection Royal.................All-time favorite
 Hotel, Copenhagen **170**

PAUL BRISLIN
ARUP
Multiple offices including London, UK

Arup is an international firm of designers, planners, engineers, consultants, and technical specialists. Paul Brislin leads Arup's Sport Architecture and Sport Venue Design teams. Brislin is also an editorial board member of *Architectural Design* journal.

Emerson Spice **348**.........................All-time favorite

FRANCESCA BUCCI
BG STUDIO INTERNATIONAL
New York City, NY, USA

Francesca Bucci is the Company President of BG Studio International is a boutique hospitality design firm, founded in 2002, which creates and manages luxury projects throughout North America and Europe.

The Brando **71**...............................All-time favorite
Canvas Club **151**..Desert
Coco Reef **464**........................Best-kept secret
The Connaught **184**.....................................Luxury
Elbow Beach **465**...Beach
Eremito **290**...............................Eco-conscious
Fairmont Southampton **465**.................Family friendly
Hotel de Russie **294**....................................Urban
Ice Hotel **163**.........................Wish I'd designed
Mandarin Oriental, New York **420**........................Spa
The Peninsula New York **424**..................Where I live
Rosapetra Spa Resort **291**.....................Mountains
The St. Regis Maldives.................Worth the travel
 Vommuli Resort **121**

HASAN ÇALIŞLAR
ERGINOĞLU & ÇALIŞLAR
Istanbul, Turkey

Founded in Istanbul in 1993 by Hasan Çalışlar and Kerem Erginoğlu, Erginoğlu & Çalışlar specializes in urban planning, architecture, and interior design. The firm has won numerous awards, including an Iconic Award for New Power Station (2013) in Baku.

7132 Hotel **227**..Spa
Amangiri **392–393**......................................Desert
Argos in Cappadocia **324**.............Worth the travel
Azulik **451**...Beach
Hacienda Temozon **453**........................Countryside
Hotel Danieli **301**.........................All-time favorite
Hotel Miró **248**..Budget
Ice Hotel **163**.........................Wish I'd designed
Kamu Lodge **126**............................Eco-conscious

RODRIGO CARAZO
CARAZO ARCHITECTURE
San José, Costa Rica
Carazo Architecture was founded by Rodrigo Carazo
in 2005. With a focus on sustainable and socially
sensitive architecture, the studio works across a
range of buildings, from residential and assisted living
facilities to institutional and mixed-used buildings.

BEPPE CATUREGLI AND GIOVANNELLA FORMICA
CATUREGLI FORMICA ARCHITETTI ASSOCIATI
Milan, Italy
Caturegli Formica Architetti Associati was formed in
1987 by Beppe Caturegli and Giovannella Formica.
Their work focuses upon the structural use of color
and light in architecture.

CRISTINA CELESTINO
CRISTINA CELESTINO
Milan, Italy
Cristina Celestino is an architect and designer who
also works as a creative director for brands. She has
received numerous accolades for her work, including
the *Elle Deco* International Design Award in the
Wallcovering category.

LUDOVICO CENTIS
THE EMPIRE
Verona, Italy
The Empire is an architecture and planning office
founded in 2013 by Ludovico Centi, who is also the
co-founder and editor of architecture magazine
San Rocco.

MANUEL CERVANTES
CC ARQUITECTOS
Mexico City, Mexico
CC Arquitectos was founded by Manuel Cervantes
in 2004. The firm works across private residences,
commercial properties, and hotels worldwide, often
drawing inspiration from Mexican Modernism.

FARID CHACÓN
NMD NOMADAS
Houston, TX, USA and Maracaibo, Venezuela
Farid Chacón is a main partner, CEO, and co-founder
with Claudia Urdaneta and Francisco Mustieles
of NMD NOMADAS. The practice has designed and
developed urban planning, architecture, interior
design, landscaping, and transport projects both
in Venezuela and throughout South America,
North America, and Europe.

JOSH CHAIKEN
KOHN PEDERSEN FOX
Multiple offices including New York City, NY, USA
Kohn Pedersen Fox Associates (KPF) is an internationally renowned architecture practice. Since joining KPF in 1986, Josh Chaiken has served as senior designer on a variety of award-winning projects including the 101-story Shanghai World Financial Center (2008), one of the world's tallest buildings.

YU-LIN CHEN
MAYU ARCHITECTS+
Kaohsiung City, Taiwan and Taipei, Taiwan
Yu-Lin Chen founded MAYU Architects+ in 2010 together with Malone Chang. The scope of MAYU's works spans from small-scale developments to large scale civic projects. Works include Dadong Art Center (2012) and Tainang Public Library in association with Mecanoo (2019).

SAM CHERMAYEFF
MEYER-GROHBRÜGGE & CHERMAYEFF
Berlin, Germany and New York City, NY, USA
The work of Meyer-Grohbrügge & Chermayeff spans a wide range of projects across diverse scales, from small gardens and bespoke furniture to office towers.

GRACE CHEUNG
XRANGE ARCHITECTURE + DESIGN
Taipei, Taiwan
XRANGE is an architecture and design firm founded in 2003 by architect Grace Cheung and industrial designer and entrepreneur Royce YC Hong. The firm operates on multiple scales, including master plans, architecture, landscape, products, and concepts.

EMANUEL CHRIST
CHRIST & GANTENBEIN
Basel, Switzerland
Christ & Gantenbein was founded by Emanuel Christ and Christoph Gantenbein in 1998. Its work ranges from cultural institutions to office spaces, luxury apartments, and social housing projects. The studio's extension of the Kunstmuseum Basel (2016) won the 2018 Wieneberger Brick Award.

MÅRTEN CLAESSON
CLAESSON KOIVISTO RUNE ARCHITECTS
Stockholm, Sweden
Architecture and design firm Claesson Koivisto Rune Architects was established in 1995 by Mårten Claesson, Eero Koivisto, and Ola Rune. Clients include Boffi, Cappellini, and Skandiform, and its work has been recognized with more than sixty international awards.

NIGEL COATES
LONDON, UK

Nigel Coates is a British architect and author.
His work spans interiors, exhibitions, strategic design,
art direction, product, and brand development.
Notable projects include the Geffrye Museum (1998)
and Hoxton Hotel (2007), both in London.

PAOLO COSSU
PAOLO COSSU ARCHITECTS
London, UK

Paolo Cossu Architects was founded in 2007. The firm's
work encompasses architecture—from small-scale
residential intervention to urban design schemes—
interior and product design, and landscaping.

MARCO COSTANZI
MARCO COSTANZI ARCHITECTS
Imola, Italy

Marco Costanzi Architects, founded in 2006, works
across design, construction, restoration, and interiors
projects spanning commercial, residential, hospitality,
and yacht design. Clients include Sergio Rossi and
Valextra.

VINCENZO DE COTIIS
VINCENZO DE COTIIS ARCHITECTS AND GALLERY
Milan, Italy

Vincenzo De Cotiis is an Italian architect, designer,
and artist. His work has been exhibited at numerous
international design fairs, such as Design Miami/
Basel, PAD London, Design Dubai, and Art Paris.

SÉBASTIEN DACHY
MAMOUT ARCHITECTES
Sint-Jans-Molenbeek, Belgium

MAMOUT Architects is led by Sébastien Dachy with
Matthieu Busana. The firm's work, which spans public
and private projects, has won a number of awards
including the Belgian Buildings Award 2019 and the
2017 Charles Duyver Award.

CIAN DEEGAN
TAKA ARCHITECTS
Dublin, Ireland

TAKA Architects was co-founded by Cian Deegan
and Alice Casey in 2006. The practice has represented
Ireland three times at the Venice Architecture Biennale
in 2008. TAKA has completed a number of award-
winning projects, including the Merrion Cricket Club
(2014).

ALJOŠA DEKLEVA AND TINA GREGORIČ
DEKLEVA GREGORIČ ARHITEKTI
Ljubljana, Slovenia

Dekleva Gregorič Arhitekti was set up by Aljoša
Dekleva and Tina Gregorič in 2003. Projects include
the Cultural Center of EU Space Technologies (2012)
in Vitanje. The duo have lectured widely, including at
the Akademie der Künste in Berlin.

DEREK DELLEKAMP
DELLEKAMP ARQUITECTOS
Mexico City, Mexico
Dellekamp Arquitectos was founded by Derek Dellekamp in 1999. Its work spans from independent research projects to social housing, interiors, commercial commissions, and exhibitions. Dellekamp has also taught at various universities.

JEAN-LOUIS DENIOT
Paris, France
Jean-Louis Deniot established his interior design firm in 2000. The studio's commissions include residential and commercial projects, including an interior for a Falcon 2000 private plane.

JACK DIAMOND
DIAMOND SCHMITT
Multiple offices including Toronto, Canada
Jack Diamond is a founding principal of Diamond Schmitt, established in 1975. Diamond is a Royal Architectural Institute of Canada Gold Medalist and an Honorary Fellow of the American Institute of Architects.

ROGER DIENER
DIENER & DIENER ARCHITEKTEN
Basel, Switzerland and Berlin, Germany
Diener & Diener was founded in 1942, and has been headed by Roger Diener, together with Terese Erngaard, Andreas Rüedi, and Michael Roth, since 2011. A notable work includes the extension to the Swiss Embassy (2000) in Berlin.

BIBA DOW
DOW JONES ARCHITECTS
London, UK
Dow Jones Architects was founded in 2000 by Biba Dow and Alun Jones. The practice works across the private, public, and commercial sectors, with clients including Tate Britain.

BERNARD DUBOIS
BERNARD DUBOIS ARCHITECTS
Brussels, Belgium
Bernard Dubois leads Bernard Dubois Architects which works across architecture, interior design, and furniture. Dubois was co-curator of the Belgian Pavillion at the Venice Biennale in 2014. Clients include Zadig & Voltaire and Aesop.

BEN DUCKWORTH
HASSELL
Multiple offices including Melbourne, Australia
Ben Duckworth is a Principal at Hassell's Melbourne office. Hassell was founded in Adelaide in 1938, and is today an international design practice. The firm consists of architects, interior designers, landscape architects, urban designers, planners, and consultants.

ROGER DUFFY
SKIDMORE, OWINGS & MERRILL
Multiple offices including New York City, NY, USA
Roger Duffy is a design partner at Skidmore, Owings & Merrill (SOM), which is one of the largest and most influential architecture, interior design, engineering, and urban planning firms in the world. He is also the Director of the SOM Foundation. SOM

CRAIG DYKERS
SNØHETTA
Multiple offices including Oslo, Norway
Snøhetta was established in 1989 by Craig Dykers and Kjetil Trædal Thorsen. Snøhetta has since grown to become one of the most important architecture practices in operation today. It won the World Architecture Award for Best Cultural Building and the Mies van der Rohe award for the Norwegian National Opera and Ballet (2008).

PETER EISENMAN
EISENMAN ARCHITECTS
New York City, NY, USA
Eisenman Architects was founded by architect Peter Eisenman, a theoretician and critic. The practice is best known for the Memorial to the Murdered Jews of Europe (2008) in Berlin.

RICHARD ENGLAND
RICHARD ENGLAND ARCHITECTS
Santa Venera, Malta
Richard England is an architect, author, sculptor, photographer, and poet. His buildings and designs have earned him numerous awards, including eleven International Academy of Architecture Awards and two Commonwealth Association of Architects Regional awards.

NILSON ARIEL ESPINO
SUMA ARQUITECTOS
Panama City, Panama
Nilson Ariel Espino founded SUMA Arquitectos in 2004. It works across restoration, interior, and landscape architecture; urban planning; and brand design.

CARLOS FERRATER
OAB
Barcelona, Spain
OAB was founded in 2005 by Carlos Ferrater, Xavier Martí-Galí, Lucía Ferrater, and Borja Ferrater. Its work spans urban planning, landscape, restoration, civic, and residential buildings.

LUIS FERREIRA-DA-SILVA
LUIS FERREIRA-DA-SILVA ARCHITECTS
Greyton, Western Cape, South Africa
Architecture and design firm Luis Ferreira-da-Silva
Architects has been featured in numerous publications,
including *The Sunday Times*, *Architectural Digest*
(USA), and *Condé Nast Traveler*.

JOB FLORIS
MONADNOCK
Rotterdam, Netherlands
Monadnock was founded by architects Job Floris
and Sandor Naus. The firm's project Landmark Nieuw
Bergen (2015) in the Netherlands was shortlisted for
the 2017 Mies van der Rohe award.

BERNARDO FORT-BRESCIA
ARQUITECTONICA
Multiple offices including Miami, FL, USA
Founded in 1977, Arquitectonica—led by principals
Bernardo Fort-Brescia and Laurinda Spear—gained
a reputation for its use of color and innovative
geometric forms, especially for the beachfront
apartments as seen in *Miami Vice*.

GIACOMO ARDESIO, ALESSANDRO BONIZZONI, NICOLA CAMPRI, VERONICA CAPRINO, AND CLAUDIA MAINARDI
FOSBURY ARCHITECTURE
Milan, Italy
Fosbury Architecture was founded in 2013, and
engages in a wide range of projects, from urban
strategies to domestic environments. The studio has
exhibited at the 2016 Venice Architecture Biennale
and the 2017 Chicago Architecture Biennial.

NORMAN FOSTER
FOSTER + PARTNERS
Multiple offices including London, UK
Norman Foster founded his practice in 1967. The
British architectural design and engineering firm
has international recognition for its innovative,
sustainable approach to design. His most important
buildings included the Hongkong and Shanghai Bank
Headquarters (1986) and Beijing Capital International
Airport (2008). In 2018 the practice won the Stirling
Prize for the Bloomberg London building (2017).

PHILLIPPE FOUCHÉ
SAOTA
Cape Town, South Africa
Phillippe Fouché is a Director of SAOTA with Stefan
Antoni, Philip Olmesdahl, Greg Truen, and Mark
Bullivant. Its projects range from residential to hospi-
tality, commercial, public, mixed-use and master
planning.

KARL FOURNIER AND OLIVIER MARTY
STUDIO KO
Paris, France and Marrakech, Morocco
Studio KO was founded in 2000 by Karl Fournier and
Olivier Marty. Its work spans private villas and
apartments, resorts, and museums. Musée Yves Saint
Laurent (2017) in Marrakech won the 2018 *Wallpaper**
magazine's Best New Public Building award.

ERIC COREY FREED
ORGANICARCHITECT
Portland, OR, USA and San Francisco, CA, USA

OrganicArchitect is a green architecture firm and
research think-tank founded in 1997 by Eric Corey
Freed. Since then, it has grown to be a national
thought-leader on sustainable and innovative design,
with clients including Pixar and Williams-Sonoma.

TONY FRETTON
TONY FRETTON ARCHITECTS
London, UK

Tony Fretton is a British architect who founded
his practice in 1982. It has gained international
recognition for its residential buildings and galleries,
including Lisson Gallery (1990) in London and the
British Embassy (2009) in Warsaw.

ANDRÉ FU
AFSO
Central, Hong Kong

AFSO was founded by architect André Fu. The studio's
interiors work—including the Fullerton Bay Hotel
(2010) and Kioku restaurant at the Four Seasons Hotel
Seoul (2015)—embraces modern luxury.

DORIANA AND MASSIMILIANO FUKSAS
STUDIO FUKSAS
Multiple offices including Rome, Italy

Studio Fuksas, led by Doriana and Massimiliano
Fuksas' works on a wide variety of projects, from
urban interventions to airports, museums, cultural
and convention centers, and offices, as well as
interiors and design collections.

MICHAEL GABELLINI AND KIMBERLY SHEPPARD
GABELLINI SHEPPARD ASSOCIATES
New York, NY, USA

Gabellini Sheppard Associates was founded in 1991.
The practice is led by three partners—Michael
Gabellini, Kimberly Sheppard, and Daniel Garbowit.
It has won numerous awards, from organizations
including the American Institute of Architects.

CRUZ GARCIA AND NATHALIE FRANKOWSKI
WAI ARCHITECTURE THINK TANK
Lincoln, NE, USA and Beijing, China

WAI Architecture Think Tank is an international studio
working across architecture, urbanism, and research.
The studio was founded in 2008 by Cruz Garcia and
Nathalie Frankowski, who are also founding curators
of Intelligentsia Gallery, an art space in Beijing.

ANGELA GARCÍA DE PAREDES
PAREDES PEDROSA ARQUITECTOS
Madrid, Spain

Paredes Pedrosa Arquitectos was founded by Angela García de Paredes and Ignacio Pedrosa in 1990, following a collaboration with José M. García de Paredes. The studio has won numerous awards, including the Spanish Fine Arts Gold Medal in 2014.

MARISOL AND UBALDO GARCÍA TORRENTE
GARCÍA TORRENTE ARQUITECTOS
Seville, Spain

García Torrente Arquitectos is led by Marisol and Ubaldo García Torrente. The firm works in architecture and landscape design across a range of sectors, including hotels, cultural centers, residences, and public spaces.

LUCA GAZZANIGA
LUCA GAZZANIGA ARCHITECTS
Lugano, Switzerland

The studio of Luca Gazzaniga initially focused on residential buildings, in particular single-family dwellings and collective housing; the studio's work now encompasses all fields. Gazzaniga often collaborates on projects with international practices, including Josep Lluis Mateo (Barcelona) and João Nunes, PROAP (Lisbon).

GUY GEIER
FXCOLLABORATIVE
Washington, D.C., USA, and New York City, NY, USA

Guy Geier is a managing partner of FXCollaborative, an architecture, planning, and interior design firm. The practice is renowned for its corporate and public projects in New York City, including the former Condé Nast building (1999) in Times Square and the renovation of the Jacob K. Javits Center (2013).

NABIL GHOLAM
NABIL GHOLAM ARCHITECTS
Beirut, Lebanon and Seville, Spain

Over the past twenty years, Nabil Gholam Architects (NGA) has worked on a range of urban design scopes, from large-scale architectural projects to private houses, interior and product design, and urban planning. In 2016 NGA won the World Architecture Festival award for Bank Headquarters Beirut (2016).

SEAN GODSELL
SEAN GODSELL ARCHITECTS
Melbourne, Australia

Sean Godsell Architects was founded in 1994 and is known for its residential projects. Godsell's work has been exhibited at the Cooper Hewitt Smithsonian Museum in New York and the Victoria and Albert Museum in London, and has been published in leading architectural journals.

LAURENT GRAVIER
FRES ARCHITECTES
Paris, France and Geneva, Switzerland

FRES was founded in 2004 by Laurent Gravier and Sara Martin Camara. Projects range from housing and urban planning to cultural, hospitality, and mixed-use buildings.

JOHANNA GRAWUNDER
San Francisco, CA, USA and Milan, Italy
Johanna Grawunder's work encompasses large-scale public lighting and color installations, architectural interventions and interiors, and limited-edition furniture and light collections. Her work has been exhibited at LACMA in Los Angeles and FNAC in Paris.

ZSOLT GUNTHER
3H ARCHITECTURE
Budapest, Hungary
3H Architecture was founded Zsolt Gunther with Katalin Csillag in 1994. The firm's work includes the design of office, residential, public, and religious buildings, and the restoration of historic buildings.

RABIH HAGE
RABIH HAGE
London, UK and New York City, NY, USA
Rabih Hage's firm delivers a wide range of private and commercial projects spanning architecture, interiors, and products. Awards include Chevalier dans l'Ordre National du Mérite in 2012, and the 2011 European Hotel Design Innovation Award.

GO HASEGAWA
GO HASEGAWA & ASSOCIATES
Tokyo, Japan
Go Hasegawa & Associates was established in 2005. Notable works include House in a Forest (2006) in Nagano and House in Sakuradai (2006) in Mie, both in Japan. Hasegawa exhibited at Venice Biennale in 2012.

MAKIO HASUIKE
MAKIO HASUIKE & CO
Milan, Italy
Makio Hasuike & Co was established in 1968 by Japanese designer Makio Hasuike, and was one of the first industrial design studios in Italy. The firm's work has been shown at exhibitions worldwide, including MoMA in New York.

LOUIS HEDGECOCK
HOK ARCHITECTS
Multiple offices including New York, NY, USA
HOK Architects was founded in St. Louis in 1955. Since then, HOK has become a global design, architecture, engineering, and planning firm, and a world leader in sustainable design. Louis Hedgecock is HOK's director of hospitality and is based in New York.

SIMON HENLEY
HENLEY HALEBROWN
London, UK
Henley Halebrown was established in 1995. The firm works across a wide range of sectors, including educational, healthcare, residential, commercial, and arts buildings. Simon Henley combines his architecture work with teaching, writing, and research.

THOMAS HERZOG
THOMAS HERZOG ARCHITEKTEN
Munich, Germany

Since its foundation in 1972, Thomas Herzog Architekten has been committed to designing buildings with technical innovation and social conscience. Notable projects include the Art Museum Guangzhou (2019) in China. In 2016, Herzog was awarded the Bavarian Order of Merit.

STEVEN HOLL
STEVEN HOLL ARCHITECTS
New York City, NY, USA and Beijing, China

Steven Holl established his practice in 1976, and has been recognized with architecture's most prestigious awards and prizes, including the 2012 AIA Gold Medal. Holl has also lectured and exhibited widely.

MATTHIAS HOLLWICH
HOLLWICH KUSHNER
New York City, NY, USA

Hollwich Kushner has designed projects at every scale, and also collaborated with creative agency KKLD in 2009 to found Architizer.com. The firm has been named one of the World's Most Innovative Companies by Fast Company. Clients include Calvin Klein, Google, and the University of Pennsylvania.

KELLY HOPPEN
KELLY HOPPEN INTERIORS
London, UK

Kelly Hoppen's interior design projects range from the homes, yachts, and jets of private clients, to luxury cruise ships and hotels.

ANTHONY HUDSON
HUDSON ARCHITECTS
Norwich, UK

Hudson Architects was founded in 2002 by Anthony Hudson, with the ambition to combine innovative and exciting design with an awareness of context and environmental responsibility. The firm's work spans one-off private houses to cultural and civic projects.

FLORIAN IDENBURG
SO–IL
New York City, NY, USA

SO–IL was founded by Florian Idenburg and Jing Liu in 2008. The studio creates refined urban spaces, residences, and cultural institutions in a variety of scales. Alongside their building works, other projects include Pole Dance (2010), a temporary structure for the PS1 courtyard at MoMA in New York, and a furniture system for Knoll (2014).

PAULO AND BERNARDO JACOBSEN
JACOBSEN ARQUITETURA
Rio de Janeiro, Brazil and Lisbon, Portugal

Jacobsen Arquitetura was founded by father and son, Paulo and Bernardo Jacobsen. It is renowned for its concept of "tropical architecture," which establishes a dialogue between Modernism and indigenous architecture. The studio works across residential, cultural, and commercial projects.

SIMON JACOBSEN
JACOBSEN ARCHITECTURE
Washington, D.C., USA

Jacobsen Architecture is the combined practice of father and son Hugh Newell Jacobsen and Simon Jacobsen. Specializing in residential and commercial projects, the firm has won more than 120 awards for excellence in architecture, interiors, and design.

HELMUT JAHN
JAHN
Chicago, IL, US and Berlin, Germany

Jahn is led by the veteran architect Helmut Jahn. The firm has more than 75 years of experience, encompassing a wide range of project typologies and scales. Notable works include Suvarnabhumi International Airport (2005) in Bangkok and the Sony Center (2000) in Berlin.

ANIA JAWORSKA
ANIA JAWORSKA & ASSOCIATES
Chicago, IL, USA

Ania Jaworska's work explores the connection between art and architecture. Her work has been exhibited in numerous exhibitions, including the Venice Biennale 2012 and the Chicago Architecture Biennial in 2015 and 2017.

TOM JESTICO
JESTICO + WHILES
London, UK and Prague, Czech Republic

Tom Jestico is now a consultant to Jestico + Whiles, which he founded with John Whiles in 1977. The firm's work spans cultural, diplomatic, hotel, and retail projects in Europe, including Hakkasan restaurant (2001) in London and Malmaison hotel (2007) at Oxford Castle.

CARLOS JIMÉNEZ
CARLOS JIMÉNEZ STUDIO
Houston, TX, USA

Carlos Jiménez Studio (CJS) is an award-winning, internationally recognized firm based in Houston, Texas. Since establishing the studio in 1983, Jiménez has been actively involved in all stages of design for each project. The projects undertaken by the studio encompass a range of scales, types, and localities, from an day-care center in Columbus to a Date Center in Houston.

TOM JORDAN
HAYBALL
Multiple offices including Melbourne, Australia

Hayball is one of Australia's largest design practices, integrating architecture, interior design, and urban design expertise. Tom Jordan is the firm's managing director, and has served as a chapter councillor and on award juries for the Australian Institute of Architects, and on design review panels for state government.

RICK JOY
STUDIO RICK JOY
Tucson, AZ, USA
Since 1993, Rick Joy has led a cooperative practice engaged in architecture, planning, and interiors projects. His residential works include Sun Valley House (2013) in Idaho. As part of i-10 studio, his hospitality projects include Amangiri (2008) in Utah.

ANNE KAESTLE
DUPLEX ARCHITEKTEN
Zurich, Switzerland
Duplex Architekten was founded by Anne Kaestle and Dan Schürch in 2007. The firm designs projects of various scales, ranging from private homes to commercial buildings.

MOMOYO KAIJIMA AND YOSHIHARU TSUKAMOTO
ATELIER BOW-WOW
Tokyo, Japan
Atelier Bow-Wow was founded in 1992 by Momoyo Kajima and Yoshiharu Tsukamoto. Their design philosophy, which they call "behaviourology," is centered on the various behaviors of three things—natural elements, human beings, and the building itself—and their architecture is known for its quirky humor.

GRACE KEELEY
GKMP ARCHITECTS
Dublin, Ireland
GKMP Architects was founded by Grace Keeley and Michael Pike. The firm largely designs residential spaces as well as larger-scale housing projects. In 2019 GKMP was nominated for the Mies van der Rohe EU Award for its Vaulted House (2018) in Dublin.

BRENT KENDLE
KENDLE DESIGN COLLABORATIVE
Scottsdale, AZ, USA
Kendle Design Collaborative was founded by Brent Kendle in 2002. Since then, it has won numerous awards for its designs which put emphasis on Regional Modernism, a movement which aims to reflect and respect the natural environment.

MATTHEW KENNEDY
STUDIO NORTH
Calgary, Canada
Studio North was established by Matthew Kennedy and Mark Erickson. The practice works on projects of a variety of scales, from flat-pack furniture and public art installations to laneway housing and hotels.

ADIL KERAI
HABIB FIDA ALI ARCHITECTS
Karachi, Pakistan

Adil Kerai joined Habib Fida Ali Architects in 1992, becoming a partner in 2001. One of Pakistan's most prominent architectural practices, Habib Fida Ali Architects is responsible for such projects as the concrete Shell House (1976) in Karachi.

DRISS KETTANI
DRISS KETTANI ARCHITECTE
Casablanca, Morocco

Driss Kettani's practice, founded in 2005, spans mainly residential and educational projects. The studio's projects include the Ecole Supérieure de Technologie de Guelmim (2011) in Morocco, designed in association with Saad El Kabbaj and Mohamed Amine Siana.

ROMI KHOSLA
ROMI KHOSLA DESIGN STUDIOS
New Delhi, India

Romi Khosla has retired from leading Romi Khosla Design Studios with Martand Khosla. The practice engages with a wide range of projects including luxury hotels, educational buildings, retail locations, interiors, and urban planning.

SEUNGHOY KIM
KYWC ARCHITECTS
Seoul, South Korea

Seunhgoy Kim established KYWC Architects in 1995. It works across numerous sectors, including educational, religious, residential, medical, public, and commercial builds. Seunhgoy Kim is currently a Professor in the Department of Architecture at Seoul National University.

STEVE KINSLER
EAST COAST ARCHITECTS
Durban, KwaZulu-Natal, South Africa

Steve Kinsler is a director of East Coast Architects, which practices social and green architecture in mainly rural environments throughout southern Africa. Honors include the 2010 SAIA Award for Excellence for Seven Fountains Primary School (2007) in Kokstad, South Africa.

WARO KISHI
K.ASSOCIATES/ARCHITECTS
Kyoto and Tokyo, Japan

K.ASSOCIATES/Architects was founded in 1993 by Waro Kishi. The firm and its founder have been honored with numerous awards for its work across architectural and interior design projects.

NICOLAS KOFF
OFFICE OU
Toronto, Canada

Office Ou is an architecture and landscape design office led by Nicolas Koff, Uros Novakovic, Sebastian Bartnicki, and Sophia Szagala.

MARCIO KOGAN
STUDIO MK27
São Paulo, Brazil

Studio MK27 is led by architect and designer Marcio Kogan. Notable projects include Gama Issa House (2001) in São Paulo.

EERO KOIVISTO
CLAESSON KOIVISTO RUNE ARCHITECTS
Stockholm, Sweden

Architecture and design firm Claesson Koivisto Rune was founded in 1995 by Mårten Claesson, Eero Koivisto, and Ola Rune. Clients include Boffi, Cappellini, and Skandiform, and their work has been recognized with more than sixty international awards.

ROBERT KONIECZNY
KWK PROMES
Katowice, Poland

KWK Promes was founded in 1999 by Robert Konieczny and Marlena Wolnik. It has been nominated for the Mies van der Rohe Award ten times, including for Konieczny's Ark (2015) in Kraków.

ANASTASIOS KOTSIOPOULOS
AM KOTSIOPOULOS & PARTNERS ARCHITECTS
Thessaloniki, Greece

AM Kotsiopoulos & Partners Architects focuses on sustainable architecture and was founded by Anastasios Kotsiopoulos in 1997. The firm has won recognition for its innovative projects.

MARGOT KRASOJEVIĆ
MARGOT KRASOJEVIĆ ARCHITECTURE
London, UK and Beijing, China

Margot Krasojević is an architect, who, having previously worked for Zaha Hadid, opened her own studio in 2000. Recent projects have focused on sustainability.

JANI KRISTOFFERSEN
GUISE
Stockholm, Sweden

Jani Kristoffersen co-founded Guise in 2008 with Andreas Ferm. Projects span hospitality, retail, residential, museums, and installations. The firm has exhibited widely, including at the Swedish Centre for Architecture and Design.

MARTIN KROGH, MARTIN LAURSEN, AND ANDERS LONKA
ADEPT
Copenhagen, Denmark

ADEPT is led by partners Martin Krogh, Martin Laursen, and Anders Lonka, as well as associate partner Simon Poulsen. The studio consists of a team of architects, landscape architects, engineers, and urban planners.

MARTIN KRUGER
MARTIN KRUGER ARCHITECTS
Cape Town, South Africa

Martin Kruger Architects was founded by Martin Kruger, who is also a founding member of the Urban Design Institute of South Africa. The studio's work spans public buildings, residential projects, and exhibition and conservation work.

KENGO KUMA
KENGO KUMA & ASSOCIATES
Tokyo, Japan and Paris, France

Kengo Kuma & Associates was founded in 1990 by internationally acclaimed architect Kengo Kuma. The firm's work includes private residences, sacred spaces, and art museums. Among Kuma's major works are the Lotus House (2005) in Japan and V&A Dundee (2018) in Scotland.

TOM KUNDIG
OLSON KUNDIG
Seattle, WA, USA

Olson Kundig is led by Jim Olson, Tom Kundig, Kirsten R. Murray, Alan Maskin, and Kevin Kudo-King. The firm's work has been recognized with numerous awards, including being named in *Architectural Digest*'s AD100 in 2016.

BRUCE KUWABARA
KPMB ARCHITECTS
Toronto, Canada

Bruce Kuwabara is a founding partner of KPMB Architects. Its work encompasses a wide range and scale of projects. He is a recipient of the RAIC Gold Medal and of the Order of Canada for his contribution to Canadian culture and society.

MARIANNE KWOK
KOHN PEDERSEN FOX
Multiple offices including New York, NY, USA

Since joining Kohn Pedersen Fox in 1994, Marianne Kwok has been the senior designer for some of the firm's most high-profile projects, including Hudson Yards, a mixed-use development in Manhattan.

RAFAEL DE LA-HOZ CASTANYS
RAFAEL DE LA-HOZ ARQUITECTOS
Multiple offices including Madrid, Spain

Founded in 1920, Rafael de la-Hoz Arquitectos was a driver for the modernization of Spanish architecture, and a pioneer of sustainable design in the country. Two generations later, Rafael de La-Hoz Castanys continues this tradition.

JOANNA LAAJISTO
STUDIO JOANNA LAAJISTO
Helsinki, Finland

Studio Joanna Laajisto was founded in 2010. The firm specializes in interiors for the retail, hospitality, and workplace sectors, as well as product design. Laajisto was named Interior Architect of the Year by the Finnish Association of Interior Architects in 2018.

HIÉRONYME LACROIX AND SIMON CHESSEX
LACROIX CHESSEX
Geneva, Switzerland

Founded in 2005 by Hiéronyme Lacroix and Simon Chessex, Lacroix Chessex has designed a wide range of projects, from private homes to apartment buildings and public structures.

MARK LANDINI
LANDINI ASSOCIATES
Sydney, Australia

The work of Landini Associates encompasses architecture as well as interior, graphic, product, furniture, and digital design. Founded in 1993 by Mark Landini, the studio has since worked with a range of clients across the food, retail, and hospitality sectors.

MARTA LAUDANI
MARTA LAUDANI DESIGN
Rome, Italy

Marta Laudani is a product, exhibition, and interior designer, with clients including Bloomberg, Driade, and Glas Italia. In collaboration with Marco Romanelli, Laudani designed the restoration of the Museum of Roman Civilization (2001) in Rome.

JOANA LEANDRO VASCONCELOS
ATELIER IN.VITRO
Porto, Portugal

Atelier in.vitro was established by Joana Leandro Vasconcelos in 2007. The studio works on architectural projects as well as furniture and graphic design. It has won a number of awards, including a National Award for Urban Rehabilitation 2019 for Casa António Patrício (2018) in Porto.

THOMAS LEESER
LEESER ARCHITECTURE
New York City, NY, USA and Shenzhen, China

Led by Thomas Leeser, Leeser Architecture often combines new media and digital technologies into its architecture. Projects include the redesign and expansion of the Museum of the Moving Image (2011) in New York.

VICTOR LEGORRETA HERNÁNDEZ
LEGORRETA
Mexico City, Mexico

Legorreta was founded in 1965 by Ricardo Legorreta, Noé Castro, and Carlos Vargas, Sr. Notable projects include the Camino Real hotels in Mexico City, Cancun, and Ixtapa; and various social housing projects. Since 2001, Ricardo's son Víctor Legorreta has led as general manager and designer.

TODD-AVERY LENAHAN
TAL STUDIO
Las Vegas, NV, USA

Founded by Todd-Avery Lenahan, TAL Studio has worked on a range of luxury projects throughout North America, the Caribbean, Asia, and Europe. Clients include Four Seasons Hotels and Resorts, Mandarin Oriental, and W Hotels.

AMANDA LEVETE
AL_A
London, UK

AL_A was founded by the Stirling Prize-winning architect Amanda Levete. Notable projects include the V&A Exhibition Road Quarter (2017) in London and MAAT (2017) in Lisbon.

HU LI
OPEN ARCHITECTURE
Beijing, China

Open was founded by Hu Li and Huang Wenjing in 2008. Notable projects include Tank Shanghai (2019), and the UCCA Dune Art Museum (2018) in Qinhuangdao, China.

JINGYU LIANG
APPROACH ARCHITECTURE STUDIO
Beijing, China

Approach Architecture Studio was founded in Beijing in 2006, its principal architect being Jingyu Liang. Notable projects include Suburb Chapel (2007) and Iberia Center for Contemporary Art (2008), both in Beijing.

DANIEL LIBESKIND
STUDIO LIBESKIND
New York City, NY, USA and Zurich, Switzerland

Studio Libeskind was established by Daniel and Nina Libeskind in Berlin in 1989. He is known for the design of the Jewish Museum (1999) in the same city. The firm has won numerous awards, including the 2012 AIA National Service Award for the World Trade Center Master Plan (2014).

ALBERTO LIEVORE
LIEVORE ALTHERR
Barcelona, Spain

Alberto Lievore specializes in product design and development, strategic consulting, creative direction, art direction, and architecture for companies including Arper and Camper.

ANTONIO G. LIÑÁN
SV60 CORDÓN & LIÑÁN ARQUITECTOS
Seville, Spain

SV60 Cordón & Liñán Arquitectos is led by Antonio González Cordón and Antonio G. Liñán. Notable projects include 317 Social Housing Units (2014) in Ceuta and the Palace of Congresses and Exhibitions (2011) in Cuenca.

PIERO LISSONI
LISSONI ASSOCIATI
Milan, Italy

Lissoni Associati was founded in 1986 by Italian architect, art director, and designer Piero Lissoni, together with Nicoletta Canesi. Clients include EDITION, Ferrari, Oberoi Hotels and Resorts, Boffi, Illy, and Kartell.

CLAUDIO LUCCHESI
URBAN FUTURE ORGANIZATION
Sicily, Italy

Urban Future Organization (UFO) was founded in 1996 as a collective of self-organized practices who share common design strategies. Claudio Lucchesi is one of its founders.

ANDREA MAFFEI
ANDREA MAFFEI ARCHITECTS
Milan, Italy

Andrea Maffei Architects works on large-scale projects, both in Italy and abroad. The practice has collaborated with architect Arata Isozaki on numerous works, including the New Bologna Central Station (2015).

RAINER MAHLAMÄKI
LAHDELMA & MAHLAMÄKI ARCHITECTS
Helsinki, Finland

Ilmari Lahdelma and Rainer Mahlamäki founded Lahdelma & Mahlamäki Architects in 1997. Their work focuses on sustainability and high-quality materials. Projects include the Finnish Nature Center Haltia (2013) in Espoo and the Vaasa City Library (2001).

FUMIHIKO MAKI
MAKI AND ASSOCIATES
Tokyo, Japan

Maki and Associates was founded in 1965, and is led by founder and principal Fumihiko Maki. The firm's expertise ranges from urban design and master planning to restorations and adaptive reuse of historic structures. Maki received the Pritzker Prize in 1993. In 2011, the American Institute of Architects honored Maki with a Gold Medal.

ANTHONY MALLOWS
WATG
Multiple offices including London, UK and Los Angeles, CA, USA

WATG stands for Wimberly, Allison, Tong, and Goo. Anthony Mallows is the President CEO, and has developed more than sixty-five projects in thirty countries for the practice.

MICHAEL MALTZAN
MICHAEL MALTZAN ARCHITECTURE
Los Angeles, CA, USA

Founded in 1995, architecture and urban design practice Michael Maltzan Architecture has been recognized with numerous awards, including the Rudy Bruner Foundation's Gold Medal for Urban Excellence. Notable clients include MoMA QNS and Museum of Contemporary Art Los Angeles, for which Michael Maltzan Architecture created the master plan.

DANIEL MANGABEIRA
BLOCO ARQUITETOS
Brasilia, Brazil

BLOCO Arquitetos consists of Daniel Mangabeira, Henrique Coutinho, and Matheus Seco. The firm is one of the founding members of Atelier Piloto, a collective that seeks to foster interaction between students, architecture schools, and professionals to promote collaborative thinking about urban design.

JOSÉ MARTINEZ SILVA
ATELIER CENTRAL
Lisbon, Portugal

Atelier Central was founded in 1996 by CEO and lead architect José Martinez Silva. The office works on projects in numerous sectors, including housing, hotels, public buildings, schools, and urban planning.

JÜRGEN MAYER H.
J. MAYER H. UND PARTNER, ARCHITEKTEN
Berlin, Germany

J. Mayer H. und Partner, Architekten was founded in 1996 by Jürgen Mayer H. Jürgen Mayer H.'s architecture can be characterized by his interest in biomorphic forms and use of concrete. The architect is known for his work in Georgia, including his observation tower (2011) at the border with Turkey.

GIANCARLO MAZZANTI
EL EQUIPO MAZZANTI
Bogotá, Colombia

El Equipo Mazzanti, founded by Giancarlo Mazzanti, specializes in socially driven design and academic research. Notable projects include Marinilla Educational Park (2015) in Colombia. Mazzanti was also made an Honorary Fellow of the American Institute of Architects in 2017.

CHRIS MCDONOUGH
THE GETTYS GROUP
Multiple offices including Chicago, IL, USA

The Gettys Group is a hotel design, branding, and development firm, which was founded in 1988. It works with brands including Accor, Shangri-La, Langham, and the Peninsula Group. Chris McDonough is a principal at the practice.

V. MITCH McEWEN
A(N) OFFICE
New York City, NY, USA

A(n) Office is a collaborative studio co-founded by V. Mitch McEwen and Marcelo López-Dinardi. The firm's portfolio includes architecture, urban, industrial, and software projects. A(n) Office has exhibited widely, including at the Venice Architecture Biennale and Museum of Contemporary Art Detroit.

RICHARD MEIER
RICHARD MEIER & PARTNERS ARCHITECTS
New York City, NY, USA and Los Angeles, CA, USA

Richard Meier & Partners has been designing high-profile buildings for more than five decades. Notable projects include the Douglas House (1973) in Harbor Springs, Michigan, and the Getty Center (1997) in Los Angeles, California.

JOÃO MENDES RIBEIRO
JOÃO MENDES RIBEIRO ARQUITECTO
Coimbra, Portugal

João Mendes Ribeiro founded his eponymous office in 1990. Awards include the 2016 RIBA Award for International Excellence for the Arquipélago—Contemporary Arts Center (2015) in Portugal.

MICHAEL MEREDITH AND HILARY SAMPLE
MOS
New York City, NY, USA

MOS was founded by Michael Meredith and Hilary Sample in 2005. The duo's work is developed through playful experimentation and serious research, and spans from houses to cultural institutions and museum installations. Alongside their architectural work, MOS also creates books, furniture, and software projects.

ADAM MESHBERG
MESHBERG GROUP
Brooklyn, NY, USA

Founded in 2006 by Adam Meshberg, the architecture and interior design firm Meshberg Group specializes in new builds and historic restorations, often incorporating principles of sustainability and utilizing contemporary materials and methods.

JOHANNA MEYER-GROHBRÜGGE
MEYER-GROHBRÜGGE
Berlin, Germany

Architecture and design office Meyer-Grohbrügge was founded by Johanna Meyer-Grohbrügge in 2015. The studio works on a range of projects, including art galleries, residential buildings, and exhibition and furniture design. Meyer-Grohbrügge has taught at several institutions, and is currently a guest professor at the Dia Dessau.

ALEX MICHAELIS
MICHAELIS BOYD
London, UK and New York City, NY, USA

Alex Michaelis and Tim Boyd founded their architecture and interior design firm Michaelis Boyd in 1995. Its work spans five continents and various sectors, including luxury residential and hospitality.

DAVID MILLER
MILLER HULL PARTNERSHIP
Seattle, WA and San Diego, CA, USA

Founded by David Miller and the late Robert Hull, architectural firm Miller Hull Partnership designs dynamic and environmentally sensitive, sustainable buildings. It also undertakes pro bono design services and the funding of scholarship programs.

SIMON MITCHELL
SYBARITE
London, UK

Sybarite was founded by Torquil McIntosh and Simon Mitchell in 2002. It has created more than 1,500 projects for global brands, for clients including Joseph, Marni, and SKP.

BRUNO MOINARD AND CLAIRE BÉTAILLE
4BI & ASSOCIÉS
Paris, France

Interior architecture studio 4BI & Associés is led by Bruno Moinard and Claire Bétaille. The practice specializes in retail, hospitality, and residential projects, with clients including Galeries Lafayette and Four Seasons at Ten Trinity Square.

ALEX MOK
LINEHOUSE
Shanghai, China and Hong Kong

Linehouse was established in 2013 by Alex Mok and Briar Hickling. The studio combines the disciplines of architecture, interiors, and product and graphic design to create work at varying scales. Clients include WeWork and Herschel Supply.

BELÉN MONEO AND JEFFREY BROCK
MONEO BROCK
Madrid, Spain and New York City, NY, USA

Founded by Belén Moneo and Jeffrey Brock, Moneo Brock is an international architecture and interior design studio. The firm has received several awards, including the Luis Moreno Mansilla Award for the Pueblo Serena Church (2016) in Monterrey, Mexico.

CHARLOTTE VON MOOS
SAUTER VON MOOS
Basel, Switzerland and Miami, FL, USA
Sauter von Moos was founded in Basel in 2001 by
Florian Sauter and Charlotte von Moos. The studio
engages in work on all scales, and both partners teach
at the University of Miami School of Architecture.

ADRIAN MORENO AND
MARIA SAMANIEGO
ARQUITECTURA X
Quito, Ecuador
Established in 1996 by Adrian Moreno and María
Samaniego, Arquitectura X has created numerous
projects throughout Ecuador. The studio is best
known for its X House (2007) in Quito.

MARCELO MORETTIN
ANDRADE MORETTIN ARQUITETOS
São Paulo, Brazil
Andrade Morettin Arquitetos was founded in 1997
by architects Vinicius Andrade and Marcelo Morettin.
The firm works across architecture and urban
planning in both the public and private sector. Clients
include Museum of Contemporary Art of Chicago
and the Iguatemi Group.

PAUL MORGAN
PAUL MORGAN ARCHITECTS
Melbourne, Australia
Founded in 1997, Paul Morgan Architects' output
spans master planning, urban design, and feasibility
studies, as well as the design of health, residential,
school, and municipal projects. Its work has received
multiple awards, including the 2007 Robin Boyd
Award for Residential Buildings by the Royal Australian
Institute of Architects for the Cape Schanck House
(2006) in Victoria.

MPHETHI MOROJELE
MMA DESIGN STUDIO
Johannesburg, South Africa
Founded by Mphethi Morojele in 1995, MMA Design
Studio works across architecture, urban regeneration,
design, research, and strategic thinking. Notable
works include the South African embassies in Berlin
(2003) and Addis Ababa (2008). The studio has
also exhibited at the 2006 and 2008 Venice Biennales.

GRACE MORTLOCK
OTHER ARCHITECTS
Sydney, Australia

Other Architects was established in 2012. The office
was awarded the 2018 INDE Prodigy award for
most promising design practice in the Asia-Pacific
region. Grace Mortlock joined Other Architects
as lead designer in 2016. In 2013 Grace co-founded
Otherothers, a design organization that operates
in parallel with Other Architects.

ALEX MUSTONEN
SNARKITECTURE
New York City, NY, USA

Design studio Snarkitecture was founded by artist
Daniel Arsham and architect Alex Mustonen. The firm
has designed installations, architecture, products,
and furniture for a diverse range of clients including
COS, Kith, Calvin Klein, the New Museum, Kartell,
and Beats by Dr. Dre.

JO NAGASAKA
SCHEMATA ARCHITECTS
Tokyo, Japan

Schemata Architects was founded by Jo Nagasaka in
1998. The studio works across architecture, interior,
and furniture design, and clients include Aesop, Vitra,
and Marimekko.

KIM HERFORTH NIELSEN
3XN
Multiple offices including Copenhagen, Denmark

3XN studio was founded in 1986 by architects Kim
Herforth Nielsen, Lars Frank Nielsen, and Hans
Peter Svendler Nielsen. Notable works include Tivoli
Concert Hall (2005) in Copenhagen and the IOC
Headquarters (2019) in Lausanne.

JO NOERO
NOERO ARCHITECTS
Cape Town, South Africa

Jo Noero founded Noero Architects in 1984. The
practice has received numerous awards, including
the Ralph Erskine Prize in 1993 and the Icon Award
for Building of the Year in 2013. Its work has also been
exhibited extensively, including at MoMA in New
York and multiple Venice Biennales.

ENRIQUE NORTEN
TEN ARQUITECTOS
Mexico City, Mexico, and New York City, NY, USA

Enrique Norten established TEN Arquitectos in 1986.
The practice specializes in architecture, design,
research, and infrastructure. Its projects range from
cultural institutions to public spaces, urban and
residential developments, and furnishings.

VALERIO OLGIATI
Flims, Switzerland

Valerio Olgiati established his practice in 1996. Notable
projects include Lucerne University (2003), the
Korean American Museum of Art and Culture (1995)
in Los Angeles, California, and the Yellow House
(1999) in Flims.

PHILIP OLMESDAHL
SAOTA
Cape Town, South Africa
Philip Olmesdahl is a director at SAOTA Stefan Antoni, Greg Truen, Phillippe Fouché, and Mark Bullivant. Its projects, which range from residential to hospitality, commercial, mixed-use, and master planning, have been widely featured in publications.

ANTONIO ORTIZ
CRUZ Y ORTIZ ARQUITECTOS
Multiple offices including Seville, Spain
Cruz y Ortiz Arquitectos was founded in 1974 by Antonio Cruz and Antonio Ortiz. The practice represented Spain at the Venice Architecture Biennale in 2014 and, in the same year, Cruz and Ortiz received the Honor Award from the American Institute of Architects.

SATYENDRA PAKHALÉ
SATYENDRA PAKHALÉ ASSOCIATES
Amsterdam, the Netherlands
Satyendra Pakhalé founded Satyendra Pakhalé Associates in 1998. Projects range from obejct design to architecture, with clients including Cappellini, Renault, and Moroso.

FELINO PALAFOX, JR.
PALAFOX ASSOCIATES
Makati, Philippines and Cebu, Philippines
Palafox Associates was founded in 1989 by Felino Palafox, Jr. The firm works on a range of diverse projects, from urban design for islands to residential and mixed-use development projects, with an emphasis on sustainability.

STÉPHANE PARMENTIER
STÉPHANE PARMENTIER
Paris, France
Stéphane Parmentier is an interior architect, designer, and creative director who also collaborates with design companies, including Maison Christofle, Vista Alegre and Bordallo, *Wallpaper**, and Hermès.

ROBIN PARTINGTON
ROBIN PARTINGTON & PARTNERS
London, UK
Apt (formerly Robin Partington & Partners) was founded by Robin Partington in 2009. Prior to forming his own studio, Partington led the design team for the 30 St. Mary Axe (2004) project at Foster + Partners.

JOHN PAWSON
London, UK
John Pawson's body of work spans a broad range of scales and typologies, including private houses, sacred commissions, galleries, museums, hotels, ballet sets, and yacht interiors.

ALFREDO PAYÁ BENEDITO
NONAME29
Alicante, Spain
Noname29 was founded by Alfredo Payá Benedito in 2006. Projects range from residential to large-scale educational institutions.

JUAN MANUEL PELÁEZ FREIDEL
JUMP/JUAN MANUEL PELÁEZ ARQUITECTOS
Medellín, Colombia

JUMP Arquitectos was founded in 1997 by Juan Manuel Peláez Freidel. The studio is divided into four sectors: residential, institutional, commercial, and cultural. Notable projects include the New Building for Arts at the National University of Colombia (2018).

DINKO PERAČIĆ
ARP AND PLATFORMA 9.81
Split, Croatia

Dinko Peračić is the founder of Platforma 9.81 and a partner in ARP. Two of his projects—Harbor Market in Vodice (2015) and the Museum of Modern and Contemporary Art in Rijeka (2017)—have been nominated for the Mies van der Rohe Award.

JOAQUÍN PÉREZ-GOICOECHEA
AGI ARCHITECTS
Madrid, Spain and Kuwait City, Kuwait

Architecture and interior design studio AGi Architects was founded in 2006 by Joaquín Pérez-Goicoechea and Nasser B. Abulhasan. Notable projects include the Ali Mohammed T. Al-Ghanim Clinic (2014) and Wafra Living (2017), both in Kuwait.

DOMINIQUE PERRAULT
DOMINIQUE PERRAULT ARCHITECTURE
Paris, France

Dominique Perrault Architecture has an inventive approach to often large-scale, technically challenging projects. Founder Dominique Perrault has been honored with many prestigious awards, including the Gold Medal by the French Academy of Architecture.

DENNIS PIEPRZ
SASAKI
Watertown, MA, USA and Shanghai, China

The work of planning and design firm Sasaki spans architecture, landscape, and urban design. Pieprz is Chair of Design. A notable project includes the urban design for the Olympic Green, the principal venue of the 2008 Beijing Olympics.

LIESBETH VAN DER POL
DOK ARCHITECTS
Amsterdam, Netherlands

Dok Architects was founded in 2007 by Liesbeth van der Pol and Patrick Cannon. The practice works on a variety of assignments, including residential dwellings, schools, and shopping centers, as well as urban development plans.

CHRISTIAN DE PORTZAMPARC
2PORTZAMPARC
Paris, France

2Portzamparc is managed by both Elizabeth and Christian de Portzamparc, alongside having their own separate studios. Christian de Portzamparc's bold designs have won him numerous awards, including the Pritzker Prize in 1994.

ANTOINE PREDOCK
ANTOINE PREDOCK ARCHITECT
Multiple offices including Albuquerque, NM, USA

Antoine Predock founded his studio in 1967. Notable projects include the La Luz Community (1967) in New Mexico and the Tacoma Art Museum (2003) in Washington. Predock has won numerous accolades, including the Smithsonian Cooper-Hewitt National Design Museum's Lifetime Achievement Award.

RON RADZINER
MARMOL RADZINER
Multiple offices including Los Angeles, CA, USA

Marmol Radziner was founded in 1989 by Leo Marmol and Ron Radziner. The firm integrates architectural design with a full range of construction services, and its work has been featured in numerous publications, including *Architectural Digest* and *Dwell*.

HANI RASHID
ASYMPTOTE ARCHITECTURE
New York City, NY, USA

Asymptote Architecture was founded in 1989 by Hani Rashid and Lise Anne Couture. The practice's projects range from architecture to art installations. The studio's early unbuilt experiments in the digital realm are still influential.

STÉPHANE RASSELET
NATUREHUMAINE
Montreal, Canada

Naturehumaine is an architecture and design firm directed by Stéphane Rasselet. The practice has created a range of projects, from residential and office buildings, to restaurants and museums. Clients include Aesop and the Guido Moreli Foundation.

SONALI RASTOGI
MORPHOGENESIS
Multiple offices including New Delhi, India

Morphogenesis was founded by Sonali Rastogi and Manit Rastogi in 1996. The practice is now one of India's largest and leading architectural firms. Morphogenesis has won numerous awards, including a World Architecture Community Award in 2010.

CARLO RATTI
CARLO RATTI ASSOCIATI
Multiple offices including Turin, Italy

Carlo Ratti leads Carlo Ratti Associati which merges design with digital technologies across a variety of scales, from furniture to urban planning. The studio has been featured twice in *TIME* magazine's "Best Inventions of the Year."

ALIREZA RAZAVI
STUDIO RAZAVI ARCHITECTURE
Multiple offices including Paris, France

Studio Razavi's projects range from residential properties to corporate interiors and multi-use centers, including the Tehran Tower (2017) and Yeoui-Naru Ferry Terminal (2017) in Seoul.

PATRICK REARDON
REARDONSMITH ARCHITECTS
London, UK

Founded in 1988, ReardonSmith Architects works across master planning, architecture, and landscape design. Projects include the restoration of the Savoy Hotel (2010) in London and Four Seasons Hotel Lion Palace (2013) in St. Petersburg.

ANDRES REMY
REMY ARCHITECTS
Buenos Aires, Argentina

After gaining international recognition at Rafael Viñoly Architects, Andrés Remy founded Remy Architects in 2003. The practice largely works across residential, commercial, and high-rise projects.

CHARLES RENFRO
DILLER SCOFIDIO + RENFRO
New York City, NY, USA

Charles Renfro is a co-founder of Diller Scofidio + Renfro. Their work spans the fields of architecture, urban design, installation art, multimedia performance, and publications. Notable projects include the Broad (2015) in Los Angeles and the High Line (2014) in New York.

MARK DE REUS
DE REUS ARCHITECTS
Waimea, HI, USA and Sun Valley, ID, USA

Founded by Mark Edison de Reus and Stephen Ewing in 2002, De Reus Architects specializes in the design of luxury resorts and residences. Clients include Four Seasons and Punta Sayulita.

SALVADOR REYES RÍOS
REYES RÍOS + LARRAÍN ARQUITECTOS
Mérida, Mexico

Reyes Ríos + Larraín Arquitectos is an architecture, furniture, interior, and landscape design studio founded by Salvador Reyes Ríos and Josefina Larraín. The firm is best known for its sensitive restoration of old mansions and haciendas in Mexico.

PATRICK REYMOND
ATELIER OÏ
La Neuveville, Switzerland

Atelier Oï was founded in 1991 by Aurel Aebi, Armand Louis, and Patrick Reymond. The practice works across architecture, interior design, product design, and scenography. Clients include B&B Italia, Moroso, Nespresso, and Zanotta.

RUDY RICCIOTTI
RUDY RICCIOTTI
Bandol, France

Architect and publisher Rudy Ricciotti creates projects that range in scale from exhibition design to the MuCEM (2013) in Marseilles. He has received numerous national honors, including the Gold Medal Foundation of the French Academy of Architecture.

IAN RITCHIE
IAN RITCHIE ARCHITECTS
London, UK

Ian Ritchie Architects (iRAL) was established in 1981. iRAL is best known for its glass structures, material and technical innovation, and sustainable design.

JOSÉ JUAN RIVERA RÍO
JJRR/ARQUITECTURA
Mexico City, Mexico

JJRR/Arquitectura is led by José Juan Rivera Río. The practice specializes in private residences and hospitality projects both in Mexico and abroad, which have been featured in publications including *Wallpaper** and *Architectural Record*.

DAVID ROCKWELL
ROCKWELL GROUP
New York City, NY, USA and Madrid, Spain

Architecture and interior design firm Rockwell Group was founded by David Rockwell in 1984. The practice specializes in hospitality, retail, public, and healthcare projects, as well as set design. Notable clients include 15 Hudson Yards in collaboration with Diller, Scofidio + Renfro and the New York EDITION.

AB ROGERS
AB ROGERS DESIGN
London, UK and Melbourne, Australia
Ab Rogers Design works across cultural, hospitality, residential, and commercial sectors. Projects range from a Comme des Garçons store in Paris (2001) to micro-living solutions for students in Melbourne (2017).

MICHEL ROJKIND
ROJKIND ARQUITECTOS
Mexico City, Mexico
Rojkind Arquitectos puts emphasis on design and experiential innovation. The firm has won many awards, including Project of the Year in the Architizer A+ Awards for Foro Boca (2017) in Mexico.

FERNANDO ROMERO
FR–EE/FERNANDO ROMERO ENTERPRISE
Mexico City, Mexico and New York City, NY, USA
Architecture and industrial design firm FR–EE was founded by Fernando Romero in 2000. The studio has been honored with numerous prestigious awards, including an AI Global Architecture Award in 2017.

NATHALIE ROSSETTI
ROSSETTI + WYSS ARCHITECTS
Zollikon, Switzerland
Rossetti + Wyss Architects was established by Nathalie Rossetti and Mark Aurel Wyss in 2000. The practice works on architectural and urban projects at various scales ranging from housing to object design.

LAUREN ROTTET
ROTTET STUDIO
Multiple offices including Houston, TX, USA
Architecture and interior design firm Rottet Studio was founded in 2008 by Lauren Rottet. The practice works across corporate, hospitality, and residential projects, as well as furniture design.

OLA RUNE
CLAESSON KOIVISTO RUNE ARCHITECTS
Stockholm, Sweden
Architecture and design firm Claesson Koivisto Rune Architects was founded in 1995 by Mårten Claesson, Eero Koivisto, and Ola Rune. Clients include Boffi, Cappellini, and Skandiform, and their work has been recognized with more than sixty international awards.

THOMAS RUUS
FRIIS & MOLTKE ARCHITECTS
Multiple offices including Aarhus, Denmark
Friis & Moltke was founded in 1954 by Knud Friis and
Elmar Moltke Nielsen, and the duo pioneered a mild
Brutalist style in Denmark. Today, Thomas Ruus is a
partner and head of concept development at the firm.

ROBERT SAKULA
ASH SAKULA ARCHITECTS
London, UK
Ash Sakula Architects was founded in 1996 by Cany
Ash and Robert Sakula. The studio works largely on
residential and community projects, and has been
honored with numerous RIBA Awards for Architecture,
including one for Exhibition Mews (2015) in Bordon.

ACHILLE SALVAGNI
SALVAGNI ARCHITETTI
Multiple offices including Rome, Italy
Architectural and design practice Salvagni Architetti
focuses on high-end residential and hospitality
projects as well as superyacht interiors. The studio's
work marries Italian craftsmanship and traditional
techniques with a passion for luxurious materials.

HENRIETTE SALVESEN
DIV.A ARKITEKTER
Oslo, Norway
Div.A Arkitekter was established in 1987. The office
works on a wide range of projects, from mountain
cabins to city planning. Henriette Salvesen is a partner
at the practice.

URKO SANCHEZ
URKO SANCHEZ ARCHITECTS
Nairobi, Kenya and Madrid, Spain
Urko Sanchez Architects specializes in hotels,
office buildings, industrial spaces, and residential
development, but also has a strong focus on social
improvement projects.

CRISTIAN SANTANDREU
A2ARQUITECTOS
Mallorca and Madrid, Spain
A2arquitectos was founded by Cristian Santandreu
and Juan Manzanares Suárez. In 2016 the studio was
selected by the European Centre for Architecture
Art Design and Urban Studies as one of the 40 most
promising architecture studios in Europe.

MATTHIAS SAUERBRUCH AND
LOUISA HUTTON
SAUERBRUCH HUTTON
Berlin, Germany
Sauerbruch Hutton is a multi-disciplinary practice
founded in 1989 by Matthias Sauerbruch and
Louisa Hutton. Major projects include the GSW
Headquarters (1999) in Berlin and the M9 Museum
District (2018) in Venice-Mestre.

HUGO SAUZAY
FESTEN ARCHITECTURE
Paris, France

Festen Architecture was founded by Charlotte de Tonnac and Hugo Sauzay in 2011. The practice largely designs interiors for private residences, offices, and hotels. Notable clients include Le Pigalle in Paris and Hôtel Les Roches Rouges on the Côte d'Azur.

UWE SCHMIDT-HESS
PATALAB ARCHITECTURE
London, UK and Berlin, Germany

Uwe Schmidt-Hess is the founding director of Patalab Architects. Their work spans residential, workplace, community, and heritage projects, as well as objects and furniture. The firm has won numerous awards, including the Surface Design Awards 2015 for Cascade House (2014) in London.

MICHAEL SCHUMACHER
SCHNEIDER + SCHUMACHER
Multiple offices including Frankfurt, Germany

Schneider + Schumacher was founded in 1988 by Till Schneider and Michael Schumacher. Notable projects include the expansion of the Städel Museum (2012) in Frankfurt and the Autobahn Church Siegerland (2013) in Wilnsdorf, Germany.

ANNABELLE SELLDORF
SELLDORF ARCHITECTS
New York City, NY, USA

Annabelle Selldorf founded Selldorf Architects in 1988. The firm came to international prominence with the opening of the Neue Galerie (2001) in New York, and has since become known for creating galleries, cultural projects, and private homes utilizing an elegant, Modernist aesthetic and subtle detailing. Selldorf was the recipient of the 2016 Medal of Honor from the AIA in 2017.

THORHALLUR SIGURDSSON
ANDERSEN & SIGURDSSON
Frederiksberg, Denmark

Andersen & Sigurdsson Architects was established in 1997 by Ene Cordt Andersen and Thorhallur Sigurdsson. The studio's expertise spans cultural, educational, residential, and public projects.

FRAN SILVESTRE
FRAN SILVESTRE ARQUITECTOS
Multiple offices including Valencia, Spain

Architecture and interior design firm Fran Silvestre Arquitectos was founded by Fran Silvestre in 2005. Major projects include House on the Cliff (2012) in Alicante and the Hofmann House (2018) in Valencia.

HAYES AND JAMES SLADE
SLADE ARCHITECTURE
New York City, NY, USA

Slade Architecture was founded in 2002 by Hayes and James Slade. The practice has worked on a range of projects that span from homeless shelters to hospitality spaces. The firm has won several NY AIA awards, among other honors.

Amangani **379**..Mountains
Parker Palm Springs **387**..............................Desert
Parker Palm Springs **387**..................................Spa
Secret Harbour Beach Resort **467**...................Beach
Secret Harbour Beach Resort **467**........Best-kept secret
Secret Harbour Beach Resort **467**.....Family friendly
Secret Harbour Beach Resort **467**........Worth the travel
The Standard High Line, NYC **426**.............Where I live
Woodstock Inn & Resort **415**........................Countryside

LEONID SLONIMSKIY
KOSMOS ARCHITECTS
Multiple offices including Geneva, Switzerland

Leonid Slonimskiy is a partner at KOSMOS Architects, which designs projects of various types and scales: from a paper podium (2017) for the Swiss Architecture Museum in Basel to the Garage Centre for Contemporary Arts Pavilion (2012) in Moscow.

7132 Hotel **227**..Spa
Argentino Hotel Casino..................All-time favorite
  & Resort **495**
Dolder Grand Hotel **231**...............................Luxury
Hans Brinker Hostel **196**.............................Budget
Historisches Alpinhotel..........................Mountains
  Grimsel Hospiz **224**
Hôtel Le Corbusier **210**..............Wish I'd designed
Heritance Kandalama **119**........................Countryside
Merzouga Desert Luxury Camp **330**.................Desert
St Gotthardo Hospiz **228**........................Countryside
The Standard High Line, NYC **426**..................Urban

GERMÁN DEL SOL
GERMÁN DEL SOL ARCHITECTS
Santiago, Chile

Germán del Sol founded his practice in 1986. His portfolio of projects includes Termas Geométricas (2009), Explora Patagonia Hotel Salto Chico (2000), and Remota (2006) in Patagonia and Atacama.

Explora Atacama **499**...................All-time favorite
Explora Atacama **499**..................................Desert
Hotel Antumalal **499**....................................Spa
Pousada Picinguaba **494**..............................Beach
Remota (Patagonia) **501**...............Family friendly
Remota (Patagonia) **501**............Wish I'd designed
Remota (Patagonia) **501**..............Worth the travel
Ski Portillo **502**....................................Mountains
W Santiago **502**................................Where I live

FERNANDO SORDO MADALENO
SORDO MADALENO
Mexico City, Mexico

Sordo Madaleno was founded in 1937 by Mexican architect Juan Sordo Madaleno (1916–1985). Fernando Sordo Madaleno is the firm's architecture director, and has overseen such projects as the Massimo Dutti flagship store (2016) in Mexico City.

&Beyond Ngorongoro Crater Lodge **347**........Mountains
Amangiri **392–393**.....................................Desert
Belmond Hotel Splendido **279**.............All-time favorite
Belmond Hotel Splendido **279**.............Best-kept secret
Chablé Resort & Spa **452**........................Countryside
Chablé Resort & Spa **452**..............................Spa
Cheval Blanc Randheli **122**........................Luxury
Cheval Blanc Randheli **122**.............Worth the travel
Four Seasons Resort Orlando.....................Family friendly
  at Walt Disney World® Resort **439**
Hotel Alfonso XIII,...Urban
  A Luxury Collection Hotel **244**
Hotel Carlota (Mexico City) **445**.............Where I live
Hotel Punta Islita **459**.......................Eco-conscious

DORIN STEFAN
DORIN STEFAN BIROU DE ARHITECTURA
Bucharest, Romania

Dorin Stefan founded his practice in 1990. Among various honors, he was awarded the Omnia Opera award by the Romanian Union of Architects in 2018.

Amangiri **392–393**.....................................Desert
Castel Mimi **311**...Spa
Éclat Hotel Taipei **83**..................................Urban
Fraţii Jderi, Utopia Verde **311**.............Family friendly
Hanging Gardens of Bali **139**.......................Luxury
Hotel Puerta América Madrid **251**........Wish I'd designed
Hotel Solar do Engenho **491**....................Countryside
Kinjohro **96**...............................All-time favorite
Mama Shelter Lyon **203**.................Best-kept secret
Sarroglia **311**.................................Where I live

MICHAEL STIFF
STIFF + TREVILLION
London, UK

Architecture and interior design practice Stiff + Trevillion was founded in 1981 by Michael Stiff and Andrew Trevillion. The firm's work spans commercial, residential, restaurant, and retail sectors. Notable clients include the Royal Academy, Selfridges, and the Wellcome Trust.

Carlisle Bay **469**..Beach
The Dusun **134**.............................Best-kept secret
The Dusun **134**.................................Countryside
The Dusun **134**.............................Eco-conscious
The Laslett **182**...............................Where I live
Mandarin Oriental Hong Kong **89**....................Luxury
Mandarin Oriental Hong Kong **89**....................Urban
The Myst Dong Khoi **133**..................Worth the travel

DANIEL SUDUCA AND THIERRY MÉRILLOU
SUDUCA & MÉRILLOU
Toulouse, France

Daniel Suduca and Thierry Mérillou are architects and specialists in decorative arts of the twentieth century. Since 1994 the duo have operated design store Galerie Saint Jacques in Toulouse.

DANIEL SUNDLIN
BJARKE INGELS GROUP
Multiple offices including New York City, NY, USA and Copenhagen, Denmark

Daniel Sundlin is a partner at Bjarke Ingels Group (BIG), which was founded by Bjarke Ingels in 2005. BIG includes architects, urbanists, landscape professionals, interior and product designers, and inventors. Sundlin has worked on many of BIG's most prominent projects, including VIA 57 West (2016) in New York.

MURAT TABANLIOĞLU
TABANLIOĞLU ARCHITECTS
Multiple offices including Istanbul, Turkey

Tabanlıoğlu Architects was established in 1990 by Murat Tabanlıoğlu and his father Hayati Tabanlıoğlu. Melkan Gürsel joined the group as partner in 1995. A major work includes the renovation of the Beyazit State Library (2016) in Istanbul.

DAVID TAJCHMAN
ARCHITECTURES DAVID TAJCHMAN
Paris, France

Architect David Tajchman has taught widely at schools and universities. The practice has several innovative architectural projects, including the Tenniscalator (2009) and the Gran Mediterraneo (2016), which won an 2017 Architizer A+ Award.

KIYOSHI SEY TAKEYAMA
AMORPHE TAKEYAMA & ASSOCIATES
Kyoto, Japan and Tokyo, Japan

Amorphe Takeyama & Associates was founded in 1983 by Kiyoshi Sey Takeyama. The practice works on a range of projects, including hotels and cultural institutions. In 1994, the practice was awarded Architecture of the Year by the Architectural Institute of Japan.

BOLLE THAM AND MARTIN VIDEGÅRD
THAM & VIDEGÅRD ARKITEKTER
Stockholm, Sweden

Tham & Videgård was founded by Bolle Tham and Martin Videgård in 1999. The practice has won numerous awards, including the 2015 Kasper Salin Prize for the KTH School of Architecture at the Royal Institute of Technology (2015) in Stockholm.

MATTEO THUN
MATTEO THUN & PARTNERS
Milan, Italy

Architecture and design firm Matteo Thun & Partners was founded in 1980. The firm employs architects, and interior, product, and graphic designers. It specializes in luxury hotel projects and residences, alongside commercial, urban design, and master planning projects.

MIA BAARUP TOFTE
NORD ARCHITECTS
Copenhagen, Denmark

NORD Architects was established in 2003 by Johannes Molander Pedersen and Morten Rask Gregersen. In 2017, Mia Baarup Tofte joined the partnership. Projects include educational buildings, day-care centers, sports facilities, and urban spaces.

ISABELLE TOLAND
AILEEN SAGE ARCHITECTS
Sydney, Australia

Aileen Sage Architects was founded by Isabelle Aileen Toland and Amelia Sage Holliday. The firm's work spans architecture, interior and urban design, and a broad range of project typologies, including private houses, galleries, and community facilities.

RANDA TUKAN
HOK ARCHITECTS
Multiple offices including Toronto, Canada

HOK Architects was founded in Missouri in 1955. Since then, HOK has become a global design, architecture, engineering, and planning firm, and a world leader in sustainable design. Randa Tukan leads the Hospitality, Retail, and Residential Commercial Interiors practice at HOK Toronto.

EMILIO TUÑÓN
TUÑÓN ARQUITECTOS
Madrid, Spain

Tuñón Architects was founded by Emilio Tuñón in 2012 as a natural transition from Mansilla+Tuñón Architects. Tuñón has also taught widely, and was previously a visiting professor at the Harvard University Graduate School of Design.

MUCH UNTERTRIFALLER
DIETRICH UNTERTRIFALLER ARCHITECTS
Multiple offices including Bregenz, Austria
Dietrich Untertrifaller Architects was founded in 1994
by Helmut Dietrich and Much Untertrifaller. Major
works include the Alice Milliat Sports Center (2016) in
Lyon and Edlach Elementary School (2016) in Austria.

CLAUDIA URDANETA
NMD NOMADAS
Maracaibo, Venezuela and Houston, TX, USA
Claudia Urdaneta is a co-founder with Farid Chacón
and Francisco Mustieles of NMD NOMADAS. The
firm's projects include urban planning, architecture,
interior design, and landscaping, throughout
Venezuela and in other countries in South America,
North America, and Europe.

MARTA URTASUN AND PEDRO RICA
MECANISMO
Madrid, Spain
Mecanismo is a Madrid-based practice founded in
2012 by Marta Urtasun and Pedro Rica. The studio
undertakes work that spans residential and public
projects. Notable projects include the Hotel Akelarre
(2017) in San Sebastián and Embolao (2017) in Madrid.

ARTEM VAKHRIN
AKZ ARCHITECTURA
Kiev, Ukraine
Architecture and design studio AKZ Architectura
was founded by Artem Vakhrin and Kateryna Zuieva.
The firm largely designs retail and hospitality spaces
throughout Kiev.

FRANÇOIS VALENTINY
VALENTINY HVP ARCHITECTS
Rëmerschen, Luxembourg
Valentiny HVP Architects was founded by François
Valentiny. One of his many major projects is the
Luxembourg Learning Center (2018) in Esch-Belval,
nominated for an EU Mies Award in 2019.

SUMAYYA VALLY
COUNTERSPACE
Johannesburg, South Africa
Counterspace is directed by Amina Kaskar, Sarah de
Villiers, and Sumayya Vally. The firm works across
a range of projects, including architecture, exhibition
design, art installation visualization, public events
curation, and urban design.

DIETER VANDER VELPEN
DIETER VANDER VELPEN ARCHITECTS
Antwerp, Belgium and New York City, NY, USA
Architecture and interior design firm Dieter Vander
Velpen Architects was founded in 2013. The firm
specializes in high-end residential projects throughout
the United States and Europe.

RUI VELOSO
ADAPTEYE
Porto, Portugal
Founded in 2017 by Rui Veloso, Adapteye spans
architecture, urban planning, and rehabilitation for
a range of typologies, including residential, health,
hospitality, and educational buildings.

INÊS VIEIRA-DA-SILVA
SAMI-ARQUITECTOS
Sétubal, Portugal
SAMI-Arquitectos was founded in 2005 by Inês Vieira
da Silva and Miguel Vieira. Notable projects include
the Gruta das Torres Visitor Centre (2006) and the E/C
House (2014), both on Pico Island in Portugal.

JEAN-PAUL VIGUIER
JEAN-PAUL VIGUIER ET ASSOCIÉS
Paris, France
Architecture, town planning, and interior design
agency Jean-Paul Viguier et Associés is led by Jean-
Paul Viguier. Notable works include the French
pavilion at the Seville World Fair (1992) and the McNay
Museum of Modern Art (2008) in San Antonio, Texas.

SARAH DE VILLIERS
COUNTERSPACE
Johannesburg, South Africa
Counterspace is a Johannesburg-based collaborative
architectural studio, directed by an all-women team
of Amina Kaskar, Sarah de Villiers, and Sumayya
Vally. The firm is dedicated to architectural projects,
exhibition design, art installation visualization, public
events curation, and urban design.

MARIA WARNER WONG
WOW ARCHITECTS | WARNER WONG DESIGN
Singapore and London, UK

WOW Architects was founded in 2000 by Wong Chiu Man and Maria Warner Wong. The studio works across architecture, interior and landscape design, and masterplanning, specializing in hospitality, residential, and commercial design.

ALEX WARNOCK-SMITH
URBAN PROJECTS BUREAU
London, UK

Urban Projects Bureau is a creative agency specializing in architecture, urbanism, spatial strategy, and design. The London-based practice has collaborated with firms including Arup, and clients include the British Council and *Blueprint* magazine.

DANIEL WELBORN
THE GETTYS GROUP
Multiple offices including Chicago, IL, USA

The Gettys Group is a hotel design, branding, and development firm, which was founded in 1988. It works with brands including Accor, Shangri-La, Langham, and the Peninsula Group. Daniel Welborn is a principal at the practice.

DAVID WELSH AND CHRIS MAJOR
WELSH + MAJOR
Surry Hills, Australia

Welsh + Major was established in 2004 by David Welsh and Chris Major. The firm's work spans across residential, public, and commercial projects. Major works include the Rocks Police Station (2014) and the Garden Room (2013), both in Sydney.

GRAHAM WEST
WEST ARCHITECTURE
London, UK

West Architecture was founded by Graham West in 2006. It focuses on residential, commercial, and public buildings. Projects include private houses, a showroom for designer Collier Webb (2018), and an installation for Dover Street Market (2014), both in London.

CHRIS WILKINSON
WILKINSON EYRE ARCHITECTS
London, UK and Hong Kong

Wilkinson Eyre was established in 1983. Notable projects include the Guangzhou International Finance Center (2010) and Gasholders London (2018). The practice has received numerous awards for its work, including the RIBA Stirling Prize in 2001 and 2002.

GERT WINGÅRDH
WINGÅRDHS
Multiple offices including Gothenburg, Sweden
Wingårdhs was founded by internationally acclaimed architect Gert Wingårdh. Notable projects include the Swedish embassies in Berlin (2000) and Washington (2006), which won Wingårdhs one of its five Kasper Salin Prizes.

ALEXANDER WONG
ALEXANDER WONG ARCHITECTS
Hong Kong and Shenzhen, China
Alexander Wong Architects is an architectural and interior design company. The studio has won numerous awards for its work across retail, residential, and hospitality sectors.

DAN WOOD
WORKAC
New York City, NY, USA
WORKac was founded by Dan Wood and Amale Andraos. The international firm's projects examine the connection between urban and natural environments. In 2015, it was named the top design firm on *Architect* magazine's Architect 50 list.

TAVIS WRIGHT
DOS ARCHITECTS
London, UK
DOS Architects was formed in 2006 by Tavis Wright and Lorenzo Grifantini. The firm's work spans residential, commercial, hospitality, and interior design. It has won numerous honors, including the 2013 Renzo Piano Foundation Award.

KEN YEANG
HAMZAH & YEANG
Kuala Lumpur, Malaysia
Hamzah & Yeang is best known for designing innovative "super-green" buildings and working with environmentally minded investors and clients. Projects include the National Library of Singapore (2005), and the Solaris Science Center (2008), both in Singapore.

GEORGE YABU AND GLENN PUSHELBERG
YABU PUSHELBERG
Toronto, Canada and New York City, NY, USA

Yabu Pushelberg was founded in 1980 by Glenn Pushelberg and George Yabu. The firm designs buildings, interiors, landscapes, lighting, products, and graphics. It has been named among the world's most influential design studios by *Wallpaper** and *The Business of Fashion*, among others.

MICHAEL YOUNG
MICHAEL YOUNG STUDIO
Hong Kong and Brussels, Belgium

Michael Young Studio was founded in Hong Kong in 2006. The studio works in the areas of product, furniture, branding, art direction, and interior design. Clients include Hennessy, Cathay Pacific, and Georg Jensen.

BUZZ YUDELL
MOORE RUBLE YUDELL
Santa Monica, CA, USA

Moore Ruble Yudell was founded by Charles Moore, John Ruble, and Buzz Yudell. Its work incorporates an extraordinary range of projects and places, such as university campuses and US embassies around the world.

ROGER ZOGOLOVITCH
SOLIDSPACE
London, UK

Solidspace was established in 2003 by Roger Zogolovitch. The firm has collaborated with a number of architects, self-builders, and other independent developers—including Groves Natcheva, MW Architects, and Stephen Taylor—on numerous split-level homes in urban locations.

CINO ZUCCHI
CZA
Milan, Italy

CZA (Cino Zucchi Architetti) works in the fields of architecture, landscape, and urban design. Notable projects include the MAUTO National Automobile Museum (2011) in Turin, Italy, and the entrance to the Vedeggio-Cassarate tunnel (2012) in Lugano, Switzerland.

KATERYNA ZUIEVA
AKZ ARCHITECTURA
Kiev, Ukraine

Architecture and design studio AKZ Architectura was founded by Artem Vakhrin and Kateryna Zuieva. The firm largely designs retail and hospitality spaces throughout Kiev.

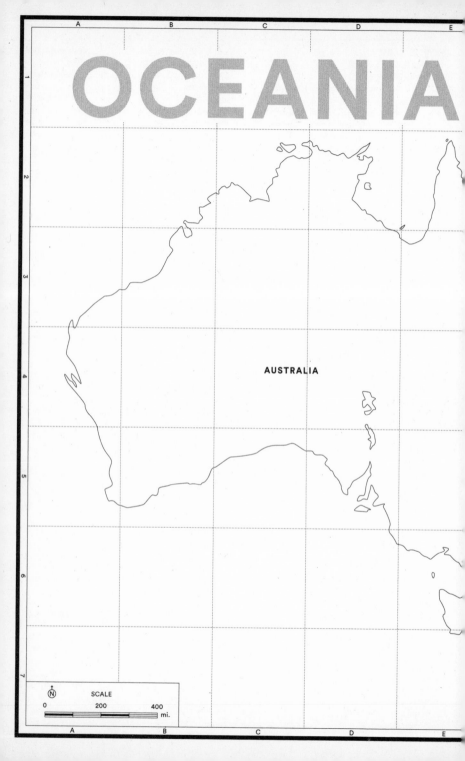

↑ GUAM

VANUATU

FIJI

FRENCH
POLYNESIA →

NEW
ZEALAND

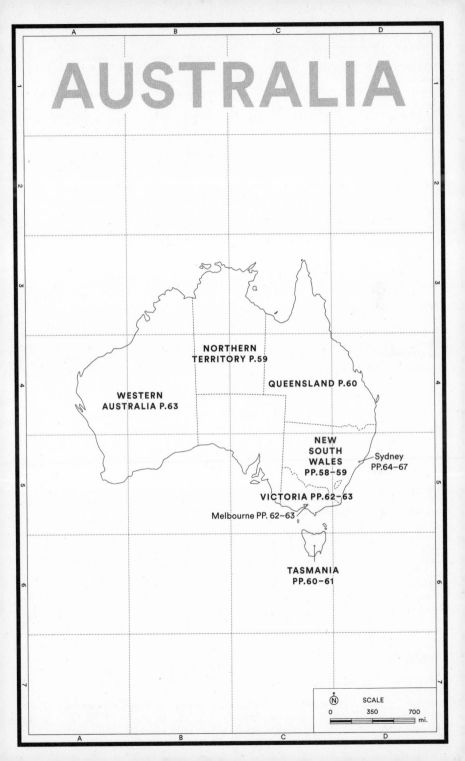

AUSTRALIA

NORTHERN
TERRITORY P.59

QUEENSLAND P.60

WESTERN
AUSTRALIA P.63

NEW
SOUTH
WALES
PP.58–59

Sydney
PP.64–67

VICTORIA PP.62–63

Melbourne PP. 62–63

TASMANIA
PP.60–61

N

SCALE

0   350   700
                        mi.

THE ENCHANTED CAVE
Berambing
Blue Mountains
New South Wales 2758, Australia
+61 409393425
lovecabins.com.au

CREDIT CARDS	Accepted but not Amex
PRICE	Mid-range
TYPE	Guesthouse
ACCOMMODATION	1 Cabin
FACILITIES	Spa, Wood-burning fireplace
GOOD TO KNOW	No pets
RECOMMENDED FOR	Mountains

"Pure mountain magic."—Mark Landini

Recommended by: Mark Landini, Landini Associates

THE ATLANTIC BYRON BAY
13 Marvell Street
Byron Bay
New South Wales 2481, Australia
+61 266855118
atlanticbyronbay.com.au

CREDIT CARDS	Accepted but not Amex
PRICE	Mid-range
TYPE	Hotel
ACCOMMODATION	15 Rooms
FACILITIES	Outdoor swimming pool, Tropical gardens
GOOD TO KNOW	BBQ, Bicycle and surfboard rentals, No pets, Shared self-catering kitchen
RECOMMENDED FOR	Best-kept secret

"Laid-back, friendly, and comfortable, all in a beautiful setting."—Alex Mok

Recommended by: Alex Mok, Linehouse

BUBBLE TENT AUSTRALIA
Capertee
New South Wales 2846, Australia
+61 412133052
bubbletentaustralia.com

CREDIT CARDS	Accepted
PRICE	Mid-range
TYPE	Tented Camp
ACCOMMODATION	3 Tents
FACILITIES	Firepits, Outdoor hot tubs
GOOD TO KNOW	Adults only, Self-catering
RECOMMENDED FOR	Eco-conscious

"Great for stargazing."—Mark Landini

A trio of transparent and inflatable tents, Bubbletent is the first of its kind in Australia. Its secluded and remote location gives the off-grid feeling of wild camping, but it has all the luxuries of glamping. Gaze upon rolling hills during the day and stargaze from the comfort of your own bed by night.

Recommended by: Mark Landini, Landini Associates

THE LITTLE BLACK SHACK
29 Ross Smith Parade
Great Mackerel Beach
New South Wales 2108
Australia
+61 400515588
thelittleblackshack.com.au

CREDIT CARDS	Accepted
PRICE	High-end
TYPE	Guesthouse
ACCOMMODATION	2 Rooms
FACILITIES	BBQ, Wood-burning fireplace
GOOD TO KNOW	Library, Shared self-catering kitchen
RECOMMENDED FOR	Best-kept secret

"The serenity! So close to Sydney, making it perfect for a weekend break."—Mark Landini

Recommended by: Mark Landini, Landini Associates

MUNGO SHEARERS' QUARTERS
Mailbox Road
Mungo National Park
New South Wales 2715
Australia
+61 350218900
nationalparks.nsw.gov.au

CREDIT CARDS	Accepted but not Amex
PRICE	Low-cost
TYPE	Former sheep station
ACCOMMODATION	5 Bunkhouses
FACILITIES	BBQ
GOOD TO KNOW	Bring your own bedding, Self-catering
RECOMMENDED FOR	Desert

"Simple accommodation set in a beautiful, remote desert location."—Tim Black

Recommended by: Tim Black, BKK Architects

SYDNEY: SEE PAGES 64–67

YARRANGOBILLY CAVES HOUSE 1917 SECTION

Yarrangobilly Caves Entrance Road
(via Snowy Mountains Highway)
Yarrangobilly
New South Wales 2720
Australia
+61 264549597
nationalparks.nsw.gov.au

CREDIT CARDS	Accepted but not Amex
PRICE	Mid-range
TYPE	Lodge
ACCOMMODATION	9 Rooms
FACILITIES	BBQ, Outdoor swimming pool
GOOD TO KNOW	Child friendly, Self-catering
RECOMMENDED FOR	Countryside

"A 1917 timber lodge set deep within the Kosciuszko National Park, and adjacent to the steaming natural outdoor thermal pool; a classic Australian bush setting."—Isabelle Toland

Recommended by: Isabelle Toland, Aileen Sage Architects

LARAPINTA TRAIL CAMPSITES

Larapinta Trail
West MacDonnell National Park
Northern Territory 0872
Australia
+61 282708455
worldexpeditions.com

CREDIT CARDS	Accepted but not Amex
PRICE	Low-cost
TYPE	Campsite trail
ACCOMMODATION	41 Tent sites
FACILITIES	Water tanks
GOOD TO KNOW	No fires, Self-catering
RECOMMENDED FOR	Desert, Eco-conscious

"The West MacDonnell Ranges are a myth-laden landscape where you can still see the furrows and peaks created by the mythical journey of the Rainbow Serpent during Aboriginal Dreamtime. The nearest town is Alice Springs, the world's most remote city, so there are no nearby lights to dim the nighttime canopy of stars. The best way to experience this is glamping in Neeson Murcutt Architects' purpose-built campsites, situated along the Larapinta Trail."—Grace Mortlock

"Eco-campsites designed by Neeson Murcutt Architects, set within a dramatic desert landscape."—Isabelle Toland

Recommended by: Grace Mortlock, Other Architects; Isabelle Toland, Aileen Sage Architects

LONGITUDE 131°

Yulara Drive
Yulara
Northern Territory 0872
Australia
+61 299184355
longitude131.com.au

CREDIT CARDS	Accepted
PRICE	Blow-out (all-inclusive)
TYPE	Resort
ACCOMMODATION	16 Luxury tents and 1 Pavilion
FACILITIES	Bar, Restaurant, Spa
GOOD TO KNOW	Near Uluru (Ayers Rock)
RECOMMENDED FOR	Desert

"Luxury-style 'camping' under the stars in this iconic landscape was an incredibly special experience."
—Mark Landini

Recommended by: Mark Landini, Landini Associates

SAILS IN THE DESERT

163 Yulara Drive
Yulara
Northern Territory 0872
Australia
+61 282968010
ayersrockresort.com.au

CREDIT CARDS	Accepted
PRICE	High-end
TYPE	Resort
ACCOMMODATION	228 Rooms and Suites
FACILITIES	Art gallery, Bar, Outdoor swimming pool, Restaurant, Spa
GOOD TO KNOW	Free parking
RECOMMENDED FOR	Desert

"Designed by Philip Cox, this hotel is near the 500-million-year-old Uluru, the largest monolithic rock on earth. The hotel has established a national training academy, so one third of the total staff are indigenous peoples."—Paul Morgan

Recommended by: Tom Jordan, Hayball; Paul Morgan, Paul Morgan Architects

INTERCONTINENTAL HAYMAN ISLAND RESORT

1 Raintree Avenue
Hayman Island
Queensland 4801
Australia
+61 755019992
hayman.com.au

CREDIT CARDS	Accepted
PRICE	High-end
TYPE	Resort
ACCOMMODATION	166 Rooms, Suites, and Villas
FACILITIES	Bar, Cafe, Gym, Outdoor swimming pool, 3 Restaurants, Spa
GOOD TO KNOW	Babysitting
RECOMMENDED FOR	Family friendly

"Great food, unbeatable location, and endless things to do."—Mark Landini

Recommended by: Mark Landini, Landini Associates

BEDARRA ISLAND RESORT

Bedarra Island
Mission Beach
Queensland 4852
Australia
+61 740688233
bedarra.com.au

CREDIT CARDS	Accepted
PRICE	Blow-out
TYPE	Resort
ACCOMMODATION	10 Villas
FACILITIES	Bar, Gym, Massage pavilion, Outdoor swimming pool, Restaurant
GOOD TO KNOW	In-room spa treatments, Water sports
RECOMMENDED FOR	Island

"Beautiful tropical setting, isolated, contemporary, context-led architecture, and individually-designed villas."
—Tom Jordan

Recommended by: Tom Jordan, Hayball

QUALIA

20 Whitsunday Boulevard
Hamilton Island
Whitsunday Islands
Queensland 4803
Australia
+61 749489222
qualia.com.au

CREDIT CARDS	Accepted
PRICE	Blow-out
TYPE	Resort
ACCOMMODATION	60 Pavilions
FACILITIES	Bar, Boutique, Golf, Gym, 2 Outdoor swimming pools, 2 Restaurants, Spa, Yoga
GOOD TO KNOW	Adults only
RECOMMENDED FOR	Island

A hotel set in the paradisiacal Whitsunday Islands, Qualia blends Chris Beckingham's harmonious design with world-class hospitality. Guests must be aged sixteen and over.

Recommended by: Adam Meshberg, Meshberg Group

BAY OF FIRES LODGE

Mount William National Park
Ansons Bay
Tasmania 7264
Australia
+61 363922211
taswalkingco.com.au

CREDIT CARDS	Accepted
PRICE	High-end (all-inclusive)
TYPE	Lodge
ACCOMMODATION	10 Rooms
FACILITIES	Spa
GOOD TO KNOW	Solar-powered lights
RECOMMENDED FOR	Beach

"Tasmania's Bay of Fires is one of the world's most beautiful and pristine coastlines, but it may not have been preserved in its current state without the Bay of Fires walk and lodge, designed by architect Tony Caro. Originally accessible only by foot, the lodge has created a new paradigm of eco-accommodation that not only provides access to a remote and spectacular location, but also helps educate visitors about the wonder and fragility of its setting. It is not just a place to stay, it is an experience."—Grace Mortlock

Recommended by: Grace Mortlock, Other Architects

MONA PAVILIONS

655 Main Road
Berriedale
Tasmania 7011
Australia
+61 362779900
mona.net.au

CREDIT CARDS..Accepted
PRICE...High-end
TYPE...Hotel
ACCOMMODATION.................................8 Pavilions
FACILITIES................................Gym, Indoor swimming pool,
Restaurant, Sauna, Spa,
Steam room, Winery
GOOD TO KNOW......................Child friendly, No pets
RECOMMENDED FOR..................................Countryside

"Since its opening in 2011, Mona (the Museum of Old and New Art) has completely transformed Tasmania's cultural landscape. Located within an active winery on a peninsula jutting into the Derwent River, Mona is a dynamic and edgy institution run by a professional gambler, and mostly hidden below ground. It's great for a day trip but even better for an overnight stay: occupying one of the luxurious pavilions enables late-night gallery visits and lazy wine-sipping evenings watching the light fade on the river." —Grace Mortlock

Recommended by: Grace Mortlock, Other Architects

FREYCINET LODGE

Coles Bay Road
Freycinet National Park
Coles Bay
Tasmania 7215
Australia
+61 362567222
freycinetlodge.com.au

CREDIT CARDS..Accepted
PRICE...Mid-range
TYPE..Lodge
ACCOMMODATION.................70 Rooms and Pavilions
FACILITIES...................................Bar, 2 Restaurants
GOOD TO KNOW......................Child friendly, No pets
RECOMMENDED FOR..Beach

"This hotel has nine architecturally designed pavilions with expansive water views, set among beautiful natural surroundings. Being situated in Freycinet National Park means there are many options for bushwalking and beach or water activities."—Tim Black

Recommended by: Tim Black, BKK Architects

FREYCINET RESORT

1799-1819 Coles Bay Road
Coles Bay
Tasmania 7215
Australia
+61 362876345
freycinet.com

CREDIT CARDS........................Accepted but not Amex
PRICE...High-end
TYPE..Resort
ACCOMMODATION....................11 Lodges and Studios
FACILITIES.............................Private walking tracks
GOOD TO KNOW.................Breakfast only, No pets
RECOMMENDED FOR.............................Eco-conscious

"The property is designated 'Land for Wildlife,' and today it forms a useful buffer for wildlife migrating in and out of the Freycinet National Park. A philosophy of do no harm, minimize waste, repair, reuse, recycle, and inculcate harmony with nature and man runs throughout the business, evidenced in the Six Green Star rating for the hotel rooms." —Paul Morgan

Recommended by: Paul Morgan, Paul Morgan Architects

PUMPHOUSE POINT

1 Lake St Clair Road
Lake St Clair
Tasmania 7140
Australia
+61 428090436
pumphousepoint.com.au

CREDIT CARDS..Accepted
PRICE...Mid-range
TYPE...Retreat
ACCOMMODATION.......................................19 Rooms
FACILITIES..Bar, Restaurant
GOOD TO KNOW......................Free parking, No pets
RECOMMENDED FOR....................Countryside, Eco-conscious

"Designed by excellent young Tasmanian architects of Cumulus Studio; try to stay in the restored industrial pumphouse or individual cabins in the wilderness." —Isabelle Toland

"Tranquility. Peace. Isolation. Luxury."—David Welsh and Chris Major

Recommended by: Isabelle Toland, Aileen Sage Architects; David Welsh and Chris Major, Welsh + Major

BRAE RESTAURANT AND GUEST SUITES

4285 Cape Otway Road
Birregurra
Victoria 3242, Australia
+61 352362226
braerestaurant.com

CREDIT CARDS	Accepted
PRICE	High-end
TYPE	Restaurant with rooms
ACCOMMODATION	6 Suites
FACILITIES	Bar, Restaurant
GOOD TO KNOW	Adults only
RECOMMENDED FOR	Countryside

"The hotel and restaurant that makes eating green ants cool!"—Mark Landini

A stay at Brae Restaurant and Guest Suites should be on every foodie's bucket list. The restaurant is run by acclaimed chef-owner Dan Hunter and incorporates organic produce from Brae Farm and local producers. The on-site guest suites are stylish, spacious, and modern, and built with sustainability in mind. Breakfast is brought to the suites each morning and, at lunch, guests have the option of ordering a shared supper plate for the evening. Bookings are available for adults only, together with a lunch or dinner reservation on the same date.

Recommended by: Mark Landini, Landini Associates

RACV CAPE SCHANCK RESORT

Trent Jones Drive (via Boneo Road)
Cape Schanck
Victoria 3939, Australia
+61 359508000
racv.com.au

CREDIT CARDS	Accepted but not Amex
PRICE	Mid-range
TYPE	Resort
ACCOMMODATION	163 Rooms, Suites, and Villas
FACILITIES	Bar, Golf, Gym, Indoor and outdoor swimming pools, Restaurant, Sauna, Spa
GOOD TO KNOW	Child friendly
RECOMMENDED FOR	Beach

"Use the Wood Marsh-designed hotel as a base to go swimming and bushwalking, viewing echidnas, kangaroos, wallabies, and Australian eagles as well as to visit the famous wineries on the Mornington Peninsula."
—Paul Morgan

Recommended by: Paul Morgan, Paul Morgan Architects

ADELPHI HOTEL

187 Flinders Lane
Central Business District
Melbourne
Victoria 3000
Australia
+61 380808888
adelphi.com.au

CREDIT CARDS	Accepted
PRICE	Mid-range
TYPE	Hotel
ACCOMMODATION	38 Rooms and Suites
FACILITIES	Bar, Outdoor swimming pool, Restaurant
GOOD TO KNOW	Child friendly, No pets
RECOMMENDED FOR	Where I live

"Great late 1980s design by Denton Corker Marshall that has stood the test of time."—Tom Jordan

Recommended by: Tom Jordan, Hayball

THE HOTEL WINDSOR

111 Spring Street
Central Business District
Melbourne
Victoria 3000
Australia
+61 396336000
thehotelwindsor.com.au

CREDIT CARDS	Accepted
PRICE	Mid-range
TYPE	Hotel
ACCOMMODATION	180 Rooms and Suites
FACILITIES	Bar, Restaurant
GOOD TO KNOW	Child friendly
RECOMMENDED FOR	Best-kept secret

"The Hotel Windsor dates back to the time of the gold and wool rushes, when Melbourne was Australia's capital and the city's Flinders Street station was the busiest train station in the entire world. The very picture of colonial grandeur, the Windsor has a vibe of faded glory; it's wonderful. You can book one of the regal many-roomed suites overlooking Parliament for a decent price."—Grace Mortlock

Recommended by: Grace Mortlock, Other Architects

QT MELBOURNE
133 Russell Street
Central Business District
Melbourne
Victoria 3000
Australia
+61 386368800
qthotelsandresorts.com

CREDIT CARDS..Accepted
PRICE..Mid-range
TYPE...Hotel
ACCOMMODATION..188 Rooms
FACILITIES...............................Bar, Cafe, Gym, Restaurant,
Rooftop terrace bar
GOOD TO KNOW.....................................Valet parking
RECOMMENDED FOR.................................Where I live

"Great location in Melbourne's Central Business District, with great views from the rooftop bar. Fun, quirky interiors in the rooms and throughout the public spaces. Great hotel to stay in or even just visit for a drink or meal."—Tim Black

Recommended by: Tim Black, BKK Architects

JACKALOPE HOTEL
166 Balnarring Road
Merricks North
Victoria 3926
Australia
+61 359312500
jackalopehotels.com

CREDIT CARDS..Accepted
PRICE...High-end
TYPE...Hotel
ACCOMMODATION................................45 Rooms and Suites
FACILITIES.....................................Art collection, Bar,
Outdoor swimming pool,
2 Restaurants, Spa, Vineyard
GOOD TO KNOW.........................Child friendly, Valet parking
RECOMMENDED FOR...Luxury

"This hotel is an easy drive from Melbourne's Central Business District, so it's a great place to escape from the city for a weekend. The interiors are enticing to many designers, but the extraordinary food and wine are what really make this a world-class destination hotel."—Tim Black

Recommended by: Tim Black, BKK Architects

THE MATADOR MOTEL
Corner Princess Highway and Raymond Street
Sale
Victoria 3850
Australia
+61 351441422
thematador.com.au

CREDIT CARDS..Accepted
PRICE..Low-cost
TYPE...Motel
ACCOMMODATION.....................54 Apartments and Rooms
FACILITIES...................BBQ, Outdoor swimming pool
GOOD TO KNOW....................................Free parking
RECOMMENDED FOR......................................Budget

"Built in the 1970s, mainly intended for American oil company workers, the Matador is designed in the Hacienda style."—Paul Morgan

Recommended by: Paul Morgan, Paul Morgan Architects

PULLMAN BUNKER BAY RESORT MARGARET RIVER REGION HOTEL
42 Bunker Bay Road (via Cape Naturaliste Road)
Western Australia 6281
Australia
+61 897569100
pullmanbunkerbayresort.com.au

CREDIT CARDS..Accepted
PRICE...High-end
TYPE...Resort
ACCOMMODATION...150 Villas
FACILITIES.......................Bar, Outdoor swimming pool,
Restaurant, Salon, Spa, Tennis
GOOD TO KNOW.........................Beach access, Child friendly
RECOMMENDED FOR..Beach

"Beautiful secluded bay, with waves, dolphins, and whales."
—Ben Duckworth

Recommended by: Ben Duckworth, Hassell

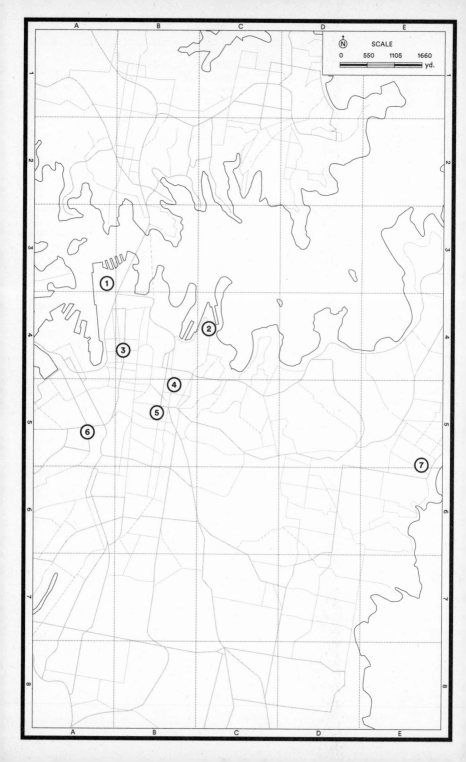

SYDNEY

HOTEL PALISADE
35 Bettington Street
Millers Point
Sydney 2000
+61 290180123
hotelpalisade.com.au

CREDIT CARDS	Accepted
PRICE	Mid-range
TYPE	Hotel
ACCOMMODATION	8 Rooms
FACILITIES	Bar
GOOD TO KNOW	No pets
RECOMMENDED FOR	Best-kept secret

"Breezy and warm service; you check in at the bar, and when it's time to leave, you just walk out, it's as simple as that."—Ben Duckworth

Recommended by: Ben Duckworth, Hassell

LARMONT SYDNEY BY LANCEMORE
2/14 Kings Cross Road
Potts Point
Sydney 2011
+61 292958888
lancemore.com.au

CREDIT CARDS	Accepted
PRICE	Mid-range
TYPE	Hotel
ACCOMMODATION	103 Rooms and Suites
FACILITIES	Gym, Yoga
GOOD TO KNOW	Child and pet friendly
RECOMMENDED FOR	Urban

"Contemporary design, walking distance to Potts Point, Kings Cross, Paddington, and the Art Gallery of New South Wales; try to get a room on the upper floors for the harbor views."—Paul Morgan

Recommended by: Paul Morgan, Paul Morgan Architects

ESTABLISHMENT HOTEL
5 Bridge Lane
Central Business District
Sydney 2000
+61 292403100
merivale.com.au

CREDIT CARDS	Accepted
PRICE	High-end
TYPE	Hotel
ACCOMMODATION	31 Suites and Penthouses
FACILITIES	3 Bars, Gym, 3 Restaurants
GOOD TO KNOW	Child friendly
RECOMMENDED FOR	Luxury

Located on Sydney's trendy Bridge Lane, the Establishment Hotel was once a prestigious publishing house. It is now a five-star hotel, which retains the charm of its period character while boasting all the comforts of a twenty-first-century, luxury hotel.

Recommended by: Tom Jordan, Hayball

MEDUSA HOTEL
267 Darlinghurst Road
Darlinghurst
Sydney 2010
+61 293311000
medusa.com.au

CREDIT CARDS	Accepted
PRICE	Mid-range
TYPE	Hotel
ACCOMMODATION	18 Rooms
FACILITIES	In-room kitchenettes
GOOD TO KNOW	Pet friendly
RECOMMENDED FOR	Best-kept secret

"This little hotel is in a great neighborhood of Sydney; friendly staff, with a retro Australian feel to the decor."
—Rodrigo Carazo

Recommended by: Rodrigo Carazo, Carazo Arquitectura

PARAMOUNT HOUSE HOTEL
80 Commonwealth Street
Surry Hills
Sydney 2010
+61 292111222
paramounthousehotel.com

CREDIT CARDS	Accepted
PRICE	Mid-range
TYPE	Hotel
ACCOMMODATION	29 Rooms and Suites
FACILITIES	Cafe, Cinema, Gym, Restaurant, Wine bar, Yoga
GOOD TO KNOW	Child friendly
RECOMMENDED FOR	Where I live

"This neighborhood is a cultural and cafe hub; the hotel itself is attached to the Golden Age Cinema and Bar. It also has easy access to the city and beach."—Mark Landini

"Designed by up-and-coming Melbourne architects Breathe, Paramount House is one of Sydney's newest boutique hotels. Breathe is renowned for its inventive reuse projects and rigorous repurposing of recycled and sustainable materials. A converted Art Deco film studio office building, the Paramount complex includes a cinema, a subterranean bar, cafe, and creative space. The hotel creates a new latticework crown for the building and features an assortment of industrial chic rooms with exposed copper fittings and terrazzo tiles."—Grace Mortlock

Recommended by: Mark Landini, Landini Associates; Grace Mortlock, Other Architects

THE OLD CLARE HOTEL
1 Kensington Street
Chippendale
Sydney 2008
+61 282778277
theoldclarehotel.com.au

CREDIT CARDS	Accepted but not Diners
PRICE	Mid-range
TYPE	Hotel
ACCOMMODATION	62 Rooms and Suites
FACILITIES	Gym, Outdoor swimming pool, 3 Restaurants, Rooftop terrace bar
GOOD TO KNOW	Babysitting, Bicycle rentals, Valet parking
RECOMMENDED FOR	Urban, Where I live

"Amazing rooms with diverse character and excellent adaptive reuse of a heritage building. At street level the public can enjoy its bar and restaurants."—Tom Jordan

"Converted old brewery buildings by Sydney architects Tonkin Zulaikha Greer. Located in Chippendale, near Central Station, Chinatown, and surrounded by great restaurants, galleries, and public spaces."—Isabelle Toland

Recommended by: Tom Jordan, Hayball; Isabelle Toland, Aileen Sage Architects

ADINA APARTMENT HOTEL BONDI BEACH SYDNEY
69-73 Hall Street
Bondi Beach
Sydney 2026
+61 293565062
adinahotels.com

CREDIT CARDS	Accepted
PRICE	Mid-range
TYPE	Apartment hotel
ACCOMMODATION	111 Apartments and Rooms
FACILITIES	Gym, Kitchenettes, Outdoor swimming pool, Spa
GOOD TO KNOW	Babysitting
RECOMMENDED FOR	Budget, Family friendly

"Close to Bondi beach, this is an ideal spot for families."
—Michael Young

Recommended by: Michael Young, Michael Young Studio

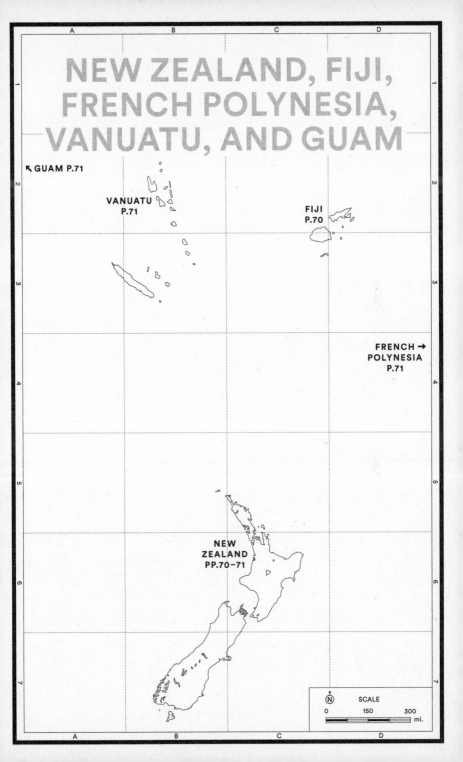

HUKA LODGE
271 Huka Falls Road
Taupo
North Island 3377
New Zealand
+64 73785791
hukalodge.co.nz

CREDIT CARDS..Accepted
PRICE...Blow-out
TYPE..Lodge
ACCOMMODATION..............22 Cottages, Lodges, and Suites
FACILITIES..Outdoor swimming pool,
Restaurant
GOOD TO KNOW..............Adventure sports, Bicycle rentals,
Child friendly
RECOMMENDED FOR...Countryside

"Sublime river setting; beautiful architecture; the cordial attitude of the staff is off the chart; they serve dinner anywhere on the property; and the area's fly-fishing is world-class."—Mark de Reus

Recommended by: Mark de Reus, de Reus Architects

CHATEAU TONGARIRO HOTEL
State Highway 48
Whakapapa Village
Mount Ruapehu
Tongariro National Park
North Island 3951
New Zealand
+64 78923809
chateau.co.nz

CREDIT CARDS..Accepted
PRICE...Mid-range
TYPE..Lodge
ACCOMMODATION...................................115 Rooms and Suites
FACILITIES........................Bar, Gym, Indoor swimming pool,
Sauna, Restaurant
GOOD TO KNOW..Babysitting
RECOMMENDED FOR...Mountains

"The Tongariro Crossing is surely the best one-day walk in the world. The route traverses a series of volcanic landscapes, encompassing red rock moonscapes and iridescent sulphur pools. It is an extraordinary adventure, but also exhausting. Where better to stay than here, a Swiss-style alpine lodge improbably relocated to Middle Earth?"—Grace Mortlock

Recommended by: Grace Mortlock, Other Architects

AZUR LODGE
23 Mackinnon Terrace
Sunshine Bay
Queenstown
South Island 9300
New Zealand
+64 34090588
azur.co.nz

CREDIT CARDS..Accepted
PRICE...High-end
TYPE..Lodge
ACCOMMODATION..9 Villas
FACILITIES...Bar, Fireplace
GOOD TO KNOW.........................Babysitting, Free parking
RECOMMENDED FOR..Eco-conscious

"Overlooking a lake and The Remarkables mountain range; it's close to Queensland's facilities but still a little isolated and tranquil."—Mark de Reus

Recommended by: Mark de Reus, de Reus Architects

WAKAYA CLUB & SPA
Wakaya Island
Lomaiviti Archipelago
Fiji
+679 7736700
wakayaresort.com

CREDIT CARDS..Accepted
PRICE...Blow-Out
TYPE..Resort
ACCOMMODATION.................................12 Bures and Villas
FACILITIES..Bar, Gym, Golf,
Outdoor swimming pool,
Restaurant, Spa
GOOD TO KNOW...Water sports
RECOMMENDED FOR..Eco-conscious

"The diving here is incredible, with completely untouched waters. The resort grows much of its produce so the food is fresh and local. It also employs people from the surrounding villages."—Antoine Predock

Recommended by: Antoine Predock, Antoine Predock Architect

JEAN-MICHEL COUSTEAU RESORT FIJI
Lesiaceva Point Road
Savusavu
Vanua Levu
Fiji
+61 398150379
fijiresort.com

CREDIT CARDS..Accepted
PRICE...Blow-out
TYPE...Resort
ACCOMMODATION...25 Bures
FACILITIES.............................Bar, Outdoor swimming pool,
Restaurant, Spa, Yoga
GOOD TO KNOW...............Babysitting, Valet parking
RECOMMENDED FOR..Island

Recommended by: Sean Godsell, Sean Godsell Architects

THE BRANDO
Tetiaroa
Arue
Society Islands 98702
French Polynesia
+689 40866300
thebrando.com

CREDIT CARDS..Accepted
PRICE...Blow-out
TYPE...Resort
ACCOMMODATION..35 Villas
FACILITIES.............................2 Bars, Boutique, Gym,
Outdoor swimming pool,
3 Restaurants, Spa
GOOD TO KNOW.....................Bicycle rentals, Child friendly,
Scuba diving, Snorkelling
RECOMMENDED FOR........................All-time favorite

"Surrounded by amazing nature, especially underwater life. The villas are luxurious and self-contained."
—Francesca Bucci

Recommended by: Francesca Bucci, BG Studio International

RATUA ISLAND RESORT AND SPA
Ratua Private Island
Luganville
Sanma 32560
Vanuatu
+678 35551
ratua.com

CREDIT CARDS..Accepted
PRICE..High-end
TYPE...Resort
ACCOMMODATION.........................17 Luxury tents and Villas
FACILITIES.........................Bar, 2 Restaurants, Spa, Yoga
GOOD TO KNOW.......................................Horse riding
RECOMMENDED FOR............................Family friendly

"An island resort surrounded by tropical gardens and beaches, with direct water access. There's also a focus on sustainable practices that support and promote the local community, culture, and enterprise."—Isabelle Toland

Recommended by: Isabelle Toland, Aileen Sage Architects

NIKKO HOTEL GUAM
Tamuning
Guam
+1 6716498815
nikkoguam.com

CREDIT CARDS..Accepted
PRICE...Mid-range
TYPE..Hotel
ACCOMMODATION.............................470 Rooms and Suites
FACILITIES....................Bar, Cafe, Outdoor swimming pool,
3 Restaurants, Spa, Yoga
GOOD TO KNOW..Child friendly
RECOMMENDED FOR..Beach

"The last hotel along the strip; remote, quiet, with a great on-site waterslide. It is walking distance to Gun Beach."
—Hu Li

Recommended by: Hu Li, Open Architecture

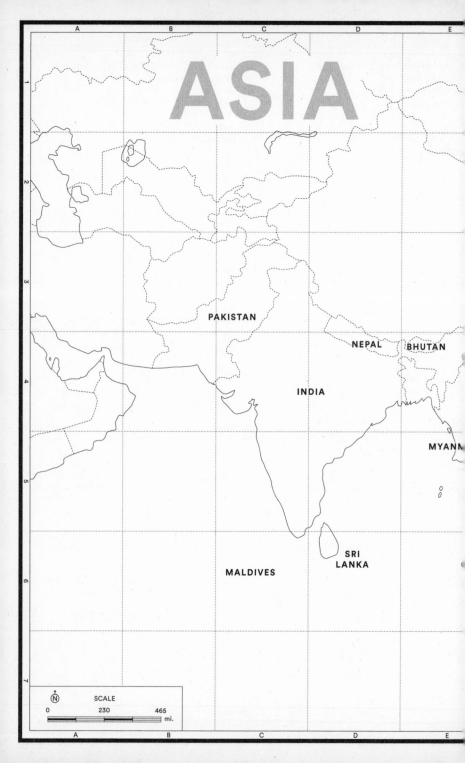

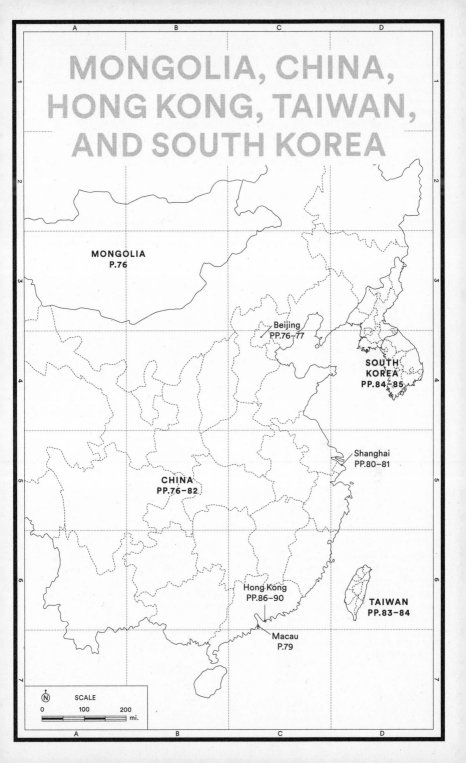

THREE CAMEL LODGE
Omnogobi Aimag
Gobi Desert
Mongolia
+976 11313396
threecamellodge.com

CREDIT CARDS	Accepted
PRICE	High-end
TYPE	Eco-lodge
ACCOMMODATION	40 Gers
FACILITIES	Bar, Restaurant, Spa
GOOD TO KNOW	Call to book
RECOMMENDED FOR	Eco-conscious

"Three Camel Lodge is the only luxury eco-lodge in the Gobi Desert and offers modern comfort that's infused with local spirit and culture."—George Yabu and Glenn Pushelberg

Recommended by: George Yabu and Glenn Pushelberg, Yabu Pushelberg

JALMAN MEADOWS WILDERNESS CAMP
Xuhui
Gorkhi Terelj National Park
Mongolia
+976 11330360
nomadicjourneys.com

CREDIT CARDS	Accepted
PRICE	Mid-range
TYPE	Tented camp
ACCOMMODATION	16 Gers
FACILITIES	Restaurant, Sauna, Wood-burning fireplace
GOOD TO KNOW	Bicycle rentals
RECOMMENDED FOR	Countryside

"Being part of a nomadic camp and traveling through such extreme terrains makes this a holiday where there is no room or time for the predictable luxuries of hotel life—this is an experiential hotel without unecessary accessories. You go back to basics in order to enjoy the treks and the amazing environment."—Margot Krasojević

Recommended by: Margot Krasojević, Margot Krasojević Architecture

AMAN SUMMER PALACE
1 Gongmenqian Street
Summer Palace
Beijing 100091
China
+86 1059879999
aman.com

CREDIT CARDS	Accepted
PRICE	High-end
TYPE	Hotel
ACCOMMODATION	51 Rooms and Suites
FACILITIES	Bar, Gym, Indoor swimming pool, 3 Restaurants, Sauna, Spa, Steam room
GOOD TO KNOW	Traditional arts workshops
RECOMMENDED FOR	All-time favorite, Luxury

"It's like staying in the midst of history."—Marianne Kwok

Recommended by: Craig Dykers, Snøhetta; Marianne Kwok, Kohn Pedersen Fox

BAMBOO WALL HOUSE: COMMUNE BY THE GREAT WALL
The Great Wall
Exit 63 at Shuiguan G6 Jingzang Highway
Beijing 100020
China
+86 1081181888
commune.sohochina.com

CREDIT CARDS	Accepted
PRICE	High-end
TYPE	House hotel
ACCOMMODATION	6 Rooms
FACILITIES	Bar, Outdoor swimming pool, Restaurant, Spa
GOOD TO KNOW	Child friendly
RECOMMENDED FOR	Mountains

"The building [designed by Kengo Kuma] is made of movable screens of glass and lean bamboo sticks, which allows you to fall asleep listening to the sound of crickets and wake up to the view of the Great Wall."
—Gert Wingårdh

Recommended by: Gert Wingårdh, Wingårdhs

BULGARI HOTEL BEIJING

Building 2, Courtyard 8, Xinyuan South Road
Chaoyang
Beijing 100027
China
+86 1085558555
bulgarihotels.com

CREDIT CARDS..Accepted
PRICE...High-end
TYPE..Hotel
ACCOMMODATION....................119 Rooms and Suites
FACILITIES..............................Bar, Indoor swimming pool,
Restaurant, Sauna, Spa, Steam room
GOOD TO KNOW....................................Child friendly
RECOMMENDED FOR..Luxury

Recommended by: Josh Chaiken, Kohn Pedersen Fox

DUGE BOUTIQUE HOTEL

26 Qianyuanensi Hutong
South Luoguo Alley
Dongcheng
Beijing 100009
China
+86 1064457463
dugehotel.com

CREDIT CARDS..Accepted
PRICE..Mid-range
TYPE...Hutong
ACCOMMODATION.......................7 Rooms and Suites
FACILITIES...Bar, Restaurant
GOOD TO KNOW.................................Inner courtyards
RECOMMENDED FOR...........................Best-kept secret

Recommended by: Margot Krasojević, Margot Krasojević
Architecture

THE OPPOSITE HOUSE

Building 1, 11 Sanlitun Road
Chaoyang
Beijing 100027
China
+86 1064176688
theoppositehouse.com

CREDIT CARDS..Accepted
PRICE...High-end
TYPE..Hotel
ACCOMMODATION.......................99 Rooms and Suites
FACILITIES.............Bar, Gym, Indoor swimming pool,
Restaurant, Spa
GOOD TO KNOW....................................Child friendly
RECOMMENDED FOR....................Urban, Where I live,
Wish I'd designed

"Well-designed, centrally located, and close to all the things
you need."—Hu Li

"Its Zen-like environment [by Kengo Kuma] manages
to wash away all of Beijing's hectic hustle and bustle."
—Charles Renfro

Recommended by: Eero Koivisto, Claesson Koivisto
Rune; Marianne Kwok, Kohn Pedersen Fox; Hu Li, Open
Architecture; Alex Mok, Linehouse; Charles Renfro,
Diller Scofidio + Renfro; Ab Rogers, Ab Rogers Design

RED CAPITAL RESIDENCE BEIJING

9 Dongsi Liutiao
Dongcheng
Beijing 100007
China
+86 1064027150
red-capital-residence-beijing.hotel-ds.com

CREDIT CARDS..Accepted
PRICE..Mid-range
TYPE..Apartment hotel
ACCOMMODATION...6 Rooms
FACILITIES.............................Bar, Library, Restaurant
GOOD TO KNOW....................Bicycle rentals, No pets
RECOMMENDED FOR..Urban

Recommended by: François Valentiny, Valentiny HVP
Architects

THE WESTIN CHONGQING LIBERATION SQUARE
222 Xin Hua Road
Yu Zhong
Chongqing 400010
China
+86 2363806666
marriott.com

CREDIT CARDS...Accepted
PRICE..Mid-range
TYPE..Hotel
ACCOMMODATION........336 Apartments, Rooms, and Suites
FACILITIES.......................Gym, Indoor swimming pool, Spa
GOOD TO KNOW..Babysitting
RECOMMENDED FOR............................Worth the travel

"In the middle of a very large city with the most comfortable beds in the world."—Will Alsop

Recommended by: Will Alsop, aLL Design

QUINSAY HOTEL
503 Bailuzhou Road
Xiamen
Fujian 361000
China
+86 18659279595
quinsay.cn

CREDIT CARDS..................................Contact property
PRICE..Mid-range
TYPE..Hotel
ACCOMMODATION..16 Rooms
FACILITIES..Restaurant
GOOD TO KNOW...Child friendly
RECOMMENDED FOR...Urban

"This boutique hotel was converted from a retail space under a high-rise residential tower. The central space is like a family living room in an indoor courtyard, and it has been a local designers' informal club since its opening. If you are staying at the weekend, don't be surprised if you encounter some kind of cultural or design event."—Jingyu Liang

Recommended by: Jingyu Liang, Approach Architecture Studio

FOUR SEASONS HOTEL GUANGZHOU
5 Zhujiang West Road, Pearl River New City
Guangzhou
Guangdong 510623
China
+86 2088833888
fourseasons.com

CREDIT CARDS...Accepted
PRICE..High-end
TYPE..Hotel
ACCOMMODATION...................................344 Rooms and Suites
FACILITIES...Bar, Cafe, Gym,
Indoor swimming pool, 4 Restaurants,
Sauna, Spa, Steam room
GOOD TO KNOW.....................Bicycle rentals, Child friendly,
Valet parking
RECOMMENDED FOR..Urban

"My favorite room is on the 93rd floor, which has full-height glazing with views over the city toward the Pearl River. There is also an excellent restaurant on the 100th floor with fantastic service."—Chris Wilkinson

Recommended by: Chris Wilkinson, Wilkinson Eyre Architects

ALILA YANGSHUO
102 Donglin Road
Guilin
Guangxi 541900
China
+86 7738883999
alilahotels.com

CREDIT CARDS...Accepted
PRICE..High-end
TYPE..Hotel
ACCOMMODATION...................................117 Rooms and Suites
FACILITIES...Bar, Gym, Restaurant,
Outdoor swimming pool, Spa
GOOD TO KNOW...Child friendly
RECOMMENDED FOR..Wish I'd designed

"Interesting play of new and old in this renovated sugar mill."
—Alex Mok

Recommended by: Alex Mok, Linehouse

XY YUNHOUSE

Yangjia Village, Xingping
Yangshuo
Guangxi 541906
China
+86 13687834347
xy-yunhouse.com

CREDIT CARDS..................................Accepted but not Amex
PRICE..Mid-range
TYPE..Hotel
ACCOMMODATION...............................25 Rooms and Villas
FACILITIES...Outdoor swimming pool,
Restaurant
GOOD TO KNOW........................Bicycle rentals, Child friendly
RECOMMENDED FOR.................Countryside, Worth the travel

"Great food and extremely comfortable."—Florian Idenburg

Recommended by: Florian Idenburg, SO–IL

HONG KONG: SEE PAGES 86–90

HYATT REGENCY WUHAN OPTICS VALLEY

1077 Luoyu Road
Wuhan
Hubei 430074
China
+86 2787781234
wuhanopticsvalley.regency.hyatt.com

CREDIT CARDS..Accepted
PRICE..Low-cost
TYPE..Hotel
ACCOMMODATION...................................318 Rooms and Suites
FACILITIES........................Bar, Gym, Indoor swimming pool,
3 Restaurants, Spa
GOOD TO KNOW.................Near East Lake and Yangtze River
RECOMMENDED FOR...Urban

"A sophisticated mixture of traditional elements and materials with modern styling."—Thomas Herzog

Recommended by: Thomas Herzog, Thomas Herzog Architekten

MARCO POLO WUHAN

159 Yanjiang Avenue
Wuhan
Hubei 430072
China
+86 2782778888
marcopolohotels.com

CREDIT CARDS..Accepted
PRICE..Mid-range
TYPE..Hotel
ACCOMMODATION...............................356 Rooms and Suites
FACILITIES.........................Bar, Gym, Indoor swimming pool,
2 Restaurants, Sauna, Steam room
GOOD TO KNOW...Child friendly
RECOMMENDED FOR...Urban

"Located near the Yangtze River with generous views over the city."—Thomas Herzog

Recommended by: Thomas Herzog, Thomas Herzog Architekten

MORPHEUS

Estrada do Istmo Cotai
Macau
China
+853 88688888
cityofdreamsmacau.com

CREDIT CARDS..Accepted
PRICE..High-end
TYPE..Hotel
ACCOMMODATION.......................770 Rooms, Suites and Villas
FACILITIES............................Bar, Gym, 4 Restaurants,
Rooftop swimming pool, Spa
GOOD TO KNOW...No pets
RECOMMENDED FOR...Wish I'd designed

Morpheus is an innovative ultra-luxury hotel, designed by Zaha Hadid, that is part of Macau's City of Dreams hotel and resort complex. Aside from the building itself—a stunning architectural feat—facilities include restaurants by Alain Ducasse and Pierre Hermé, an award-winning art collection, spa, and rooftop pool.

Recommended by: Claudio Lucchesi, Urban Future Organization

ANDAZ XINTIANDI, SHANGHAI

88 Songshan Road
Huangpu
Shanghai 200021
China
+86 2123101234
hyatt.com

CREDIT CARDS...Accepted
PRICE..Mid-range
TYPE..Hotel
ACCOMMODATION..................................307 Rooms and Suites
FACILITIES.........................Bar, Gym, Indoor swimming pool,
3 Restaurants, Spa
GOOD TO KNOW...No pets
RECOMMENDED FOR...Urban

Recommended by: Josh Chaiken, Kohn Pedersen Fox

BELLAGIO SHANGHAI

188 Beisuzhou Road
Hongkou
Shanghai 200080
China
+86 2086009099
bellagioshanghaihotel.com

CREDIT CARDS...Accepted
PRICE..Mid-range
TYPE..Hotel
ACCOMMODATION..................................162 Rooms and Suites
FACILITIES................................Gym, Indoor swimming pool,
Restaurant, Sauna, Spa
GOOD TO KNOW...Five event venues
RECOMMENDED FOR...Urban

Bellagio Shanghai is the first Bellagio hotel outside North
America. This Art Deco-inspired hotel is situated on the
North Bund, next to the historic Waibaidu Bridge. Rooms
are spacious—some with expansive private terraces—
and restaurants include Mansion on One, which recaptures
the elegance of 1920's Shanghai.

Recommended by: Anthony Mallows, WATG

GRAND HYATT SHANGHAI

Jin Mao Tower, 88 Century Avenue
Pudong
Shanghai 200121
China
+86 2150491234
hyatt.com

CREDIT CARDS...Accepted
PRICE..Mid-range
TYPE..Hotel
ACCOMMODATION..................................548 Rooms and Suites
FACILITIES..............................3 Bars, Indoor swimming pool,
Patisserie, 5 Restaurants, Spa, Yoga
GOOD TO KNOW...........................Free parking, Skyline views
RECOMMENDED FOR...Worth the travel

Grand Hyatt Shanghai is situated at the top of the
eighty-eight-story Jin Mao Tower and has stunning views of
the Shanghai cityscape. Rooms are spacious and refined,
and dining options are extensive. Take the time to visit the
swimming pool, one of the highest in the world, if only to
look at the bustle on the Bund below.

Recommended by: Waro Kishi, K.ASSOCIATES/Architects

HENGSHAN PICARDIE HOTEL

534 Hengshan Road
Xuhui
Shanghai 200030
China
+86 2164377050
hengshanhotel.com

CREDIT CARDS...Accepted
PRICE..Mid-range
TYPE..Hotel
ACCOMMODATION..................................236 Rooms and Suites
FACILITIES...............................Bakery, Bar, Boutique,
Gym, 3 Restaurants, Salon
GOOD TO KNOW...Six event venues
RECOMMENDED FOR...........................Best-kept secret, Urban

"Historical colonial hotel located in one of the best
neighborhoods of Shanghai."—Hu Li

Recommended by: Hu Li, Open Architecture

HOTEL INDIGO SHANGHAI ON THE BUND

585 Zhongshan Dong Er Road
Huangpu
Shanghai 200010
China
+86 2133029999
hotelindigo.com

CREDIT CARDS	Accepted
PRICE	Mid-range
TYPE	Hotel
ACCOMMODATION	184 Rooms and Suites
FACILITIES	Bar, Gym, Indoor swimming pool, Restaurant
GOOD TO KNOW	Babysitting, No pets
RECOMMENDED FOR	All-time favorite, Family friendly, Urban

"Located in the heart of Shanghai, with a spectacular view of the typical utopian urban future—it feels like you are in a movie."—Nathalie Frankowski and Cruz Garcia

Recommended by: Nathalie Frankowski and Cruz Garcia, WAI Architecture Think Tank; François Valentiny, Valentiny HVP Architects

THE PENINSULA SHANGHAI

32 The Bund 32 Zhongshan Dong Yi Road
Huangpu
Shanghai 200002
China
+86 2123272888
peninsula.com

CREDIT CARDS	Accepted
PRICE	High-end
TYPE	Hotel
ACCOMMODATION	235 Rooms and Suites
FACILITIES	Bar, Gym, Indoor swimming pool, 3 Restaurants, Rooftop terrace bar, Sauna, Spa
GOOD TO KNOW	Child friendly
RECOMMENDED FOR	Urban

"A perfect location in a great city, with beautiful and lively public rooms downstairs and up, paired with private, discreet, perfectly designed guest accommodation."
—Louis Hedgecock

Recommended by: Louis Hedgecock, HOK Architects

THE PULI HOTEL AND SPA

1 Changde Road
Jing'an
Shanghai 200040
China
+86 2132039999
thepuli.com

CREDIT CARDS	Accepted
PRICE	Mid-range
TYPE	Hotel
ACCOMMODATION	229 Rooms and Suites
FACILITIES	Bar, Gym, Indoor swimming pool, Restaurant, Sauna, Spa
GOOD TO KNOW	No pets
RECOMMENDED FOR	Luxury, Spa

"One of the world's most elegant hotels, the PuLi also has an amazingly serene and well-staffed spa. The changing rooms are luxurious and huge, with giant hot baths; the massages are otherworldly. The long pool, facing a bank of windows looking out on to a small park in the center of Shanghai, provides a relaxing and enchanting end to a day."
—Dan Wood

Recommended by: Florian Idenburg, SO–IL; Christian de Portzamparc, 2 Portzamparc; Ab Rogers, Ab Rogers Design; Dan Wood, WORKac

THE WATERHOUSE AT SOUTH BUND

1-3 Maojiayuan Road
Huangpu
Shanghai 200010
China
+86 2160802988
marriott.com

CREDIT CARDS	Accepted
PRICE	Mid-range
TYPE	Hotel
ACCOMMODATION	19 Rooms and Suites
FACILITIES	Bar, Restaurant
GOOD TO KNOW	No pets
RECOMMENDED FOR	Wish I'd designed

"The contrast between old and new architecture is masterfully resolved here—both remain recognizable and in tension. The hotel was built within a disused 1930s Japanese army headquarters. The original concrete building has been restored, while new additions are housed beneath a Cor-Ten steel roof extension."—Marta Laudani

Recommended by: Marta Laudani, Marta Laudani Design; Alex Mok, Linehouse

THE TEMPLE HOUSE

81 Bitieshi Street
Chengdu
Sichuan 610021
China
+86 2866369999
thetemplehousehotel.com

CREDIT CARDS...Accepted
PRICE...Mid-range
TYPE...Hotel
ACCOMMODATION...................142 Apartments, Penthouses,
Rooms, and Suites
FACILITIES.....................Bar, Gym, Indoor swimming pool,
3 Restaurants, Spa, Steam room
GOOD TO KNOW....................................Child friendly
RECOMMENDED FOR.........................Wish I'd designed

"The Temple House's blend of new and old, its restaurant
design, and the way it melts into the city are all things that
make me extremely jealous not to have designed it myself."
—Forth Bagley

Recommended by: Forth Bagley, Kohn Pedersen Fox;
Marcelo Morettin, Andrade Morettin Arquitetos

AMANFAYUN

22 Fayun Lane, West Lake Street
Hangzhou
Zhejiang 310013
China
+86 57187329999
aman.com

CREDIT CARDS...Accepted
PRICE...High-end
TYPE...Hotel
ACCOMMODATION...................46 Rooms, Suites, and Villas
FACILITIES.....................Bar, Gym, Outdoor swimming pool,
5 Restaurants, Spa,
Traditional bathhouse, Yoga
GOOD TO KNOW...........................Situated in a wooded valley
RECOMMENDED FOR...................................Best-kept secret

"In the heart of a forest, surrounded by temples, nearby
lakes—you can lose all concept of time."—Claire Bétaille
and Bruno Moinard

Recommended by: Claire Bétaille and Bruno Moinard,
4BI & Associés

FOUR SEASONS HOTEL HANGZHOU AT WEST LAKE

5 Lingyin Road
Hangzhou
Zhejiang 310013
China
+86 57188298888
fourseasons.com

CREDIT CARDS...Accepted
PRICE...High-end
TYPE...Hotel
ACCOMMODATION........................78 Rooms, Suites, and Villas
FACILITIES..Bar, Gym,
Indoor and outdoor swimming pools,
2 Restaurants, Yoga
GOOD TO KNOW....................................Babysitting
RECOMMENDED FOR.......All-time favorite, Wish I'd designed

"Simple, and really beautiful."—Michael Schumacher

"A wonderful base, this hotel allows guests to experience
the city's rich Buddhist history, resources, and Chinese
tranquility in one place."—Sonali Rastogi

Recommended by: Sonali Rastogi, Morphogenesis;
Michael Schumacher, Schneider+Schumacher

WILD HOMESTAY

Yingchuan Village
Yellow Mountains
Zhejiang
China
+86 13601855447
wildhomestay.com

CREDIT CARDS...Accepted
PRICE...Low-cost
TYPE...Guesthouse
ACCOMMODATION...4 Cottages
FACILITIES.......................................Restaurant, Yoga
GOOD TO KNOW.........................Bicycle rentals, Pet friendly
RECOMMENDED FOR...Mountains

"A humble retreat in a genuine Chinese village with a
beautiful mountain backdrop. Great for cycling."—Alex Mok

Recommended by: Alex Mok, Linehouse

SILKS PLACE TAROKO

18 Tianxiang Road
Xiulin
Hualien 972
Taiwan
+886 38691155
taroko.silksplace.com

CREDIT CARDS	Accepted
PRICE	Mid-range
TYPE	Resort
ACCOMMODATION	160 Rooms and Suites
FACILITIES	Bar, Gym, Indoor and outdoor swimming pools, 2 Restaurants, Sauna, Spa, Tennis, Yoga
GOOD TO KNOW	Bicycle rentals, Child friendly
RECOMMENDED FOR	Countryside, Mountains

"Incredibly peaceful hotel 'floating' in a deep ravine inside the dramatic and endless Tarok Gorge on Taiwan's eastern coast. It feels like the edge of the world, completely secret and completely hidden. The hotel has a rooftop garden and pool where you can swim alongside the mountain walls or relax at night by the fireside under the stars."
—Alex Warnock-Smith

Recommended by: Alex Warnock-Smith, Urban Projects Bureau

AMBA TAIPEI XIMENDING

Section 77, 2 Wuchang Street
Taipei 10843
Taiwan
+886 223755111
amba-hotels.com

CREDIT CARDS	Accepted
PRICE	Mid-range
TYPE	Hotel
ACCOMMODATION	160 Rooms
FACILITIES	Bakery, Bar, Restaurant
GOOD TO KNOW	Child friendly
RECOMMENDED FOR	Where I live

"Great locale and casual vibe."—Grace Cheung

Recommended by: Grace Cheung, XRANGE Architecture + Design

ÉCLAT HOTEL TAIPEI

Section 1, 370 Dunhua South Road
Taipei 106, Taiwan
+886 227848888
eclathotels.com

CREDIT CARDS	Accepted
PRICE	Mid-range
TYPE	Hotel
ACCOMMODATION	60 Rooms and Suites
FACILITIES	2 Restaurants
GOOD TO KNOW	Babysitting
RECOMMENDED FOR	Urban

Recommended by: Dorin Stefan, Dorin Stefan Birou de Arhitectura

WOOLLOOMOOLOO ZZZZZ

3F, 385 Section 4, Xinyi Road
Taipei 11051, Taiwan
+886 287893978
woolloomooloo.tw

CREDIT CARDS	Accepted
PRICE	Mid-range
TYPE	Bed and Breakfast
ACCOMMODATION	6 Rooms
FACILITIES	Bar, Delicatessen, Restaurant
GOOD TO KNOW	Call or email to book
RECOMMENDED FOR	Best-kept secret

Recommended by: Grace Cheung, XRANGE Architecture + Design

HOTEL DÙA

165 Linsen 1st Road
Kaohsiung 800, Taiwan
+886 72722999
hoteldua.com

CREDIT CARDS	Accepted
PRICE	Low-cost
TYPE	Hotel
ACCOMMODATION	145 Rooms
FACILITIES	Bar, Gym, 3 Restaurants
GOOD TO KNOW	Near a traditional market
RECOMMENDED FOR	Where I live

An elegant oasis of calm in the heart of the city's bustling Kaohsiung district, Hotel Dùa is a perfect base for exploration, with a wellness-focused restaurant and a more traditional dim sum option.

Recommended by: Yu-lin Chen, MAYU Architects+

GLORIA MANOR
101 Gongyuan Road
Kenting
Pingtung 946
Taiwan
+886 88863666
gloriamanor.com

CREDIT CARDS..Accepted
PRICE...Mid-range
TYPE..House hotel
ACCOMMODATION.......................................60 Rooms
FACILITIES...............................Bar, Outdoor swimming pool,
Restaurant, Spa, Yoga
GOOD TO KNOW.......................Chiang Kai-shek's study room
open to the public
RECOMMENDED FOR..Countryside

Formerly Kenting House and revamped as Gloria Manor in 2012, the design concept for the hotel is inspired by nature and the local environment, from the interior accents to the design and construction. Hot water is provided by solar energy, and an elaborate handmade bamboo weave structure built by six craftsmen is the centerpiece of the lobby.

Recommended by: Yu-lin Chen, MAYU Architects+

BAEKYANGSA
1239 Baekyang-ro
Bukha-myeon
Jangseong
Jeollanam
South Korea
+82 613920434
baekyangsa.templestay.com

CREDIT CARDS..Accepted
PRICE..Low-cost
TYPE..Temple
ACCOMMODATION..............................Communal living
FACILITIES..Cookery class,
Worship programmes
GOOD TO KNOW......................Buddhist temple rules
RECOMMENDED FOR..Countryside

"Baekyangsa temple holds a special place in my heart: from the early morning walks through stunning forests, to the absolute privilege of cooking and learning from the generous, welcoming [Zen Buddhist nun and chef] Jeong Kwan."—Nicolas Koff

Recommended by: Nicolas Koff, Office Ou

MILLENNIUM SEOUL HILTON
50 Sowol-ro, Jung-gu
Seoul 04637
South Korea
+82 27537788
hilton.com

CREDIT CARDS..Accepted
PRICE...Mid-range
TYPE..Hotel
ACCOMMODATION................................709 Rooms and Suites
FACILITIES.........................Bar, Driving range, Gym,
Indoor swimming pool,
4 Restaurants, Spa
GOOD TO KNOW....................................Free parking
RECOMMENDED FOR...............................Where I live

Millennium Seoul Hilton's downtown location and range of facilities—which include an award-winning medi-spa and even a driving range for golf enthusiasts—make it an ideal base for tourists and business travelers alike.

Recommended by: Seunghoy Kim, KYWC Architects

NOOK
6-2 Sowol-ro, 2 Na-gil, Yongsan-gu
Seoul 04326
South Korea
nookseoul.com

CREDIT CARDS..Accepted
PRICE..Low-cost
TYPE..Home rental
ACCOMMODATION...2 Rooms
FACILITIES...Kitchen
GOOD TO KNOW.......................................Self-catering
RECOMMENDED FOR....................................Budget, Urban

Nook is a small yet perfectly formed, three-story historic wooden house in the heart of Seoul. It is a self-catering home, and guests have access to kitchen and laundry facilities. For its design, the hotel received the Seoul Architecture Award in 2016.

Recommended by: Seunghoy Kim, KYWC Architects

PARK HYATT SEOUL

606 Teheran-ro, Gangnam-gu
Seoul 06174
South Korea
+82 220161234
hyatt.com

CREDIT CARDS	Accepted
PRICE	Mid-range
TYPE	Hotel
ACCOMMODATION	185 Rooms and Suites
FACILITIES	Bar, Gym, Indoor swimming pool, 3 Restaurants, Sauna, Spa, Yoga
GOOD TO KNOW	Babysitting, Valet parking
RECOMMENDED FOR	Spa

"Designed to be slick and modern with a nod to Korean history and traditions... it's up high over the city so completely surreal and otherworldly."—Hani Rashid

Recommended by: Hani Rashid, Asymptote Architecture

SHILLA STAY GURO SEOUL

210 Dasan-ro
Seoul 04856
South Korea
+82 222300700
shillastay.com

CREDIT CARDS	Accepted
PRICE	Low-cost
TYPE	Hotel
ACCOMMODATION	310 Rooms
FACILITIES	Bar, Gym
GOOD TO KNOW	Free parking
RECOMMENDED FOR	Budget

Shilla Stay Guro Seoul is an elegant business hotel, conveniently situated in the city's tech hub. Although the hotel is designed primarily for business travelers, children are welcome.

Recommended by: Piero Lissoni, Lissoni Associati

LOTTE BUYEO RESORT BAEKSANGWON

400 Baekjemun-ro, Gyuam-myeon
Buyeo
South Chungcheong 33115
South Korea
+82 419391000
lottebuyeoresort.com

CREDIT CARDS	Accepted
PRICE	Mid-range
TYPE	Resort
ACCOMMODATION	300 Rooms and Suites
FACILITIES	Indoor and outdoor swimming pools, Restaurant, Sauna
GOOD TO KNOW	Pet friendly
RECOMMENDED FOR	Family friendly

A large resort with more than 300 guest rooms, Lotte Buyeo Resort Baeksangwon plays with the internal and external space with balcony-style corridors and provides a pop of color in its urban surroundings. The resort is an ideal base from which to explore the historic city of Buyeo, and welcomes both dogs and children.

[This hotel was designed by KYWC Architects.]

Recommended by: Seunghoy Kim, KYWC Architects

PARADISE HOTEL BUSAN

1408-5 Jung-dong Haeundae-gu
Busan
Yeongnam
South Korea
+82 517422121
busanparadisehotel.co.kr

CREDIT CARDS	Accepted
PRICE	Mid-range
TYPE	Resort
ACCOMMODATION	532 Rooms and Suites
FACILITIES	Bakery, 2 Bars, Hot-spring bath, Outdoor swimming pool, 4 Restaurants, Sauna, Spa
GOOD TO KNOW	Child friendly
RECOMMENDED FOR	Beach

Located on Haeundae Beach and framed by the mountains, Paradise Hotel Busan is a family friendly coastal retreat with truly comprehensive facilities. There are ten on-site restaurants, outdoor oceanic hot springs, and a casino. For younger guests, the Kids' Village includes a PlayStation lounge and a driving zone presented by BMW.

Recommended by: Seunghoy Kim, KYWC Architects

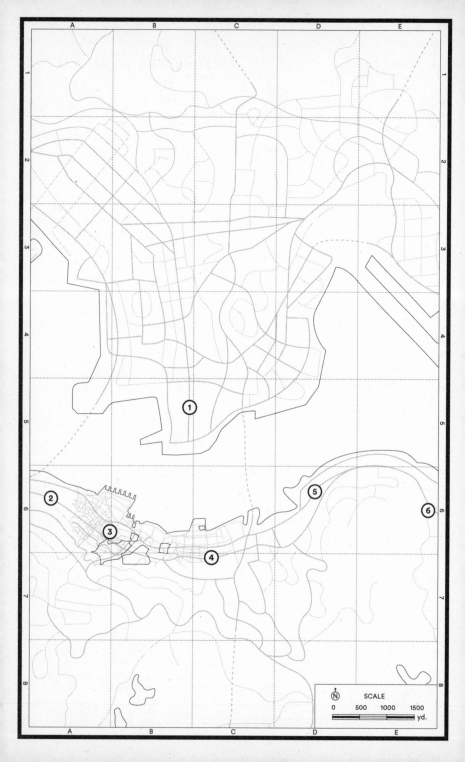

HONG KONG

HOTEL ICON
17 Science Museum Road
Tsim Sha Tsui, Hong Kong
+852 34001000
hotel-icon.com

CREDIT CARDS	Accepted
PRICE	Mid-range
TYPE	Hotel
ACCOMMODATION	262 Rooms and Suites
FACILITIES	Bar, Gym, Outdoor swimming pool, 3 Restaurants, Spa
GOOD TO KNOW	Babysitting
RECOMMENDED FOR	Best-kept secret

Recommended by: Matthias Sauerbruch and Louisa Hutton, Sauerbruch Hutton

INTERCONTINENTAL HONG KONG
18 Salisbury Road
Tsim Sha Tsui, Hong Kong
+852 27211211
ihg.com

CREDIT CARDS	Accepted
PRICE	Mid-range
TYPE	Hotel
ACCOMMODATION	503 Rooms and Suites
FACILITIES	Bar, Gym, Outdoor swimming pool, 5 Restaurants, Sauna, Spa
GOOD TO KNOW	Babysitting, Valet parking
RECOMMENDED FOR	Spa

"Knowledgeable staff and excellent tea."—Anthony Mallows

Recommended by: Anthony Mallows, WATG

THE PENINSULA HONG KONG
Salisbury Road
Tsim Sha Tsui, Hong Kong
+852 29202888
peninsula.com

CREDIT CARDS	Accepted
PRICE	High-end
TYPE	Hotel
ACCOMMODATION	300 Rooms and Suites
FACILITIES	Bar, Gym, Indoor swimming pool, 8 Restaurants, Sauna, Spa, Steam room
GOOD TO KNOW	Child friendly
RECOMMENDED FOR	Luxury, Worth the travel

"This iconic landmark truly understands how to deliver on a luxury experience and timeless design."—Daniel Welborn

The oldest hotel in Hong Kong, and affectionately referred to as the "Grand Dame of the Far East," The Peninsula Hong Kong remains a byword for timeless glamour and a benchmark for impeccable hospitality.

Recommended by: Nabil Gholam, Nabil Gholam Architects; Jean-Paul Viguier, Jean-Paul Viguier et Associés; Daniel Welborn, The Gettys Group; Ken Yeang, Hamzah & Yeang

THE RITZ-CARLTON, HONG KONG
1 Austin Road West, International Commerce Centre
Tsim Sha Tsui, Hong Kong
+85 222632263
ritzcarlton.com

CREDIT CARDS	Accepted
PRICE	High-end
TYPE	Hotel
ACCOMMODATION	312 Rooms and Suites
FACILITIES	Bar, Gym, Indoor swimming pool, 3 Restaurants, Sauna, Spa, Steam room
GOOD TO KNOW	Child friendly
RECOMMENDED FOR	Luxury

"Exquisite rooms with unmatched views, from one of the tallest hotel's in the world."—Rodrigo Carazo

Recommended by: Rodrigo Carazo, Carazo Architecture

W HONG KONG
1 Austin Road West
Tsim Sha Tsui, Hong Kong
+852 37172222
w-hongkong.com

CREDIT CARDS	Accepted
PRICE	Mid-range
TYPE	Hotel
ACCOMMODATION	393 Rooms and Suites
FACILITIES	Bar, Gym, Outdoor swimming pool, 3 Restaurants, Rooftop terrace bar, Sauna, Spa
GOOD TO KNOW	Valet parking
RECOMMENDED FOR	Urban, Worth the travel

"Amazing design, technology, and views over Hong Kong city and the sea."—Farid Chacon

Recommended by: Ludovico Centis, The Empire; Farid Chacon, NMD NOMADAS

HOTEL JEN HONG KONG BY SHANGRI-LA
508 Queen's Road West
Sheung Wan
Hong Kong
+852 29741234
hoteljen.com

CREDIT CARDS..Accepted
PRICE..Mid-range
TYPE..Hotel
ACCOMMODATION..................................283 Rooms and Suites
FACILITIES..Bar, Gym,
                              Outdoor swimming pool, Restaurant
GOOD TO KNOW..Babysitting
RECOMMENDED FOR...Urban

Hotel Jen Hong Kong has a less formal atmosphere than other more traditional Shangri-La hotels, but it still boasts the world-class facilities and warm hospitality that the group has built its reputation upon. Highlights include a rooftop pool (closed during the winter months) and the concierge gives hints and tips for making the most of a stay in Hong Kong.

Recommended by: Kiyoshi Sey Takeyama, Amorphe Takeyama & Associates

MANDARIN ORIENTAL, HONG KONG
5 Connaught Road Central
Central
Hong Kong
+852 25220111
mandarinoriental.com

CREDIT CARDS..Accepted
PRICE..High-end
TYPE..Hotel
ACCOMMODATION..................................499 Rooms and Suites
FACILITIES..2 Bars, Bakery, Gym,
                                            Indoor swimming pool,
                                            7 Restaurants, Sauna, Spa
GOOD TO KNOW..Child friendly
RECOMMENDED FOR...Luxury, Urban

"Absolutely the best service."—Michael Stiff

Recommended by: Michael Stiff, Stiff + Trevillion

THE LANDMARK MANDARIN ORIENTAL
15 Queen's Road Central
Central
Hong Kong
+852 21320188
mandarinoriental.com

CREDIT CARDS..Accepted
PRICE..High-end
TYPE..Hotel
ACCOMMODATION..................................111 Rooms and Suites
FACILITIES..................2 Bars, Gym, Indoor swimming pool,
                              4 Restaurants, Sauna, Spa, Yoga
GOOD TO KNOW..................................Personal chefs available,
                                                          Valet parking
RECOMMENDED FOR...Luxury, Urban

"As a frequent guest, there is no better level of service and no place with a warmer welcome."—Forth Bagley

"You can feel you are in the heart of the city; the hospitality is typically Asian in terms of attention to detail and care."—Waro Kishi

Recommended by: Forth Bagley, Kohn Pedersen Fox; Waro Kishi, K.ASSOCIATES/Architects

GRAND HYATT HONG KONG
1 Harbour Road
Wan Chai
Hong Kong
+852 25881234
hyatt.com

CREDIT CARDS..Accepted
PRICE..High-end
TYPE..Hotel
ACCOMMODATION..................................542 Rooms and Suites
FACILITIES..2 Bars, Gym,
                                            Outdoor swimming pool,
                                            8 Restaurants, Spa
GOOD TO KNOW..On the waterfront,
                                                          Valet parking
RECOMMENDED FOR...Urban

"The very best service you can get from any hotel in the world (and the food is not bad either)."—Alexander Wong

Recommended by: Alexander Wong, Alexander Wong Architects

THE FLEMING
41 Fleming Road
Wan Chai
Hong Kong
+852 36072288
thefleming.com

CREDIT CARDS..Accepted
PRICE..Mid-range
TYPE...Hotel
ACCOMMODATION.....................................66 Rooms
FACILITIES..........................Bar, Gym, Restaurant
GOOD TO KNOW................Near Hong Kong Convention and
Exhibition Centre
RECOMMENDED FOR...Urban

"Stylish and playful on a smaller scale for an urban environment."—Alex Mok

Recommended by: Alex Mok, Linehouse

THE UPPER HOUSE
Pacific Place, 88 Queensway
Wan Chai
Hong Kong
+852 29181838
upperhouse.com

CREDIT CARDS..Accepted
PRICE..High-end
TYPE...Hotel
ACCOMMODATION..........117 Rooms, Penthouses, and Suites
FACILITIES...................Bar, Gym, Restaurant, Yoga
GOOD TO KNOW.....................In-room spa treatments
RECOMMENDED FOR.........................All-time favorite,
Luxury, Urban, Where I live,
Wish I'd designed, Worth the travel

"The upper suites with corner views are quite spectacular, as is the service. I was handed a croissant and coffee as I left for a very early flight—an unexpected and thoughtful gesture."—Amanda Levete

"Stay here for the rooms—you look down at the city below and it's like being in the movie Tron. A former office building, it's astringent and minimalist."—Antoine Predock

"Located in Central Hong Kong, this boutique hotel is a great example of simple, modern luxury. Café Grey is one of the best places in the city for a drink with a view."—Daniel Welborn

[This hotel was designed by AFSO.]

Recommended by: Bernardo Fort-Brescia, Arquitectonica; André Fu, AFSO; Kelly Hoppen, Kelly Hoppen Interiors; Amanda Levete, AL_A; Antoine Predock, Antoine Predock Architect; Charles Renfro, Diller Scofidio + Renfro; David Rockwell, Rockwell Group; Daniel Welborn, The Gettys Group; Michael Young, Michael Young Studio

TUVE
16 Tsing Fung Street
Causeway Bay
Hong Kong
+852 39958899
tuve.hk

CREDIT CARDS..Accepted
PRICE..Mid-range
TYPE...Hotel
ACCOMMODATION.....................................64 Rooms
FACILITIES..Restaurant
GOOD TO KNOW...................."handy Smartphones" available
RECOMMENDED FOR.............................All-time favorite

"Incredible sequence of spaces. It makes you feel calm in the midst of the intense energy of Hong Kong."—Ben Duckworth

Recommended by: Ben Duckworth, Hassell

EAST, HONG KONG
29 Tai Koo Shing Road
Quarry Bay
Hong Kong
+852 39683968
east-hongkong.com

CREDIT CARDS..Accepted
PRICE..Mid-range
TYPE...Hotel
ACCOMMODATION...................................345 Rooms and Suites
FACILITIES.....................Bar, Gym, Outdoor swimming pool,
Restaurant, Spa
GOOD TO KNOW...................................Bicycle rentals
RECOMMENDED FOR...Urban

"EAST is a business-minded hotel that's human in every way, taking all needs of the guest into account with plenty of personality, excellent spa and gym facilities, and high-end tech facilities."—Satyendra Pakhalé

Recommended by: Satyendra Pakhalé, Satyendra Pakhalé Associates

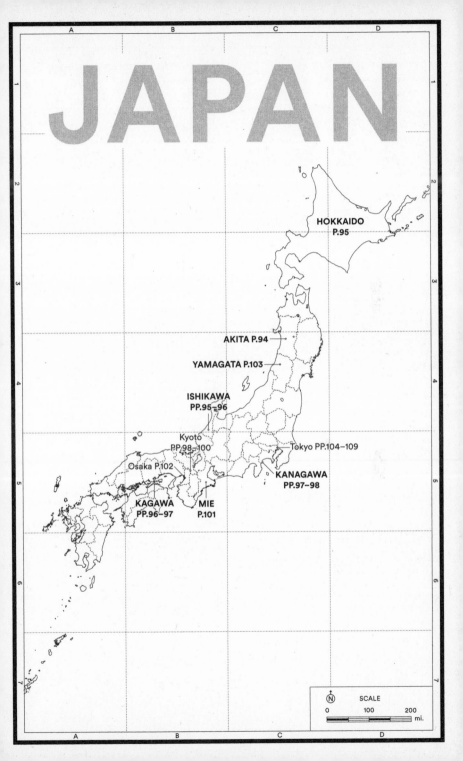

KUROYU ONSEN
Tazawako obonai aza kuroyuzawa 2-1
Semboku
Akita 014-1201
Japan
+81 187462214
kuroyu.com

CREDIT CARDS	Accepted
PRICE	Mid-range
TYPE	Onsen resort
ACCOMMODATION	16 Rooms
FACILITIES	Hot-spring and open-air baths, Restaurant, Sauna, Spa
GOOD TO KNOW	Free parking
RECOMMENDED FOR	Spa

"There is nothing quite like taking a hot spring bath in the middle of nature, steam rising into the cold fall air."
—Nicolas Koff

Recommended by: Nicolas Koff, Office Ou

TSURUNOYU
50 Kokuyurin
Semboku
Akita 014-1204
Japan
+81 187462139
tsurunoyu.com

CREDIT CARDS	Not accepted
PRICE	Mid-range
TYPE	Onsen resort
ACCOMMODATION	34 Rooms
FACILITIES	Hot-spring and open-air baths, Restaurant
GOOD TO KNOW	Cash payments only
RECOMMENDED FOR	Eco-conscious

"Huge outdoor hot spring surrounded by nature."
—Kiyoshi Sey Takeyama

Recommended by: Kiyoshi Sey Takeyama, Amorphe Takeyama & Associates

SETOUCHI RETREAT AONAGI
794-1 Yanaidani-cho
Matsuyama
Ehime 799-2641
Japan
+81 899779500
setouchi-aonagi.com

CREDIT CARDS	Accepted
PRICE	High-end
TYPE	Boutique hotel
ACCOMMODATION	7 Suites
FACILITIES	Boutique, Hot-spring bath, Indoor and outdoor swimming pools, Restaurant, Sauna, Spa
GOOD TO KNOW	Free parking
RECOMMENDED FOR	Worth the travel, Wish I'd designed

Tadao Ando's seven-suite retreat is a minimalist's dream, where contemporary lines and raw finishes do all the talking. In a mountainous location, Setouchi Retreat Aonagi looks out over the calm Seto Inland Sea, from which the hotel's seafood is sourced daily. The sea is also visible from the hotel's private spa.

Recommended by: Boris Bernaskoni, BERNASKONI; Anastasios Kotsiopoulos, AM Kotsiopoulos & Partners Architects

GRAND HYATT FUKUOKA
1-2-82 Sumiyoshi
Hakata-ku
Fukuoka 812-0018
Japan
+81 922821234
hyatt.com

CREDIT CARDS	Accepted
PRICE	Mid-range
TYPE	Hotel
ACCOMMODATION	370 Rooms and Suites
FACILITIES	2 Bars, Gym, Indoor swimming pool, 3 Restaurants, Spa
GOOD TO KNOW	No pets
RECOMMENDED FOR	Best-kept secret

Recommended by: Felino Palafox, Jr., Palafox Associates

KURAYADO IROHA RYOKAN

589-4 Miyajima
Hatsukaichi
Hiroshima 739-0559
Japan
+81 829440168
iroha.to

CREDIT CARDS	Accepted
PRICE	Mid-range
TYPE	Ryokan
ACCOMMODATION	18 Rooms
FACILITIES	Open-air bath, Restaurant, Spa
GOOD TO KNOW	Near Itsukushima Shrine
RECOMMENDED FOR	Countryside

Recommended by: Bruce Kuwabara, KPMB Architects

ZABORIN RYOKAN

76-4 Hanazono Kutchan-cho
Abuta
Hokkaido 044-0084
Japan
+81 136230003
zaborin.com

CREDIT CARDS	Accepted
PRICE	Blow-out
TYPE	Ryokan
ACCOMMODATION	15 Villas
FACILITIES	Bar, Hot-spring and open-air baths, Library, Restaurant
GOOD TO KNOW	Near one of Japan's largest ski resorts, Valet parking
RECOMMENDED FOR	Eco-conscious

Zaborin prides itself on the peace and tranquility it offers
to guests. Each villa has its own private indoor and outdoor
bath with spring water fed directly from a hot spring.

Recommended by: Piero Lissoni, Lissoni Associati

ARAYA TOTOAN

Yamashiro Onsen Yunogawa
Kaga
Ishikawa 922-0242
Japan
+81 761770010
araya-totoan.com

CREDIT CARDS	Accepted
PRICE	High-end
TYPE	Onsen resort
ACCOMMODATION	18 Rooms
FACILITIES	Hot-spring bath, Restaurant
GOOD TO KNOW	Dinner reservations in advance
RECOMMENDED FOR	Best-kept secret

"One of the world's most culturally rich hospitality
experiences; worth traveling for."—Deborah Berke

Recommended by: Deborah Berke, Deborah Berke Partners

BENIYA MUKAYU

55-1-3 Yamashiro Onsen
Kaga
Ishikawa 922-0242
Japan
+81 761771340
mukayu.com

CREDIT CARDS	Accepted
PRICE	High-end
TYPE	Onsen resort
ACCOMMODATION	16 Rooms
FACILITIES	Boutique, Hot-spring and open-air baths, Restaurant, Sauna, Spa, Yoga
GOOD TO KNOW	Child friendly (7 and over)
RECOMMENDED FOR	All-time favorite, Countryside

Recommended by: Kiyoshi Sey Takeyama, Amorphe
Takeyama & Associates

KINJOHRO
2-23 Hashibacho
Kanazawa
Ishikawa 920-0911
Japan
+81 762218188
kinjohro.co.jp

CREDIT CARDS..Accepted
PRICE...High-end
TYPE..Ryokan
ACCOMMODATION.......................................6 Rooms
FACILITIES..Restaurant
GOOD TO KNOW........................Free parking, Smoking rooms
RECOMMENDED FOR............................All-time favorite

A traditional Japanese ryokan featuring six guest rooms,
Kinjohro is a space designed for the purpose of unwinding
and reflecting. Many of the bathtubs in the rooms are
made with wood from the prized Japanese Hinoki tree,
which releases a soothing cypress scent.

**Recommended by: Dorin Stefan, Dorin Stefan Birou
de Arhitectura**

AUBERGE DE OISHI
65 Yashimanishi-machi
Takamsatsu
Kagawa 761-0113
Japan
+81 878432235
auberge-de-oishi.jp

CREDIT CARDS..Accepted
PRICE..Mid-range
TYPE..Ryokan
ACCOMMODATION...5 Rooms
FACILITIES.........................Delicatessen, Restaurant
GOOD TO KNOW.......Near Open Air Architectural Museum,
No televisions
RECOMMENDED FOR............................Best-kept secret

This ryokan is a little piece of France on Japan's Shikoku
Island. Auberge de Oishi features an on-site, European-
inspired delicatessen that sells local produce and freshly
baked bread. The restaurant also draws inspiration from
French culinary traditions.

Recommended by: Patrick Reymond, Atelier Oï

BENESSE HOUSE
Gotanji
Naoshima
Kagawa 761-3110
Japan
+81 878923223
benesse-artsite.jp

CREDIT CARDS..Accepted
PRICE..Mid-range
TYPE...Hotel
ACCOMMODATION......................65 Rooms and Suites
FACILITIES...Restaurant, Spa
GOOD TO KNOW............................Child friendly (5 and over)
RECOMMENDED FOR..........................All-time favorite, Island,
Mountains, Spa,
Wish I'd designed,
Worth the travel

"The small remote island of Naoshima is the most sublime
combination of art and nature. The island offers some of
the world's greatest art experiences, as well as impressive
nature. Benesse House offers something truly original;
to be alone with some of the greatest pieces of art one
can find."—Jani Kristoffersen

"This hotel is designed by Tadao Ando and feels more like
a gallery than hotel, with its minimal design, natural light,
and contemporary art. We love the concept of a museum
where visitors can sleep surrounded by nature—it's a
magical opportunity."—Belén Moneo and Jeffrey Brock

"Beautifully simple hotel set within easy walking or cycling
distance of Naoshima's museums and pavilions. You get
to spend the night in a Tadao Ando-designed building."
—Graham West

**Recommended by: Thomas Bartlett, Waldo Works;
Manuel Cervantes, CC Arquitectos; Jack Diamond,
Diamond Schmitt; Biba Dow, Dow Jones Architects;
Norman Foster, Foster + Partners; Bernardo and Paulo
Jacobsen, Jacobsen Arquitetura; Jani Kristoffersen,
Guise; Bruce Kuwabara, KPMB Architects; Belén Moneo
and Jeffrey Brock, Moneo Brock; Adrian Moreno and
Maria Samaniego, Arquitectura X; Ron Radziner, Marmol
Radziner; Salvador Reyes Ríos, Reyes Ríos + Larraín
Arquitectos; Patrick Reymond, Atelier Oï; José Juan Rivera
Rio, JJRR/Arquitectura; Michel Rojkind, Rojkind Arquitectos;
Cristian Santandreu, A2arquitectos; Daniel Suduca and
Thierry Mérillou, Suduca & Mérillou; Mia Baarup Tofte,
NORD Architects; Isabelle Toland, Aileen Sage Architects;
Graham West, West Architecture**

KOTOHIRA KADAN

1241-5 Kotohira-cho
Nakatado
Kagawa 766-0001
Japan
+81 877753232
kotohira-kadan.jp

CREDIT CARDS..Accepted
PRICE..High-end
TYPE...Ryokan
ACCOMMODATION.....................................3 Houses, 43 Rooms
FACILITIES..........................Hot-spring bath, Open-air bath,
Outdoor restaurant, Sauna, Spa
GOOD TO KNOW....................Karaoke available, Free parking
RECOMMENDED FOR...Spa

A traditional ryokan and houses dating back 400 years,
Kotohira Kadan has 43 guest rooms—some include private
open-air baths with views of Mount Fuji—and three special
Sukiya-zukuri houses. Highly regarded for its hospitality,
the ryokan is a stone's throw from Kotohira's shrines and
renowned dining scene.

Recommended by: Giancarlo Mazzanti, El Equipo Mazzanti

YAEDAKE SANSO LODGE

2191 Miyanoura
Yakushima-cho
Kumage
Kagoshima 891-4205
Japan
+81 997421551
yaedake.jp

CREDIT CARDS.....................................Accepted but not Amex
PRICE..Low-cost
TYPE...Lodge
ACCOMMODATION..9 Cabins
FACILITIES...........................Open-air bath, Restaurant
GOOD TO KNOW..Forest hiking
RECOMMENDED FOR..Eco-conscious

"Retreat into your own private forest with deer and fireflies
that light up at night."—Alex Mok

Recommended by: Alex Mok, Linehouse

HAKONE RETREAT (FORMERLY NEST INN HAKONE)

1286-116 Sengokuhara
Hakone
Ashigarashimo
Kanagawa 250-0631
Japan
+81 460839090
hakone-retreat.com

CREDIT CARDS..Accepted
PRICE..High-end
TYPE...Onsen resort
ACCOMMODATION.....................................37 Rooms and Villas
FACILITIES...Bakery,
Hot-spring and open-air baths,
2 Restaurants, Spa
GOOD TO KNOW.............................Child friendly (12 and over)
RECOMMENDED FOR.....................................Worth the travel

Whether you choose to stay in the Hakone Retreat's Före
or Villa, the warm welcome and smells from the on-site
bakery make for a homely feel. Immersed in the forest, an
outdoor hot spring bath is accessible by a wooden walkway;
in colder weather, take in panoramic views of the woods and
mountains from the indoor public bath.

Recommended by: Patrick Reymond, Atelier Oï

HOSHINO RESORTS KAI ATAMI

750-6 Izusan
Atami
Shizuoka 413-0002
Japan
+81 570073011
kai-ryokan.jp

CREDIT CARDS..Accepted
PRICE..High-end
TYPE...Ryokan
ACCOMMODATION...................................16 Cottages and Suites
FACILITIES.....................................Hot-spring bath, Restaurant
GOOD TO KNOW.................. Closed for renovation until 2022
RECOMMENDED FOR...All-time favorite

"Because I feel a marvelous combination of tropical climate
and Japanese tradition there."—Kengo Kuma

Recommended by: Kengo Kuma, Kengo Kuma & Associates

GORA HANAOUGI
1300-681 Gora
Hakone
Ashigarashimo
Kanagawa 250-0408
Japan
+81 460877715
gorahanaougi.com

CREDIT CARDS..Accepted
PRICE..High-end
TYPE..Onsen resort
ACCOMMODATION..13 Rooms
FACILITIES.........................Hot-spring bath, Open-air bath,
Restaurant
GOOD TO KNOW..Free parking
RECOMMENDED FOR...................All-time favorite, Spa

"Visit for the total onsen experience, with private
outdoor bath."—Mårten Claesson

Recommended by: Mårten Claesson, Claesson Koivisto
Rune; Eero Koivisto, Claesson Koivisto Rune

GORA KADAN
1300 Gora
Hakone
Ashigarashimo
Kanagawa 250-0408
Japan
+81 460823331
gorakadan.com

CREDIT CARDS..Accepted
PRICE..High-end
TYPE..Ryokan
ACCOMMODATION................................20 Rooms and Suites
FACILITIES.........................Bar, Gym, Indoor swimming pool,
Open-air bath, Restaurant, Spa
GOOD TO KNOW..Child friendly
RECOMMENDED FOR...Spa

Gora Kadan is the former summer retreat of the Imperial
Family, and offers all the comfort and hospitality one expects
of a traditional Japanese ryokan. It is located in the Hakone
National Park, an area renowned for its hot springs, some of
which feed the mineral-rich, open-air pools on-site.

Recommended by: Kiyoshi Sey Takeyama, Amorphe
Takeyama & Associates

FOUR SEASONS HOTEL KYOTO
445-3 Myohoin Maekawa-cho
Higashiyama-ku
Kyoto 605-0932
+81 755418288
Japan
fourseasons.com

CREDIT CARDS..Accepted
PRICE..Blow-out
TYPE...Hotel
ACCOMMODATION..............................163 Rooms and Suites
FACILITIES.........................Bar, Gym, Indoor swimming pool,
2 Restaurants, Spa, Yoga
GOOD TO KNOW..........................Babysitting, Bicycle rentals
RECOMMENDED FOR.......................Wish I'd designed

"A beautiful contemporary Japanese masterpiece."
—Victor Legorreta Hernández

Recommended by: Victor Legorreta Hernández, Legorreta

HIIRAGIYA
Nakahakusan-cho
Fuyacho Anekoji-agaru
Nakagyo-ku
Kyoto 604-8094
Japan
+81 752211136
hiiragiya.co.jp

CREDIT CARDS..Accepted
PRICE..High-end
TYPE..Ryokan
ACCOMMODATION..28 Rooms
FACILITIES...Restaurant
GOOD TO KNOW...Garden
RECOMMENDED FOR........All-time favorite, Countryside, Spa

"This exquisite traditional inn dates from the 1800s when
it served traveling Samurai. Its quiet, rustic elegance creates
an extraordinary experience for all the senses. The food is
rarefied in its beauty and subtlety. The staff seem psychic
in their ability to anticipate your needs, and all this set in the
historic district of Kyoto."—Buzz Yudell

Dating back to 1818, Hiiragiya has been under the ownership
of the same family for six generations and has become
one of Japan's most beloved traditional ryokans. Each of
the property's twenty-eight rooms are unique in their
design.

Recommended by: Manuel Cervantes, CC Arquitectos;
Buzz Yudell, Moore Ruble Yudell

KYOMACHIYA HOTEL SHIKI JURAKU

165 Konoecho
Kamigyo-ku
Kyoto 602-8046, Japan
+81 754170210
shikijuraku.com

CREDIT CARDS	Accepted
PRICE	High-end
TYPE	Hotel
ACCOMMODATION	10 Rooms
FACILITIES	Bar
GOOD TO KNOW	No pets
RECOMMENDED FOR	Urban

"The rooms by Kengo Kuma are beautiful."—Mårten Claesson

Recommended by: Mårten Claesson, Claesson Koivisto Rune

KYOTO HOTEL OKURA

Kawaramachi-Oike
Nakagyo-ku
Kyoto 604-8558, Japan
+81 752232333
hotel.kyoto

CREDIT CARDS	Accepted
PRICE	Mid-range
TYPE	Hotel
ACCOMMODATION	322 Rooms and Suites
FACILITIES	Bar, Gym, Indoor swimming pool, 6 Restaurants, Sauna
GOOD TO KNOW	Babysitting, Free parking
RECOMMENDED FOR	Family friendly

Recommended by: Waro Kishi, K.ASSOCIATES/Architects

MIYAMASOU

375 Daihizan, Hanaseharachi-cho
Sakyo-ku
Kyoto 601-1102, Japan
+81 757460231
miyamasou.jp

CREDIT CARDS	Accepted
PRICE	High-end
TYPE	Hotel
ACCOMMODATION	8 Rooms
FACILITIES	Restaurant, Wood-burning fireplace
GOOD TO KNOW	Call or email to book
RECOMMENDED FOR	Best-kept secret

Recommended by: Kiyoshi Sey Takeyama, Amorphe
Takeyama & Associates

PIECE HOSTEL SANJO

531 Asakura-cho
Nakagyo-ku
Kyoto 604-8074
Japan
+81 757463688
piecehostel.com

CREDIT CARDS	Accepted
PRICE	Low-cost
TYPE	Hostel
ACCOMMODATION	13 Dorms and Private rooms
FACILITIES	Cafe, Self-service laundry
GOOD TO KNOW	Bicycle rentals
RECOMMENDED FOR	Budget

PIECE is a collection of elegantly designed and conveniently located hostels with a range of accommodation options. It has two Sanjo hostels—the original, Sanjo West, is a renovated traditional ryokan, and Sanjo East opened in 2018 across the road, just two minutes from Nishiki Food Market.

Recommended by: Kiyoshi Sey Takeyama, Amorphe
Takeyama & Associates

THE RITZ-CARLTON, KYOTO

Kamogawa Nijo-Ohashi Hotori
Nakagyo-ku
Kyoto 604-0902
Japan
+81 757465555
ritzcarlton.com

CREDIT CARDS	Accepted
PRICE	High-end
TYPE	Hotel
ACCOMMODATION	134 Rooms and Suites
FACILITIES	2 Bars, Gym, Indoor swimming pool, 2 Restaurants, Spa
GOOD TO KNOW	Babysitting, Bicycle rentals
RECOMMENDED FOR	Luxury

"Kyoto is one of the world's most amazing cities, and the Ritz-Carlton, Kyoto is one of the world's most refined hotels, which reflects the elegance and sophistication of this remarkable place."—Deborah Berke

Recommended by: Deborah Berke, Deborah Berke Partners

SEN HOUSE KYOTO

15-6 Uzumasa Yasui Kasuga-cho
Ukyo-ku
Kyoto 616-8062, Japan
+81 757088030
shikiproperties.com

CREDIT CARDS	Accepted but not Amex
PRICE	Mid-range
TYPE	Home rental
ACCOMMODATION	3 Rooms
FACILITIES	Zen garden
GOOD TO KNOW	Self-catering
RECOMMENDED FOR	Best-kept secret

Recommended by: Waro Kishi, K.ASSOCIATES/Architects

SHIRAUME

Shirakawa-hotori
Higashiyama-ku
Kyoto 605-0085, Japan
+81 755611459
shiraume-kyoto.jp

CREDIT CARDS	Accepted
PRICE	Mid-range
TYPE	Ryokan
ACCOMMODATION	5 Rooms
FACILITIES	Bar, Restaurant
GOOD TO KNOW	Near Downtown Kyoto
RECOMMENDED FOR	Urban

"Beautiful and spacious rooms, great service, and a wonderfully welcoming staff."—Nicolas Koff

Recommended by: Nicolas Koff, Office Ou

SUMIYA RYOKAN KYOTO

Fuyacho-dori Sanjo Sagaru
Nakagyo-ku
Kyoto 604-8075, Japan
+81 752212188
www2.odn.ne.jp

CREDIT CARDS	Accepted
PRICE	Mid-range
TYPE	Ryokan
ACCOMMODATION	23 Rooms
FACILITIES	Restaurant
GOOD TO KNOW	Onsen packages
RECOMMENDED FOR	Worth the travel

Recommended by: Raúl de Armas, MdeAS Architects

TAWARAYA RYOKAN

2-7-8 Nakahakusancho
Nakagyo-ku
Kyoto 604-8094
Japan
+81 752115566

CREDIT CARDS	Accepted
PRICE	High-end
TYPE	Ryokan
ACCOMMODATION	18 Rooms
FACILITIES	Hot-spring and Open-air baths, Restaurant, Sauna
GOOD TO KNOW	Call or fax to book
RECOMMENDED FOR	All-time favorite, Urban, Where I live, Worth the travel

"The best hotel I have stayed in. The rooms are super traditional and adapt around the guest's daily needs. The attention to detail and the curious and brilliant Japanese aesthetic makes it visually arresting, and the service is above anything comparable."—Thomas Bartlett

Recommended by: Thomas Bartlett, Waldo Works; Bernard Dubois, Bernard Dubois Architects; Bernardo Fort-Brescia, Arquitectonica; Michael Gabellini and Kimberly Sheppard, Gabellini Sheppard Associates; Waro Kishi, K.ASSOCIATES/Architects; Andrea Maffei, Andrea Maffei Architects; Stéphane Parmentier; Dominique Perrault, Dominique Perrault Architecture; Dan Wood, WORKac; George Yabu and Glenn Pushelberg, Yabu Pushelberg

UTANO YOUTH HOSTEL

29 Uzumasa Nakayama-cho
Ukyo-ku
Kyoto 616-8191
Japan
+81 754622288
yh-kyoto.or.jp

CREDIT CARDS	Accepted
PRICE	Low-cost
TYPE	Hostel
ACCOMMODATION	6 Dorms and Rooms
FACILITIES	Restaurant
GOOD TO KNOW	Self-service laundry
RECOMMENDED FOR	Budget

"Modest serenity to set you in the mood for Zen gardens."
—Charlotte von Moos

Recommended by: Charlotte von Moos, Sauter von Moos

MIYAKO RESORT SHIMA BAYSIDE TERRACE

3618-33 Ugata Ago-cho
Shima
Mie 517-0501
Japan
+81 599437211
miyakohotels.ne.jp

CREDIT CARDS...Accepted
PRICE...Mid-range
TYPE...Resort
ACCOMMODATION...................108 Rooms, Suites, and Villas
FACILITIES.....................Bar, Gym, Outdoor swimming pool,
3 Restaurants, Sauna, Spa, Tennis
GOOD TO KNOW...............................Pool open in summer only
RECOMMENDED FOR...Family friendly

Recommended by: Kiyoshi Sey Takeyama, Amorphe
Takeyama & Associates

MOMONOURA VILLAGE

Ishinomaki-shi
Miyagi 6986-2353
Japan
+81 225256870
momonouravillage.com

CREDIT CARDS...Not accepted
PRICE..Low-cost
TYPE...Village (curated festival)
ACCOMMODATION.................6 Campsites, Huts, and Rooms
FACILITIES...Shared bathrooms
GOOD TO KNOW...Cookery classes,
Fishing, Self-catering
RECOMMENDED FOR...Countryside

Recommended by: Momoyo Kaijima and Yoshiharu
Tsukamoto, Atelier Bow-Wow

HENN NA HOTEL

6-5 Huis Ten Bosch-cho
Sasebo
Nagasaki 859-3293
Japan
+81 956270604
h-n-h.jp

CREDIT CARDS...Accepted
PRICE...Low-cost
TYPE...Hotel
ACCOMMODATION...140 Rooms
FACILITIES...Bar, Restaurant
GOOD TO KNOW..Robot staff
RECOMMENDED FOR...Budget

"Groundbreaking concept for a budget hotel."
—Grace Cheung

Recommended by: Grace Cheung, XRANGE
Architecture + Design

YOSHINO CEDAR HOUSE

624 Yoshino-cho Iigai
Yoshino
Nara 639-3113
Japan
yoshinocedarhouse.com

CREDIT CARDS...Accepted
PRICE...Mid-range
TYPE...House rental
ACCOMMODATION..1 Room
FACILITIES..Yoga
GOOD TO KNOW...................................Bicycle rentals, No pets
RECOMMENDED FOR...All-time favorite,
Wish I'd designed

"A twist on the Airbnb concept, the process of materializing
the idea, using local cedar construction and sparse detailing,
make this a perfect pl0ace to stay."—Adrian Moreno and
Maria Samaniego

[This property was designed by Go Hasegawa.]

Recommended by: Go Hasegawa, Go Hasegawa &
Associates; Adrian Moreno and Maria Samaniego,
Arquitectura X

HOUSE OF LIGHT
2891 Ueno
Tokamachi
Niigata 948-0122, Japan
+81 257611090
hikarinoyakata.com

CREDIT CARDS	Not accepted
PRICE	Mid-range
TYPE	Guesthouse
ACCOMMODATION	3 Family rooms
FACILITIES	Open-air bath
GOOD TO KNOW	On-site light installation, Self-catering
RECOMMENDED FOR	Countryside

"Experimental work from James Turrell."
—Joaquín Pérez-Goicoechea

Inspired by Junichiro Tanizaki's novel *In Praise of Shadows* and the traditional architecture of the Echigo-Tsumari region, the House of Light was designed by artist James Turrell as a space for blending light and shadow, the modern and traditional, and Eastern and Western design sensibilities. This exchange of ideas is reflected in the accommodation; its common areas are intended to be shared by up to three families.

Recommended by: Joaquín Pérez-Goicoechea, AGi Architects

HOSHINOYA TAKETOMI ISLAND
Taketomi Island
Yaeyama
Okinawa 907-1101, Japan
+81 5037861144
hoshinoya.com

CREDIT CARDS	Accepted
PRICE	Mid-range
TYPE	Resort
ACCOMMODATION	48 Villas
FACILITIES	Outdoor swimming pool, Restaurant, Spa
GOOD TO KNOW	Child friendly
RECOMMENDED FOR	Beach

Hoshinoya Taketomi Island offers guests the opportunity to slow down and experience traditional Japanese island life. The design principles of its pavilions reflect time-honored methods, as do cultural experiences including minsa weaving and water buffalo wagon tours.

Recommended by: Jo Nagasaka, Schemata Architects

CONRAD OSAKA
3-2-4 Nakanoshima
Kita-ku
Osaka 530-0005
Japan
+81 662220111
conradosaka.jp

CREDIT CARDS	Accepted
PRICE	Mid-range
TYPE	Hotel
ACCOMMODATION	164 Rooms and Suites
FACILITIES	Bar, Indoor swimming pool, Restaurant, Spa
GOOD TO KNOW	Child friendly
RECOMMENDED FOR	Where I live

Recommended by: Kiyoshi Sey Takeyama, Amorphe Takeyama & Associates

TOKYO: SEE PAGES 104-109

KITA ONSEN
151 Yumoto Nasu-machi
Nasu
Tochigi 325-0301
Japan
+81 287762008
kitaonsen.com

CREDIT CARDS	Not accepted
PRICE	Low-cost
TYPE	Onsen resort
ACCOMMODATION	44 Rooms
FACILITIES	Hot-spring bath, Open-air bath, Restaurant
GOOD TO KNOW	On-site waterfall, Free parking
RECOMMENDED FOR	Spa

A visit to Kita Onsen is like stepping back in time—it takes its name from the ancient hot springs that were first discovered 1,200 years ago. Rooms are simple yet comfortable, and the Edo-period dining room is warmed by fire-lit hearths during winter.

Recommended by: Johanna Meyer-Grohbrügge, Meyer-Grohbrügge

KOYASAN ONSEN FUKUCHIIN

6-5-7 Koyasan, Koya-cho
Ito
Wakayama 648-0211, Japan
+81 736562021
fukuchiin.com

CREDIT CARDS	Accepted but not Amex
PRICE	Mid-range
TYPE	Onsen resort
ACCOMMODATION	60 Rooms
FACILITIES	Hot-spring bath, Restaurant, Sauna
GOOD TO KNOW	Free parking
RECOMMENDED FOR	Mountains

"This thirteenth-century temple with elegant rooms is a short walk from the Kongōbu-ji temple."—Cristian Santandreu

Recommended by: Cristian Santandreu, A2arquitectos

FUJIYA INN

443 Ginzanshinhata
Obanazawa
Yamagata 999-4333, Japan
+81 237282141
selected-ryokan.com

CREDIT CARDS	Accepted but not Amex
PRICE	Mid-range
TYPE	Inn
ACCOMMODATION	8 Rooms
FACILITIES	Hot-spring bath, Restaurant
GOOD TO KNOW	Free parking
RECOMMENDED FOR	Wish I'd designed

"Kengo Kuma's design [for the Ginzan Onsen] keeps things simple yet creates unforgettable spaces."—Nicolas Koff

Recommended by: Nicolas Koff, Office Ou

SHONAI HOTEL SUIDEN TERRASSE

23-1 Kitakyoden Shimotorinosu
Tsuruoka
Yamagata 997-0053, Japan
+81 235257424
suiden-terrasse.yamagata-design.com

CREDIT CARDS	Accepted
PRICE	Low-cost
TYPE	Hotel
ACCOMMODATION	143 Rooms and Suites
FACILITIES	Hot-spring bath, Restaurant, Spa
GOOD TO KNOW	Child friendly
RECOMMENDED FOR	Countryside

The design concept behind Suiden Terrasse was inspired by the scenic countryside and rice fields which surround it. Produce served in the restaurant—including the wines—is locally sourced. There is also a hot spring in the fitness center.

Recommended by: Shigeru Ban, Shigeru Ban Architects

BETTEI OTOZURE

2208 Fukawayumoto
Nagato
Yamaguchi 759-4103, Japan
+81 837253377
otozure.jp

CREDIT CARDS	Accepted
PRICE	Blow-out
TYPE	Onsen resort
ACCOMMODATION	18 Rooms
FACILITIES	Gym, Hot-spring bath, Open-air bath, Restaurant
GOOD TO KNOW	Child friendly (13 and over)
RECOMMENDED FOR	All-time favorite

"Surrounded by nature, the mountains, a beautiful landscape, and the River Otuzure, which allows you to experience a traditional atmosphere in a setting unique to Japan. The service is based on what the staff proudly call omotenashi—hospitality from the heart."
—Marcelo Morettin

Recommended by: Marcelo Morettin, Andrade Morettin Arquitetos

KOZANTEI UBUYA

10 Azagawa, Fujikawaguchiko-machi
Minamitsuru
Yamanashi 401-0303, Japan
+81 555721145
ubuya.co.jp

CREDIT CARDS	Accepted
PRICE	High-end
TYPE	Onsen resort
ACCOMMODATION	51 Rooms
FACILITIES	Hot-spring bath, Open-air bath, Restaurant, Sauna, Spa
GOOD TO KNOW	Free parking, Overlooks Lake Kawaguchi
RECOMMENDED FOR	Spa

"Mount Fuji is your scenery; what more could you want?"
—Ludovico Centis

Recommended by: Ludovico Centis, The Empire

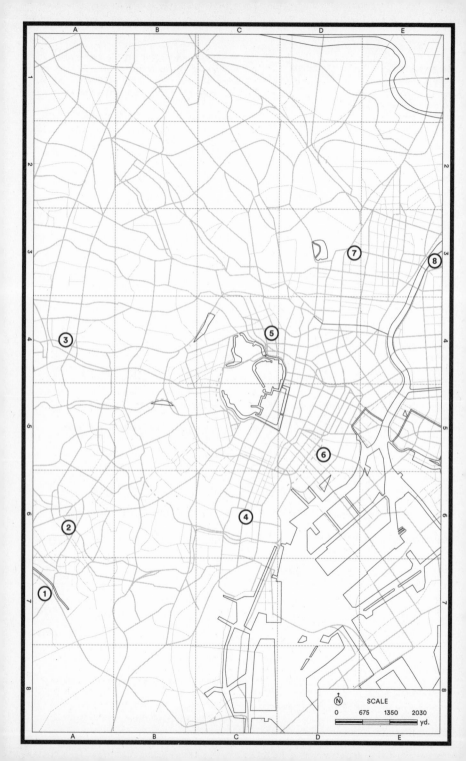

TOKYO

CLASKA
1-3-18 Chuo-cho
Meguro
Tokyo 152-0001
+81 337198121
claska.com

CREDIT CARDS...Accepted
PRICE...Mid-range
TYPE..Hotel
ACCOMMODATION..20 Rooms
FACILITIES............................Restaurant, Rooftop terrace bar
GOOD TO KNOW.........................Bicycle rentals, Free parking
RECOMMENDED FOR...Best-kept secret

This 1969 block was turned into Tokyo's first boutique
property by Intentionallies in 2003. Each of Claska's twenty
rooms has been designed by a celebrated designer or
architect representing Japan, and is characterized by four
distinct themes including Tatami and Contemporary, so
guests may choose their preferred design experience during
their stay. Claska also houses the gallery and lifestyle
store Do.

Recommended by: Flavio Albanese, ASA Studio

DO-C EBISU
1-8-1 Ebisu
Shibuya
Tokyo 150-0013
+81 334495255
do-c.jp

CREDIT CARDS...Accepted
PRICE...Low-cost
TYPE..Hotel
ACCOMMODATION..162 Pods
FACILITIES...Sauna
GOOD TO KNOW....................................Guests must check-out
daily to allow for cleaning
RECOMMENDED FOR...Wish I'd designed

As a "sauna+sleep" hotel, Do-c Ebisu is a simple yet stylish
concept—guests can choose to book an overnight stay in a
pod, or a nap plan which charges by the hour (both of which
include access to the saunas). Towels and loungewear are
also provided.

Recommended by: Marcio Kogan, Studio MK27

TRUNK HOTEL
5-31 Jingumae
Shibuya
Tokyo 150-0001
+81 357663210
trunk-hotel.com

CREDIT CARDS...Accepted
PRICE...Mid-range
TYPE..Hotel
ACCOMMODATION.................................15 Rooms and Suites
FACILITIES....................................Bar, Restaurant, Spa
GOOD TO KNOW..............................Tsukiji Fish Market tours
RECOMMENDED FOR..Urban

"Visit for its welcoming and relatable architecture, its scale,
permeability, and relationship to the neighborhood, and
for all the design features related to the local producers
and products."—Adrian Moreno and Maria Samaniego

Recommended by: Adrian Moreno and Maria Samaniego,
Arquitectura X

HOTEL GRACERY
1-19-1 Kabukicho
Shinjuku
Tokyo 160-8466
+81 368332489
gracery.com

CREDIT CARDS...Accepted
PRICE...Mid-range
TYPE..Hotel
ACCOMMODATION..970 Rooms
FACILITIES............................Restaurant, Rooftop terrace bar
GOOD TO KNOW...Child friendly
RECOMMENDED FOR............................All-time favorite, Urban

"A comfortable basic hotel, hermetically sealed from the
chaos of Shinjuku immediately outside. Disproportionately
large, immaculately designed bathrooms."—Graham West

Recommended by: Graham West, West Architecture

PARK HYATT TOKYO
3-7-1-2 Nishi-Shinjuku
Shinjuku
Tokyo 163-1055
+81 353221234
tokyo.park.hyatt.com

CREDIT CARDS..Accepted
PRICE..High-end
TYPE..Hotel
ACCOMMODATION................................177 Rooms and Suites
FACILITIES.......................Bar, Gym, Indoor swimming pool,
3 Restaurants, Sauna,
Spa, Steam room
GOOD TO KNOW.......................................Valet parking
RECOMMENDED FOR..............All-time favorite, Luxury, Urban

"A resort within a sanctuary within a hotel."—Sean Godsell

"Park Hyatt Tokyo doesn't feel like a big hotel—checking
in and out happens while you're sitting at a table and chair.
The sensitive interior planning means you have little
opportunity to bump into other guests. Public spaces offer
plenty of privacy, but when you enter your room, the whole
of Tokyo spreads out in front of your eyes, as the hotel
occupies the highest floors of a skyscraper in Shinjuku."
—Waro Kishi

Recommended by: Cian Deegan, TAKA Architects;
André Fu, AFSO; Sean Godsell, Sean Godsell Architects;
Waro Kishi, K.ASSOCIATES/Architects; Nicolas Koff,
Office Ou; Isabelle Toland, Aileen Sage Architects

ANDAZ TOKYO TORANOMON HILLS
1-23-4 Toranomon
Minato
Tokyo 105-0001
+81 368301234
tokyo.andaz.hyatt.com

CREDIT CARDS..Accepted
PRICE..High-end
TYPE..Hotel
ACCOMMODATION................................164 Rooms and Suites
FACILITIES...Bar, Gym, 5 Restaurants,
Rooftop terrace bar
GOOD TO KNOW...Babysitting
RECOMMENDED FOR...Urban

Recommended by: Marcio Kogan, Studio MK27

THE OKURA TOKYO
2-10-4 Toranomon
Minato
Tokyo 105-0001
+81 335820111
hotelokura.co.jp

CREDIT CARDS..Accepted
PRICE..High-end
TYPE..Hotel
ACCOMMODATION................................380 Rooms and Suites
FACILITIES.......................Bar, Gym, Indoor swimming pool,
6 Restaurants, Sauna
GOOD TO KNOW.......................................Valet parking
RECOMMENDED FOR.........................All-time favorite,
Luxury, Urban,
Wish I'd designed

"The legendary Hotel Okura, originally designed in the
late 1950s by Yoshiro Taniguchi. Visit for its sublimely
beautiful entrance hall with suspended hexahedral okura
lamps, beautiful wall patterns, materials, and textures,
as well as its ingenious illusion of limitless garden behind
low-level windows set into the rear shoji screen."
—Matthias Sauerbruch and Louisa Hutton

Recommended by: Claire Bétaille and Bruno Moinard,
4BI & Associés; Bernard Dubois, Bernard Dubois Architects;
Doriana and Massimiliano Fuksas, Studio Fuksas; Makio
Hasuike, Makio Hasuike & Co; Alireza Razavi, Studio Razavi
Architecture; Matthias Sauerbruch and Louisa Hutton,
Sauerbruch Hutton

THE ROYAL PARK HOTEL TOKYO SHIODOME
1-6-3 Higashi-Shinbashi
Minato
Tokyo 105-8333
+81 362531111
royal-park-the-shiodome.intokyohotels.com

CREDIT CARDS..Accepted
PRICE..Mid-range
TYPE..Hotel
ACCOMMODATION................................490 Rooms and Suites
FACILITIES.......................Bar, Gym, Restaurant, Sauna, Spa
GOOD TO KNOW...No pets
RECOMMENDED FOR...Urban

"Good location, essential and functional interior design,
and good service."—Makio Hasuike

Recommended by: Makio Hasuike, Makio Hasuike & Co

AMAN TOKYO

The Otemachi Tower, 1-5-6 Otemachi
Chiyoda
Tokyo 100-0004
+81 0352243333
aman.com

CREDIT CARDS	Accepted
PRICE	Blow-out
TYPE	Hotel
ACCOMMODATION	84 Rooms and Suites
FACILITIES	Bar, Gym, Indoor swimming pool, Restaurant, Spa, Yoga
GOOD TO KNOW	Babysitting
RECOMMENDED FOR	Luxury, Urban, Spa

"Minimalist, chic, contemporary, and recommended for
the views of the city from the swimming pool."
—Marco Costanzi

"Near perfection: *wabi sabi* personified."
—Todd-Avery Lenahan

Recommended by: Marco Costanzi, Marco Costanzi
Architects; Waro Kishi, K.ASSOCIATES/Architects; Tom
Kundig, Olson Kundig; Todd-Avery Lenahan, TAL
Studio; Michel Rojkind, Rojkind Arquitectos; George Yabu
and Glenn Pushelberg, Yabu Pushelberg

HOSHINOYA TOKYO

1-9-1 Otemachi
Chiyoda
Tokyo 100-0004
+81 5037861144
hoshinoya.com

CREDIT CARDS	Accepted
PRICE	High-end
TYPE	Onsen resort
ACCOMMODATION	84 Rooms
FACILITIES	Gym, Hot-spring and open-air baths, Restaurant, Spa
GOOD TO KNOW	Child friendly
RECOMMENDED FOR	Best-kept secret, Luxury

"Brings the relaxed onsen experience into an urban setting."
—André Fu

Recommended by: André Fu, AFSO; Stéphane Parmentier

IMPERIAL HOTEL

1-1-1 Uchisaiwai-cho
Chiyoda
Tokyo 100-8558
+81-335041111
imperialhotel.co.jp

CREDIT CARDS	Accepted
PRICE	High-end
TYPE	Hotel
ACCOMMODATION	931 Rooms and Suites
FACILITIES	Bar, Gym, 14 Restaurants, Sauna, Spa
GOOD TO KNOW	Babysitting
RECOMMENDED FOR	All-time favorite, Wish I'd designed, Worth the travel

Recommended by: Carlos Ferrater, OAB; Alfredo Payá
Benedito, Noname29; Ken Yeang, Hamzah & Yeang

THE PENINSULA TOKYO

1-8-1 Yurakucho
Chiyoda
Tokyo 100-0006
+81 362702888
peninsula.com

CREDIT CARDS	Accepted
PRICE	High-end
TYPE	Hotel
ACCOMMODATION	314 Rooms and Suites
FACILITIES	Bar, Gym, Indoor swimming pool, 4 Restaurants, Sauna, Spa, Steam room
GOOD TO KNOW	Small pets only
RECOMMENDED FOR	Luxury

The five-star Peninsula Tokyo is one of the city's finest
hotels. The hotel is both family and pet friendly (15kg limit)
and has a range of dedicated children's facilities. It also runs
a "Keys to the City" program which offers insider access to
unique Tokyo experiences and highlights such as culture,
tradition, art, history, night life, and cuisine.

Recommended by: Nabil Gholam, Nabil Gholam Architects

MANDARIN ORIENTAL, TOKYO
2-1-1 Nihonbashi Muromachi
Chūō
Tokyo 103-8328
+81 332708188
mandarinoriental.com

CREDIT CARDS	Accepted
PRICE	High-end
TYPE	Hotel
ACCOMMODATION	178 Rooms and Suites
FACILITIES	Bar, Gym, 8 Restaurants, Sauna, Spa, Yoga
GOOD TO KNOW	Pet friendly
RECOMMENDED FOR	Luxury

"Standing in the sauna on the thirty-eighth floor looking through floor-to-ceiling windows at the city of Tokyo below is a pretty memorable experience."—Graham West

Recommended by: Johanna Meyer-Grohbrügge, Meyer-Grohbrügge; Graham West, West Architecture

ANDON RYOKAN
2-34-10 Nihonzutsumi
Taito
Tokyo 111-0021
+81 338738611
andon.co.jp

CREDIT CARDS	Accepted but not Amex
PRICE	Low-cost
TYPE	Ryokan
ACCOMMODATION	24 Rooms
FACILITIES	Rooftop terrace
GOOD TO KNOW	Bicycle rentals, Tea ceremonies
RECOMMENDED FOR	Budget

"Not a square inch is wasted in this architecturally designed but modest Tokyo ryokan. Ingenious contemporary steel detailing abounds; the traditional futon rooms are tiny but comfortable. Staff are friendly and there's a cheeky little communal spa bath on the top floor. Andon is located in a central but low-key area with a neighborhood feel, an easy metro ride from historic Asakusa and bustling Ueno."
—Grace Mortlock

Recommended by: Grace Mortlock, Other Architects

ONE@TOKYO
1-19-3 Oshiage
Sumida
Tokyo 131-0045
+81 356301193
onetokyo.com

CREDIT CARDS	Accepted
PRICE	Low-cost
TYPE	Hotel
ACCOMMODATION	139 Rooms and Suites
FACILITIES	Bar, Restaurant
GOOD TO KNOW	Child friendly
RECOMMENDED FOR	Eco-conscious

The facade and interiors of One@Tokyo are the mastermind of Kengo Kuma. Its design is inspired by the surrounding neighborhood of Oshiage, in which the charm of the old Edo period sits comfortably alongside modern innovation. The result is a timelessly, effortlessly cool art hotel—each room also comes equipped with a smartphone that can be linked to guests' own apps, allowing free calls to anywhere in Japan.

Recommended by: Patrick Reymond, Atelier Oï

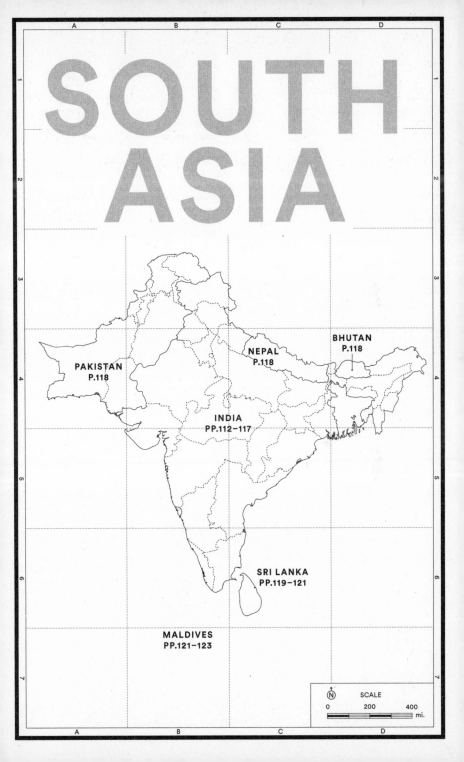

SOUTH
ASIA

PAKISTAN
P.118

NEPAL
P.118

BHUTAN
P.118

INDIA
PP.112–117

SRI LANKA
PP.119–121

MALDIVES
PP.121–123

N
SCALE
0   200   400
mi.

THE PARK NEW DELHI
15 Parliament Street
New Delhi 110001, India
+91 1123743000
theparkhotels.com

CREDIT CARDS	Accepted
PRICE	Mid-range
TYPE	Hotel
ACCOMMODATION	220 Rooms and Suites
FACILITIES	Bar, Boutique, 3 Restaurants, Rooftop pool
GOOD TO KNOW	24-hour butler service
RECOMMENDED FOR	Wish I'd designed

The Park Hotel's eye-catching interiors have cemented its reputation as one of New Delhi's most iconic five-star hotels. Including a rooftop pool, complete with bar and restaurant, The Park is frequently rated as one of the city's sleekest and most stylish destinations, whether for rest and relaxation or a little indulgence.

Recommended by: Romi Khosla, Romi Khosla Design Studios

THE HOUSE OF MANGALDAS GIRDHARDAS
Opposite Sidi Saiyad Jali
Ahmedabad
Gujarat 380001, India
+91 7925506946
houseofmg.com

CREDIT CARDS	Accepted
PRICE	Low-cost
TYPE	Hotel
ACCOMMODATION	38 Rooms
FACILITIES	Boutique, Gym, Indoor swimming pool, 2 Restaurants, Spa
GOOD TO KNOW	The property once hosted Mahatma Gandhi
RECOMMENDED FOR	Urban

"The House of Mangaldas Girdhardas is a mysterious place to stay. It has a wonderful collection of traditional fabrics, and dining on the roof terrace is a fantastic experience too: there's one elegant vegetarian menu and nobody to explain anything in English."—Roger Diener

Recommended by: Roger Diener, Diener & Diener Architekten

THE DIVINE HIMA
Opposite Norbulingka Institute Sidhpur
Dharamshala
Himachal Pradesh 176057
India
+91 8626983777
thedivinehima.com

CREDIT CARDS	Accepted but not Amex
PRICE	Mid-range
TYPE	Guesthouse
ACCOMMODATION	7 Rooms and Suites
FACILITIES	Cafe, Restaurant, Yoga
GOOD TO KNOW	Free parking, Meditation classes
RECOMMENDED FOR	Eco-conscious

"The personal care given by the owner is a memorable touch here."—Romi Khosla

Recommended by: Romi Khosla, Romi Khosla Design Studios

RAKKH RESORT
Ghamrota Village
Kangra
Himachal Pradesh 176061
India
+91 8800409567
rakkh.com

CREDIT CARDS	Accepted but not Amex
PRICE	Mid-range
TYPE	Resort
ACCOMMODATION	17 Cottages and Rooms
FACILITIES	Bar, Gym, Restaurant, Rooftop terrace bar, Steam room, Yoga
GOOD TO KNOW	Bicycle rentals, Child friendly, Free parking
RECOMMENDED FOR	Mountains

"One of the finest luxury resorts I have come across, Rakkh is an an idyllic retreat for those who want to get close to nature, surrounded by panoramic views and terraced hillsides. The resort has been designed using local materials, with all the modern facilities of a boutique hotel."
—Sonali Rastogi

Recommended by: Sonali Rastogi, Morphogenesis

KUMARAKOM LAKE RESORT
North Post
Kottayam
Kerala 686563
India
+91 4812524900
kumarakomlakeresort.in

CREDIT CARDS	Accepted
PRICE	Mid-range
TYPE	Resort
ACCOMMODATION	1 Houseboat, 65 Suites and Villas
FACILITIES	Bar, Gym, Outdoor swimming pool, 4 Restaurants, Spa
GOOD TO KNOW	Coconut groves, Valet parking
RECOMMENDED FOR	Beach

"Built in the style of a traditional homestead of Kerala, the Heritage Villas offer views of exquisite lotus-strewn canals; the interiors exude splendors of a prosperous bygone era."—Sonali Rastogi

Recommended by: Sonali Rastogi, Morphogenesis

AHILYA FORT
Ahilya Wada
Maheshwar
Madhya Pradesh 451224
India
+91 1141551575
ahilyafort.com

CREDIT CARDS	Accepted
PRICE	Blow out (all-inclusive)
TYPE	Fort hotel
ACCOMMODATION	19 Rooms
FACILITIES	Bar, Outdoor swimming pool, Restaurant, Yoga
GOOD TO KNOW	Child friendly
RECOMMENDED FOR	Countryside

Located in the central Indian town of Maheshwar, Ahilya Fort Hotel overlooks the Narmada River. A hotel with ample history and charm, it is owned and managed by Prince Richard Holkar, son of the last Maharaja of Indore and descendant of the fort's eighteenth-century creator, Maharani Ahilyabai Holkar.

Recommended by: Robert Sakula, Ash Sakula Architects

ABODE BOMBAY
Lansdowne House, MB Marg (near Regal Cinema)
Mumbai
Maharashtra 400001
India
+91 8080234066
abodeboutiquehotels.com

CREDIT CARDS	Accepted but not Amex
PRICE	Low-cost
TYPE	Hotel
ACCOMMODATION	20 Rooms
FACILITIES	Gym, Spa, Yoga
GOOD TO KNOW	Babysitting
RECOMMENDED FOR	Urban

"A charming and calm oasis in the middle of the city." —Johanna Meyer-Grohbrügge

Recommended by: Johanna Meyer-Grohbrügge, Meyer-Grohbrügge

THE TAJ MAHAL PALACE
Apollo Bunder
Mumbai
Maharashtra 400001
India
+91 2266653333
tajhotels.com

CREDIT CARDS	Accepted
PRICE	High-end
TYPE	Palace hotel
ACCOMMODATION	543 Rooms and Suites
FACILITIES	Bar, Outdoor swimming pool, Patisserie, 6 Restaurants, Salon, Spa, Yoga
GOOD TO KNOW	Child friendly, Valet parking
RECOMMENDED FOR	All-time favorite, Luxury, Urban, Worth the travel

"The hotel is located in an area that embodies all of my favorite things about walking in Mumbai—Apollo Bunder has the best little art and fashion stores and is completely colorful. A clash of many different worlds all in one place." —Sumayya Vally

"Charming with a sense of history, and perfect service." —Roger Zogolovitch

Recommended by: Thomas Bartlett, Waldo Works; Doriana and Massimiliano Fuksas, Studio Fuksas; Dennis Pieprz, Sasaki; Sumayya Vally, Counterspace; Roger Zogolovitch, Solidspace

AMANBAGH
Ajabgarh Village
Alwar District
Rajasthan 301027
India
+91 1465223333
aman.com

CREDIT CARDS..Accepted
PRICE...High-end
TYPE..Resort
ACCOMMODATION.........................37 Pavilions and Suites
FACILITIES.............................Gym, Outdoor swimming pool,
Restaurant, Spa, Yoga
GOOD TO KNOW..Free parking,
Near the Aravalli Range
RECOMMENDED FOR..Worth the travel

"Located among the Aravalli mountain range, this hotel offers incredible, discreet service and the Sariska National Park is just a short drive away."—Murat Tabanlıoğlu

Recommended by: Murat Tabanlıoğlu, Tabanlıoğlu Architects

DEOGARH MAHAL
Palace Road
Deogarh
Rajasthan 313331
India
+91 9928834777
deogarhmahal.com

CREDIT CARDS..Accepted
PRICE...High-end
TYPE..Palace hotel
ACCOMMODATION.....................................50 Rooms and Suites
FACILITIES...Bar, Gym,
Outdoor swimming pool, Restaurant
GOOD TO KNOW...Babysitting
RECOMMENDED FOR...All-time favorite

"Owned by a local family, this is a magical palace with quirky rooms, excellent service, and extravagant architecture."—Tom Jestico

Recommended by: Tom Jestico, Jestico + Whiles

THE OBEROI RAJVILAS
Babaji Ka Modh, Goner Road
Jaipur
Rajasthan 302031
India
+91 1412680101
oberoihotels.com

CREDIT CARDS..Accepted
PRICE..Mid-range
TYPE..Hotel
ACCOMMODATION.........................71 Rooms, Tents, and Villas
FACILITIES....................Bar, Gym, Outdoor swimming pool,
2 Restaurants, Spa, Steam room, Yoga
GOOD TO KNOW..Child friendly
RECOMMENDED FOR...................Countryside, Luxury, Urban,
Worth the travel

"This hotel is a beautiful example of traditional architecture adorned with Mughal arches, gold-leaf frescoes, high-domed ceilings, and magnificent crystal chandeliers. An amalgamation of Rajasthani charm and luxury, this hotel also offers a look into the way of life of a community."
—Sonali Rastogi

"A remarkable place to visit—particularly for the tent accommodation."—Salvador Reyes Ríos

Recommended by: Hasan Çalışlar, Erginoğlu & Çalışlar; Jean-Louis Deniot, Jean-Louis Deniot; Sonali Rastogi, Morphogenesis; Salvador Reyes Ríos, Reyes Ríos + Larraín Arquitectos

SAMODE HAVELI
Jorawar Singh Gate, Gangapole Road
Jaipur
Rajasthan 302002
India
+91 1412632407
samode.com

CREDIT CARDS..Accepted
PRICE..Mid-range
TYPE...Haveli
ACCOMMODATION.....................................50 Rooms and Suites
FACILITIES....................Bar, Gym, Outdoor swimming pool,
Restaurant, Spa, Steam room
GOOD TO KNOW.......................................Ayurvedic massage
RECOMMENDED FOR...Urban

"A fantastic oasis in the middle of bustling Jaipur with large outdoor terraces for dining."—Anthony Hudson

Recommended by: Anthony Hudson, Hudson Architects

SAMODE PALACE
Village Samode
Jaipur
Rajasthan 303806
India
+91 1412632407
samode.com

CREDIT CARDS	Accepted
PRICE	Mid-range
TYPE	Palace hotel
ACCOMMODATION	42 Suites
FACILITIES	Bar, Outdoor swimming pool, 2 Restaurants, Spa
GOOD TO KNOW	Free parking
RECOMMENDED FOR	Mountains

A popular choice among celebrities and royalty, the Palace is more than 450 years old, and, although it has high-end, modern facilities, such as a rooftop infinity pool, the interiors retain an historical sense of ancient grandeur. The "Pink City" of Jaipur is just an hour's drive away.

Recommended by: Sumayya Vally, Counterspace

SURYAGARH JAISALMER
Kahala Phata, Sam Road
Jaisalmer
Rajasthan 345001
India
+91 7827151151
suryagarh.com

CREDIT CARDS	Accepted
PRICE	Low-cost
TYPE	Haveli
ACCOMMODATION	72 Rooms and Suites
FACILITIES	Bar, Indoor and outdoor swimming pools, 2 Restaurants, Sauna, Spa
GOOD TO KNOW	Child friendly
RECOMMENDED FOR	Desert

"Drawing on history and fashioned on native wisdom and lore, this hotel celebrates a community's way of life, having preserved the traditions of the past yet framing them in a modern idiom. The sandstone Thar Haveli evokes a profound nostalgia."—Sonali Rastogi

Recommended by: Sonali Rastogi, Morphogenesis

MIHIR GARH
Khandi Village
Jodhpur
Rajasthan 306421
India
+91 1244654330
houseofrohet.com

CREDIT CARDS	Accepted but not Amex
PRICE	Mid-range
TYPE	Hotel
ACCOMMODATION	8 Suites
FACILITIES	Bar, Outdoor swimming pool, Restaurant, Spa
GOOD TO KNOW	Culinary workshops, Local safaris
RECOMMENDED FOR	Desert

"This fantasy of a building could only be in India. It is so hot that you spend your evening sitting in your room's small pool with your head at ground level. You look out across the colorless, baking desert at brightly clad guides leading their camels to an oasis. The integration of the hotel with the local community is memorable, and it is a part of Rajasthan that people perhaps miss between the glories of the region's towns."—Thomas Bartlett

Recommended by: Thomas Bartlett, Waldo Works

RAAS
Tunwar ji ka Jhalra, Makrana Mohalla
Jodhpur
Rajasthan 342001
India
+91 2912636455
raasjodhpur.com

CREDIT CARDS	Accepted
PRICE	Mid-range
TYPE	Haveli
ACCOMMODATION	40 Rooms and Suites
FACILITIES	Outdoor swimming pool, 2 Restaurants, Rooftop terrace bar, Spa, Yoga
GOOD TO KNOW	Babysitting, Pet friendly
RECOMMENDED FOR	Wish I'd designed

"Perfect alliance between traditional Indian architecture and soft Modernism."—Daniel Suduca and Thierry Mérillou

Recommended by: Sonali Rastogi, Morphogenesis; Daniel Suduca and Thierry Mérillou, Suduca & Mérillou

SAMSARA DESERT CAMP & RESORT
115km Milestone Post-Dechu, Jodhpur
Jaisalmer Highway
Jodhpur
Rajasthan 342314
India
+91 9829091100
samsaradechu.com

CREDIT CARDS	Accepted but not Amex
PRICE	Mid-range
TYPE	Tented camp resort
ACCOMMODATION	21 Rooms and Suites
FACILITIES	Bar, Outdoor swimming pool, Restaurant, Spa
GOOD TO KNOW	Free parking
RECOMMENDED FOR	Desert

"Bird-watching and dinner on the sand dunes or in the bush."
—Satyendra Pakhalé

Recommended by: Satyendra Pakhalé, Satyendra Pakhalé Associates

UMAID BHAWAN PALACE, JODHPUR
Circuit House Road
Jodhpur
Rajasthan 342006
India
+91 2912510101
tajhotels.com

CREDIT CARDS	Accepted
PRICE	High-end
TYPE	Palace hotel
ACCOMMODATION	70 Rooms and Suites
FACILITIES	Bar, Indoor and outdoor swimming pools, 2 Restaurants, Spa, Yoga
GOOD TO KNOW	Free parking
RECOMMENDED FOR	Worth the travel

The last of the great palaces of India, the exterior of the Umaid Bhawan Palace hotel is an imposing facade for the warm, world-class hospitality that lies within. History and heritage are entrenched within the building itself; the palm court marble used in its construction is the same as that of the Taj Mahal, and even the views are epic— its location atop Chittar Hill means the Palace benefits from views across the "Blue City" of Jodhpur and Mehrangarh Fort.

Recommended by: Bernardo and Paulo Jacobsen, Jacobsen Arquitetura

RANVAS-NAGAUR
Ahhichatragarh Fort
Nagpur
Rajasthan 341001
India
+91 1582241271
ranvasnagaur.com

CREDIT CARDS	Accepted but not Amex
PRICE	Mid-range
TYPE	Residence
ACCOMMODATION	10 Havelis
FACILITIES	Outdoor swimming pool, 2 Restaurants, Spa, Steam room
GOOD TO KNOW	Near Ahhichatragarh Fort
RECOMMENDED FOR	Desert

"The conservation and restoration of this palace, in the heart of the twelfth-century Ahhichatragarh Fort, has created a truly stunning setting. The hotel is located within the ten havelis, originally built for the Maharaja of Jodhpur's queens. Each haveli has its own courtyard, an open-air living room, and spacious bedroom with en suite marble bathrooms."—Robin Partington

Recommended by: Robin Partington, Robin Partington & Partners

AMAN-I-KHÁS
Sherpur Khiljipur, Ranthambhore Road
Sawai Madhopur
Rajasthan 322001
India
+91 7462252052
aman.com

CREDIT CARDS	Accepted
PRICE	Blow-out
TYPE	Tented camp resort
ACCOMMODATION	10 Tents
FACILITIES	Outdoor swimming pool, Restaurant, Spa, Yoga
GOOD TO KNOW	Air-conditioning, Child friendly
RECOMMENDED FOR	Countryside, Mountains

"A wonderful place to stay in rural India."—Ron Radziner

"Mysterious, magical, romantic: this is the ultimate waking dream. You'll experience a tiger safari, champagne under the stars, tents nestled among tall grasses, mountaintop temples with monkeys and barefoot pilgrims, pagodas, and ruins of the Maharajas."—Grace Cheung

Recommended by: Grace Cheung, XRANGE Architecture + Design; Ron Radziner, Marmol Radziner

TAJ LAKE PALACE HOTEL
Lake Pichola
Udaipur
Rajasthan 313001
India
+91 2942428800
tajhotels.com

CREDIT CARDS...Accepted
PRICE...High-end
TYPE...Palace hotel
ACCOMMODATION..65 Rooms
FACILITIES.................Outdoor restaurant, Restaurant, Spa
GOOD TO KNOW...Babysitting
RECOMMENDED FOR.........................Luxury, Worth the travel

"This hotel is like an apparition, appearing to float in the middle of Lake Pichola. The Lake Palace was built in the 1740s as a summer retreat for royalty. Its white-and-black marble walls are ornamented with semi-precious stones, which reflect the lake. The upper terrace is organized around gardens, fountains, courts, and colonnades."—Buzz Yudell

Recommended by: Will Alsop, aLL Design; Enrique Norten, TEN Arquitectos; Buzz Yudell, Moore Ruble Yudell; Cino Zucchi, CZA

ANANDA IN THE HIMALAYAS
The Palace Estate, Narendra Nagar Tehri
Garhwal
Uttarakhand 249175
India
+91 1244516650
anandaspa.com

CREDIT CARDS...Accepted
PRICE...High-end
TYPE...Destination spa resort
ACCOMMODATION......................78 Rooms, Suites, and Villas
FACILITIES...........................Gym, Outdoor swimming pool,
Restaurant, Spa, Yoga
GOOD TO KNOW............................Spa programmes available
RECOMMENDED FOR...Spa

Ananda In the Himalayas is one of India's most renowned luxury spa and wellness retreats. Situated on a hundred-acre (forty-hectare) Maharaja's Palace Estate in the Himalayan foothills of northern India, it offers a range of programs, from stress management and weight loss to yoga and Ayurvedic rejuvenation.

Recommended by: Anthony Hudson, Hudson Architects

THE KUMAON
Village Gadholi, Kasar Devi
Almora
Uttarakhand 263601
India
+91 9411736084
thekumaon.com

CREDIT CARDS.............................Accepted but not Amex
PRICE...Mid-range
TYPE..Hotel
ACCOMMODATION..10 Suites
FACILITIES.................................Luxury, Restaurant
GOOD TO KNOW..Free parking
RECOMMENDED FOR......................................Mountains

"Amazing location and experience overlooking the Himalayas."—Andres Remy

Recommended by: Andres Remy, Remy Architects

VANA
Mussoorie Road
Dehradun
Uttarakhand 248001
India
+91 1353911114
vana.co.in

CREDIT CARDS...Accepted
PRICE...High-end
TYPE..Hotel
ACCOMMODATION...............................82 Rooms and Suites
FACILITIES..Restaurant, Sauna, Spa,
Steam room, Tennis, Yoga
GOOD TO KNOW.................................Airport transfers
RECOMMENDED FOR..Best-kept secret,
Worth the travel

"Vana is a harmonious retreat near the foothills of the Himalayan mountains, near the source of the Ganges river."—George Yabu and Glenn Pushelberg

"Vana is a place to raise your spirits."—Tavis Wright

Recommended by: Tavis Wright, Dos Architects Ltd; George Yabu and Glenn Pushelberg, Yabu Pushelberg

PEARL CONTINENTAL HOTEL KARACHI
Club Road
Karachi
Sindh, Pakistan
+92 21111505505
pchotels.com

CREDIT CARDS	Accepted but not Amex
PRICE	Mid-range
TYPE	Hotel
ACCOMMODATION	286 Rooms and Suites
FACILITIES	Bar, Gym, Indoor swimming pool, 5 Restaurants, Sauna
GOOD TO KNOW	24-hour butler service
RECOMMENDED FOR	Where I live

Recommended by: Adil Kerai, Habib Fida Ali Architects

SWAT SERENA HOTEL
Officers Colony Road
Saidu Sharif
Swat, Pakistan
+92 94671163741
serenahotels.com

CREDIT CARDS	Accepted but not Amex
PRICE	Low-cost
TYPE	Hotel
ACCOMMODATION	49 Rooms and Suites
FACILITIES	Outdoor swimming pool, Restaurant
GOOD TO KNOW	Airport transfers
RECOMMENDED FOR	Mountains

Recommended by: Alfredo Payá Benedito, Noname29

HOTEL ANNAPURNA VIEW
Sarangkot, Pokhara
Kaski 33700
Nepal
+977 61506000
annapurnaview.com

CREDIT CARDS	Accepted
PRICE	Mid-range
TYPE	Hotel
ACCOMMODATION	150 Rooms and Suites
FACILITIES	Bar, Outdoor pool, Restaurant, Spa, Yoga
GOOD TO KNOW	Bicycle rentals
RECOMMENDED FOR	Mountains

"Visit for astounding views of the Himalayas."
—Kiyoshi Sey Takeyama

Situated in lush green hills with spectacular views of the Nepalese countryside, Hotel Annapurna View offers mountainside meditation sessions, off-road cycling, and the opportunity to watch the sunrise over the Himalayas.

Recommended by: Kiyoshi Sey Takeyama, Amorphe Takeyama & Associates

AMANKORA, PARO LODGE
Paro Valley
Bhutan
+975 2331333
aman.com

CREDIT CARDS	Accepted
PRICE	High-end (all-inclusive)
TYPE	Resort lodge
ACCOMMODATION	24 Suites
FACILITIES	Bar, Outdoor restaurant, Sauna, Spa, Steam room, Yoga
GOOD TO KNOW	Tailor-made guided excursions
RECOMMENDED FOR	Mountains, Worth the travel

"An amazingly stylish way to explore a kingdom that's not easily accessible."—Marianne Kwok

"It's like you're on the roof of the world."
—Stéphane Parmentier

[There are five lodges that form Amankora: the editors have chosen Paro Lodge.]

Recommended by: Marianne Kwok, Kohn Pedersen Fox; Stéphane Parmentier

COMO UMA PARO
Paro Valley
Bhutan
+975 8271597
comohotels.com

CREDIT CARDS	Accepted but not Amex
PRICE	High-end
TYPE	Hotel
ACCOMMODATION	29 Rooms and Villas
FACILITIES	Bar, Gym, Indoor swimming pool, Restaurant, Steam room, Yoga
GOOD TO KNOW	Visiting external yoga experts
RECOMMENDED FOR	Mountains, Spa

"A calm and mystical experience in the middle of one of the most unspoiled places on the planet."—Rodrigo Carazo

Recommended by: Rodrigo Carazo, Carazo Architecture; Kelly Hoppen, Kelly Hoppen Interiors

HERITANCE KANDALAMA
Dambulla
Central Province 21106
Sri Lanka
+94 665555000
heritancehotels.com

CREDIT CARDS	Accepted
PRICE	Mid-range
TYPE	Hotel
ACCOMMODATION	152 Rooms and Suites
FACILITIES	Bar, Gym, Outdoor swimming pool, 2 Restaurants, Spa
GOOD TO KNOW	Babysitting, Bicycle rentals
RECOMMENDED FOR	Countryside, Eco-conscious, Mountains, Wish I'd designed, Worth the travel

"The Kandalama is extraordinary. Geoffrey Bawa's concrete megastructure—Park Hill in the jungle—with its open decks, rooftop restaurant, the pools and terraces, and giant overgrown pergola, is home to a troop of monkeys that peer through the full-height windows to watch you shower. I plan to retire here for six months of the year."
—Simon Henley

Recommended by: Rodrigo Carazo, Carazo Architecture; Cian Deegan, TAKA Architects; Biba Dow, Dow Jones Architects; Tony Fretton, Tony Fretton Architects; Simon Henley, Henley Halebrown; Anthony Hudson, Hudson Architects; Rick Joy, Studio Rick Joy; Grace Mortlock, Other Architects; Dennis Pieprz, Sasaki; Carlo Ratti, Carlo Ratti Associati; Uwe Schmidt-Hess, Patalab Architecture; Leonid Slonimskiy, KOSMOS Architects; Mia Baarup Tofte, NORD Architects; Buzz Yudell, Moore Ruble Yudell

HIDEAWAY RESORT
Arugam Bay
Pottuvil
Eastern Province
Sri Lanka
+94 774596670
hideawayarugambay.com

CREDIT CARDS	Accepted but not Amex
PRICE	Low-cost
TYPE	Resort
ACCOMMODATION	14 Bungalows and Rooms
FACILITIES	Bar, Outdoor swimming pool, Restaurant, Yoga
GOOD TO KNOW	Child friendly
RECOMMENDED FOR	Beach

"Concrete pavilions in a beautiful garden."—Simon Henley

Hideaway is a boutique, family run resort offering a range of yoga and surf classes, and retreats. The service is warm, and the resort is well known for its delicious food and chilled-out cocktail bar.

Recommended by: Simon Henley, Henley Halebrown

TURTLE BAY
Gurupokuna Road
Tangalle
Southern Province 82200
Sri Lanka
+94 477887853
turtlebay.lk

CREDIT CARDS	Accepted but not Amex
PRICE	Low-cost
TYPE	Hotel
ACCOMMODATION	7 Rooms
FACILITIES	Bar, Outdoor swimming pool, Restaurant
GOOD TO KNOW	Child friendly
RECOMMENDED FOR	Beach

"A small, remote beach hotel with great service and food, and nice architecture."—Mia Baarup Tofte

Recommended by: Mia Baarup Tofte, NORD Architects

ONE WORLD FOUNDATION: AYURVEDA GUESTHOUSE & RESORT
162/45 Wathuregama
Ahungalla
Southern Province
Sri Lanka
+94 912264147
owf.at

CREDIT CARDS	Accepted
PRICE	Mid-range (all-inclusive)
TYPE	Guesthouse
ACCOMMODATION	13 Bungalows
FACILITIES	Outdoor swimming pool, Restaurant, Yoga
GOOD TO KNOW	Child friendly
RECOMMENDED FOR	Eco-conscious

"This is the most inspiring place we've ever stayed—we have already returned twice. Sustainability is taken seriously; all profits from this guesthouse go straight into running a neighboring non-profit school set up by the owners. The various bungalows are dotted between palm trees that host squirrels, birds, and monkeys. The fantastic service, long green swimming pool, delicious food, yoga, Ayurvedic treatments, and massages; and conversations with [founder] Katrin Messner, tempt us every February."
—Matthias Sauerbruch and Louisa Hutton

Recommended by: Matthias Sauerbruch and Louisa Hutton, Sauerbruch Hutton

LUNUGANGA COUNTRY ESTATE

Lunuganga Estate, Dedduwa Lake
Bentota
Southern Province 32350
Sri Lanka
+94 112589212
geoffreybawa.com

CREDIT CARDS.....................................Accepted but not Amex
PRICE...Mid-range
TYPE...Country estate hotel
ACCOMMODATION.......................................6 Rooms
FACILITIES...Restaurant
GOOD TO KNOW..............................Former country home of
Geoffrey Bawa
RECOMMENDED FOR..Wish I'd designed

Recommended by: Hugo Sauzay, Festen Architecture

GALLE FORT HOTEL

28 Church Street
Galle
Southern Province 80000
Sri Lanka
+94 766658080
galleforthotel.com

CREDIT CARDS...Accepted
PRICE...Mid-range
TYPE...Hotel
ACCOMMODATION..................................13 Rooms and Suites
FACILITIES..................Outdoor swimming pool, Restaurant
GOOD TO KNOW............................Child friendly (6 and over)
RECOMMENDED FOR...Luxury

"Originally a Dutch mansion and warehouse, this hotel is truly luxurious, with more staff than guests."—Simon Henley

Recommended by: Simon Henley, Henley Halebrown

JETWING LIGHTHOUSE

433 A Dadella
Galle
Southern Province 80000
Sri Lanka
+94 114709400
jetwinghotels.com

CREDIT CARDS...Accepted
PRICE...Mid-range
TYPE...Hotel
ACCOMMODATION..................................63 Rooms and Suites
FACILITIES.....................Bar, Gym, Outdoor swimming pool,
6 Restaurants, Spa, Tennis, Yoga
GOOD TO KNOW..............................Babysitting, Free parking
RECOMMENDED FOR..Beach

Designed by Geoffrey Bawa, the Jetwing Lighthouse hotel remains one of Galle's most iconic buildings. There's a wide range of luxury facilities, including a library, wine cellar, and Ayurvedic spa treatments, as well as sublime Sri Lankan hospitality.

Recommended by: Carlo Ratti, Carlo Ratti Associati

TAPROBANE ISLAND

23 Upper Dickson Road
Galle
Southern Province 80000
Sri Lanka
+94 914380275
taprobaneisland.com

CREDIT CARDS...Accepted
PRICE...Blow-out
TYPE...Resort
ACCOMMODATION...1 Villa
FACILITIES.................................Bar, Restaurant, Yoga
GOOD TO KNOW...Bicycle rentals,
No transport to island
RECOMMENDED FOR..Beach

"The adventure begins when staff walk you through the ocean carrying your luggage on their heads, while you wade toward the island. This is the only way to get to the resort, which is its own island. Need we say more?"
—George Yabu and Glenn Pushelberg

Recommended by: George Yabu and Glenn Pushelberg, Yabu Pushelberg

AMBA ESTATE

Ambadandegam
Bandarawella
Uva Province 90108
Sri Lanka
+94 573575489
ambaestate.com

CREDIT CARDS..Not accepted
PRICE..Low-cost
TYPE..Tea plantation estate
ACCOMMODATION...4 Bungalows
FACILITIES......................................Badminton, Restaurant
GOOD TO KNOW................................Free parking, Pet friendly
RECOMMENDED FOR...Countryside

"A quiet, refreshing stay in an Edwardian tea plantation bungalow with fabulous views, and delicious meals that you can eat in the garden."—Biba Dow

Recommended by: Biba Dow, Dow Jones Architects

FOUR SEASONS RESORT MALDIVES AT LANDAA GIRAAVARU

Landaa Giraavaru
Baa Atoll 20215
Maldives
+960 6600888
fourseasons.com

CREDIT CARDS...Accepted
PRICE...Blow-out
TYPE..Resort
ACCOMMODATION...106 Villas
FACILITIES.....................Bar, Gym, Outdoor swimming pool,
4 Restaurants, Salon,
Spa, Steam room, Yoga
GOOD TO KNOW..Babysitting
RECOMMENDED FOR...Worth the travel

In the heart of the Baa Atoll UNESCO World Biosphere Reserve, this resort is an island retreat that epitomizes a luxury hideaway experience, from moonlight spa rituals in the island's jungle to the Rossano Ferreti hair salon and wealth of children's facilities.

Recommended by: Antoine Predock, Antoine Predock Architect

SONEVA FUSHI

Kunfunadhoo Island
Baa Atoll 06170, Maldives
+960 6600304
soneva.com

CREDIT CARDS...Accepted
PRICE...Blow-out
TYPE..Resort
ACCOMMODATION..62 Villas
FACILITIES..............................Bar, Gym, Restaurant,
Spa, Tennis, Yoga
GOOD TO KNOW...............................Babysitting, Water sports
RECOMMENDED FOR.............................Eco-conscious, Island

"You are in a UNESCO biosphere reserve, with barefoot luxury in every detail."—Luca Gazzaniga

"Stay within the confines of your villa in splendid isolation, or enjoy the wide range of facilities on the island. Activities are a comfortable cycle ride away and include an excellent diving center, and an outdoor cinema. You can even spend a night under the stars on your own island in the middle of the ocean. Bliss!"—Robin Partington

Recommended by: Luca Gazzaniga, Luca Gazzaniga Architects; Robin Partington, Robin Partington & Partners

THE ST. REGIS MALDIVES VOMMULI RESORT

Vommuli Island
Dhaalu Atoll 13080, Maldives
+960 6766333
marriott.com

CREDIT CARDS...Accepted
PRICE...Blow-out
TYPE..Resort
ACCOMMODATION..77 Villas
FACILITIES.....................Bar, Gym, Outdoor swimming pool,
Restaurant, Sauna, Spa,
Steam room, Tennis, Yoga
GOOD TO KNOW.......................Bicycle rentals, Child friendly
RECOMMENDED FOR...........................All-time favorite, Island,
Spa, Worth the travel

"The resort is private and bespoke with a deep respect for the environment."—Francesca Bucci

"Spa treatment rooms are embedded in the natural surroundings—you can watch dolphins swimming nearby!"—Maria Warner Wong

Recommended by: Francesca Bucci, BG Studio International; Maria Warner Wong, WOW Architects | Warner Wong Design

CHEVAL BLANC RANDHELI

Randheli
Noonu Atoll 11111
Maldives
+960 6561515
chevalblanc.com

CREDIT CARDS..Accepted
PRICE..Blow-out
TYPE..Resort
ACCOMMODATION......................................45 Villas
FACILITIES......................Bar, Gym, Outdoor swimming pool,
5 Restaurants, Sauna, Spa,
Steam room, Tennis, Yoga
GOOD TO KNOW................................Child friendly
RECOMMENDED FOR.................Luxury, Spa, Worth the travel

"An ultimate escape experience composed of multiple private islands."—André Fu

Recommended by: André Fu, AFSO; Alireza Razavi, Studio Razavi Architecture; Fernando Sordo Madaleno, Sordo Madaleno

THE SUN SIYAM IRU FUSHI

Sun Siyam Iru Fushi
Noonu Atoll 02036
Maldives
+960 6560591
sunsiyam.com

CREDIT CARDS..Accepted
PRICE..Blow-out
TYPE..Resort
ACCOMMODATION......................221 Retreats and Villas
FACILITIES..........................4 Bars, Gym, Outdoor swimming
pool, 10 Restaurants, Sauna,
Spa, Steam room, Yoga
GOOD TO KNOW..Child friendly
RECOMMENDED FOR..Luxury

"A magical location."—Stephen Barrett

Recommended by: Stephen Barrett, Rogers Stirk Harbour + Partners

FOUR SEASONS RESORT MALDIVES AT KUDA HURAA

Kuda Huraa
North Malé Atoll 20097
Maldives
+960 6644888
fourseasons.com

CREDIT CARDS..Accepted
PRICE..Blow-out
TYPE..Resort
ACCOMMODATION................98 Bungalows, Suites, and Villas
FACILITIES..2 Bars, Gym,
Outdoor swimming pool,
4 Restaurants, Spa, Yoga
GOOD TO KNOW................................Child friendly
RECOMMENDED FOR..........................All-time favorite, Luxury,
Worth the travel

"Pure luxury. Beautiful chalets, each with a private pool and ocean views. The whole setting is heavenly. Service is excellent and the restaurants serve amazing food." —Adil Kerai

Recommended by: Adil Kerai, Habib Fida Ali Architects

HUVAVEN FUSHI MALDIVES

Huvaven Fushi
North Malé Atoll 08390
Maldives
+960 6644222
huvafenfushi.com

CREDIT CARDS..Accepted
PRICE..Blow-out
TYPE..Resort
ACCOMMODATION..................................45 Pavilions and Villas
FACILITIES..Bar, Cafe, Gym,
Outdoor swimming pool,
4 Restaurants, Spa, Yoga
GOOD TO KNOW..Diving
RECOMMENDED FOR...Spa

"A surreal underwater spa experience: fish swim by while you enjoy the wonderful, relaxing treatments." —Grace Cheung

Recommended by: Grace Cheung, XRANGE Architecture + Design

ONE&ONLY REETHI RAH
Reethi Rah
Malé
North Malé Atoll 08440
Maldives
+971 44261099
oneandonlyresorts.com

CREDIT CARDS	Accepted
PRICE	Blow-out
TYPE	Resort
ACCOMMODATION	122 Villas
FACILITIES	3 Bars, Gym, Outdoor swimming pool, 6 Restaurants, Salon, Sauna, Spa, Steam room, Tennis
GOOD TO KNOW	Child friendly
RECOMMENDED FOR	Island, Spa

"There are stand-alone suites and full facilities. The white sand beach is amazing."—Rick Joy

Recommended by: Rick Joy, Studio Rick Joy; Patrick Reymond, Atelier Oï

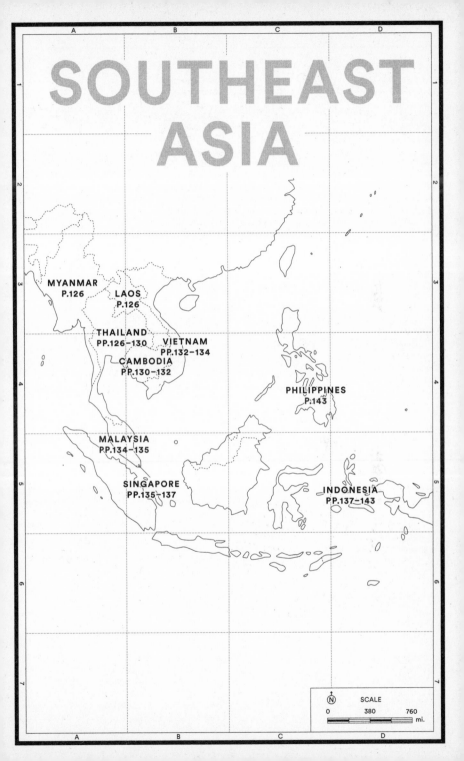

SOUTHEAST ASIA

MYANMAR
P.126

LAOS
P.126

THAILAND
PP.126–130

VIETNAM
PP.132–134

CAMBODIA
PP.130–132

PHILIPPINES
P.143

MALAYSIA
PP.134–135

SINGAPORE
PP.135–137

INDONESIA
PP.137–143

N

SCALE

0   380   760
mi.

PLEASANT VIEW RESORT
Mya Pyin Main Street
Thandwe Township
Ngapali 07171
Myanmar
+95 4342224
pleasant-view-resort-ngapali-beach.business.site

CREDIT CARDS	Accepted but not Amex
PRICE	Low-cost
TYPE	Resort
ACCOMMODATION	56 Rooms
FACILITIES	Swimming pool, Restaurant, Spa
GOOD TO KNOW	Closed from May to September
RECOMMENDED FOR	Beach

"This little-known hotel is close to a charming fishing village."—Beppe Caturegli and Giovannella Formica

Recommended by: Beppe Caturegli and Giovannella Formica, Caturegli Formica Architetti Associati

BELMOND LA RÉSIDENCE PHOU VAO
Phou Vao Road
Luang Prabang 84330, Laos
+856 71212530
belmond.com

CREDIT CARDS	Accepted
PRICE	Mid-range
TYPE	Hotel
ACCOMMODATION	34 Suites
FACILITIES	Bar, Gym, Outdoor swimming pool, Restaurant, Sauna, Spa
GOOD TO KNOW	Bicycle rentals, Child friendly
RECOMMENDED FOR	Mountains

Belmond La Résidence Phou Vao, situated in a UNESCO Heritage Site, is regarded as one of the finest and most serene hotels in Luang Prabang. Experiences include taking part in early morning almsgiving with local monks, before enjoying a sunrise breakfast cruise.

Recommended by: José Juan Rivera Rio, JJRR/Arquitectura

KAMU LODGE
Ban Nioy Hai
Muang Nga District
Luang Prabang 06000, Laos
+856 2056032365
kamulodge.com

CREDIT CARDS	Accepted
PRICE	Mid-range
TYPE	Tented lodge
ACCOMMODATION	20 Tents
FACILITIES	Bar, Outdoor restaurant, Spa
GOOD TO KNOW	Child friendly
RECOMMENDED FOR	Eco-conscious

"Very calm and authentic experience of local rural life with lots of excursions on offer."—Hasan Çalışlar

Recommended by: Hasan Çalışlar, Erginoğlu & Çalışlar

THE ATLANTA HOTEL
78 Soi 2 Sukhumvit Road
Bangkok 10110, Thailand
+66 22526069
theatlantahotelbangkok.com

CREDIT CARDS	Not Accepted
PRICE	Low-cost
TYPE	Hotel
ACCOMMODATION	49 Rooms
FACILITIES	Outdoor swimming pool, Restaurant
GOOD TO KNOW	No pets
RECOMMENDED FOR	Budget

"This place has remained unchanged since it was built in the 1960s. No frills, but plenty of character."—Isabelle Toland

Recommended by: Isabelle Toland, Aileen Sage Architects

MANDARIN ORIENTAL, BANGKOK
48 Oriental Avenue
Bangkok 10500, Thailand
+66 26599000
mandarin-bkk.com

CREDIT CARDS	Accepted
PRICE	High-end
TYPE	Hotel
ACCOMMODATION	347 Rooms and Suites
FACILITIES	Bar, Gym, Outdoor swimming pool, Patisserie, 9 Restaurants, Spa, Yoga
GOOD TO KNOW	Free parking
RECOMMENDED FOR	Luxury, Spa, Urban

"Breakfast on the river-facing terrace."—Mårten Claesson

Recommended by: Rodrigo Carazo, Carazo Architecture; Mårten Claesson, Claesson Koivisto Rune; Doriana and Massimiliano Fuksas, Studio Fuksas; Thomas Leeser, Leeser Architecture; Claudio Lucchesi, Urban Future Organization

PARK HYATT BANGKOK
Central Embassy, 88 Wireless Road
Bangkok 10330
Thailand
+66 20121234
hyatt.com

CREDIT CARDS	Accepted
PRICE	High-end
TYPE	Hotel
ACCOMMODATION	222 Rooms and Suites
FACILITIES	Bar, Gym, Outdoor swimming pool, 3 Restaurants, Spa, Yoga
GOOD TO KNOW	Babysitting, Valet parking
RECOMMENDED FOR	Spa, Worth the travel

"The pool and spa are sculpturally refined. Treatment rooms and suites are curated on an intimate scale with a soft, residential quality thanks to the furnishings and finishes."—George Yabu and Glenn Pushelberg

Recommended by: Amanda Levete, AL_A; George Yabu and Glenn Pushelberg, Yabu Pushelberg

SILOM VILLAGE INN
286 Silom Road, Suriyawong
Bangkok 10500
Thailand
+66 26356810
silomvillage.co.th

CREDIT CARDS	Accepted but not Amex
PRICE	Low-cost
TYPE	Hotel
ACCOMMODATION	65 Rooms
FACILITIES	Restaurant
GOOD TO KNOW	Near Patpong Night Market
RECOMMENDED FOR	Budget

"Nice, clean, and large rooms. Very basic hotel, but set in a lovely courtyard nearby a shopping zone with restaurants, art galleries, and a spa."—Adil Kerai

Recommended by: Adil Kerai, Habib Fida Ali Architects

SUKHOTHAI BANGKOK
13/3 South Sathorn Road
Bangkok 10120
Thailand
+66 23448888
sukhothai.com

CREDIT CARDS	Accepted
PRICE	High-end
TYPE	Hotel
ACCOMMODATION	214 Rooms and Suites
FACILITIES	Bar, Outdoor swimming pool, Restaurant, Spa
GOOD TO KNOW	Child friendly
RECOMMENDED FOR	All-time favorite, Luxury

"The bathroom in the guest rooms is large and luxurious. Its teak detailing, earthy Thai ceramic tiles, and upholstered furniture rival any spa interior."—David Rockwell

With its sleek architecture by Kerry Hill and Edward Tuttle, it's hard to believe that the lush green spaces of The Sukothai are in the center of Bangkok. The hotel also has excellent spa programs and an impressive eighty-foot (twenty-five-meter) infinity pool.

Recommended by: Carlo Ratti, Carlo Ratti Associati; David Rockwell, Rockwell Group; Uwe Schmidt-Hess, Patalab Architecture

TAMARIND VILLAGE
50/1 Rajdamnoen Road
Chiang Mai 50200
Thailand
+66 534188969
tamarindvillage.com

CREDIT CARDS	Accepted
PRICE	Mid-range
TYPE	Hotel
ACCOMMODATION	46 Rooms and Suites
FACILITIES	Restaurant, Spa
GOOD TO KNOW	Babysitting
RECOMMENDED FOR	Spa

An enchanting boutique hotel in the heart of Chiang Mai, Tamarind Village is an ideal base from which to explore all that the city has to offer. A number of local excursions are available to book through the hotel concierge. However, for those looking for a spot of relaxation, the spa has a wide range of excellent wellness treatments such as traditional Thai massage.

Recommended by: Dinko Peračić, ARP and Platforma 9.81

FOUR SEASONS TENTED CAMP GOLDEN TRIANGLE

499 Moo 1, Vieng Road
Chiang Rai 57150
Thailand
+66 53910200
fourseasons.com

CREDIT CARDS	Accepted
PRICE	High-end (all-inclusive)
TYPE	Tented Camp
ACCOMMODATION	16 Tents and Villas
FACILITIES	2 Bars, Restaurant
GOOD TO KNOW	Child friendly (10 and over)
RECOMMENDED FOR	Worth the travel

"Arriving by water and ascending the steep hillside stairs to the jaw-droppingly beautiful open-air reception deck sets the scene for this fantastical tented camp that elevates the term 'glamping' to an unprecedented level. Set within a spectacular Thai jungle elephant sanctuary, the site design and tent structures are a childhood tree-house fantasy come to life in a very, very grown-up way. From its exquisite cultural context to its extraordinary culinary experiences, the property is splendid in every dimension imaginable."
—Todd-Avery Lenahan

Recommended by: Todd-Avery Lenahan, TAL Studio

THE TUBKAAK KRABI BOUTIQUE RESORT

123 Moo 3, Tumbol Nongtalay
Amphur Muang
Krabi 81180
Thailand
+66 7562 8456
tubkaakresort.com

CREDIT CARDS	Accepted
PRICE	Mid-range
TYPE	Resort
ACCOMMODATION	28 Rooms, Suites, and Villas
FACILITIES	Gym, Outdoor swimming pool, 2 Restaurants, Spa, Yoga
GOOD TO KNOW	Bicycle rentals, Child friendly (10 and over), Cookery classes
RECOMMENDED FOR	Beach

"Peaceful location, fantastic service, beautiful spa, and designed to minimize environmental impact and maximize visitor experience."—Ab Rogers

Recommended by: Ab Rogers, Ab Rogers Design

SIX SENSES YAO NOI

56 Moo 5, Tambol Koh Yao Noi
Amphur Koh Yao
Phang Nga 82160
Thailand
+66 76418500
sixsenses.com

CREDIT CARDS	Accepted
PRICE	High-end
TYPE	Resort
ACCOMMODATION	56 Suites and Villas
FACILITIES	Bar, Gym, Outdoor swimming pool, 2 Restaurants, Spa, Yoga
GOOD TO KNOW	Child friendly, Water sports
RECOMMENDED FOR	Beach

"Breathtaking views from your villa, with a contrast between the jungle and the ocean."—Bernardo and Paulo Jacobsen

Recommended by: Bernardo and Paulo Jacobsen, Jacobsen Arquitetura

HAADSON RESORT

30 Moo 7, BangMuang
Takuapa
Phang Nga 82190
Thailand
+66 76406450
haadsonresort.com

CREDIT CARDS	Accepted but not Amex
PRICE	Mid-range
TYPE	Resort
ACCOMMODATION	45 Rooms
FACILITIES	Bar, Outdoor restaurant and swimming pools
GOOD TO KNOW	Bicycle rentals
RECOMMENDED FOR	Eco-conscious, Family friendly

"Located within a palm plantation close to the sea, this resort is great, with safe, calm outdoor facilities—ideal for families."—Uwe Schmidt-Hess

Recommended by: Uwe Schmidt-Hess, Patalab Architecture

IUDIA

Moo 4, 11-12 Utong Road
Pratuchai
Phra Nakhon Si Ayutthaya 13000
Thailand
+66 860801888
iudia.com

CREDIT CARDS	Accepted
PRICE	Low-cost
TYPE	Hotel
ACCOMMODATION	13 Rooms
FACILITIES	Cafe, Outdoor swimming pool
GOOD TO KNOW	Ancient ruins
RECOMMENDED FOR	Wish I'd designed

"Very beautiful, small hotel on the river in the ancient World Heritage Site of Ayutthaya. An understated and contemporary reinterpretation of traditional Thai architecture, Iudia is formed from a beautiful sequence of courtyards, terraces, gardens, and buildings that open up and appear to tumble into the river, framing views of an ancient temple across the water."—Alex Warnock-Smith

Recommended by: Alex Warnock-Smith, Urban Projects Bureau

ROSEWOOD PHUKET

88/28 Muen-Ngern Road
Patong
Phuket 83150
Thailand
+66 76356888
rosewoodhotels.com

CREDIT CARDS	Accepted
PRICE	High-end
TYPE	Resort
ACCOMMODATION	71 Rooms
FACILITIES	Bar, Gym, Outdoor swimming pool, 3 Restaurants, Yoga
GOOD TO KNOW	Pet friendly, Valet parking
RECOMMENDED FOR	Family friendly

"Our best family vacation. Situated on one of Phuket's nicest beaches, the hotel has a fantastic rustic Thai restaurant, a sprawling set of pools, and a dedicated (and discrete) kids' zone. It was so perfect for the whole family that we hardly left the beautifully landscaped grounds."—Forth Bagley

Recommended by: Forth Bagley, Kohn Pedersen Fox

AMANPURI

Thalang District
Phuket 83110, Thailand
+66 76324333
aman.com

CREDIT CARDS	Accepted
PRICE	High-end
TYPE	Resort
ACCOMMODATION	83 Pavilions and Villas
FACILITIES	3 Bars, Gym, Outdoor swimming pool, 5 Restaurants, Spa, Tennis
GOOD TO KNOW	Child friendly
RECOMMENDED FOR	Island, Luxury, Spa

"Impeccable design and stunning natural environment."
—Bruce Kuwabara

The original Aman resort, Amanpuri is situated among a secluded grove of coconut trees on the shores of Phuket. It takes full advantage of its private beachside location, from high-adrenaline Flyboard and jet skiing to sea kayaking.

Recommended by: Luca Gazzaniga, Luca Gazzaniga Architects; Bruce Kuwabara, KPMB Architects; Michael Young, Michael Young Studio

EVASON HUA HIN

9 Moo 5, Paknampran Beach
Pranburi
Prachuap Khirikhan 77220, Thailand
+66 32632111
sixsenses.com

CREDIT CARDS	Accepted
PRICE	Low-cost
TYPE	Resort
ACCOMMODATION	196 Suites and Villas
FACILITIES	Bar, Gym, Outdoor swimming pool, 3 Restaurants, Sauna, Spa, Steam room, Tennis, Yoga
GOOD TO KNOW	Complimentary beach shuttle service
RECOMMENDED FOR	Spa

"Very beautiful, secluded villas nestled into stunning Thai gardens with pools, spas, tree-lined walkways, and lily ponds. Family villas have terraces, pools, and baths. The spa is amazing, with thatched-cottage massage parlors. The family center has a pool for kids."
—Alex Warnock-Smith

Recommended by: Alex Warnock-Smith, Urban Projects Bureau

BANYAN TREE SAMUI

99 Moo 4
Samui
Surat Thani 84310
Thailand
+66 77915333
banyantree.com

CREDIT CARDS	Accepted
PRICE	High-end
TYPE	Resort
ACCOMMODATION	88 Villas
FACILITIES	3 Bars, Gym, Outdoor swimming pool, 4 Restaurants, Spa, Yoga
GOOD TO KNOW	Child friendly
RECOMMENDED FOR	Spa

Banyan Tree Samui is situated in a secluded cove and offers guests stunning views of the surrounding bay. Each villa has a private pool, and highlights of the luxury spa include The Rainforest, a hydrotherapy experience that de-stresses and soothes.

Recommended by: Seunghoy Kim, KYWC Architects

SHANTAA KOH KOOD

20/3 Moo 2, Tambol
Koh Kood
Trat 23000
Thailand
+668 15660607
shantaakohkood.com

CREDIT CARDS	Accepted but not Amex
PRICE	Low-cost
TYPE	Resort
ACCOMMODATION	19 Huts
FACILITIES	Bar, 2 Restaurants
GOOD TO KNOW	Closed from June to September, No pets
RECOMMENDED FOR	Island

"A very relaxed, beautiful, and charming property by the sea on the lesser-known Thai island of Koh Kood. Not commercial or 'resorty' in the slightest. Simple A-frame huts for bedrooms, with private tropical gardens, an outdoor bathroom, and showers. It has all the must-have expectations of a Thai-island resort without the commercial atmosphere or scale."—Alex Warnock-Smith

Recommended by: Alex Warnock-Smith, Urban Projects Bureau

SONEVA KIRI

110 Moo 4
Koh Kood
Trat 23000
Thailand
+66 822088888
soneva.com

CREDIT CARDS	Accepted
PRICE	Blow-out
TYPE	Resort
ACCOMMODATION	35 Villas
FACILITIES	Bar, Gym, 4 Restaurants, Spa
GOOD TO KNOW	Child friendly, Cookery classes
RECOMMENDED FOR	Island, Spa

"After arriving at Suvarnabhumi airport, you take the private plane to Soneva Kiri—the flight makes you feel you're escaping far from busy Bangkok and daily life. The resort is understated, with low-key guests."
—Waro Kishi

"The spa treatments are amazing. Great jungle and fantastic beaches, and only a short flight from Bangkok."
—Murat Tabanlıoğlu

Recommended by: Waro Kishi, K.ASSOCIATES/Architects; Murat Tabanlıoğlu, Tabanlıoğlu Architects

SONG SAA COLLECTIVE

Koh Ouen Private Island
Koh Rong Archipelago
Cambodia
+855 23886750
songsaacollective.com

CREDIT CARDS	Accepted
PRICE	Blow-out
TYPE	Resort
ACCOMMODATION	24 Villas
FACILITIES	Bar, Gym, Outdoor swimming pool, Restaurant, Spa, Yoga
GOOD TO KNOW	Scuba diving, Water sports
RECOMMENDED FOR	Island

"Its remote location, world-class food, beautiful rooms, and down-to-earth ease make this one of the most unforgettable stays. The ecological and conservation initiatives of the hotel, their projects with local artisans, and their commitment to the land is very impressive. Everything here comes together beautifully."
—Grace Cheung

Recommended by: Grace Cheung, XRANGE Architecture + Design

THE PLANTATION URBAN RESORT AND SPA
28 Street 184
Phnom Penh 12206
Cambodia
+855 23215151
theplantation.asia

CREDIT CARDS...Accepted
PRICE...Low-cost
TYPE..Resort
ACCOMMODATION...84 Rooms
FACILITIES...Bar, Boutique,
Outdoor swimming pool,
2 Restaurants, Sauna, Spa,
Steam room
GOOD TO KNOW.......................................Child friendly
RECOMMENDED FOR..Urban

"A small oasis in the center of town. The hotel has a nice pool surrounded by palm trees, and the architecture is a mix of modern and colonial style. The small compound has several outdoor spaces with lush tropical gardens."
—Mia Baarup Tofte

Recommended by: Mia Baarup Tofte, NORD Architects

RAFFLES HOTEL LE ROYAL
92 Rukhak Vithei Daun Penh
Phnom Penh 12202
Cambodia
+855 23981888
raffles.com

CREDIT CARDS...Accepted
PRICE...Mid-range
TYPE...Hotel
ACCOMMODATION................................175 Rooms and Suites
FACILITIES...................Bar, Gym, Outdoor swimming pool,
2 Restaurants, Spa
GOOD TO KNOW.......................................Child friendly
RECOMMENDED FOR..........................All-time favorite

"My most memorable hotel stay; it feels perfectly relaxed within a vibrant city. A cocktail never tasted or looked so good as the one I sipped on the covered stucco porch after a long, hot day of sightseeing."—Forth Bagley

Recommended by: Forth Bagley, Kohn Pedersen Fox

AMANSARA
Road to Angkor
Siem Reap 17250
Cambodia
+855 63760333
aman.com

CREDIT CARDS...Accepted
PRICE...Blow-out
TYPE...Hotel
ACCOMMODATION..24 Suites
FACILITIES................Bar, Gym, Outdoor swimming pool,
Restaurant, Spa, Steam Room, Yoga
GOOD TO KNOW.....................Bicycle rentals, Child friendly
RECOMMENDED FOR..................................Luxury, Spa

A masterpiece of 1960s New Khmer architecture, the hotel's unabashedly modern yet thoughtfully considered design contrasts pleasantly with its ancient surroundings. A former residence for guests of the King, Amansara is now the ideal base from which to explore the nearby Angkor Wat complex; its bespoke itineraries take guests away from the crowds and toward less-explored areas. Its spa and wellness programs—a highlight of any Aman experience—draw upon Khmer traditions, complemented by sunrise yoga sessions.

Recommended by: Adam Meshberg, Meshberg Group; José Juan Rivera Rio, JJRR/Arquitectura

FCC ANGKOR
Pokambor Avenue (next to the Royal Residence)
Siem Reap
Cambodia
+855 63760280
fcccollection.com

CREDIT CARDS...Accepted
PRICE...Mid-range
TYPE...Hotel
ACCOMMODATION................................80 Rooms and Suites
FACILITIES...................Bar, Gym, Outdoor swimming pool,
2 Restaurants, Spa, Yoga
GOOD TO KNOW.......................................Child friendly
RECOMMENDED FOR..........................Best-kept secret, Urban

"Beautiful restoration of the existing Foreign Correspondents Club."—Joana Leandro Vasconcelos

"Unpretentious, with just the right amount of luxury."
—David Welsh and Chris Major

Recommended by: Joana Leandro Vasconcelos, Atelier In.vitro; David Welsh and Chris Major, Welsh + Major

PHUM BAITANG RESORT
Sangkat Svaydangkum
Siem Reap 17000
Cambodia
+855 63961111
zannierhotels.com

CREDIT CARDS	Accepted
PRICE	High-end
TYPE	Resort
ACCOMMODATION	45 Villas
FACILITIES	Bar, Gym, Outdoor swimming pool, 2 Restaurants, Sauna, Spa, Steam room, Yoga
GOOD TO KNOW	Babysitting, Free parking
RECOMMENDED FOR	All-time favorite, Countryside, Luxury, Spa

"The hotel is designed to give an experience of rural Cambodian lifestyle, and within that they give you an extremely luxurious experience. One gets a glimpse of the architectural vestige of Angkor with views overlooking the rice paddies and gardens."—Sonali Rastogi

Recommended by: Sonali Rastogi, Morphogenesis

VIROTH'S HOTEL
Street 24
Wat Bo Village Siem Reap Angkor
Siem Reap 17252
Cambodia
+855 63766107
viroth-hotel.com

CREDIT CARDS	Accepted but not Amex
PRICE	Mid-range
TYPE	Hotel
ACCOMMODATION	35 Rooms and Suites
FACILITIES	Bar, Gym, Outdoor swimming pool, 2 Restaurants, Spa
GOOD TO KNOW	Child friendly (12 and over)
RECOMMENDED FOR	All-time favorite

Recommended by: Claudio Lucchesi, Urban Future Organization

SIX SENSES CON DAO
Con Dao Island
Ba Ria—Vung Tau 74000
Vietnam
+84 2543831222
sixsenses.com

CREDIT CARDS	Accepted
PRICE	High-end
TYPE	Resort
ACCOMMODATION	50 Villas
FACILITIES	Bar, Outdoor swimming pool, 2 Restaurants, Spa, Yoga
GOOD TO KNOW	Bicycle rentals, Water sports
RECOMMENDED FOR	Spa, Worth the travel

"Amazing, unique location and great architecture."
—Tavis Wright

Inspired by the design of a traditional Vietnamese fishing villages, Six Senses Con Dao is a relaxed yet elegant retreat with a focus on wellbeing. Facilities include a spa, yoga, and experiences such as snorkeling and diving trips, plus excursions into the surrounding rainforest.

Recommended by: Kelly Hoppen, Kelly Hoppen Interiors; Tavis Wright, Dos Architects

CINNAMON CATHEDRAL HOTEL
38 Autrieu Street
Hoan Kiem
Hanoi
Vietnam
+84 2439386761
cinnamonhotel.net

CREDIT CARDS	Accepted but not Amex
PRICE	Low-cost
TYPE	Hotel
ACCOMMODATION	10 Rooms
FACILITIES	Bar, Restaurant
GOOD TO KNOW	Close to night markets
RECOMMENDED FOR	Urban

"Stay here for Vietnamese contemporary design style influenced by tradition."—Laurent Gravier

Recommended by: Laurent Gravier, FRES architectes

SOFITEL LEGEND METROPOLE HANOI HOTEL

15 Ngo Quyen Street
Hoan Kiem
Hanoi
Vietnam
+84 2438266919
accorhotels.com

CREDIT CARDS	Accepted
PRICE	High-end
TYPE	Hotel
ACCOMMODATION	364 Rooms and Suites
FACILITIES	4 Bars, Gym, Outdoor swimming pool, 3 Restaurants
GOOD TO KNOW	Babysitting
RECOMMENDED FOR	Urban

Set in a colonial, Neo-Classical building in the heart of
the old city, Sofitel Legend Metropole Hanoi offers guests
a glimpse of Hanoi's past while providing five-star comfort
and facilities. Rooms and suites are spread across two wings:
the historic Metropole Wing and the newer Opera Wing.

Recommended by: Jean-Paul Viguier, Jean-Paul Viguier
et Associés

THE MYST DONG KHOI

6-8 Ho Huan Nghiep Street, District 1
Ho Chi Minh City
Vietnam
+84 2835203040
themystdongkhoihotel.com

CREDIT CARDS	Accepted
PRICE	Mid-range
TYPE	Hotel
ACCOMMODATION	108 Rooms
FACILITIES	Bar, Cafe, Outdoor swimming pool, Restaurant, Rooftop terrace bar
GOOD TO KNOW	Child friendly
RECOMMENDED FOR	Worth the travel

Rising high above the streets of Ho Chi Minh, The Myst
Dong Khoi is a calm retreat in the center of the city.
The interior design is thoughtful, and the antiques and
objets d'art give this modern space a sense of place
and context within its historic surroundings.

Recommended by: Michael Stiff, Stiff + Trevillion

SIX SENSES NIHN VAN BAY

Nihn Van Bay
Ninh Hoa
Khanh Hoa
Vietnam
+84 2583524268
sixsenses.com

CREDIT CARDS	Accepted
PRICE	High-end
TYPE	Resort
ACCOMMODATION	59 Villas
FACILITIES	3 Bars, Gym, Outdoor swimming pool, 3 Restaurants, Spa, Yoga
GOOD TO KNOW	Child friendly, Cooking classes, Water sports
RECOMMENDED FOR	Eco-conscious

"Ocean-front villas and pools are one step away from
the ocean, where you can snorkel. Cooking classes in the
organic vegetable gardens and the hotel's sustainability
pledge are great examples of hospitality with a conscience."
—Grace Cheung

Recommended by: Grace Cheung, XRANGE Architecture +
Design

CHEN SEA RESORT AND SPA

Cua Duong Village
Phu Quoc
Kien Giang
Vietnam
+84 2973995895
chensea-resort.com

CREDIT CARDS	Accepted
PRICE	Mid-range
TYPE	Resort
ACCOMMODATION	36 Villas
FACILITIES	Bar, Gym, Outdoor swimming pool, Restaurant, Spa, Yoga
GOOD TO KNOW	Child friendly, Water sports
RECOMMENDED FOR	Island

Recommended by: Beppe Caturegli and Giovannella
Formica, Caturegli Formica Architetti Associati

EAST WEST VILLAS HOI AN
294 Cua Dai Street
Hoi An
Quang Nam
Vietnam
+84 2353929988
eastwesthoianvillas.com

CREDIT CARDS	Accepted
PRICE	Low-cost
TYPE	Hotel
ACCOMMODATION	14 Villas
FACILITIES	Outdoor swimming pool
GOOD TO KNOW	Bicycle rentals, Child friendly
RECOMMENDED FOR	Countryside

"The natural stone pool is a highlight, but especially good is the breakfast, which is served in your room, with the most amazing tropical fresh juices and fruits."
—Dieter Vander Velpen

Recommended by: Dieter Vander Velpen, Dieter Vander Velpen Architects

FOUR SEASONS RESORT THE NAM HAI, HOI AN
Block Ha My Dong B, Dien Duong Ward
Hoi An
Quang Nam
Vietnam
+84 2353940000
fourseasons.com

CREDIT CARDS	Accepted
PRICE	High-end
TYPE	Resort
ACCOMMODATION	100 Villas
FACILITIES	2 Bars, Gym, 2 Restaurants, Sauna, Spa, Steam room, Tennis, Yoga
GOOD TO KNOW	Child friendly, Water sports
RECOMMENDED FOR	Luxury

"Probably the best hotel landscape and pool design I've seen—the combination of strong lines, natural materials, and water features makes it a perfect resort."
—Dieter Vander Velpen

Recommended by: Dieter Vander Velpen, Dieter Vander Velpen Architects

THE DATAI LANGKAWI
Jalan Teluk Datai
Langkawi
Kedah 07000
Malaysia
+60 49500500
thedatai.com

CREDIT CARDS	Accepted
PRICE	High-end
TYPE	Resort
ACCOMMODATION	112 Rooms and Suites
FACILITIES	Bar, Gym, Golf, Nature center, Outdoor swimming pool, 4 Restaurants, Spa
GOOD TO KNOW	Bicycle rentals, Child friendly
RECOMMENDED FOR	Beach, Best-kept secret, Wish I'd designed

"Originally designed by Kerry Hill, this is superb architecture on every scale, carefully refurbished by Didier Lefort."
—Jack Diamond

"A beautiful hotel inspired by local building traditions and climate, built with local materials."—Henriette Salvesen

Recommended by: Stefan Antoni, SAOTA; Jack Diamond, Diamond Schmitt; Amanda Levete, AL_A; Henriette Salvesen, Div.A Arkitekter; Ken Yeang, Hamzah & Yeang

THE DUSUN
3437, Jalan, Mukim, Kampung Baru Pantai
Negeri Sembilan 71770
Malaysia
+60 126162585
thedusun.com.my

CREDIT CARDS	Not Accepted
PRICE	Mid-range
TYPE	Resort
ACCOMMODATION	7 Cabins
FACILITIES	Outdoor swimming pool
GOOD TO KNOW	Free parking, Self-catering
RECOMMENDED FOR	Best-kept secret, Countryside, Eco-conscious

"Pure tranquility."—Michael Stiff

Recommended by: Michael Stiff, Stiff + Trevillion

THE FRAME GUESTHOUSE

168 Chulia Street
George Town
Penang 10200
Malaysia
+60 42638807
theframeguesthouse.com

CREDIT CARDS.....................................Accepted but not Amex
PRICE...Low-cost
TYPE..Guesthouse
ACCOMMODATION....................................15 Dorms and Rooms
FACILITIES...Lockers, Lounge
GOOD TO KNOW...Laundry service,
Linen and towels provided
RECOMMENDED FOR...Budget

Situated in a former framemaker shop, the industrial-chic
accommodation makes an ideal base from which to explore
George Town's famous food stalls.

Recommended by: Robert Konieczny, KWK Promes

FLAMINGO HOTEL BY THE LAKE

5 Tasik Ampang
Jalan Hulu Kelang
Ampang
Selangor 68000
Malaysia
+60 342563288
flamingo.com.my

CREDIT CARDS....................................Accepted but not Amex
PRICE...Low-cost
TYPE..Hotel
ACCOMMODATION....................Chalet, 228 Rooms and Suites
FACILITIES...Bar, Bakery,
Outdoor swimming pool, Restaurant
GOOD TO KNOW...Child friendly
RECOMMENDED FOR...Budget

Recommended by: Ken Yeang, Hamzah & Yeang

SHANGRI-LA HOTEL, KUALA LUMPUR

11 Jalan Sultan Ismail
Kuala Lumpur
Selangor 50250
Malaysia
+60 320322388
shangri-la.com

CREDIT CARDS...Accepted
PRICE...Mid-range
TYPE..Hotel
ACCOMMODATION.............................662 Rooms and Suites
FACILITIES.......................................2 Bars, Florist, Gym,
Outsoor swimming pool, 5 Restaurants,
Salon, Sauna, Spa, Steam room
GOOD TO KNOW...Child friendly
RECOMMENDED FOR...Where I live

"This is an oldie but goodie."—Ken Yeang

Recommended by: Ken Yeang, Hamzah & Yeang

THE FULLERTON HOTEL SINGAPORE

1 Fullerton Square
Downtown Core
Singapore 049178
+65 67338388
fullertonhotels.com

CREDIT CARDS...Accepted
PRICE...Mid-range
TYPE..Hotel
ACCOMMODATION.............................399 Rooms and Suites
FACILITIES...2 Bars, Gym,
Outdoor swimming pool,
Patisserie, 4 Restaurants,
Sauna, Spa, Steam room
GOOD TO KNOW...Child friendly
RECOMMENDED FOR...All-time favorite

**"The service at this hotel is the best I have ever encountered.
It feels like being at home when I stay here. It is truly special."
—Ben van Berkel**

Recommended by: Ben van Berkel, UNStudio

MARINA BAY SANDS SINGAPORE
10 Bayfront Avenue
Downtown Core
Singapore 018956
+65 66888888
marinabaysands.com

CREDIT CARDS	Accepted
PRICE	High-end
TYPE	Hotel
ACCOMMODATION	2,561 Rooms and Suites
FACILITIES	Bar, Florist, Gym, Outdoor swimming pool, 60 Restaurants, Sauna, Spa, Steam room, Yoga
GOOD TO KNOW	Valet parking
RECOMMENDED FOR	Urban, Worth the travel

"Take in the views from the rooftop pool!"—Randa Tukan

Marina Bay Sands, designed by Moshe Safdie, is one of the world's most iconic hotels, renowned for its huge rooftop infinity pool and world-class service. It also has more than 80 dining choices.

Recommended by: Andres Remy, Remy Architects; Randa Tukan, HOK Architects; Fosbury Architecture

PARK ROYAL ON PICKERING
3 Upper Pickering Street
Downtown Core
Singapore 058289
+65 68098888
panpacific.com

CREDIT CARDS	Accepted
PRICE	Mid-range
TYPE	Hotel
ACCOMMODATION	367 Rooms and Suites
FACILITIES	Bar, Gym, Outdoor swimming pool, Restaurant, Spa, Steam room
GOOD TO KNOW	Child friendly, Free parking
RECOMMENDED FOR	Urban

"In a dense urban setting, the hotel has floors of hanging gardens, lush green walls, and huge areas of landscaped pools."—Grace Cheung

Recommended by: Grace Cheung, XRANGE Architecture + Design; Dennis Pieprz, Sasaki

RAFFLES HOTEL
1 Beach Road
Downtown Core
Singapore 189673
+65 63371886
raffles.com

CREDIT CARDS	Accepted
PRICE	High-end
TYPE	Hotel
ACCOMMODATION	103 Suites
FACILITIES	2 Bars, Gym, Outdoor swimming pool, 6 Restaurants, Spa
GOOD TO KNOW	No pets
RECOMMENDED FOR	All-time favorite, Urban

"Ground-floor rooms are best, as they face a tropical landscaped courtyard. Their internal layout makes the most of a small space, and are like single-bedroom apartments with multi-zoned areas. Rooms open to a wide corridor and the courtyard, with tables for breakfast or tea."—Ken Yeang

Raffles is not just an iconic hotel, but a Singaporean landmark in its own right. After extensive restoration works, it reopened in 2019 and has retained its signature charm. To step across its teakwood floors, past its charming verandas and through its lush courtyard gardens to the famous Long Bar, is like taking a (glamorous) step back in time.

Recommended by: Jean-Paul Viguier, Jean-Paul Viguier et Associés; Ken Yeang, Hamzah & Yeang

THE WAREHOUSE HOTEL
320 Havelock Road
Robertson Quay
Singapore 169628
+65 68280000
thewarehousehotel.com

CREDIT CARDS	Accepted
PRICE	Mid-range
TYPE	Hotel
ACCOMMODATION	37 Rooms and Suites
FACILITIES	Bar, Rooftop swimming pool, Restaurant
GOOD TO KNOW	Near Singapore River
RECOMMENDED FOR	Where I live

Recommended by: Maria Warner Wong, WOW Architects | Warner Wong Design

CAPELLA RESORT SINGAPORE
1 The Knolls
Sentosa Island
Singapore 098297
+65 63778888
capellahotels.com

CREDIT CARDS	Accepted
PRICE	High-end
TYPE	Resort
ACCOMMODATION	1 Manor, 112 Suites and Villa
FACILITIES	Outdoor swimming pool, 3 Restaurants, Spa, Steam room
GOOD TO KNOW	Pet friendly
RECOMMENDED FOR	Family friendly

"A genuine urban resort with a layered and truly mesmerizing pool experience."—André Fu

Recommended by: André Fu, AFSO

ALILA VILLAS ULUWATU
Jalan Belimbing Sari
Banjar Tambiyak
Bali 80364
Indonesia
+62 3618482166
alilahotels.com

CREDIT CARDS	Accepted
PRICE	High-end
TYPE	Resort
ACCOMMODATION	65 Villas
FACILITIES	Bar, Outdoor swimming pool, 4 Restaurants, Spa, Yoga
GOOD TO KNOW	Free Parking
RECOMMENDED FOR	Beach, Eco-conscious, Luxury, Wish I'd designed

"Sustainable architecture combining vernacular and Modernist styles with an amazing sea view."—Andres Remy

"The combination of modern clean lines and warm, natural materials is incredible. Perfect symbiosis of Asian design influences and contemporary luxuries."
—Dieter Vander Velpen

Recommended by: André Fu, AFSO; Alex Mok, Linehouse; Stéphane Parmentier; Andres Remy, Remy Architects; Dieter Vander Velpen, Dieter Vander Velpen Architects

HOTEL TUGU BALI
Jalan Pantai Batu Bolong
Canggu
Bali 80361
Indonesia
+62 3614731701
tuguhotels.com

CREDIT CARDS	Accepted
PRICE	Mid-range
TYPE	Resort
ACCOMMODATION	21 Rooms and Suites
FACILITIES	Bar, Outdoor swimming pool, 3 Restaurants, Spa
GOOD TO KNOW	Owner's art and antique collection
RECOMMENDED FOR	Luxury

Hotel Tugu is one of a boutique collection of art hotels founded by the owner of a large collection of fine Indonesian art and cultural antiquities, many of which are on display. A love story to Indonesia, the resort is a visual celebration of the finest in traditional Balinese design, wellness, and culture.

Recommended by: Patrick Reymond, Atelier Oï

PLANTA VILLA
Jalan Batu Mejan 11D
Canggu
Bali 80351
Indonesia
+62 3618445650
plantabali.com

CREDIT CARDS	Accepted
PRICE	Mid-range
TYPE	Resort
ACCOMMODATION	5 Suites
FACILITIES	Massage hut, Outdoor swimming pool, Yoga
GOOD TO KNOW	Butler service, Child friendly
RECOMMENDED FOR	Countryside

"Beautiful five-room resort set within a rice paddy field."
—Alex Mok

Recommended by: Alex Mok, Linehouse

THE SLOW
Jalan Batu Bolong 97
Canggu
Bali 80361
Indonesia
+62 3612099000
theslow.id

CREDIT CARDS...Accepted
PRICE...Mid-range
TYPE...Hotel
ACCOMMODATION.......................................12 Suites
FACILITIES......................................Bar, Restaurant
GOOD TO KNOW.........................Near spas and a yoga studio
RECOMMENDED FOR..............................Worth the travel

Aptly named and achingly cool, The Slow offers guests a truly immersive holiday experience. The project of fashion designer George Gorrow, facilities range from a gallery with a rotating art collection and a soundtrack by LA-based Reverberation Studio, to all-day dining options, including one of Canggu's best breakfasts.

Recommended by: Juan Manuel Peláez Freidel, JUMP/Juan Manuel Peláez Arquitectos

FOUR SEASONS RESORT BALI AT JIMBARAN BAY
Jimbaran
Bali 80361
Indonesia
+62 361701010
fourseasons.com

CREDIT CARDS...Accepted
PRICE...Blow-out
TYPE...Resort
ACCOMMODATION......................................137 Villas
FACILITIES....................Bar, Gym, Outdoor swimming pool, 3 Restaurants, Spa, Yoga
GOOD TO KNOW...........................Babysitting, Child friendly, Water sports
RECOMMENDED FOR..Beach

"Frangipani-lined walkways lead to secluded villas and the resort has the most attentive staff."—Luis Ferreira-da-Silva

Recommended by: Luis Ferreira-da-Silva, Luis Ferreira-da-Silva Architects

AMANKILA
Jalan Raya Manggis
Manggis
Bali 80871
Indonesia
+62 36341333
aman.com

CREDIT CARDS...Accepted
PRICE...High-end
TYPE...Resort
ACCOMMODATION.......................................33 Suites
FACILITIES......................................Bar, Restaurant, Outdoor swimming pool, Spa
GOOD TO KNOW.........................Babysitting, Child friendly, Cookery classes
RECOMMENDED FOR...........................Wish I'd designed

Designed by architect Ed Tuttle, Amankila overlooks Bali's east coast beaches, providing breathtaking views. The hotel's aesthetic nods to traditional Balinese design, from the subtle accents in its well-appointed rooms to the three-tier, rice paddy-inspired infinity pool, which looks out across the sea to distant Lombok.

Recommended by: Roger Duffy, Skidmore, Owings & Merrill

ALILA UBUD
Melinggih Kelod
Payangan
Bali 80572
Indonesia
+62 361975963
alilahotels.com

CREDIT CARDS...Accepted
PRICE...Mid-range
TYPE...Hotel
ACCOMMODATION..74 Villas
FACILITIES..................2 Restaurants, Swimming pool, Yoga
GOOD TO KNOW.........................Babysitting, Cookery classes
RECOMMENDED FOR.................Countryside, Worth the travel

"A serene, rustic destination."—André Fu

Recommended by: André Fu, AFSO; Alex Mok, Linehouse

HANGING GARDENS OF BALI
Buahan
Payangan
Bali 80571, Indonesia
+62 361982700
hanginggardensofbali.com

CREDIT CARDS	Accepted
PRICE	High-end
TYPE	Resort
ACCOMMODATION	44 Villas
FACILITIES	Bar, Restaurant, Spa, Swimming pool
GOOD TO KNOW	Handcrafted furniture
RECOMMENDED FOR	Luxury

One of the highlights of the Hanging Gardens of Bali is the striking infinity pool, which affords swimmers the unique sensation of floating above the rainforest.

Recommended by: Dorin Stefan, Dorin Stefan Birou de Arhitectura

ALILA SEMINYAK
Jalan Taman Ganesha 9
Seminyak
Bali 80361, Indonesia
+62 3613021888
alilahotels.com

CREDIT CARDS	Accepted
PRICE	Mid-range
TYPE	Hotel
ACCOMMODATION	Penthouse, 240 Suites
FACILITIES	3 Bars, Outdoor swimming pool, 2 Restaurants, Spa, Yoga
GOOD TO KNOW	Babysitting
RECOMMENDED FOR	Eco-conscious

Recommended by: Andres Remy, Remy Architects

THE ELYSIAN BOUTIQUE VILLAS
Jalan Sari Dewi 18
Seminyak
Bali 80361, Indonesia
+62 361730999
theelysian.com

CREDIT CARDS	Accepted
PRICE	Mid-range
TYPE	Resort
ACCOMMODATION	27 Villas
FACILITIES	Restaurant, Spa
GOOD TO KNOW	Airport transfers
RECOMMENDED FOR	Beach

"Stay here for the privacy—every room is a beautiful villa with its own pool."—Mårten Claesson

Recommended by: Mårten Claesson, Claesson Koivisto Rune

KATAMAMA
Jalan Petitenget 51B
Seminyak
Bali 80361
Indonesia
+62 3613029999
katamama.com

CREDIT CARDS	Accepted
PRICE	Mid-range
TYPE	Hotel
ACCOMMODATION	56 Suites
FACILITIES	2 Bars, Gym, Outdoor swimming pool, Restaurant, Yoga
GOOD TO KNOW	Surfing
RECOMMENDED FOR	Beach

Recommended by: Alexander Wong, Alexander Wong Architects

MUNDUK MODING PLANTATION NATURE SPA AND RESORT
Jalan Asah Gobleg
Singaraja
Bali 81152
Indonesia
+62 811385059
mundukmodingplantation.com

CREDIT CARDS	Accepted
PRICE	Mid-range
TYPE	Boutique hotel
ACCOMMODATION	26 Suites and Villas
FACILITIES	Outdoor swimming pool, Restaurant, Spa, Tennis
GOOD TO KNOW	Coffee plantation
RECOMMENDED FOR	Countryside

"A boutique hotel situated away from the tourist tracks of Bali. A place for relaxation and for enjoying splendid views of the mountains and rural surroundings. The rooms are situated in the middle of the nature and have oversized, luxurious bathrooms."—Mia Baarup Tofte

Recommended by: Mia Baarup Tofte, NORD Architects

CONRAD BALI
Jalan Pratama 168
Tanjung Benoa
Bali 80363
Indonesia
+62 361778788
conradbali.com

CREDIT CARDS	Accepted
PRICE	Mid-range
TYPE	Hotel
ACCOMMODATION	358 Suites and Villas
FACILITIES	2 Bars, Gym, Outdoor swimming pool, 3 Restaurants, Spa, Tennis, Yoga
GOOD TO KNOW	Babysitting
RECOMMENDED FOR	Wish I'd designed

"The whole setting of the resort is amazing, and the use of water elements and greenery is very calming and soothing."
—Adil Kerai

Recommended by: Adil Kerai, Habib Fida Ali Architects

AMANDARI
Kedewatan
Ubud
Bali 80571
Indonesia
+62 361975333
aman.com

CREDIT CARDS	Accepted
PRICE	High-end
TYPE	Resort
ACCOMMODATION	30 Suites
FACILITIES	Bar, Outdoor swimming pool, Restaurant, Rooftop terrace bar, Sauna, Spa, Steam Room
GOOD TO KNOW	Near Goa Gajah caves
RECOMMENDED FOR	Countryside, Eco-conscious, Wish I'd designed, Worth the travel

"Situated in Ubud, the hotel blends into the local culture and architecture of a traditional Balinese village, giving an authentic experience of Indonesia's countryside."
—Bernardo and Paulo Jacobsen

Recommended by: Doriana and Massimiliano Fuksas, Studio Fuksas; Bernardo and Paulo Jacobsen, Jacobsen Arquitetura; Mark de Reus, de Reus Architects; Pedro Rica and Marta Urtasun, Mecanismo; Buzz Yudell, Moore Ruble Yudell

THE CHEDI CLUB TANAH GAJAH
Jalan Goa Gajah, Tengkulak Kaja
Ubud
Bali 80571
Indonesia
+62 361975685
ghmhotels.com

CREDIT CARDS	Accepted
PRICE	High-end
TYPE	Hotel
ACCOMMODATION	20 Suites and Villas
FACILITIES	Bar, Gym, Outdoor swimming pool, Restaurant, Spa
GOOD TO KNOW	Hot-air ballooning
RECOMMENDED FOR	Best-kept secret

The Chedi Club Tanah Gajah is a former private estate, and has only twenty villas, all with personal butler service. It prides itself on tailor-made experiences, and guests can request anything from a romantic dinner for two overlooking the rice paddies to an excursion to meet a local shaman— or even admire the sunrise from a hot-air balloon.

Recommended by: Carlo Ratti, Carlo Ratti Associati

COMO UMA UBUD
Jalan Raya Sanggingan
Ubud
Bali 80571
Indonesia
+62 361972448
comohotels.com

CREDIT CARDS	Accepted
PRICE	Mid-range
TYPE	Resort
ACCOMMODATION	46 Suites and Villas
FACILITIES	Bar, Outdoor swimming pool, 2 Restaurants, Spa, Yoga
GOOD TO KNOW	Bicycle rentals, Valet parking
RECOMMENDED FOR	Countryside

"It feels like paradise. A cluster of small houses in a tropical garden centered around a swimming pool, lake, restaurant, and other facilities. It is quiet and relaxing with magnificent service. The rooms have outside bathrooms and compact private gardens."—Chris Wilkinson

Recommended by: Chris Wilkinson, Wilkinson Eyre Architects

FOUR SEASONS RESORT BALI AT SAYAN

Sayan
Ubud
Bali 80571
Indonesia
+62 361977577
fourseasons.com

CREDIT CARDS	Accepted
PRICE	Blow-out
TYPE	Resort
ACCOMMODATION	60 Suites and Villas
FACILITIES	Bar, Gym, Outdoor swimming pool, 3 Restaurants, Sauna, Salon, Spa, Steam room, Yoga
GOOD TO KNOW	Child friendly, Cookery classes
RECOMMENDED FOR	Mountains

"A resort that is thoughtfully integrated into the surrounding landscape."—André Fu

Recommended by: André Fu, AFSO

HOTEL TJAMPUHAN SPA

Jalan Raya Tjampuhan
Ubud
Bali 80571
Indonesia
+62 361975368
tjampuhan-bali.com

CREDIT CARDS	Accepted
PRICE	Mid-range
TYPE	Hotel
ACCOMMODATION	67 Rooms
FACILITIES	Bar, Hot-spring bath, Outdoor restaurant, 2 Restaurants, Sauna, Spa, Steam room
GOOD TO KNOW	Child friendly
RECOMMENDED FOR	Budget

"On a hillside within a river and jungle setting, this hotel is close to Ubud but outside of the hectic tourist zone. Rooms offer privacy and are naturally ventilated."
—Mark de Reus

Recommended by: Mark de Reus, de Reus Architects

THE KAYON RESORT UBUD BY PRAMANA

Banjar Kepitu
Ubud
Bali 80572
Indonesia
+62 36147925523
thekayonresort.com

CREDIT CARDS	Accepted
PRICE	High-end
TYPE	Resort
ACCOMMODATION	23 Suites and Villas
FACILITIES	Bar, Outdoor swimming pool, Restaurant, Spa, Yoga
GOOD TO KNOW	Adults only, Bicycle rentals, Free parking
RECOMMENDED FOR	Mountains, Spa

"Situated on a mountain with a river flowing at the bottom, the views from the rooms are magnificent. Bathrooms are spacious, and the whole environment is quiet and serene."
—Adil Kerai

Recommended by: Adil Kerai, Habib Fida Ali Architects

MANDAPA, A RITZ-CARLTON RESERVE

Jalan Raya Kedewatan
Ubud
Bali 80571
Indonesia
+62 3614792777
ritzcarlton.com

CREDIT CARDS	Accepted
PRICE	Blow-out
TYPE	Resort
ACCOMMODATION	60 Suites and Villas
FACILITIES	Bar, Gym, Outdoor swimming pool, 3 Restaurants, Sauna, Spa, Steam room, Yoga
GOOD TO KNOW	Child friendly
RECOMMENDED FOR	Spa

"The pool villa is a special experience. The basic spa treatment was delightful."—Satyendra Pakhalé

Recommended by: Satyendra Pakhalé, Satyendra Pakhalé Associates

BULGARI RESORT BALI
Jalan Goa Lempeh
Uluwatu
Bali 80364
Indonesia
+62 3618471000
bulgarihotels.com

CREDIT CARDS..Accepted
PRICE..High-end
TYPE..Resort
ACCOMMODATION...................................63 Villas
FACILITIES...................Bar, Gym, Outdoor swimming pool,
3 Restaurants, Spa, Yoga
GOOD TO KNOW.....................................Private beach
RECOMMENDED FOR............Beach, Countryside, Luxury, Spa

"This is luxury countryside hotel living at its apotheosis.
It has everything—a semi-enclosed outside lounge, a private
pool, beds facing the sea, a spacious Balinese open-air
shower—total privacy."—Ken Yeang

Recommended by: Vincenzo De Cotiis, Vincenzo De Cotiis
Architects and Gallery; Bernardo Fort-Brescia,
Arquitectonica; Kiyoshi Sey Takeyama, Amorphe Takeyama
& Associates; Ken Yeang, Hamzah & Yeang

SILOLONA YACHT
Komodo Island
Indonesia
+62 361286682
silolona.com

CREDIT CARDS..Mid-range
PRICE..Blow-out
TYPE..Sailing yacht
ACCOMMODATION..5 Berths
FACILITIES....................................Diving, Restaurant, Spa,
Water sports
GOOD TO KNOW...16 crew members,
Sails in Indonesia from April to
November; Malaysia, Thailand, and
Myanmar from December to March
RECOMMENDED FOR..Worth the travel

"This yacht cruise brings together modern technology and
local traditions: a trip to see the ancient and majestic
Komodo dragons is a bucket-list entry."—Grace Cheung

Recommended by: Grace Cheung, XRANGE Architecture
+ Design

THE OBEROI BEACH RESORT, LOMBOK
Medana Beach
Lombok 83352
Indonesia
+62 3706138444
oberoihotels.com

CREDIT CARDS..Accepted
PRICE..Mid-range
TYPE...Hotel
ACCOMMODATION...................50 Rooms and Suites
FACILITIES.....................................Bar, Cafe, Gym,
Outdoor swimming pool,
2 Restaurants, Spa, Steam room
GOOD TO KNOW...................................Child friendly
RECOMMENDED FOR........................Best-kept secret,
Worth the travel

"Lombok, compared to Bali, remains relatively unspoiled,
so this is a magnificent place to really unwind, eat fresh
seafood, and relax in the sun."—Achille Salvagni

Recommended by: Achille Salvagni, Salvagni Architetti

AMANWANA
Moyo Island
Indonesia
+62 37122233
aman.com

CREDIT CARDS..Accepted
PRICE..Blow-out
TYPE...Tented resort
ACCOMMODATION..................................20 Tented suites
FACILITIES............................Dive center, Restaurant, Spa
GOOD TO KNOW...............Babysitting, Child friendly, Sailing
RECOMMENDED FOR..Island

"This complex is right on the edge of the Flores Sea, on
an island off the coast of Sumbawa Island, where packs of
monkeys gather around. We took a seaplane to one of the
hotel's boats, a fabulous old wooden freighter, which meant
we could dive in the most remote and untouched areas."
—Antoine Predock

Recommended by: Antoine Predock, Antoine Predock
Architect

NIHI SUMBA
Nihi Sumba Island
Indonesia
+62 361757149
nihi.com

CREDIT CARDS..Accepted
PRICE...Blow-out (all-inclusive)
TYPE...Resort
ACCOMMODATION...33 Villas
FACILITIES...........................2 Bars, Outdoor swimming pool,
3 Restaurants, Spa, Yoga
GOOD TO KNOW...Child friendly
RECOMMENDED FOR...Island

"The entire experience is out of this world!"
—Jean-Louis Deniot

Recommended by: Jean-Louis Deniot

SHANGRI-LA'S MACTAN RESORT AND SPA, CEBU
Punta Engaño Road
Lapu-Lapu
Cebu 6015
Philippines
+63 322310288
shangri-la.com

CREDIT CARDS..Accepted
PRICE...Mid-range
TYPE...Resort
ACCOMMODATION..................................530 Rooms and Suites
FACILITIES..4 Bars, Gym,
Outdoor swimming pool,
4 Restaurants, Sauna,
Spa, Steam room, Tennis
GOOD TO KNOW............................Child friendly, Water sports
RECOMMENDED FOR...............................Family friendly, Island

"This resort has its own beach and a coral reef for snorkeling and diving."—Alex Mok

"A tropical island resort with a wonderful ambience."
—Felino Palafox, Jr.

Recommended by: Alex Mok, Linehouse; Felino Palafox, Jr., Palafox Associates

AMANPULO
Pamalican Island
Philippines
+63 29765200
aman.com

CREDIT CARDS..Accepted
PRICE...Blow-out
TYPE...Resort
ACCOMMODATION.................................51 Casitas and Villas
FACILITIES..................................2 Bars, Dive center,
Outdoor swimming pool,
4 Restaurants, Spa, Tennis
GOOD TO KNOW...Babysitting
RECOMMENDED FOR...Worth the travel

"You're trapped: here, that's a good thing."
—Michael Young

A truly luxurious "castaway" destination, Amanpulo is situated on the private island of Pamalican. Little more than an hour away from the frenetic energy of Manila, it is accessible only by private plane. Teeming with marine life, Pamalican boasts four and a half miles (seven kilometers) of reef; each Casita and Villa comes with a dune buggy for exploring the island.

Recommended by: Michael Young, Michael Young Studio

SHANGRI-LA'S BORACAY RESORT & SPA
Barangay Yapak
Boracay
Western Visayas 5608
Philippines
+63 362884988
shangri-la.com

CREDIT CARDS..Accepted
PRICE...High-end
TYPE...Resort
ACCOMMODATION......................................219 Suites and Villas
FACILITIES..............................Bar, Dive center, Gym,
Outdoor swimming pool,
4 Restaurants, Sauna, Spa, Tennis
GOOD TO KNOW...Child friendly
RECOMMENDED FOR...Family friendly

"Great activities for kids with gaming rooms, nursery, and many activities such as kayaking and other water sports. Two separate pool areas with beach access."—Adil Kerai

Recommended by: Adil Kerai, Habib Fida Ali Architects

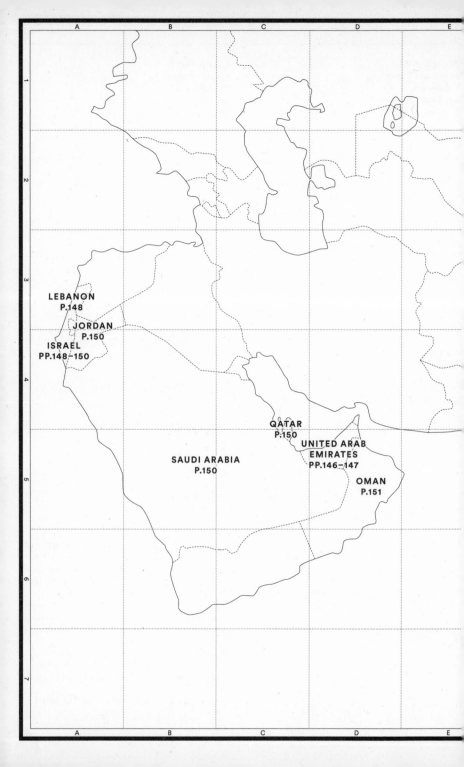

LEBANON
P.148

JORDAN
P.150

ISRAEL
PP.148-150

QATAR
P.150

UNITED ARAB
EMIRATES
PP.146-147

SAUDI ARABIA
P.150

OMAN
P.151

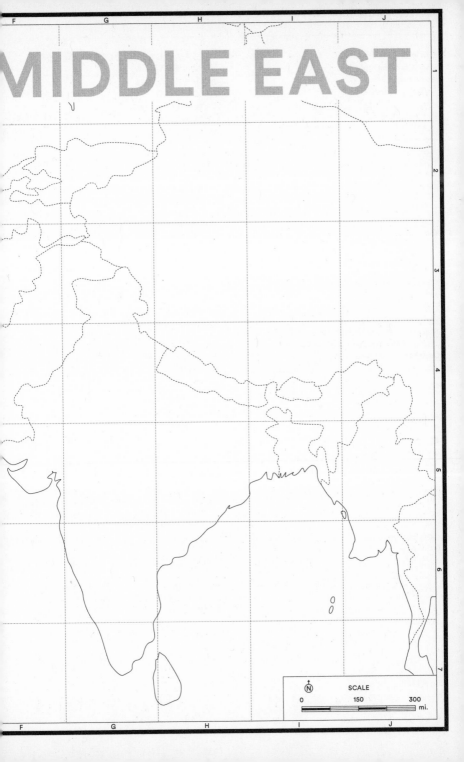

EMIRATES PALACE

West Corniche Road
Abu Dhabi
United Arab Emirates
+971 26909000
kempinski.com

CREDIT CARDS..Accepted
PRICE...High-end
TYPE..Hotel
ACCOMMODATION....................................362 Rooms and Suites
FACILITIES...3 Bars, Cafe, Gym,
2 Outdoor swimming pools,
7 Restaurants, Spa, Yacht marina
GOOD TO KNOW...........................Child friendly, Water sports
RECOMMENDED FOR...............................Beach, Desert, Luxury

"It feels like you are not in the desert."—Daniel Libeskind

"The level of service at the Emirates Palace is
extraordinary."—David Rockwell

Recommended by: Olajumoke Adenowo, AD Consulting;
Simon Jacobsen, Jacobsen Architecture; Thomas Leeser,
Leeser Architecture; Daniel Libeskind, Studio Libeskind;
David Rockwell, Rockwell Group

FOUR SEASONS HOTEL ABU DHABI AT AL MARYAH ISLAND

Abu Dhabi Global Market Street
Al Maryah Island
Abu Dhabi
United Arab Emirates
+971 23332222
fourseasons.com

CREDIT CARDS..Accepted
PRICE...High-end
TYPE..Hotel
ACCOMMODATION.........324 Residences, Rooms, and Suites
FACILITIES..2 bars, Cafe, 2 Gyms,
Outdoor swimming pool,
3 Restaurants, Spa
GOOD TO KNOW...............................Babysitting, Child friendly
RECOMMENDED FOR...Desert

Recommended by: Achille Salvagni, Salvagni Architetti

QASR AL SARAB DESERT RESORT BY ANANTARA

1 Qasr Al Sarab Road
Abu Dhabi
United Arab Emirates
+971 2 886 2088
anantara.com

CREDIT CARDS..Accepted
PRICE...High-end
TYPE..Resort
ACCOMMODATION....................206 Rooms, Suites, and Villas
FACILITIES....................Bar, Cafe, Gym, 3 Restaurants, Spa,
Outdoor swimming pool
GOOD TO KNOW..Child friendly
RECOMMENDED FOR...Desert

"Stunning setting, design, and service."
—Anthony Mallows

Recommended by: Anthony Mallows, WATG; Murat
Tabanlıoğlu, Tabanlıoğlu Architects

YAS HOTEL ABU DHABI

Yas Island
Abu Dhabi
United Arab Emirates
+971 2656000
marriott.com

CREDIT CARDS..Accepted
PRICE...Mid-range
TYPE..Hotel
ACCOMMODATION....................................499 Rooms and Suites
FACILITIES..Gym, 3 Restaurants, Spa,
Swimming pool
GOOD TO KNOW..........Connected to the Yas Marina Circuit
(used for Abu Dhabi Formula One),
Free Parking
RECOMMENDED FOR....................................Family friendly, Spa

"Very cosy and relaxing environment."—Andres Remy

Recommended by: Hani Rashid, Asymptote Architecture;
Andres Remy, Remy Architects; Sumayya Vally,
Counterspace

AL MAHA, A LUXURY COLLECTION DESERT RESORT & SPA, DUBAI

Dubai Desert Conservation Reserve
Al Ain Road
Dubai
United Arab Emirates
+971 48329900
marriott.com

CREDIT CARDS..Accepted
PRICE...Blow-out
TYPE..Resort
ACCOMMODATION...42 Suites
FACILITIES...Bar, Gym,
Outdoor swimming pool,
Restaurant, Sauna, Spa
GOOD TO KNOW....................................Horse riding, No pets
RECOMMENDED FOR...Desert

"This property is in stark contrast to the crazy world of Dubai—even though it is only 45 minutes from the city. Herds of Arabian oryx roam near the hotel. You might think of the desert as barren, but when you wake up in the morning you can see all the tracks made by snakes and foxes. There's an ambient haze around the desert, and a certain beauty and poetry."—Antoine Predock

Recommended by: Michel Abboud, SOMA; Claudio Lucchesi, Urban Future Organization; Antoine Predock, Antoine Predock Architect Studio

ARMANI HOTEL DUBAI

Burj Khalifa
Sheikh Mohammed bin Rashid Boulevard
Dubai
United Arab Emirates
+971 48883999
armanihoteldubai.com

CREDIT CARDS..Accepted
PRICE..High-end
TYPE..Hotel
ACCOMMODATION.......................................160 Suites
FACILITIES................Bar, Boutique, Indoor swimming pool,
7 Restaurants, Spa
GOOD TO KNOW...Free parking
RECOMMENDED FOR.....................Family friendly, Spa, Urban
Wish I'd Designed

"Outstanding design in the world's tallest tower [at the time of going to print]! Every detail is perfect."—Michel Abboud

Recommended by: Michel Abboud, SOMA; Bernardo and Paulo Jacobsen, Jacobsen Arquitetura; Anthony Mallows, WATG

BURJ AL ARAB JUMEIRAH

Jumeirah Street
Dubai
United Arab Emirates
+971 43017777
jumeirah.com

CREDIT CARDS..Accepted
PRICE...Blow-out
TYPE..Hotel
ACCOMMODATION.......................................201 Suites
FACILITIES.................................Bar, Gym, Indoor and outdoor
swimming pools, 9 Restaurants, Spa
GOOD TO KNOW.....................Chauffeur-driven Rolls-Royce
available, Child friendly,
Complimentary access
to Wild Wadi Waterpark™,
Private beach
RECOMMENDED FOR.........All-time favorite, Worth the travel

"The luxury amenities by Hermès are a very cool touch. Also recommended for the sheer space, the grand staircase in the room, and the view over the sea from your bed."— Olajumoke Adenowo

Recommended by: Olajumoke Adenowo, AD Consulting; Felino Palafox, Jr., Palafox Associates

ONE&ONLY ROYAL MIRAGE DUBAI

King Salman Bin Abdulaziz Al Saud Street
Dubai
United Arab Emirates
+971 43999999
oneandonlyresorts.com

CREDIT CARDS..Accepted
PRICE..High-end
TYPE..Resort
ACCOMMODATION..........................452 Residences, Rooms,
Suites, and Villas
FACILITIES..Gym, Hammam,
2 Outdoor swimming pools,
8 Restaurants, Spa
GOOD TO KNOW..........................Child friendly, Water Sports
RECOMMENDED FOR...Luxury

Recommended by: Marta Laudani, Marta Laudani Design

HOTEL ALBERGO

137 Abdel Wahab El Inglizi Street
Sodeco
Beirut, Lebanon
+961 1339797
albergobeirut.com

CREDIT CARDS...Accepted
PRICE..Mid-range
TYPE..Hotel
ACCOMMODATION......................................33 Suites
FACILITIES.....................Gym, Outdoor swimming pool,
Restaurant, Rooftop terrace bar, Spa
GOOD TO KNOW.......................................Valet parking
RECOMMENDED FOR.....................Luxury, Urban, Where I live

"A small peaceful haven in a chaotic city, in one of Beirut's
most charming neighborhoods."—Nabil Gholam

"Absolute perfection: a cross between Mediterranean Art
Deco, Beirut's crazy rooftop nightlife, and a Wes Anderson
movie. The Hotel Albergo is an extremely special place. The
rooms are quirky but comfortable and tasteful. The rooftop
pool and the amazing restaurant and bar are where to watch
the sunset over the city."—Dan Wood

Recommended by: Beppe Caturegli and Giovannella
Formica, Caturegli Formica Architetti Associati;
Nabil Gholam, Nabil Gholam Architects; Dan Wood,
WORKac

ELMA ARTS COMPLEX LUXURY HOTEL

1 Ya'ir Street
Zihron Ya'akov
Haifa 3094260, Israel
+972 46300111
elma-hotel.com

CREDIT CARDS...Accepted
PRICE..Mid-range
TYPE..Hotel
ACCOMMODATION.........................95 Rooms and Suites
FACILITIES..Gym,
Indoor and outdoor swimming pools,
2 Restaurants, Spa
GOOD TO KNOW..Child friendly
RECOMMENDED FOR................................Worth the travel

"An exceptional building by one of the greatest Israeli
architects, Yaakov Rechter, situated on a hill above the
Roman city of Caeserae."—David Tajchman

Recommended by: David Tajchman, Architectures
David Tajchman

THE AMERICAN COLONY HOTEL

1 Louis Vincent Street
American Colony
Jerusalem 97200
Israel
+972 26279777
americancolony.com

CREDIT CARDS...Accepted
PRICE..Mid-range
TYPE..Hotel
ACCOMMODATION......................................94 Suites
FACILITIES..........................2 Bars, Boutique, Cafe, Gym,
Outdoor swimming pool,
3 Restaurants
GOOD TO KNOW.................................Babysitting, Free parking
RECOMMENDED FOR...Urban

"I always try to get the bedroom of the second of the pasha's
four wives. From its domed, dark blue and gold-starred
ceiling and generosity of space to its situation in the internal
court, it seemed to me that this must have been for a wife
married for love, rather than one for dynastic or other
practical reasons. The scale of the hotel is perfect—not too
large, but big enough to offer fine cuisine, which you can
eat either inside the restaurant or in the charming central
courtyard. This building has its own authenticity, not
having been built as a commercial enterprise, but for the
satisfaction of the owner-inhabitant."—Jack Diamond

Recommended by: Jack Diamond, Diamond Schmitt;
Massimiliano and Doriana Fuksas, Studio Fuksas

WALDORF ASTORIA JERUSALEM

26–28 Gershon Agron Street
Mamilla
Jerusalem 9419008
Israel
+972 25423333
waldorfastoria3.hilton.com

CREDIT CARDS...Accepted
PRICE...High-end
TYPE..Hotel
ACCOMMODATION.........................226 Rooms and Suites
FACILITIES..Bar, 2 Restaurants
GOOD TO KNOW...........................Child friendly, No pets
RECOMMENDED FOR.............................All-time favorite

Recommended by: Olajumoke Adenowo, AD Consulting

BERESHEET
1 Derech Beresheet
Mitzpe Ramon 80600, Israel
+972 86598000
isrotel.com

CREDIT CARDS	Accepted
PRICE	High-end
TYPE	Hotel
ACCOMMODATION	111 Rooms and Villas
FACILITIES	Bar, Indoor and outdoor swimming pools, Restaurant, Spa
GOOD TO KNOW	Babysitting
RECOMMENDED FOR	Desert

Recommended by: David Tajchman, Architectures
David Tajchman

HOTEL CARLTON
10 Eliezer Peri Street
Tayelet
Tel Aviv 6357325, Israel
+972 35201818
carlton.co.il

CREDIT CARDS	Accepted
PRICE	High-end
TYPE	Hotel
ACCOMMODATION	268 Rooms and Suites
FACILITIES	2 Bars, Gym, Outdoor swimming pool, 3 Restaurants, Spa
GOOD TO KNOW	Child friendly
RECOMMENDED FOR	Beach

"The best beach promenade in the world—better than Rio!"
—Daniel Libeskind

Recommended by: Daniel Libeskind, Studio Libeskind

HOTEL SAUL
17 Tshernichowski Street
Lev Hair
Tel Aviv 6329132, Israel
+972 35277700
hotelsaul.com

CREDIT CARDS	Accepted
PRICE	Mid-range
TYPE	Hotel
ACCOMMODATION	34 Rooms
FACILITIES	Rooftop terrace cafe
GOOD TO KNOW	Child friendly
RECOMMENDED FOR	Urban

"Nice interior design."— David Tajchman

Recommended by: David Tajchman, Architectures
David Tajchman

THE JAFFA
2 Louis Pasteur Street
Jaffa
Tel Aviv 6803602
Israel
+972 35042000
marriott.co.uk

CREDIT CARDS	Accepted but not Diners
PRICE	High-end
TYPE	Hotel
ACCOMMODATION	120 Rooms and Suites
FACILITIES	Bar, Gym, Outdoor swimming pool, 2 Restaurants, Spa
GOOD TO KNOW	Child friendly
RECOMMENDED FOR	Urban

The Jaffa hotel is situated within the walls of a nineteenth-century complex that once housed Jaffa's French Hospital and combines heritage architecture with the finest elements of modern design in the heart of Tel Aviv's historic centre. The building was restored by Ramy Gill with stunning minimalist design by John Pawson, and has a range of dining options including Golda's Delicatessen for a stylish take on New York classics.

Recommended by: Paolo Cossu, Paolo Cossu Architects

MONTEFIORE
36 Montefiore Street
Lev Hair
Tel Aviv 6520105
Israel
+972 35646100
hotelmontefiore.co.il

CREDIT CARDS	Accepted
PRICE	High-end
TYPE	Hotel
ACCOMMODATION	12 Rooms
FACILITIES	Bar, Restaurant
GOOD TO KNOW	Free parking
RECOMMENDED FOR	Urban

"A former private residence in the Bauhaus district [White City]—a little gem."—Piero Lissoni

Recommended by: Piero Lissoni, Lissoni Associati

THE NORMAN
23–25 Nachmani Street
Lev Hair
Tel Aviv 6579441
Israel
+972 35435555
thenorman.com

CREDIT CARDS..Accepted
PRICE...High-end
TYPE..Hotel
ACCOMMODATION.....................................50 Rooms and Suites
FACILITIES...Bar, Gym,
Outdoor swimming pool,
2 Restaurants, Spa, Yoga
GOOD TO KNOW....................................Valet parking
RECOMMENDED FOR.............Beach, Best-kept secret, Luxury

"It has a great blend of Mediterranean influences and is in
one of Tel Aviv's most vibrant neighborhoods."
—Forth Bagley

"It's a rare treat to stay in such a Modernist gem. The public
spaces are filled with Bauhaus-influenced artwork by
contemporary Israeli artists, so you feel like you are
spending time at home in an amazing private residence."
—David Rockwell

Recommended by: Forth Bagley, Kohn Pedersen Fox;
Charles Renfro, Diller Scofidio + Renfro; David Rockwell,
Rockwell Group; David Tajchman, Architectures
David Tajchman

KEMPINSKI HOTEL AQABA RED SEA
King Hussein Street
Aqaba 77110
Jordan
+962 32090888
kempinski.com

CREDIT CARDS..Accepted
PRICE..Mid-range
TYPE..Hotel
ACCOMMODATION.....................200 Rooms and Suites
FACILITIES...3 Bars, Gym,
Outdoor swimming pool,
3 Restaurants, Spa
GOOD TO KNOW...No pets
RECOMMENDED FOR.........................Wish I'd designed

"There is not a single room without an amazing sea
view."—Nabil Gholam

Recommended by: Nabil Gholam, Nabil Gholam Architects

SHAZA AL MADINA
Building 2943, King Fahd Road
Central Medina 41476
Saudi Arabia
+971 44376460
shazahotels.com

CREDIT CARDS..Accepted
PRICE..Mid-range
TYPE..Hotel
ACCOMMODATION...................................469 Rooms and Suites
FACILITIES...Gym, 2 Restaurants
GOOD TO KNOW..Child friendly
RECOMMENDED FOR.........................All-time favorite

Recommended by: Michel Abboud, SOMA

SHARQ VILLAGE & SPA
Ras Abu Abboud Street
Doha 26662
Qatar
+974 44256666
ritzcarlton.com

CREDIT CARDS..Accepted
PRICE..Mid-range
TYPE..Resort
ACCOMMODATION.....................174 Rooms and Suites
FACILITIES...............................Bar, Boutique, Gym,
Outdoor swimming pool,
3 Restaurants, Spa
GOOD TO KNOW..Child friendly
RECOMMENDED FOR.......................................Desert

"Go for the Arabian-inspired architecture, the landscaping,
the stunning site layout, and the location by the gentle
waters of the Arabian Gulf Sea. The combination of the
desert, the beach, and the sea is rare!"
—Olajumoke Adenowo

Recommended by: Olajumoke Adenowo, AD Consulting

SIX SENSES ZIGHY BAY

Zighy Bay
Dibba
Musandam Peninsula 800
Oman
+968 26735555
sixsenses.com

CREDIT CARDS	Accepted
PRICE	Blow-out
TYPE	Resort
ACCOMMODATION	82 Villas
FACILITIES	2 Bars, Gym, Hammam, Outdoor swimming pool, 3 Restaurants, Spa
GOOD TO KNOW	Babysitting
RECOMMENDED FOR	Desert, Eco-conscious, Family friendly, Spa, Worth the travel

"It's the only place where I have been barefoot all day long. Feeling the sand beneath your toes was a real experience for the family. We enjoyed every moment."—Murat Tabanlioglu

"Ultimate pampering, locally grown and organically prepared food, and in-villa services."—Randa Tukan

Recommended by: Tom Kundig, Olson Kundig; Stéphane Parmentier; Patrick Reymond, Atelier Oï; Murat Tabanlıoğlu, Tabanlıoğlu Architects; Randa Tukan, HOK Architects

THE CHEDI MUSCAT

18 November Street
Al Ghubrah
Muscat 133
Oman
+968 24524400
ghmhotels.com

CREDIT CARDS	Accepted
PRICE	High-end
TYPE	Resort
ACCOMMODATION	158 Rooms and Villas
FACILITIES	Bar, Gym, 3 Outdoor swimming pools, 6 Restaurants, Spa, Yoga
GOOD TO KNOW	Babysitting
RECOMMENDED FOR	All-time favorite, Desert, Urban, Worth the travel

"This is a prime example of an 'oasis' concept. Located on a tranquil beach, the hotel has six restaurants, twenty-one acres (nine hectares) of gardens, three swimming pools, and a Balinese spa."—Vincenzo De Cotiis

Recommended by: Vincenzo De Cotiis, Vincenzo De Cotiis Architects and Gallery; Dominique Perrault, Dominique Perrault Architecture

SHANGRI-LA BARR AL JISSAH RESORT & SPA

Barr Al Jissah
Muscat 100
Oman
+968 24776666
shangri-la.com

CREDIT CARDS	Accepted
PRICE	Mid-range
TYPE	Resort
ACCOMMODATION	460 Rooms and Suites
FACILITIES	4 Bars, Gym, Outdoor swimming pool, 11 Restaurants, Spa, Tennis
GOOD TO KNOW	Adults-only wing
RECOMMENDED FOR	Spa

"A hedonistic experience with discreet, impeccable service and warmth and privacy. Chi, the spa, affords breathtaking sea views."—Nabil Gholam

Recommended by: Nabil Gholam, Nabil Gholam Architects

CANVAS CLUB

Wahiba Sands
Oman
+49 21197533323
canvascluboman.com

CREDIT CARDS	Accepted
PRICE	High-end (all-inclusive)
TYPE	Tented camp
ACCOMMODATION	Tents
FACILITIES	Restaurant
GOOD TO KNOW	Candlelight only
RECOMMENDED FOR	Desert

"Five-star camping in the desert. The tents are a sanctuary, perfectly styled and furnished with everything you need. Very authentic."—Francesca Bucci

"The outside air, the sand, and the starry sky!"
—Liesbeth van der Pol

Recommended by: Francesca Bucci, BG Studio International; Liesbeth van der Pol, Dok Architects

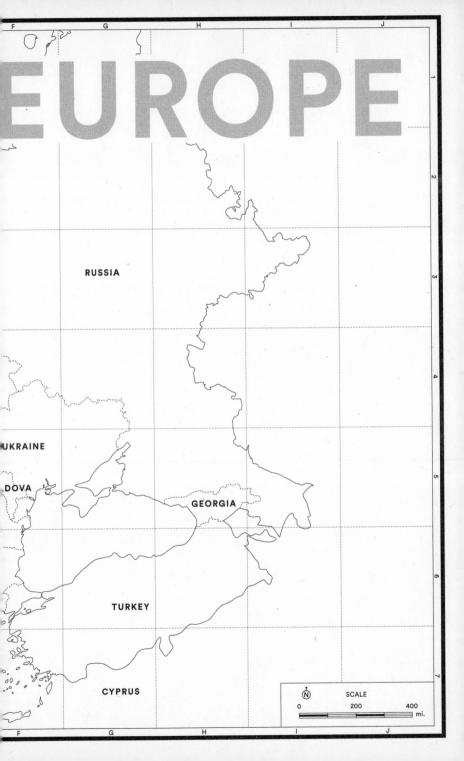

GREENLAND, ICELAND, AND FAROE ISLANDS

GREENLAND P.156

ICELAND P.156

FAROE ISLANDS P.157 ↘

N

SCALE

0   125   250 mi.

HOTEL ARCTIC

Mittarfimmut B1128
Ilulissat
Avannaata DK-3952
Greenland
+29 9944153
hotelarctic.com

CREDIT CARDS...Accepted
PRICE...Mid-range
TYPE..Hotel
ACCOMMODATION.................................90 Rooms and Suites
FACILITIES......................Bar, Gym, Igloos, 2 Restaurants
GOOD TO KNOW...Airport transfer,
Optional arrival by dogsled
RECOMMENDED FOR...Worth the travel

Since opening, Hotel Arctic has hosted royalty and rock stars alike. Its restaurant serves "Greenland cuisine," and accommodation ranges from simple yet comfortable guest rooms to seasonal aluminum "igloos" which afford fantastic views of Disko Bay.

Recommended by: Roger Duffy, Skidmore, Owings & Merrill

BLÁBJÖRG GUESTHOUSE

Gamla Frystihusid 720
Borgarfjarðarhreppur
Iceland
+354 8611792
blabjorg.com

CREDIT CARDS...Accepted
PRICE...Mid-range
TYPE...Guesthouse
ACCOMMODATION............................11 Apartments and Rooms
FACILITIES...................................Bar, Restaurant, Sauna
GOOD TO KNOW...Child friendly,
Shared bathrooms
RECOMMENDED FOR.......................................Countryside

"Falling asleep to the sound of the ocean and waking up to sunrise over the mountains and the calls of seabirds is spectacular. The hotel has a simple outdoor spa area with a wooden hot tub, cold pool, and a sauna, all with views. Bathing in the ocean and a spell in the hot tub afterwards is a must. The surrounding landscape is absolutely stunning, so take advantage of experiences such as hiking, horse riding, and sailing."—Thorhallur Sigurdsson

Recommended by: Thorhallur Sigurdsson, Andersen & Sigurdsson

ION ADVENTURE HOTEL

Nesjavellir 801
Thingvellir National Park
Iceland
+354 4823415
ionadventure.ioniceland.is

CREDIT CARDS...Accepted
PRICE...Mid-range
TYPE..Hotel
ACCOMMODATION...................................27 Rooms and Suites
FACILITIES.............................Bar, Outdoor swimming pool,
Restaurant, Sauna, Yoga
GOOD TO KNOW...............................Active volcano, Wildlife
RECOMMENDED FOR...Mountains

A Modernist masterpiece with excellent sustainability credentials, ION Adventure Hotel is the place for once-in-a-lifetime opportunities: viewing the Northern Lights, and glacier treks, with all the luxury comforts and facilities required for an enjoyable stay. These include an award-winning restaurant, tranquil spa, and stylish rooms, some of which enjoy views of Thingvellir National Park.

Recommended by: Flavio Albanese, ASA Studio

HOTEL BÚÐIR

Snæfellsnes 356
Ólafsvík
Western Region
Iceland
+354 4356700
hotelbudir.is

CREDIT CARDS...Accepted
PRICE...Mid-range
TYPE..Hotel
ACCOMMODATION...................................28 Rooms and Suites
FACILITIES...Bar, Restaurant
GOOD TO KNOW.................March is Northern Lights season
RECOMMENDED FOR...Best-kept secret,
Worth the travel

"Beautiful rooms and an incredible restaurant. Sit by the fireplace and wait for time to stop."—Dan Wood

Recommended by: Marianne Kwok, Kohn Pedersen Fox; Dan Wood, WORKac

HOTEL FØROYAR
45 Oyggjarvegur
Tórshavn 100
Faroe Islands
+29 8317500
hotelforoyar.fo

CREDIT CARDS..Accepted
PRICE..Mid-range
TYPE..Hotel
ACCOMMODATION...................................106 Rooms and Suites
FACILITIES...Bar, Gym, Restaurant
GOOD TO KNOW..Free parking
RECOMMENDED FOR..Countryside

With its grass roof and stylish design, Hotel Føroyar blends effortlessly into the rugged surrounding landscape. Inside, the Philippe Starck-designed rooms are light, bright, and spacious, and the restaurant benefits from panoramic views of Tórshavn and beyond.

[This hotel was designed by Friis & Moltke Architects.]

Recommended by: Thomas Ruus, Friis & Moltke Architects

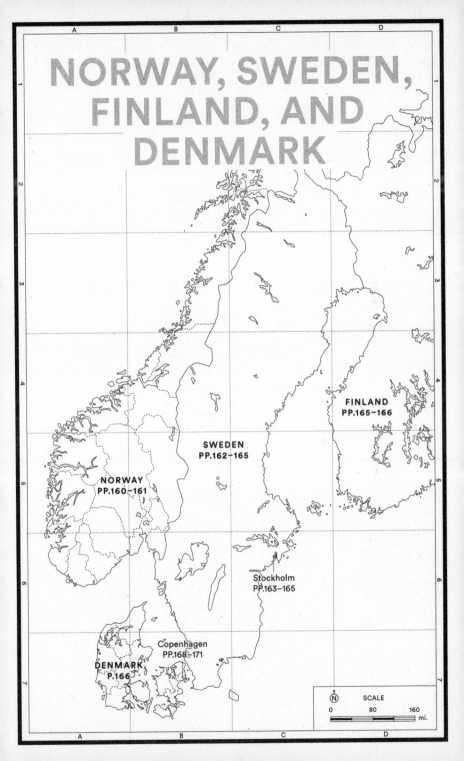

NORWAY, SWEDEN, FINLAND, AND DENMARK

FINLAND
PP.165–166

SWEDEN
PP.162–165

NORWAY
PP.160–161

Stockholm
PP.163–165

Copenhagen
PP.168–171

DENMARK
P.166

SCALE

0   80   160
mi.

SNOWHOTEL KIRKENES
Sandnesdalen 14
Bjørnevatn
Finnmark 9910
Norway
+47 78970540
snowhotelkirkenes.com

CREDIT CARDS.....................................Accepted but not Amex
PRICE...Mid-range
TYPE...Hotel
ACCOMMODATION..................................20 Cabins and Rooms
FACILITIES...Bar, Restaurant
GOOD TO KNOW.....................Husky safaris, Northern Lights
RECOMMENDED FOR...Wish I'd designed

Twenty rooms decorated with snow and ice kept at -4°C
(24°F), and warm, thick sleeping bags make this hotel an
extraordinary experience. It is ideally located for embarking
upon Nordic adventures: the Northern Lights, a snowmobile
safari in winter, or king crab fishing in summer.

Recommended by: Dinko Peračić, ARP and Platforma 9.81

ZANDER K HOTEL
Zander Kaaes Gate 8
Bergen
Hordaland 5015
Norway
+47 55362040
zanderk.no

CREDIT CARDS..Accepted
PRICE...Mid-range
TYPE...Hotel
ACCOMMODATION...................................249 Rooms and Suites
FACILITIES..Bar, Gym, Restaurant
GOOD TO KNOW..Bicycle rentals
RECOMMENDED FOR...Urban

"The Scandinavian ideal of luxury."—Eero Koivisto

Recommended by: Mårten Claesson and Eero Koivisto,
Claesson Koivisto Rune Architects

HOTEL BROSUNDET
Apotekergata 1-5
Ålesund
Møre og Romsdal 6004
Norway
+47 70103300
brosundet.no

CREDIT CARDS..Accepted
PRICE...Mid-range
TYPE...Hotel
ACCOMMODATION......................131 Apartment, Guesthouse,
Lighthouse, Rooms, and Suites
FACILITIES...Bar, Restaurant
GOOD TO KNOW....................................Boat and fishing trips
RECOMMENDED FOR..................Countryside, Family friendly

"Stay in Room 47—the Molja Lighthouse. Downstairs is an
elegant and amazingly compact bathroom, while upstairs
is a circular bedroom with a custom-fitted bed. A lovely
experience, especially for a family with children."
—Satyendra Pakhalé

Recommended by: Craig Dykers, Snøhetta; Satyendra
Pakhalé, Satyendra Pakhalé Associates

STORFJORD HOTEL
Øvre Glomset
Storfjord
Møre og Romsdal 6260
Norway
+47 70274922
storfjordhotel.com

CREDIT CARDS..Accepted
PRICE...Mid-range
TYPE...Hotel
ACCOMMODATION...................................30 Rooms and Suites
FACILITIES.......................Bar, Restaurant, Sauna, Wellness
area
GOOD TO KNOW...Kayaking
RECOMMENDED FOR...Mountains

"Atop a mountain, with a view over the fjords—in a
place that's both authentic and chic. Breathtaking."
—Claire Bétaille and Bruno Moinard

Recommended by: Claire Bétaille and Bruno Moinard,
4BI & Associés

JUVET LANDSCAPE HOTEL
Valldal
Møre og Romsdal 6210
Norway
+47 95032010
juvet.com

CREDIT CARDS	Accepted
PRICE	High-end
TYPE	Hotel
ACCOMMODATION	9 Rooms
FACILITIES	Restaurant, Spa, Steam room, Wood-burning fireplace
GOOD TO KNOW	No pets
RECOMMENDED FOR	All-time favorite, Best-kept secret, Eco-conscious, Mountains, Wish I'd designed, Worth the travel

"Probably the best architecture in the woods."
—Paolo Brambilla

Recommended by: Boris Bernaskoni, Bernaskoni; Paolo Brambilla, Calvi Brambilla; Robert Konieczny, KWK Promes; João Mendes Ribeiro, João Mendes Ribeiro Arquitecto; Ron Radziner, Marmol Radziner; Thomas Ruus, Friis & Moltke Architects; Maria Warner Wong, WOW Architects | Warner Wong Design; Graham West, West Architecture

MANSHAUSEN HOTEL
Lille Manshausen
Manshausen Island
Nordland 8283
Norway
+47 90363616
manshausen.no

CREDIT CARDS	Accepted but not Amex
PRICE	Mid-range
TYPE	Hotel
ACCOMMODATION	7 Huts
FACILITIES	Bar, Open-air bath, Restaurant, Saltwater swimming pool, Sauna
GOOD TO KNOW	Bicycles and Kayaks available, Child friendly
RECOMMENDED FOR	Island

"Its sense of 'floating' over water instills calm and serenity, even when a storm rages outside the windows. On the north side of Manshausen there is a private beach with lovely white sand. The area has lots of exciting things to do, from catching crabs and fish to climbing trees and swimming. Naturally, it's a family hotel."—Satyendra Pakhalé

Recommended by: Satyendra Pakhalé, Satyendra Pakhalé Associates

KVIKNES HOTEL
Kviknevegen 8
Balestrand
Sogn og Fjordane 6899
Norway
+47 57694200
kviknes.no

CREDIT CARDS	Accepted
PRICE	Mid-range
TYPE	Hotel
ACCOMMODATION	190 Rooms and Suites
FACILITIES	Bar, 2 Restaurants
GOOD TO KNOW	Kayaking
RECOMMENDED FOR	Worth the travel

"This hotel, designed in nineteenth-century Swiss style, is set in beautiful Norwegian scenery, where the Sognefjord forks into two branches. Its old-world charm is enhanced by an extensive collection of artworks and antiques. When darkness falls, it is exciting to see the lights of the boats sailing and crossing the Sognefjord. Ask for a room in the old building, overlooking the water."—Marta Laudani

Recommended by: Marta Laudani, Marta Laudani Design

WALAKER HOTELL
Solvorn
Glomset
Sogn og Fjordane 6879
Norway
+47 57682080
walaker.com

CREDIT CARDS	Accepted but not Amex
PRICE	Mid-range
TYPE	Hotel
ACCOMMODATION	38 Rooms
FACILITIES	Restaurant
GOOD TO KNOW	Private beach, Set menu from 7.30pm
RECOMMENDED FOR	Mountains

"Tucked away and hard to get to, it's the perfect mountain getaway with stunning views. We stayed one night and wished we had booked seven."—Forth Bagley

Recommended by: Forth Bagley, Kohn Pedersen Fox

DJUPVIK HOTEL

Eksta Bopparve 233
Klintehamn
Gotland 62354
Sweden
+46 498244272
djupvikhotel.com

CREDIT CARDS	Accepted but not Diners
PRICE	Mid-range
TYPE	Hotel
ACCOMMODATION	8 Rooms
FACILITIES	Bar, Outdoor swimming pool, Restaurant
GOOD TO KNOW	Near nature reserve
RECOMMENDED FOR	Worth the travel

"An oasis by the sea on a very special island. You have to travel by plane, then car, then boat to get there—but it is very much worth the effort!"—Ben van Berkel

Recommended by: Ben van Berkel, UNStudio

FABRIKEN FURILLEN

Rute Furilden 870
Lärbro
Gotland 62458
Sweden
+46 498223040
furillen.com

CREDIT CARDS	Accepted
PRICE	Mid-range
TYPE	Hotel
ACCOMMODATION	16 Cabins and Rooms
FACILITIES	Bar, Restaurant
GOOD TO KNOW	Child friendly
RECOMMENDED FOR	Beach, Countryside

"Converted quarry structures with industrial raw charm and amazing food."—Daniel Sundlin

"Furillen is raw concrete heaven in the middle of a wild and untamed landscape. A perfect setting for long walks among wind-battered trees, cliffs, and pebble beaches."
—Gert Wingårdh

Recommended by: Daniel Sundlin, Bjarke Ingels Group; Gert Wingårdh, Wingårdhs

STEDSANS IN THE WOODS

Bohult 109
Hyltebruk
Halland 31491
Sweden
+46 704849749
stedsans.org

CREDIT CARDS	Accepted but not Amex
PRICE	High-end
TYPE	Restaurant with rooms
ACCOMMODATION	15 Cabins, 1 Tent
FACILITIES	Restaurant, Sauna, Spa
GOOD TO KNOW	Compost toilets
RECOMMENDED FOR	Eco-conscious

"A great combination of simple, sustainable living combined with delicious food and breathtaking nature. Everything is completely organic. It is almost an out-of-body experience staying in the middle of a Swedish forest with no electricity, just candlelight. The floating sauna on the lake is irresistible."—Kim Herforth Nielsen

Recommended by: Kim Herforth Nielsen, 3XN

TREEHOTEL

Edeforsväg 2A
Harads
Norrbotten 96024
Sweden
+46 92810300
treehotel.se

CREDIT CARDS	Accepted
PRICE	High-end
TYPE	Tree hotel
ACCOMMODATION	7 Treehouses
FACILITIES	Bar, Restaurant, Sauna, Yoga
GOOD TO KNOW	Child friendly
RECOMMENDED FOR	Best-kept secret, Countryside, Eco-conscious, Mountains, Wish I'd designed

"A perfect example of how iconic architecture can seamlessly integrate with nature."—Boris Bernaskoni

Recommended by: Boris Bernaskoni, Bernaskoni; Craig Dykers, Snøhetta; Stéphane Rasselet, Naturehumaine; João Mendes Ribeiro, João Mendes Ribeiro Arquitecto; Pedro Rica and Marta Urtasun, Mecanismo; Cristian Santandreu, A2arquitectos; Bolle Tham and Martin Videgård, Tham & Videgård Arkitekter; Kateryna Zuieva, AKZ Architectura

ICE HOTEL

Marknadsvägen 63
Jukkasjärvi
Norrbotten 98191
Sweden
+46 98066800
icehotel.com

CREDIT CARDS	Accepted
PRICE	Mid-range
TYPE	Ice hotel
ACCOMMODATION	137 Chalets, Rooms, and Suites
FACILITIES	Bar, Restaurant, Sauna
GOOD TO KNOW	Bicycle rentals, No pets
RECOMMENDED FOR	All-time favorite, Spa, Wish I'd designed

"I had the best sleep of my life there, on a block of ice. You can see the Aurora Borealis, and do Swedish sauna rituals like plunging into the Torne river after taking a sauna. Go in January, when it's coldest."—Rick Joy

Recommended by: Kelly Bair, Central Standard Office of Design; Francesca Bucci, BG Studio International; Hasan Çalışlar, Erginoğlu & Çalışlar; Eric Corey Freed, OrganicArchitect; Rick Joy, Studio Rick Joy

WANÅS RESTAURANT HOTEL

Hässleholmsvägen
Knislinge
Skåne 28990
Sweden
+46 442531581
wanasrh.se

CREDIT CARDS	Accepted but not Amex
PRICE	Mid-range
TYPE	Restaurant with rooms
ACCOMMODATION	11 Rooms
FACILITIES	Bar, Restaurant
GOOD TO KNOW	Free parking
RECOMMENDED FOR	Worth the travel

"Modern refurbished estate with a great sculpture park of contemporary art."—Mia Baarup Tofte

Recommended by: Mia Baarup Tofte, NORD Architects

HOTEL TEGNÉRLUNDEN

Tegnérlunden 8
Vasastan
Stockholm 113 59
Sweden
+46 854545550
hoteltegnerlunden.se

CREDIT CARDS	Accepted
PRICE	Mid-range
TYPE	Hotel
ACCOMMODATION	102 Rooms and Suites
FACILITIES	Bar, Breakfast, Gym
GOOD TO KNOW	Child and pet friendly
RECOMMENDED FOR	Urban

"Very sophisticated small hotel with personal service and centrally located in beautiful Stockholm."—Martin Kruger

Recommended by: Martin Kruger, Martin Kruger Architects

NOBIS HOTEL STOCKHOLM

Norrmalmstorg 2-4
Norrmalm
Stockholm 111 86
Sweden
+46 86141000
nobishotel.se

CREDIT CARDS	Accepted
PRICE	Mid-range
TYPE	Hotel
ACCOMMODATION	201 Rooms and Suites
FACILITIES	Bar, Gym, 2 Restaurants, Sauna
GOOD TO KNOW	24-hour room service
RECOMMENDED FOR	Where I live

Nobis is a super-stylish design hotel in the center of Stockholm. Rooms are furnished with natural materials in neutral tones, with toiletries by Swedish luxury brand Byredo.

Recommended by: Mårten Claesson, Claesson Koivisto Rune Architects

ETT HEM
Sköldungagatan 2
Östermalm
Stockholm 114 27
Sweden
+46 8200590
etthem.se

CREDIT CARDS..Accepted
PRICE...High-end
TYPE...Boutique hotel
ACCOMMODATION..12 Rooms and Suites
FACILITIES..............................Bar, Gym, Restaurant, Sauna,
Spa, Wood-burning fireplace
GOOD TO KNOW..Child friendly
RECOMMENDED FOR...........All-time favorite, Luxury, Urban,
Where I live, Worth the travel

"Amazing concept, atmosphere, and hospitality, plus
interiors by Ilse Crawford. Recommended for a pampering
escape from the routines of everyday life."—Joanna
Laajisto

"The ultimate boutique hotel."—Ola Rune

Recommended by: Marco Costanzi, Marco Costanzi
Architects; Joanna Laajisto, Studio Joanna Laajisto; Michel
Rojkind, Rojkind Arquitectos; Ola Rune, Claesson Koivisto
Rune Architects; Gert Wingårdh, Wingårdhs

STORY HOTEL
Riddargatan 6
Östermalm
Stockholm 114 35
Sweden
+46 854503940
storyhotels.com

CREDIT CARDS..Accepted
PRICE...Mid-range
TYPE..Hotel
ACCOMMODATION..............................83 Rooms and Suites
FACILITIES...Bar, Restaurant
GOOD TO KNOW...Pet friendly
RECOMMENDED FOR..Urban

"Smart and chic."—Marcio Kogan

Recommended by: Marcio Kogan, Studio MK27

HOTEL SKEPPSHOLMEN
Gröna gången 1
Skeppsholmen
Stockholm 111 49
Sweden
+46 84072300
hotelskeppsholmen.se

CREDIT CARDS..Accepted
PRICE...Mid-range
TYPE..Hotel
ACCOMMODATION........................78 Rooms and Suites
FACILITIES...Restaurant
GOOD TO KNOW...................Byredo toiletries, Duxiana beds
RECOMMENDED FOR...........................Family friendly, Urban,
Where I live, Worth the travel

"Archipelago ambience in the center of the city."
—Eero Koivisto

"A great restaurant and outdoor terrace during
summertime. I also love the island location in the heart
of the city. It works for both business and pleasure."
—Joanna Laajisto

Recommended by: Eero Koivisto, Claesson Koivisto
Rune Architects; Joanna Laajisto, Studio Joanna Laajisto;
Patrick Reymond, Atelier Oï; Gert Wingårdh, Wingårdhs

STF VANDRARHEM AF CHAPMAN & SKEPPSHOLMEN
Flaggmansvägen 8
Skeppsholmen
Stockholm 111 49
Sweden
+46 84632280
vandrarhemstockholm.se

CREDIT CARDS..Accepted
PRICE...Low-cost
TYPE...Ship hostel
ACCOMMODATION...............................77 Cabins and Dorms
FACILITIES...................................Bar, Cafe, Grocery store
GOOD TO KNOW.......................................Self-catering kitchen
RECOMMENDED FOR.......................................Best-kept secret

"In the center of Skeppsholmen island, where the Moderna
Museet by Rafael Moneo is also situated, this is a unique
experience aboard an old three-masted schooner. The ship's
comfortable cabins are restored to their original style."
—Belén Moneo and Jeffrey Brock

Recommended by: Belén Moneo and Jeffrey Brock,
Moneo Brock

HOTEL RIVAL
Mariatorget 3
Södermalm
Stockholm 118 48
Sweden
+46 854578900
rival.se

CREDIT CARDS	Accepted
PRICE	Mid-range
TYPE	Hotel
ACCOMMODATION	99 Rooms and Suites
FACILITIES	3 Bars, Restaurant
GOOD TO KNOW	No pets, Valet parking
RECOMMENDED FOR	All-time favorite

"It's my second home, in my second hometown. Everything works, everything is familiar, and everyone knows me. And you get the perfect poached eggs for breakfast every time."—Gert Wingårdh

Recommended by: Gert Wingårdh, Wingårdhs

VILLA SJÖTORP HOTEL
Dirhuvudsvägen
Ljungskile
Västra Götaland 45933
Sweden
+46 52220174
villasjotorp.se

CREDIT CARDS	Accepted
PRICE	Mid-range
TYPE	Hotel
ACCOMMODATION	14 Rooms
FACILITIES	Cafe, Restaurant
GOOD TO KNOW	Child and pet friendly
RECOMMENDED FOR	Best-kept secret

"A small and ancient villa on the bank of the Havstesfjord, with a garden that reaches to the sea. During summer evenings, it's lovely to have dinner sitting on the porch—and the food is absolutely excellent. You can take trips to Bohuslän, a very nice stretch of the Swedish coast, north of Gothenburg."—Marta Laudani

Recommended by: Marta Laudani, Marta Laudani Design

TOFTA HERRGÅRD
Tofta 200
Lycke
Västra Götaland 44275
Sweden
+46 303225805
toftaherrgard.se

CREDIT CARDS	Accepted
PRICE	Mid-range
TYPE	Manor house hotel
ACCOMMODATION	14 Rooms
FACILITIES	Games room, Restaurant
GOOD TO KNOW	Child friendly, No pets
RECOMMENDED FOR	Countryside

"Close to birds (it's a national preservation area), the archipelago, and clean water. Listen to the sound of silence."—Gert Wingårdh

Recommended by: Gert Wingårdh, Wingårdhs

TERTIN KARTANO
Kuopiontie 68
Mikkeli
Etelä-Savo 50350
Finland
+358 15176012
tertinkartano.fi

CREDIT CARDS	Accepted
PRICE	Low-cost
TYPE	Manor house hotel
ACCOMMODATION	5 Rooms
FACILITIES	Restaurant
GOOD TO KNOW	Free parking
RECOMMENDED FOR	Family friendly

"A lovely late nineteenth-century manor and gardens in the Finnish lake district, this hotel is a functioning farm with herb, vegetable, and rose gardens, and even a secret garden inside old stonewalls. The grains and vegetables served at the restaurant are grown here. Guest rooms are located in a separate guest house, near the manor."—Marta Laudani

Recommended by: Marta Laudani, Marta Laudani Design

RANTALINNA HOTEL
Rantalinnantie 127
Ruokolahti
South Karelia 56100
Finland
+358 401528150
rantalinna.eu

CREDIT CARDS	Accepted
PRICE	Mid-range
TYPE	Hotel
ACCOMMODATION	8 Rooms and Suites
FACILITIES	Restaurant, Sauna
GOOD TO KNOW	Free parking
RECOMMENDED FOR	Countryside

"Art Nouveau style, dating back to 1912, this former Romanov royal holiday villa sits on the banks of a lake surrounded by birches. The Prince and Princess suites still have the original furniture and regal atmosphere. Nearby, you can enjoy the historic park and a marina."
—Marta Laudani

Recommended by: Marta Laudani, Marta Laudani Design

HOTEL KÄMP
Pohjoisesplanadi 29
Helsinki
Uusimaa 00100
Finland
+358 9576111
hotelkamp.com

CREDIT CARDS	Accepted
PRICE	High-end
TYPE	Hotel
ACCOMMODATION	179 Rooms and Suites
FACILITIES	Bar, Restaurant, Sauna, Spa
GOOD TO KNOW	Valet parking
RECOMMENDED FOR	Luxury

"Classic luxury in the middle of Helsinki, this hotel echoes the elegance of one of the most beautifully designed cities in the world."—Carlos Jimenez

Recommended by: Carlos Jiménez, Carlos Jiménez Studio

COPENHAGEN: SEE PAGES 168–171

HOTEL HAVEN
Unioninkatu 17
Helsinki
Uusimaa 00130
Finland
+358 9681930
hotelhaven.fi

CREDIT CARDS	Accepted
PRICE	Mid-range
TYPE	Hotel
ACCOMMODATION	137 Rooms and Suites
FACILITIES	Bar, Gym, 2 Restaurants
GOOD TO KNOW	Child friendly
RECOMMENDED FOR	Where I live

"Nice atmosphere and a good location."
—Rainer Mahlamäki

Recommended by: Rainer Mahlamäki, Lahdelma & Mahlamäki Architects

COPENHAGEN

CABINN CITY HOTEL
Mitchellsgade 14
København V
Copenhagen 1568
+45 33461616
cabinn.com

CREDIT CARDS	Accepted
PRICE	Low-cost
TYPE	Hotel
ACCOMMODATION	352 Rooms
FACILITIES	Breakfast cafe
GOOD TO KNOW	24-hour reception
RECOMMENDED FOR	Budget

Cabinn is a low-cost base within easy reach of many of Copenhagen's top attractions. There are simple, wallet-friendly rooms and a 24-hour reception that sells snacks.

Recommended by: Daniel Libeskind, Studio Libeskind

NIMB HOTEL
Bernstorffsgade 5
København V
Copenhagen 1577
+45 88700000
nimb.dk

CREDIT CARDS	Accepted
PRICE	Blow-out
TYPE	Hotel
ACCOMMODATION	38 Rooms and Suites
FACILITIES	2 Bars, Gym, Outdoor swimming pool, 4 Restaurants, Rooftop terrace bar, Spa, Wellness area, Yoga
GOOD TO KNOW	Child and pet friendly
RECOMMENDED FOR	Best-kept secret

A stylish boutique hotel with views of the adjacent Tivoli Gardens, which hotel guests can access freely during operational hours. Each room features a unique and thoughtfully curated piece of art, and guests can also enjoy views of the city from the Rooftop pool.

Recommended by: Matteo Thun, Matteo Thun & Partners

NOBIS HOTEL COPENHAGEN
Niels Brocks Gade 1
København V
Copenhagen 1574
+45 78741400
nobishotel.dk

CREDIT CARDS	Accepted
PRICE	High-end
TYPE	Hotel
ACCOMMODATION	75 Rooms and Suites
FACILITIES	Bar, Gym, Restaurant, Sauna
GOOD TO KNOW	Bicycle rentals, Valet parking
RECOMMENDED FOR	Urban

Recommended by: Gert Wingårdh, Wingårdhs

RADISSON COLLECTION ROYAL HOTEL, COPENHAGEN
Hammerichsgade 1
København V
Copenhagen 1611
+45 33426000
radissoncollection.com

CREDIT CARDS	Accepted
PRICE	Mid-range
TYPE	Hotel
ACCOMMODATION	261 Rooms and Suites
FACILITIES	Bar, Gym, Restaurant, Sauna
GOOD TO KNOW	Babysitting
RECOMMENDED FOR	All-time favorite, Luxury, Wish I'd designed, Worth the travel

"A lot of this fantastic project was lost when it was refurbished. [It was originally named the SAS Royal Hotel.] Nonetheless, Room 606 has been saved with its masterful Arne Jacobsen interiors and details."—Marcio Kogan

"Beautiful design in classic Scandinavian style by Arne Jacobsen."—Stéphane Rasselet

Recommended by: Ludovico Centis, The Empire; Nuno Brandão Costa, Brandão Costa Arquitectos; Bernardo and Paulo Jacobsen, Jacobsen Arquitetura; Marcio Kogan, Studio MK27; Rafael de La-Hoz Castanys, Rafael de La-Hoz Arquitectos; Stéphane Rasselet, Naturehumaine; Fran Silvestre, Fran Silvestre Arquitectos

BABETTE

Bredgade 78
Indre By
Copenhagen 1260
+45 33141500
guldsmedenhotels.com

CREDIT CARDS...Accepted
PRICE...Mid-range
TYPE...Hotel
ACCOMMODATION...98 Rooms
FACILITIES..............................Bar, Restaurant, Sauna
GOOD TO KNOW................................Charger available
for electric vehicles
RECOMMENDED FOR..Eco-conscious

"Unpretentious atmosphere and uncompromising
sustainability in the heart of Copenhagen."—Gert Wingårdh

Recommended by: Gert Wingårdh, Wingårdhs

HOTEL SANDERS

Tordenskjoldsgade 15
Indre By
Copenhagen 1055
+45 46400040
hotelsanders.com

CREDIT CARDS.....................................Accepted but not Diners
PRICE..High-end
TYPE...Hotel
ACCOMMODATION.....................................53 Rooms and Suites
FACILITIES...........................Restaurant, Rooftop terrace bar
GOOD TO KNOW...Child friendly
RECOMMENDED FOR...Where I live

"A great spot to enjoy a drink in the center of Copenhagen.
This is an elegant place where you're surrounded by
high-quality design, giving it a distinctively cool ambience."
—Kim Herforth Nielsen

Recommended by: Kim Herforth Nielsen, 3XN

HOTEL CPH LIVING

Langebrogade 1A
København K
Copenhagen 1411
+45 61608546
cphliving.com

CREDIT CARDS...Accepted
PRICE...Mid-range
TYPE...Boat
ACCOMMODATION...12 Cabins
FACILITIES...Sun terrace
GOOD TO KNOW...Floating hotel
RECOMMENDED FOR...Urban

"A small hotel in the middle of Copenhagen. Being moored
to the east side of Inderhavnen and adjacent to the Langebro
bridge puts most destinations within walking distance.
Accommodation is arranged over two levels with the roof
acting as a sun terrace. The rooms are large and clean with
stunning views over the water."—Robin Partington

Recommended by: Robin Partington, Robin Partington
& Partners

REPUBLIC OF IRELAND AND UNITED KINGDOM

SCALE

0   55   110
mi.

BOTHAR BUI

Ardgroom
Beara Peninsula
County Cork
Republic of Ireland
+353 868902338
botharbui.com

CREDIT CARDS	Accepted
PRICE	Mid-range
TYPE	Home rental
ACCOMMODATION	5 Rooms
FACILITIES	Private beach, Woodlands
GOOD TO KNOW	Boat trips, Child friendly, Self-catering
RECOMMENDED FOR	Countryside

"An incredible collection of small buildings, both modern and vernacular, designed by Robin Walker. A great place to retreat from the world."—Cian Deegan

Recommended by: Cian Deegan, TAKA Architects

CLARENCE HOTEL

6-8 Wellington Quay
Temple Bar
Dublin D02 HT44
Republic of Ireland
+353 14070800
theclarence.ie

CREDIT CARDS	Accepted
PRICE	Mid-range
TYPE	Hotel
ACCOMMODATION	51 Rooms and Suites
FACILITIES	Bar, Restaurant
GOOD TO KNOW	Valet parking
RECOMMENDED FOR	Wish I'd designed

Recommended by: Kiyoshi Sey Takeyama, Amorphe Takeyama & Associates

THE MERRION HOTEL

21-24 Merrion Street Upper
Dublin D02 KF79, Republic of Ireland
+353 16030600
merrionhotel.com

CREDIT CARDS	Accepted
PRICE	High-end
TYPE	Hotel
ACCOMMODATION	143 Rooms and Suites
FACILITIES	Bar, Gym, Indoor swimming pool, Restaurant, Sauna, Spa, Steam room
GOOD TO KNOW	Bicycle rentals, Valet parking
RECOMMENDED FOR	Spa, Where I live

Recommended by: Cian Deegan, TAKA Architects; Roger Duffy, Skidmore, Owings & Merrill

NUMBER 31

31 Leeson Close
Dublin D02 CP70, Republic of Ireland
+353 16765011
number31.ie

CREDIT CARDS	Accepted but not Amex
PRICE	Mid-range
TYPE	Townhouse hotel
ACCOMMODATION	21 Rooms
FACILITIES	Honesty Bar
GOOD TO KNOW	Airport transfers
RECOMMENDED FOR	Where I live

Recommended by: Grace Keeley, GKMP Architects

INIS MEAIN RESTAURANT & SUITES

Inis Meáin
Aran Islands
County Galway H91 NX86, Republic of Ireland
inismeain.com

CREDIT CARDS	Accepted
PRICE	High-end
TYPE	Restaurant with rooms
ACCOMMODATION	5 Suites
FACILITIES	Restaurant
GOOD TO KNOW	Email to book, Open March to September
RECOMMENDED FOR	All-time favorite

"An island escape."—Shane de Blacam

Recommended by: Shane de Blacam, de Blacam and Meagher

BALLYFIN DEMESNE
Ballyfin
County Laois R32 PN34
Republic of Ireland
+353 578755866
ballyfin.com

CREDIT CARDS	Accepted
PRICE	Blow-out
TYPE	Country house hotel
ACCOMMODATION	21 Cottages and Rooms
FACILITIES	Bar, Gym, Indoor swimming pool, Restaurant, Sauna, Spa, Steam room
GOOD TO KNOW	Bicycle rentals, Child friendly (9 and over), Clay pigeon shooting, Horse riding, Rowing boats
RECOMMENDED FOR	Countryside

Considered one of Ireland's finest country houses, a stay at Ballyfin is like stepping back in time. Following its restoration in 2011, each of its rooms has been tastefully and individually designed to reflect the character of the house. The hotel's culinary philosophy is "local, natural, and seasonal," and showcases the best of Irish produce.

Recommended by: Kelly Hoppen, Kelly Hoppen Interiors

CASTLE LESLIE ESTATE
Glaslough
County Monaghan H18 FY04
Republic of Ireland
+353 4788100
castleleslie.com

CREDIT CARDS	Accepted
PRICE	Mid-range
TYPE	Country estate hotel
ACCOMMODATION	70 Rooms
FACILITIES	Bar, Open-air bath, 2 Restaurants, Spa
GOOD TO KNOW	Horse riding
RECOMMENDED FOR	All-time favorite

"The perfect blend of a comfortable hotel and feeling like you are a guest in a (rich) friend's home—try to stay in the main house. The breakfast room overlooking the grounds is sublime."—Cian Deegan

Recommended by: Cian Deegan, TAKA Architects

THE MACHRIE HOTEL & GOLF LINKS
Isle of Islay
Port Ellen
Argyll and Bute PA42 7AN
Scotland
+44 1496302310
campbellgrayhotels.com

CREDIT CARDS	Accepted
PRICE	Mid-range
TYPE	Hotel
ACCOMMODATION	47 Rooms and Suites
FACILITIES	Bar, Cinema, Golf, Gym, Outdoor restaurant, Restaurant, Spa
GOOD TO KNOW	Pet friendly
RECOMMENDED FOR	Countryside

"Remote Islay is one of Scotland's most beautiful islands, and the Machrie brings contemporary luxury and style to a stunning location overlooking the Atlantic: an ideal base for exploring Islay's rugged landscape or its many famous distilleries."—Anthony Hudson

[This hotel was designed by Hudson Architects.]

Recommended by: Anthony Hudson, Hudson Architects

THE FIFE ARMS
Mar Road
Braemar
Aberdeenshire AB35 5YN
Scotland
+44 1339720200
thefifearms.com

CREDIT CARDS	Accepted
PRICE	High-end
TYPE	Hotel
ACCOMMODATION	46 Rooms and Suites
FACILITIES	Bar, Gym, Restaurant, Spa
GOOD TO KNOW	Art tours, Foraging walks, Helicopter rides, Picnics
RECOMMENDED FOR	Worth the travel

The Fife Arms is warm Scottish hospitality at its best. The former coaching inn has been imaginatively yet sensitively restored—sumptuous yet cozy with special touches. All guestrooms and suites are individually decorated and named after a local figure, place, event, or theme, while showcasing the work of local craftsmen and the rich history of Braemar.

Recommended by: Paolo Cossu, Paolo Cossu Architects

GREYWALLS HOTEL & CHEZ ROUX
Gullane
East Lothian EH31 2EG, Scotland
+44 1620842144
greywalls.co.uk

CREDIT CARDS	Accepted
PRICE	Mid-range
TYPE	Country house hotel
ACCOMMODATION	23 Cottages and Rooms
FACILITIES	Bar, Golf, Restaurant
GOOD TO KNOW	Designed by Sir Edwin Lutyens
RECOMMENDED FOR	Countryside, Family friendly

Recommended by: Jack Diamond, Diamond Schmitt;
Simon Henley, Henley Halebrown

THE WEST END HOTEL
35 Palmerston Place
Edinburgh EH12 5AU, Scotland
+44 1312253656
thewestendhotel.co.uk

CREDIT CARDS	Accepted but not Amex
PRICE	Low-cost
TYPE	Hostel
ACCOMMODATION	10 Dorms
FACILITIES	Bar, Restaurant
GOOD TO KNOW	Live music at weekends
RECOMMENDED FOR	Budget

Recommended by: Claudia Urdaneta, NMD NOMADAS

BABBITY BOWSTER
16-18 Blackfriars Street
Glasgow G1 1PE, Scotland
+44 1415525055
babbitybowster.com

CREDIT CARDS	Accepted
PRICE	Mid-range
TYPE	Pub with rooms
ACCOMMODATION	5 Rooms
FACILITIES	Bar, Restaurant
GOOD TO KNOW	Free parking
RECOMMENDED FOR	Best-kept secret

"Small and comfortable rooms, and a rollicking good pub
downstairs for good food and a friendly atmosphere."
—Biba Dow

Recommended by: Biba Dow, Dow Jones Architects

HOTEL TRESANTON
27 Lower Castle Road
St Mawes
Cornwall TR25DR, England
+44 1326270055
tresanton.com

CREDIT CARDS	Accepted
PRICE	Mid-range
TYPE	Hotel
ACCOMMODATION	30 Rooms and Suites
FACILITIES	Bar, Restaurant
GOOD TO KNOW	Child and pet friendly
RECOMMENDED FOR	Beach

"The hotel [designed by Olga Polizzi] is small but
wonderfully elegant, overlooking the Cornish coastline."
—Dennis Pieprz

Recommended by: Dennis Pieprz, Sasaki

THE NOBODY INN
Doddiscombsleigh
Exeter
Devon EX6 7PS, England
+44 1647252394
nobodyinn.co.uk

CREDIT CARDS	Accepted
PRICE	Low-cost
TYPE	Inn
ACCOMMODATION	5 Rooms
FACILITIES	Bar, Restaurant
GOOD TO KNOW	Homemade ale, More than 250 wines and whiskeys
RECOMMENDED FOR	Countryside

Recommended by: Simon Mitchell, Sybarite

HOTEL ENDSLEIGH
Milton Abbot
Devon PL19 0PQ, England
+44 1822870000
hotelendsleigh.com

CREDIT CARDS	Accepted
PRICE	Mid-range
TYPE	Country house hotel
ACCOMMODATION	18 Rooms
FACILITIES	Bar, 2 Restaurants
GOOD TO KNOW	Babysitting
RECOMMENDED FOR	Countryside

Recommended by: Flavio Albanese, ASA Studio

HOTEL DU VIN POOLE

7-11 Thames Street
Poole
Dorset BH15 1JN
England
+44 1305819027
hotelduvin.com

CREDIT CARDS	Accepted
PRICE	Mid-range
TYPE	Townhouse hotel
ACCOMMODATION	38 Rooms and Suites
FACILITIES	Bar, Restaurant
GOOD TO KNOW	Child friendly
RECOMMENDED FOR	Urban

"A small Georgian building in the historic harbor area of Poole, stylishly furnished, and a warm, friendly atmosphere."
—Chris Wilkinson

Recommended by: Chris Wilkinson, Wilkinson Eyre Architects

COWLEY MANOR

Cheltenham
Gloucestershire GL53 9NL
England
+44 1242870900
cowleymanor.com

CREDIT CARDS	Accepted
PRICE	Mid-range
TYPE	Manor house hotel
ACCOMMODATION	31 Rooms
FACILITIES	Bar, Gym, Indoor and outdoor swimming pools, Restaurant, Sauna, Spa, Steam room
GOOD TO KNOW	Child and pet friendly
RECOMMENDED FOR	Countryside

"Beautiful, romantic hotel tucked away in the gorgeous Gloucestershire countryside."—Alex Michaelis

Recommended by: Alex Michaelis, Michaelis Boyd

LONDON: SEE PAGES 180–187

THE PIG

Beaulieu Road
Brockenhurst
Hampshire SO42 7QL
England
+44 1590622354
thepighotel.com

CREDIT CARDS	Accepted
PRICE	Mid-range
TYPE	Country house hotel
ACCOMMODATION	32 Rooms
FACILITIES	Bar, Restaurant, Spa
GOOD TO KNOW	Child friendly, Free parking
RECOMMENDED FOR	Family friendly

The Pig is in the heart of the England's New Forest, and exploring the grounds is a treat in itself. This property is the original of the hotel group, which is a charming collection of hip, shabby-chic retreats, with a focus on farm-to-fork dining. Any produce not grown on-site is sourced within a twenty-five-mile (forty kilometer) radius. Spa treatments use Bamford and Oskia products.

Recommended by: Alex Michaelis, Michaelis Boyd

THE GUNTON ARMS

Cromer Road
Thorpe Market
Norfolk NR11 8TZ
England
+44 1263832010
theguntonarms.co.uk

CREDIT CARDS	Accepted
PRICE	Mid-range
TYPE	Pub with rooms
ACCOMMODATION	16 Rooms
FACILITIES	Bar, Restaurant
GOOD TO KNOW	Contemporary art collection
RECOMMENDED FOR	Family friendly, Where I live

"Venison cooked over an open fire and raunchy artworks."
—Will Alsop

"Atmospheric hunting lodge in a deer park with fabulous food and work by young British artists."—Anthony Hudson

Recommended by: Will Alsop, aLL Design; Anthony Hudson, Hudson Architects

SOHO FARMHOUSE
Great Tew
Chipping Norton
Oxfordshire OX7 4JS
England
+44 1608691000
sohofarmhouse.com

CREDIT CARDS	Accepted
PRICE	High-end
TYPE	Members' club
ACCOMMODATION	92 Cabins, Cottage, Rooms, and Suites
FACILITIES	Bar, Gym, Outdoor swimming pool, Restaurant, Sauna, Spa, Steam room
GOOD TO KNOW	Free parking
RECOMMENDED FOR	Countryside, Luxury

"I like the surrounding countryside. The service is professional, and it's an ideal place to escape the hustle and bustle of London."—Murat Tabanlıoğlu

Recommended by: Anne Kaestle, Duplex Architekten; Murat Tabanlıoğlu, Tabanlıoğlu Architects

BABINGTON HOUSE
Babington
Somerset BA11 3RW
England
+44 1373812266
babingtonhouse.co.uk

CREDIT CARDS	Accepted
PRICE	Mid-range
TYPE	Hotel (and Members' club)
ACCOMMODATION	32 Rooms and Suites
FACILITIES	Bar, Gym, Indoor and outdoor swimming pools, Restaurant, Sauna, Spa, Steam room
GOOD TO KNOW	Child friendly, Free parking
RECOMMENDED FOR	Countryside

An original of the Soho House group, Babington House is a stylish and sensitively restored hotel and spa retreat set among the green fields and rolling hills of the English countryside. Facilities include a spa, cinema, children's entertainment, indoor and outdoor pools, and a bar and restaurant.

[Soho House Group is a client of Michaelis Boyd.]

Recommended by: Alex Michaelis, Michaelis Boyd

THE SWAN HOTEL
Market Place
Southwold
Suffolk IP18 6EG
England
+44 1502722186
theswansouthwold.co.uk

CREDIT CARDS	Accepted but not Amex
PRICE	Mid-range
TYPE	Hotel
ACCOMMODATION	35 Rooms
FACILITIES	Bar, Restaurants
GOOD TO KNOW	Child and pet friendly
RECOMMENDED FOR	Best-kept secret

"Great location in a beautiful town near a great coastline." —Will Alsop

Recommended by: Will Alsop, aLL Design

THE BISHOPS TABLE HOTEL
27 West Street
Farnham
Surrey GU9 7DR
England
+44 1252710222
bishopstable.com

CREDIT CARDS	Accepted
PRICE	Low-cost
TYPE	Hotel
ACCOMMODATION	24 Rooms
FACILITIES	Bar
GOOD TO KNOW	Weddings and special events
RECOMMENDED FOR	Countryside

"Lovely staff and a great location."—Claudia Urdaneta

Recommended by: Claudia Urdaneta, NMD NOMADAS

AMBERLEY CASTLE

Church Street
Arundel
West Sussex BN18 9LT
England
+44 1798831992
amberleycastle.co.uk

CREDIT CARDS	Accepted
PRICE	High-end
TYPE	Castle hotel
ACCOMMODATION	19 Rooms
FACILITIES	Bar, Golf, Restaurant
GOOD TO KNOW	Free parking
RECOMMENDED FOR	Countryside

"A brilliant way to escape the pace of London. Book a room within the castle walls and enjoy delicious food and seclusion, with lots to do and see during the day in the surrounding countryside."—Robin Partington

Recommended by: Robin Partington, Robin Partington & Partners

DUMBLETON HALL HOTEL

Evesham
Worcestershire WR11 7TS
England
+44 1386881240
dumbletonhall.co.uk

CREDIT CARDS	Accepted but not Amex
PRICE	Mid-range
TYPE	Manor house hotel
ACCOMMODATION	38 Rooms
FACILITIES	Bar, Restaurant
GOOD TO KNOW	Pet friendly
RECOMMENDED FOR	Countryside

"If you think a manor house hotel near a tiny Cotswolds village with a cricket oval, church, and winding lanes exists only in fiction, think again! A great base from which to go rambling through fields."—Paul Morgan

Recommended by: Paul Morgan, Paul Morgan Architects

PEN-Y-GWRYD HOTEL

Nant Gwynant
Gwynedd LL55 4NT
Wales
+44 1286870211
pyg.co.uk

CREDIT CARDS	Accepted
PRICE	Low-cost
TYPE	Hotel
ACCOMMODATION	20 Rooms
FACILITIES	Restaurant
GOOD TO KNOW	Free parking, Pet friendly
RECOMMENDED FOR	Mountains

"A traditional and friendly hotel in fabulous countryside, with a mountaineering legend."—Biba Dow

Recommended by: Biba Dow, Dow Jones Architects

HOTEL PORTMEIRION

Portmeirion
Gwynedd LL48 6ER
Wales
+44 1766772440
portmeirion.wales

CREDIT CARDS	Accepted but not Amex
PRICE	Mid-range
TYPE	Hotel
ACCOMMODATION	14 Rooms and Suites
FACILITIES	Bar, Outdoor swimming pool, Restaurant, Spa
GOOD TO KNOW	Child friendly
RECOMMENDED FOR	Family friendly

"With a fantasy village, wilderness, and beautiful beaches, it makes an extraordinary impression and provides lots of exciting things to do."—Anthony Hudson

Recommended by: Anthony Hudson, Hudson Architects

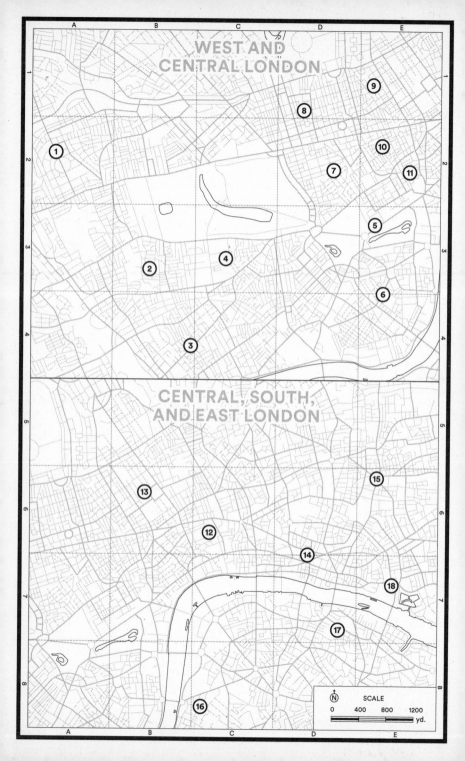

LONDON

THE LASLETT
8 Pembridge Gardens
Notting Hill
London W2 4DU
+44 2077926688
living-rooms.co.uk

CREDIT CARDS..Accepted
PRICE...Mid-range
TYPE..Townhouse hotel
ACCOMMODATION.......................................51 Rooms and Suites
FACILITIES...Bar, Restaurant
GOOD TO KNOW........................Curated library and shop
RECOMMENDED FOR....................................Where I live

Recommended by: Michael Stiff, Stiff + Trevillion

NUMBER SIXTEEN
16 Sumner Place
South Kensington
London SW7 3EG
+44 2075895232
firmdalehotels.com

CREDIT CARDS..Accepted
PRICE...High-end
TYPE..Townhouse hotel
ACCOMMODATION.......................................41 Rooms
FACILITIES...Bar, Restaurant
GOOD TO KNOW..Child friendly
RECOMMENDED FOR............................All-time favorite

Recommended by: Marcio Kogan, Studio MK27

THE PELHAM HOTEL
15 Cromwell Place
South Kensington
London SW7 2LA
+44 2075898288
starhotelscollezione.com

CREDIT CARDS..Accepted
PRICE...Mid-range
TYPE..Townhouse hotel
ACCOMMODATION............1 Penthouse, 52 Rooms and Suites
FACILITIES...Gym, Restaurant
GOOD TO KNOW..........................Babysitting, Child friendly
RECOMMENDED FOR....................................Where I live

"Impeccable service in a quintessential London townhouse."
—Simon Mitchell

Recommended by: Simon Mitchell, Sybarite

11 CADOGAN GARDENS
11 Cadogan Gardens
Chelsea
London SW3 2RJ
+44 2077307000
11cadogangardens.com

CREDIT CARDS..Accepted
PRICE...High-end
TYPE..Townhouse hotel
ACCOMMODATION.......................................56 Rooms and Suites
FACILITIES....................................2 Bars, Gym, Restaurant
GOOD TO KNOW..Child friendly
RECOMMENDED FOR............................All-time favorite

Recommended by: Will Alsop, aLL Design

SAN DOMENICO HOUSE HOTEL
29-31 Draycott Place
Chelsea
London SW3 2SH
+44 2075815757
sandomenicohouse.com

CREDIT CARDS..Accepted
PRICE...Mid-range
TYPE..Hotel
ACCOMMODATION.......................................19 Rooms and Suites
FACILITIES................Air-conditioning, In-room dining
GOOD TO KNOW..................Babysitting, Child friendly
RECOMMENDED FOR....................................Urban

"I stay here whenever I visit London: it's well-connected,
and quiet, affording a great night's sleep."—Achille Salvagni

Recommended by: Achille Salvagni, Salvagni Architetti

BULGARI HOTEL LONDON
171 Knightsbridge
Knightsbridge
London SW7 1DW
+44 2071511010
bulgarihotels.com

CREDIT CARDS..Accepted
PRICE...Blow-out
TYPE..Hotel
ACCOMMODATION.......................................85 Rooms and Suites
FACILITIES...................Bar, Gym, Indoor swimming pool,
Restaurant, Spa
GOOD TO KNOW..Child friendly
RECOMMENDED FOR....................................Urban

Recommended by: Emre Arolat, EAA

MANDARIN ORIENTAL HYDE PARK, LONDON
66 Knightsbridge
Knightsbridge
London SW1X 7LA
+44 2072352000
mandarinoriental.com

CREDIT CARDS...Accepted
PRICE...High-end
TYPE...Hotel
ACCOMMODATION....................................181 Rooms and Suites
FACILITIES.........................Bar, Gym, Indoor swimming pool,
3 Restaurants, Sauna,
Spa, Steam room
GOOD TO KNOW...Babysitting
RECOMMENDED FOR...Luxury

Mandarin Oriental Hyde Park reopened in the exclusive Knightsbridge district in 2019 following a fire. Its rooms, suites, and public areas, designed by Joyce Wang, take inspiration from the natural beauty of Hyde Park and the Golden Age of Travel. Art Deco accents, carefully curated artwork, and custom-designed furniture feature in rooms and suites. Dining experiences showcase the finest of French and British culinary traditions—including, of course, afternoon tea.

Recommended by: Marta Urtasun and Pedro Rica, Mecanismo

DUKE'S LONDON
35 St James's Place
St James's
London SW1A 1NY
+44 2074914840
dukeshotel.com

CREDIT CARDS...Accepted
PRICE...High-end
TYPE...Hotel
ACCOMMODATION....................................87 Rooms and Suites
FACILITIES...Bar, Gym, Restaurant,
Spa, Steam room
GOOD TO KNOW...Child friendly
RECOMMENDED FOR...Urban

Tucked behind St James's Palace in London's exclusive Mayfair district, Duke's is a five-star hotel renowned for its martini bar and discreet, impeccable service. It is family friendly and, with notice, also caters for dog owners.

Recommended by: Raúl de Armas, MdeAS Architects

SOFITEL LONDON ST JAMES
6 Waterloo Place
St James's
London SW1Y 4AN
+44 2077472200
sofitelstjames.com

CREDIT CARDS...Accepted
PRICE...High-end
TYPE...Hotel
ACCOMMODATION....................................186 Rooms and Suites
FACILITIES.........................Bar, Gym, Jacuzzi, Restaurant,
Spa, Steam room
GOOD TO KNOW...Child friendly
RECOMMENDED FOR...Luxury

"Elegance, location, luxury, and comfort that is top top top."
—Jean-Paul Viguier

Recommended by: Jean-Paul Viguier, Jean-Paul Viguier et Associés

THE GORING HOTEL
15 Beeston Place
Westminster
London SW1W 0JW
+44 2073969000
thegoring.com

CREDIT CARDS...Accepted
PRICE...High-end
TYPE...Hotel
ACCOMMODATION....................................69 Rooms and Suites
FACILITIES...Bar, Gym, 2 Restaurants
GOOD TO KNOW...Child friendly,
Michelin-starred restaurant
RECOMMENDED FOR...........................All-time favorite, Luxury

"Like staying in a luxurious, large family home. It has friendly, helpful staff, excellent food and drink, and all of London outside the door."—Louis Hedgecock

Recommended by: Louis Hedgecock, HOK Architects; Daniel Libeskind, Studio Libeskind

THE BEAUMONT

8 Balderton Street, Brown Hart Gardens
Mayfair
London W1K 6TF
+44 2074991001
thebeaumont.com

CREDIT CARDS	Accepted
PRICE	High-end
TYPE	Hotel
ACCOMMODATION	73 Rooms and Suites
FACILITIES	Bar, Gym, Plunge pool, Restaurant, Sauna, Spa, Steam room
GOOD TO KNOW	Child friendly
RECOMMENDED FOR	Luxury, Urban

"Forty-plus years in the international hotel industry, and I find it simply the best in the world."—Patrick Reardon

[ReardonSmith Architects were the architects for this hotel.]

Recommended by: Patrick Reardon, ReardonSmith Architects

CLARIDGE'S

Brook Street
Mayfair
London W1K 4HR
+44 2076298860
claridges.co.uk

CREDIT CARDS	Accepted
PRICE	Blow-out
TYPE	Hotel
ACCOMMODATION	203 Penthouses, Rooms, and Suites
FACILITIES	2 Bars, Gym, Restaurant, Spa
GOOD TO KNOW	Babysitting
RECOMMENDED FOR	All-time favorite, Luxury, Urban, Where I live

"The Art Deco design is breathtaking. The hotel's history and specific cultural references create a beautiful place to linger in. I love the hotel's detailing—a fine balance of elegance and precision, which makes you want to idle away the hours."—Margot Krasojevic

"For old school glamour and exceptional, discreet service."
—Amanda Levete

Recommended by: Margot Krasojevic, Margot Krasojevic Architecture; Amanda Levete, AL_A; Ken Yeang, Hamzah & Yeang

THE CONNAUGHT

Carlos Place
Mayfair
London W1K 2AL
+44 2074997070
the-connaught.co.uk

CREDIT CARDS	Accepted
PRICE	Blow-out
TYPE	Hotel
ACCOMMODATION	121 Apartments, Rooms, and Suites
FACILITIES	Bar, Gym, 2 Restaurants, Sauna, Spa, Steam room
GOOD TO KNOW	Child friendly
RECOMMENDED FOR	All-time favorite, Luxury, Spa, Urban

"A hotel that takes you back to London's Gilded Age where service and attention were the marks of excellence. Great location and architecture—ideal for a romantic trip to the city."—Simon Jacobsen

Recommended by: Flavio Albanese, ASA Studio; Francesca Bucci, BG Studio International; Manuel Cervantes, CC Arquitectos; Doriana and Massimiliano Fuksas, Studio Fuksas; Simon Jacobsen, Jacobsen Architecture; Rick Joy, Studio Rick Joy; Mark de Reus, de Reus Architects; Daniel Suduca and Thierry Mérillou, Suduca & Mérillou

CHILTERN FIREHOUSE

1 Chiltern Street
Marylebone
London W1U 7PA
+44 2070737676
chilternfirehouse.com

CREDIT CARDS	Accepted
PRICE	High-end
TYPE	Hotel
ACCOMMODATION	26 Lofts, Rooms, and Suites
FACILITIES	Bar, Restaurant
GOOD TO KNOW	Child friendly
RECOMMENDED FOR	All-time favorite, Best-kept secret, Luxury, Urban

"Great bars and lobby, amazing history and location."
—Craig Dykers

Recommended by: Craig Dykers, Snøhetta; Bernardo Fort-Brescia, Arquitectonica; Alex Mustonen, Snarkitecture; Hugo Sauzay, Festen Architecture

DURRANTS HOTEL

32 George Street
Marylebone
London W1H 5BJ
+44 2079358131
durrantshotel.co.uk

CREDIT CARDS	Accepted
PRICE	Mid-range
TYPE	Hotel
ACCOMMODATION	90 Rooms and Suites
FACILITIES	Bar, Gym, Restaurant
GOOD TO KNOW	Family owned
RECOMMENDED FOR	Best-kept secret

"A classic London urban hotel in a fantastic location opposite the Wallace Collection."—Dennis Pieprz

Recommended by: Dennis Pieprz, Sasaki

CHARLOTTE STREET HOTEL

15-17 Charlotte Street
Fitzrovia
London W1T 1RJ
+44 2078062000
firmdalehotels.com

CREDIT CARDS	Accepted
PRICE	High-end
TYPE	Hotel
ACCOMMODATION	52 Rooms and Suites
FACILITIES	Bar, Gym, Restaurant, Screening room
GOOD TO KNOW	Afternoon tea, Child friendly
RECOMMENDED FOR	Urban

Recommended by: Jack Diamond, Diamond Schmitt

THE GROUCHO CLUB

45 Dean Street
Soho
London W1D 4QB
+44 2074394685
thegrouchoclub.com

CREDIT CARDS	Accepted
PRICE	Mid-range
TYPE	Members' club
ACCOMMODATION	20 Rooms
FACILITIES	Bar, Restaurant
GOOD TO KNOW	No mobile devices after 5pm
RECOMMENDED FOR	Urban

The Groucho Club—also known as the maverick, "anti-traditionalist" members' club—has maintained its reputation as a hedonistic haven for the creative industries since its opening in 1985. Room bookings are open to club members and their guests, who receive temporary membership for the duration of their stay.

Recommended by: Matthias Sauerbruch and Louisa Hutton, Sauerbruch Hutton

HAZLITT'S

6 Frith Street
Soho
London W1D 3JA
+44 2074341771
hazlittshotel.com

CREDIT CARDS	Accepted
PRICE	Mid-range
TYPE	Townhouse hotel
ACCOMMODATION	30 Rooms and Suites
FACILITIES	Honesty bar
GOOD TO KNOW	Child friendly, Breakfast served in guest's rooms
RECOMMENDED FOR	Urban

Hazlitt's is a boutique townhouse hotel in the heart of London's Soho district. It combines quirky British spirit and genial hospitality with lavishly appointed rooms inspired by the hotel's Georgian-era heritage.

Recommended by: Flavio Albanese, ASA Studio

HOTEL CAFÉ ROYAL

10 Air Street
Soho
London W1B 4DY
+44 2074063333
hotelcaferoyal.com

CREDIT CARDS	Accepted
PRICE	High-end
TYPE	Hotel
ACCOMMODATION	160 Rooms and Suites
FACILITIES	2 Bars, Gym, Hammam, Indoor swimming pool, Jacuzzi, 3 Restaurants, Sauna, Spa, Steam room, Yoga
GOOD TO KNOW	Child friendly, No pets
RECOMMENDED FOR	Urban, Wish I'd designed

"Great design and comfortable rooms."—Ola Rune

Recommended by: Marta Urtasun and Pedro Rica, Mecanismo; Ola Rune, Claesson Koivisto Rune Architects

THE SOHO HOTEL
4 Richmond Mews
Soho
London W1D 3DH
+44 2075593000
firmdalehotels.com

CREDIT CARDS	Accepted
PRICE	High-end
TYPE	Townhouse hotel
ACCOMMODATION	96 Rooms and Suites
FACILITIES	Bar, Gym, Restaurant, Screening rooms, Spa, Steam room
GOOD TO KNOW	Afternoon tea
RECOMMENDED FOR	Urban

"Great location and value for money."—Sean Godsell

Recommended by: Sean Godsell, Sean Godsell Architects

ST MARTINS LANE
45 St Martin's Lane
Covent Garden
London WC2N 4HX
+44 2073005500
morganshotelgroup.com

CREDIT CARDS	Accepted
PRICE	High-end
TYPE	Hotel
ACCOMMODATION	204 Apartments, Rooms, and Suites
FACILITIES	Bar, Gym, Restaurant
GOOD TO KNOW	Bicycle rentals
RECOMMENDED FOR	Where I live

Recommended by: Uwe Schmidt-Hess, Patalab Architecture

ROSEWOOD LONDON
252 High Holborn
Holborn
London WC1V 7EN
+44 2077818888
rosewoodhotels.com

CREDIT CARDS	Accepted
PRICE	High-end
TYPE	Hotel
ACCOMMODATION	314 Residences, Rooms, and Suites
FACILITIES	Bar, Gym, 2 Restaurants, Sauna, Spa, Steam room
GOOD TO KNOW	Child and pet friendly
RECOMMENDED FOR	Urban, Where I live, Wish I'd designed

Rosewood London is one of the city's finest ultra-luxury hotels but it is far from stuffy. Service is warm and genuine, and artwork by caricaturist Gerald Scarfe in Scarfe's Bar is a great conversation starter. The hotel also goes the extra mile for families of all ages.

Recommended by: Kelly Hoppen, Kelly Hoppen Interiors; Maria Warner Wong, WOW Architects | Warner Wong Design

MY BLOOMSBURY
11-13 Bayley Street
Bloomsbury
London WC1B 3HD
+44 2030046000
myhotels.com

CREDIT CARDS	Accepted
PRICE	Mid-range
TYPE	Hotel
ACCOMMODATION	86 Rooms and Suites
FACILITIES	Bar, Restaurant, Spa
GOOD TO KNOW	Near British Museum
RECOMMENDED FOR	Best-kept secret

"Compact and in a great location in Bloomsbury."
—Ken Yeang

Recommended by: Ken Yeang, Hamzah & Yeang

FOUR SEASONS HOTEL LONDON AT TEN TRINITY SQUARE
10 Trinity Square
City of London
London EC3N 4AJ
+44 2032979200
fourseasons.com

CREDIT CARDS	Accepted
PRICE	High-end
TYPE	Hotel
ACCOMMODATION	100 Residences, Rooms, and Suites
FACILITIES	Bar, Gym, Indoor swimming pool, 2 Restaurants, Salon, Sauna, Spa
GOOD TO KNOW	Child friendly, Valet parking
RECOMMENDED FOR	Urban

"Visit for its architecture and location in an historic area of London. It has a strong thematic experience that operates as a link between the classical building and its contemporary reinterpretation."
—Claire Bétaille and Bruno Moinard

Recommended by: Claire Bétaille and Bruno Moinard, 4BI & Associés

ACE HOTEL LONDON SHOREDITCH

100 Shoreditch High Street
Shoreditch
London E1 6JQ
+44 2076139800
acehotel.com

CREDIT CARDS..Accepted
PRICE...Mid-range
TYPE...Hotel
ACCOMMODATION.....................258 Rooms and Suites
FACILITIES...............................Bar, Gym, Restaurant,
Rooftop terrace bar, Sauna
GOOD TO KNOW......................On-site nightclub, Pet friendly
RECOMMENDED FOR...Urban

The Ace Hotel is situated in London's vibrant East End, and is popular with locals who come to enjoy the lobby vibe.

Recommended by: Hiéronyme Lacroix and Simon Chessex, Lacroix Chessex

TULSE HILL HOTEL

150 Norwood Road
Lambeth
London SE24 9AY
+44 2086717499
tulsehillhotel.com

CREDIT CARDS..Accepted
PRICE...Mid-range
TYPE...Hotel
ACCOMMODATION..9 Rooms
FACILITIES.............................Bar, Pub, Restaurant
GOOD TO KNOW..Garden
RECOMMENDED FOR..................................Where I live

Recommended by: Biba Dow, Dow Jones Architects

CITIZENM LONDON BANKSIDE

20 Lavington Street
Southwark
London SE1 0NZ
+44 2035191680
citizenm.com

CREDIT CARDS..Accepted
PRICE...Mid-range
TYPE...Hotel
ACCOMMODATION..192 Rooms
FACILITIES...Bar, Cafe
GOOD TO KNOW.................................Near Tate Modern
RECOMMENDED FOR...Urban

"Centrally located near the Tate Modern, Borough Market, the Thames River Walk, and The Shard, this hotel may have petite rooms, but the heart of the hotel is the large communal area that is a bustling hub of activity. Active throughout the day, it invites guests to get out of their room and do something, seamlessly transitioning from day to night. Recommended for urban adventurers who need a base camp."—Daniel Welborn

Recommended by: Daniel Welborn, The Gettys Group

SHANGRI-LA HOTEL AT THE SHARD

31 St Thomas Street
Southwark
London SE1 9QU
+44 2072348000
shangri-la.com

CREDIT CARDS..Accepted
PRICE...High-end
TYPE...Hotel
ACCOMMODATION.....................202 Rooms and Suites
FACILITIES..................2 Bars, Gym, Indoor swimming pool,
2 Restaurants
GOOD TO KNOW..............................Babysitting, Child friendly
RECOMMENDED FOR..........................Wish I'd designed

"Nice panoramic views and good design."
—Felino Palafox, Jr.

Recommended by: Felino Palafox, Jr., Palafox Associates

ROCKWELL EAST

99 Mansell Street
Whitechapel
London E1 8AX
+44 2070140250
rockwelleast.com

CREDIT CARDS..Accepted
PRICE...Mid-range
TYPE...Apartment hotel
ACCOMMODATION...................................57 Apartments
FACILITIES.................................Bar, Restaurant
GOOD TO KNOW.......................................Child friendly
RECOMMENDED FOR...Urban

Recommended by: Thomas Bartlett, Waldo Works

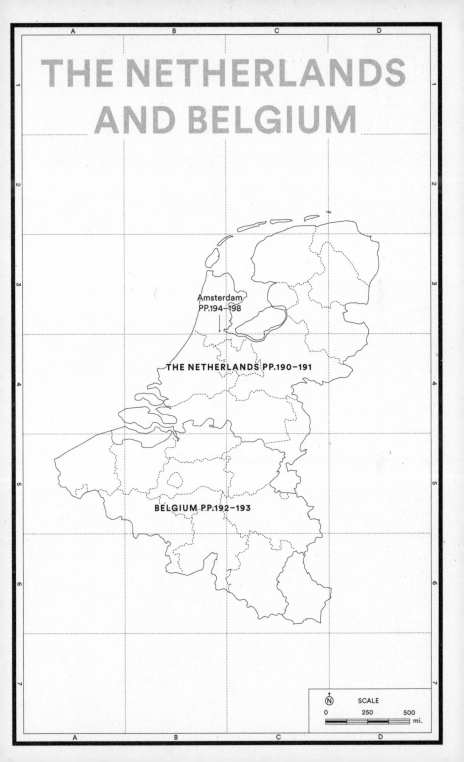

BITTER EN ZOET

Hospitaallaan 16
Veenhuizen
Drenthe 9341, The Netherlands
+31 592385002
bitterenzoet.nl

CREDIT CARDS	Accepted
PRICE	Low-cost
TYPE	Hotel
ACCOMMODATION	15 Rooms
FACILITIES	Restaurant, Sauna
GOOD TO KNOW	Bicycle rentals
RECOMMENDED FOR	Countryside

Recommended by: Liesbeth van der Pol, Dok Architects

KASTEEL ENGELENBURG

Eerbeekseweg 6
Brummen
Gelderland 6971, The Netherlands
+31 575569999
engelenburg.com

CREDIT CARDS	Accepted
PRICE	Mid-range
TYPE	Country estate hotel
ACCOMMODATION	41 Rooms and Suites
FACILITIES	Bar, 2 Restaurants
GOOD TO KNOW	On-site castle, Child friendly
RECOMMENDED FOR	Luxury

Recommended by: Liesbeth van der Pol, Dok Architects

OORTJESHEKKEN

Erlecomsedam 4
Ooij
Gelderland 6576, The Netherlands
+31 246631288
oortjeshekken.nl

CREDIT CARDS	Accepted
PRICE	Low-cost
TYPE	Restaurant with rooms
ACCOMMODATION	13 Rooms
FACILITIES	Bar, Restaurant
GOOD TO KNOW	Child friendly
RECOMMENDED FOR	Family friendly

"Built on a former dike, Oortjeshekken consists of two very distinctive levels facing either the garden, the water, or the grassland. Sociable ambience, pleasantly chaotic, and entertaining—a great hotel to stay at with family."
—Liesbeth van der Pol

Recommended by: Liesbeth van der Pol, Dok Architects

AMSTERDAM: SEE PAGES 194–198

MONUMENT EN BED, HUIS DIJKSTRA

Nieuweweg 2
Groet
Noord-Holland
The Netherlands
+31 205210645
monumentenbed.nl

CREDIT CARDS	Accepted
PRICE	Mid-range
TYPE	Home rental
ACCOMMODATION	1 Room
FACILITIES	Kitchen, Wood-burning stove
GOOD TO KNOW	No pets
RECOMMENDED FOR	Wish I'd designed

"A chance to stay in a selection of historical monuments. My absolute favorite is Huis Dijkstra in Groet: a typical, tiny, square house with two teal doors that, when open, function as windscreens for the terrace."—Liesbeth van der Pol

Recommended by: Liesbeth van der Pol, Dok Architects

ML IN HAARLEM

Klokhuisplein 9
Haarlem
Noord-Holland 2011
The Netherlands
+31 235123910
mlinhaarlem.nl

CREDIT CARDS	Accepted
PRICE	Mid-range
TYPE	Hotel
ACCOMMODATION	17 Rooms and Suites
FACILITIES	Bar, 2 Restaurants
GOOD TO KNOW	Local markets
RECOMMENDED FOR	Best-kept secret

Recommended by: Florian Idenburg, SO–IL

HOTEL NEW YORK

Koninginnenhoofd 1
Rotterdam
Noord-Holland 3072
The Netherlands
+31 104390500
hotelnewyork.com

CREDIT CARDS...Accepted
PRICE...Mid-range
TYPE...Hotel
ACCOMMODATION.....................................72 Rooms and Suites
FACILITIES....................Bar, Barbershop, Bookshop,
2 Restaurants
GOOD TO KNOW...Former head office of
Holland America Line
RECOMMENDED FOR...........................Best-kept secret, Urban,
Where I live, Worth the travel

"A former Holland America Line HQ, the hotel features a
range of rooms from one to four stars; the main collective
space hosts a cafe and design shop."—Cino Zucchi

Recommended by: Emre Arolat, EAA; Job Floris,
Monadnock; Liesbeth van der Pol, Dok Architects; Fran
Silvestre, Fran Silvestre Arquitectos; Cino Zucchi, CZA

INNTEL HOTELS ROTTERDAM CENTRE (FORMERLY GOLDEN TULIP ROTTERDAM CENTRE)

Leuvehaven 80
Rotterdam
Noord-Holland 3011
The Netherlands
+31 104134139
inntelhotelsrotterdamcentre.nl

CREDIT CARDS...Accepted
PRICE...Mid-range
TYPE...Hotel
ACCOMMODATION...265 Suites
FACILITIES......................Bar, Gym, Indoor swimming pool,
Restaurant, Sauna, Spa, Steam room
GOOD TO KNOW.......................................Near Erasmus Bridge
RECOMMENDED FOR...Best-kept secret

"The best view of postwar architecture in the Netherlands."
—Cruz Garcia and Nathalie Frankowski

Recommended by: Cruz Garcia and Nathalie Frankowski,
WAI Architecture Think Tank

BUITENLUST

Burgemeester Jonkheer H van Den Boschstraat 13
Amerongen
Utrecht 3958, The Netherlands
+31 343451692
buitenlust-amerongen.nl

CREDIT CARDS..Not accepted
PRICE...Low-cost
TYPE....................................Restaurant with rooms
ACCOMMODATION..13 Rooms
FACILITIES...Restaurant
GOOD TO KNOW..Pet friendly
RECOMMENDED FOR...Budget

Recommended by: Liesbeth van der Pol, Dok Architects

VILLA AUGUSTUS

Oranjelaan 7
Dordrecht
Zuid-Holland 3311, The Netherlands
+31 786393111
villa-augustus.nl

CREDIT CARDS...Accepted
PRICE...Mid-range
TYPE...Hotel
ACCOMMODATION.....................................45 Rooms and Suites
FACILITIES...Restaurant
GOOD TO KNOW.......................................Former water tower
RECOMMENDED FOR...................................Worth the travel

"Views from the lantern room in the former water tower
are spectacular."—Liesbeth van der Pol

Recommended by: Liesbeth van der Pol, Dok Architects

THERMAE 2000

Cauberg 25-27
Valkenburg
Zuid-Holland 6301, The Netherlands
+31 436092000
thermae-2000.co.uk

CREDIT CARDS...Accepted
PRICE...Mid-range
TYPE..Spa resort
ACCOMMODATION..62 Rooms
FACILITIES....................................Bar, Gym, Swimming pools,
2 Restaurants, Sauna, Steam room
GOOD TO KNOW.....................Swimwear and unclothed days
RECOMMENDED FOR...Spa

Recommended by: Sébastien Dachy, MAMOUT architectes

GRAANMARKT 13 THE APARTMENT
Graanmarkt 13
Antwerp 2000, Belgium
+32 33377991
graanmarkt13.com

CREDIT CARDS	Accepted
PRICE	High-end
TYPE	Serviced apartment
ACCOMMODATION	4 Bedrooms
FACILITIES	Restaurant
GOOD TO KNOW	Situated above a shop and restaurant
RECOMMENDED FOR	Family friendly

Recommended by: Marco Costanzi, Marco Costanzi Architects

HOSTEL PULCINELLA
Bogaardplein 1
Antwerp 2000, Belgium
+32 32340314
jeugdherbergen.be

CREDIT CARDS	Accepted but not Amex
PRICE	Low-cost
TYPE	Hostel
ACCOMMODATION	209 Dorms and Rooms
FACILITIES	Bar
GOOD TO KNOW	No pets
RECOMMENDED FOR	Wish I'd designed

"The austere yet intimate style of Vincent van Duysen makes this hotel extremely appealing."—Zsolt Gunther

Recommended by: Zsolt Gunther, 3H Architecture

HOTEL JULIEN
Korte Nieuwstraat 24
Antwerp 2000, Belgium
+32 32290600
hotel-julien.com

CREDIT CARDS	Accepted
PRICE	Mid-range
TYPE	Townhouse hotel
ACCOMMODATION	21 Rooms and Suites
FACILITIES	Bar, Rooftop terrace bar, Sauna, Spa
GOOD TO KNOW	Chauffeured cars
RECOMMENDED FOR	Where I live

Recommended by: Dieter Vander Velpen, Dieter Vander Velpen Architects

HOTEL PILAR
Leopold de Waelplaats 34
Antwerp 2000
Belgium
+32 32926510
hotelpilar.be

CREDIT CARDS	Accepted
PRICE	Mid-range
TYPE	Hotel
ACCOMMODATION	17 Rooms and Suites
FACILITIES	Bar, Restaurant
GOOD TO KNOW	Near Museum of Fine Arts
RECOMMENDED FOR	Urban

Recommended by: Artem Vakhrin, AKZ Architectura

LE DIXSEPTIEME
Rue de la Madeleine 25
Brussels 1000
Belgium
+32 25171717
ledixseptieme.be

CREDIT CARDS	Accepted
PRICE	Mid-range
TYPE	Hotel
ACCOMMODATION	37 Rooms and Suites
FACILITIES	Bar, Gym, Sauna
GOOD TO KNOW	No pets
RECOMMENDED FOR	Urban

"Massive rooms, and at great prices."—Michael Young

Recommended by: Michael Young, Michael Young Studio

THE HOTEL BRUSSELS
Boulevard de Waterloo 38
Brussels 1000
Belgium
+32 25041111
thehotel-brussels.be

CREDIT CARDS	Accepted
PRICE	Mid-range
TYPE	Hotel
ACCOMMODATION	420 Rooms and Suites
FACILITIES	Bar, Gym, Restaurant, Sauna, Spa, Steam room
GOOD TO KNOW	Near European Parliament
RECOMMENDED FOR	Best-kept secret

Recommended by: Jean-Paul Viguier, Jean-Paul Viguier et Associés

HOTEL METROPOLE
Place de Brouckère 31
Brussels 1000
Belgium
+32 22172300
metropolehotel.com

CREDIT CARDS...Accepted
PRICE..Mid-range
TYPE..Hotel
ACCOMMODATION....................284 Rooms and Suites
FACILITIES................................Bar, Gym, Restaurant
GOOD TO KNOW..............................Babysitting, Pet friendly,
Valet parking
RECOMMENDED FOR....................................Urban, Where I live

Hotel Metropole Brussels, dating back to 1894, is a luxury hotel in the city center with a rich history and lavishly appointed rooms. Even better is that pets are welcome.

Recommended by: Sébastien Dachy, MAMOUT architectes; Bernard Dubois, Bernard Dubois Architects; Cruz Garcia and Nathalie Frankowski, WAI Architecture Think Tank

DOMAINE LA BUTTE AUX BOIS
Paalsteenlaan 90
Lanaken
Limburg 3620
Belgium
+32 89739770
labutteauxbois.be

CREDIT CARDS...Accepted
PRICE..High-end
TYPE..Hotel
ACCOMMODATION......................59 Rooms, Suites, and Villas
FACILITIES...............................Bar, Gym, Indoor pool,
2 Restaurants, Sauna, Spa,
Wood-burning fireplace, Yoga
GOOD TO KNOW..No pets
RECOMMENDED FOR..................................Countryside

Domaine La Butte aux Bois is highly regarded for its luxurious spa, elegant rooms, and award-winning dining options. For those looking to indulge in retail therapy, it is a ten-minute drive from Maasmechelen Village, a luxury shopping outlet.

Recommended by: Dominique Perrault, Dominique Perrault Architecture

THERMAE PALACE
Koningin Astridlaan 7
Oostende
West-Vlaanderen 8400
Belgium
+32 59806644
thermaepalace.be

CREDIT CARDS...Accepted
PRICE..Mid-range
TYPE..Palace hotel
ACCOMMODATION.....................................130 Rooms
FACILITIES........................Gym, Restaurant, Sauna
GOOD TO KNOW................................Bicycle rentals
RECOMMENDED FOR..........................All-time favorite, Beach,
Best-kept secret

"A timeless classic."—Sébastien Dachy

Recommended by: Sébastien Dachy, MAMOUT architectes; Antonio Ortiz, Cruz y Ortiz Arquitectos

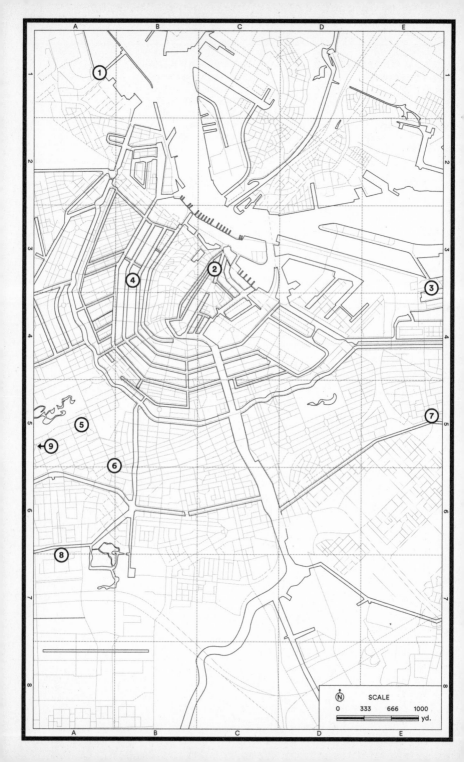

AMSTERDAM

MOXY AMSTERDAM HOUTHAVENS
Danzigerkade 175
Houthavens
Amsterdam 1013 AP
+31 203081780
moxy-hotels.marriott.com

CREDIT CARDS...Accepted
PRICE...Mid-range
TYPE...Hotel
ACCOMMODATION...150 Rooms
FACILITIES...Bar, Gym,
Indoor swimming pool, Sauna
GOOD TO KNOW..........................Bicycle rentals, Pet friendly
RECOMMENDED FOR...Urban

A modern, reasonably priced hotel, Moxy Amsterdam
Houthavens' warm hospitality and quirky interiors
encapsulate the spirit of the city.

Recommended by: Alex Michaelis, Michaelis Boyd

AMBASSADE HOTEL
Herengraat 341
Centrum
Amsterdam 1016
+31 205550222
ambassade-hotel.nl

CREDIT CARDS...Accepted
PRICE..High-end
TYPE...Townhouse hotel
ACCOMMODATION.................................56 Rooms and Suites
FACILITIES...Bar
GOOD TO KNOW............................Babysitting, Bicycle rentals
RECOMMENDED FOR..............................Urban, All-time favorite

"In the best part of the city center, this hotel is created from
a number of townhouses. Each room has its own character
and the service is impeccable."—Tony Fretton

"A home from home."—Antonio Ortiz

Recommended by: Tony Fretton, Tony Fretton Architects;
Antonio Ortiz, Cruz y Ortiz Arquitectos

DYLAN HOTEL
Keizersgracht 384
Centrum
Amsterdam 1016
+31 205302010
dylanamsterdam.com

CREDIT CARDS...Accepted
PRICE..High-end
TYPE..Townhouse hotel
ACCOMMODATION...40 Rooms
FACILITIES...Bar, Gym, 2 Restaurants
GOOD TO KNOW...Valet parking
RECOMMENDED FOR...............................Best-kept secret,
Wish I'd designed

"We love it—it is small, well-located with great service and
food, and a lovely bar."—Mark de Reus

Recommended by: Mark de Reus, de Reus Architects; Maria
Warner Wong, WOW Architects | Warner Wong Design

HANS BRINKER HOSTEL
Kerkstraat 136-138
Centrum
Amsterdam 1017 GR
+31 206220687
hansbrinker.eu

CREDIT CARDS....................................Accepted but not Amex
PRICE...Low-cost
TYPE..Hostel
ACCOMMODATION...................Dorms and Rooms (550 Beds)
FACILITIES..Bar, Restaurant
GOOD TO KNOW.....................................Near the Rijksmuseum
RECOMMENDED FOR...Budget

Recommended by: Leonid Slonimskiy, KOSMOS Architects

WALDORF ASTORIA AMSTERDAM
Herengracht 542-556
Centrum
Amsterdam 1017 CG
+31 207184600
waldorfastoria.hilton.com

CREDIT CARDS...Accepted
PRICE..High-end
TYPE...Hotel
ACCOMMODATION.................................93 Rooms and Suites
FACILITIES......................Bar, Gym, Indoor swimming pool,
3 Restaurants, Sauna, Spa
GOOD TO KNOW...Valet parking
RECOMMENDED FOR...Where I live

"The Waldorf Astoria is a good combination of the historic and modern. It was formerly a bank, and in the Vault Bar they still have the original safety deposit boxes. The entrance features a majestic carved staircase designed by Daniel Marot, architect to King Willem III. The rooms have elegant, high ceilings and period features typical of Amsterdam. The lobby is a perfect place for working, or to have breakfast or lunch meetings."
—Ben van Berkel

Recommended by: Ben van Berkel, UNStudio

ZOKU AMSTERDAM

Weesperstraat 105
Centrum
Amsterdam 1018
+31 208112811
livezoku.com

CREDIT CARDS...Accepted
PRICE...Mid-range
TYPE...Apartment hotel
ACCOMMODATION...133 Lofts
FACILITIES..Bar, Restaurant
GOOD TO KNOW..................Co-working and meeting spaces
RECOMMENDED FOR............................All-time favorite, Urban

A sleek, modern apartment hotel designed for both short and long-term stays. With communal dining and co-working spaces, it is ideal for business travelers.

Recommended by: Matthias Hollwich, Hollwich Kushner

LLOYD HOTEL

Oostelijke Handelskade 34
Eastern Docklands
Amsterdam 1019 BN
+31 205613636
lloydhotel.com

CREDIT CARDS...Accepted
PRICE...Mid-range
TYPE...Hotel
ACCOMMODATION....................................117 Rooms and Suites
FACILITIES..Bar, Restaurant
GOOD TO KNOW..Near Central Station
RECOMMENDED FOR...............................Family friendly, Urban,
Where I live, Wish I'd designed

"It's a unique experience to have breakfast amid hipsters and regular European business folks and rockers from Japan. There are lots of cultural activities as it was created as a home for travelers of all stripes. Wonderfully refreshing."
—Satyendra Pakhalé

Recommended by: Nathalie Frankowski and Cruz Garcia, WAI Architecture Think Tank; Martin Kruger, Martin Kruger Architects; Mark Landini, Landini Associates; Satyendra Pakhalé, Satyendra Pakhalé Associates

LINDEN

Lindengracht 251
Jordaan
Amsterdam 1015 KH
+31 206221460
lindenhotel.nl

CREDIT CARDS...Accepted
PRICE...Mid-range
TYPE...Hotel
ACCOMMODATION..25 Rooms
FACILITIES..Bar, Restaurant
GOOD TO KNOW.......................................Bicycle rentals,
Near the Linden Market
RECOMMENDED FOR..Budget

A stylish boutique hotel located in a nineteenth-century redbrick building just twenty minutes from the center of Amsterdam, Linden is the perfect base for a short city break.

Recommended by: Uwe Schmidt-Hess, Patalab Architecture

CONSCIOUS HOTEL MUSEUM SQUARE

De Lairessestraat 7
Museumkwartier
Amsterdam 1071
+31 208203333
conscioushotels.com

CREDIT CARDS...Accepted
PRICE...Mid-range
TYPE...Hotel
ACCOMMODATION..36 Rooms
FACILITIES..Bar, Restaurant
GOOD TO KNOW...Bicycle rentals
RECOMMENDED FOR................................Eco-conscious

A hip, contemporary, and eco-conscious hotel within walking distance of many of Amsterdam's major cultural highlights. There are also express check-ins and check-outs, and a courtyard garden.

Recommended by: Joana Leandro Vasconcelos, Atelier In.vitro

CONSERVATORIUM HOTEL

Van Baerlestraat 27
Oud Zuid
Amsterdam 1071 AN
+31 205700000
conservatoriumhotel.com

CREDIT CARDS	Accepted
PRICE	High-end
TYPE	Hotel
ACCOMMODATION	128 Rooms and Suites
FACILITIES	Bar, Gym, Indoor swimming pool, 2 Restaurants, Sauna, Spa, Steam room
GOOD TO KNOW	Child friendly
RECOMMENDED FOR	All-time favorite, Urban

"A great mix of modern and historic elements in a city I love."—Ron Radziner

Recommended by: Piero Lissoni, Lissoni Associati; Ron Radziner, Marmol Radziner

HOTEL ARENA

's-Gravesandestraat 55
Oost
Amsterdam 1092 AA
+31 208502400
hotelarena.nl

CREDIT CARDS	Accepted
PRICE	High-end
TYPE	Hotel
ACCOMMODATION	139 Rooms and Suites
FACILITIES	Bar, Restaurant
GOOD TO KNOW	Bicycle rentals
RECOMMENDED FOR	Where I live

"Hotel Arena faces the lively and green Oosterpark. Originally built as an orphanage, the hotel's disco is located in the site's former chapel. My visits to Hotel Arena are often spontaneous and for a night or two. Kind of like a second home; it's a nice place to eat, work, sleep, and dance."—Liesbeth van der Pol

Recommended by: Liesbeth van der Pol, Dok Architects

CITIZENM AMSTERDAM

Prinses Irenestraat 30
Zuid
Amsterdam 1077
+31 208117090
citizenm.com

CREDIT CARDS	Accepted
PRICE	Mid-range
TYPE	Hotel
ACCOMMODATION	215 Rooms
FACILITIES	Bar, Restaurant
GOOD TO KNOW	Bicycle rentals
RECOMMENDED FOR	Urban

Situated fifteen minutes from the city center, CitizenM Amsterdam is a fun, young hotel with a focus on low-cost luxury. There's a big emphasis on a "home from home" feel with a comfortable living room instead of a lobby. The key elements of a good hotel stay—and a good night's sleep—are all here: express check-ins and check-outs, a 24-hour bar, homely communal areas, and XL king size beds.

Recommended by: Bernardo Fort-Brescia, Arquitectonica

WESTCORD FASHION HOTEL AMSTERDAM

Hendrikje Stoffelsstraat 1
Nieuw-West
Amsterdam 1058 GC
+31 208100800
westcordhotels.com

CREDIT CARDS	Accepted
PRICE	Low-cost
TYPE	Hotel
ACCOMMODATION	260 Rooms and Suites
FACILITIES	Bar, Gym, Indoor swimming pool, Restaurant, Sauna, Steam room
GOOD TO KNOW	Near Schipol Airport
RECOMMENDED FOR	Budget

"Funky, wacky, budget hotel on the way to Schipol airport."
—Martin Kruger

Recommended by: Martin Kruger, Martin Kruger Architects

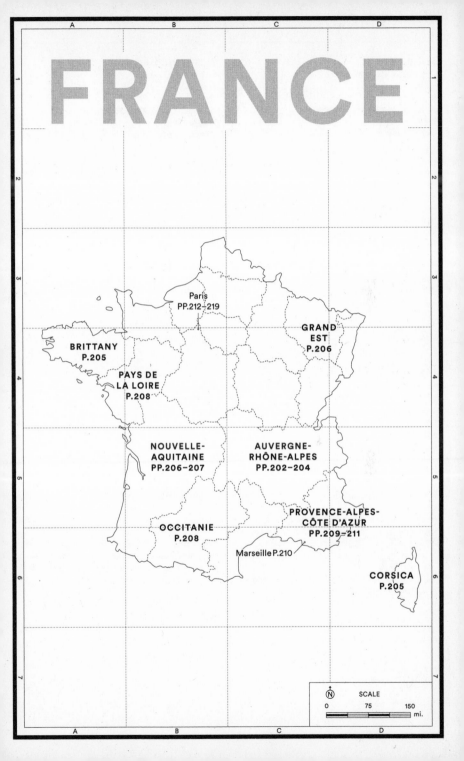

MAISON PIC
285 avenue Victor Hugo
Valence
Drôme
Auvergne-Rhône-Alpes 26000
France
+33 475441532
anne-sophie-pic.com

CREDIT CARDS	Accepted
PRICE	High-end
TYPE	Hotel
ACCOMMODATION	15 Rooms
FACILITIES	Bar, 2 Restaurants
GOOD TO KNOW	Babysitting, No pets
RECOMMENDED FOR	Family friendly

"A great place for sharing moments at the heart of a family history. This is the source from which all [chef] Anne-Sophie Pic's gastronomic projects originate."—Claire Bétaille and Bruno Moinard

Recommended by: Claire Bétaille and Bruno Moinard, 4BI & Associés

HOTEL TERMINAL NEIGE TOTEM
Flaine
Haute-Savoie
Auvergne-Rhône-Alpes 74300
France
+33 430050340
totem.terminal-neige.com

CREDIT CARDS	Accepted
PRICE	Mid-range
TYPE	Hotel
ACCOMMODATION	96 Rooms and Suites
FACILITIES	Bar, Gym, Restaurant, Sauna, Spa
GOOD TO KNOW	Child friendly
RECOMMENDED FOR	All-time favorite, Mountains, Wish I'd designed

"For any architect, the idea of staying at a resort designed by Modern master, Marcel Breuer, is a real pleasure." —Paul Morgan

Recommended by: Paolo Brambilla, Calvi Brambilla; Paul Morgan, Paul Morgan Architects

FLOCONS DE SEL
1775 route du Leutaz
Megève
Haute-Savoie
Auvergne-Rhône-Alpes 74120
France
+33 450214999
floconsdesel.com

CREDIT CARDS	Accepted
PRICE	Mid-range
TYPE	Hotel
ACCOMMODATION	10 Apartments, Rooms, and Suites
FACILITIES	Bar, Indoor swimming pool, 2 Restaurants, Sauna, Spa, Wood-burning fireplace
GOOD TO KNOW	Pet friendly
RECOMMENDED FOR	Mountains

Recommended by: Laurent Gravier, FRES Architectes

LA MAISON TROISGROS
728 route de Villerest
Ouches
Loire
Auvergne-Rhône-Alpes 42155
France
+33 477716697
troisgros.com

CREDIT CARDS	Accepted
PRICE	Mid-range
TYPE	Restaurant with rooms
ACCOMMODATION	15 Rooms
FACILITIES	Outdoor swimming pool, Restaurant
GOOD TO KNOW	Free parking, No pets
RECOMMENDED FOR	All-time favorite, Countryside

"Just like its [three-Michelin-starred] restaurant next door, also called Troisgros, it's the family's attention to detail, service, and taste that create unforgettable experiences." —Nathalie Frankowski and Cruz Garcia

Recommended by: Nathalie Frankowski and Cruz Garcia, WAI Architecture Think Tank

MAMA SHELTER LYON

13 rue Domer
Lyon
Auvergne-Rhône-Alpes 69007
France
+33 478025800
mamashelter.com

CREDIT CARDS...Accepted
PRICE...Low-cost
TYPE...Hotel
ACCOMMODATION.....................156 Rooms and Suites
FACILITIES..Bar, Restaurant
GOOD TO KNOW....................Child and pet friendly
RECOMMENDED FOR............................Best-kept secret

Rooms at the Lyon outpost of the ultra-hip Mama Shelter
Hotel Group are both stylish and low-cost, and each is
equipped with a twenty-seven-inch (sixty-eight-centimeter)
iMac with TV and free films. The hotel is also family
friendly and has a range of activities—board games, video
games, and pinball—to keep younger guests entertained.

Recommended by: Dorin Stefan, Dorin Stefan Birou
de Arhitectura

CHÂTEAU DE BAGNOLS

Le Bourg
Bagnols
Rhône
Auvergne-Rhône-Alpes 69920
France
+33 474714000
chateaudebagnols.com

CREDIT CARDS...Accepted
PRICE..Mid-range
TYPE...Château hotel
ACCOMMODATION...27 Suites
FACILITIES..Bar, Gym,
Indoor and outdoor swimming pools,
Restaurant, Spa
GOOD TO KNOW....................Child friendly, Free parking
RECOMMENDED FOR...................................Worth the travel

An elegant, five-star château located in the heart of
Beaujolais. Suites are divided into three themes, in three
areas: the opulent and historic Suites Château, the
contemporary Suites Chai in the former cellar building,
and the spacious Suites Jardin.

Recommended by: Rudy Ricciotti

COUVENT DE LA TOURETTE

Route de la Tourette
Éveux
Rhône
Auvergne-Rhône-Alpes 69210, France
+33 472191090
couventdelatourette.fr

CREDIT CARDS...Not accepted
PRICE...Low-cost
TYPE...Convent (annexe)
ACCOMMODATION...9 Cells
FACILITIES..Canteen
GOOD TO KNOW............Reservations two weeks in advance
RECOMMENDED FOR.........................All-time favorite, Budget,
Countryside, Mountains,
Wish I'd designed

"To stay in a Dominican convent designed by Le Corbusier
at a bargain price. Need I say more?"—Gert Wingårdh

This priory was designed by Le Corbusier, and opened in
1961. For those wishing to immerse themselves, there are
single rooms designed by Renzo Piano to stay in.

Recommended by: Aljoša Dekleva and Tina Gregorič,
Dekleva Gregorič Architects; Bernard Dubois, Bernard
Dubois Architects; Marianne Kwok, Kohn Pedersen Fox;
Hu Li, Open Architecture; Michael Meredith and Hilary
Sample, MOS; Dennis Pieprz, Sasaki; Daniel Sundlin, Bjarke
Ingels Group; Gert Wingårdh, Wingårdhs

L'APOGÉE COURCHEVEL

5 rue Emile Allais
Courchevel
Savoie
Auvergne-Rhône-Alpes 73120, France
+33 479040104
oetkercollection.com

CREDIT CARDS...Accepted
PRICE...Blow-out
TYPE...Hotel
ACCOMMODATION.....................53 Chalets and Rooms
FACILITIES...................Bar, Gym, 2 Restaurants, Sauna, Spa
GOOD TO KNOW............................Child friendly, Free parking
RECOMMENDED FOR.......................................Mountains

"The combination of two top designers, architect Joseph
Dirand and interior designer India Madhavi, creates a
sublime, rich interior with sharp details and a refined but
colorful material palette."—Dieter Vander Velpen

Recommended by: Dieter Vander Velpen, Dieter Vander
Velpen Architects

HOTEL LE CHABICHOU
Route des Chenus
Courchevel
Savoie
Auvergne-Rhône-Alpes 73120
France
+33 479080055
chabichou-courchevel.com

CREDIT CARDS	Accepted
PRICE	High-end
TYPE	Hotel
ACCOMMODATION	42 Rooms and Suites
FACILITIES	Bar, Indoor swimming pool, 2 Restaurants, Sauna, Spa
GOOD TO KNOW	Child and pet friendly
RECOMMENDED FOR	Mountains

"The founding hotel of the Courchevel resort; the Rochedy family have become friends. The two-starred Michelin restaurant is excellent."—Jean-Paul Viguier

<u>Recommended by</u>: Jean-Paul Viguier, Jean-Paul Viguier et Associés

SIX SENSES RESIDENCES COURCHEVEL
Rue des Tovets
Courchevel
Savoie
Auvergne-Rhône-Alpes 73120
France
+33 649474058
sixsenses.com

CREDIT CARDS	Accepted
PRICE	High-end
TYPE	Serviced apartments
ACCOMMODATION	24 Apartments
FACILITIES	Bar, Indoor swimming pool, Restaurant, Sauna, Spa, Steam room
GOOD TO KNOW	Babysitting, Pet friendly, Self-catering
RECOMMENDED FOR	Family friendly

<u>Recommended by</u>: Bernardo and Paulo Jacobsen, Jacobsen Arquitetura

ALPINA LODGE
Rue Principale
Val d'Isère
Savoie
Auvergne-Rhône-Alpes 73150
France
+33 479416000
alpina-lodge.com

CREDIT CARDS	Accepted
PRICE	Mid-range
TYPE	Serviced apartments
ACCOMMODATION	44 Apartments
FACILITIES	Kitchens, Ski lockers
GOOD TO KNOW	Child and pet friendly
RECOMMENDED FOR	Family friendly

"Very nice, comfortable rooms and superb service. The surroundings are cozy and they make the whole family feel welcome."—Kim Herforth Nielsen

<u>Recommended by</u>: Kim Herforth Nielsen, 3XN

HÔTEL LE BLIZZARD
Avenue Olympique
Val-d'Isère
Savoie
Auvergne-Rhône-Alpes 73150
France
+33 479060207
hotelblizzard.com

CREDIT CARDS	Accepted
PRICE	High-end
TYPE	Chalet
ACCOMMODATION	70 Rooms and Suites
FACILITIES	Gym, Outdoor swimming pool, 2 Restaurants, Sauna, Spa, Yoga
GOOD TO KNOW	Babysitting, Free parking
RECOMMENDED FOR	Mountains

"A hotel with a homely feeling in a great location. The spa with an outdoor hot tub right at the foot of the ski slope is amazing."—Kim Herforth Nielsen

<u>Recommended by</u>: Kim Herforth Nielsen, 3XN

LES MAISONS DE BRICOURT, LA FERME DU VENT

Ferme du Vent, Langavant
Ille-et-Vilaine
Brittany 35350
France
+33 299896476
maisons-de-bricourt.com

CREDIT CARDS	Accepted
PRICE	Mid-range
TYPE	Gîte
ACCOMMODATION	6 Kled
FACILITIES	Indoor and outdoor swimming pools, Patisserie, Restaurant, Sauna, Spa, Steam room
GOOD TO KNOW	No Television or Wifi
RECOMMENDED FOR	Spa

Part of Les Maisons de Bricourt, a beautiful boutique collection of restored properties, La Ferme du Vent enjoys breathtaking views of Mont-Saint-Michel Bay, as well as facilities including the Maison de Bricourt spa, swimming pool, and on-site patisserie.

Recommended by: Hugo Sauzay, Festen Architecture

LES MAISONS DE BRICOURT, LES RIMAINS

62 rue des Rimains
Ille-et-Vilaine
Brittany 35260
France
+33 299896476
maisons-de-bricourt.com

CREDIT CARDS	Accepted
PRICE	Mid-range
TYPE	Cottage
ACCOMMODATION	4 Rooms
FACILITIES	Indoor and outdoor swimming pools, Restaurant, Sauna, Spa, Steam room
GOOD TO KNOW	No wifi
RECOMMENDED FOR	Beach

Les Maisons de Bricourt is a family run collection of beautiful residences on the Brittany coastline. It is a space for switching off from the outside world and reconnecting with "the true art of living".

Recommended by: Joaquín Pérez-Goicoechea, AGi Architects

BOUTIQUE-HÔTEL ARTEMISIA

Boccialacce
Corse-du-Sud
Corsica 20119
France
+33 495281913
hotel-artemisia.com

CREDIT CARDS	Accepted but not Amex
PRICE	Mid-range
TYPE	Hotel
ACCOMMODATION	8 Rooms and Suites
FACILITIES	Bar, Gym, Outdoor swimming pool, Restaurant, Sauna
GOOD TO KNOW	Restaurant open seasonally
RECOMMENDED FOR	Best-kept secret

Boutique-Hôtel Artemisia blends old and new architecture and interior design. Located in the historic commune of Bastelica, near Lac de Tolla, it's an ideal base for exploring—from beaches and mountain trails during the summer to skiing at Val d'Ese during the winter months.

Recommended by: Much Untertrifaller, Dietrich Untertrifaller Architects

HOTEL CASE LATINE

Route du Haut Village
Haute-Corse
Corsica 20218
France
+33 622371416
caselatine.com

CREDIT CARDS	Accepted but not Amex
PRICE	Mid-range
TYPE	Hotel
ACCOMMODATION	8 Rooms and Suites
FACILITIES	Bar, Outdoor swimming pool, Restaurant
GOOD TO KNOW	Medieval village
RECOMMENDED FOR	Countryside

"Small family run hotel nestling on a wild Corsican hillside, with some nice beaches close by. Each room is situated in its own stone building, some with small pools. A fantastic breakfast is served on the terrace with fabulous views stretching out over the landscape."— Matthias Sauerbruch and Louisa Hutton

Recommended by: Matthias Sauerbruch and Louisa Hutton, Sauerbruch Hutton

MGALLERY HÔTEL COUR DU CORBEAU

6–8 rue des Couples
Strasbourg
Bas-Rhin
Grand Est 67000
France
+33 390002626
cour-corbeau.com

CREDIT CARDS	Accepted
PRICE	Mid-range
TYPE	Hotel
ACCOMMODATION	63 Rooms and Suites
FACILITIES	Bar, Spa
GOOD TO KNOW	Near Cathédrale Notre Dame de Strasbourg
RECOMMENDED FOR	Family friendly

A charming sixteenth-century hotel—and a fine example of
Renaissance architecture—MGallery Hôtel Cour du Corbeau
provides guests with a beautiful boutique stay in the heart
of historical Strasbourg. Interiors are modern yet not at odds
with the building's exterior, and no two rooms are the same.

Recommended by: Nicolas Koff, Office Ou

HOTEL LES BAS RUPTS

181 route de la Bresse
Vosges
Grand Est 88402
France
+33 329630925
bas-rupts.com

CREDIT CARDS	Accepted but not Amex
PRICE	Mid-range
TYPE	Hotel
ACCOMMODATION	24 Rooms and Suites
FACILITIES	Bar, Indoor and outdoor swimming pools, Restaurant, Sauna
GOOD TO KNOW	Bicycle rentals, Child and pet friendly
RECOMMENDED FOR	Mountains

"The journey here is a wonderful drive through the Alps."
—Michael Young

Recommended by: Michael Young, Michael Young Studio

PARIS: SEE PAGES 212–219

DOMAINE DES ETANGS

Domaine des Etangs
Charente
Nouvelle-Aquitaine 16310
France
+33 545618500
domainedesetangs.com

CREDIT CARDS	Accepted
PRICE	High-end
TYPE	Château hotel
ACCOMMODATION	17 Cottages, Rooms, and Suites
FACILITIES	Bar, Gym, Indoor and outdoor swimming pools, Restaurant, Sauna, Spa, Steam room
GOOD TO KNOW	Child friendly
RECOMMENDED FOR	Wish I'd designed

"Staying here is a fairy tale."—Stéphane Parmentier

Recommended by: Stéphane Parmentier

CHÂTEAU DE GAUBERT

Lieu dit Gaubert
Dordogne
Nouvelle-Aquitaine 24120
France
+33 613253800
chateau-de-gaubert.com

CREDIT CARDS	Accepted
PRICE	Mid-range
TYPE	Bed and Breakfast (Chambres d'hôtes)
ACCOMMODATION	3 Rooms
FACILITIES	Gardens, Terrace
GOOD TO KNOW	Free parking, Near Lascaux Cave, No children or pets
RECOMMENDED FOR	Countryside

"In the French countryside near Terrasson-Lavilledieu,
the Périgord region of France, the historic sixteenth-century
Château de Gaubert is a gem overlooking two valleys and
is a firm countryside favorite hotel of mine for the beauty
of its setting and rooms, and its classic architecture."
—Ian Ritchie

Recommended by: Ian Ritchie, Ian Ritchie Architects

LE MOULIN DE L'ABBAYE

1 route de Bourdeilles
Brantôme
Dordogne
Nouvelle-Aquitaine 24310
France
+33 553058022
moulinabbaye.com

CREDIT CARDS..Accepted
PRICE..Mid-range
TYPE..Hotel
ACCOMMODATION.......................................20 Suites and Rooms
FACILITIES....................Bar, Outdoor restaurant, Restaurant
GOOD TO KNOW......................................Child and pet friendly
RECOMMENDED FOR..Countryside

"Intimate, individual, spacious accommodation overlooking the river and millpond in a small, remote French village, with an exquisite restaurant."—Louis Hedgecock

Recommended by: Louis Hedgecock, HOK Architects

LA MAISON DU BASSIN

5 rue des Pionniers
Lège Cap-Ferret
Gironde
Nouvelle-Aquitaine 33970
France
+33 556606063
lamaisondubassin.com

CREDIT CARDS..Accepted
PRICE..Mid-range
TYPE..Restaurant with rooms
ACCOMMODATION...11 Rooms
FACILITIES...Bar, Outdoor restaurant,
Restaurant
GOOD TO KNOW......................................Near the seaside
RECOMMENDED FOR..Family friendly

A charming former home surrounded by woodland and ten minutes from the ocean, La Maison du Bassin is a boutique hotel that retains many of its original, classic features.

Recommended by: Hugo Sauzay, Festen Architecture

LE SAINT JAMES

3 place Camille Hostein
Bouliac
Gironde
Nouvelle-Aquitaine 33270
France
+33 557970600
saintjames-bouliac.com

CREDIT CARDS..Accepted
PRICE..Mid-range
TYPE..Hotel
ACCOMMODATION.......................................18 Rooms and Suites
FACILITIES................................Bar, Outdoor swimming pool,
Restaurant, Sauna
GOOD TO KNOW......................................Free parking
RECOMMENDED FOR...............All-time favorite, Countryside,
Wish I'd designed

"Very relaxing, with wild strawberries for breakfast."
—Will Alsop

Recommended by: Will Alsop, aLL Design; Diego Arraigada, Diego Arraigada Arquitectos; Stephen Barrett, Rogers Stirk Harbour + Partners; Makio Hasuike, Makio Hasuike & Co; Giancarlo Mazzanti, El Equipo Mazzanti

LES SOURCES DE CAUDALIE

Chemin de Smith Haut Lafitte
Martillac
Gironde
Nouvelle-Aquitaine 33650
France
+33 557838383
sources-caudalie.com

CREDIT CARDS..Accepted
PRICE..High-end
TYPE..Spa hotel
ACCOMMODATION.......................................74 Rooms and Suites
FACILITIES..Bar, Gym,
Indoor and outdoor swimming pools,
2 Restaurants, Spa, Wine bar, Yoga
GOOD TO KNOW..........................Babysitting, Bicycle rentals
RECOMMENDED FOR..Spa

"Lovely French countryside in which you can walk between spa experiences; try to stay in the little cabin on the lake."
—Lauren Rottet

Recommended by: Lauren Rottet, Rottet Studio

LA FORGE DE MONTOLIEU

676 chemin La Forge
Aude
Occitanie 11170
France
+33 468766053
forgedemontolieu.com

CREDIT CARDS	Accepted
PRICE	Low-cost
TYPE	Bed and Breakfast
ACCOMMODATION	8 Caravan, Gîtes, Rooms, and Treetent
FACILITIES	Restaurant
GOOD TO KNOW	Camping available, Child friendly
RECOMMENDED FOR	Best-kept secret, Family friendly

"Enormous and extremely beautiful grounds including a river, lake, and forest. Hosts are friendly and knowledgable." —Yu-lin Chen

Recommended by: Yu-lin Chen, MAYU Architects+

BAUDON DE MAUNY

1 rue de la Carbonnerie
Montpellier
Hérault
Occitanie 34000
France
+33 467022177
baudondemauny.com

CREDIT CARDS	Accepted
PRICE	Mid-range
TYPE	Townhouse hotel
ACCOMMODATION	10 Rooms and Suites
FACILITIES	Babysitting
GOOD TO KNOW	Transfers available
RECOMMENDED FOR	Urban

"Hidden in the narrow streets of Montpellier's historic center, this hotel is in an eighteenth-century townhouse. There's plenty of space and a relaxing mix of contemporary design. It's intimate, but feels grand."—Jürgen Mayer H.

Recommended by: Jürgen Mayer H., J. Mayer H. und Partner, Architekten

CHATEAU DE MERCUÈS

Route du Château
Lot
Occitanie 46090
France
+33 565200001
chateaudemercues.com

CREDIT CARDS	Accepted
PRICE	Mid-range
TYPE	Château hotel
ACCOMMODATION	30 Rooms
FACILITIES	Bar, Outdoor swimming pool, 2 Restaurants, Spa
GOOD TO KNOW	Babysitting, Free parking, Pet friendly
RECOMMENDED FOR	Countryside

"Quiet medieval castle with excellent food and wine." —Thomas Leeser

Recommended by: Thomas Leeser, Leeser Architecture

FONTEVRAUD L'HÔTEL

38 rue Saint-Jean de l'Habit
Maine-et-Loire
Pays de la Loire 49590
France
+33 246461010
hotel-fontevraud.com

CREDIT CARDS	Accepted
PRICE	Low-cost
TYPE	Hotel
ACCOMMODATION	54 Rooms
FACILITIES	Bar, Restaurant
GOOD TO KNOW	No pets,
RECOMMENDED FOR	Countryside

"The hotel is located inside the Abbaye Royale; it is a spiritual experience exploring the cloisters at night. Designed by Jouin-Manku, the hotel is monastic yet contemporary, combining natural materials and a sensitive color palette with well-designed furniture."—Yu-lin Chen

Recommended by: Yu-lin Chen, MAYU Architects+

LA BASTIDE DE MOUSTIERS

Chemin de Quinson
Moustiers-Sainte-Marie
Alpes-de-Haute-Provence
Provence-Alpes-Côte d'Azur 04360
France
+33 492704747
bastide-moustiers.com

CREDIT CARDS	Accepted
PRICE	Mid-range
TYPE	Bastide
ACCOMMODATION	13 Rooms and Suites
FACILITIES	Bar, Outdoor restaurant and swimming pool
GOOD TO KNOW	Electric boat rides
RECOMMENDED FOR	Countryside

"Run by Alain Ducasse, a near relation; we won't betray a secret saying this place is his and our favorite."
—Claire Bétaille and Bruno Moinard

Recommended by: Claire Bétaille and Bruno Moinard, 4BI & Associés

HÔTEL DU CAP-EDEN-ROC

Boulevard J. F. Kennedy
Antibes
Alpes-Maritimes
Provence-Alpes-Côte d'Azur 06605
France
+33 493613901
oetkercollection.com

CREDIT CARDS	Accepted
PRICE	Blow-out
TYPE	Hotel
ACCOMMODATION	118 Rooms and Villas
FACILITIES	Bar, Gym, Outdoor swimming pool, 2 Restaurants, Spa, Yoga
GOOD TO KNOW	Private villas also for rent
RECOMMENDED FOR	Spa, Luxury

"Modernity perched on a cliff."—Bernardo Fort-Brescia

"French luxury. An iconic destination!"—Matteo Thun

Recommended by: Luis Ferreira-da-Silva, Luis Ferreira-da-Silva Architects; Bernardo Fort-Brescia, Arquitectonica; Matteo Thun, Matteo Thun & Partners; Alexander Wong, Alexander Wong Architects

LA COLOMBE D'OR

Place du Général de Gaulle
Saint-Paul-de-Vence
Alpes-Maritimes
Provence-Alpes-Côte d'Azur 06570
France
+33 493328002
la-colombe-dor.com

CREDIT CARDS	Accepted
PRICE	High-end
TYPE	Hotel
ACCOMMODATION	24 Rooms and Suites
FACILITIES	Bar, Outdoor restaurant and swimming pool
GOOD TO KNOW	Famous art collection
RECOMMENDED FOR	All-time favorite, Countryside, Family friendly, Luxury

"A beautiful family run hotel, La Colombe d'Or is home to amazing artworks collected since the 1920s. Breakfast under the fig tree facing the Fernand Léger ceramic mural; lunch in the restaurant under Picasso's painted vase. The hotel is a five-minute walk from Fondation Maeght, a wonderful private museum."—Rabih Hage

Recommended by: Sam Chermayeff, Meyer-Grohbrügge & Chermayeff; Rabih Hage; Johanna Meyer-Grohbrügge, Meyer-Grohbrügge; ; Charlotte von Moos, Sauter von Moos; Hugo Sauzay, Festen Architecture; Daniel Suduca and Thierry Mérillou, Suduca & Mérillou

HÔTEL NORD PINUS

14 place du Forum
Arles
Bouches-du-Rhône
Provence-Alpes-Côte d'Azur 13200
France
+33 490934444
nord-pinus.com

CREDIT CARDS	Accepted
PRICE	Mid-range
TYPE	Hotel
ACCOMMODATION	1 Apartment and 25 Rooms
FACILITIES	Bar, Restaurant
GOOD TO KNOW	Pet friendly
RECOMMENDED FOR	Best-kept secret, Urban

"This comfortable hotel houses a wonderful cocktail bar off the Place du Forum."—Grace Keeley

Recommended by: Grace Keeley, GKMP Architects; Hugo Sauzay, Festen Architecture

L'HÔTEL PARTICULIER
4 rue de la Monnaie
Arles
Bouches-du-Rhône
Provence-Alpes-Côte d'Azur 13200
France
+33 490525140
hotel-particulier.com

CREDIT CARDS	Accepted
PRICE	Mid-range
TYPE	Hotel
ACCOMMODATION	10 Rooms and Suites
FACILITIES	Bar, Gym, Outdoor swimming pool, Restaurant, Sauna, Spa, Steam room
GOOD TO KNOW	Free parking, Pet friendly
RECOMMENDED FOR	Countryside

Recommended by: Rudy Ricciotti

VILLA LA COSTE
2750 route de la Cride
Le Puy-Sainte-Réparade
Bouches-du-Rhône
Provence-Alpes-Côte d'Azur 13610
France
+33 442505000
villalacoste.com

CREDIT CARDS	Accepted
PRICE	High-end
TYPE	Hotel
ACCOMMODATION	28 Villas
FACILITIES	Outdoor swimming pool, Restaurant, Sauna, Spa, Yoga
GOOD TO KNOW	Art park, On-site vineyard
RECOMMENDED FOR	Worth the travel

Recommended by: André Fu, AFSO

LES LODGES SAINTE VICTOIRE
2250 route Cézanne
Le Tholonet
Bouches-du-Rhône
Provence-Alpes-Côte d'Azur 13100
France
+33 442248040
leslodgessaintevictoire.com

CREDIT CARDS	Accepted
PRICE	Mid-range
TYPE	Spa hotel
ACCOMMODATION	39 Rooms, Villas, and Suites
FACILITIES	Bar, Gym, Outdoor swimming pool, 2 Restaurants, Sauna, Spa
GOOD TO KNOW	Cézanne painted here
RECOMMENDED FOR	Countryside

"A gorgeous setting for this old bastide, refurbished with absolute taste and comfort."—Jean-Paul Viguier

Recommended by: Jean-Paul Viguier, Jean-Paul Viguier et Associé

HÔTEL LE CORBUSIER
280 boulevard Michelet
Sainte-Anne
Marseille
Bouches-du-Rhône
Provence-Alpes-Côte d'Azur 13008
France
+33 428313922
hotellecorbusier.com

CREDIT CARDS	Accepted
PRICE	Low-cost
TYPE	Hotel
ACCOMMODATION	22 Rooms and Suites
FACILITIES	Outdoor swimming pool, Restaurant, Rooftop terrace
GOOD TO KNOW	Child friendly, Free parking
RECOMMENDED FOR	Urban, Wish I'd designed

"For a 1950s-style experience in the amazing Cité Radieuse by Le Corbusier."—Daniel Suduca and Thierry Mérillou

Recommended by: Leonid Slonimskiy, KOSMOS Architects; Daniel Suduca and Thierry Mérillou, Suduca & Mérillou

LES ROCHES ROUGES

90 boulevard de la 36ème Division du Texas
Saint-Raphaël
Var
Provence-Alpes-Côte d'Azur 83530
France
+33 489814060
hotellesrochesrouges.com

CREDIT CARDS	Accepted
PRICE	High-end
TYPE	Hotel
ACCOMMODATION	45 Rooms and Suites
FACILITIES	Bar, Outdoor swimming pool, 2 Restaurants, Spa, Yoga
GOOD TO KNOW	Pet friendly, Valet parking
RECOMMENDED FOR	Beach, Wish I'd designed

"Many of the bedrooms have a view of the sea, and there is also a seawater pool. This Modernist building style is rare on the Côte d'Azur."—Karl Fournier and Olivier Marty

Recommended by: Bernard Dubois, Bernard Dubois Architects; Karl Fournier and Olivier Marty, Studio KO; Hugo Sauzay, Festen Architecture

HÔTEL CRILLON LE BRAVE

Place de l'Eglise
Crillon-le-Brave
Vaucluse
Provence-Alpes-Côte d'Azur 84410
France
+33 490656161
crillonlebrave.com

CREDIT CARDS	Accepted
PRICE	High-end
TYPE	Hotel
ACCOMMODATION	32 Rooms and Suites
FACILITIES	Bar, Outdoor restaurant and swimming pool, Spa
GOOD TO KNOW	Babysitting, Bicycle rentals
RECOMMENDED FOR	Countryside

"A chilled place to stop after a long drive."—Michael Young

Recommended by: Michael Young, Michael Young Studio

DOMAINE DE FONTENILLE

Route de Roquefraiche
Lauris
Vaucluse
Provence-Alpes-Côte d'Azur 84360
France
+33 413980000
domainedefontenille.com

CREDIT CARDS	Accepted
PRICE	Mid-range
TYPE	Hotel
ACCOMMODATION	Apartment, 19 Suites and Villas
FACILITIES	Bar, Gym, Outdoor swimming pool, Restaurant, Sauna, Spa, Steam room
GOOD TO KNOW	Free parking, On-site vineyard, Pet friendly
RECOMMENDED FOR	Luxury, Worth the travel

"This hotel combines relaxation and sophistication in one perfect environment. Rooms and facilities are designed with natural materials and are full of character. Very good restaurants and friendly service."—Yu-lin Chen

Recommended by: Yu-lin Chen, MAYU Architects+

DOMAINE DES ANDEOLS

Les Andéols
Saint-Saturnin-lès-Apt
Vaucluse
Provence-Alpes-Côte d'Azur 84490
France
+33 490755063
andeols.com

CREDIT CARDS	Accepted
PRICE	High-end
TYPE	Hotel
ACCOMMODATION	11 Guesthouses and Suites
FACILITIES	Bar, Outdoor swimming pool, 2 Restaurants
GOOD TO KNOW	No pets
RECOMMENDED FOR	Countryside

Recommended by: Patrick Reymond, Atelier Oï

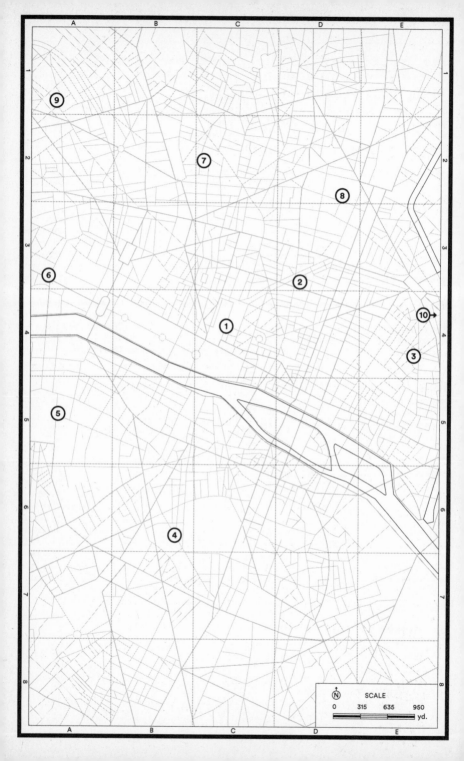

PARIS

HÔTEL COSTES

239-241 rue Saint-Honoré
1er arrondissement
Paris 75001
+33 142445000
hotelcostes.com

CREDIT CARDS..Accepted
PRICE...High-end
TYPE..Hotel
ACCOMMODATION..........................84 Rooms and Suites
FACILITIES................................Bar, Gym, Restaurant,
Spa, Steam room
GOOD TO KNOW..................Babysitting, Pet friendly,
Valet parking
RECOMMENDED FOR......................Urban, Where I live

"Great location, friendly staff, and a wonderful restaurant."
—Fernando Romero

Recommended by: Stéphane Parmentier; Fernando Romero,
FR–EE/Fernando Romero Enterprise

HÔTEL RITZ PARIS

15 place Vendôme
1er arrondissement
Paris 75001
+33 143163030
ritzparis.com

CREDIT CARDS..Accepted
PRICE...Blow-out
TYPE..Hotel
ACCOMMODATION........................142 Rooms and Suites
FACILITIES..3 Bars, Gym,
Indoor swimming pool,
2 Restaurants, Sauna, Spa
GOOD TO KNOW.............................Child and pet friendly
RECOMMENDED FOR......................Urban, Where I live

"The ultimate institution."—Karl Fournier and Olivier Marty

"Visit for the location, the bar, the service, the history,
and its outrageousness."—Simon Jacobsen

Recommended by: Karl Fournier and Olivier Marty,
Studio KO; Simon Jacobsen, Jacobsen Architecture, LLC

LE MEURICE

228 rue de Rivoli
1er arrondissement
Paris 75001
+33 144581010
dorchestercollection.com

CREDIT CARDS..Accepted
PRICE...Blow-out
TYPE..Hotel
ACCOMMODATION........................160 Rooms and Suites
FACILITIES............................Bar, Gym, 2 Restaurants,
Sauna, Spa, Steam room
GOOD TO KNOW..........................Child and pet friendly
RECOMMENDED FOR...........Luxury, Urban, Wish I'd designed

"Sophisticated luxury in a proud building."—Craig Dykers

"A stunning historic landmark brought up to date with an
artful eye. Period opulence meets imaginative modernity.
It is magnificent."—Todd-Avery Lenahan

Recommended by: Craig Dykers, Snøhetta; Todd-Avery
Lenahan, TAL Studio; Daniel Libeskind, Studio Libeskind

MANDARIN ORIENTAL, PARIS

251 rue Saint-Honoré
1er arrondissement
Paris 75001
+33 170987888
mandarinoriental.com

CREDIT CARDS..Accepted
PRICE...High-end
TYPE..Hotel
ACCOMMODATION........................138 Rooms and Suites
FACILITIES......................Bar, Gym, Indoor swimming pool,
3 Restaurants, Rooftop terrace bar,
Sauna, Spa
GOOD TO KNOW.........................Babysitting, Small pets only
RECOMMENDED FOR..Urban

Recognized as one of the ten most exclusive hotels in the
capital, this Mandarin Oriental combines Parisian chic with
the hotel group's signature style. Some of the penthouse
and terrace suites include pergolas, private gyms, and steam
rooms. It is also located just moments away from Place
Vendôme and some of Paris's most fashionable addresses.

Recommended by: Stefan Antoni, SAOTA

THE NOLINSKI PARIS

16 avenue de l'Opéra
1er arrondissement
Paris 75001
+33 142861010
nolinskiparis.com

CREDIT CARDS..Accepted
PRICE..High-end
TYPE...Hotel
ACCOMMODATION.....................................45 Rooms
FACILITIES.....................................Bar, Indoor swimming pool,
2 Restaurants, Sauna,
Spa, Steam room
GOOD TO KNOW........................Child and pet friendly
RECOMMENDED FOR..................................Where I live

"The ultimate Parisian experience in the center of the city; everything is within walking distance."—Jean-Louis Deniot

Recommended by: Jean-Louis Deniot

HÔTEL EDGAR

31 rue d'Alexandrie
2e arrondissement
Paris 75002
+33 140410519
edgarparis.com

CREDIT CARDS..Accepted
PRICE..Mid-range
TYPE...Hotel
ACCOMMODATION.......................................13 Rooms
FACILITIES...Bar, Restaurant
GOOD TO KNOW.................Individually designed rooms
RECOMMENDED FOR..Urban

Recommended by: Dinko Peračić, ARP and Platforma 9.81

THE HOXTON, PARIS

30-32 rue du Sentier
2e arrondissement
Paris 75002
+33 185657500
thehoxton.com

CREDIT CARDS..Accepted
PRICE..Mid-range
TYPE...Hotel
ACCOMMODATION.....................................172 Rooms
FACILITIES..4 Bars, Restaurant
GOOD TO KNOW..................Bicycle rentals, Pet friendly
RECOMMENDED FOR...................Urban, Where I live

"Ideal for families or groups of friends. Smart, comfortable, and welcoming."—Claire Bétaille and Bruno Moinard

"A remarkable renovation of several historic buildings in the heart of the city. The place functions as a collection of spaces, of programs and experiences."—Alireza Razavi

Recommended by: Claire Bétaille and Bruno Moinard, 4BI & Associés; Alireza Razavi, Studio Razavi Architecture

HÔTEL NATIONAL DES ARTS ET MÉTIERS

243 rue Saint Martin
3e arrondissement
Paris 75003
+33 180972280
hotelnational.paris

CREDIT CARDS..Accepted
PRICE..Mid-range
TYPE...Hotel
ACCOMMODATION.......................................66 Rooms
FACILITIES.................................Bar, Gym, Restaurant,
Rooftop terrace bar, Spa, Yoga
GOOD TO KNOW................................Small pets only
RECOMMENDED FOR.....................Wish I'd designed

A design hotel situated between Le Marais and Montorgueil. Rooms by designer Raphael Navot are contemporary and stylish, and the three separate bar and restaurant areas have become must-visit Parisian destinations in their own right.

Recommended by: Makio Hasuike, Makio Hasuike & Co

LE PAVILLON DE LA REINE

28 place des Vosges
3e arrondissement
Paris 75003
+33 140291919
pavillon-de-la-reine.com

CREDIT CARDS..Accepted
PRICE..High-end
TYPE...Hotel
ACCOMMODATION.......................................56 Rooms
FACILITIES................................Bar, Gym, Restaurant, Spa,
Steam room
GOOD TO KNOW.....................Child friendly, Valet parking
RECOMMENDED FOR...........................Best-kept secret

"Delicate lodgings in Le Marais, a favorite Parisian district." —Craig Dykers

Recommended by: Emanuel Christ, Christ & Gantenbein; Craig Dykers, Snøhetta

HOTEL BEL AMI

7-11 rue St. Benoît
6e arrondissement, Paris 75006
+33 142615353
hotelbelami-paris.com

CREDIT CARDS	Accepted
PRICE	Mid-range
TYPE	Hotel
ACCOMMODATION	108 Rooms and Suites
FACILITIES	Bar, Gym, Restaurant, Sauna, Spa
GOOD TO KNOW	Babysitting, Small pets allowed
RECOMMENDED FOR	Urban

"Best-value hotel in Paris."—Sean Godsell

Recommended by: Sean Godsell, Sean Godsell Architects

HÔTEL ODÉON SAINT GERMAIN

13 rue Saint Sulpice
6e arrondissement, Paris 75006
+33 143257011
hotelparisodeonsaintgermain.com

CREDIT CARDS	Accepted
PRICE	Mid-range
TYPE	Hotel
ACCOMMODATION	27 Rooms and Suites
FACILITIES	Honesty bar
GOOD TO KNOW	Babysitting, Pet friendly
RECOMMENDED FOR	Urban

"Beautiful and cozy, in one of the most charming neighborhood's of Paris."—Nuno Brandão Costa

Recommended by: Nuno Brandão Costa, Brandão Costa Arquitectos

L'HÔTEL

13 rue des Beaux-Arts
6e arrondissement, Paris 75006
+33 144419900
l-hotel.com

CREDIT CARDS	Accepted
PRICE	High-end
TYPE	Hotel
ACCOMMODATION	20 Rooms
FACILITIES	Bar, Indoor swimming pool, Restaurant, Spa, Steam room
GOOD TO KNOW	Last home of Oscar Wilde
RECOMMENDED FOR	Luxury, Where I live

An intimate and opulent retreat, L'Hôtel is regarded as the world's first boutique hotel, and remains one of the finest. Famous former patrons include Oscar Wilde, Salvador Dalí, and Elizabeth Taylor.

Recommended by: Alex Michaelis, Michaelis Boyd; Hugo Sauzay, Festen Architecture; Matteo Thun, Matteo Thun & Partners

HOTEL MONTALEMBERT

3 rue Montalembert
7e arrondissement
Paris 75007
+33 145496868
hotelmontalembert-paris.fr

CREDIT CARDS	Accepted
PRICE	Mid-range
TYPE	Hotel
ACCOMMODATION	50 Rooms
FACILITIES	Bar, Restaurant, Spa
GOOD TO KNOW	Babysitting, Small pets only
RECOMMENDED FOR	All-time favorite, Best-kept secret

"Located near boulevard Saint Germain-des-Pres, this is the heart of my 'real' Paris. The hotel can best be described as boutique, but no expense is spared in the high modern design of its rooms. Some of the city's best restaurants and cafes are just a few feet away."—Simon Jacobsen

Recommended by: Simon Jacobsen, Jacobsen Architecture; Bruce Kuwabara, KPMB Architects

FOUR SEASONS HOTEL GEORGE V, PARIS

31 avenue George V
8e arrondissement
Paris 75008
+33 149527000
fourseasons.com

CREDIT CARDS	Accepted
PRICE	Blow-out
TYPE	Hotel
ACCOMMODATION	244 Rooms and Suites
FACILITIES	Bar, Gym, 4 Restaurants, Indoor swimming pool, Sauna, Spa, Steam room
GOOD TO KNOW	Babysitting, Valet parking
RECOMMENDED FOR	All-time favorite, Luxury

Recommended by: Anastasios Kotsiopoulos, AM Kotsiopoulos & Partners Architects; David Miller, Miller Hull Partnership

HÔTEL DE CRILLON

10 place de la Concorde
8e arrondissement
Paris 75008
+33 144711500
rosewoodhotels.com

CREDIT CARDS	Accepted
PRICE	Blow-out
TYPE	Hotel
ACCOMMODATION	125 Rooms and Suites
FACILITIES	Bar, Gym, 3 Restaurants, Spa, Yoga
GOOD TO KNOW	Child and pet friendly
RECOMMENDED FOR	All-time favorite

"A masterpiece in restoration from a very forward-thinking team with a generous budget!"—Achille Salvagni

Recommended by: Achille Salvagni, Salvagni Architetti

HÔTEL SAN RÉGIS

12 rue Jean Goujon
8e arrondissement
Paris 75008
+33 144951616
hotel-sanregis.fr

CREDIT CARDS	Accepted
PRICE	High-end
TYPE	Hotel
ACCOMMODATION	42 Rooms
FACILITIES	Bar, Restaurant
GOOD TO KNOW	Babysitting, Valet parking
RECOMMENDED FOR	Worth the travel

"Traditional Parisian luxury."—Tom Jordan

Recommended by: Tom Jordan, Hayball

LA RÉSERVE PARIS HOTEL AND SPA

42 avenue Gabriel
8e arrondissement
Paris 75008
+33 158366060
lareserve-paris.com

CREDIT CARDS	Accepted
PRICE	Blow-out
TYPE	Townhouse hotel
ACCOMMODATION	40 Rooms and Suites
FACILITIES	Bar, Gym, Indoor swimming pool, 2 Restaurants, Spa, Steam room
GOOD TO KNOW	Babysitting, Pet friendly
RECOMMENDED FOR	Urban

"An exceptional Haussmann-style mansion, the hotel was formerly designer Pierre Cardin's Paris mansion. With forty suites and nearly as many butlers, it offers a level of personal service that's as gracious and as opulent as the Jacques Garcia-designed interiors."—Todd-Avery Lenahan

"It is like coming home in a very busy town."—Matteo Thun

Recommended by: Todd-Avery Lenahan, TAL Studio; Matteo Thun, Matteo Thun & Partners

LE BRISTOL PARIS

112 rue du Faubourg Saint-Honoré
8e arrondissement
Paris 75008
+33 153434300
oetkercollection.com

CREDIT CARDS	Accepted
PRICE	Blow-out
TYPE	Hotel
ACCOMMODATION	190 Rooms and Suites
FACILITIES	2 Bars, Gym, Indoor swimming pool, 2 Restaurants, Spa
GOOD TO KNOW	Babysitting, Small pets only
RECOMMENDED FOR	All-time favorite, Luxury, Spa

"Charm and class in a historic property."—Mark de Reus

Recommended by: Stéphane Parmentier; Carlo Ratti, Carlo Ratti Associati; Mark de Reus, de Reus Architects

LE ROYAL MONCEAU RAFFLES PARIS

37 avenue Hoche
8e arrondissement
Paris 75008
+33 142998800
raffles.com

CREDIT CARDS	Accepted
PRICE	Blow-out
TYPE	Hotel
ACCOMMODATION	149 Rooms and Suites
FACILITIES	Bar, Gym, Indoor swimming pool, 3 Restaurants, Spa
GOOD TO KNOW	Child and pet friendly
RECOMMENDED FOR	Luxury

Designed by Philippe Starck, Le Royal Monceau Raffles Paris is a five-star piece of Parisian history that has been sensitively restored. The hotel regularly hosts world-renowned chefs for culinary events and residencies.

Recommended by: Bernardo and Paulo Jacobsen, Jacobsen Arquitetura

MAISON ASTOR, CURIO COLLECTION, PARIS
11 rue d'Astorg
8e arrondissement
Paris 75008
+33 153050505
curiocollection.hilton.com

CREDIT CARDS	Accepted
PRICE	High-end
TYPE	Hotel
ACCOMMODATION	150 Rooms
FACILITIES	Bar, Gym, Restaurant
GOOD TO KNOW	Babysitting, Small pets only, Valet parking
RECOMMENDED FOR	Best-kept secret

"Situated in the 8th arrondissement, almost everywhere I need to go is within walking distance. It's small and private, and the design style is a contemporary interpretation of Parisian decor. You can see the rooftops of Paris from the room's terraces."—Olajumoke Adenowo

Recommended by: Olajumoke Adenowo, AD Consulting

PLAZA ATHÉNÉE
25 avenue Montaigne
8e arrondissement
Paris 75008
+33 153676665
dorchestercollection.com

CREDIT CARDS	Accepted
PRICE	Blow-out
TYPE	Hotel
ACCOMMODATION	250 Rooms and Suites
FACILITIES	Bar, Gym, Outdoor restaurant, 3 Restaurants, Spa, Steam room
GOOD TO KNOW	Babysitting, Pet friendly
RECOMMENDED FOR	All-time favorite, Where I live

"This is almost like home. It has a heart-filled history where we find a warm welcome like nowhere else."
—Claire Bétaille and Bruno Moinard

"A lovely spot for tea."—Roger Duffy

Recommended by: Claire Bétaille and Bruno Moinard, 4BI & Associés; Roger Duffy, Skidmore, Owings & Merrill; Nabil Gholam, Nabil Gholam Architects

9 HOTEL OPÉRA
14 rue Papillon
9e arrondissement
Paris 75009
+33 147707834
9-hotel-opera-paris.fr

CREDIT CARDS	Accepted
PRICE	Mid-range
TYPE	Boutique hotel
ACCOMMODATION	48 Rooms and Suites
FACILITIES	Bar
GOOD TO KNOW	Babysitting, No pets
RECOMMENDED FOR	Urban

"Conveniently located within walking distance to the Gare du Nord, a simple but elegant hotel that has been a mainstay for many working visits to Paris."—Stephen Barrett

Recommended by: Stephen Barrett, Rogers Stirk Harbour + Partners

HÔTEL DU TEMPS
11 rue de Montholon
9e arrondissement
Paris 75009
+33 147703716
hotel-du-temps.fr

CREDIT CARDS	Accepted
PRICE	Mid-range
TYPE	Hotel
ACCOMMODATION	23 Rooms and Suites
FACILITIES	Bar
GOOD TO KNOW	Near Gare du Nord
RECOMMENDED FOR	Best-kept secret

Recommended by: David Tajchman, Architectures David Tajchman

9 HOTEL RÉPUBLIQUE
7-9 rue Pierre Chausson
10e arrondissement
Paris 75010
+33 140181100
9-hotel-republique-paris.fr

CREDIT CARDS	Accepted
PRICE	Low-cost
TYPE	Boutique hotel
ACCOMMODATION	48 Rooms
FACILITIES	Bar, Gym
GOOD TO KNOW	Child friendly
RECOMMENDED FOR	Budget

A boutique hotel located a short distance from Le Marais,
9 Hotel République has plenty of perks, including a
24-hour bar and a well-equipped shared working space.

Recommended by: Patrick Reymond, Atelier Oï

HÔTEL RÉGENCE ETOILE
24 avenue Carnot
17e arrondissement
Paris 75017
+33 158054242
hotelregenceetoile.com

CREDIT CARDS	Accepted
PRICE	Mid-range
TYPE	Hotel
ACCOMMODATION	40 Rooms and Suites
FACILITIES	Bar, Gym
GOOD TO KNOW	No pets
RECOMMENDED FOR	Family friendly

"It's right behind the Arc de Triomphe...Great location and
cozy."—Nilson Ariel Espino

Recommended by: Nilson Ariel Espino, Suma Arquitectos

RENAISSANCE PARIS ARC DE TRIOMPHE HOTEL
39 Avenue de Wagram
17e arrondissement
Paris 75017
+33 155375537
marriott.com

CREDIT CARDS	Accepted
PRICE	High-end
TYPE	Hotel
ACCOMMODATION	118 Rooms and Suites
FACILITIES	Bar, Gym, Restaurant
GOOD TO KNOW	Babysitting, Valet parking
RECOMMENDED FOR	Where I live

Recommended by: Christian de Portzamparc, 2Portzamparc

MAMA SHELTER PARIS
109 Rue de Bagnolet
20e arrondissement
Paris 75020
+33 143484848
mamashelter.com

CREDIT CARDS	Accepted
PRICE	Low-cost
TYPE	Hotel
ACCOMMODATION	149 Rooms and Suites
FACILITIES	Bar, Restaurant, Rooftop terrace bar
GOOD TO KNOW	Child and pet friendly
RECOMMENDED FOR	Budget

Designed by Philippe Starck, this is the original Parisian
property of the perennially cool hotel brand. Restaurant
dishes have been created by Guy Savoy, and rooms are
low-cost yet contain added perks, such as minibars and
office spaces in larger suites. The Rooftop bar is the
perfect place to unwind on a sunny evening.

Recommended by: Hiéronyme Lacroix and Simon Chessex,
Lacroix Chessex

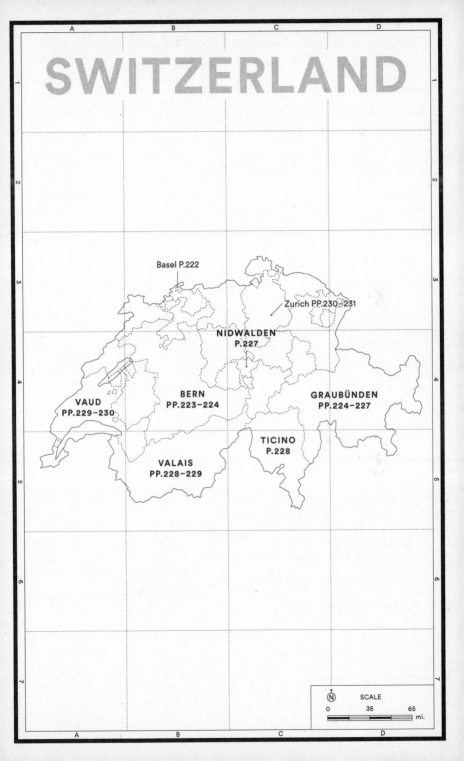

DER TEUFELHOF

Leonhardsgraben 47-49
Altstadt Grossbasel
Basel 4051
Switzerland
+41 612611010
teufelhof.com

CREDIT CARDS..Accepted
PRICE..Mid-range
TYPE..Townhouse hotel
ACCOMMODATION.......................................33 Rooms
FACILITIES...............................Bar, Library, 2 Restaurants,
Theater, Wine store
GOOD TO KNOW...........................Babysitting, Bicycle rentals,
On-site brewery, Pet friendly
RECOMMENDED FOR...Urban

Renowned as a pioneer of the art hotel trend, Der Teufelhof is located in an eighteenth-century townhouse in the heart of the city's Old Town.

Recommended by: Antonio Ortiz, Cruz y Ortiz Arquitectos

HOTEL KRAFFT

Rheingasse 12
Altstadt Kleinbasel
Basel 4058
Switzerland
+41 616909130
krafftbasel.ch

CREDIT CARDS..Accepted
PRICE..Mid-range
TYPE...Hotel
ACCOMMODATION.......................................48 Rooms
FACILITIES...............................Wine bar, Restaurant
GOOD TO KNOW...................Bicycle rentals, Child friendly
RECOMMENDED FOR...........................Where I live

"A pure classic on the Rhine."—Charlotte von Moos

Situated in the heart of Basel's Old Town, the building's classic townhouse exterior conceals its modern interiors. This hotel is a favorite with the art and design crowd—small touches make the difference, such as the Brompton folding bikes provided for guests to explore the city.

Recommended by: Emanuel Christ, Christ & Gantenbein; Charlotte von Moos, Sauter von Moos

JUGENDHERBERGE

St. Alban-Kirchrain 10
Vorstädte
Basel 4052
Switzerland
+41 612720572
youthhostel.ch

CREDIT CARDS..Accepted
PRICE..Low-cost
TYPE...Bed and Breakfast
ACCOMMODATION.......................................66 Rooms
FACILITIES...................Bar, Games room, Restaurant
GOOD TO KNOW...........................Child friendly, No pets
RECOMMENDED FOR...Urban

"In a wonderfully connected world with traditional ideas of luxury, this is a refreshing place that is innovative, cool, and in the center of Basel."—Satyendra Pakhalé

Recommended by: Satyendra Pakhalé, Satyendra Pakhalé Associates

NOMAD

Brunngässlein 8
Vorstädte
Basel 4052
Switzerland
+41 616909160
nomad.ch

CREDIT CARDS..Accepted
PRICE..Mid-range
TYPE...Hotel
ACCOMMODATION.......................................65 Rooms
FACILITIES...............................Bar, Gym, Library,
Restaurant, Sauna, Spa
GOOD TO KNOW...................Bicycle rentals, Child friendly
RECOMMENDED FOR...Urban

"A stone's throw from the new Kunstmuseum, this terrific hotel is an exemplar of 1960s adaptive reuse."—Anne Kaestle

Recommended by: Anne Kaestle, Duplex Architekten

HOTEL SCHWEIZERHOF BERN & THE SPA
Bahnhofplatz 11
Bern 3001
Switzerland
+41 313268080
schweizerhof-bern.ch

CREDIT CARDS	Accepted
PRICE	High-end
TYPE	Hotel
ACCOMMODATION	99 Rooms
FACILITIES	Bar, Gym, Hammam, Hot-spring bath, Indoor swimming pool, 3 Restaurants, Sauna, Spa
GOOD TO KNOW	Child and pet friendly
RECOMMENDED FOR	Urban

"This hotel dates back to the early twentieth century, which gives it a classical feel."—Mario Botta

Recommended by: Mario Botta, Mario Botta Architetti

GRANDHOTEL GIESSBACH
Axalpstrasse
Brienz
Bern 3855
Switzerland
+41 339522525
giessbach.ch

CREDIT CARDS	Accepted
PRICE	Mid-range
TYPE	Hotel
ACCOMMODATION	70 Rooms and Suites
FACILITIES	Bar, 3 Restaurants, Outdoor swimming pool
GOOD TO KNOW	Bicycle rentals, Pet friendly
RECOMMENDED FOR	Mountains

"The Grandhotel Giessbach is a unique place to visit, representing the golden era of high society. Set above Lake Brienz, its historical bones retain the charm and unique expression of its past, creating a place to escape all sense of time and space."—Nathalie Rossetti

Recommended by: Nathalie Rossetti, Rossetti + Wyss Architects

HOTEL BELLEVUE DES ALPES
Kleine Scheidegg
Bern 3801
Switzerland
+41 338551212
scheidegg-hotels.ch

CREDIT CARDS	Accepted
PRICE	High-end
TYPE	Hotel
ACCOMMODATION	60 Rooms
FACILITIES	Bar, Restaurant, Wood-burning fireplace
GOOD TO KNOW	Child and pet friendly
RECOMMENDED FOR	Mountains

"A perfect place to take in the dramatic landscape. The hotel has a long history and the renovation is thoughtfully done. New architectural interventions have been done carefully and in good spirit—no unnecessary fuss, no trying to be modern, simply beautiful attention to detail."
—Michael Schumacher

Recommended by: Michael Schumacher, Schneider + Schumacher

HISTORISCHES ALPINHOTEL GRIMSEL HOSPIZ
Grimselpass
Interlaken-Oberhasli
Bern 3864
Switzerland
+41 339824611
grimselwelt.ch

CREDIT CARDS	Accepted
PRICE	Mid-range
TYPE	Hotel
ACCOMMODATION	28 Rooms
FACILITIES	Bar, Open-air bath, Restaurant, Steam room, Wood-burning fireplace
GOOD TO KNOW	Free parking, Pet friendly
RECOMMENDED FOR	Mountains

"A beautiful historical building in an amazing, remote location."—Leonid Slonimskiy

Recommended by: Leonid Slonimskiy, KOSMOS Architects

HOTEL REGINA MÜRREN
Hauptstrasse
Mürren
Interlaken-Oberhasli
Bern 3825
Switzerland
+41 338554242
reginamuerren.ch

CREDIT CARDS	Accepted
PRICE	Low-cost
TYPE	Hotel
ACCOMMODATION	52 Rooms
FACILITIES	Bar, Resaurant
GOOD TO KNOW	Child and pet friendly
RECOMMENDED FOR	Family friendly

"Imparts a James Bond feeling with great views of the Eiger, Mönch, and Jungfrau mountains."—Anne Kaestle

Recommended by: Anne Kaestle, Duplex Architekten

GUARDA VAL
Voa Sporz 85
Lenzerheide
Albula
Graubünden 7078
Switzerland
+41 813858585
guardaval.ch

CREDIT CARDS	Accepted
PRICE	Mid-range
TYPE	Hotel
ACCOMMODATION	50 Rooms
FACILITIES	Bar, Golf, Gym, Open-air baths, 2 Restaurants, Sauna
GOOD TO KNOW	Horse riding, Michelin-starred restaurant
RECOMMENDED FOR	Countryside

"You will have the best sleep here, ever!"—Anne Kaestle

Recommended by: Anne Kaestle, Duplex Architekten

HOTEL VILLA GARBALD
Via Principale 9
Graubünden 7608
Switzerland
+41 818381515
garbald.ch

CREDIT CARDS	Accepted
PRICE	Mid-range
TYPE	Campus with rooms
ACCOMMODATION	14 Rooms
FACILITIES	Auditorium, Libary, Seminar spaces
GOOD TO KNOW	Retreats, Seminars, Workshops
RECOMMENDED FOR	Mountains

"A beautiful nineteenth-century villa with a modern extension in a small alpine village."—Ahmed Belkhodja

Recommended by: Ahmed Belkhodja, Fala Atelier

BADRUTT'S PALACE
Via Serlas 27
Saint Moritz
Maloja
Graubünden 7500
Switzerland
+41 818371000
badruttspalace.com

CREDIT CARDS..Accepted
PRICE..Blow-out
TYPE..Hotel
ACCOMMODATION...................................120 Rooms and Suites
FACILITIES..Bar, Golf, Gym,
Hot-spring bath, Ice rink,
Indoor and outdoor swimming pools,
3 Restaurants, Spa, Tennis
GOOD TO KNOW.....................................Child and pet friendly
RECOMMENDED FOR...Spa

"This hotel is especially beautiful in winter. You can swim outside, between the mountains and spectacular lake views, which makes the spa even more relaxing."—Ben van Berkel

Recommended by: Ben van Berkel, UNStudio

VILLA FLOR
Somvih 19
S-Chanf
Maloja
Graubünden 7525
Switzerland
+41 818512230
villaflor.ch

CREDIT CARDS..Accepted
PRICE..High-end
TYPE..Guesthouse
ACCOMMODATION...7 Rooms
FACILITIES..Bar, Gallery, Library
GOOD TO KNOW.............Child and pet friendly, Free parking
RECOMMENDED FOR...Countryside

"In the heart of an unspoiled village called S-Chanf, this is a simple but sophisticated guest house. Its corridors host exhibitions by artists, many of whom are frequent guests. It is discreet and unpretentious without any signs to advertise its presence."—Norman Foster

Recommended by: Norman Foster, Foster + Partners

HOTEL WALDHAUS SILS-MARIA
Fexerstrasse 3
Sils im Engadin
Maloja
Graubünden 7514, Switzerland
+41 818385100
waldhaus-sils.ch

CREDIT CARDS..Accepted
PRICE..Blow-out
TYPE..Hotel
ACCOMMODATION...140 Rooms
FACILITIES.....................Bar, Gym, Indoor swimming pool,
2 Restaurants, Spa, Steam room,
Tennis, Yoga
GOOD TO KNOW.....................................Child and pet friendly
RECOMMENDED FOR...All-time favorite,
Family friendly, Mountains

"This hotel has been run by the same family since 1908, offering old-school luxury. Its rooms are intimate and cozy. You're transported to a place where time stands still." —Rabih Hage

Recommended by: Sam Chermayeff, Meyer-Grohbrügge & Chermayeff; Emanuel Christ, Christ & Gantenbein; Rabih Hage; Jürgen Mayer H., J. Mayer H. und Partner, Architekten; Johanna Meyer-Grohbrügge, Meyer-Grohbrügge; Charlotte von Moos, Sauter von Moos

HOTEL PALAZZO SALIS
Villaggio 131
Soglio
Maloja
Graubünden 7610, Switzerland
+41 818221208
palazzo-salis.ch

CREDIT CARDS.....................................Accepted but not Amex
PRICE..Mid-range
TYPE..Hotel
ACCOMMODATION...14 Rooms
FACILITIES..Bar, Restaurant
GOOD TO KNOW...Child friendly
RECOMMENDED FOR....................Mountains, Worth the travel

A friendly boutique hotel high in the Bregaglia Valley, Palazzo Salis embraces warm hospitality and local produce. Each room is unique, yet all are elegant, and in keeping with the "old-world" feel—you won't find any phones or televisions.

Recommended by: Emanuel Christ, Christ & Gantenbein; Much Untertrifaller, Dietrich Untertrifaller Architects

HOTEL CASTELL ZUOZ
Via Castell 300
Zuoz
Maloja
Graubünden 7524
Switzerland
+41 818515253
hotelcastell.ch

CREDIT CARDS...Accepted
PRICE...Mid-range
TYPE..Hotel
ACCOMMODATION..68 Rooms
FACILITIES.........................Bar, Hammam, Ice rink,
Restaurant, Sauna, Spa, Yoga
GOOD TO KNOW...........................Babysitting, Bicycle rentals,
Pet friendly
RECOMMENDED FOR...Mountains

"Children love the Castell! All the little extras ensure
relaxation and quality time for parents, too. They have
family rooms at family prices, professionally supervised
day care, a hotel park with a large playground in the
summer and an ice rink in winter."—Ben van Berkel

Recommended by: Ben van Berkel, UNStudio; Anne Kaestle,
Duplex Architekten

TSCHUGGEN GRAND HOTEL
Tschuggentorweg 1
Arosa
Plessur
Graubünden 7050
Switzerland
+41 813789999
tschuggen.ch

CREDIT CARDS...Accepted
PRICE...High-end
TYPE..Hotel
ACCOMMODATION......................................128 Rooms
FACILITIES...........................Bar, Gym, Hot-spring bath,
Indoor and outdoor swimming pools,
5 Restaurants, Sauna, Spa, Yoga
GOOD TO KNOW..............................Pet friendly, Valet parking
RECOMMENDED FOR...Mountains

"Stay here for Mario Botta's spectacular and unique
architecture, where you can enjoy the poetry of the hotel
with glass sails rising dramatically from the roof."
—Stéphane Rasselet

Recommended by: Stéphane Rasselet, Naturehumaine

SCHATZALP
Promenade 65
Davos
Prättigau/Davos
Graubünden 7270
Switzerland
+41 814155151
schatzalp.ch

CREDIT CARDS...Accepted
PRICE...Mid-range
TYPE..Hotel
ACCOMMODATION..92 Rooms
FACILITIES.....................Bar, Games room, Gym, Hammam,
4 Restaurants, Sauna,
Spa, Steam room, Yoga
GOOD TO KNOW...Babysitting
RECOMMENDED FOR...Mountains

"Wonderful hotel of the late eighteenth-century in Art
Nouveau style. Built as a sanatorium, the hotel reflects
the classic Swiss 'Mountain Hotel' era. Extensively and
sensitively preserved, it remains a spacious and cozy
place with a memorable atmosphere."—Nathalie Rossetti

Recommended by: Ian Ritchie, Ian Ritchie Architects;
Nathalie Rossetti, Rossetti + Wyss Architects

ROCKSRESORT
Via Murschetg 17
Laax
Surselva
Graubünden 7032
Switzerland
+41 819279797
rocksresort.com

CREDIT CARDS...Accepted
PRICE...Mid-range
TYPE...Serviced apartments
ACCOMMODATION.........143 Apartments, Rooms, and Suites
FACILITIES.........................Bar, Gym, Indoor swimming pool,
8 Restaurants, Sauna, Yoga
GOOD TO KNOW...Bicycle rentals,
Child and pet friendly, Skiing
RECOMMENDED FOR.............All-time favorite, Family friendly

A chic, child-friendly ski resort with direct access to the
LAAX lift station. It was voted World's Best Green Ski Hotel
in 2018.

Recommended by: Robert Konieczny, KWK Promes

GASTHAUS AM BRUNNEN

Hauptstrasse 61
Valendas
Surselva
Graubünden 7122, Switzerland
+41 819202122
gasthausambrunnen.ch

CREDIT CARDS	Accepted
PRICE	Mid-range
TYPE	Guesthouse
ACCOMMODATION	7 Rooms
FACILITIES	Bar, Restaurant
GOOD TO KNOW	Child and pet friendly
RECOMMENDED FOR	Best-kept secret

Recommended by: Sam Chermayeff, Meyer-Grohbrügge
& Chermayeff

7132 HOTEL

Postrasse 560
Vals
Surselva
Graubünden 7132, Switzerland
+41 587132000
7132.com

CREDIT CARDS	Accepted
PRICE	High-end
TYPE	Hotel
ACCOMMODATION	90 Houses and Rooms
FACILITIES	Bar, Indoor and outdoor swimming pools, 3 Restaurants, Sauna, Spa, Steam room, Wood-burning fireplace
GOOD TO KNOW	Child and pet friendly
RECOMMENDED FOR	Countryside, Family friendly, Mountains, Spa, Wish I'd designed, Worth the travel

"Peter Zumthor's thermal baths will never go out of style."
—Gert Wingårdh

[Recommended for the architecture of Therme Vals.]

Recommended by: Emre Arolat, EAA; Diego Arraigada,
Diego Arraigada Arquitectos; Kelly Bair, Central Standard
Office of Design; Paul Bernier, Paul Bernier Architecte;
Tim Black, BKK Architects; Nuno Brandão Costa, Brandão
Costa Arquitectos; Hasan Çalışlar, Erginoğlu & Çalışlar;
Beppe Caturegli and Giovannella Formica, Caturegli
Formica Architetti Associati; Cristina Celestino; Farid
Chacon, NMD NOMADAS; Sébastien Dachy, MAMOUT
architectes; Bernard Dubois, Bernard Dubois Architects;
Karl Fournier and Olivier Marty, Studio KO; Tony Fretton,
Tony Fretton Architects; Makio Hasuike, Makio Hasuike &
Co; Simon Henley, Henley Halebrown; Kim Herforth Nielsen,
3XN; Waro Kishi, K.ASSOCIATES/Architects; Eero Koivisto
and Ola Rune, Claesson Koivisto Rune Architects; Robert
Konieczny, KWK Promes; Marianne Kwok, Kohn Pedersen
Fox; Rafael de La-Hoz Castanys, Rafael de La-Hoz
Arquitectos; Joana Leandro Vasconcelos, Atelier in.vitro;
Victor Legorreta Hernández, Legorreta; Antonio G. Liñán,
SV60 Cordón & Liñán Arquitectos; Andrea Maffei, Andrea
Maffei Architects; José Martinez-Silva, Atelier Central;
Giancarlo Mazzanti, El Equipo Mazzanti; Alex Michaelis,
Michaelis Boyd; David Miller, Miller Hull Partnership; Alex
Mok, Linehouse; Grace Mortlock, Other Architects;
Alfredo Payá Benedito, Noname29; Juan Manuel Peláez
Freidel, JUMP/Juan Manuel Peláez Arquitectos; Joaquín
Pérez-Goicoechea, AGi Architects; Ron Radziner, Marmol
Radziner; Stéphane Rasselet, Naturehumaine; Carlo
Ratti, Carlo Ratti Associati; Alireza Razavi, Studio Razavi
Architecture; Patrick Reymond, Atelier Oï; João Mendes
Ribeiro, João Mendes Ribeiro Arquitecto; Michel Rojkind,
Rojkind Arquitectos; Nathalie Rossetti, Rossetti + Wyss
Architects; Urko Sanchez, Urko Sanchez Architects; Cristian
Santandreu, A2arquitectos; Uwe Schmidt-Hess, Patalab
Architecture; Fran Silvestre, Fran Silvestre Arquitectos;
Leonid Slonimskiy, KOSMOS Architects; Daniel Suduca
and Thierry Mérillou, Suduca & Mérillou; Daniel Sundlin,
Bjarke Ingels Group; David Tajchman, Architectures David
Tajchman; Mia Baarup Tofte, NORD Architects; Isabelle
Toland, Aileen Sage Architects; Gert Wingårdh, Wingårdhs

HOTEL VILLA HONNEG

Honegg
Ennetbürgen
Nidwalden 6373
Switzerland
+41 416183200
villa-honegg.ch

CREDIT CARDS	Accepted
PRICE	Blow-out
TYPE	Hotel
ACCOMMODATION	23 Rooms and Suites
FACILITIES	Bar, Gym, Hammam, Indoor and outdoor swimming pools, Library, Restaurant, Sauna, Spa, Wood-burning fireplace
GOOD TO KNOW	Bicycle rentals, Child friendly, No pets
RECOMMENDED FOR	Countryside, Mountains, Spa

"Visit for the calm environment in a beautiful landscape
setting."—Bernard Dubois

Recommended by: Bernard Dubois, Bernard Dubois
Architects; Daniel Libeskind, Studio Libeskind

ST. GOTTHARDO HOSPIZ

Passo del San Gottardo
Airolo
Leventina
Ticino 6780
Switzerland
+41 918691235
passosangottardo.ch

CREDIT CARDS.....................................Accepted but not Amex
PRICE...Mid-range
TYPE...Hotel
ACCOMMODATION...14 Dorms and Rooms
FACILITIES...Bar, 3 Restaurants
GOOD TO KNOW...........................Child friendly, Free parking
RECOMMENDED FOR............................Countryside, Mountains

"Incredible! It's in the middle of the mountains and the
renovation by Miller and Maranta is impressive."
—Hiéronyme Lacroix and Simon Chessex

Recommended by: Hiéronyme Lacroix and Simon Chessex,
Lacroix Chessex; Leonid Slonimskiy, KOSMOS Architects;
Bolle Tham and Martin Videgård, Tham & Videgård
Arkitekter

HOTEL MONTE VERITÀ

Strauss Collina 84
Ascona
Locarno
Ticino 6612
Switzerland
+41 917854040
monteverita.org

CREDIT CARDS...Accepted
PRICE...Low-cost
TYPE...Hotel
ACCOMMODATION..52 Rooms
FACILITIES...........................Bar, Tea house, Restaurant
GOOD TO KNOW......................................Child and pet friendly
RECOMMENDED FOR...Countryside

"Far away from everyday life, this hotel is a wonderful oasis
designed in an impressive Bauhaus style. Its original
furnished quality offers unique charm."—Nathalie Rossetti

Recommended by: Nathalie Rossetti, Rossetti +
Wyss Architects

THE CHEDI ANDERMATT

Gotthardstrasse 4
Andermatt
Uri 6490
Switzerland
+41 418887488
thechediandermatt.com

CREDIT CARDS...Accepted
PRICE...High-end
TYPE...Hotel
ACCOMMODATION..............................123 Rooms and Suites
FACILITIES..........................2 Bars, 3 Cafes, Golf, Gym,
Indoor and outdoor pools,
2 Restaurants, Spa
GOOD TO KNOW...................Alpine bar The Chalet operates
during the winter months
RECOMMENDED FOR..Luxury, Mountains

"Real alpine chic with a touch of Asian expression; deluxe
treatment in the middle of the Alps."—Luca Gazzaniga

Recommended by: Luca Gazzaniga, Luca Gazzaniga
Architects; Alexander Wong, Alexander Wong Architects

MONTAGNE ALTERNATIVE

Commeire
Orsières
Entremont
Valais 1937
Switzerland
+41 212130280
montagne-alternative.co

CREDIT CARDS...........................Accepted but not Amex
PRICE...Mid-range
TYPE...Lodge
ACCOMMODATION..28 Rooms
FACILITIES.......................................Bar, Restaurant,
Wood-burning fireplace, Yoga
GOOD TO KNOW....................................Child and pet friendly,
Free parking
RECOMMENDED FOR.......................Eco-conscious, Mountains

"This chalet in the MittelEuropa mountains has wonderful
facilities and services, including a chalet dedicated to yoga,
and chefs at your disposal."—Karl Fournier and Olivier Marty

A stylish collection of restored chalets with a strong focus
on nature and sustainable practices.

Recommended by: Bernard Dubois, Bernard Dubois
Architects; Karl Fournier and Olivier Marty, Studio KO

HOTEL WHITEPOD
Les Cerniers
Monthey
Valais 1871, Switzerland
+41 244713838
whitepod.com

CREDIT CARDS	Accepted
PRICE	High-end
TYPE	Hotel
ACCOMMODATION	18 Pods
FACILITIES	Bar, Cafe, Restaurant, Sauna, Wood-burning fireplace
GOOD TO KNOW	Bicycle rentals
RECOMMENDED FOR	Eco-conscious, Family friendly, Mountains

"This 'eco-luxury' hotel in the Swiss Alps offers a unique, sustainable alpine experience. Guests stay in pods with minimal environmental impact, made from self-supporting frameworks to minimize the use of building materials."
—Paolo Brambilla

Recommended by: Flavio Albanese, ASA Studio; Boris Bernaskoni, Bernaskoni; Paolo Brambilla, Calvi Brambilla; Marcelo Morettin, Andrade Morettin Arquitetos; Satyendra Pakhalé, Satyendra Pakhalé Associates

CHETZERON
Rue de Chetzeron 2112
Crans-Montana
Sierre
Valais 3963
Switzerland
+41 274850800
chetzeron.ch

CREDIT CARDS	Accepted
PRICE	High-end
TYPE	Hotel
ACCOMMODATION	16 Rooms
FACILITIES	Bar, Gym, Outdoor swimming pool, Restaurant, Sauna, Spa, Steam room
GOOD TO KNOW	Child friendly, No pets
RECOMMENDED FOR	Mountains

Recommended by: Alex Michaelis, Michaelis Boyd

MONTE ROSA HÜTTE
Sennereiweg
Baltschieder
Visp
Valais 3937
Switzerland
+41 279672115
monterosahuette.ch

CREDIT CARDS	Accepted but not Amex
PRICE	Low-cost
TYPE	Mountain hut
ACCOMMODATION	120 Sleeping spots
FACILITIES	Communal dining room
GOOD TO KNOW	Pet friendly
RECOMMENDED FOR	All-time favorite, Budget, Countryside, Eco-conscious, Mountains, Wish I'd designed, Worth the travel

"To reach the hotel it is a solid four-hour ascent over the Gorner glacier...but the effort is worth it."—Anne Kaestle

Recommended by: Anne Kaestle, Duplex Architekten; Robert Konieczny, KWK Promes; Henriette Salvesen, Div.A Arkitekter

CERVO MOUNTAIN BOUTIQUE RESORT
Riedweg 156
Zermatt
Visp
Valais 3920
Switzerland
+41 279681212
cervo.ch

CREDIT CARDS	Accepted
PRICE	Blow-out
TYPE	Chalet
ACCOMMODATION	36 Rooms and Suites
FACILITIES	Bar, Gym, Jacuzzi, 2 Restaurants, Sauna, Spa, Steam room, Yoga
GOOD TO KNOW	Child friendly, No pets
RECOMMENDED FOR	Mountains

CERVO's approach is authentically hospitable and elegantly fuss-free. It has rooms and suites in six chalets and its restaurants showcase the best of Swiss cuisine. Its sun terrace is the ideal spot for après-ski drinks and alpine tapas.

Recommended by: Dominique Perrault, Dominique Perrault Architecture

CABANE DE MOIRY

Chemin de la Valerette 15
Ollon
Aigle
Vaud 1867
Switzerland
+41 274754534
cabane-moiry.ch

CREDIT CARDS	Accepted
PRICE	Low-cost
TYPE	Guesthouse
ACCOMMODATION	10 Dorms
FACILITIES	Restaurant
GOOD TO KNOW	Accessible by hike, Mountaineering
RECOMMENDED FOR	Best-kept secret

"If you are delighted by the Alps and mountain surroundings, it is great to hike to this simple but extraordinary place."—Nathalie Rossetti

Recommended by: Nathalie Rossetti, Rossetti + Wyss Architects

TROIS COURONNES

Rue d'Italie 49
Vevey
Lake Geneva
Vaud 1800
Switzerland
+41 219233200
hoteltroiscouronnes.ch

CREDIT CARDS	Accepted
PRICE	Mid-range
TYPE	Spa hotel
ACCOMMODATION	71 Rooms and Suites
FACILITIES	Bar, Gym, Indoor swimming pool, Jacuzzi, Restaurant, Sauna, Spa, Steam room
GOOD TO KNOW	Pet friendly, Valet parking
RECOMMENDED FOR	Spa

A luxurious spa hotel on the waterfront of Lake Geneva, Trois Couronnes is ideally located for exploring the Swiss Riviera of Vevey, as well as Gruyère and the vineyards of Lavaux. The hotel restaurant also holds a Michelin star.

Recommended by: Emanuel Christ, Christ & Gantenbein

BEAU-RIVAGE PALACE

Chemin de Beau-Rivage 21
Lausanne
Vaud 1006
Switzerland
+41 216133333
brp.ch

CREDIT CARDS	Accepted
PRICE	High-end
TYPE	Hotel
ACCOMMODATION	168 Rooms and Suites
FACILITIES	Bar, Gym, Hammam, Indoor and outdoor swimming pools, Jacuzzi, 6 Restaurants, Spa, Tennis
GOOD TO KNOW	Child and pet friendly
RECOMMENDED FOR	Luxury

"Enjoy famous Swiss hospitality in classic rooms by Lake Geneva."—Nuno Brandão Costa

Recommended by: Nuno Brandão Costa, Brandão Costa Arquitectos; Dominique Perrault, Dominique Perrault Architecture

B2 BOUTIQUE HOTEL AND SPA

Brandschenkestrasse 152
Enge
Zurich 8002
Switzerland
+41 445676767
b2boutiquehotels.com

CREDIT CARDS	Accepted
PRICE	Mid-range
TYPE	Hotel
ACCOMMODATION	60 Rooms and Suites
FACILITIES	Bar, Gym, Indoor and outdoor swimming pools, Library, Spa, Thermal baths
GOOD TO KNOW	Child and pet friendly
RECOMMENDED FOR	Where I live

"This urban hotel is situated in the former Hürlimann brewery. It stands out for its industrial character."
—Nathalie Rossetti

Recommended by: Nathalie Rossetti, Rossetti + Wyss Architects

DOLDER GRAND HOTEL
Kurhausstrasse 65
Hottingen
Zurich 8032
Switzerland
+41 444566000
thedoldergrand.com

CREDIT CARDS	Accepted
PRICE	Blow-out
TYPE	Hotel
ACCOMMODATION	176 Rooms
FACILITIES	Bar, Golf, Gym, Indoor and outdoor swimming pools, 2 Restaurants, Sauna, Spa, Tennis
GOOD TO KNOW	Bicycle rentals, Child and pet friendly
RECOMMENDED FOR	Luxury, Mountains

"The renovated historic Dolder Grand by Foster + Partners has incredible views over Lake Zurich. Highlights include contemporary artworks, an amazing spa, and a Michelin-starred restaurant."—Bernardo and Paulo Jacobsen

Recommended by: Bernardo and Paulo Jacobsen, Jacobsen Arquitetura; Charles Renfro, Diller Scofidio + Renfro; Leonid Slonimskiy, KOSMOS Architects

HOTEL HELVETIA
Stauffacherquai 1
Kreis 4
Zurich 8004
Switzerland
+41 442979999
hotel-helvetia.ch

CREDIT CARDS	Accepted
PRICE	Mid-range
TYPE	Hotel
ACCOMMODATION	37 Apartments and Rooms
FACILITIES	Bar, Gym, Restaurant, Rooftop terrace bar
GOOD TO KNOW	Pet friendly
RECOMMENDED FOR	Where I live

Recommended by: Anne Kaestle, Duplex Architekten

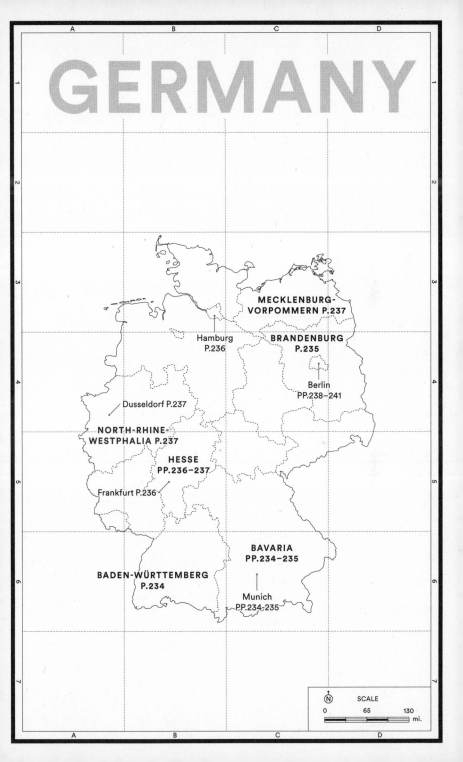

GERMANY

MECKLENBURG-
VORPOMMERN P.237

Hamburg
P.236

BRANDENBURG
P.235

Berlin
PP.238–241

Dusseldorf P.237

NORTH-RHINE-
WESTPHALIA P.237

HESSE
PP.236–237

Frankfurt P.236

BAVARIA
PP.234–235

BADEN-WÜRTTEMBERG
P.234

Munich
PP.234–235

Ⓝ   SCALE

0   65   130
                        mi.

ARTHOTEL HEIDELBERG
Grabengasse 7
Heidelberg
Baden-Württemberg 69117
Germany
+49 622165006
arthotel.de

CREDIT CARDS	Accepted
PRICE	Mid-range
TYPE	Hotel
ACCOMMODATION	24 Rooms
FACILITIES	Bar, Restaurant, Rooftop terrace bar
GOOD TO KNOW	Child and pet friendly
RECOMMENDED FOR	Urban

"Smartly renovated in good taste, the contrast between old
and new elements is successful. The charming courtyard
you enter on arrival has a poetic feeling, reflective of
Heidelberg as a whole."—Yu-lin Chen

Recommended by: Yu-lin Chen, MAYU Architects+

DAS KRANZBACH
Kranzbach 1
Krün
Bavaria 82493
Germany
+49 8823928000
daskranzbach.de

CREDIT CARDS	Accepted but not Amex
PRICE	Mid-range
TYPE	Hotel
ACCOMMODATION	137 Rooms
FACILITIES	Bar, Gym, Indoor and outdoor swimming pools, 2 Restaurants, Sauna, Spa, Steam room, Yoga
GOOD TO KNOW	Pet friendly
RECOMMENDED FOR	Luxury, Spa

"Lovely winter stop-off after skiing."—Michael Young

Recommended by: Carlo Baumschlager, Baumschlager
Hutter Partners; Michael Young, Michael Young Studio

HOTEL MARIANDL
Goethestrasse 51
Munich
Bavaria 80336
Germany
+49 895529100
mariandl.com

CREDIT CARDS	Accepted
PRICE	Low-cost
TYPE	Hotel
ACCOMMODATION	30 Rooms
FACILITIES	Bar, Restaurant
GOOD TO KNOW	Child friendly
RECOMMENDED FOR	Budget

Housed in a listed Belle Époque building, Hotel Mariandl
is a beautiful yet laid-back hotel where check-in takes place
in the cafe. For one week every year, international artists
take residence in the hotel's rooms to seek inspiration from
its history and develop a series of installations.

Recommended by: Johanna Meyer-Grohbrügge,
Meyer-Grohbrügge

LANSERHOF TEGERNSEE
Gut Steinberg 1–4
Munich
Bavaria 83666
Germany
+49 802218800
lanserhof.com

CREDIT CARDS	Accepted
PRICE	High-end
TYPE	Medical destination spa
ACCOMMODATION	70 Rooms and Suites
FACILITIES	Bar, Gym, Indoor and outdoor swimming pools, Restaurant, Sauna, Spa, Yoga
GOOD TO KNOW	Over 16s only
RECOMMENDED FOR	Wish I'd designed

Renowned for its highly effective medi-spa, holistic
treatments, and sleek interiors, Lanserhof Tegernsee
places emphasis upon mental and physical tranquility.

Recommended by: Alex Michaelis, Michaelis Boyd

LIVING HOTEL DAS VIKTUALIENMARKT

Frauenstrasse 4
Munich
Bavaria 80469
Germany
+49 898856560
living-hotels.com

CREDIT CARDS..Accepted
PRICE...Low-cost
TYPE..Apartment hotel
ACCOMMODATION...83 Rooms and
Serviced apartments
FACILITIES....................................Bar, Gym, Restaurant
GOOD TO KNOW..Child friendly
RECOMMENDED FOR...Budget

Recommended by: Victor Legorreta Hernández, Legorreta

LOUIS HOTEL

Viktualienmarkt 6
Munich
Bavaria 80331
Germany
+49 8941119080
louis-hotel.com

CREDIT CARDS..Accepted
PRICE...Mid-range
TYPE..Hotel
ACCOMMODATION...72 Rooms
FACILITIES.....................................Bar, Restaurant,
Rooftop terrace bar
GOOD TO KNOW.............................Near Deutsches Museum
RECOMMENDED FOR...............................Family friendly

"Close to the Deutsches Museum and right on the Munich food market. Perfect for a weekend."—Gert Wingård

Recommended by: Ben Duckworth, Hassell; Gert Wingård, Wingårdhs

RUBY LILLY HOTEL

Dachauer Strasse 37
Munich
Bavaria 80335
Germany
+49 89954570320
ruby-hotels.com

CREDIT CARDS..Accepted
PRICE...Mid-range
TYPE..Hotel
ACCOMMODATION...174 Rooms
FACILITIES..........................Bar, Rooftop terrace bar
GOOD TO KNOW..No pets
RECOMMENDED FOR..Urban

A modern hotel with light, bright rooms affording stunning city views, Ruby Lilly is just a stone's throw from many of Munich's top locations, including Königsplatz. The Rooftop terrace view is a panoramic spectacular.

Recommended by: Phillippe Fouché, SAOTA

BERLIN: SEE PAGES 238–241

BLEICHE RESORT & SPA

Bleichestrasse 16
Burg
Brandenburg 03096
Germany
+49 35603620
bleiche.de

CREDIT CARDS...Not accepted
PRICE...Mid-range
TYPE..Hotel
ACCOMMODATION.............................98 Rooms and Suites
FACILITIES..Bar, Gym,
Indoor and outdoor swimming pools,
8 Restaurants, Sauna, Spa,
Steam room, Wellness bath
GOOD TO KNOW......................Bicycle rentals, Child friendly,
Payment only by cash
or debit card at hotel
RECOMMENDED FOR..Spa

"A fabulous setting in the watery Spreewald landscape. Many treatments and massages on offer, and incredibly delicious meals—that's without even trying its gourmet restaurant."—Matthias Sauerbruch and Louisa Hutton

Recommended by: Matthias Sauerbruch and Louisa Hutton, Sauerbruch Hutton

THE WESTIN HAMBURG
Platz der Deutschen Einheit 2
Hafencity
Hamburg 20457
Germany
+49 408000100
marriott.com

CREDIT CARDS..Accepted
PRICE...Mid-range
TYPE..Hotel
ACCOMMODATION...................................244 Rooms and Suites
FACILITIES........................Bar, Gym, Indoor swimming pool,
Restaurant, Spa
GOOD TO KNOW.................................Child and pet friendly
RECOMMENDED FOR..Wish I'd designed

A landmark of the city skyline, the Westin Hamburg is
a sleek and modern hotel that is well-suited for business
travelers and holiday-makers alike. Rooms are chic and
spacious, and all benefit from the hotel chain's trademark
Heavenly beds and showers, for the ultimate night's sleep.

Recommended by: Yu-lin Chen, MAYU Architects+

EMPIRE RIVERSIDE HOTEL
Bernhard-Nocht-Strasse 97
St.Pauli
Hamburg 20359
Germany
+49 40311190
empire-riverside.de

CREDIT CARDS..Accepted
PRICE...Mid-range
TYPE..Hotel
ACCOMMODATION..............................,.................286 Rooms
FACILITIES..Bar, Gym, Restaurant,
Rooftop terrace bar,
Sauna, Spa, Steam room
GOOD TO KNOW...Pet friendly
RECOMMENDED FOR...Urban

Recommended by: Thomas Ruus, Friis & Moltke Architects

HOTEL NIZZA
Elbestrasse 10
Bahnhofsviertel
Frankfurt
Hesse 60329
Germany
+49 692425380
hotelnizza.de

CREDIT CARDS..Accept
PRICE...Low-c
TYPE..Bed and Breakf
ACCOMMODATION.......................................26 Roo
FACILITIES...............................Bar, Rooftop terrace
GOOD TO KNOW................................Child and pet frien
RECOMMENDED FOR....................................Where I

"An old building, where all the rooms are different. It's not
renovated to death, and it's good value."
—Michael Schumacher

Recommended by: Michael Schumacher, Schneider
+ Schumacher

LIBERTINE LINDENBERG
Frankensteiner Strasse 20
Sachsenhausen
Frankfurt
Hesse 60594
Germany
+49 6966161550
das-lindenberg.de

CREDIT CARDS..Accept
PRICE...Mid-rar
TYPE..Apartment ho
ACCOMMODATION.......................................27 Roo
FACILITIES..Bar, G
GOOD TO KNOW......................................Bicycle renta
Shared cooking facilit
RECOMMENDED FOR.............................All-time favor

Recommended by: Anne Kaestle, Duplex Architekten

HOTEL KLEMM

Kapellenstrasse 9
Wiesbaden
Hesse 65193
Germany
+49 6115820
hotel-klemm.de

CREDIT CARDS	Accepted
PRICE	Low-cost
TYPE	Bed and Breakfast
ACCOMMODATION	63 Rooms
FACILITIES	Breakfast bar
GOOD TO KNOW	Child and pet friendly
RECOMMENDED FOR	Urban

"The city has a very strong aristocratic character; this small hotel is its condensed version."—Zsolt Gunther

Recommended by: Zsolt Gunther, 3H Architecture

GRAND HOTEL HEILIGENDAMM

Prof.-Dr.-Vogel-Strasse 6
Rostock
Mecklenburg-Vorpommern 18209
Germany
+49 382037400
grandhotel-heiligendamm.de

CREDIT CARDS	Accepted
PRICE	Mid-range
TYPE	Hotel
ACCOMMODATION	199 Rooms and Suites
FACILITIES	Bar, Gym, Indoor swimming pool, Outdoor restaurant, Sauna, Spa, Yoga
GOOD TO KNOW	Babysitting, Pet friendly, Valet parking
RECOMMENDED FOR	Where I live

"This is all about the location on Germany's coast—take fantastic breezy beach walks in both directions, enjoying the sand dunes and mature beech trees. It also has an excellent small restaurant."—Matthias Sauerbruch and Louisa Hutton

Recommended by: Matthias Sauerbruch and Louisa Hutton, Sauerbruch Hutton

RELAIS & CHÂTEAUX SCHLOSSHOTEL BURG SCHLITZ

Burg Schlitz 2
Rostock
Mecklenburg-Vorpommern 17166, Germany
+49 399612700
burg-schlitz.de

CREDIT CARDS	Accepted
PRICE	Mid-range
TYPE	Hotel
ACCOMMODATION	20 Rooms and Suites
FACILITIES	Bar, Indoor swimming pool, 2 Restaurants, Sauna, Spa, Steam room
GOOD TO KNOW	Child friendly
RECOMMENDED FOR	Countryside

Recommended by: Uwe Schmidt-Hess, Patalab Architecture

INNSIDE DÜSSELDORF SEESTERN

Niederkasseler Lohweg 18a
Düsseldorf
North Rhine-Westphalia 40547, Germany
+49 211522990
melia.com

CREDIT CARDS	Accepted
PRICE	Low-cost
TYPE	Hotel
ACCOMMODATION	126 Rooms
FACILITIES	Bar, Gym, Restaurant, Sauna, Spa
GOOD TO KNOW	Child and pet friendly
RECOMMENDED FOR	Wish I'd designed

Recommended by: Michael Schumacher, Schneider + Schumacher

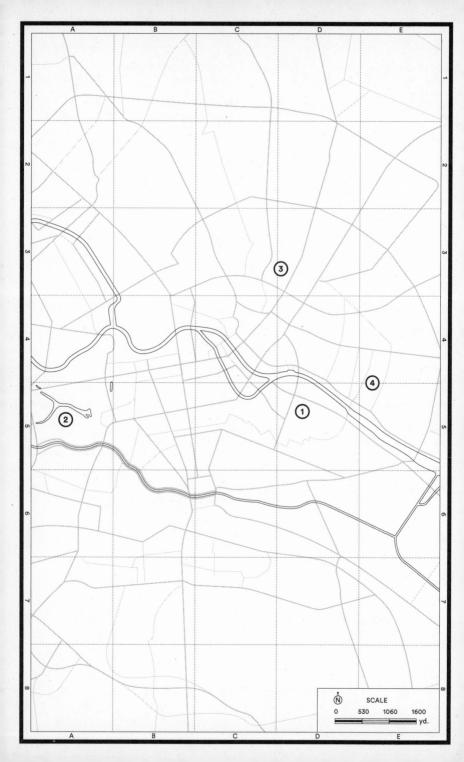

BERLIN

CASA CAMPER
Weinmeisterstrasse 1
Mitte, Berlin 10178
+49 3020003410
casacamper.com

CREDIT CARDS	Accepted
PRICE	Mid-range
TYPE	Hotel
ACCOMMODATION	54 Rooms
FACILITIES	Bar, Gym, Rooftop terrace bar
GOOD TO KNOW	Child friendly, No pets
RECOMMENDED FOR	Urban

Recommended by: Yu-lin Chen, MAYU Architects+

DAS STUE
Drakestrasse 1
Mitte, Berlin 10787
+49 303117220
das-stue.com

CREDIT CARDS	Accepted
PRICE	Mid-range
TYPE	Hotel
ACCOMMODATION	78 Rooms and Suites
FACILITIES	Bar, Gym, Outdoor restaurant, 2 Restaurants, Sauna, Spa
GOOD TO KNOW	Park setting, Pet friendly
RECOMMENDED FOR	Best-kept secret, Where I live

Recommended by: Johanna Meyer-Grohbrügge, Meyer-Grohbrügge; Uwe Schmidt-Hess, Patalab Architecture; Maria Warner Wong, WOW Architects | Warner Wong Design

HOTEL ADLON KEMPINSKI BERLIN
Unter den Linden 77
Mitte, Berlin 10117
+49 3022610
kempinski.com

CREDIT CARDS	Accepted
PRICE	Blow-out
TYPE	Hotel
ACCOMMODATION	385 Rooms and Suites
FACILITIES	Bar, Gym, Indoor swimming pool, 3 Restaurants, Sauna, Spa, Steam room
GOOD TO KNOW	Pet friendly
RECOMMENDED FOR	Family friendly, Luxury, Urban

"Multi-zoned room layout in a perfect location near the Brandenberg Gate."—Ken Yeang

Recommended by: Peter Eisenman, Eisenman Architects; Christian de Portzamparc, 2Portzamparc; Ken Yeang, Hamzah & Yeang

HOTEL ROSSI
Botschaft für Kinder, Lehrter Strasse 66
Mitte
Berlin 10557
+49 30330993800
hotel-rossi.de

CREDIT CARDS	Accepted
PRICE	Low-cost
TYPE	Hotel
ACCOMMODATION	28 Rooms
FACILITIES	Restaurant, Rooftop terrace bar
GOOD TO KNOW	Child and pet friendly
RECOMMENDED FOR	Budget

"A hotel with a social message, good design, and simple style. It is luxury at a low-cost price."—Zsolt Gunther

Recommended by: Zsolt Gunther, 3H Architecture

SHERATON BERLIN GRAND HOTEL ESPLANADE
Lützowufer 15
Mitte
Berlin 10785
+49 30254780
esplanade.de

CREDIT CARDS	Accepted
PRICE	Mid-range
TYPE	Hotel
ACCOMMODATION	394 Rooms and Suites
FACILITIES	Bar, Gym, Indoor swimming pool, Restaurant
GOOD TO KNOW	Bicycle rentals, Pet friendly
RECOMMENDED FOR	Urban

Considered Germany's first design hotel, it has hosted an impressive list of famous guests since it opened in 1988.

Recommended by: Helmut Jahn, Jahn

25HOURS HOTEL BIKINI BERLIN

Budapester Strasse 40
Tiergarten
Berlin 10787
+49 301202210
25hours-hotels.com

CREDIT CARDS	Accepted
PRICE	Mid-range
TYPE	Hotel
ACCOMMODATION	149 Rooms
FACILITIES	Bar, Gym, Restaurant, Sauna
GOOD TO KNOW	Pet friendly
RECOMMENDED FOR	Urban

"Great location and attitude."—Ben Duckworth

Recommended by: Ben Duckworth, Hassell; Jean-Paul Viguier, Jean-Paul Viguier et Associés

WALDORF ASTORIA BERLIN

Hardenbergstrasse 28
Tiergarten
Berlin 10623
+49 308140000
waldorfastoria.hilton.com

CREDIT CARDS	Accepted
PRICE	High-end
TYPE	Hotel
ACCOMMODATION	232 Rooms and Suites
FACILITIES	2 Bars, Gym, Indoor swimming pool, Restaurant, Sauna, Spa, Steam room
GOOD TO KNOW	Pet friendly, Valet parking
RECOMMENDED FOR	Worth the travel

The luxurious, five-star Waldorf Astoria Berlin is sleek and modern, with design features inspired by the Art Deco glamour of the original Waldorf Astoria. Facilities include a Guerlain spa and four elegant dining-and-bar experiences.

Recommended by: François Valentiny, Valentiny HVP Architects

SOHO HOUSE

Torstrasse 1
Kollwitzkiez
Berlin 10119
+49 304050440
sohohouseberlin.com

CREDIT CARDS	Accepted
PRICE	Mid-range
TYPE	Members' club
ACCOMMODATION	89 Apartments, Lofts, and Rooms
FACILITIES	Bar, Gym, Outdoor swimming pool, 3 Restaurants, Rooftop terrace bar, Sauna, Spa
GOOD TO KNOW	No pets
RECOMMENDED FOR	All-time favorite, Where I live

Recommended by: Jürgen Mayer H., J. Mayer H. und Partner, Architekten; Kateryna Zuieva, AKZ Architectura

MICHELBERGER HOTEL

Warschauer Strasse 39-40
Friedrichshain
Berlin 10243
+49 3029778590
michelbergerhotel.com

CREDIT CARDS	Accepted
PRICE	Mid-range
TYPE	Hotel
ACCOMMODATION	134 Rooms and Suites
FACILITIES	Bar, Restaurant, Sauna, Spa
GOOD TO KNOW	Pet friendly
RECOMMENDED FOR	Urban

"Cool, no-fuss design with an urban vibe. Nice rooms, nice location, nice restaurant, and nice bar."—Martin Krogh and Martin Laursen

Recommended by: Flavio Albanese, ASA Studio; Sam Chermayeff, Meyer-Grohbrügge & Chermayeff; Karl Fournier and Olivier Marty, Studio KO; Martin Krogh, Martin Laursen, and Anders Lonka, ADEPT; Cristian Santandreu, A2arquitectos

HOTEL LA CASA DEL CALIFA
Plaza de España 16
Cádiz
Andalusia 11150
Spain
+34 956447730
califavejer.com

CREDIT CARDS..Accepted
PRICE...Low-cost
TYPE...Townhouse hotel
ACCOMMODATION....................................20 Rooms and Suites
FACILITIES..Bar, Restaurant
GOOD TO KNOW...No pets
RECOMMENDED FOR...Urban

"A quiet, ancient house subtly camouflaged in the Old Town."
—Antonio G. Liñán

Recommended by: Antonio G. Liñán, SV60 Cordón &
Liñán Arquitectos

PARADOR DE CÁDIZ
Avenida Duque de Nájera 9
Cádiz
Andalusia 11002
Spain
+34 956226905
parador.es

CREDIT CARDS..Accepted
PRICE..Mid-range
TYPE..Parador
ACCOMMODATION...124 Rooms
FACILITIES....................Bar, Gym, Outdoor swimming pool,
2 Restaurants, Sauna, Spa
GOOD TO KNOW.................................Bicycle rentals, No pets
RECOMMENDED FOR...Urban

"Cádiz is a stunning city, layered with history and diverse
cultural influences. The hotel is perfectly located, and the
rooms are beautiful with fantastic views."—Stephen Barrett

Recommended by: Stephen Barrett, Rogers Stirk Harbour
+ Partners

PARADOR DE GRANADA
Calle Real de la Alhambra S/N
Granada
Andalusia 18009
Spain
+34 958221440
parador.es

CREDIT CARDS..Accepted
PRICE..Mid-range
TYPE..Parador
ACCOMMODATION...40 Rooms
FACILITIES..Bar, Restaurant
GOOD TO KNOW..........................Child friendly, No pets
RECOMMENDED FOR..............................All-time favorite,
Worth the travel

"The hotel occupies a former monastery within the grounds
of the Alhambra UNESCO World Heritage Site. Guests can
savor the sublime Moorish architecture, gardens, and
fountains throughout the day, but also in the evening after
visitors have left."—Buzz Yudell

Recommended by: Alfredo Payá Benedito, Noname29;
Carlos Ferrater, OAB; Buzz Yudell, Moore Ruble Yudell

HOTEL ALFONSO XIII,
A LUXURY COLLECTION HOTEL
Calle San Fernando 2
Seville
Andalusia 41004
Spain
+34 954917000
marriott.com

CREDIT CARDS..Accepted
PRICE...High-end
TYPE..Hotel
ACCOMMODATION...148 Rooms
FACILITIES....................Bar, Gym, Outdoor swimming pool,
2 Restaurants, Sauna
GOOD TO KNOW...................................Bicycle rentals,
Child and pet friendly, Valet parking
RECOMMENDED FOR...............................Luxury, Urban

"Incredible Moorish architecture, luxury accommodation,
and fine dining in a great location."—Claudia Urdaneta

Recommended by: Fernando Sordo Madaleno,
Sordo Madaleno; Emilio Tuñón, Tuñón Arquitectos;
Claudia Urdaneta, NMD NOMADAS

HOTEL MERCER SEVILLA

Calle Castelar 26
Seville
Andalusia 41001
Spain
+34 954223004
mercersevilla.com

CREDIT CARDS..Accepted
PRICE...High-end
TYPE...Hotel
ACCOMMODATION....................................12 Rooms and Suites
FACILITIES................................Bar, Outdoor swimming pool,
Restaurant, Rooftop terrace bar
GOOD TO KNOW...................................Child friendly, No pets
RECOMMENDED FOR..................................Where I live

[Cruz y Ortiz Arquitectos were the executive architects on this hotel.]

Recommended by: Antonio G. Liñán, SV60 Cordón & Liñán Arquitectos; Antonio Ortiz, Cruz y Ortiz Arquitectos

GRAN HOTEL BALNEARIO DE PANTICOSA

Carretera Balneario km10
Huesca
Aragon 22661
Spain
+34 974487161
panticosa.com

CREDIT CARDS..Accepted
PRICE...Low-cost
TYPE...Hotel
ACCOMMODATION..250 Rooms
FACILITIES........................Bar, Gym, Indoor swimming pool,
Restaurant, Spa, Thermal bath
GOOD TO KNOW..........................Child friendly, Free parking
RECOMMENDED FOR..............................Mountains, Spa

"Next to a spa designed by Rafael Moneo, this is a great location for setting out on a hike in the mountains (and then recovering afterwards)."—Stephen Barrett

Recommended by: Stephen Barrett, Rogers Stirk Harbour + Partners; Belén Moneo and Jeffrey Brock, Moneo Brock; Emilio Tuñón, Tuñón Arquitectos

LA TORRE DEL VISCO

Partida Torre del Visco S/N
Teruel
Aragon 44587, Spain
+34 978769015
torredelvisco.com

CREDIT CARDS..Accepted
PRICE..Mid-range
TYPE...Hotel
ACCOMMODATION....................................17 Rooms and Suites
FACILITIES................................Bar, Outdoor swimming pool,
Restaurant, Wood-burning fireplace
GOOD TO KNOW..........................Bicycle rentals, Free parking
RECOMMENDED FOR..................................Countryside

"La Torre is in the middle of nowhere. You first drive on a highway, then a local road, and finally a forest track. The effort is worth it: a library of over 3,000 books; an honor system for wine; and a large table laden with good things to eat. Luxury in remote, primitive vastness makes for a satisfying contrast."—Jack Diamond

Recommended by: Jack Diamond, Diamond Schmitt

CAP ROCAT

Carretera d'Enderrocat S/N
Cala Blava
Mallorca
Balearic Islands 07609, Spain
+34 971747878
caprocat.com

CREDIT CARDS..Accepted
PRICE...Blow-out
TYPE..Fortress hotel
ACCOMMODATION....................................30 Rooms and Suites
FACILITIES....................Bar, Gym, Outdoor swimming pool,
2 Restaurants, Sauna,
Spa, Steam room, Yoga
GOOD TO KNOW..........................Bicycle rentals, Valet parking
RECOMMENDED FOR..........................All-time favorite, Beach,
Luxury, Wish I'd designed,
Worth the travel

"Cap Rocat is a rare hotel experience. The old fortress has been carefully restored with inventive design solutions and quality materials. Its ingenious transformation is unique and there are exceptional sea views from the rooms, restaurant, and infinity pool."—Kim Herforth Nielsen

Recommended by: Bernard Dubois, Bernard Dubois Architects; Rafael de La-Hoz Castanys, Rafael de La-Hoz Arquitectos; Kim Herforth Nielsen, 3XN; Tavis Wright, Dos Architects

HOTEL PLETA DE MAR
Via de les Cales S/N
Canyamel
Mallorca
Balearic Islands 07580
Spain
+34 871515340
pletademar.com

CREDIT CARDS	Accepted
PRICE	High-end
TYPE	Hotel
ACCOMMODATION	30 Suites
FACILITIES	Bar, Gym, Golf, Outdoor restaurant and swimming pool, Sauna, Spa, Steam room, Yoga
GOOD TO KNOW	Boats available, Free parking
RECOMMENDED FOR	Beach, All-time favorite

Recommended by: Tavis Wright, Dos Architects

BELMOND LA RESIDENCIA
Son Canals S/N
Deià
Mallorca
Balearic Islands 07179
Spain
+34 971639011
belmond.com

CREDIT CARDS	Accepted
PRICE	High-end
TYPE	Hotel
ACCOMMODATION	72 Rooms and Suites
FACILITIES	Bar, Gym, Indoor and outdoor swimming pools, 2 Restaurants, Sauna, Spa, Steam room
GOOD TO KNOW	Babysitting
RECOMMENDED FOR	Luxury

Mallorca's creative soul permeates Belmond La Residencia, which blends into the surrounding Tramuntana Mountains and picturesque village of Deià. In addition to crafted antiques and furnishings in the rooms, it has more than 750 works from local painters, and a gallery that hosts exhibitions and performances throughout the year.

Recommended by: Kelly Hoppen, Kelly Hoppen Interiors

AGROTURISMO S'OLIVAR
Carretera Al Mar km93 5
Estellencs
Mallorca
Balearic Islands 07192, Spain
+34 629266035
fincaolivar.org

CREDIT CARDS	Accepted but not Amex
PRICE	Low-cost
TYPE	Finca
ACCOMMODATION	4 Cottages
FACILITIES	Outdoor swimming pool
GOOD TO KNOW	No pets, Self-catering
RECOMMENDED FOR	Countryside

Recommended by: Stephen Barrett, Rogers Stirk Harbour + Partners

HM BALANGUERA
Calle Balanguera 37
Palma de Mallorca
Mallorca
Balearic Islands 07011, Spain
+34 971456152
hmbalanguera.com

CREDIT CARDS	Accepted
PRICE	Low-cost
TYPE	Hotel
ACCOMMODATION	40 Rooms
FACILITIES	Bar, Outdoor swimming pool, Restaurant, Rooftop terrace bar
GOOD TO KNOW	No pets
RECOMMENDED FOR	Where I live

Recommended by: Cristian Santandreu, A2arquitectos

HOTEL CORT
Plaça de Cort 11
Palma de Mallorca
Mallorca
Balearic Islands 07001, Spain
+34 971213333
hotelcort.com

CREDIT CARDS	Accepted
PRICE	Mid-range
TYPE	Hotel
ACCOMMODATION	16 Rooms and Suites
FACILITIES	Bar, Outdoor swimming pool, Restaurant
GOOD TO KNOW	Babysitting
RECOMMENDED FOR	Urban

"Eclectic style, food, location, and staff."—Tavis Wright

Recommended by: Tavis Wright, Dos Architects

SON BRULL HOTEL & SPA
Carretera Palma a Pollença km50
Pollença
Mallorca
Balearic Islands 07460
Spain
+34 971535353
sonbrull.com

CREDIT CARDS	Accepted
PRICE	High-end
TYPE	Hotel
ACCOMMODATION	27 Suites and Villas
FACILITIES	Bar, Gym, 2 Restaurants, Sauna, Spa, Steam room, Yoga
GOOD TO KNOW	Bicycle rentals, Child friendly
RECOMMENDED FOR	Beach, Countryside

"This renovated eighteenth-century Jesuit Monastery is nestled in the foothills of northern Mallorca's Serra de Tramuntana. It is also close to the island's exquisite coves and sandy beaches."—Belén Moneo and Jeffrey Brock

Recommended by: Belén Moneo and Jeffrey Brock, Moneo Brock; Emilio Tuñón, Tuñón Arquitectos; Tavis Wright, Dos Architects

HOTEL ESPLÉNDIDO
Es Traves 5
Port de Sóller
Mallorca
Balearic Islands 07108
Spain
+34 971631850
esplendidohotel.com

CREDIT CARDS	Accepted
PRICE	Mid-range
TYPE	Hotel
ACCOMMODATION	74 Rooms
FACILITIES	Bar, Gym, Indoor and outdoor swimming pools, Restaurant, Sauna, Spa, Steam room, Yoga
GOOD TO KNOW	Bicycle rentals, Child friendly
RECOMMENDED FOR	Beach

"Light, airy, and well-designed with a view of the fishing village's charming bay."—Grace Keeley

Recommended by: Grace Keeley, GKMP Architects

HOTEL CASTELL DELS HAMS
Carretera Manacor km10
Porto Cristo
Mallorca
Balearic Islands 07680, Spain
+34 971820007
castellhotels.com

CREDIT CARDS	Accepted but not Amex
PRICE	Mid-range
TYPE	Hotel
ACCOMMODATION	280 Rooms
FACILITIES	Bar, Gym, Indoor and outdoor swimming pools, Restaurant, Sauna, Spa
GOOD TO KNOW	On-site disco
RECOMMENDED FOR	Family friendly

Recommended by: Cristian Santandreu, A2arquitectos

SON GENER
Carretera Ma-4031 km3
Son Servera
Mallorca
Balearic Islands 07550
Spain
+34 971183612
songener.com

CREDIT CARDS	Accepted but not Amex
PRICE	Mid-range
TYPE	Finca
ACCOMMODATION	15 Rooms
FACILITIES	Golf, Indoor and outdoor swimming pools, 2 Restaurants, Sauna, Spa, Yoga
GOOD TO KNOW	Free parking
RECOMMENDED FOR	Where I live

"Once a rustic eighteenth-century farm house surrounded by an exceptional environment, the building has been transformed into a luminous and rarefied space loaded with great art and antiques. The project is a celebration of the island's essence."—Belén Moneo and Jeffrey Brock

Recommended by: Belén Moneo and Jeffrey Brock, Moneo Brock

HOTEL TORRALBENC
Carretera Maó Cala'n Porter km10
Menorca
Balearic Islands 07730
Spain
+34 971377211
torralbenc.com

CREDIT CARDS...Accepted
PRICE...Mid-range
TYPE..Country estate hotel
ACCOMMODATION...............................27 Cottages and Rooms
FACILITIES.....................................Bar, Outdoor restaurant and
swimming pool, Spa
GOOD TO KNOW..Yoga retreats
RECOMMENDED FOR............................Beach, Best-kept secret

Torralbenc is a charming and serene collection of white-washed, carefully restored farm buildings dating from the nineteenth and early twentieth century. The restaurant is advised by Michelin-star chef Gorka Txapartegi and combines Basque and Minorcan culinary tradition with locally sourced produce, including Torralbenc's own wines. Torralbenc also runs yoga retreats.

Recommended by: Pedro Rica and Marta Urtasun, Mecanismo

HOTEL AKELARRE
Padre Orcolaga 56
San Sebastian
Gipuzkoa
Basque Country 20008
Spain
+34 943311208
akelarre.net

CREDIT CARDS...Accepted
PRICE...High-end
TYPE..Hotel
ACCOMMODATION.......................................22 Rooms
FACILITIES...Gym, Restaurant, Sauna,
Spa, Steam room
GOOD TO KNOW......................................Free parking
RECOMMENDED FOR...............All-time favorite, Countryside,
Spa, Where I live, Worth the travel

"It has a fabulous spa, a three Michelin-starred restaurant, and incredible views."—Pedro Rica and Marta Urtasun

Recommended by: Joaquín Pérez-Goicoechea, AGi Architects; Pedro Rica and Marta Urtasun, Mecanismo

HOTEL MIRÓ
Alameda Mazarredo 77
Bilbao
Basque Country 48009, Spain
+34 946611880
mirohotelbilbao.com

CREDIT CARDS...Accepted
PRICE...Low-cost
TYPE..Hotel
ACCOMMODATION.......................................50 Rooms
FACILITIES....................Bar, Gym, Sauna, Spa, Steam room
GOOD TO KNOW.......................Bicycle rentals, Child friendly
RECOMMENDED FOR..Budget

"Smart room designs for rooms with non-expensive materials and details—they aren't big and fancy, but they are chic and classy."—Hasan Çalışlar

Recommended by: Hasan Çalışlar, Erginoğlu & Çalışlar

HOTEL MÉDANO
Paseo Picacho 2
Tenerife
Canary Islands 38612, Spain
+34 922177000
medano.es

CREDIT CARDS.....................................Accepted but not Amex
PRICE...Low-cost
TYPE..Hotel
ACCOMMODATION.......................................90 Rooms
FACILITIES...Bar, Restaurant
GOOD TO KNOW......................................Bicycle rentals
RECOMMENDED FOR..Budget

Recommended by: Carlos Ferrater, OAB

VILLA SLOW
San Roque de Riomiera
Cantabria 39728, Spain
+34 615298655
villaslow.com

CREDIT CARDS...Not accepted
PRICE...Mid-range
TYPE..House rental
ACCOMMODATION...1 Room
FACILITIES........................Hot tub, Wood-burning fireplace
GOOD TO KNOW..Self-catering
RECOMMENDED FOR....................................Mountains

Recommended by: Antonio Ortiz, Cruz y Ortiz Arquitectos

SAN GIL PLAZA
Plaza Maestro Haedo 5
Zamora
Castile and León 49003
Spain
+34 980048470
sangilplaza.es

CREDIT CARDS..Accepted
PRICE...Low-cost
TYPE...Hotel
ACCOMMODATION........................7 Rooms and Suites
FACILITIES..Free wifi
GOOD TO KNOW..Wine tasting
RECOMMENDED FOR..................................Worth the travel

The San Gil Plaza hotel is ideally situated for exploring the historic city of Zamora. The original townhouse building has rooms that are bright and modern, with furniture from designers such as Eero Saarinen and Arne Jacobsen. Contemporary Spanish artwork hangs on the walls of communal staircases and the hotel periodically organizes wine tastings.

<u>Recommended by:</u> Rafael de La-Hoz Castanys, Rafael de La-Hoz Arquitectos

BARCELONA: SEE PAGES 252–257

LES COLS PAVELLONS
Avinguda de les Cols 2
Girona
Catalonia 17800
Spain
+34 699813817
lescolspavellons.com

CREDIT CARDS..Accepted
PRICE..High-end
TYPE...Hotel
ACCOMMODATION...5 Pavilions
FACILITIES..Restaurant
GOOD TO KNOW....................Free parking, No pets
RECOMMENDED FOR..............Best-kept secret, Countryside, Eco-conscious

"This hotel is an experience of the senses; it demonstrates the beauty of emptiness."—Alfredo Payá Benedito

<u>Recommended by:</u> Alfredo Payá Benedito, Noname29; Carlos Ferrater, OAB; Nabil Gholam, Nabil Gholam Architects; Stéphane Rasselet, Naturehumaine; Fran Silvestre, Fran Silvestre Arquitectos; Emilio Tuñón, Tuñón Arquitectos

HOSTAL EMPURIES
Platja de Portitxol S/N
Girona
Catalonia 17130
Spain
+34 972770207
hostalempuries.com

CREDIT CARDS..Accepted
PRICE..Mid-range
TYPE...Hotel
ACCOMMODATION......................55 Rooms and Suites
FACILITIES..Bar, Gym,
Indoor and outdoor swimming pools,
2 Restaurants, Spa, Yoga
GOOD TO KNOW................................Child friendly
RECOMMENDED FOR...Beach

"Perfectly located in a small cave, next to some of Europe's greatest Roman ruins, this is a stylish eco hotel that serves brilliant food and has a great spa."—Stephen Barrett

<u>Recommended by:</u> Stephen Barrett, Rogers Stirk Harbour + Partners

RAFAELHOTELES BY LA PLETA
Carretera de Baqueira a Beret, Cota 1
Lérida
Catalonia 25598
Spain
+34 973645550
lapleta.com

CREDIT CARDS..Accepted
PRICE..Mid-range
TYPE...Hotel
ACCOMMODATION......................69 Rooms and Suites
FACILITIES.................................Bar, Cigar bar, Gym,
Indoor swimming pool,
Restaurant, Sauna, Spa
GOOD TO KNOW..................Babysitting, Valet parking
RECOMMENDED FOR.......................................Mountains

Rafaelhoteles by La Pleta is a luxury ski and spa hotel in the Spanish Pyrenees with plenty of facilities to keep avid sporty types and après-skiers alike entertained. Dining ranges from Catalan cuisine to sushi, and activities include helicopter tours, and food and wine tastings.

<u>Recommended by:</u> Tavis Wright, Dos Architects

ATRIO RESTAURANT HOTEL

Plaza de San Mateo 1
Cáceres
Extremadura 10003
Spain
+34 927242928
restauranteatrio.com

CREDIT CARDS..Accepted
PRICE...High-end
TYPE..Hotel
ACCOMMODATION......................................14 Rooms and Suites
FACILITIES.............................Bar, Outdoor swimming pool,
Restaurant
GOOD TO KNOW...............................Babysitting, Valet parking
RECOMMENDED FOR........All-time favorite, Best-kept secret,
Countryside, Wish I'd designed,
Worth the travel

"The beautiful contemporary intervention by Mansilla and
Tuñón enhances the monastery-like quality of the existing
stone building—it's a delightful retreat."—Cino Zucchi

Recommended by: Angela García de Paredes, Paredes
Pedrosa Arquitectos; Rafael de La-Hoz Castanys,
Rafael de La-Hoz Arquitectos; Joaquín Pérez-Goicoechea,
AGi Architects; Emilio Tuñón, Tuñón Arquitectos;
Cino Zucchi, CZA

LA HOSPEDERÍA CONVENTUAL SIERRA DE GATA

Camino del Convento 39
Cáceres
Extremadura 10892
Spain
+34 927144279
hospederiasdeextremadura.es

CREDIT CARDS..Accepted
PRICE..Low-cost
TYPE..Hotel
ACCOMMODATION......................................30 Rooms and Suites
FACILITIES..........................Gym, Outdoor swimming pool,
Restaurant, Sauna, Spa
GOOD TO KNOW..Pet friendly
RECOMMENDED FOR...Budget

La Hospedería, a sensitively restored fifteenth-century
Franciscan convent, has simple rooms, yet its remote
location and spa facilities make this hotel an ideal place
for disconnecting from the outside world.

Recommended by: Joaquín Pérez-Goicoechea,
AGi Architects

BARCELÓ TORRE DE MADRID

Plaza de España 18
Malasaña
Madrid 28008
Spain
+34 915242399
barcelo.com

CREDIT CARDS..Accepted
PRICE...Mid-range
TYPE..Hotel
ACCOMMODATION....................................258 Rooms and Suites
FACILITIES............................Bar, Indoor swimming pool,
Restaurant, Sauna, Spa
GOOD TO KNOW..Babysitting
RECOMMENDED FOR..............Where I live, Wish I'd designed

Barceló Torre de Madrid is situated in an iconic high-rise
overlooking the Plaza de España. Rooms are stylish with
cutting-edge technology. The hotel also has a large
Wellness Area.

Recommended by: Belén Moneo and Jeffrey Brock,
Moneo Brock; Joaquín Pérez-Goicoechea, AGi architects

SLEEP'N ATOCHA

Doctor Drumen 4
Atocha
Madrid 28012
Spain
+34 915399807
sleepnatocha.com

CREDIT CARDS.....................................Accepted but not Amex
PRICE..Low-cost
TYPE..Hotel
ACCOMMODATION...80 Rooms
FACILITIES...Rooftop bar
GOOD TO KNOW..Breakfast buffet
RECOMMENDED FOR...Budget

"Excellent architectural and interior design in a budget
hotel."—Rafael de La-Hoz Castanys

Recommended by: Rafael de La-Hoz Castanys, Rafael de
La-Hoz Arquitectos

HOTEL PUERTA AMÉRICA MADRID
Avenida de América 41
Prosperidad
Madrid 28002
Spain
+34 917445400
hotelpuertamerica.com

CREDIT CARDS...Accepted
PRICE...Mid-range
TYPE..Hotel
ACCOMMODATION........................315 Rooms and Suites
FACILITIES...3 bars, Cafe,
Outdoor Swimming Pool,
2 Restaurants
GOOD TO KNOW.............................Free parking (book direct)
RECOMMENDED FOR...Wish I'd designed

"Zaha Hadid's pure organic forms and integrated
systems are merged into biophilic shapes that morph
into a functional space. I love it. I wish I had designed it!"
—Eric Corey Freed

Recommended by: Eric Corey Freed, OrganicArchitect;
Cristian Santandreu, A2arquitectos; Dorin Stefan,
Dorin Stefan Birou de Arhitectura

HOTEL AIRE DE BARDENAS
Carretera de Ejea km1.5
Tudela
Navarre 31500
Spain
+34 948116666
airebardenas.com

CREDIT CARDS...Accepted
PRICE...High-end
TYPE..Hotel
ACCOMMODATION........................28 Bubbles, Cubes,
Rooms and Suites
FACILITIES...............................Bar, Outdoor swimming pool,
Restaurant
GOOD TO KNOW...No pets
RECOMMENDED FOR..............................Countryside, Desert,
Eco-conscious,
Luxury, Wish I'd designed,
Worth the travel

"The austerity of this peaceful, rural hotel is contemplative
and invigorating. The noise of the world seems far away,
and each room has a window onto the soothing landscape.
A marvelous stay, any time."—Carlos Jiménez

Recommended by: Paolo Brambilla, Calvi Brambilla;
Carlos Jiménez, Carlos Jiménez Studio; Rafael de La-Hoz

Castanys, Rafael de La-Hoz Arquitectos; Belén Moneo and
Jeffrey Brock, Moneo Brock; Antonio Ortiz, Cruz y Ortiz
Arquitectos; Angela García de Paredes, Paredes Pedrosa
Arquitectos; Joaquín Pérez-Goicoechea, AGi architects;
Stéphane Rasselet, Naturehumaine; Cristian Santandreu,
A2arquitectos; Fran Silvestre, Fran Silvestre Arquitectos;
Daniel Suduca and Thierry Mérillou, Suduca & Mérillou;
Emilio Tuñón, Tuñón Arquitectos; Claudia Urdaneta, NMD
NOMADAS; Artem Vakhrin, AKZ Architectura

VIVOOD LANDSCAPE HOTEL
Carretera Guadalest-Alcoy 10
Benimantell
Alicante
Valencia 03516
Spain
+34 966318585
vivood.com

CREDIT CARDS...Accepted
PRICE...Mid-range
TYPE..Hotel
ACCOMMODATION........................25 Suites and Villas
FACILITIES...............................Bar, Outdoor swimming pool,
Restaurant, Sauna, Spa,
Steam room, Yoga
GOOD TO KNOW.......................................Free parking
RECOMMENDED FOR.....................................Mountains

Recommended by: Fran Silvestre, Fran Silvestre Arquitectos

HOTEL MARQUÉS DE RISCAL, A LUXURY COLLECTION HOTEL, ELCIEGO
Calle Torrea 1
Álava
Basque Country 01340
Spain
+34 945180880
marriott.com

CREDIT CARDS...Accepted
PRICE...High-end
TYPE..Hotel
ACCOMMODATION........................43 Rooms and Suites
FACILITIES......................Bar, Gym, Indoor swimming pool,
2 Restaurants, Spa, Winery
GOOD TO KNOW.......................................Bicycle rental
RECOMMENDED FOR...............All-time favorite, Countryside,
Wish I'd designed

Recommended by: Emre Arolat, EAA; Emilio Tuñón, Tuñón
Arquitectos; Tavis Wright, Dos Architects

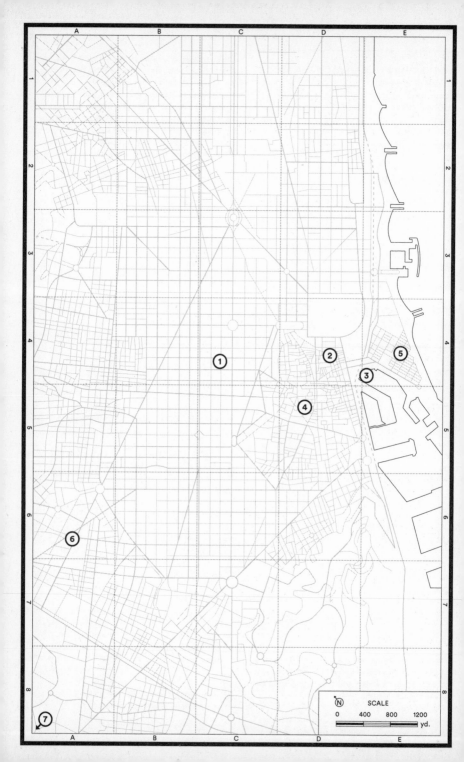

BARCELONA

CASA BONAY

Gran Via de les Corts Catalanes 700
Eixample
Barcelona 08008
+34 935458070
casabonay.com

CREDIT CARDS	Accepted
PRICE	Low-cost
TYPE	Hotel
ACCOMMODATION	67 Rooms
FACILITIES	Bar, 2 Restaurants, Rooftop terrace bar, Yoga
GOOD TO KNOW	Child and pet friendly
RECOMMENDED FOR	Budget

"It's budget but does not compromise on hospitality. The strong design balances the minimal service; the location is excellent, and it has a fantastic bar and restaurants."
—Ab Rogers

Recommended by: Ab Rogers, Ab Rogers Design

COTTON HOUSE HOTEL, AUTOGRAPH COLLECTION

Gran Via de les Corts Catalanes 670
Eixample
Barcelona 08010
+34 934505045
hotelcottonhouse.com

CREDIT CARDS	Accepted
PRICE	Mid-range
TYPE	Hotel
ACCOMMODATION	83 Rooms and Suites
FACILITIES	Bar, Gym, Outdoor restaurant, Restaurant, Spa
GOOD TO KNOW	Babysitting, Valet parking
RECOMMENDED FOR	Urban

"The interior of this hotel, an old cotton foundation HQ converted by Lazaro Rosa Violan, is stunning in every detail. The real showstopper is the original six-story suspended spiral staircase!"—Dieter Vander Velpen

Recommended by: Dieter Vander Velpen, Dieter Vander Velpen Architects

HOTEL CASA FUSTER

Passeig de Gràcia 132
Eixample
Barcelona 08008
+34 932553000
hotelcasafuster.com

CREDIT CARDS	Accepted
PRICE	Mid-range
TYPE	Hotel
ACCOMMODATION	105 Rooms and Suites
FACILITIES	Bar, Outdoor swimming pool, Restaurant, Rooftop terrace bar
GOOD TO KNOW	No pets, On-site jazz club
RECOMMENDED FOR	Urban

"Amazing Modernist building by Lluís Domènech i Montaner, with a relaxed, elegant lobby and cafe."—Claudia Urdaneta

Recommended by: Claudia Urdaneta, NMD NOMADAS

HOTEL CRAM

Aribau 54
Eixample
Barcelona 08011
+34 932167700
hotelcram.com

CREDIT CARDS	Accepted
PRICE	Mid-range
TYPE	Hotel
ACCOMMODATION	67 Rooms and Suites
FACILITIES	Bar, Outdoor swimming pool, 2 Restaurants, Rooftop terrace bar
GOOD TO KNOW	Chef master classes, No pets
RECOMMENDED FOR	Urban

Recommended by: Robert Konieczny, KWK Promes

HOTEL PRAKTIK RAMBLA

Rambla de Catalunya 27
Eixample
Barcelona 08007
+34 933436690
hotelpraktikrambla.com

CREDIT CARDS	Accepted
PRICE	Low-cost
TYPE	Hotel
ACCOMMODATION	43 Rooms
FACILITIES	Bar, Outdoor showers
GOOD TO KNOW	Bicycle rentals, No pets
RECOMMENDED FOR	Best-kept secret, Urban

Hotel Praktik Rambla is a stylishly restored townhouse hotel situated on Barcelona's famous Rambla Catalunya. Original elements, including mosaic floors, have been lovingly preserved, and its outdoor terrace is a calm space in which to unwind.

Recommended by: Paolo Brambilla, Calvi Brambilla; Dieter Vander Velpen, Dieter Vander Velpen Architects

MANDARIN ORIENTAL, BARCELONA
Passeig de Gràcia 38-40
Eixample
Barcelona 08007
+34 931518888
mandarinoriental.com

CREDIT CARDS	Accepted
PRICE	High-end
TYPE	Hotel
ACCOMMODATION	144 Penthouses, Rooms, and Suites
FACILITIES	Bar, Gym, Indoor swimming pool, 2 Restaurants, Rooftop terrace bar, Spa, Steam room
GOOD TO KNOW	Child friendly
RECOMMENDED FOR	Luxury, Urban, Where I live

Recommended by: Carlos Ferrater, OAB; Joaquín Pérez-Goicoechea, AGi Architects; Fran Silvestre, Fran Silvestre Arquitectos

YÖK CASA + CULTURA
Carrer de Trafalgar 39
Eixample
Barcelona 08010
+34 640625313
helloyok.com

CREDIT CARDS	Accepted
PRICE	Mid-range
TYPE	Apartment rental
ACCOMMODATION	3 Apartments
FACILITIES	Rooftop terrace
GOOD TO KNOW	No pets, Self-catering
RECOMMENDED FOR	Eco-conscious

"Refurbished traditional apartments with sustainable, locally produced furniture. Your water consumption is displayed in the corridor, which makes a great conversation piece." —Daniel Sundlin

Recommended by: Daniel Sundlin, Bjarke Ingels Group

YURBANN TRAFALGAR
Carrer de Trafalgar 30
Eixample
Barcelona 08010
+34 932680727
yurbbantrafalgar.com

CREDIT CARDS	Accepted
PRICE	Mid-range
TYPE	Hotel
ACCOMMODATION	56 Rooms and Suites
FACILITIES	Bar, Gym, Outdoor swimming pool, Restaurant, Rooftop terrace bar
GOOD TO KNOW	Bicycle rentals, Child friendly
RECOMMENDED FOR	Budget

"Beautiful interior design with gorgeous details like the Jules Wabbes lamps lining the hallway. And of course the Rooftop deck with a swimming pool and incredible views over Barcelona."—Dieter Vander Velpen

Recommended by: Rodrigo Carazo, Carazo Architecture; Dieter Vander Velpen, Dieter Vander Velpen Architects

YURBBAN PASSAGE HOTEL & SPA
Carrer de Trafalgar 26
Eixample
Barcelona 08010
+34 938828977
yurbbanpassage.com

CREDIT CARDS	Accepted
PRICE	Mid-range
TYPE	Hotel
ACCOMMODATION	59 Rooms
FACILITIES	Bar, Gym, Indoor and outdoor swimming pools, Restaurant, Rooftop terrace bar, Spa, Steam room
GOOD TO KNOW	Bicycle rentals
RECOMMENDED FOR	Spa

"There's a beautiful little spa in the basement of the hotel. Its design is thoughtful, in a warm, minimal style, which continues into the spa's indoor pool."—Dieter Vander Velpen

Recommended by: Dieter Vander Velpen, Dieter Vander Velpen Architects

GRAND HOTEL CENTRAL
Vía Laietana 30
Born
Barcelona 08003
+34 932957900
grandhotelcentral.com

CREDIT CARDS	Accepted
PRICE	Mid-range
TYPE	Hotel
ACCOMMODATION	147 Rooms and Suites
FACILITIES	Bar, Gym, Outdoor restaurant and swimming pool, Rooftop terrace bar, Sauna, Spa, Steam room
GOOD TO KNOW	Near Las Ramblas
RECOMMENDED FOR	Spa

Recommended by: Aljoša Dekleva and Tina Gregorič, Dekleva Gregorič Architects

HOTEL BANYS ORIENTALS
Carrer de l'Argenteria 37
Born
Barcelona 08003
+34 932688460
hotelbanysorientals.com

CREDIT CARDS	Accepted
PRICE	Mid-range
TYPE	Inn
ACCOMMODATION	43 Rooms
FACILITIES	Bar, Restaurant
GOOD TO KNOW	Near La Sagrada Família
RECOMMENDED FOR	Where I live

Recommended by: Alberto Lievore, Lievore Altherr

CASA CAMPER
Carrer d'Elisabets 11
Ciutat Vella
Barcelona 08001
+34 933426280
casacamper.com

CREDIT CARDS	Accepted
PRICE	Mid-range
TYPE	Hotel
ACCOMMODATION	40 Rooms and Suites
FACILITIES	Bar, Gym, Restaurant, Rooftop terrace bar
GOOD TO KNOW	Child friendly
RECOMMENDED FOR	Urban

Casa Camper Barcelona is a boutique design hotel created by cult shoe brand Camper. It is situated just two minutes from Plaza Cataluña. Facilities include Michelin-starred restaurant Dos Palillos, and a terrace with an honesty bar. Thoughtful touches include the "tentempié," a 24-hour complimentary buffet service which replaces a traditional room minibar.

Recommended by: Eric Corey Freed, OrganicArchitect

HOTEL SANTA MARTA
Carrer del General Castaños 14
Ciutat Vella
Barcelona 08003
+34 933194427
hotelsantamartabcn.com

CREDIT CARDS	Accepted but not Amex
PRICE	Mid-range
TYPE	Hotel
ACCOMMODATION	47 Rooms
FACILITIES	Bar, Cafe, Private parking
GOOD TO KNOW	Near the seaside
RECOMMENDED FOR	Family friendly

Recommended by: Carlos Ferrater, OAB

MERCER HOTEL BARCELONA
Carrer dels Lledó 7
Ciutat Vella
Barcelona 08002
+34 933107480
mercerbarcelona.com

CREDIT CARDS	Accepted
PRICE	High-end
TYPE	Hotel
ACCOMMODATION	28 Rooms
FACILITIES	Bar, Outdoor swimming pool, 2 Restaurants, Rooftop terrace bar
GOOD TO KNOW	Near Museu Picasso
RECOMMENDED FOR	All-time favorite, Urban

Recommended by: Belén Moneo and Jeffrey Brock, Moneo Brock; Emilio Tuñón, Tuñón Arquitectos

HOTEL BRUMMELL

Carrer Nou de la Rambla 174
El Poble-Sec
Barcelona 08004
+34 931258622
hotelbrummell.com

CREDIT CARDS	Accepted
PRICE	Mid-range
TYPE	Hotel
ACCOMMODATION	20 Rooms
FACILITIES	Outdoor swimming pool, Sauna, Yoga
GOOD TO KNOW	Bicycle rentals
RECOMMENDED FOR	Urban

Hotel Brummell is a hip boutique hotel situated in Barcelona's charming Poble Sec district. The beautifully restored townhouse dates back to the 1800s, and the rooms have design details influenced by Geoffrey Bawa's "tropical Modernism." The in-room amenities include yoga mats and homemade toiletries and there is also free access for guests to the sauna and swimming pool.

Recommended by: Joanna Laajisto, Studio Joanna Laajisto

W BARCELONA

Plaça Rosa dels Vents 1, Passeig de Joan de Borbó
La Barceloneta
Barcelona 08039
+34 932952800
marriott.com

CREDIT CARDS	Accepted
PRICE	High-end
TYPE	Hotel
ACCOMMODATION	473 Rooms and Suites
FACILITIES	Bar, Gym, Indoor and outdoor swimming pools, 2 Restaurants, Rooftop terrace bar, Spa
GOOD TO KNOW	Near Olympic Village beaches
RECOMMENDED FOR	Beach, Wish I'd designed

W Barcelona, designed by Ricardo Bofill, is a five-star hotel situated on the Barceloneta Boardwalk and has panoramic views of the Mediterranean Sea and Barcelona from each of its rooms. The hotel also features a range of dining options including Michelin-starred La Barra by Chef Carles Abellan.

Recommended by: Farid Chacon, NMD NOMADAS;
Mark Landini, Landini Associates

PRIMERO PRIMERA

Carrer del Doctor Carulla 25
Tres Torres
Barcelona 08017
+34 934175600
primeroprimera.com

CREDIT CARDS	Accepted
PRICE	Mid-range
TYPE	Hotel
ACCOMMODATION	30 Rooms and Suites
FACILITIES	Bar, Gym, Outdoor swimming pool, Restaurant
GOOD TO KNOW	Babysitting, Pet friendly
RECOMMENDED FOR	Urban

Primero Primera is just ten minutes from Barcelona's city center. An ultimate boutique hotel, it is designed to evoke the glamour and exclusivity of a British private members' club.

Recommended by: Phillippe Fouché, SAOTA

RENAISSANCE BARCELONA FIRA HOTEL

Plaza Europa 50-52
L'Hospitalet de Llobregat
Barcelona 08902
+34 932618000
marriott.com

CREDIT CARDS	Accepted
PRICE	Mid-range
TYPE	Hotel
ACCOMMODATION	357 Rooms and Suites
FACILITIES	Bar, Gym, Indoor and outdoor swimming pools, Restaurant
GOOD TO KNOW	Babysitting
RECOMMENDED FOR	Wish I'd designed

Recommended by: Luca Gazzaniga, Luca Gazzaniga Architects

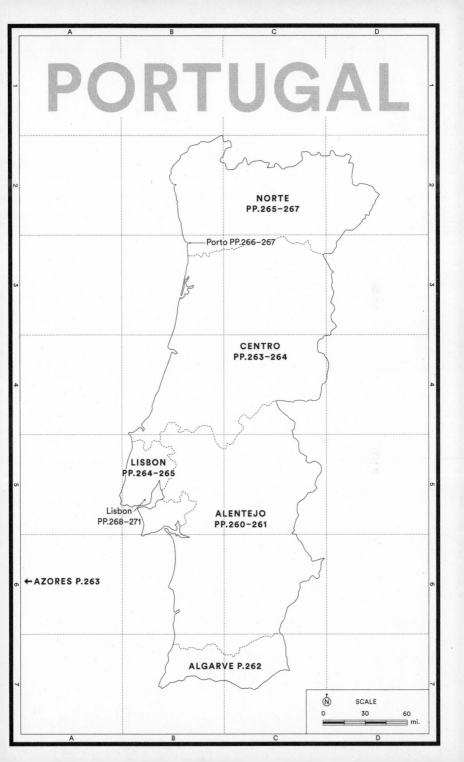

CASA DA COMPORTA

Alameda da Praia do Pego Lote 3
Comporta
Alentejo 7570-781
Portugal
+351 962048447
casadacomporta.net

CREDIT CARDS	Accepted
PRICE	Blow-out
TYPE	House rental
ACCOMMODATION	5 Rooms
FACILITIES	Outdoor swimming pool
GOOD TO KNOW	Babysitting, Bicycle rentals, Call to book, Self-catering, Horse riding
RECOMMENDED FOR	Family friendly

"Unique atmosphere and beautiful beaches in an amazing, undiscovered place."—Luis Ferreira-da-Silva

Recommended by: Luis Ferreira-da-Silva, Luis Ferreira-da-Silva Architects

CASAS NA AREIA

Sítio da Carrasqueira
Comporta
Alentejo 7580-613
Portugal
+351 964362816
silentliving.pt

CREDIT CARDS	Accepted
PRICE	Mid-range
TYPE	Beachhouse rental
ACCOMMODATION	4 Houses (4 Bedrooms)
FACILITIES	Outdoor swimming pool
GOOD TO KNOW	3–7 night minimum stay according to season
RECOMMENDED FOR	Beach

Casas na Areia was originally designed as a vacation home and is now a collection of four thatched-roof houses inspired by traditional fishermens' cottages. The region is renowned for its wines and seafood, white sand beaches, and birdwatching. Casas na Areia is only an hour's drive south of Lisbon.

Recommended by: José Martinez-Silva, Atelier Central

CABANAS NO RIO

Sítio da Carrasqueira
Comporta
Alentejo 7580-613
Portugal
+351 964362816
silentliving.pt

CREDIT CARDS	Accepted
PRICE	Mid-range
TYPE	Cabin
ACCOMMODATION	1 Room
FACILITIES	Outdoor shower
GOOD TO KNOW	Horse riding
RECOMMENDED FOR	All-time favorite, Beach

Designed by Lisbon studio Aires Mateus, Cabanas no Rio is an ideal base for a romantic retreat. There are just two waterfront cabins, one of which is a living area and the other a bedroom, en suite bathroom, and sheltered outdoor shower. The cabins were constructed from recycled wood in a demonstration of respect for nature and simplicity.

Recommended by: Fran Silvestre, Fran Silvestre Arquitectos

TORRE DE PALMA, WINE HOTEL

Herdade de Torre de Palma
Monforte
Alentejo 7450-250
Portugal
+351 245038890
torredepalma.com

CREDIT CARDS	Accepted
PRICE	Mid-range
TYPE	Wine hotel
ACCOMMODATION	19 Rooms
FACILITIES	Bar, Indoor and outdoor swimming pools, Restaurant, Spa
GOOD TO KNOW	Horse riding, On-site vineyard
RECOMMENDED FOR	Family friendly

Torre de Palma is renowned for its winery. A beautifully restored fourteenth-century manor house, it also has a spa, a restaurant highlighting the best of Alentejo cuisine, and a horse-riding center.

Recommended by: Fran Silvestre, Fran Silvestre Arquitectos

SÃO LOURENÇO DO BARROCAL

Herdade do Barrocal
Monsaraz
Alentejo 7200-177
Portugal
+351 266247140
barrocal.pt

CREDIT CARDS	Accepted
PRICE	High-end
TYPE	Farm estate
ACCOMMODATION	40 Cottages and Rooms
FACILITIES	Gym, Outdoor Swimming pool, Restaurant, Sauna, Spa
GOOD TO KNOW	Bicycle rentals, Horse riding, No pets, On-site vineyard
RECOMMENDED FOR	Best-kept secret, Wish I'd designed, Worth the travel

Recommended by: Eero Koivisto, Claesson Koivisto Rune Architects; Marcelo Morettin, Andrade Morettin Arquitetos; João Mendes Ribeiro, João Mendes Ribeiro Arquitecto

L'AND VINEYARDS

Herdade das Valadas
Montemor-o-Novo
Alentejo 7050-909
Portugal
+351 266242400
l-and.com

CREDIT CARDS	Accepted
PRICE	High-end
TYPE	Wine hotel
ACCOMMODATION	26 Suites
FACILITIES	Indoor swimming pool, Restaurant, Sauna, Spa
GOOD TO KNOW	On-site vineyard
RECOMMENDED FOR	Spa

"Visit for the landscape, the spa, and the architecture."
—Angela García de Paredes

Recommended by: Angela García de Paredes, Paredes Pedrosa Arquitectos

CASA NO TEMPO

Herdade do Carvalho
Sabugueiro
Alentejo 7040-404
Portugal
+351 964362816
silentliving.pt

CREDIT CARDS	Accepted
PRICE	Mid-range
TYPE	House rental
ACCOMMODATION	4 Suites
FACILITIES	Outdoor swimming pool
GOOD TO KNOW	Bicycle rentals, Horse riding, No pets
RECOMMENDED FOR	Best-kept secret, Spa

Casa no Tempo is a celebration of simplicity and refinement. Redefined as a hotel by architect Manuel Aires Mateus, this former farmhouse is situated among the golden plains and cork groves of Alentejo. The owners also provide bikes for exploring the surrounding countryside.

Recommended by: Joaquín Pérez-Goicoechea, AGi Architects; Emilio Tuñón, Tuñón Arquitectos

TRÊS MARIAS

Ribeira da Azenha
Vila Nova de Milfontes
Alentejo 7645-909
Portugal
+351 965666231
tres-marias-pt.book.direct

CREDIT CARDS	Accepted but not Amex
PRICE	Mid-range
TYPE	Hotel
ACCOMMODATION	10 Rooms and Suites
FACILITIES	Bar, Restaurant
GOOD TO KNOW	Bicycle rentals, No pets
RECOMMENDED FOR	Family friendly

Recommended by: Joana Leandro Vasconcelos, Atelier In.vitro

FORTE DE SÃO JOÃO DA BARRA
Sítio da Fortaleza
Cabanas de Tavira
Algarve 8800-595
Portugal
+351 960375419
fortesaojoaodabarra.com

CREDIT CARDS	Accepted but not Amex
PRICE	Mid-range
TYPE	Hotel
ACCOMMODATION	10 Rooms
FACILITIES	Outdoor swimming pool
GOOD TO KNOW	Horse riding, No pets
RECOMMENDED FOR	Beach

"Secluded with great views."—Aljoša Dekleva and
Tine Gregorič

Recommended by: Aljoša Dekleva and Tina Gregorič,
Dekleva Gregorič Architects

CASA MODESTA
Quatrim do sul, Moncarapacho
Olhão
Algarve 8700-128
Portugal
+351 289701096
casamodesta.pt

CREDIT CARDS	Accepted
PRICE	Mid-range
TYPE	Hotel
ACCOMMODATION	9 Rooms
FACILITIES	Outdoor swimming pool
GOOD TO KNOW	Free parking
RECOMMENDED FOR	Countryside

"A small and interesting piece of architecture integrated
with the natural landscape."—Antonio G. Liñán

Recommended by: Antonio G. Liñán, SV60 Cordón & Liñán
Arquitectos

MARTINHAL SAGRES FAMILY RESORT
Quinta do Martinhal, Apartado 54
Sagres
Algarve 8650-908
Portugal
+351 282240200
martinhal.com

CREDIT CARDS	Accepted
PRICE	Mid-range
TYPE	Resort hotel
ACCOMMODATION	169 Apartments, Suites, Rooms, and Villa
FACILITIES	Bar, Gym, Indoor and outdoor swimming pools, 3 Restaurants, Sauna, Spa
GOOD TO KNOW	Bicycle rental
RECOMMENDED FOR	Family friendly

"Lovely setting by the ocean with good food and service.
It's both family friendly and elegant."—Nabil Gholam

Recommended by: Nabil Gholam, Nabil Gholam Architects;
Tavis Wright, Dos Architects

RESORT PEDRAS D'EL REI
Aldeamento Pedras D'el Rei
Santa Luzia
Algarve 8800-531, Portugal
+351 259437140
pedrasdelrei.com

CREDIT CARDS	Accepted
PRICE	Low-cost
TYPE	Resort
ACCOMMODATION	Apartments, Studios, and Villas
FACILITIES	Bar, Gym, Restaurant, Outdoor swimming pool
GOOD TO KNOW	Babysitting, Bicycle rentals, Pet friendly
RECOMMENDED FOR	Family friendly, Beach

Recommended by: José Martinez-Silva, Atelier Central;
Rui Veloso, Adapteye

CASA DO FERREIRO
Rua de Baixo 15
São Roque do Pico
Pico Island
Azores 9940-312, Portugal
+351 911553466
atlanticdays.net

CREDIT CARDS	Not accepted
PRICE	Mid-range
TYPE	House rental
ACCOMMODATION	1 Villa (4 Bedrooms)
FACILITIES	BBQ, Garden, Terrace
GOOD TO KNOW	No pets
RECOMMENDED FOR	Beach, Countryside, Mountains

Recommended by: Inês Vieira-da-Silva, SAMI-Arquitectos

7 CIDADES LAKE LODGE
Rua das Lavadeiras 2
Sete Cidades
São Miguel Island
Azores 9555-194, Portugal
+351 918304014
7cidadeslakelodge.com

CREDIT CARDS	Accepted but not Amex
PRICE	Low-cost
TYPE	House rental
ACCOMMODATION	7 Bungalows and House
FACILITIES	Self-catering
GOOD TO KNOW	Lagoon
RECOMMENDED FOR	Best-kept secret

7 Cidades Lake Lodge is a collection of bungalows situated in the stunning Sete Cidades, in the Azores archipelago. Each has been designed with the surrounding scenery in mind, with wide windows and porches. Each property also features a fireplace for cozy nights in.

Recommended by: Nuno Brandão Costa, Brandão Costa Arquitectos

CURIA PALACE HOTEL SPA & GOLF
Tamengos
Anadia
Centro 3780-541
Portugal
+351 231510300
almeidahotels.pt

CREDIT CARDS	Accepted
PRICE	Low-cost
TYPE	Palace hotel
ACCOMMODATION	100 Rooms
FACILITIES	Bar, Golf, Indoor and outdoor swimming pools, Restaurant, Sauna, Spa, Steam room
GOOD TO KNOW	On-site vineyard
RECOMMENDED FOR	Budget

Curia Palace is a grand, 1920s manor house hotel which has retained the charm and glamour of the Belle Époque. The restaurant serves traditional Portuguese cuisine and wines from the palace's own winery. It is also ideally situated for exploring the region's famous wine route and Atlantic beaches.

Recommended by: João Mendes Ribeiro, João Mendes Ribeiro Arquitecto

LONGROIVA HOTEL & THERMAL SPA
Lugar do Rossio
Longroiva
Centro 6430-071
Portugal
+351 279149020
hoteldelongroiva.com

CREDIT CARDS	Accepted but not Amex
PRICE	Low-cost
TYPE	Spa resort
ACCOMMODATION	14 Rooms and Suites
FACILITIES	Bar, Hot-spring bath, Indoor swimming pool, Restaurant, Spa
GOOD TO KNOW	Near Parque Arqueológico do Vale do Côa
RECOMMENDED FOR	Countryside, Spa

Designed by Luís Rebelo de Andrade, Longroiva is built upon the existing Neo-Classical spa. The result is a chic retreat that takes advanage of local hot springs for its holistic spa experience of combining natural therapies with modern innovation.

Recommended by: Carlo Ratti, Carlo Ratti Associati; Rui Veloso, Adapteye

PALACE HOTEL DO BUÇACO
Luso
Centro 3050-261
Portugal
+351 231937970
almeidahotels.pt

CREDIT CARDS	Accepted
PRICE	Mid-range
TYPE	Palace hotel
ACCOMMODATION	60 Rooms and Suites
FACILITIES	Bar, Restaurant
GOOD TO KNOW	In Buçaco Forest
RECOMMENDED FOR	Countryside, Luxury

"Manuelino-style palatial hunting lodge with fascinating decorations and *azulejos* [Portuguese tiles]. Built for the last King of Portugal in 1885, it has vaulted ceilings, peaceful swan ponds, and is surrounded by an enormous ancient forest."—Luis Ferreira-da-Silva

Recommended by: João Mendes Ribeiro, João Mendes Ribeiro Arquitecto; Luis Ferreira-da-Silva, Luis Ferreira-da-Silva Architects

CASA DAS PENHAS DOURADAS
Penhas Douradas
Manteigas
Centro 6260-200
Portugal
+351 275981045
casadaspenhasdouradas.pt

CREDIT CARDS	Accepted but not Amex
PRICE	Mid-range
TYPE	Resort
ACCOMMODATION	18 Rooms
FACILITIES	Bar, Indoor swimming pool, Restaurant, Sauna
GOOD TO KNOW	Free parking, 1,500m (5,000ft) above sea level
RECOMMENDED FOR	Family friendly

Recommended by: João Mendes Ribeiro, João Mendes Ribeiro Arquitecto

CASA DO RIO
Quinta do Orgal km213 222
Villa Nova de Foz Côa
Centro 5150-145
Portugal
+351 279764339
quintadovallado.com

CREDIT CARDS	Accepted but not Amex
PRICE	Mid-range
TYPE	Wine hotel
ACCOMMODATION	8 Rooms and Suites
FACILITIES	Bar, Outdoor swimming pool, Restaurant
GOOD TO KNOW	Bicycle rentals, Child friendly (12 and over)
RECOMMENDED FOR	Countryside

Recommended by: João Mendes Ribeiro, João Mendes Ribeiro Arquitecto

LISBON: SEE PAGES 268–271

PALACIO ESTORIL GOLF & SPA HOTEL
Rua Particular
Estoril
Cascais
Lisbon 2769-504
Portugal
+351 214648000
palacioestorilhotel.com

CREDIT CARDS	Accepted
PRICE	High-end
TYPE	Golf hotel
ACCOMMODATION	161 Rooms and Suites
FACILITIES	Bar, Golf, Gym, Indoor and outdoor swimming pools, 3 Restaurants, Sauna, Spa, Yoga
GOOD TO KNOW	Golf and wellness packages
RECOMMENDED FOR	Luxury

Recommended by: Alfredo Payá Benedito, Noname29

TIVOLI PALÁCIO DE SETEAIS

Rua Barbosa Du Bocage 8
Sintra
Lisbon 2710-517
Portugal
+351 219233200
tivolihotels.com

CREDIT CARDS	Accepted
PRICE	High-end
TYPE	Palace hotel
ACCOMMODATION	30 Rooms and Suites
FACILITIES	Bar, Outdoor swimming pool, Restaurant, Spa
GOOD TO KNOW	Wine tastings
RECOMMENDED FOR	Countryside

"Impressive palatial building with beautiful gardens; summer concerts and ballet performances are held in the Orangerie."—Luis Ferreira-da-Silva

Recommended by: Luis Ferreira-da-Silva, Luis Ferreira-da-Silva Architects

PEDRAS SALGADAS SPA & NATURE PARK

Parque Pedras Salgadas
Bornes de Aguiar
Norte 5450-140
Portugal
pedrassalgadaspark.com

CREDIT CARDS	Accepted
PRICE	Mid-range
TYPE	Spa hotel
ACCOMMODATION	16 Eco- and Tree-houses
FACILITIES	Indoor and outdoor swimming pools, Natural springs, Restaurant, Sauna, Spa, Steam room
GOOD TO KNOW	In Parque Termal de Pedras Salgadas
RECOMMENDED FOR	Eco-conscious, Family friendly, Mountains

"Wonderful accommodation with remarkable tree- and eco-houses. Great kids' activities."—Nathalie Rossetti

Recommended by: José Martinez-Silva, Atelier Central; João Mendes Ribeiro, João Mendes Ribeiro Arquitecto; Nathalie Rossetti, Rossetti + Wyss Architects; Rui Veloso, Adapteye

SIX SENSES DOURO VALLEY

Quinta Vale de Abrão
Lamego
Norte 5100-758
Portugal
+351 254660600
sixsenses.com

CREDIT CARDS	Accepted
PRICE	High-end
TYPE	Resort
ACCOMMODATION	57 Rooms, Suites, and Villa
FACILITIES	Bar, Gym, Indoor and outdoor swimming pools, Restaurant, Sauna, Spa, Wine library, Yoga
GOOD TO KNOW	Babysitting
RECOMMENDED FOR	Spa

A restored nineteenth-century manor house overlooking the rolling hills of the Douro Valley. The hotel has a wine library, swimming pools, excellent dining experiences, a kitchen garden, and world-class spa facilities.

Recommended by: Dominique Perrault, Dominique Perrault Architecture

HOTEL RURAL QUINTA DE NOVAIS

Novais
Santa Eulália
Norte 4540-540
Portugal
+351 256940100
quintadenovais.com

CREDIT CARDS	Accepted
PRICE	Low-cost
TYPE	Hotel
ACCOMMODATION	16 Rooms
FACILITIES	Bar, Gym, Outdoor swimming pool, Restaurant
GOOD TO KNOW	Canyoning, Mountain biking, Rafting
RECOMMENDED FOR	Worth the travel

Located in the heart of Arouca Geopark, Hotel Rural Quinta de Novais is a simple yet charming retreat from urban life in the countryside, south of the cultural hub of Porto.

Recommended by: Rui Veloso, Adapteye

HOTEL SANTA MARIA DE BOURO
Largo do Terreiro
Santa Maria do Bouro
Norte 4720-633, Portugal
+351 258821751
pousadasofportugal.com

CREDIT CARDS	Accepted but not Amex
PRICE	Mid-range
TYPE	Hotel
ACCOMMODATION	32 Rooms
FACILITIES	Bar, Outdoor swimming pool, Restaurant
GOOD TO KNOW	Child and pet friendly
RECOMMENDED FOR	All-time favorite, Best-kept secret, Countryside, Luxury, Mountains, Wish I'd designed, Worth the travel

"The experience of being a guest in the former Santa Maria do Bouro monastery is a memorable one. Surrounded by the region's misty mountains... it simply it does not get better than this."—Carlos Jiménez

"Great Modern architecture by Eduardo Souto de Moura. Calm and peaceful."—Daniel Suduca and Thierry Mérillou

Recommended by: Nuno Brandão Costa, Brandão Costa Arquitectos; Aljoša Dekleva and Tina Gregorič, Dekleva Gregorič Architects; Angela García de Paredes, Paredes Pedrosa Arquitectos; Zsolt Gunther, 3H Architecture; Carlos Jiménez, Carlos Jiménez Studio; Anne Kaestle, Duplex Architekten; Grace Keeley, GKMP Architects; Eero Koivisto, Claesson Koivisto Rune Architects; João Mendes Ribeiro, João Mendes Ribeiro Arquitecto; Salvador Reyes Ríos, Reyes Ríos + Larraín Arquitectos; Nathalie Rossetti, Rossetti + Wyss Architects; Daniel Suduca and Thierry Mérillou, Suduca & Mérillou

HOTEL FEELVIANA
Rua Brás de Abreu Soares 222
Viana do Castelo
Norte 4935-159, Portugal
+351 258330330
hotelfeelviana.com

CREDIT CARDS	Accepted but not Amex
PRICE	Mid-range
TYPE	Wellness resort
ACCOMMODATION	55 Bungalows and Rooms
FACILITIES	Bar, Gym, Indoor and outdoor swimming pools, Restaurant, Spa, Yoga
GOOD TO KNOW	Bicycle rentals, Child friendly
RECOMMENDED FOR	Eco-conscious

Hotel FeelViana is a sports and wellness retreat for those looking to switch off, unwind, and re-energize; take part in a range of water sports, explore the wild beaches and forests by bike, and unwind in the hotel spa. Room interiors are pared-back yet stylish. The overall ambience is a laid-back connection with the stunning surrounding natural environment.

Recommended by: José Martinez-Silva, Atelier Central

VIDAGO PALACE HOTEL
Parque de Vidago
Vidago
Vila Real
Norte 5425-307, Portugal
+351 276990920
vidagopalace.com

CREDIT CARDS	Accepted
PRICE	Mid-range
TYPE	Hotel
ACCOMMODATION	70 Rooms and Suites
FACILITIES	Bar, Golf, Gym, Indoor and outdoor swimming pools, Restaurant, Sauna, Spa, Steam room, Tennis
GOOD TO KNOW	Child and pet friendly
RECOMMENDED FOR	Worth the travel

The Vidago Palace Hotel was originally commissioned by King Carlos I who wanted to build a spa hotel to rival the finest in Europe. To this day, it is recognized as an award-winning five-star retreat, renowned for its thermal spa and charming period features. The hotel is both family and pet-friendly.

Recommended by: Diego Arraigada, Diego Arraigada Arquitectos

CASA DO CONTO
Rua da Boavista 703
Boavista
Porto 4050-110, Portugal
+351 222060340
casadoconto.com

CREDIT CARDS	Accepted
PRICE	Mid-range
TYPE	Guesthouse
ACCOMMODATION	6 Suites
FACILITIES	Garden, Library, Lounge, Shared kitchen
GOOD TO KNOW	Babysitting
RECOMMENDED FOR	Urban

"Casa do Conto is a little infill building—a combination of great design and craftsmanship in a unique setting. The hotel is a few steps from one of the world's modern architectural masterpieces, Casa da Música by OMA."
—Thomas Birkkjær

Recommended by: Thomas Birkkjær, Arkitema Architects; José Martinez-Silva, Atelier Central; João Mendes Ribeiro, João Mendes Ribeiro Arquitecto

HOTEL VINCCI PORTO
Alameda de Basílio Teles 29
Massarelos
Porto 4150-127
Portugal
+351 220439620
vincciporto.com

CREDIT CARDS	Accepted
PRICE	Mid-range
TYPE	Hotel
ACCOMMODATION	95 Rooms and Suites
FACILITIES	Bar, Restaurant
GOOD TO KNOW	Babysitting
RECOMMENDED FOR	Where I live

Situated in a refurbished building that formerly housed a fish market, Vinnci Porto is a bright, spacious design hotel with character.

Recommended by: Rui Veloso, Adapteye

DUAS PORTAS
Ruas das Sobreiras 516
Ouro
Porto 4150-713
Portugal
+351 914786518
duasportas.com

CREDIT CARDS	Accepted but not Amex
PRICE	Mid-range
TYPE	Guesthouse
ACCOMMODATION	8 Rooms
FACILITIES	Bar
GOOD TO KNOW	Bicycle rentals
RECOMMENDED FOR	Best-kept secret, Budget, Family friendly, Urban

"It's easy to feel at home here, in the city, by the Douro River."—Nuno Brandão Costa

Recommended by: Nuno Brandão Costa, Brandão Costa Arquitectos; Manuel Cervantes, CC Arquitectos; Marcio Kogan, Studio MK27; Fran Silvestre, Fran Silvestre Arquitectos

GRAND HOTEL DE PARIS
Rua da Fábrica 27
Vitória
Porto 4000-196
Portugal
+351 222073140
hotelparis.pt

CREDIT CARDS	Accepted
PRICE	Low-cost
TYPE	Hotel
ACCOMMODATION	45 Rooms
FACILITIES	Bar, Restaurant
GOOD TO KNOW	No pets
RECOMMENDED FOR	Budget

"Central, cheerful, and characterful, with generous breakfasts and a grand dining room."—Biba Dow

Recommended by: Biba Dow, Dow Jones Architects

PORTO A.S. 1829 HOTEL
Largo São Domingos 45-55
Vitória
Porto 4050-097
Portugal
+351 223402740
as1829.luxhotels.pt

CREDIT CARDS	Accepted
PRICE	Mid-range
TYPE	Hotel
ACCOMMODATION	41 Rooms
FACILITIES	Restaurant
GOOD TO KNOW	Babysitting, Bicycle rentals, No pets
RECOMMENDED FOR	Urban

Once home to the renowned stationery shop Papelaria Araújo e Sobrinho, Porto AS 1829 is a charming hotel with interiors that pay respectful homage to its past.

Recommended by: Rui Veloso, Adapteye

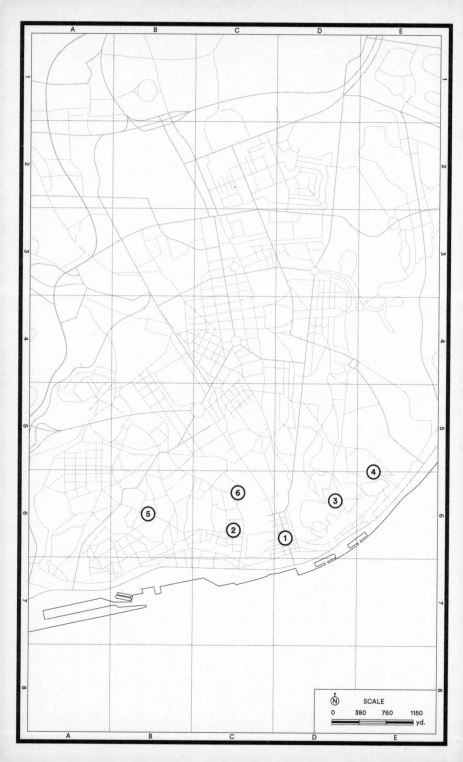

LISBON

FOUR SEASONS HOTEL RITZ LISBON

Rua Rodrigo da Fonseca 88
Baixa
Lisbon 1099-039
+351 213811400
fourseasons.com

CREDIT CARDS...Accepted
PRICE..High-end
TYPE..Hotel
ACCOMMODATION..................................282 Rooms and Suites
FACILITIES..Bar, Gym,
Indoor and outdoor swimming pools,
Pilates studio, 2 Restaurants,
Running track, Sauna,
Spa, Steam room
GOOD TO KNOW.................................Babysitting, Valet parking
RECOMMENDED FOR..Wish I'd designed

Recommended by: Nuno Brandão Costa, Brandão Costa Arquitectos

DEAR LISBON PALACE CHIADO

Rua Ivens 35
Chiado
Lisbon 1200-226
+351 211547832
dearlisbon.com

CREDIT CARDS...Accepted
PRICE...Mid-range
TYPE...Guesthouse
ACCOMMODATION...9 Suites
FACILITIES...............................Near Museu Nacional de Arte
Contemporânea do Chiado
GOOD TO KNOW...Bicycle rentals
RECOMMENDED FOR..Best-kept secret

"In the Chiado district, this beautifully restored nineteenth-century noblehouse has wonderful views of Lisbon and its extraordinary southern light."—Amanda Levete

Recommended by: Amanda Levete, AL_A

VALVERDE HOTEL

Avenida da Liberdade 164
Chiado
Lisbon 1250-146
+351 210940300
valverdehotel.com

CREDIT CARDS...Accepted
PRICE...Mid-range
TYPE..Townhouse hotel
ACCOMMODATION....................................25 Rooms and Suites
FACILITIES...Bar, Gym,
Outdoor swimming pool, Restaurant
GOOD TO KNOW...Screening room
RECOMMENDED FOR..Urban

"This hotel is homey and intimate. Its elegant style combines contemporary furniture, art and antiques, which reminds us of London and New York townhouses, even though it's in Lisbon."—Belén Moneo and Jeffrey Brock

Recommended by: Belén Moneo and Jeffrey Brock, Moneo Brock

HOTEL PALACIO BELMONTE

Pátio de Dom Fradique 14
Alfama
Lisbon 1100-624
+351 218816600
palaciobelmonte.com

CREDIT CARDS...Accepted
PRICE..High-end
TYPE...Palace hotel
ACCOMMODATION...11 Suites
FACILITIES..................Outdoor swimming pool, Restaurant,
Sauna, Wood-burning fireplace
GOOD TO KNOW.................................Babysitting, Pet friendly
RECOMMENDED FOR............................Best-kept secret, Luxury

"Graceful; the perfect styling of an historic palace built on ancient ruins."—Lauren Rottet

Recommended by: Lauren Rottet, Rottet Studio

MEMMO ALFAMA HOTEL LISBOA

Travessa das Merceeiras 27
Alfama
Lisbon 1100-348
+351 210495660
memmohotels.com

CREDIT CARDS...Accepted
PRICE...Mid-range
TYPE..Hotel
ACCOMMODATION...42 Rooms
FACILITIES...................Bar, Gym, Outdoor swimming pool,
Rooftop terrace bar
GOOD TO KNOW..............................Near the Lisbon Cathedral
RECOMMENDED FOR.......................................Wish I'd designed

"The hotel's design incorporates and preserves original
details of the old bakery, which give it a distinct character.
There's a great buffet breakfast, which you can take upstairs
to the terrace overlooking Alfama and the waterfront."
—Josh Chaiken

Recommended by: Josh Chaiken, Kohn Pedersen Fox

SANTA CLARA 1728

Campo de Santa Clara 128
Graça & São Vicente
Lisbon 1100-470
+351 964362816
silentliving.pt

CREDIT CARDS...Accepted
PRICE..High-end
TYPE..Townhouse hotel
ACCOMMODATION...6 Suites
FACILITIES...Communal dining
GOOD TO KNOW...Near flea market
RECOMMENDED FOR...........................Best-kept secret, Urban,
Wish I'd designed

Santa Clara 1728 is a charming eighteenth-century
townhouse in the heart of Lisbon's old cultural quarter.
It has been thoughtfully restored under the guidance
of Manuel Aires Mateus. Interiors are serenely minimalist,
and each of the six suites is bright and spacious.

Recommended by: Manuel Aires Mateus, Aires Mateus
e Associados; Mårten Claesson, Claesson Koivisto Rune
Architects; Bolle Tham and Martin Videgård, Tham
& Videgård Arkitekter; Emilio Tuñón, Tuñón Arquitectos

HOTEL YORK HOUSE LISBON

Rua das Janelas Verdes
Lapa, Lisbon 1200-691
+351 213962435
yorkhouselisboa.com

CREDIT CARDS...Accepted
PRICE...Mid-range
TYPE..Townhouse hotel
ACCOMMODATION................................33 Rooms and Suites
FACILITIES..Restaurant
GOOD TO KNOW............................Near National Museum
of Ancient Art
RECOMMENDED FOR..Urban

Recommended by: Luis Ferreira-da-Silva, Luis Ferreira-da-
Silva Architects

PALACIO RAMALHETE

Rua das Janelas Verdes 92
Lapa, Lisbon 1200-692
+351 213931380
palacio-ramalhete.com

CREDIT CARDS...Accepted
PRICE...Mid-range
TYPE...Palace hotel
ACCOMMODATION................................16 Rooms and Suites
FACILITIES...Bar, Courtyard,
Outdoor swimming pool, Restaurant
GOOD TO KNOW..........Near Museu Nacional de Arte Antiga
RECOMMENDED FOR..Urban

Recommended by: Rick Joy, Studio Rick Joy

PESTANA PALACE LISBOA

Rua Jau 54
Alcântara, Lisbon 1300-312
+351 21 361 5600
pestanacollection.com

CREDIT CARDS...Accepted
PRICE...Mid-range
TYPE...Palace hotel
ACCOMMODATION................................193 Rooms and Suites
FACILITIES..Bar, Gym,
Indoor and outdoor swimming pools,
Restaurant, Sauna, Spa, Steam room
GOOD TO KNOW.......................................Near Tower of Belém
RECOMMENDED FOR.......................................Spa, Urban

Recommended by: Nathalie Frankowski and Cruz Garcia,
WAI Architecture Think Tank; Grace Keeley, GKMP
Architects

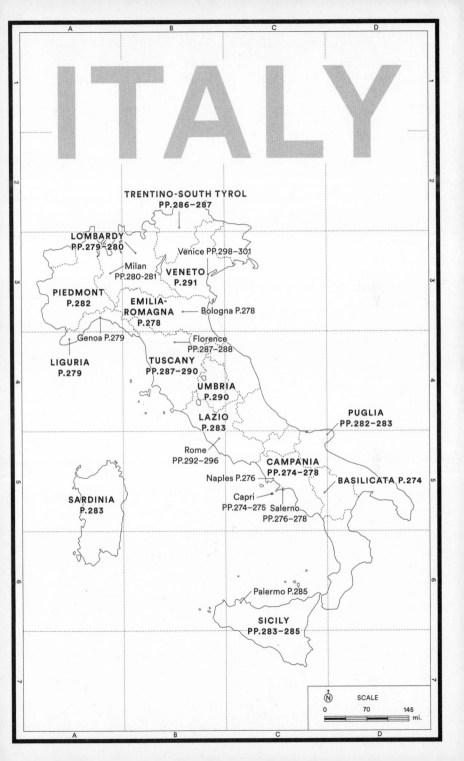

ITALY

TRENTINO-SOUTH TYROL
PP.286–287

LOMBARDY
PP.279–280

Venice PP.298–301

Milan
PP.280–281

VENETO
P.291

PIEDMONT
P.282

EMILIA-
ROMAGNA
P.278

Bologna P.278

Genoa P.279

Florence
PP.287–288

LIGURIA
P.279

TUSCANY
PP.287–290

UMBRIA
P.290

LAZIO
P.283

PUGLIA
PP.282–283

Rome
PP.292–296

CAMPANIA
PP.274–278

Naples P.276

BASILICATA P.274

Capri
PP.274–275

Salerno
PP.276–278

SARDINIA
P.283

Palermo P.285

SICILY
PP.283–285

N

SCALE

0   70   145
mi.

CAVEOSO HOTEL
Rione Pianelle, 26 Piazza San Pietro Caveoso
Matera 75100
Basilicata
Italy
+39 0835310931
caveosohotel.com

CREDIT CARDS	Accepted
PRICE	Mid-range
TYPE	Hotel
ACCOMMODATION	14 Rooms and Suites
FACILITIES	Bar
GOOD TO KNOW	No pets, Valet parking
RECOMMENDED FOR	Worth the travel

Recommended by: Flavio Albanese, ASA Studio

SEXTANTIO LE GROTTE DELLA CIVITA
Via Civita 28
Matera 75100
Basilicata
Italy
+39 0835332744
legrottedellacivita.sextantio.it

CREDIT CARDS	Accepted
PRICE	High-end
TYPE	Hotel
ACCOMMODATION	18 Rooms and Suites
FACILITIES	Restaurant
GOOD TO KNOW	Babysitting, In-room massage
RECOMMENDED FOR	All-time favorite, Countryside, Eco-conscious, Luxury

"One of southern Italy's most charming hotels set within ancient caves where people lived until the 1950s. It faces an amazing canyon; the atmosphere is intense, almost spiritual."
—Paolo Brambilla

Recommended by: Paolo Brambilla, Calvi Brambilla; Marco Costanzi, Marco Costanzi Architects; David Miller, Miller Hull Partnership; Dominique Perrault, Dominique Perrault Architecture; Nathalie Rossetti, Rossetti + Wyss Architects

CAPRI PALACE HOTEL
Via Capodimonte 14
Anacapri 80071
Campania
Italy
+39 0819780111
capripalace.com

CREDIT CARDS	Accepted
PRICE	High-end
TYPE	Spa hotel
ACCOMMODATION	69 Rooms and Suites
FACILITIES	Bar, Gym, Indoor and outdoor swimming pools, 2 Restaurants, Spa
GOOD TO KNOW	Babysitting, Pet friendly
RECOMMENDED FOR	Family friendly, Spa

Recommended by: Michel Abboud, SOMA; Will Alsop, aLL Design

GRAND HOTEL QUISISANA
Via Camerelle 2
Capri 80073
Campania
Italy
+39 0810901333
quisisana.com

CREDIT CARDS	Accepted
PRICE	High-end
TYPE	Hotel
ACCOMMODATION	147 Rooms and Suites
FACILITIES	Bar, Gym, Indoor swimming pool, 3 Restaurants, Sauna, Spa
GOOD TO KNOW	Child friendly, No pets
RECOMMENDED FOR	Island

A landmark in its own right, Grand Hotel Quisisana is located at the top of the picturesque Via Camerelle. Its terraces overlook the dramatic landscape and glimmering sea beyond.

Recommended by: Doriana and Massimiliano Fuksas, Studio Fuksas

HOTEL LUNA
Viale Matteotti 3
Capri 80073
Campania
Italy
+39 0818370433
lunahotel.com

CREDIT CARDS..Accepted
PRICE...Mid-range
TYPE...Hotel
ACCOMMODATION...................................56 Rooms and Suites
FACILITIES...............................Gym, Outdoor swimming pool,
2 Restaurants, Rooftop terrace bar
GOOD TO KNOW....................................Child friendly, No pets
RECOMMENDED FOR..Best-kept secret

"Fantastic value in a premier location in Capri, with beautiful views and a great pool."—Louis Hedgecock

Recommended by: Louis Hedgecock, HOK Architects

JK PLACE CAPRI
Via Marina Grande 225
Capri 80073
Campania
Italy
+39 0818384001
jkcapri.com

CREDIT CARDS..Accepted
PRICE...Blow-out
TYPE...Hotel
ACCOMMODATION...........................22 Penthouses and Rooms
FACILITIES.......................Bar, Gym, Outdoor restaurant and
swimming pool, Sauna,
Spa, Steam room
GOOD TO KNOW...Pet friendly
RECOMMENDED FOR..Worth the travel

An elegant designer retreat overlooking the Bay of Naples, JK Place is a boutique hotel that prides itself on its warm hospitality and classic style.

Recommended by: José Juan Rivera Rio, JJRR/Arquitectura

LA SCALINATELLA
Via Tragara 8
Capri 80073
Campania
Italy
+39 0818370633
scalinatella.com

CREDIT CARDS..Accepted
PRICE...High-end
TYPE...Hotel
ACCOMMODATION.......................32 Rooms, Suites, and Villas
FACILITIES.....................Bar, Gym, Outdoor swimming pool,
Restaurant
GOOD TO KNOW...No pets
RECOMMENDED FOR..Best-kept secret

An elegant yet intimate family run boutique hotel, La Scalinatella is the sister of the Grand Hotel Quisisana. It has bright and spacious rooms and suites, as well as two villas.

Recommended by: Kelly Hoppen, Kelly Hoppen Interiors

MEZZATORRE HOTEL & THERMAL SPA
Via Mezzatorre 23
Forio d'Ischia 80075
Ischia
Campania
Italy
+39 081986111
mezzatorre.it

CREDIT CARDS..Accepted
PRICE...Mid-range
TYPE...Hotel
ACCOMMODATION................57 Cottages, Rooms, and Suites
FACILITIES...Bar,
Indoor and outdoor swimming pools,
2 Restaurants, Spa
GOOD TO KNOW...Pet friendly
RECOMMENDED FOR..Family friendly

Recommended by: David Tajchman, Architectures David Tajchman

DIMORA DORIA D'ANGRI
Piazza Sette Settembre 28
Naples 80134
Campania
Italy
+39 03334079529
dimoradoriadangri.it

CREDIT CARDS...Not accepted
PRICE...Low-cost
TYPE...Bed and Breakfast
ACCOMMODATION...4 Rooms and Suites
FACILITIES..Valet parking
GOOD TO KNOW...Near Center
RECOMMENDED FOR...Urban

Recommended by: Jo Noero, Noero Architects

HOTEL PARCO DEI PRINCIPI
Via Rota 44
Sorrento 80067
Campania
Italy
+39 0818784644
royalgroup.it

CREDIT CARDS...Accepted
PRICE...High-end
TYPE...Hotel
ACCOMMODATION.....................................96 Rooms and Suites
FACILITIES...Bar, Gym,
Outdoor swimming pool, 2 Restaurants
GOOD TO KNOW...Free parking
RECOMMENDED FOR.........................Beach, Wish I'd designed

"Immerse yourself in the fabulous 1960s white-and-blue world of Gio Ponti—he designed absolutely everything in the building, from furniture to doorstops."—Amanda Levete

Recommended by: Beppe Caturegli and Giovannella Formica, Caturegli Formica Architetti Associati; Nigel Coates; Richard England, Richard England Architects; André Fu, AFSO; Angela García de Paredes, Paredes Pedrosa Arquitectos; Grace Keeley, GKMP Architects; Eero Koivisto, Claesson Koivisto Rune Architects; Amanda Levete, AL_A; Johanna Meyer-Grohbrügge, Meyer-Grohbrügge; Charlotte von Moos, Sauter von Moos; Patrick Reymond, Atelier Oï; Daniel Suduca and Thierry Mérillou, Suduca & Mérillou

IL CANNITO
Via Cannito
Paestum
Salerno 84047
Campania
Italy
+39 08281962277
ilcannito.com

CREDIT CARDS.............................Accepted but not Amex
PRICE...Mid-range
TYPE...Hotel
ACCOMMODATION..4 Rooms
FACILITIES...................Outdoor swimming pool, Restaurant
GOOD TO KNOW..Child friendly
RECOMMENDED FOR.......................................Countryside

"Remote and tiny with incredibly warm hospitality. It's a medieval stone monastery sensitively renovated to blend in with the surrounding landscape."—Marianne Kwok

Recommended by: Marianne Kwok, Kohn Pedersen Fox

HOTEL PALAZZO MURAT
Via dei Mulini 23
Positano
Salerno 84017
Campania
Italy
+39 089875177
palazzomurat.it

CREDIT CARDS...Accepted
PRICE...High-end
TYPE...Hotel
ACCOMMODATION..31 Rooms
FACILITIES...Bar, Outdoor restaurant
and swimming pool
GOOD TO KNOW...Private parking
RECOMMENDED FOR...Best-kept secret

"The beautiful garden provides privacy and relaxing surroundings. Along with the astonishing Mediterranean Sea views, it's a great place to unwind."—Kim Herforth Nielsen

Recommended by: Kim Herforth Nielsen, 3XN

LE SIRENUSE

Via Cristoforo Colombo 30
Positano
Salerno 84017
Campania
Italy
+39 089875066
sirenuse.it

CREDIT CARDS...Accepted
PRICE...Blow-out
TYPE..Hotel
ACCOMMODATION.....................58 Rooms and Suites
FACILITIES..3 Bars, Gym,
Outdoor swimming pool,
2 Restaurants, Sauna, Spa
GOOD TO KNOW...No pets
RECOMMENDED FOR...........................Beach, Wish I'd designed

"The vibe at Le Sirenuse is classic *la dolce vita*. Located in a spectacular UNESCO World Heritage location, the hotel is beautifully styled by the family who have owned it for decades. Rooms are sensational and sun-washed, and the bars and dining venues are stunning."—Todd-Avery Lenahan

Recommended by: Bernardo Fort-Brescia, Arquitectonica; André Fu, AFSO; Doriana and Massimiliano Fuksas, Studio Fuksas; Marta Laudani, Marta Laudani Design; Todd-Avery Lenahan, TAL Studio; Giancarlo Mazzanti, El Equipo Mazzanti

VILLA TRE VILLE

Via Arienzo 30
Positano
Salerno 84017
Campania
Italy
+39 0898122411
villatreville.com

CREDIT CARDS...Accepted
PRICE...Blow-out
TYPE..Hotel
ACCOMMODATION.............................14 Suites and Villas
FACILITIES........................Bar, Gym, Outdoor restaurant
and swimming pool
GOOD TO KNOW..................Free parking, Pet friendly
RECOMMENDED FOR..Beach

Recommended by: Matteo Thun, Matteo Thun & Partners

CASA ANGELINA

Via Capriglione 147
Praiano
Salerno 84010
Campania
Italy
+39 0898131333
casangelina.com

CREDIT CARDS...Accepted
PRICE...High-end
TYPE..Hotel
ACCOMMODATION.....................40 Rooms and Suites
FACILITIES...................Bar, Gym, Indoor and outdoor
swimming pool, 2 Restaurants, Spa
GOOD TO KNOW..............................Private chauffeur
RECOMMENDED FOR...................All-time favorite, Beach,
Worth the travel

"Excellent balance between simplicity and sophistication; visit for striking views of the Mediterranean and Positano." —Gaston Atelman

Recommended by: Gaston Atelman, AFT Arquitectos

VILLA MARIA PIA

Via Roma 17
Praiano
Salerno 84010
Campania
Italy
+39 0899840032
villamariapia-praiano.com

CREDIT CARDS...Accepted
PRICE..Mid-range
TYPE..Hotel
ACCOMMODATION.....................16 Rooms and Suites
FACILITIES...Bar
GOOD TO KNOW....................................Free parking
RECOMMENDED FOR..Beach

"Set between stone cliffs, at Villa Maria Pia the landscape is everything. A stone staircase of 170 steps leads down the cliff to the sea, where there is a grotto in which to swim in complete darkness."—Felipe Assadi

Recommended by: Felipe Assadi, Felipe Assadi Architects

BELMOND HOTEL CARUSO

Piazza San Giovanni del Toro 2
Ravello
Salerno 84010
Campania
Italy
+39 089858801
belmond.com

CREDIT CARDS..Accepted
PRICE...Blow-out
TYPE..Hotel
ACCOMMODATION........................52 Rooms and Suites
FACILITIES.....................Bar, Gym, Outdoor swimming pool,
Restaurant, Spa
GOOD TO KNOW......................................Child friendly
RECOMMENDED FOR.........................All-time favorite,
Luxury, Urban

"A discreet hideaway set on a cliff edge at the top of the town, it is perfection in terms of comfort, service, luxury, views, romance, food, and history."—Simon Mitchell

Recommended by: Doriana and Massimiliano Fuksas, Studio Fuksas; Simon Mitchell, Sybarite

RAVELLO HOTEL MARMORATA

Via Bizantina 3
Ravello
Salerno 84010
Campania
Italy
+39 089877777
marmorata.it

CREDIT CARDS..Accepted
PRICE...Mid-range
TYPE..Hotel
ACCOMMODATION..........37 Apartments, Rooms, and Suites
FACILITIES.....................Bar, Gym, Outdoor swimming pool,
Restaurant
GOOD TO KNOW................Free parking (book through hotel)
RECOMMENDED FOR.........................Best-kept secret

A beautiful, fifteenth-century former paper mill on the Amalfi Coast, rooms at Hotel Marmorata are bright and cheery, with charming nautical design touches.

Recommended by: Gaston Atelman, AFT Arquitectos

I PORTICI HOTEL BOLOGNA

Via dell'Indipendenza 69
Bologna 40121
Emilia-Romagna, Italy
+39 05142185
iporticihotel.com

CREDIT CARDS..Accepted
PRICE...Mid-range
TYPE..Hotel
ACCOMMODATION...............................91 Rooms and Suites
FACILITIES...4 Restaurants
GOOD TO KNOW.................................Bicycle rentals,
Child and pet friendly
RECOMMENDED FOR...........................Best-kept secret

I Portici Hotel is situated in the historic center of Bologna, in a restored nineteenth-century townhouse. Rooms vary from minimalist to classic with traditional Bolognese design features, and some have substantial balconies. I Portici Restaurant has a Michelin star, and the hotel also operates a seasonal pizzeria on the Terrace.

Recommended by: Prof. Thomas Herzog, Thomas Herzog Architekten

LA FATTORIA DELL'AUTOSUFFICIENZA

Strada Provinciale 43
Forlì-Cesena 47021
Emilia-Romagna, Italy
+39 0543918302
autosufficienza.it

CREDIT CARDS.....................................Accepted but not Amex
PRICE...Mid-range
TYPE...Agriturismo
ACCOMMODATION...............4 Rooms and Studio apartments
FACILITIES...Restaurant
GOOD TO KNOW...................................Child and pet friendly,
Communal vegetarian buffet on
weekends from May to October
RECOMMENDED FOR...........................Eco-conscious

La Fattoria dell'Autosufficienza is an agriturismo in the Apennine mountains. It is run by a warm, passionate, and dedicated team who host a variety of workshops. All furniture is constructed from natural materials, and the energy used comes from renewable resources. Breakfast is organic and included; vegetarian lunches and dinners are served buffet-style on weekends from May to October upon request.

Recommended by: Beppe Caturegli and Giovannella Formica, Caturegli Formica Architetti Associati

ROME: SEE PAGES 292–296

HOTEL CENOBIO DEI DOGI
Via Niccolò Cuneo 34
Camogli
Genoa 16032
Liguria
Italy
+39 01857241
cenobio.it

CREDIT CARDS	Accepted
PRICE	Mid-range
TYPE	Hotel
ACCOMMODATION	100 Rooms
FACILITIES	Bar, Outdoor swimming pool, 3 Restaurants
GOOD TO KNOW	Free parking, Pet friendly
RECOMMENDED FOR	Best-kept secret

Recommended by: Makio Hasuike, Makio Hasuike & Co

BELMOND HOTEL SPLENDIDO
Salita Baratta 16
Portofino
Genoa 16034
Liguria
Italy
+39 0185267801
belmond.com

CREDIT CARDS	Accepted
PRICE	Blow-out
TYPE	Hotel
ACCOMMODATION	70 Rooms and Suites
FACILITIES	Bar, Gym, Outdoor swimming pool, 2 Restaurants, Sauna, Spa, Steam room
GOOD TO KNOW	Child and pet friendly
RECOMMENDED FOR	All-time favorite, Best-kept secret, Luxury

"A luxury European classic in a stunning setting."
—Dennis Pieprz

Recommended by: Will Alsop, aLL Design; Dennis Pieprz, Sasaki; Fernando Sordo Madaleno, Sordo Madaleno; Randa Tukan, HOK Architects

HOTEL VILLA D'ESTE
Via Regina 40
Cernobbio
Como 22012
Lombardy
Italy
+39 0313481
villadeste.com

CREDIT CARDS	Accepted
PRICE	Blow-out
TYPE	Hotel
ACCOMMODATION	152 Rooms and Suites
FACILITIES	2 Bars, Gym, Indoor swimming pool, 3 Restaurants, Sauna, Spa, Steam room
GOOD TO KNOW	Child friendly, Free parking
RECOMMENDED FOR	All-time favorite, Family friendly, Luxury, Worth the travel

Recommended by: Hans Baldauf, BCV Architecture + Interiors; Beppe Caturegli and Giovannella Formica, Caturegli Formica Architetti Associati; Bernard Dubois, Bernard Dubois Architects; Bruce Kuwabara, KPMB Architects; Mark Landini, Landini Associates; Piero Lissoni, Lissoni Associati; Dominique Perrault, Dominique Perrault Architecture; Lauren Rottet, Rottet Studio

IL SERENO HOTEL
Via Torrazza 10
Torno
Como 22020
Lombardy
Italy
+39 0315477800
serenohotels.com

CREDIT CARDS	Accepted
PRICE	Blow-out
TYPE	Hotel
ACCOMMODATION	30 Suites
FACILITIES	2 Bars, Gym, Outdoor swimming pool, Restaurant, Spa
GOOD TO KNOW	Child and pet friendly
RECOMMENDED FOR	Countryside, Wish I'd designed

"Located on Lake Como and designed by Patricia Urquiola."
—Lauren Rottet

Recommended by: Marcio Kogan, Studio MK27; Pedro Rica and Marta Urtasun, Mecanismo; Lauren Rottet, Rottet Studio

EDEN HOTEL
Via Funivie 3
Bormio
Sondrio 23032
Lombardy
Italy
+39 0342911669
edenbormio.it

CREDIT CARDS..Accepted
PRICE...Mid-range
TYPE...Hotel
ACCOMMODATION.........................27 Rooms and Suites
FACILITIES..Bar
GOOD TO KNOW...Pet friendly
RECOMMENDED FOR................................Mountains

"Design meets tradition at this hotel in the center of
the small town of Bormio, just in front of the Stelvio
National Park."—Paolo Brambilla

Recommended by: Paolo Brambilla, Calvi Brambilla

BULGARI HOTEL MILANO
Via Privata Fratelli Gabba 7b
Brera
Milan 20121
Italy
+39 028058051
bulgarihotels.com

CREDIT CARDS..Accepted
PRICE..Blow-out
TYPE...Hotel
ACCOMMODATION.........................58 Rooms and Suites
FACILITIES.........................Bar, Gym, Indoor swimming pool,
Restaurant, Sauna, Spa,
Wood-burning fireplace, Yoga
GOOD TO KNOW..Garden
RECOMMENDED FOR........................Spa, Where I live

"It is a great hotel, quietly elegant, and the rooms face a
lovely garden in the heart of Milan."—Piero Lissoni

Recommended by: Vincenzo De Cotiis, Vincenzo De Cotiis
Architects and Gallery; Piero Lissoni, Lissoni Associati;
Andrea Maffei, Andrea Maffei Architects

OSTELLO BELLO
Via Medici 4
Carrobbio
Milan 20123
Italy
+39 0236582720
ostellobello.com

CREDIT CARDS.........................Accepted but not Amex
PRICE...Mid-range
TYPE..Hostel
ACCOMMODATION..................................12 Dorms and Rooms
FACILITIES.......................................Bar, Restaurant
GOOD TO KNOW...Pet friendly
RECOMMENDED FOR...............................Where I live

A hip and characterful hostel on one of Milan's oldest
streets. Rooms are clean, bright, and stylish (some private
rooms are en suite), and there are plenty of lively communal
spaces.

Recommended by: Fosbury Architecture

ROOM MATE GIULIA
Via Silvio Pellico 4
Duomo
Milan 20121
Italy
+39 0280888900
room-matehotels.com

CREDIT CARDS..Accepted
PRICE...Mid-range
TYPE...Hotel
ACCOMMODATION.........................85 Rooms and Suites
FACILITIES..................................Bar, Gym, Sauna,
Spa, Steam room
GOOD TO KNOW...Babysitting
RECOMMENDED FOR............................All-time favorite,
Luxury, Urban, Where I live

"In the global design capital, where better to stay than the
ultimate design hotel? With interiors by legendary Spanish
designer Patricia Urquiola, Room Mate Giulia is a dream.
Right on the doorstep of the Duomo and Galleria Vittorio
Emanuele II, this is not just Milan's best-designed hotel, but
also its best appointed."—Grace Mortlock

Recommended by: Paolo Brambilla, Calvi Brambilla; Grace
Mortlock, Other Architects; Mia Baarup Tofte, NORD
Architects; Artem Vakhrin, AKZ Architectura

FOUR SEASONS HOTEL MILAN
Via Gesù 6–8
Quadrilatero della Moda
Milan 20121
Italy
+39 0277088
fourseasons.com

CREDIT CARDS..Accepted
PRICE...High-end
TYPE..Hotel
ACCOMMODATION.....................................118 Rooms and Suites
FACILITIES.........................Bar, Gym, Indoor swimming pool,
Restaurant, Spa
GOOD TO KNOW..Pet friendly
RECOMMENDED FOR......................Babysitting, Child friendly,
Valet parking

Recommended by: Doriana and Massimiliano Fuksas, Studio
Fuksas; David Rockwell, Rockwell Group; Lauren Rottet,
Rottet Studio; Matteo Thun, Matteo Thun & Partners

GRAND HOTEL ET DE MILAN
Via Manzoni 29
Quadrilatero della Moda
Milan 20121
Italy
+39 02723141
grandhoteletdemilan.it

CREDIT CARDS..Accepted
PRICE...High-end
TYPE..Hotel
ACCOMMODATION.....................................94 Rooms and Suites
FACILITIES....................................Bar, Gym, 2 Restaurants
GOOD TO KNOW..Pet friendly
RECOMMENDED FOR...All-time favorite,
Luxury, Where I live

"Old-style, low-key luxury, and the best-looking doormen
in the world."—Amanda Levete

Recommended by: Peter Eisenman, Eisenman Architects;
Amanda Levete, AL_A; Carlo Ratti, Carlo Ratti Associati

PALAZZO MATTEOTTI
Corso Matteotti 4/6
Quadrilatero della Moda
Milan 20121, Italy
+39 0277679611
dahotels.com

CREDIT CARDS..Accepted
PRICE...Mid-range
TYPE..Hotel
ACCOMMODATION.....................................154 Rooms and Suites
FACILITIES.................................Bar, Gym, Hammam,
Indoor swimming pool, Restaurant
GOOD TO KNOW.......................................Child friendly
RECOMMENDED FOR...Spa

Recommended by: Claudia Urdaneta, NMD NOMADAS

HOTEL PALAZZO DELLE STELLINE
Corso Magenta 61
San Vittore
Milan 20123, Italy
+39024818431
hotelpalazzostelline.it

CREDIT CARDS..Accepted
PRICE...Low-cost
TYPE..Hotel
ACCOMMODATION.....................................105 Rooms and Suites
FACILITIES...Bar
GOOD TO KNOW...No pets
RECOMMENDED FOR...........................Budget, Family friendly

"A former monastery across the street from Michelangelo's
Last Supper."—Thomas Leeser

Recommended by: Thomas Leeser, Leeser Architecture

SENATO HOTEL MILANO
Via Senato 22
Porta Nuova
Milan 20121, Italy
+39 02781236
senatohotelmilano.it

CREDIT CARDS..Accepted
PRICE...Mid-range
TYPE..Hotel
ACCOMMODATION.....................................41 Rooms, 2 Suites
FACILITIES...Bar, Gym
GOOD TO KNOW...................................Child and pet friendly
RECOMMENDED FOR..Where I live

Recommended by: Cristina Celestino

RELAIS SAN MAURIZIO

Località San Maurizio 39
Santo Stefano Belbo 12058
Cuneo
Piedmont, Italy
+39 0141841900
relaissanmaurizio.it

CREDIT CARDS	Accepted
PRICE	Mid-range
TYPE	Hotel
ACCOMMODATION	36 Rooms and Suites
FACILITIES	Bar, 2 Restaurants, Sauna, Spa, Swimming pools, Yoga
GOOD TO KNOW	Seasonal truffle hunting
RECOMMENDED FOR	Countryside

Recommended by: Michael Young, Michael Young Studio

CAPANNA MARGHERITA

Punta Gnifetti 4554m
Alagna Valsesia 13021
Vercelli
Piedmont, Italy
rifugimonterosa.it

CREDIT CARDS	Accepted but not Amex
PRICE	Low-cost
TYPE	Lodge
ACCOMMODATION	12 Rooms
FACILITIES	Bar, Library, Restaurant
GOOD TO KNOW	Email to book, Shared bathrooms
RECOMMENDED FOR	Mountains

Europe's highest refuge hut, the Capanna Margherita is an eco-friendly building for up to seventy people.

Recommended by: Carlo Ratti, Carlo Ratti Associati

MASSERIA LE CARRUBE

Contrada Spennati, SS Fasano-Ostuni km873
Ostuni 72017
Brindisi
Puglia, Italy
+39 0831342595
masserialecarrubeostuni.it

CREDIT CARDS	Accepted but not Amex
PRICE	Mid-range
TYPE	Masseria
ACCOMMODATION	19 Rooms
FACILITIES	Outdoor swimming pool, Restaurant
GOOD TO KNOW	Babysitting, Free parking
RECOMMENDED FOR	Countryside

"The height of simplicity; the vegan food is amazing."
—Stéphane Parmentier

Recommended by: Stéphane Parmentier

MASSERIA MOROSETA

Contrada Lamacavallo
Ostuni 72017
Brindisi
Puglia, Italy
+39 3381899199
masseriamoroseta.it

CREDIT CARDS	Accepted
PRICE	Mid-range
TYPE	Masseria
ACCOMMODATION	6 Rooms
FACILITIES	Bar, Outdoor swimming pool, Restaurant, Sauna, Spa, Steam room, Yoga
GOOD TO KNOW	Free parking
RECOMMENDED FOR	Best-kept secret

"A delicate, intelligent, and refined country house in a relatively undiscovered corner of Italy. The nature, calm, and serenity make for a healing stay."—Nabil Gholam

Recommended by: Nabil Gholam, Nabil Gholam Architects

BORGO EGNAZIA

Strada Comunale Egnazia
Savelletri di Fasano 72015
Brindisi
Puglia, Italy
+39 0802255000
borgoegnazia.com

CREDIT CARDS	Accepted
PRICE	High-end
TYPE	Village resort
ACCOMMODATION	191 Duplexes, Rooms, Suites, and Villas
FACILITIES	Bar, Gym, Indoor and outdoor swimming pools, 5 Restaurants, Sauna, Spa, Steam room, Yoga
GOOD TO KNOW	Miniature farm, Pet friendly
RECOMMENDED FOR	Beach, Family friendly

"You won't want to leave—it has everything you could imagine and more."—Achille Salvagni

Recommended by: Rafael de La-Hoz Castanys, Rafael de La-Hoz Arquitectos; Achille Salvagni, Salvagni Architetti

MASSERIA CIMINO

Contrada Masciola
Savelletri di Fasano 72010
Brindisi
Puglia, Italy
+39 0804827886
masseriacimino.com

CREDIT CARDS	Accepted
PRICE	Low-cost
TYPE	Masseria
ACCOMMODATION	14 Rooms and Suites
FACILITIES	Outdoor swimming pool, Restaurant
GOOD TO KNOW	Free parking
RECOMMENDED FOR	Budget

Recommended by: Stéphane Parmentier

MASSERIA POTENTI

Contrada Potenti
Manduria 74024
Taranto
Puglia, Italy
+39 0999735408
masseriapotenti.it

CREDIT CARDS	Accepted
PRICE	Mid-range
TYPE	Masseria
ACCOMMODATION	23 Rooms and Suites
FACILITIES	Bar, Outdoor swimming pool, 2 Restaurants, Yoga
GOOD TO KNOW	Free parking
RECOMMENDED FOR	Countryside

Recommended by: Jürgen Mayer H., J. Mayer H. und Partner, Architekten

HOTEL CALA DI VOLPE

Costa Smeralda
Porto Cervo 07020
Sassari
Sardinia, Italy
+39 0789976111
caladivolpe.com

CREDIT CARDS	Accepted
PRICE	Mid-range
TYPE	Hotel
ACCOMMODATION	121 Rooms
FACILITIES	Bar, Gym, Outdoor swimming pool, 2 Restaurants, Spa
GOOD TO KNOW	Babysitting, Bicycle rentals
RECOMMENDED FOR	Beach, Wish I'd designed

"A legendary 1960s hotel by Jacques Couëlle. With the history and the beauty of the area, it is no coincidence that many movies have been shot here."—Claire Bétaille and Bruno Moinard

Recommended by: Claire Bétaille and Bruno Moinard, 4BI & Associés; Matteo Thun, Matteo Thun & Partners

VILLA ATHENA HOTEL

Via Passeggiata Archeologica 33
Agrigento 92100
Sicily, Italy
+39 0922596288
hotelvillaathena.it

CREDIT CARDS	Accepted but not Amex
PRICE	Mid-range
TYPE	Hotel
ACCOMMODATION	27 Rooms and Suites
FACILITIES	Bar, Outdoor swimming pool, 2 Restaurants, Spa
GOOD TO KNOW	Free parking, Pet friendly
RECOMMENDED FOR	Best-kept secret

"This fantastic hotel allows you to visit the Agrigento Greek Temples by night."—Alfredo Payá Benedito

Recommended by: Alfredo Payá Benedito, Noname29

VERDURA RESORT

Strada Statale 115 km131
Sciacca 92019
Agrigento
Sicily, Italy
+39 0925998180
roccofortehotels.com

CREDIT CARDS	Accepted
PRICE	High-end
TYPE	Resort
ACCOMMODATION	200 Rooms and Suites
FACILITIES	4 Bars, Gym, Indoor and outdoor swimming pools, 3 Restaurants, Sauna, Spa
GOOD TO KNOW	Babysitting, Kids' club
RECOMMENDED FOR	Beach

A member of the Rocco Forte collection, Verdura Resort is a five-star retreat on Sicily's south coast. An idyllic holiday destination for keen golfers, sun-seekers, and gourmands alike, it has a Kyle Phillips eighteen-hole golf course, a selection of excellent dining experiences and cookery classes. The spa has extensive wellness treatments.

Recommended by: Flavio Albanese, ASA Studio

MUSEO ALBERGO ATELIER SUL MARE
Via Cesare Battisti 4
Castel di Tusa 98079
Messina
Sicily, Italy
+39 0921334295
ateliersulmare.com

CREDIT CARDS	Accepted but not Amex
PRICE	Low-cost
TYPE	Inn
ACCOMMODATION	40 Rooms
FACILITIES	Bar, Restaurant, Sauna
GOOD TO KNOW	Child and pet friendly, Free parking
RECOMMENDED FOR	Wish I'd designed

Recommended by: Carlos Ferrater, OAB

CAPOFARO
Via Faro 3
Salina Isole Eolie 98050
Messina
Sicily, Italy
+39 0909844330
capofaro.it

CREDIT CARDS	Accepted
PRICE	Mid-range
TYPE	Hotel
ACCOMMODATION	27 Rooms
FACILITIES	Bar, Outdoor swimming pool, Restaurant, Spa, Yoga
GOOD TO KNOW	Child friendly, Free parking
RECOMMENDED FOR	Island

Recommended by: Paolo Brambilla, Calvi Brambilla

BELMOND GRAND HOTEL TIMEO
Via Teatro Greco 59
Taormina 98039
Messina
Sicily, Italy
+39 09426270200
belmond.com

CREDIT CARDS	Accepted
PRICE	High-end
TYPE	Hotel
ACCOMMODATION	80 Rooms
FACILITIES	Bar, Gym, Outdoor swimming pool, Restaurant, Sauna, Spa
GOOD TO KNOW	Child friendly, Free parking
RECOMMENDED FOR	Island

Belmond Grand Hotel Timeo is a hotel that embraces the glamour and opulence of Sicilian design. It looks over the Taormina rooftops and out to the Ionian Sea. Treatments at the spa and wellness center feature natural and organic products prepared with local herbs and flowers.

Recommended by: Doriana and Massimiliano Fuksas, Studio Fuksas

HOTEL BEL SOGGIORNO
Via Luigi Pirandello 60
Taormina 98039
Messina
Sicily, Italy
+39 094223342
belsoggiorno.com

CREDIT CARDS	Accepted
PRICE	Low-cost
TYPE	Hotel
ACCOMMODATION	33 Rooms and Suites
FACILITIES	Bar
GOOD TO KNOW	Free parking, Pet friendly
RECOMMENDED FOR	Budget

"Old-school Italian hotel with great views of the sea and Mount Etna."—Mia Baarup Tofte

Recommended by: Mia Baarup Tofte, NORD Architects

THERASIA RESORT
Isola di Vulcano
Vulcanello 98050
Messina
Sicily, Italy
+39 0909852555
therasiaresort.it

CREDIT CARDS	Accepted
PRICE	Mid-range
TYPE	Resort
ACCOMMODATION	95 Rooms
FACILITIES	Bar, Indoor and outdoor swimming pools, 3 Restaurants, Sauna, Spa, Steam room
GOOD TO KNOW	Free parking, No pets
RECOMMENDED FOR	Beach

"Quiet location and a Michelin-starred restaurant."
—Claudio Lucchesi

Recommended by: Claudio Lucchesi, Urban Future Organization

GRAND HOTEL VILLA IGIEA PALERMO

Salita Belmonte 43
Palermo 90142
Sicily
Italy
+39 0916312111
villa-igiea.com

CREDIT CARDS	Accepted
PRICE	High-end
TYPE	Hotel
ACCOMMODATION	115 Rooms and Suites
FACILITIES	Bar, Gym, Outdoor swimming pool, 2 Restaurants
GOOD TO KNOW	Babysitting, Free parking, Small pets only
RECOMMENDED FOR	Luxury

This charming hotel retains many original features following its nineteenth-century restoration by the pioneering Art Nouveau architect Ernesto Basile. It also offers guests Sicilian cooking courses and walking tours of Palermo.

Recommended by: Raúl de Armas, MdeAS Architects

RELAIS SANTA ANASTASIA

Contrada Santa Anastasia
Castelbuono 90013
Sicily
Italy
+39 0921672233
abbaziasantanastasia.com

CREDIT CARDS	Accepted
PRICE	Mid-range
TYPE	Hotel
ACCOMMODATION	28 Rooms and Suites
FACILITIES	Bar, Gym, Outdoor swimming pool, Restaurant
GOOD TO KNOW	Child friendly
RECOMMENDED FOR	Countryside

Recommended by: Ludovico Centis, The Empire

CAVE BIANCHE HOTEL

Strada Comunale Fanfalo
Favignana 91023
Trapani
Sicily
Italy
+39 0923925451
cavebianchehotel.it

CREDIT CARDS	Accepted
PRICE	Low-cost
TYPE	Hotel
ACCOMMODATION	50 Rooms
FACILITIES	Bar, Outdoor swimming pool, Restaurant
GOOD TO KNOW	Free parking
RECOMMENDED FOR	All-time favorite, Island, Worth the travel

Recommended by: Makio Hasuike, Makio Hasuike & Co

TONNARA DI SCOPELLO

Largo Tonnara
Scopello 91014
Trapani
Sicily
Italy
+39 03888299472
latonnaradiscopello.it

CREDIT CARDS	Accepted but not Amex
PRICE	Mid-range
TYPE	House rental
ACCOMMODATION	14 Apartments
FACILITIES	Museum
GOOD TO KNOW	Free parking, No pets, Self-catering
RECOMMENDED FOR	Best-kept secret, Budget

A thirteenth-century house with an extensive history at the heart of a fishing community, Tonnara di Scopello now houses a museum and a collection of beautifully restored rooms and apartments. There is no television or telephone—ideal for those looking to escape the stresses of the modern world.

Recommended by: Hugo Sauzay, Festen Architecture

ADLER LODGE ALPE
Via Piz 11
Castelrotto 39040
Alpe di Siusi
Trentino-South Tyrol
Italy
+39 0471723000
adler-lodge.com

CREDIT CARDS...Accepted
PRICE...Mid-range
TYPE...Lodge
ACCOMMODATION...................................30 Chalets and Suites
FACILITIES..Bar, Gym,
Indoor and outdoor swimming pools,
Restaurant, Sauna,
Spa, Wood-burning fireplace
GOOD TO KNOW.....................Bicycle rentals, Nordic walking
RECOMMENDED FOR..........Mountains, Spa, Worth the travel

"This brilliantly designed contemporary lodge caught my attention while hiking in the Dolomites. It offers a truly otherworldly experience, and is a stunning picture frame for the extraordinary landscape. Interiors are comfortable, convivial, and artful; every dimension of this lodge comes together perfectly."—Todd-Avery Lenahan

Recommended by: Hans Baldauf, BCV Architecture + Interiors; Todd-Avery Lenahan, TAL Studio

HOTEL BRIOL
Via Briol 1
Barbiano
Bolzano
Trentino-South Tyrol 39040
Italy
+39 0471650125
briol.it

CREDIT CARDS...Accepted
PRICE...Low-cost
TYPE...Hotel
ACCOMMODATION..........................10 Apartments and Houses
FACILITIES...................Outdoor swimming pool, Restaurant
GOOD TO KNOW...........Child and pet friendly, Free parking,
RECOMMENDED FOR...........Best-kept secret, Eco-conscious,
Mountains

Recommended by: Paolo Brambilla, Calvi Brambilla; Much Untertrifaller, Dietrich Untertrifaller Architects

MIRAMONTI BOUTIQUE HOTEL
Via Santa Caterina 14
Avalengo
Merano
Trentino-South Tyrol 39010
Italy
+39 0473279335
hotel-miramonti.com

CREDIT CARDS...Accepted
PRICE...Mid-range
TYPE...Hotel
ACCOMMODATION......................................43 Rooms and Suites
FACILITIES...Bar, Jacuzzi,
Outdoor swimming pool,
3 Restaurants, Sauna, Steam room
GOOD TO KNOW.................................Babysitting, Pet friendly,
Valet parking
RECOMMENDED FOR...Spa

Recommended by: Robert Konieczny, KWK Promes

VIGILIUS MOUNTAIN RESORT
Via Villa 3
Lana 39011
Bolzano
Trentino-South Tyrol
Italy
+39 0473556600
vigilius.it

CREDIT CARDS...Accepted
PRICE...High-end
TYPE..Resort
ACCOMMODATION......................................41 Rooms and Suites
FACILITIES...Outdoor swimming pool,
2 Restaurants, Sauna, Spa, Yoga
GOOD TO KNOW...Arrival by cable car
RECOMMENDED FOR...Mountains

"Beautifully designed by Matteo Thun in a magical setting where you feel at one with nature."—Amanda Levete

[This hotel was designed by Matteo Thun & Partners.]

Recommended by: Amanda Levete, AL_A; Giancarlo Mazzanti, El Equipo Mazzanti; Matteo Thun, Matteo Thun & Partners

WHITE DEER SAN LORENZO MOUNTAIN LODGE

Località Elle 23
San Lorenzo di Sebato 39030
Bolzano
Trentino-South Tyrol, Italy
+39 0474404042
sanlorenzolodges.com

CREDIT CARDS	Accepted
PRICE	High-end
TYPE	Lodge
ACCOMMODATION	4 Rooms
FACILITIES	Outdoor swimming pool, Sauna
GOOD TO KNOW	Must book entire lodge
RECOMMENDED FOR	Mountains

Recommended by: Marcio Kogan, Studio MK27

SMART HOTEL SASLONG

Strasse Pallua 40
Santa Cristina Valgardena 39047
Bolzano
Trentino-South Tyrol, Italy
+39 0471774444
saslong.eu

CREDIT CARDS	Accepted but not Amex
PRICE	Low-cost
TYPE	Hotel
ACCOMMODATION	50 Rooms
FACILITIES	Bar, Restaurant
GOOD TO KNOW	Pet friendly, Ski bus
RECOMMENDED FOR	Mountains

Recommended by: Claudio Lucchesi, Urban Future Organization

CASTELLO DI GARGONZA

Località Gargonza
Monte San Savino 52048
Tuscany, Italy
+39 0575847021
gargonza.it

CREDIT CARDS	Accepted
PRICE	Mid-range
TYPE	Hotel
ACCOMMODATION	47 Apartments and Rooms
FACILITIES	Bar, Outdoor swimming pool, Restaurant
GOOD TO KNOW	Bicycle rentals, Child friendly
RECOMMENDED FOR	Countryside

"A magical enclave in a well-preserved thirteenth-century hamlet. All rooms and suites are unique."—Buzz Yudell

Recommended by: Buzz Yudell, Moore Ruble Yudell

BELMOND VILLA SAN MICHELE

Via Doccia 4
Fiesole 50014
Tuscany
Italy
+39 0555678200
belmond.com

CREDIT CARDS	Accepted
PRICE	Blow-out
TYPE	Hotel
ACCOMMODATION	45 Rooms and Suites
FACILITIES	Bar, Gym, Outdoor swimming pool, 2 Restaurants
GOOD TO KNOW	Child friendly
RECOMMENDED FOR	Luxury

With a facade attributed to Michelangelo, Belmond Villa San Michele is a masterpiece in a former monastery situated in the Tuscan hills overlooking Florence. From the attentive concierge team to a host of intimate dining options, it provides an experience of supreme luxury and tranquility.

Recommended by: Emanuel Christ, Christ & Gantenbein

LOGGIATO DEI SERVITI

Piazza della Santissima Annunziata 3
Florence 50122
Tuscany
Italy
+39 055289592
loggiatodeiservitihotel.it

CREDIT CARDS	Accepted
PRICE	Low-cost
TYPE	Hotel
ACCOMMODATION	42 Rooms
FACILITIES	Bar
GOOD TO KNOW	Child friendly, Valet parking
RECOMMENDED FOR	Budget

"Originally designed by Antonio da Sangallo. Some rooms face the Academy of Fine Arts' garden."—Andrea Maffei

Recommended by: Andrea Maffei, Andrea Maffei Architects

AL PALAZZO DEL MARCHESE DI CAMUGLIANO

Via del Moro 15
Florence 50123
Tuscany, Italy
+39 0552654578
palazzodicamugliano.com

CREDIT CARDS...Accepted
PRICE...Mid-range
TYPE...Hotel
ACCOMMODATION.....................................13 Rooms and Suites
FACILITIES...Bar, Gym
GOOD TO KNOW.................................Child friendly
RECOMMENDED FOR...Urban

"A great boutique hotel with a rich history and a garden in a tiny street in the middle of Florence."—Nilson Ariel Espino

Recommended by: Nilson Ariel Espino, Suma Arquitectos

PORTRAIT FIRENZE

Lungarno degli Acciaiuoli 4
Florence 50123
Tuscany, Italy
+39 05527268000
lungarnocollection.com

CREDIT CARDS...Accepted
PRICE...High-end
TYPE...Hotel
ACCOMMODATION...37 Suites
FACILITIES...........................Bar, Restaurant, Spa
GOOD TO KNOW.................................Child friendly
RECOMMENDED FOR...............................All-time favorite

Recommended by: Waro Kishi, K.ASSOCIATES/Architects

TERME DI SATURNIA

Saturnia
Tuscany 58014, Italy
+39 0564600111
termedisaturnia.it

CREDIT CARDS...Accepted
PRICE...High-end
TYPE...Spa resort
ACCOMMODATION.....................................128 Rooms and Suites
FACILITIES.................................Bar, Hot-spring bath,
Outdoor swimming pool,
Restaurant, Spa
GOOD TO KNOW.................................Pet friendly, Valet parking
RECOMMENDED FOR.......................................Countryside, Spa

"Great for recharging body and mind."—Achille Salvagni

Recommended by: Achille Salvagni, Salvagni Architetti

HOTEL IL PELLICANO

Località Sbarcatello
Porto Ercole 58019
Tuscany
Italy
+39 0564858111
hotelilpellicano.com

CREDIT CARDS...Accepted
PRICE...Blow-out
TYPE...Hotel
ACCOMMODATION.....................................50 Rooms and Suites
FACILITIES...2 Bars, Gym,
Outdoor swimming pool,
2 Restaurants, Spa, Yoga
GOOD TO KNOW.........................Bicycle rentals, Pet friendly
RECOMMENDED FOR...............................Beach, Worth the travel

A legend. This effortlessly stylish boutique hotel on the Tuscan coast is a glamorous holiday destination near Porto Ercole, just ninety minutes from Rome.

Recommended by: Emanuel Christ, Christ & Gantenbein; Peter Eisenman, Eisenman Architects

AGRITURISMO BIOLOGICO SANT'EGLE

Via Case Sparse Sant'Egle 18
Sorano 58010
Tuscany
Italy
+39 03294250285
agriturismobiologicotoscana.it

CREDIT CARDS.....................................Accepted but not Amex
PRICE...Mid-range
TYPE...Agriturismo
ACCOMMODATION.................................8 Apartments, Rooms,
Suites, and Tents
FACILITIES.....................Bar, Outdoor swimming pool, Yoga
GOOD TO KNOW.........................Child friendly (14 and over),
No pets
RECOMMENDED FOR.......................................Eco-conscious

An eco-centric holiday destination with a sustainable and organic ethos. Rooms are simple yet stylish, and there are plenty of wellness-focused activities available, including massages, yoga, nature walks, and cookery classes.

Recommended by: Beppe Caturegli and Giovannella Formica, Caturegli Formica Architetti Associati

BORGO PIGNANO
Località Pignano 6
Volterra 56048
Tuscany
Italy
+39 058835032
borgopignano.com

CREDIT CARDS	Accepted
PRICE	High-end
TYPE	Country estate hotel
ACCOMMODATION	32 Cottages, Maisonettes, Rooms, Suites, and VIllas
FACILITIES	Bar, Gym, Outdoor swimming pool, 2 Restaurants, Sauna, Spa, Steam room, Yoga
GOOD TO KNOW	Child friendly
RECOMMENDED FOR	Spa

Situated in 750 acres (300 hectares) of Tuscan countryside, Borgo Pignano is a sensitively restored estate that prides itself on its credentials of sustainable living. Accommodation includes rooms in the manor house and surrounding cottages, which are stylishly pared-back. The majority of ingredients used in the restaurant and spa are grown on the estate.

Recommended by: Yu-lin Chen, MAYU Architects+

LA BANDITA COUNTRYHOUSE
Podere La Bandita
Pienza 53026
Siena
Tuscany
Italy
+39 3334046704
la-bandita.com

CREDIT CARDS	Accepted
PRICE	High-end
TYPE	Bed and Breakfast and Villa
ACCOMMODATION	12 Rooms
FACILITIES	Outdoor swimming pool, Wine cellar
GOOD TO KNOW	Bicycle rental, Private chef available on request
RECOMMENDED FOR	Worth the travel

"For its intimate scale and how you feel lost in Tuscany's Val d'Orcia. Incredible views, phenomenal color palette, materials, and attention to detail."—Ab Rogers

Recommended by: Ab Rogers, Ab Rogers Design

TENUTA DI SPANNOCCHIA
Località Spannocchia 167
Chiusdino 53012
Siena
Tuscany
Italy
+39 0577752601
spannocchia.com

CREDIT CARDS	Accepted but not Amex
PRICE	Low-cost
TYPE	Farm rentals and Bed and Breakfast
ACCOMMODATION	14 Farmhouses and Rooms
FACILITIES	Outdoor swimming pool
GOOD TO KNOW	Child friendly, Self-catering
RECOMMENDED FOR	Eco-conscious

"Historic Tuscan villa within a working organic farm, set on a nature reserve."—Hans Baldauf

Recommended by: Hans Baldauf, BCV Architecture + Interiors

BADIA A COLTIBUONO
Località Badia a Coltibuono
Gaiole in Chianti 53013
Siena
Tuscany
Italy
+39 057774481
coltibuono.com

CREDIT CARDS	Accepted but not Amex
PRICE	Mid-range
TYPE	Hotel
ACCOMMODATION	15 Apartments and Rooms
FACILITIES	Bar, Outdoor swimming pool, Restaurant
GOOD TO KNOW	Child and pet friendly, Free parking
RECOMMENDED FOR	Worth the travel

Recommended by: Hani Rashid, Asymptote Architecture

MONTEVERDI
Via di Mezzo
Castiglioncello del Trinoro 53047
Siena
Tuscany
Italy
+39 0578268146
monteverdituscany.com

CREDIT CARDS..Accepted
PRICE..Blow-out
TYPE...Hotel
ACCOMMODATION.......................11 Rooms and Villas
FACILITIES........................Bar, Gym, Indoor swimming pool,
2 Restaurants, Spa
GOOD TO KNOW...........................Child friendly, Valet parking
RECOMMENDED FOR.......................................Countryside

"The owner has renovated the hotel, situated in the peaceful medieval village of Castiglioncello del Trinoro, but has also brought new life to this almost deserted little place. The village is part of the whole experience. Interior design by Ilaria Miani is second to none; bedrooms have a uniquely Tuscan character; and the spa is exquisite."—Ben van Berkel

Recommended by: Ben van Berkel, UNStudio

HOTEL PALAZZO RAVIZZA
Pian dei Mantellini 34
Siena 53100
Tuscany
Italy
+39 0577280462
palazzoravizza.it

CREDIT CARDS..Accepted
PRICE...Mid-range
TYPE...Hotel
ACCOMMODATION...............................40 Rooms and Suites
FACILITIES...Bar
GOOD TO KNOW...........................Child friendly, Free parking
RECOMMENDED FOR...................................All-time favorite

"In Siena's ancient center, this hotel has a small garden overlooking the hills, a private chapel, and a Steinway piano in the great hall. Popular with musicians from the nearby Accademia Chigiana, past guests of the hotel have included composers, writers, and historians such as Bernard Berenson, Aldous Huxley, and Alfredo Casella. Room 5 is my favorite for its very nice frescoes."—Marta Laudani

Recommended by: Marta Laudani, Marta Laudani Design

NUN ASSISI RELAIS & SPA MUSEUM
Via Eremo delle Carceri 1A
Assisi 06081
Perugia
Umbria
Italy
+39 0758155150
nunassisi.com

CREDIT CARDS..Accepted
PRICE...High-end
TYPE...Hotel
ACCOMMODATION...18 Suites
FACILITIES.........................Bar, Gym, Restaurant, Sauna,
Spa, Steam room
GOOD TO KNOW...Child friendly
RECOMMENDED FOR.......................................Countryside

Recommended by: Emre Arolat, EAA

EREMITO
Località Tarina 2
Parrano 05010
Terni
Umbria
Italy
+39 0763891010
eremito.com

CREDIT CARDS..Accepted
PRICE...Mid-range
TYPE...Hotel
ACCOMMODATION...12 Rooms
FACILITIES....................Indoor swimming pool, Restaurant,
Spa, Steam room, Yoga
GOOD TO KNOW...................Access by private transfer only
RECOMMENDED FOR....................................Eco-conscious

"An old monastery fully restored as an eco-resort. Rooms are carved from local stone slabs, which also insulates the building and saves energy. Every aspect of the hotel is sustainable, from the food to the textiles decorating the public spaces. The view are stunning."—Francesca Bucci

Recommended by: Francesca Bucci, BG Studio International; Lauren Rottet, Rottet Studio

MERCURE DOLOMITI HOTEL BOITE
Via Ravenna 297
Borca di Cadore 32040
Belluno
Veneto
Italy
+39 0435482156
hotelboitedolomiti.it

CREDIT CARDS.....................................Accepted but not Amex
PRICE...Low-cost
TYPE...Hotel
ACCOMMODATION...84 Rooms
FACILITIES...Bar, Restaurant
GOOD TO KNOW..........................Babysitting, Pet friendly
RECOMMENDED FOR...Mountains

"This hotel was originally designed by Edoardo Gellner in the 1960s, commissioned by Enrico Mattei as a tourist village for Eni's workers. Its architecture remains unchanged; visitors can breathe in the authentic atmosphere of the past and enjoy the idealist design."—Cristina Celestino

Recommended by: Cristina Celestino

ROSAPETRA SPA RESORT
Località Zuel di Sopra 1
Cortina d'Ampezzo 32043
Belluno
Veneto
Italy
+39 0436869062
rosapetracortina.it

CREDIT CARDS...Accepted
PRICE...High-end
TYPE...Spa resort
ACCOMMODATION..................................29 Rooms and Suites
FACILITIES.....................................Bar, Indoor swimming pool,
Restaurant, Sauna, Spa
GOOD TO KNOW..Child friendly
RECOMMENDED FOR...Mountains

"Rooms are simple but carefully detailed and each has a view to the Dolomites. It is relaxing to watch the colour of the mountains turn orange–pink at sunset."
—Francesca Bucci

Recommended by: Francesca Bucci, BG Studio International

HOTEL VILLA CIPRIANI
Via Canova 298
Asolo 31011
Treviso
Veneto
Italy
+39 0423523411
villaciprianiasolo.com

CREDIT CARDS...Accepted
PRICE...Mid-range
TYPE...Hotel
ACCOMMODATION..................................29 Rooms and Suites
FACILITIES.....................Bar, Gym, Outdoor swimming pool,
Restaurant
GOOD TO KNOW..Bicycle rentals
RECOMMENDED FOR.................................Best-kept secret

"An elegant, intimate hotel with a stunning garden, in a beautiful town with views to the Tuscan hills."—Buzz Yudell

Recommended by: Buzz Yudell, Moore Ruble Yudell

DUE TORRI HOTEL
Piazza Sant'Anastasia 4
Verona 37121
Veneto
Italy
+39 045595044
hotelduetorri.duetorrihotels.com

CREDIT CARDS...Accepted
PRICE...High-end
TYPE...Hotel
ACCOMMODATION..................................78 Rooms and Suites
FACILITIES...Restaurant
GOOD TO KNOW..............Babysitting, Child and pet friendly
RECOMMENDED FOR.................................Where I live

"It has interesting 1950s frescoes by Pino Casarini, one of the few twentieth-century Italian fresco painters who also worked with Gio Ponti. In addition, the rooftop terrace of the hotel has wonderful views of old Verona."—Marta Laudani

Recommended by: Ludovico Centis, The Empire; Marta Laudani, Marta Laudani Design

VENICE: SEE PAGES 298–301

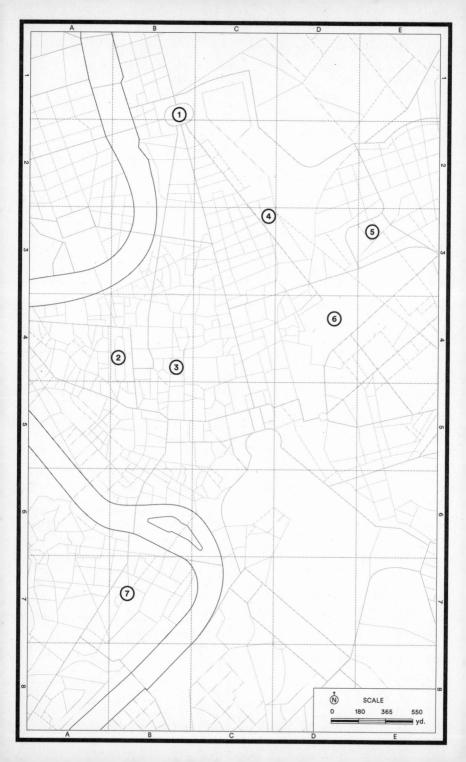

ROME

HOTEL DE RUSSIE
Via del Babuino 9
Piazza del Popolo
Rome 00187
+39 06328881
roccofortehotels.com

CREDIT CARDS	Accepted
PRICE	High-end
TYPE	Hotel
ACCOMMODATION	120 Rooms and Suites
FACILITIES	Bar, Gym, Indoor swimming pool, Restaurant, Sauna, Spa, Steam room
GOOD TO KNOW	Child friendly
RECOMMENDED FOR	Urban

"This hotel is the perfect blend of cultural heritage and modern luxury. Located between Villa Borghese park and fifteenth-century Bernini churches, it blends Italian fashion with touches of eclecticism."—Francesca Bucci

"From its upper-level suites (with terraces), you're looking down on Via del Babuino, one of Rome's best shopping streets. The inner courtyard is spectacular. Breakfast is fabulous, served on a multi-level terrace. Be sure to seek out the hotel's concierge, Salvatore—he's a great guy, and he knows every inch of the city."—Antoine Predock

Recommended by: Francesca Bucci, BG Studio International; Antoine Predock, Antoine Predock Architect

HOTEL LOCARNO
Via della Penna 22
Piazza del Popolo
Rome 00186
+39 063610841
hotellocarno.com

CREDIT CARDS	Accepted
PRICE	Mid-range
TYPE	Hotel
ACCOMMODATION	44 Rooms and Suites
FACILITIES	Bar
GOOD TO KNOW	Babysitting, Bicycle rentals, Child and pet friendly, Limousine and valet service
RECOMMENDED FOR	Urban

"The elevator, the courtyard, the breakfast."
—Charlotte von Moos

Recommended by: Charlotte von Moos, Sauter von Moos

HOTEL RAPHAËL
Largo Febo 2
Piazza Navona
Rome 00186
+39 06682831
raphaelhotel.com

CREDIT CARDS	Accepted
PRICE	High-end
TYPE	Hotel
ACCOMMODATION	51 Rooms and Suites
FACILITIES	Bar, Restaurant, Terrace
GOOD TO KNOW	Concierge
RECOMMENDED FOR	All-time favorite, Urban

Recommended by: Steven Holl, Steven Holl Architects; Richard Meier, Richard Meier & Partners Architect

FENDI PRIVATE SUITES
Via della Fontanella di Borghese 48
Pantheon
Rome 00186
+39 0697798080
fendiprivatesuites.com

CREDIT CARDS	Accepted
PRICE	Blow-out
TYPE	Hotel
ACCOMMODATION	7 Suites
FACILITIES	Bar, Restaurant
GOOD TO KNOW	Child friendly, Free parking
RECOMMENDED FOR	Urban

[This hotel was designed by Marco Costanzi Architects.]

Recommended by: Marco Costanzi, Marco Costanzi Architects

HOTEL ABBRUZZI
Piazza della Rotonda 69
Pantheon
Rome 00186
+39 0697841351
hotelabruzzi.it

CREDIT CARDS	Accepted
PRICE	Mid-range
TYPE	Hotel
ACCOMMODATION	26 Rooms
FACILITIES	Restaurant
GOOD TO KNOW	Near Trevi Fountain
RECOMMENDED FOR	Urban

A family run hotel in the heart of Rome that's just a short walk from the Pantheon and Piazza Navona. Each of the rooms is equipped with a "handy" smartphone, which allows guests to make unlimited national calls and is also pre-loaded with a complimentary city guide.

Recommended by: Emanuel Christ, Christ & Gantenbein

HOTEL ALBERGO DEL SOLE AL PANTHEON
Piazza della Rotonda 63
Pantheon
Rome 00186
+39 066780441
hotelsolealpantheon.com

CREDIT CARDS	Accepted
PRICE	Mid-range
TYPE	Hotel
ACCOMMODATION	25 Rooms and Suites
FACILITIES	Bar, Motorbike rentals
GOOD TO KNOW	Babysitting
RECOMMENDED FOR	Urban

"Having a view to the Pantheon from your room has no price." —Luca Gazzaniga

Recommended by: Luca Gazzaniga, Luca Gazzaniga Architects

HOTEL NAZIONALE ROMA
Piazza Montecitorio 131
Pantheon
Rome 00186
+39 06695001
hotelnazionale.it

CREDIT CARDS	Accepted
PRICE	Mid-range
TYPE	Hotel
ACCOMMODATION	100 Apartments, Rooms, and Suites
FACILITIES	Bar
GOOD TO KNOW	Babysitting, Child friendly
RECOMMENDED FOR	Urban

Located in an eighteenth-century building in Rome's historic center, Hotel Nazionale Roma is a four-star hotel featuring bright, contemporary rooms with stunning views of the surrounding area.

Recommended by: Giancarlo Mazzanti, El Equipo Mazzanti

HASSLER ROMA
Piazza della Trinità dei Monti 6
Spanish Steps
Rome 00187
+39 06699340
hotelhasslerroma.com

CREDIT CARDS	Accepted
PRICE	High-end
TYPE	Hotel
ACCOMMODATION	87 Rooms and Suites
FACILITIES	Bar, Barber, Gym, 2 Restaurants, Salon, Sauna, Spa, Steam room
GOOD TO KNOW	Babysitting, Bicycle rentals, No pets
RECOMMENDED FOR	Where I live

"Set on top of the Spanish Steps with one of the most beautiful views of Rome, this is one of the world's few hotels that has managed to maintain its unique style over time, with a service of the highest level that's always discreet and refined. It has been a mainstay for royal families, presidents, writers, artists, musicians, film stars, and directors from all over the world."—Marta Laudani

Recommended by: Marta Laudani, Marta Laudani Design; Achille Salvagni, Salvagni Architetti

HOTEL D'INGHILTERRA ROMA
Via Bocca di Leone 14
Spanish Steps
Rome 00187
+39 06699811
starhotelscollezione.com

CREDIT CARDS	Accepted
PRICE	Mid-range
TYPE	Hotel
ACCOMMODATION	88 Rooms and Suites
FACILITIES	Bar, Restaurant
GOOD TO KNOW	Babysitting, Child and pet friendly, Personal shopper
RECOMMENDED FOR	Best-kept secret

Recommended by: Raúl de Armas, MdeAS Architects

PORTRAIT ROMA
Via Bocca di Leone 23
Spanish Steps
Rome 00187
+39 0669380742
lungarnocollection.com

CREDIT CARDS...Accepted
PRICE...High-end
TYPE...Hotel
ACCOMMODATION..................................14 Rooms and Suites
FACILITIES.......................................Rooftop terrace bar
GOOD TO KNOW...Personal shopper
RECOMMENDED FOR..Luxury

"Spectacular views in a romantic setting with impecable haute couture interiors and exquisite amenities."
—Maria Warner Wong

Recommended by: Maria Warner Wong, WOW Architects | Warner Wong Design

HOTEL EDEN
Via Ludovisi 49
Via Veneto
Rome 00187
+39 06478121
dorchestercollection.com

CREDIT CARDS...Accepted
PRICE...Blow-out
TYPE...Hotel
ACCOMMODATION...................................98 Rooms and Suites
FACILITIES..Bar, Gym, 2 Restaurants,
                                                Spa, Steam room
GOOD TO KNOW...Child friendly
RECOMMENDED FOR..Luxury

"Italian charm and Roman emotions without a pastiche of the past. Amazing, timeless views over the Eternal City and the neighbouring Villa Medici."—Claire Bétaille and Bruno Moinard

Recommended by: Claire Bétaille and Bruno Moinard, 4BI & Associés; Roger Duffy, Skidmore, Owings & Merrill; Peter Eisenman, Eisenman Architects

HOTEL ST. REGIS ROME
Via Vittorio Emanuele Orlando 3
Quirinale
Rome 00185
+39 0647091
marriott.co.uk

CREDIT CARDS...Accepted
PRICE...High-end
TYPE...Hotel
ACCOMMODATION.................................161 Rooms and Suites
FACILITIES...Bar, Gym, Restaurant
GOOD TO KNOW...Child friendly
RECOMMENDED FOR.................................All-time favorite

"It is a beautiful hotel in an ancient city. You feel the presence of Rome in every detail. I have stayed here only once, and like any true luxury, once is enough as the memory lasts a lifetime."—Carlos Jiménez

Recommended by: Carlos Jiménez, Carlos Jiménez Studio

VOI DONNA CAMILLA SAVELLI HOTEL
Via Garibaldi 27
Trastevere
Rome 00153
+39 06588861
voihotels.com

CREDIT CARDS................................Accepted but not Amex
PRICE...Mid-range
TYPE...Hotel
ACCOMMODATION...................................78 Rooms and Suites
FACILITIES...Bar, Restaurant
GOOD TO KNOW...Babysitting,
                                    Barber and hairdresser available
RECOMMENDED FOR............................Best-kept secret, Urban

Recommended by: Daniel Libeskind, Studio Libeskind; Michael Maltzan, Michael Maltzan Architecture

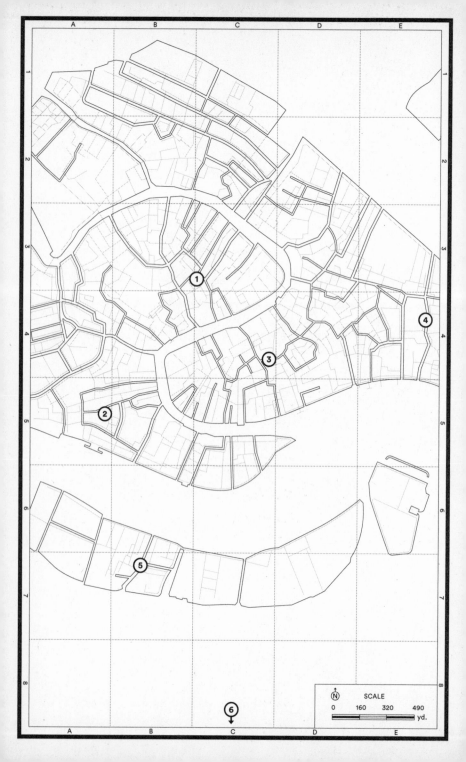

VENICE

AMAN VENICE
Palazzo Papadopoli, Calle Tiepolo 1364
San Polo
Venice 30125
+39 0412707333
aman.com

CREDIT CARDS...Accepted
PRICE..Blow-out
TYPE..Palazzo hotel
ACCOMMODATION.....................................24 Rooms and Suites
FACILITIES...Bar, Gym, Restaurant, Spa
GOOD TO KNOW...Child friendly
RECOMMENDED FOR...........................Luxury, Worth the travel

Recommended by: Emre Arolat, EAA

OLTRE IL GIARDINO
Fondamenta Contarini 2542
San Polo
Venice 30125
+39 0412750015
oltreilgiardino-venezia.com

CREDIT CARDS...Accepted
PRICE...Mid-range
TYPE...Bed and Breakfast
ACCOMMODATION..6 Rooms and Suites
FACILITIES:...Garden
GOOD TO KNOW...Child friendly
RECOMMENDED FOR..Island

Recommended by: Angela García de Paredes,
Paredes Pedrosa Arquitectos

CHARMING HOUSE DD724
Dorsoduro 724
Venice 30124
+39 0412770262
thecharminghouse.com

CREDIT CARDS...Accepted
PRICE..High-end
TYPE..Hotel
ACCOMMODATION..9 Rooms and Suites
FACILITIES...Breakfast room
GOOD TO KNOW...........Near Peggy Guggenheim Collection
RECOMMENDED FOR......................................Best-kept secret

Recommended by: Michel Rojkind, Rojkind Arquitectos

HOTEL LA CALCINA
Fondamenta Zattere Ai Gesuati 780
Dorsoduro
Venice 30123
+39 0415206466
lacalcina.com

CREDIT CARDS...Accepted
PRICE...Mid-range
TYPE..Hotel
ACCOMMODATION...29 Rooms
FACILITIES..Bar, Restaurant
GOOD TO KNOW...Child friendly
RECOMMENDED FOR................................Family friendly, Island

Overlooking the Giudecca Canal, Hotel La Calcina is a
former seventeenth-century limestone warehouse, which
has hosted many travelers and writers including John Ruskin
and Philippe Sollers.

Recommended by: Flavio Albanese, ASA Studio; Alberto
Lievore, Lievore Altherr

BAUER PALAZZO
Calle Giovanni Legrenzi
San Marco
Venice 1459
+39 0415207022
bauervenezia.com

CREDIT CARDS...Accepted
PRICE..High-end
TYPE..Palazzo hotel
ACCOMMODATION..................................243 Rooms and Suites
FACILITIES...........................2 Bars, Gym, 3 Restaurants, Spa
GOOD TO KNOW...................................Near St Mark's Square
RECOMMENDED FOR.............All-time favorite, Luxury, Urban

Recommended by: Ludovico Centis, The Empire; Emanuel
Christ, Christ & Gantenbein; Doriana and Massimiliano
Fuksas, Studio Fuksas; Matthias Sauerbruch and Louisa
Hutton, Sauerbruch Hutton

THE GRITTI PALACE

Campo Santa Maria del Giglio 2467
San Marco
Venice 30124
+39 041794611
thegrittipalace.com

CREDIT CARDS..Accepted
PRICE...Blow-out
TYPE...Palazzo hotel
ACCOMMODATION......................82 Rooms and Suites
FACILITIES....................Bar, Gym, Restaurant, Spa
GOOD TO KNOW.....................Child and pet friendly,
Valet parking
RECOMMENDED FOR...........All-time favorite, Luxury

"Rich with history and with excellent rooms; the hotel bar has one of my favorite views in the world, looking across the Grand Canal to Santa Maria Della Salute."—Adam Meshberg

Recommended by: Job Floris, Monadnock; Piero Lissoni, Lissoni Associati; Adam Meshberg, Meshberg Group

HOTEL DANIELI

Riva degli Schiavoni 4196
Castello
Venice 30122
+39 0415226480
danielihotelvenice.com

CREDIT CARDS..Accepted
PRICE..High-end
TYPE...Palazzo hotel
ACCOMMODATION....................204 Rooms and Suites
FACILITIES.........................Bar, Gym, 2 Restaurants
GOOD TO KNOW..........................Babysitting, Pet friendly,
Valet parking
RECOMMENDED FOR.............................All-time favorite,
Luxury, Wish I'd designed

"This old palazzo in my favorite city has an amazing interior and staircases, as well as a beautiful terrace with great views. It makes you feel as if you're a Venetian duke." —Hasan Çalışlar

Recommended by: Hasan Çalışlar, Erginoğlu & Çalışlar; Carlos Ferrater, OAB; Andrea Maffei, Andrea Maffei Architects; Gert Wingårdh, Wingårdhs

BELMOND HOTEL CIPRIANI

Giudecca 10
Venice 30133
+39 041240801
belmond.com

CREDIT CARDS..Accepted
PRICE...Blow-out
TYPE..Hotel
ACCOMMODATION......................96 Rooms and Suites
FACILITIES....................Bar, Gym, Outdoor swimming pool,
4 Restaurants, Sauna,
Spa, Steam room
GOOD TO KNOW.......................................Child friendly
RECOMMENDED FOR.............All-time favorite, Island, Luxury

"Situated on Giudecca Island, with fantastic views of St. Mark's Square and Palladio San Giorgio Maggiore, and a twenty-four-hour water taxi service to and from St. Mark's. Incredible service and amazing food." —Chris Wilkinson

Recommended by: Bernardo Fort-Brescia, Arquitectonica; Amanda Levete, AL_A; David Rockwell, Rockwell Group; Chris Wilkinson, Wilkinson Eyre Architects

JW MARRIOTT VENICE RESORT & SPA

Isola delle Rose
Laguna di San Marco
Venice 30133
+39 0418521300
jwvenice.com

CREDIT CARDS..Accepted
PRICE..High-end
TYPE..Hotel
ACCOMMODATION.............266 Duplexes, Rooms, and Suites
FACILITIES..Bar, Gym,
Indoor and outdoor swimming pools,
3 Restaurants, Sauna, Spa
GOOD TO KNOW.......................................Child friendly
RECOMMENDED FOR...Spa

[This hotel was designed by Matteo Thun & Partners.]

Recommended by: Matteo Thun, Matteo Thun & Partners

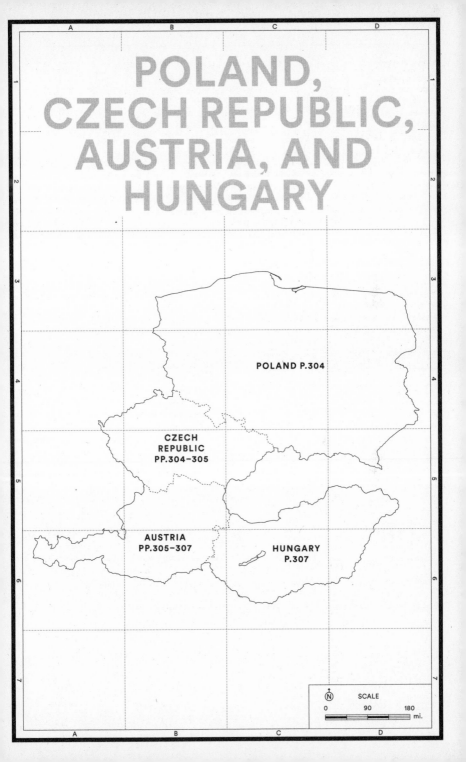

POLAND,
CZECH REPUBLIC,
AUSTRIA, AND
HUNGARY

POLAND P.304

CZECH
REPUBLIC
PP.304–305

AUSTRIA
PP.305–307

HUNGARY
P.307

SCALE

0   90   180

mi.

MONOPOL

Dworcowa 5
Katowice
Silesia 40001
Poland
+48 327828282
monopolkatowice.hotel.com.pl

CREDIT CARDS	Accepted
PRICE	Mid-range
TYPE	Hotel
ACCOMMODATION	108 Rooms and Suites
FACILITIES	Bar, Gym, Indoor swimming pool, 2 Restaurants, Sauna, Spa, Steam room
GOOD TO KNOW	Pet friendly
RECOMMENDED FOR	Where I live

"I always recommend this to friends or people who visit. A fantastic combination of old and new, in the center of industrial Katowice near the railway station and Mariacka Street, full of cafes and pubs."—Robert Konieczny

Recommended by: Robert Konieczny, KWK Promes

HT HOUSEBOATS

6 Marca 2
Mielno
West Pomerania 76032
Poland
+48 669855769
hthouseboats.com

CREDIT CARDS	Accepted
PRICE	Mid-range
TYPE	Houseboat
ACCOMMODATION	10 Berths
FACILITIES	Sauna, Spa
GOOD TO KNOW	Bicycle rentals, Child friendly
RECOMMENDED FOR	Beach

"Charming and cozy house boats."—Robert Konieczny

Recommended by: Robert Konieczny, KWK Promes

HOTEL JEŠTĚD

Horni Hanychov 153
Liberec 46008
Czech Republic
+42 0485104291
jested.cz

CREDIT CARDS	Accepted
PRICE	Low-cost
TYPE	Hotel
ACCOMMODATION	22 Rooms and Suites
FACILITIES	Restaurant
GOOD TO KNOW	Child and pet friendly, Free parking
RECOMMENDED FOR	Mountains, Worth the travel

"This space age 'rocket' tower was designed by Karel Hubáček and built between 1963 and 1968. It was once the future. You wake up above the clouds and look out of airplane windows."—Simon Henley

Recommended by: Simon Henley, Henley Halebrown

BREWERY TRAUTENBERK

Horní Malá Úpa 87
Hradec Králové 54227
Czech Republic
+42 733746444
pivovartrautenberk.cz

CREDIT CARDS	Accepted
PRICE	Low-cost
TYPE	Lodge
ACCOMMODATION	21 Lofts
FACILITIES	Games room, Restaurant, Sauna
GOOD TO KNOW	On-site microbrewery
RECOMMENDED FOR	Eco-conscious

"This brewery is a renovated, traditional wooden building with loft rooms and bunk beds. It has a touch of contemporary architecture without being obtrusive. Everything is minimal, except for the drinks. The beers produced are definitely worth traveling for."—Zsolt Gunther

Recommended by: Zsolt Gunther, 3H Architecture

HOTEL STAJNHAUS

Alfonse Muchy 13
Mikulov
Moravia 69201
Czech Republic
+518 324106
stajnhaus.cz

CREDIT CARDS	Accepted but not Amex
PRICE	Low-cost
TYPE	Hotel
ACCOMMODATION	5 Rooms
FACILITIES	Kitchenette
GOOD TO KNOW	Wine tastings
RECOMMENDED FOR	Best-kept secret

"This small Baroque town is crowded with tiny houses. One of them is Hotel Stajnhaus, which has rooms where each has a different atmosphere. It's austere yet inviting and evokes living in an old city."—Zsolt Gunther

Recommended by: Zsolt Gunther, 3H Architecture

SCHLOSSWIRT ZU ANIF

Salzachtalbundesstraße 7
Anif
Salzburg 5081
Austria
+43 624672175
schlosswirt-anif.at

CREDIT CARDS	Accepted
PRICE	Low-cost
TYPE	Hotel
ACCOMMODATION	29 Rooms
FACILITIES	Restaurant
GOOD TO KNOW	Free parking, Pet friendly
RECOMMENDED FOR	Mountains

"Perfect for enjoying Salzburg's summer festivals."
—François Valentiny

Recommended by: François Valentiny, Valentiny HVP Architects

STEIRERECK CHALETS

Pogusch 21
Turnau
Styria 8625
Austria
+43 386320000
steirereck.at

CREDIT CARDS	Accepted but not Amex
PRICE	Mid-range
TYPE	Hotel
ACCOMMODATION	11 Cottages, Houses, and Rooms
FACILITIES	Restaurant, Sauna
GOOD TO KNOW	Restaurant closed from Monday to Wednesday
RECOMMENDED FOR	Mountains

Steirereck Chalets, built as an extension to the award-winning Wirsthaus Steirereck restaurant, are a collection of modern, eco-conscious alpine chalets designed for stunning views of the surrounding mountain landscapes. Panoramic windows frame the countryside from vantage points including the living rooms, bedrooms, bathrooms, and even the sauna.

Recommended by: Hasan Çalışlar, Erginoğlu & Çalışlar

HOTEL SACHER WIEN

Philharmoniker Straße 4
Innere Stadt
Vienna 1010
Austria
+43 1514560
sacher.com

CREDIT CARDS	Accepted
PRICE	High-end
TYPE	Hotel
ACCOMMODATION	150 Rooms and Suites
FACILITIES	Bar, Gym, 2 Restaurants, Sauna, Spa, Steam room
GOOD TO KNOW	Babysitting
RECOMMENDED FOR	Urban

An iconic luxury hotel in the heart of Vienna, which has hosted key historical figures such as JFK. It is also renowned as the birthplace of the notoriously indulgent Sacher Torte, a rich chocolate cake made from a carefully guarded recipe.

Recommended by: Doriana and Massimiliano Fuksas, Studio Fuksas

ALTSTADT VIENNA

Kirchengasse 41
Neubau
Vienna 1070
Austria
+43 15226666
altstadt.at

CREDIT CARDS	Accepted
PRICE	Mid-range
TYPE	Hotel
ACCOMMODATION	49 Rooms and Suites
FACILITIES	Bar
GOOD TO KNOW	Child and pet friendly, Valet parking
RECOMMENDED FOR	Urban, Where I live

"An innovative hotel concept: set across several floors of
an early twentieth-century building. Adapting the former
apartments into hotel rooms affords a casual touch and
a homey feeling. Rooms and suites are each different,
designed by architects, and product and fashion designers."
—Marta Laudani

Recommended by: Marta Laudani, Marta Laudani Design;
Much Untertrifaller, Dietrich Untertrifaller Architects

HOTEL & CHALET AURELIO

Tannberg 130
Lech
Vorarlberg 6764
Austria
+43 55832214
aureliolech.com

CREDIT CARDS	Accepted
PRICE	Blow-out
TYPE	Hotel
ACCOMMODATION	18 Rooms and Suites
FACILITIES	Bar, Gym, Indoor pool, Restaurant, Sauna, Spa, Steam room, Wood-burning fireplace, Yoga
GOOD TO KNOW	Babysitting, No pets
RECOMMENDED FOR	Mountains

Recommended by: Piero Lissoni, Lissoni Associati

HOTEL ALMHOF SCHNEIDER

Tannberg 59
Lech
Vorarlberg 6764
Austria
+43 55833500
almhof.at

CREDIT CARDS	Accepted but not Amex
PRICE	Blow-out
TYPE	Hotel
ACCOMMODATION	53 Rooms and Suites
FACILITIES	Bar, Gym, Indoor swimming pool, 2 Restaurants, Sauna, Spa, Steam room, Yoga
GOOD TO KNOW	Babysitting, Cinema, No pets
RECOMMENDED FOR	Mountains

"You can't beat old-world Austrian skiing traditions: great
service, coziness, warmth, wonderful food, and facilities.
A heartwarming winter experience."—Nabil Gholam

Recommended by: Nabil Gholam, Nabil Gholam Architects;
Charlotte von Moos, Sauter von Moos

PENSION FORTUNA

Anger 384
Lech
Vorarlberg 6764
Austria
+43 558324240
fortuna-lech.com

CREDIT CARDS	Accepted
PRICE	Low-cost
TYPE	Guesthouse
ACCOMMODATION	11 Rooms
FACILITIES	Restaurant, Sauna
GOOD TO KNOW	Bicycle rentals, No pets
RECOMMENDED FOR	Family friendly

Pension Fortuna is a charming, family run guesthouse in the
village and ski resort of Lech am Arlberg. Ideally suited for
both winter ski excursions and summer hiking retreats. The
guesthouse also benefits from a sauna and summer terrace.

Recommended by: Jean-Paul Viguier, Jean-Paul Viguier
et Associés

ROTE WAND
Zug 5
Lech
Vorarlberg 6764
Austria
+43 558334350
rotewand.com

CREDIT CARDS	Accepted but not Amex
PRICE	Mid-range
TYPE	Hotel
ACCOMMODATION	50 Rooms and Suites
FACILITIES	Bar, Gym, Indoor and outdoor swimming pool, Restaurant, Sauna, Spa, Steam room, Wood-burning fireplace, Yoga
GOOD TO KNOW	Bicycle rentals, Pet friendly
RECOMMENDED FOR	All-time favorite, Countryside, Family friendly, Spa

"The attitude toward kids is friendly, relaxed, and respectful."
—Much Untertrifaller

Recommended by: Much Untertrifaller, Dietrich
Untertrifaller Architects

R40 VENDÉGHÁZ
Rákóczi utca 40
Mád
Borsod-Abaúj-Zemplén 3909
Hungary
+36 303016533
r40.hu

CREDIT CARDS	Accepted
PRICE	Low-cost
TYPE	Cottage
ACCOMMODATION	4 Rooms
FACILITIES	Shared kitchen
GOOD TO KNOW	Free parking, No pets
RECOMMENDED FOR	Countryside

"This small village house reflects all the spatial qualities
of the region. The interior is nostalgic, like your grandma's
house."—Zsolt Gunther

Recommended by: Zsolt Gunther, 3H Architecture

ALMAGYAR BORTERASZ
Szeszfőzde utca
Eger
Heves 3300, Hungary
+36 302780715
almagyar.hu

CREDIT CARDS	Not accepted
PRICE	Low-cost
TYPE	Winery
ACCOMMODATION	1 Campsite, 3 Huts
FACILITIES	Bar, Outdoor swimming pool, Restaurant
GOOD TO KNOW	Terrace closed from October to April
RECOMMENDED FOR	Mountains

Recommended by: Zsolt Gunther, 3H Architecture

BRODY HOUSE
Bródy Sándor utca 10
Budapest 1088, Hungary
+36 15507363
brody.land

CREDIT CARDS	Accepted
PRICE	Mid-range
TYPE	Hotel
ACCOMMODATION	11 Rooms, Studios, and Suites
FACILITIES	Bar, Restaurant
GOOD TO KNOW	A "BrodyLand Visa" gives access to affiliate global clubs
RECOMMENDED FOR	Wish I'd designed

Recommended by: Martin Krogh, Martin Laursen,
and Anders Lonka, ADEPT

FOUR SEASONS HOTEL GRESHAM PALACE BUDAPEST
Széchenyi István tér 5
Budapest 1051, Hungary
+36 12686000
fourseasons.com

CREDIT CARDS	Not accepted
PRICE	High-end
TYPE	Hotel
ACCOMMODATION	179 Rooms and Suites
FACILITIES	Bar, Indoor swimming pool, Restaurant, Sauna, Spa, Steam room
GOOD TO KNOW	Babysitting, Valet parking
RECOMMENDED FOR	Luxury

Recommended by: Cristian Santandreu, A2arquitectos

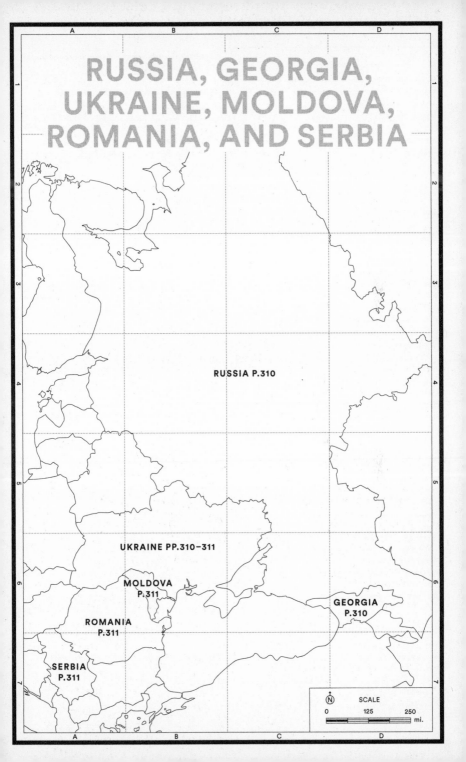

MOSS BOUTIQUE HOTEL
Building 4, Krivokolennyy Pereulok 10
Moscow 101000, Russia
+7 4951145572
mosshotel.ru

CREDIT CARDS	Accepted
PRICE	Mid-range
TYPE	Hotel
ACCOMMODATION	31 Rooms
FACILITIES	Bar, Gym, Restaurant
GOOD TO KNOW	Art for sale
RECOMMENDED FOR	Where I live

Recommended by: Boris Bernaskoni, Bernaskoni

HOTEL ASTORIA
Bolshaya Morskaya 39
Saint Petersburg 190000, Russia
+7 8124945757
roccofortehotels.com

CREDIT CARDS	Accepted
PRICE	Mid-range
TYPE	Hotel
ACCOMMODATION	83 Rooms and Suites
FACILITIES	Bar, Gym, Indoor swimming pool, Restaurant, Sauna, Spa, Steam room
GOOD TO KNOW	Child friendly
RECOMMENDED FOR	All-time favorite

"The lobby is a popular meeting place for the powerful, and where a great afternoon tea is served."—Jack Diamond

Recommended by: Jack Diamond, Diamond Schmitt

ROOMS HOTEL KAZBEGI
1 V.Gorgasali Street
Stepantsminda
Mtskheta-Mtianeti, Georgia
+995 322710099
roomshotels.com

CREDIT CARDS	Accepted
PRICE	Mid-range
TYPE	Hotel
ACCOMMODATION	155 Rooms
FACILITIES	Bar, Gym, Indoor swimming pool, Restaurant, Sauna, Spa
GOOD TO KNOW	Free parking
RECOMMENDED FOR	Countryside, Mountains

"Beautiful mountain retreat with fabulous view of Gergeti Trinity Church."—Guy Geier

Recommended by: Guy Geier, FXCollaborative; Artem Vakhrin and Kateryna Zuieva, AKZ Architectura

HILTON KYIV
Tarasa Shevchenko Boulevard 30
Kiev 01030
Ukraine
+380 443935400
www.hilton.com

CREDIT CARDS	Accepted
PRICE	Mid-range
TYPE	Hotel
ACCOMMODATION	262 Rooms and Suites
FACILITIES	Bar, Gym, Indoor swimming pool, Restaurant, Sauna, Spa, Steam room
GOOD TO KNOW	Babysitting
RECOMMENDED FOR	Where I live

Hilton Kyiv is a modern hotel, situated within walking distance of many of the city's major tourist attractions. The rooms and suites are spacious and have floor-to-ceiling windows. During the summer months, the hotel opens a roof terrace where guests can enjoy views overlooking the Old Botanical Gardens.

Recommended by: Kateryna Zuieva, AKZ Architectura

PREMIER HOTEL LYBID
Peremohy Square 1
Kiev 01135
Ukraine
+380 445979027
lybid-hotel.phnr.com

CREDIT CARDS	Accepted but not Amex
PRICE	Low-cost
TYPE	Hotel
ACCOMMODATION	274 Rooms and Suites
FACILITIES	Bar, Restaurant
GOOD TO KNOW	Child and pet friendly
RECOMMENDED FOR	Wish I'd designed

"One of the oldest hotels in Kiev."—Artem Vakhrin

Recommended by: Artem Vakhrin, AKZ Architectura

VOLIA VASHA APARTMENT

672 Verkhovyna
Verkhovyna
Ivano-Frankivsk Oblast 78704, Ukraine
+380 962425519
voliavasha.info

CREDIT CARDS	Not accepted
PRICE	Mid-range
TYPE	Cottage (rental)
ACCOMMODATION	1 Room
FACILITIES	Mini kitchen
GOOD TO KNOW	Near Museum of Gutsulsk Magic
RECOMMENDED FOR	Best-kept secret, Countryside

"Set in a quiet, very picturesque corner of the Ukrainian Carpathian mountains."—Artem Vakhrin

Recommended by: Artem Vakhrin, AKZ Architectura

CASTEL MIMI

1 Dacia Street
Bulboaca
Anenii Noi 6512, Moldova
+373 62001893
castelmimi.md

CREDIT CARDS	Accepted
PRICE	Mid-range
TYPE	Resort hotel
ACCOMMODATION	21 Bungalows and Suites
FACILITIES	Bar, Outdoor swimming pool, Restaurant, Sauna, Spa
GOOD TO KNOW	Child friendly, On-site vineyard
RECOMMENDED FOR	Spa

Recommended by: Dorin Stefan, Dorin Stefan Birou de Arhitectura

SARROGLIA

Strada Vasile Lascăr 59
Bucharest 20493, Romania
+40 314126000
sarrogliahotel.com

CREDIT CARDS	Accepted but not Amex
PRICE	Low-cost
TYPE	Hotel
ACCOMMODATION	33 Rooms and Suites
FACILITIES	Bar, Gym, Jacuzzi, Restaurant
GOOD TO KNOW	No pets
RECOMMENDED FOR	Where I live

Sarroglia is a stylish, modern design hotel in the center of Bucharest. The hotel's lounge area also functions as an art gallery, featuring the work of both well-known and up-and-coming artists. Guests are welcome to purchase pieces from the exhibition during their stay.

Recommended by: Dorin Stefan, Dorin Stefan Birou de Arhitectura

FRAȚII JDERI

Sat Pascoaia 123
Păscoaia
Vâlcea 245505, Romania
+40 744509123
fratiijderi.ro

CREDIT CARDS	Not accepted
PRICE	Low-cost
TYPE	Resort
ACCOMMODATION	35 Cottages, Huts, Rooms, and Villas
FACILITIES	Outdoor swimming pool
GOOD TO KNOW	Children's camps
RECOMMENDED FOR	Family friendly

A tranquil mountain resort with simple, rustic rooms. The convivial staff are more than happy to arrange a variety of outdoor excursions, such as hiking and kayaking.

Recommended by: Dorin Stefan, Dorin Stefan Birou de Arhitectura

SQUARE NINE

Studentski Trg 9
Belgrade 103933, Serbia
+381 113333500
squarenine.rs

CREDIT CARDS	Accepted
PRICE	Mid-range
TYPE	Hotel
ACCOMMODATION	45 Rooms and Suites
FACILITIES	Bar, Gym, Indoor swimming pool, Restaurant, Sauna, Spa, Steam room
GOOD TO KNOW	Valet parking
RECOMMENDED FOR	Urban

"Belgrade is vibrant and full of possibilities. Square Nine is impeccably designed and is situated in the heart of city. Building and room size, rooftop, lounge area, and pool are all sensitively balanced; nothing is overdone."
—Alireza Razavi

Recommended by: Sam Chermayeff, Meyer-Grohbrügge & Chermayeff; Alireza Razavi, Studio Razavi Architecture

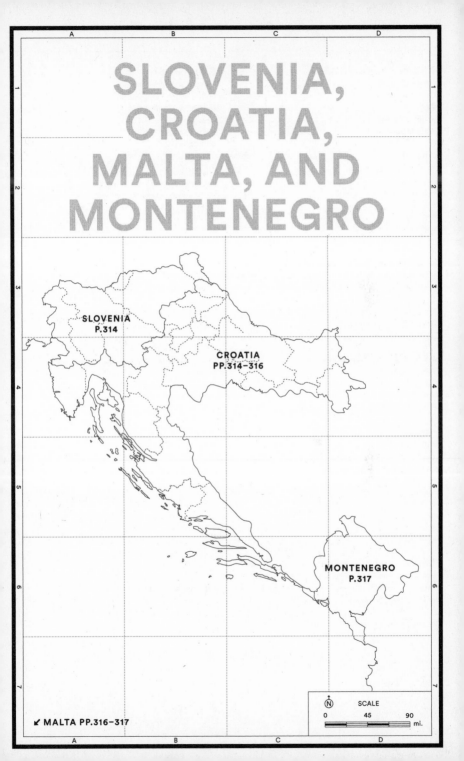

ANTIQ PALACE HOTEL

Gosposka Ulica 10
Ljubljana 1000
Slovenia
+386 83896700
antiqpalace.com

CREDIT CARDS	Accepted
PRICE	Mid-range
TYPE	Hotel
ACCOMMODATION	18 Residences, Rooms, and Suites
FACILITIES	2 Bars, Gym, Spa
GOOD TO KNOW	Near city center
RECOMMENDED FOR	Urban

A grand sixteenth-century mansion located in the historic
city center, this classically decorated boutique hotel has
suites and duplex residences for longer stays. It also has a
private garden, two bars, and a fitness and spa center.

Recommended by: Aljoša Dekleva and Tina Gregorič,
Dekleva Gregorič Architects

ART HOTEL TARTINI

Tartinijev Trg 15
Old Town
Piran
Primorska 6330
Slovenia
+386 56711000
arthoteltartini.com

CREDIT CARDS	Accepted but not Amex
PRICE	Mid-range
TYPE	Hotel
ACCOMMODATION	45 Rooms and Suites
FACILITIES	Bar, Restaurant
GOOD TO KNOW	Pet friendly
RECOMMENDED FOR	Beach

"It is worth going to the seaside in November; foggy days
with sudden minutes of strong sunshine recall Hiroshi
Sugimoto's photography. The hotel is a perfect background
for this melancholy feeling."—Zsolt Gunther

Recommended by: Zsolt Gunther, 3H Architecture

GOLI+BOSI

Morpurgova Poljana 2
Split
Dalmatian Coast 21000
Croatia
+385 21510999
gollybossy.com

CREDIT CARDS	Accepted but not Amex
PRICE	Mid-range
TYPE	Hostel
ACCOMMODATION	29 Dorms, Rooms, and Suites
FACILITIES	Bar
GOOD TO KNOW	Child friendly
RECOMMENDED FOR	Where I live

A design hostel, with a range of rooms and beds for a variety
of budgets. Staff are available to arrange local itineraries,
including olive-oil tasting and diving trips.

Recommended by: Dinko Peračić, ARP and Platforma 9.81

HOTEL ADRIATIC

Obala Pina Budicina 16
Rovinj
Istria 52210
Croatia
+385 52800250
maistra.com

CREDIT CARDS	Accepted
PRICE	Mid-range
TYPE	Hotel
ACCOMMODATION	18 Rooms and Suites
FACILITIES	Bar, Restaurant
GOOD TO KNOW	Free parking, No pets
RECOMMENDED FOR	Luxury

Hotel Adriatic is a stylish hotel with plenty of warmth and
character. Each room contains contemporary art created
exclusively for the hotel.

Recommended by: Dinko Peračić, ARP and Platforma 9.81

HOTEL NEBODER

Strossmayerova 1
Rijeka
Kvarner Bay 51000
Croatia
+385 51373538
jadran-hoteli.hr

CREDIT CARDS..Accepted
PRICE...Low-cost
TYPE..Hotel
ACCOMMODATION.....................................54 Rooms
FACILITIES..Bar
GOOD TO KNOW.................................Free parking
RECOMMENDED FOR.................................Budget

A simple yet reasonably priced hotel with panoramic views of the city of Rijeka and Kvarner Bay. Centrally located, Hotel Neboder is moments from attractions such as the Croatian National Theatre.

Recommended by: Dinko Peračić, ARP and Platforma 9.81

LAFODIA SEA RESORT

Iva Kuljevana 51
Lopud Island 20222
Croatia
+385 20450300
lafodiahotel.com

CREDIT CARDS..Accepted
PRICE..Mid-range
TYPE..Resort
ACCOMMODATION....................185 Apartments and Rooms
FACILITIES....................Bar, Gym, Outdoor swimming pool, 3 Restaurants, Sauna, Spa, Yoga
GOOD TO KNOW.......................Bicycle rentals, Child friendly
RECOMMENDED FOR..........................Best-kept secret

"The island itself is really the secret; it's a half-hour ferry ride from Dubrovnik, with no cars and a cluster of very good restaurants. Once you get to the island the hotel is the draw, it has a private beach with terraces and pine trees, and this alone makes it worth the stay."—Graham West

Recommended by: Graham West, West Architecture

LIGHTHOUSE PALAGRUŽA

Palagruža Island
Croatia
adriagate.com

CREDIT CARDS..Accepted
PRICE..Mid-range
TYPE...Lighthouse
ACCOMMODATION...................................2 Bedrooms
FACILITIES..Email to book
GOOD TO KNOW..................Accessible by chartered motor boat
RECOMMENDED FOR.................................Island

Recommended by: Dinko Peračić, ARP and Platforma 9.81

CAMP PONTA

Mokalo
Orebić
Pelješac 20250
Croatia
+385 20713104
ponta.com.hr

CREDIT CARDS..Accepted
PRICE...Low-cost
TYPE..Campsite
ACCOMMODATION...............................30 Camping units
FACILITIES.................Mini golf, Outdoor swimming pool
GOOD TO KNOW................................Pet friendly
RECOMMENDED FOR...............................Family friendly

"Very relaxed, sporty environment."—Dinko Peračić

Recommended by: Dinko Peračić, ARP and Platforma 9.81

LITTLE GREEN BAY HOTEL

6 Uvala Lozna
Hvar
Split-Dalmatia 21450
Croatia
+385 996034693
littlegreenbay.com

CREDIT CARDS	Accepted
PRICE	High-end
TYPE	Hotel
ACCOMMODATION	15 Rooms
FACILITIES	Bar, Restaurant, Spa
GOOD TO KNOW	Island transfers
RECOMMENDED FOR	Beach

Little Green Bay is a picturesque boutique hotel in a tiny bay on Hvar. This tranquil retreat is ideal for those seeking sun, sea, and sand, and also has an outdoor spa terrace.

Recommended by: Philip Olmesdahl, SAOTA

HOTEL JULIANI

25 St George's Road
Saint Julian's
Central STJ3208
Malta
+356 21388000
hoteljuliani.com

CREDIT CARDS	Accepted
PRICE	Mid-range
TYPE	Hotel
ACCOMMODATION	47 Rooms and Suites
FACILITIES	Bar, Gym, Outdoor swimming pool, Restaurant, Rooftop terrace bar
GOOD TO KNOW	Free parking
RECOMMENDED FOR	Where I live

Recommended by: Richard England, Richard England Architects

THE VICTORIA HOTEL

Gorg Borg Olivier Street
Sliema
Central 1807
Malta
+356 21334711
victoriahotel.com

CREDIT CARDS	Accepted
PRICE	Mid-range
TYPE	Hotel
ACCOMMODATION	137 Rooms and Suites
FACILITIES	Bar, Gym, Indoor and outdoor swimming pools, 2 Restaurants, Rooftop terrace bar, Spa
GOOD TO KNOW	Babysitting
RECOMMENDED FOR	Family friendly

"The Victoria is a four-star hotel with some five-star advantages, including several pools on the upper floors with views of the Mediterranean."—Paul Morgan

Recommended by: Paul Morgan, Paul Morgan Architects

HOTEL TA' CENC & SPA

Triq Ta Cenc, Ta' Sannat
Sannat
Gozo SNT9049
Malta
+356 22191000
tacenc.com

CREDIT CARDS	Accepted
PRICE	Mid-range
TYPE	Hotel
ACCOMMODATION	83 Rooms, Suites, and Trulli
FACILITIES	Bar, Gym, Indoor and outdoor swimming pool, 3 Restaurants, Sauna, Spa
GOOD TO KNOW	Babysitting
RECOMMENDED FOR	Countryside, Spa

"Isolated accommodation with superb gardens and excellent surroundings for countryside walks."—Richard England

Recommended by: Richard England, Richard England Architects

SAINT PATRICK'S HOTEL GOZO

Pjazza Amphora
Xlendi
Gozo XLN1150
Malta
+356 21562951
stpatrickshotel.com

CREDIT CARDS	Accepted
PRICE	Low-cost
TYPE	Hotel
ACCOMMODATION	64 Rooms
FACILITIES	Bar, Outdoor restaurant
GOOD TO KNOW	Bicycle rentals
RECOMMENDED FOR	Family friendly

"Small, in a good way, and on the water's edge."
—Richard England

Recommended by: Richard England, Richard England Architects

THE XARA PALACE RELAIS & CHATEAUX

Misrah Il Kunsill
Mdina
Northern MDN1050
Malta
+356 21450560
xarapalace.com.mt

CREDIT CARDS	Accepted
PRICE	Mid-range
TYPE	Hotel
ACCOMMODATION	17 Rooms and Suites
FACILITIES	Bar, Cafe, 2 Restaurants
GOOD TO KNOW	Pet friendly
RECOMMENDED FOR	Beach

"Close to the water, and set on an island with an unusual history."—Craig Dykers

Recommended by: Craig Dykers, Snøhetta

SU29 HOTEL VALLETTA

29 St Ursula Steps
Malta 1230
+356 21242929
su29hotel.com

CREDIT CARDS	Accepted
PRICE	Mid-range
TYPE	Hotel
ACCOMMODATION	8 Rooms
FACILITIES	Bar
GOOD TO KNOW	No pets
RECOMMENDED FOR	Worth the travel

"Chic and eclectic, this hotel in Malta's capital is close to St. John's Co-Cathedral, which houses Caravaggio's painting *The Beheading of Saint John the Baptist* (1608)."
—Paul Morgan

Recommended by: Paul Morgan, Paul Morgan Architects

AMAN SVETI STEFAN

Sveti Stefan
Coastal Region 85315
Montenegro
+382 33420000
aman.com

CREDIT CARDS	Accepted
PRICE	Blow-out
TYPE	Hotel
ACCOMMODATION	58 Houses, Rooms, and Suites
FACILITIES	Bar, Gym, Indoor and outdoor swimming pool, Restaurant, Sauna, Spa, Steam room, Yoga
GOOD TO KNOW	Babysitting
RECOMMENDED FOR	Island

"The island's environment is stunning; the natural coastline and pine forest remind me of my childhood on Sveti Stefan. The hotel has preserved the village's original features while turning it into an elegant, understated series of spaces. Its natural lighting mimics the dynamic shadows of the granite coastline."—Margot Krasojevic

Recommended by: Margot Krasojevic, Margot Krasojevic Architecture

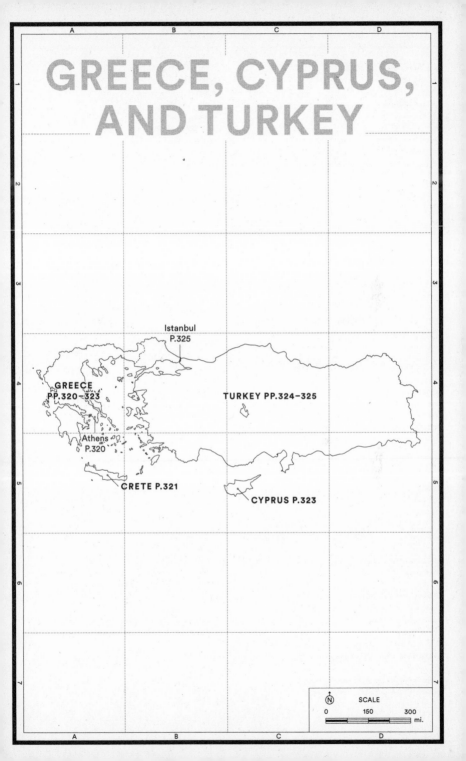

GREECE, CYPRUS, AND TURKEY

N

SCALE

0   150   300
mi.

18 MICON STREET
Esopou 14
Psiri
Athens 10554
Greece
+30 2103235307
18miconstr.com

CREDIT CARDS.....................................Accepted but not Amex
PRICE..Mid-range
TYPE...Hotel
ACCOMMODATION............................15 Rooms and Suites
FACILITIES...Lounge
GOOD TO KNOW.............................Babysitting, Child friendly,
"handy Smartphones" available
RECOMMENDED FOR................................Eco-conscious

A former warehouse where each of the rooms has been
individually and thoughtfully designed to provide guests
with a quality setting at an affordable price.

Recommended by: Carlo Baumschlager, Baumschlager
Hutter Partners

HOTEL GRANDE BRETAGNE
1 Vasileos Georgiou A
Synma Square
Athens 10564
Greece
+30 2103330000
marriott.com

CREDIT CARDS...Accepted
PRICE...High-end
TYPE...Hotel
ACCOMMODATION................................320 Rooms and Suites
FACILITIES..Bar, Gym,
Indoor and outdoor swimming pools,
Restaurant, Rooftop terrace bar,
Sauna, Spa
GOOD TO KNOW..Babysitting
RECOMMENDED FOR..Luxury

Since 1874, the Hotel Grande Bretagne has set the
benchmark for luxury hotels across the capital. The hotel
is so full of antiquities and masterpieces that there is
a special tour for its guests every Thursday. It also has
a rooftop garden restaurant, lavishly appointed rooms,
and a tranquil spa tucked away in the heart of the hotel.

Recommended by: Anastasios Kotsiopoulos,
AM Kotsiopoulos & Partners Architects

SPETSES HOTEL
Anargirou
Spetses
Attica 18050
Greece
+30 2298072602
spetses-hotel.gr

CREDIT CARDS...Accepted
PRICE..Low-cost
TYPE...Hotel
ACCOMMODATION............................77 Rooms and Villas
FACILITIES...Bar, Restaurant
GOOD TO KNOW................................Private beach, Yacht hire
RECOMMENDED FOR.............................Family friendly

"Right on the water, accompanied by a small beach, great
deck, and an incredible bar, this hotel accommodates and
welcomes all ages."—Anthony Mallows

Recommended by: Anthony Mallows, WATG

SANI RESORT
Kassandra
Halkidiki
Central Macedonia 63077
Greece
+30 2374099503
sani-resort.com

CREDIT CARDS...Accepted
PRICE...Mid-range
TYPE..Resort
ACCOMMODATION..........944 Bungalows, Rooms, and Suites
FACILITIES.......................16 Bars, Gym, Private beach,
Outdoor swimming pool,
23 Restaurants, Sauna, Spa,
Steam room, Yoga
GOOD TO KNOW................................Babysitting, Pet friendly
RECOMMENDED FOR.............................Family friendly

A family owned collection of luxury coastal hotels, all within
walking distance of the resort's excellent bars, restaurants,
and boutiques.

Recommended by: Anastasios Kotsiopoulos,
AM Kotsiopoulos & Partners Architects

THE EXCELSIOR HOTEL THESSALONIKI
10 Komninon Street and 23 Mitropoleos Avenue
Upper Town
Thessaloniki
Central Macedonia 54624
Greece
+30 2310021020
excelsiorhotel.gr

CREDIT CARDS	Accepted
PRICE	High-end
TYPE	Hotel
ACCOMMODATION	34 Rooms and Suites
FACILITIES	Bar, Gym, Restaurant
GOOD TO KNOW	Pet friendly
RECOMMENDED FOR	Where I live

Excelsior Hotel Thessaloniki is a five-star boutique hotel just a few minutes' walk from the beachfront. Its easy, modern elegance provides a little serenity amidst the hustle and bustle of the surrounding city.

Recommended by: Anastasios Kotsiopoulos,
AM Kotsiopoulos & Partners Architects

DAIOS COVE LUXURY RESORT & VILLAS
Vathi
Agios Nikolaos
Crete 72100
Greece
+30 2841888029
daioscovecrete.com

CREDIT CARDS	Accepted
PRICE	High-end
TYPE	Resort
ACCOMMODATION	300 Rooms and Villas
FACILITIES	3 Bars, Gym, Outdoor swimming pool, 3 Restaurants, Sauna, Spa, Steam room, Tennis, Yoga
GOOD TO KNOW	Babysitting
RECOMMENDED FOR	Spa

Daios Cove Luxury Resort & Villas is situated on a hillside overlooking its own private bay. Rooms are well-appointed and have been designed with natural materials and a focus on the flow of sunlight and outdoor areas. There are tailor-made excursions, a constantly evolving line-up of visiting artists and musicians, and a range of dining experiences.

Recommended by: Anastasios Kotsiopoulos,
AM Kotsiopoulos & Partners Architects

MILIA MOUNTAIN RETREAT
Vlatos
Chania
Crete 73012
Greece
+30 2821046774
milia.gr

CREDIT CARDS	Accepted but not Amex
PRICE	Low-cost
TYPE	Lodge
ACCOMMODATION	14 Apartments, Rooms, and Suites
FACILITIES	Restaurant
GOOD TO KNOW	Child and pet friendly
RECOMMENDED FOR	Eco-conscious

Milia Mountain Retreat is a tranquil eco-lodge situated in the rugged beauty of the Kissamos province. The mountain settlement dates back to the seventeenth century.

Recommended by: Anastasios Kotsiopoulos,
AM Kotsiopoulos & Partners Architects

THALORI TRADITIONAL VILLAGE
Kapetaniana
Heraklion
Crete 70016
Greece
+30 2893041762
thalori.com

CREDIT CARDS	Accepted but not Amex
PRICE	Mid-range
TYPE	Village
ACCOMMODATION	20 Houses
FACILITIES	Outdoor swimming pool, Restaurant, Wood-burning fireplace
GOOD TO KNOW	Bicycle rentals, Child friendly
RECOMMENDED FOR	Mountains

"A stunning, completely isolated environment."
—Thomas Leeser

Recommended by: Thomas Leeser, Leeser Architecture

ARISTI MOUNTAIN RESORT + VILLAS
Artisti
Zagori
Epirus 44016
Greece
+30 2653041330
aristi.eu

CREDIT CARDS..Accepted
PRICE..High-end
TYPE...Resort
ACCOMMODATION...24 Rooms and Villas
FACILITIES.......................................Bar, Indoor swimming pool,
Restaurant, Sauna,
Spa, Steam room, Yoga
GOOD TO KNOW...Child friendly
RECOMMENDED FOR...Mountains

High in the Pindus mountains, Aristi is an exceptional resort,
far from the tourist-driven Greek islands. Rooms have an
ambience of rustic luxury, featuring wood and stone details,
and afford views of the local villages and nearby cliffs.
Activities include rock climbing and rafting, as well as more
relaxed pursuits such as cookery classes.

Recommended by: Anastasios Kotsiopoulos,
AM Kotsiopoulos & Partners Architects

PELECAS COUNTRY CLUB
Eparchiaki Odos Pelekas-kastellanion
Pelecas
Corfu
Ionian Islands 49100
Greece
+30 2661052918
country-club.gr

CREDIT CARDS..Accepted
PRICE..High-end
TYPE...Country club
ACCOMMODATION...................................15 Rooms and Suites
FACILITIES..................................Bar, Outdoor swimming pool
GOOD TO KNOW..Babysitting
RECOMMENDED FOR..Best-kept secret

A beautiful, family owned, eighteenth-century stone
mansion house set in fifty acres (twenty hectares) of land.
Breakfast is homemade with produce from the estate,
which also has its own stables and olive press.

Recommended by: Anastasios Kotsiopoulos,
AM Kotsiopoulos & Partners Architects

PERANTZADA 1811
Odyssea Androutsou Street
Vathi
Ithaca
Ionian Islands 28300, Greece
+30 2674033496
perantzadahotel.com

CREDIT CARDS..Accepted
PRICE..Low-cost
TYPE..Hotel
ACCOMMODATION...17 Rooms
FACILITIES.............................Bar, Outdoor swimming pool
GOOD TO KNOW..Bicycle rentals
RECOMMENDED FOR..Beach

Recommended by: Anastasios Kotsiopoulos,
AM Kotsiopoulos & Partners Architects

GRACE MYKONOS
Agios Stefanos
Mykonos
South Aegean 84600, Greece
+30 2289020100
aubergeresorts.com

CREDIT CARDS..Accepted
PRICE..High-end
TYPE..Hotel
ACCOMMODATION.................................32 Rooms and Suites
FACILITIES..............................Bar, Outdoor swimming pool,
Restaurant, Sauna, Spa, Steam room
GOOD TO KNOW..Boat trips
RECOMMENDED FOR.....................................Family friendly

Recommended by: Kelly Hoppen, Kelly Hoppen Interiors

CASA COOK RHODES
European Union Street
Kolympia
Rhodes
South Aegean 85102, Greece
+49 234961038606
casacook.com

CREDIT CARDS................................Accepted but not Amex
PRICE..Mid-range
TYPE..Hotel
ACCOMMODATION.................................90 Rooms and Suites
FACILITIES....................Bar, Gym, Outdoor swimming pool,
Restaurant, Yoga
GOOD TO KNOW..No children
RECOMMENDED FOR..Beach

Stylish and effortlessly cool, Casa Cook has yoga classes, nature hikes, and a sailboat for lazy days out on the sea.

Recommended by: Kateryna Zuieva, AKZ Architectura

ARTEMIS SUITES
Megalochori
Santorini
South Aegean 84700
Greece
+30 2286081922
artemissuites.com

CREDIT CARDS	Accepted
PRICE	Mid-range
TYPE	Hotel
ACCOMMODATION	15 Rooms and Suites
FACILITIES	Bar, Outdoor swimming pool, Restaurant
GOOD TO KNOW	Free parking
RECOMMENDED FOR	Urban, Worth the travel

"Excellent accommodation, isolated, and perched on the lava cliffs with splendid views over the caldera."
—Richard England

Recommended by: Richard England, Richard England Architects

PERIVOLAS
Oía
Santorini
South Aegean 84702
Greece
+30 2286071308
perivolas.gr

CREDIT CARDS	Accepted
PRICE	High-end
TYPE	Hotel
ACCOMMODATION	20 Suites
FACILITIES	Bar, Gym, Restaurant, Sauna, Spa, Steam room
GOOD TO KNOW	No pets
RECOMMENDED FOR	All-time favorite, Beach, Wish I'd designed

"Hillside location overlooking the sea and peaks of the submerged caldera; incredible food and lots of history in the wonderfully quaint villages."—Mark de Reus

Recommended by: Mark de Reus, de Reus Architects; David Tajchman, Architectures David Tajchman

THE CHATZIGAKI MANOR
Pertouli
Trikala
Thessaly 42032
Greece
+30 2434091146
chatzigaki.gr

CREDIT CARDS	Accepted
PRICE	Low-cost
TYPE	Country estate hotel
ACCOMMODATION	36 Rooms and Suites
FACILITIES	Bar, Outdoor swimming pool, Restaurant
GOOD TO KNOW	Child and pet friendly
RECOMMENDED FOR	Countryside

Situated among the surrounding mountains and forest, the Chatzigaki Manor is a traditional estate, ideally located for nearby ski resorts. Rooms and suites are cosy and traditional, and facilities include saunas, an outdoor summer pool, and a playroom for children.

Recommended by: Anastasios Kotsiopoulos, AM Kotsiopoulos & Partners Architects

THE CLASSIC HOTEL
94 Rigenis Street
Tophane
Nicosia 1513
Cyprus
+357 22664006
classic.com.cy

CREDIT CARDS	Accepted
PRICE	Low-cost
TYPE	Hotel
ACCOMMODATION	57 Rooms
FACILITIES	Bar, Gym, Restaurant
GOOD TO KNOW	Bicycle rentals
RECOMMENDED FOR	Budget

Recommended by: Anastasios Kotsiopoulos, AM Kotsiopoulos & Partners Architects

ARGOS IN CAPPADOCIA
Kayabaşı Street 23
Uçhisar
Cappadocia
Central Anatolia 50240
Turkey
+90 3842193130
argosincappadocia.com

CREDIT CARDS	Accepted
PRICE	Mid-range
TYPE	Hotel
ACCOMMODATION	51 Rooms and Suites
FACILITIES	Bar, Restaurant
GOOD TO KNOW	Wine tastings
RECOMMENDED FOR	Worth the travel

"Amazing rooms carved into the mountains and integrated with the small town overlooking Cappadocia."
—Hasan Çalışlar

Recommended by: Hasan Çalışlar, Erginoğlu & Çalışlar

AMANRUYA
Bülent Ecevit Cad
Göltürkbükü
Muğla
Aegean 48483
Turkey
+90 2523111212
aman.com

CREDIT CARDS	Accepted
PRICE	Blow-out
TYPE	Hotel
ACCOMMODATION	36 Villas
FACILITIES	Bar, Gym, Outdoor swimming pool, 4 Restaurants, Sauna, Spa, Steam room, Yoga
GOOD TO KNOW	Closed from November to March
RECOMMENDED FOR	All-time favorite, Beach, Family friendly

"Fantastic private villa accommodation, perfectly pitched beach club, seamless and invisible service, and ingenious and classic locally inspired design."—Louis Hedgecock

Recommended by: Louis Hedgecock, HOK Architects; Ian Ritchie, Ian Ritchie Architects

MAÇAKIZI
Kesire Mevkii Narçiçegi Sok
Bodrum
Muğla
Aegean 48400
Turkey
+90 2523112400
macakizi.com

CREDIT CARDS	Accepted
PRICE	High-end
TYPE	Hotel
ACCOMMODATION	74 Rooms and Suites
FACILITIES	Bar, Gym, Outdoor swimming pool, Restaurant, Sauna, Spa, Steam room, Yoga
GOOD TO KNOW	Babysitting
RECOMMENDED FOR	All-time favorite, Beach, Best-kept secret

"The hotel has the perfect mix of everything for summer fun."
—Murat Tabanlıoğlu

Recommended by: Murat Tabanlıoğlu, Tabanlıoğlu Architects

SIX SENSES KAPLANKAYA
Bozbük Mahallesi, Merkez Sokak 198
Milas
Muğla
Aegean 48200
Turkey
+90 2525110051
sixsenses.com

CREDIT CARDS	Accepted
PRICE	Mid-range
TYPE	Hotel
ACCOMMODATION	291 Residences, Rooms, Suites, and Villas
FACILITIES	3 Bars, Gym, Indoor swimming pool, 3 Restaurants, Sauna, Spa, Steam room, Yoga
GOOD TO KNOW	Child friendly
RECOMMENDED FOR	Spa

A luxury coastal spa retreat which is also in close proximity to major archeological sites. Tours of the surrounding area—including helicopter experiences —are easily arranged.

Recommended by: Marco Costanzi, Marco Costanzi Architects

MANICI KASRI

Yeşilyurt Köyü 16
Ayvacık
Çanakkale
Marmara 17980
Turkey
+90 2867521731
manicikasri.com

CREDIT CARDS..Accepted
PRICE...Mid-range
TYPE..Hotel
ACCOMMODATION........................16 Rooms, Suites, and Villas
FACILITIES...........................Bar, Open-air bath, Restaurant,
Wood-burning fireplace
GOOD TO KNOW...Child friendly
RECOMMENDED FOR.......................................Family friendly

Recommended by: Emre Arolat, EAA

EMPRESS ZOE

Akbıyık Cad 10
Istanbul
Marmara 34122
Turkey
+90 2124585880
emzoe.com

CREDIT CARDS.....................Accepted but not Amex
PRICE...Low-cost
TYPE...Townhouse hotel
ACCOMMODATION.....................25 Rooms and Suites
FACILITIES..Bar
GOOD TO KNOW................................Child friendly
RECOMMENDED FOR...................................Urban

Empress Zoe is a charming boutique townhouse hotel
located within walking distance of some of Istanbul's
major cultural highlights. It is centered around a private
archaeological garden which borders the ruins of a
fifteenth-century bath house. Each of the guestrooms and
suites is individually decorated and features elements
of traditional Turkish art and craftwork. Some of the rooms
also have terraces with stunning views of the ancient
city and Marmara Sea.

Recommended by: Biba Dow, Dow Jones Architects

FOUR SEASONS HOTEL ISTANBUL AT THE BOSPHORUS

Çırağan Cad 28
Istanbul
Marmara 34349
Turkey
+90 2123814000
fourseasons.com

CREDIT CARDS..Accepted
PRICE...High-end
TYPE..Hotel
ACCOMMODATION....................................170 Rooms and Suites
FACILITIES...Bar, Gym,
Indoor and outdoor swimming pools,
3 Restaurants, Sauna,
Spa, Steam room, Yoga
GOOD TO KNOW..Babysitting
RECOMMENDED FOR...............Where I live, Wish I'd designed

"The hotel is next to the Bosphorus. You can see the Asian
side of Istanbul and magnificent views of the Hagia Sophia
and the Topkapi Palace."—Murat Tabanlıoğlu

Recommended by: Murat Tabanlıoğlu, Tabanlıoğlu
Architects

SUMAHAN ON THE WATER

Kuleli Cad 43
Istanbul
Marmara 34684
Turkey
+90 2164228000
sumahan.com

CREDIT CARDS..Accepted
PRICE...Mid-range
TYPE..Hotel
ACCOMMODATION.....................................13 Rooms and Suites
FACILITIES...............................Bar, Gym, Restaurant,
Spa, Steam room
GOOD TO KNOW..Babysitting
RECOMMENDED FOR..................................Where I live

Recommended by: Hasan Çalışlar, Erginoğlu & Çalışlar

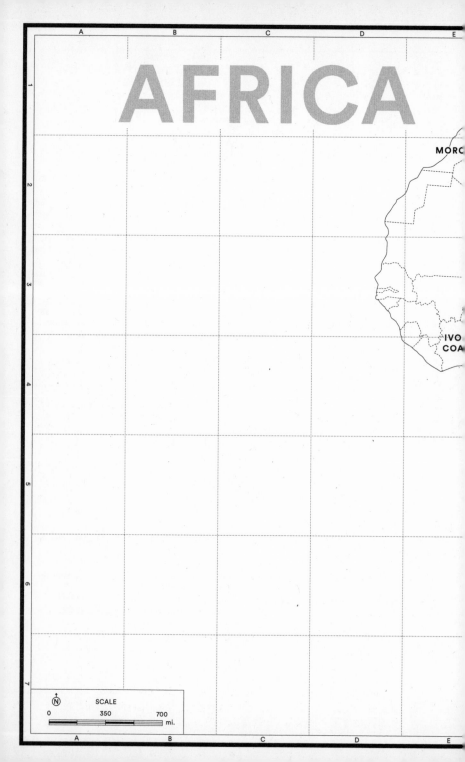

AFRICA

MORC

IVO
COA

N
SCALE
0   350   700
mi.

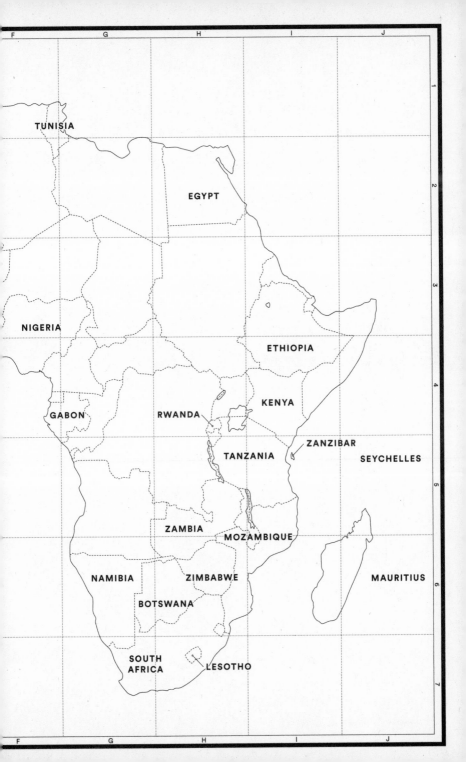

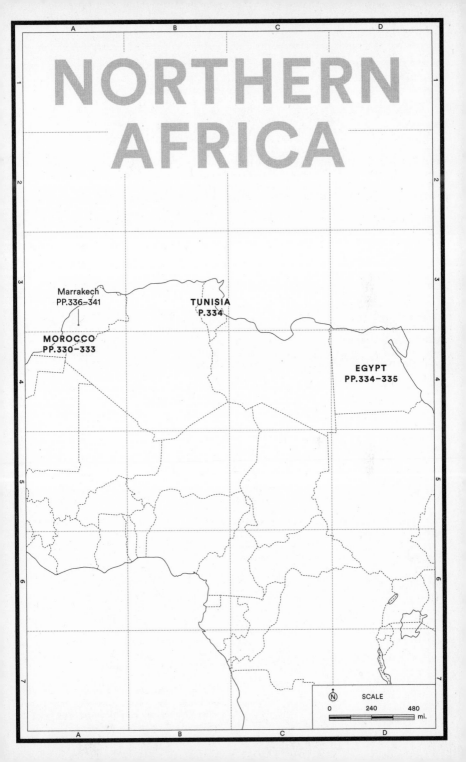

HYATT REGENCY CASABLANCA
Place des Nations Unies
Casablanca 20000
Morocco
+212 522431234
hyatt.com

CREDIT CARDS	Accepted
PRICE	Mid-range
TYPE	Hotel
ACCOMMODATION	255 Rooms and Suites
FACILITIES	Bar, Gym, Outdoor swimming pool, 3 Restaurants, Spa
GOOD TO KNOW	Babysitting
RECOMMENDED FOR	Countryside

Recommended by: Christian de Portzamparc,
2Portzamparc

LA SULTANA OUALIDIA
3 Parc à huîtres
Oualidia
Casablanca-Settat 24252
Morocco
+212 523366595
lasultanahotels.com

CREDIT CARDS	Accepted
PRICE	High-end
TYPE	Hotel
ACCOMMODATION	12 Rooms and Suites
FACILITIES	Bar, Gym, Outdoor swimming pool, Private beach, Restaurant, Spa
GOOD TO KNOW	Horse riding
RECOMMENDED FOR	Beach

"Perfect nest on the lagoon with lovely service and spot-on food."—Nabil Gholam

Recommended by: Nabil Gholam, Nabil Gholam Architects

MERZOUGA DESERT LUXURY CAMP
Erg Chebbi
Merzouga Desert
Drâa-Tafilalet 52002
Morocco
+212 662344816
merzougaluxurydesertcamps.com

CREDIT CARDS	Not accepted
PRICE	Mid-range
TYPE	Tented camp
ACCOMMODATION	15 tents
FACILITIES	Bar, Restaurant, Yoga
GOOD TO KNOW	Camel trekking, Child and pet friendly, Desert picnics, Stargazing
RECOMMENDED FOR	Desert

"Berber luxury in the middle of nowhere."
—Leonid Slonimskiy

Recommended by: Leonid Slonimskiy, KOSMOS Architects

DAR AHLAM
Douar Oulad Cheik Ali
Skoura
Ouarzazate
Drâa-Tafilalet 45502
Morocco
+212 524852239
darahlam.com

CREDIT CARDS	Accepted
PRICE	High-end
TYPE	Hotel
ACCOMMODATION	14 Rooms
FACILITIES	Bar, Hammam, Outdoor swimming pool, Restaurant
GOOD TO KNOW	4×4 with chauffeur, Babysitting, Traditional tea ceremonies
RECOMMENDED FOR	Desert, Worth the travel

"It's the final point of the 'Route du Sud'; staff meet you at the last gas station and guide you back by motorbike through dry riverbeds, fields, villages, and palmgroves. When you leave they offer you a basket with water, fruits, and sandwiches for your onward journey. It's the only opportunity we know of that allows you to live in a real Kasbah—it's almost like a dream."
—Karl Fournier and Olivier Marty

"This place is both inspiration and retreat—a 200-year-old rammed-earth Kasbah with a traditional hammam. You can see the Atlas Mountains and eat in private dining 'rooms' within groves of palm trees."—Rick Joy

"Simple luxury in desert surroundings"
—Daniel Suduca and Thierry Mérillou

Recommended by: Rick Joy, Studio Rick Joy; Charles
Renfro, Diller Scofidio + Renfro; Daniel Suduca and Thierry
Mérillou, Suduca & Mérillou

LA ROSE DU SABLE

Kasbah Ait Ben Haddou
Aït Benhaddou
Ouarzazate
Drâa-Tafilalet 45122, Morocco
+212 524890022
larosedusable.com

CREDIT CARDS	Not accepted
PRICE	Low-cost
TYPE	Hotel
ACCOMMODATION	18 Rooms
FACILITIES	Outdoor swimming pool, Restaurant
GOOD TO KNOW	Child friendly, Near Ait-Ben-Haddou
RECOMMENDED FOR	Desert

"Oasis in the desert, surrounded by cultural treasures."
—Luca Gazzaniga

Recommended by: Luca Gazzaniga, Luca Gazzaniga
Architects

KASBAH OUZINA

Dunas de Ouzina BP 7
Rissani
Drâa-Tafilalet 52450
Morocco
+212 668986500
ouzina.com

CREDIT CARDS	Accepted but not Amex
PRICE	Low-cost
TYPE	Hotel
ACCOMMODATION	21 Rooms
FACILITIES	Bar, Restaurant
GOOD TO KNOW	Camel riding, Child and pet friendly, Quadbike rentals
RECOMMENDED FOR	Desert

"Traditional kasbah in a desert setting."—Antonio G. Liñán

Recommended by: Antonio G. Liñán, SV60 Cordón &
Liñán Arquitectos

ERG CHIGAGA LUXURY DESERT CAMP

Erg Chigaga
Sahara Desert
Drâa-Tafilalet 40007
Morocco
+212 654398520
desertcampmorocco.com

CREDIT CARDS	Not accepted
PRICE	Mid-range (all-inclusive)
TYPE	Tented camp
ACCOMMODATION	17 tents
FACILITIES	Lounge, Outdoor restaurant
GOOD TO KNOW	Camel rides, Quad biking, Sandboarding, Stargazing
RECOMMENDED FOR	Desert

Situated across three distinctive camps—the Berber-
inspired Main Camp, the Private Camp, and a Nomadic
Private Camp ideal for couples—the resort captures the
rugged romance of a truly remote desert experience.

Recommended by: Dinko Peračić, ARP and Platforma 9.81

HOTEL XALUCA DADES

Boumalne Dades
Tinghir
Drâa-Tafilalet 45150
Morocco
+212 524830060
xaluca.com

CREDIT CARDS	Accepted but not Amex
PRICE	Low-cost
TYPE	Hotel
ACCOMMODATION	106 Rooms and Suites
FACILITIES	Bar, Gym, Outdoor swimming pool, Restaurant, Spa
GOOD TO KNOW	4WD excursions, Trekking
RECOMMENDED FOR	Desert

"Wonderful 1970s Abdeslam Faraoui and Patrice de
Mazières architecture blending marvelously with the
surrounding desert terrain."—Richard England

Recommended by: Richard England, Richard England
Architects

PALAIS FARAJ SUITES & SPA

16–18 Derb Bensouda
Bab Ziat
Fes 30000
Morocco
+212 535635356
palaisfaraj-fes.com

CREDIT CARDS	Accepted but not Amex
PRICE	Mid-range
TYPE	Hotel
ACCOMMODATION	25 Rooms and Suites
FACILITIES	2 Bars, Outdoor swimming pool, 2 Restaurants, Spa
GOOD TO KNOW	Free parking
RECOMMENDED FOR	Family friendly

"In the heart of the beautiful Fez medina."—Driss Kettani

Recommended by: Driss Kettani, Driss Kettani Architecte

RYAD MABROUKA

Derb El Miter No 25 Talaa Kbira
Fes el Bali
Fes 30110
Morocco
+212 535636345
ryadmabrouka.com

CREDIT CARDS	Accepted
PRICE	Low-cost
TYPE	Riad
ACCOMMODATION	8 Rooms and Suites
FACILITIES	Outdoor swimming pool, Restaurant, Spa
GOOD TO KNOW	Bicycle rentals, Child friendly
RECOMMENDED FOR	Best-kept secret

"Hidden away at the end of a labyrinth of alleyways, this riad, run by a French couple, has only a handful of rooms around a central atrium. The garden is also home to two tortoises."—Simon Henley

Recommended by: Simon Henley, Henley Halebrown

KASBAH TAMADOT

Kasbah Tamadot BP 67
Asni
Atlas Mountains
Marrakech-Safi 42152
Morocco
+44 2071938093
kasbahtamadot.icastelli.net

CREDIT CARDS	Accepted
PRICE	Blow-out
TYPE	Hotel
ACCOMMODATION	28 Rooms and Suites
FACILITIES	Indoor and outdoor swimming pools, Spa
GOOD TO KNOW	Babysitting, Cooking lessons, Mule trekking
RECOMMENDED FOR	Countryside

"Wonderful, not least because of the context, the food, and the people."—Fernando Romero

Recommended by: Fernando Romero, FR–EE/Fernando Romero Enterprise

KASBAH DU TOUBKAL

Toubkal National Park
Imlil
Atlas Mountains
Marrakech-Safi 42152
Morocco
+44 1883744667
kasbahtoubkal.com

CREDIT CARDS	Accepted but not Amex
PRICE	Mid-range
TYPE	Lodge
ACCOMMODATION	14 Rooms
FACILITIES	Restaurant, Steam room
GOOD TO KNOW	Pet friendly
RECOMMENDED FOR	Best-kept secret

Kasbah du Toubkal is situated in the Atlas Mountains above the village of Imlil. It has a delightful garden and large terraces with unparalleled views of the surrounding mountains. The hotel can arrange trekking packages as well as tailor-made tours around Morocco.

Recommended by: Luca Gazzaniga, Luca Gazzaniga Architects

KASBAH BAB OURIKA

Ourika Valley
Tnine Ourika
Atlas Mountains
Marrakech-Safi 42452
Morocco
+212 668749547
kasbahbabourika.com

CREDIT CARDS	Accepted but not Amex
PRICE	Mid-range
TYPE	Hotel
ACCOMMODATION	26 Rooms
FACILITIES	Bar, Outdoor swimming pool, Restaurant, Spa
GOOD TO KNOW	Babysitting, Camel trekking, Pet friendly, Waterfall trips
RECOMMENDED FOR	Desert, Mountains

"Amazing suites, food, and the best Bloody Mary made with fresh tomatoes from the garden."—Cian Deegan

Recommended by: Emanuel Christ, Christ & Gantenbein; Cian Deegan, TAKA Architects

MARRAKECH: SEE PAGES 336–341

MAISON ROUGE

Aojou
Awju Valley
Souss-Massa
Morocco
+212 524852239
darahlam.com

CREDIT CARDS	Accepted
PRICE	Blow-out
TYPE	Riad
ACCOMMODATION	13 Rooms and Suites
FACILITIES	Restaurant
GOOD TO KNOW	Camel rides, Views of Awju Valley
RECOMMENDED FOR	Desert

"The architecture [by Studio KO] is the outcome of thousands of years of dwelling traditions in the desert."
—Alireza Razavi

Recommended by: Alireza Razavi, Studio Razavi Architecture

HOTEL CONTINENTAL

36 rue Dar Baroud
Tangier 90000
Morocco
+212 539931024
hotel-tanger.com

CREDIT CARDS	Accepted but not Amex
PRICE	Low-cost
TYPE	Hotel
ACCOMMODATION	56 Rooms
FACILITIES	Restaurant
GOOD TO KNOW	Free parking
RECOMMENDED FOR	Urban

"Travelers like us, who are faithful to the mythical (though distant) legend of Tangier, will find ideal accommodation in the rundown Hotel Continental. The hotel continues to be one of our favorite places in the city. The energy of its Atlantic light at dawn, the clear views of Europe from its terrace, and the relaxing cup of tea served in the evening in its dining room compensate for its ageing demeanor."
—Marisol and Ubaldo García Torrente

Recommended by: Marisol and Ubaldo García Torrente, García Torrente Arquitectos

VILLA JOSÉPHINE

231 rue Sidi Mesmoudi
Tangier 90000
Morocco
+212 539334535
villajosephine-tanger.com

CREDIT CARDS	Accepted
PRICE	High-end
TYPE	Villa
ACCOMMODATION	10 Rooms and Suites
FACILITIES	Bar, Outdoor swimming pool, Restaurant
GOOD TO KNOW	Free parking
RECOMMENDED FOR	Mountains

"Refined hospitality and a sophisticated atmosphere."
—Carlos Ferrater

Recommended by: Carlos Ferrater, OAB

SANGHO PRIVILEGE TATAOUINE
Route De Chenini el Farch BP 186
Tataouine 3200
Tunisia
+216 75860102
sanghoprivilegetataouine.info

CREDIT CARDS......................................Accepted but not Amex
PRICE...Low-cost
TYPE..Hotel
ACCOMMODATION..86 Rooms
FACILITIES..................................Bar, Outdoor swimming pool,
3 Restaurants
GOOD TO KNOW...Bicycle tours, Hiking
RECOMMENDED FOR..Desert

"The architecture includes underground houses that stay cool and fortified *ksour*, or storage enclaves, built of the local earth. When a group of us stayed there it coincided with my wife's birthday. The hosts were so accommodating that we were able to organize, at short notice, a wonderfully festive surprise party for her with traditional live music provided by local artists. They even helped us learn traditional dances."—Buzz Yudell

Recommended by: Buzz Yudell, Moore Ruble Yudell

DAR EL JELD HOTEL & SPA
5 rue Dar El Jeld
Tunis 1006
Tunisia
+216 70016190
dareljeld.com

CREDIT CARDS..Accepted
PRICE..Mid-range
TYPE..Hotel
ACCOMMODATION..16 Suites
FACILITIES........................Bar, Hammam, 2 Restaurants, Spa
GOOD TO KNOW....................Bespoke tours can be arranged
RECOMMENDED FOR..Spa

"The renovation of this old palace into a hotel has been done extremely well. After the hammam, go to the rooftop terrace with a nice view of the Medina."—Cino Zucchi

Recommended by: Cino Zucchi, CZA

SOFITEL LEGEND OLD CATARACT ASWAN
Abtal el Tahrir Street
Aswan 81511
Egypt
+20 1022229071
accorhotels.com

CREDIT CARDS..Accepted
PRICE...High-end
TYPE..Hotel
ACCOMMODATION................................76 Rooms and Suites
FACILITIES...4 Bars, Gym,
Outdoor swimming pool,
4 Restaurants, Spa
GOOD TO KNOW..Babysitting
RECOMMENDED FOR............................Desert, Worth the travel

"*Death on the Nile*, anyone?"—Craig Dykers

"We stayed at the Old Cataract on our honeymoon in a grand room the size of a squash court."—Simon Henley

Recommended by: Craig Dykers, Snøhetta; Simon Henley, Henley Halebrown; Jean-Paul Viguier, Jean-Paul Viguier et Associés

MARRIOTT MENA HOUSE
6 Pyramids Road
Giza
Cairo 12556
Egypt
+20 233773222
marriott.com

CREDIT CARDS..Accepted
PRICE..Mid-range
TYPE..Hotel
ACCOMMODATION..............................331 Rooms and Suites
FACILITIES............................Gym, Outdoor swimming pool,
4 Restaurants, Spa
GOOD TO KNOW...............Near Giza pyramids, Valet parking
RECOMMENDED FOR..Desert

"The old wing of the house has rooms with a view of the pyramids of Giza and Khafre."—Beppe Caturegli and Giovannella Formica

Recommended by: Raúl de Armas, MdeAS Architects; Beppe Caturegli and Giovannella Formica, Caturegli Formica Architetti Associati

HOTEL SOFITEL WINTER PALACE LUXOR

Corniche el Nile
Luxor 11432
Egypt
+20 952380422
accorhotels.com

CREDIT CARDS..Accepted
PRICE...Mid-range
TYPE..Hotel
ACCOMMODATION...................................92 Rooms and Suites
FACILITIES...4 Bars, Gym, Outdoor
swimming pool, 3 Restaurants
GOOD TO KNOW...............................Babysitting, Water sports
RECOMMENDED FOR...All-time favorite

"It reminds me of the most beautiful, enriching journey that
I have ever made—it was almost like a dream."
—Alfredo Payá Benedito

Recommended by: Alfredo Payá Benedito, Noname29

ADRÈRE AMELLAL

Sidi al-Ja'afar
Siwa Oasis 11211
Egypt
+20 22736 7879
adrereamellal.net

CREDIT CARDS..Accepted
PRICE...High-end
TYPE..Hotel
ACCOMMODATION...40 Rooms
FACILITIES..........................2 Bars, Outdoor swimming pool,
Restaurant, Library
GOOD TO KNOW...Dune hiking,
Horse riding, No electricity
RECOMMENDED FOR..Desert

"It is located in an oasis between the Qattara Depression
and the Egyptian Sand Sea in the Western Desert—truly,
it's unlike anywhere else on earth."—Jean-Louis Deniot

"This place has no electricity and the best food."
—Matteo Thun

Recommended by: Jean-Louis Deniot; Marcio Kogan,
Studio MK27; Stéphane Parmentier; Matteo Thun, Matteo
Thun & Partners

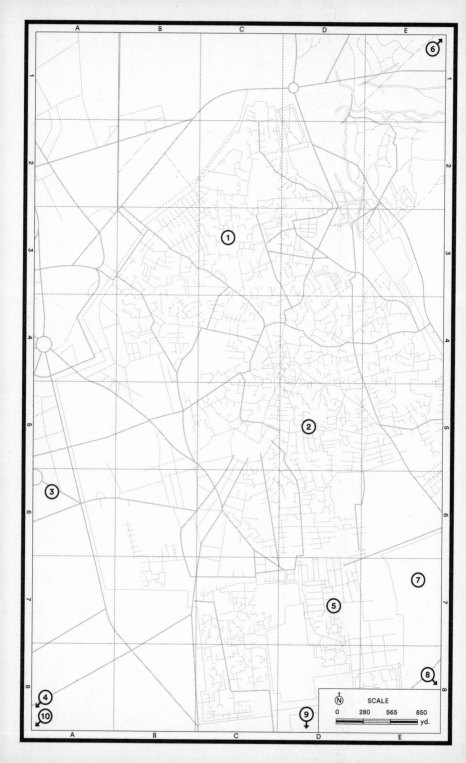

MARRAKECH

DAR RBAA LAROUB

61 Derb Abid Allah Quartier Mouassine
North Medina
Marrakech 40000
+212 524390716
darrbaalaroub.com

CREDIT CARDS	Accepted
PRICE	Low-cost
TYPE	Riad
ACCOMMODATION	7 Rooms and Suites
FACILITIES	Restaurant, Roof terrace
GOOD TO KNOW	Picnics, Views of Atlas Mountains
RECOMMENDED FOR	Best-kept secret

"A typical Moroccan house. You will be welcomed by
the landlord, who will proceed to give you the best travel
tips for the city—and the rest of the country."
—Karl Fournier and Olivier Marty

Recommended by: Karl Fournier and Olivier Marty,
Studio KO

RIAD 72

72 Arset Awzel
North Medina
Marrakech 40000
+212 524387629
riad72.com

CREDIT CARDS	Accepted but not Amex
PRICE	Mid-range
TYPE	Riad
ACCOMMODATION	7 Rooms and Suites
FACILITIES	Restaurant, Rooftop terrace bar, Spa
GOOD TO KNOW	Bicycle rentals, Pet friendly
RECOMMENDED FOR	Desert

"Huge rooms and sensitive attention to detail where old
meets new."—Ab Rogers

Recommended by: Ab Rogers, Ab Rogers Design

EL FENN

Derb Moullay Abdullah Ben Hussain, Bab El Ksour
South Medina
Marrakech 40000
+212 524441280
el-fenn.com

CREDIT CARDS	Accepted but not Amex
PRICE	Mid-range
TYPE	Riad
ACCOMMODATION	28 Rooms and Suites
FACILITIES	Outdoor swimming pool, Restaurant, Rooftop terrace bar, Spa
GOOD TO KNOW	Near Jemaa el-Fnaa
RECOMMENDED FOR	Wish I'd designed

"A masterpiece."—Anne Kaestle

El Fenn is a luxurious retreat in the heart of Marrakech,
just a short walk from Jemaa el-Fnaa (the main square).
The converted riad has individually styled rooms and suites,
tree-filled courtyards, a large roof terrace and a family
of resident tortoises. There is also a spa and pool, and yoga
can be organised on the roof terrace.

Recommended by: Anne Kaestle, Duplex Architekten

HOTEL CTM

Rue El Ksour, Jemaa el-Fna
South Medina
Marrakech 40000
+212 524442325

CREDIT CARDS	Not accepted
PRICE	Low-cost
TYPE	Hotel
ACCOMMODATION	21 Rooms
FACILITIES	Restaurant
GOOD TO KNOW	No alcohol
RECOMMENDED FOR	Budget

"From the terrace rooms of the hotel you can witness
the comings and goings of daily life in the Jemaa el-Fna
square."—Alfredo Payá Benedito

Recommended by: Alfredo Payá Benedito, Noname29

LA MAMOUNIA
Avenue Bab Jdid
South Medina
Marrakech 40040
+212 524388600
mamounia.com

CREDIT CARDS..Accepted
PRICE..High-end
TYPE..Hotel
ACCOMMODATION.......................209 Rooms and Suites
FACILITIES.................Indoor and outdoor swimming pools,
4 Restaurants, Spa, Yoga
GOOD TO KNOW...Babysitting
RECOMMENDED FOR...Luxury

The legendary five-star La Mamounia is one of Marrakech's finest hotels. The property has extensive private gardens, a wellness centre, and a range of rooms and suites designed by Jacques Garcia, as well as four separate restaurants which serve Moroccan and European cuisine.

Recommended by: Giancarlo Mazzanti, El Equipo Mazzanti

ROYAL MANSOUR MARRAKECH
Rue Abou El Abbas Sebti
South Medina
Marrakech 40000
+212 529808080
royalmansour.com

CREDIT CARDS..Accepted
PRICE..Blow-out
TYPE...Riad
ACCOMMODATION............53 Residences, Rooms, and Suites
FACILITIES...................................Bar, Gym, 3 Restaurants, Spa
GOOD TO KNOW...Babysitting
RECOMMENDED FOR.................Desert, Spa, Worth the travel

"Authentic Moorish architecture, contemporary interior design, and incredible food."—Maria Warner Wong

Recommended by: Driss Kettani, Driss Kettani Architecte; Fernando Romero, FR–EE/Fernando Romero Enterprise; Maria Warner Wong, WOW Architects | Warner Wong Design

THE PEARL
Corner Avenue Echouhada and Rue des Temples
Hivernage
Marrakech 40000
+212 524424242
thepearlmarrakech.com

CREDIT CARDS..Accepted
PRICE...Mid-range
TYPE..Hotel
ACCOMMODATION......................71 Rooms and Suites
FACILITIES...Bar, Gym,
Indoor and outdoor swimming pools,
4 Restaurants, Spa
GOOD TO KNOW...................Babysitting, Pet friendly
RECOMMENDED FOR..Wish I'd designed

"This is an example of optimal use of a tight urban plot to create a vibrant, detailed design with sensory experiences at every turn."—Olajumoke Adenowo

Recommended by: Olajumoke Adenowo, AD Consulting

BELDI COUNTRY CLUB
Route de Barrage km6
Chrifia
Marrakech 40000
+212 524383950
beldicountryclub.com

CREDIT CARDS..Accepted
PRICE...Mid-range
TYPE..Hotel
ACCOMMODATION...38 Suites
FACILITIES...Bar,
Indoor and outdoor swimming pools,
2 Restaurants, Spa, Tennis
GOOD TO KNOW.......................Cooking and pottery classes,
Child friendly, Horse riding
RECOMMENDED FOR...Worth the travel

Beldi Country Club is a green oasis on the outskirts of bustling Marrakech with views across the rose gardens to the Atlas Mountains. Within the extensive landscaped grounds are four swimming pools, a tennis court, and a garden restaurant. The hotel's suites have been designed to resemble a Moroccan village. There is a range of activities for children and adults alike, including pottery courses, horse riding, and the opportunity to bake your own morning bread with the hotel's baker.

Recommended by: Aljoša Dekleva and Tina Gregorič, Dekleva Gregorič Architects

RIAD AZOULAY

3 Derb Jamaa El Kbir
Mellah
Marrakech 40000
+212 524383729
riad-azoulay.com

CREDIT CARDS	Accepted but not Amex
PRICE	Low-cost
TYPE	Riad
ACCOMMODATION	9 Rooms and Suites
FACILITIES	Restaurant, Spa, Swimming pool
GOOD TO KNOW	Child friendly, Cooking classes
RECOMMENDED FOR	Urban

"A little oasis in a bustling city."—Simon Henley

Recommended by: Simon Henley, Henley Halebrown

LES DEUX TOURS

Circuit de la Palmeraie
Douar Abiad
Marrakech 40000
+212 524329525
les-deux-tours.com

CREDIT CARDS	Accepted but not Amex
PRICE	Mid-range
TYPE	Hotel
ACCOMMODATION	40 Rooms and Suites
FACILITIES	Bar, Outdoor swimming pool, 2 Restaurants, Spa, Yoga
GOOD TO KNOW	Babysitting, Guided tours of souks, Pet friendly
RECOMMENDED FOR	Desert

"On the edge of the Marrakech desert, but twenty minutes' drive from the center of the city. The resort is akin to a small campus of traditional buildings, set in a palm forest with a Michelin-star restaurant. What could be better?"
—Chris Wilkinson

Recommended by: Chris Wilkinson, Wilkinson Eyre Architects

PALAIS NAMASKAR

88/69 Route de Bab Atlas
Syba
Marrakech 40000
+212 524299800
palaisnamaskar.com

CREDIT CARDS	Accepted
PRICE	Mid-range
TYPE	Hotel
ACCOMMODATION	41 Palaces, Rooms, Suites, and Villas
FACILITIES	Gym, Outdoor swimming pool, 2 Restaurants, Spa, Yoga
GOOD TO KNOW	Babysitting, Bicycle rentals, Pet friendly
RECOMMENDED FOR	Best-kept secret

Palais Namaskar is a landmark destination in Marrakech's La Palmeraie, with its accommodations situated along meandering waterways. The spa has a range of wellness packages and each of the bars and restaurants uses organic produce from the hotel's own gardens and local producers.

Recommended by: Hani Rashid, Asymptote Architecture

AMANJENA

Route de Ouarzazate km12
Marrakech 40000
+212 524399000
aman.com

CREDIT CARDS	Accepted
PRICE	High-end
TYPE	Hotel
ACCOMMODATION	32 Maisons and Pavilions
FACILITIES	Gym, Outdoor swimming pool, 3 Restaurants, Spa
GOOD TO KNOW	Babysitting, Hiking
RECOMMENDED FOR	Desert

"A majestic resort set within a peaceful, lush, tropical landscape. Luxurious simplicity."—Bruce Kuwabara

Recommended by: Bruce Kuwabara, KPMB Architects

BERBER LODGE

Douar Oumnes
Al Haouz
Marrakech 42312
+212 662049043
berberlodge.net

CREDIT CARDS	Accepted
PRICE	Mid-range
TYPE	Lodge
ACCOMMODATION	9 Lodges
FACILITIES	Bar, Outdoor swimming pool, Restaurant
GOOD TO KNOW	Free parking
RECOMMENDED FOR	Family friendly

Berber Lodge is situated amongst tranquil olive groves and is twenty minutes by car from Marrakech. The charming collection of cottages has been constructed using traditional Berber techniques and at each of their cores is a large lounge with a fireplace, library, bar, and dining room. There is also an outdoor bar adjoining the pool, as well as gardens from which the Lodge's chefs source much of the restaurant's organic produce.

[Studio KO conceived the original plans for this hotel.]

Recommended by: Karl Fournier and Olivier Marty, Studio KO

LA PAUSE

Douar Lmih Laroussiene
Désert Agafay
Marrakech 40000
+212 610772240
lapause-marrakech.com

CREDIT CARDS	Not accepted
PRICE	Mid-range
TYPE	Lodge
ACCOMMODATION	10 Lodges and Tent
FACILITIES	Bar, Outdoor swimming pool, Restaurant
GOOD TO KNOW	Bicycle rentals, Camel trekking, Horse riding, Mountain biking
RECOMMENDED FOR	Desert

"Quirky, original, and secluded."—Tavis Wright

Recommended by: Tavis Wright, Dos Architects

SCARABEO CAMP

Désert Agafay
Marrakech 40000
+212 662800823
scarabeocamp.com

CREDIT CARDS	Accepted but not Amex
PRICE	Mid-range
TYPE	Tented camp
ACCOMMODATION	15 Tents
FACILITIES	Restaurant, Yoga
GOOD TO KNOW	Camel and horse riding, Heated tents in winter, Stargazing, Trekking
RECOMMENDED FOR	Desert

"Glamping in a desert less than one hour from Marrakech."
—Anne Kaestle

Recommended by: Anne Kaestle, Duplex Architekten; Maria Warner Wong, WOW Architects | Warner Wong Design

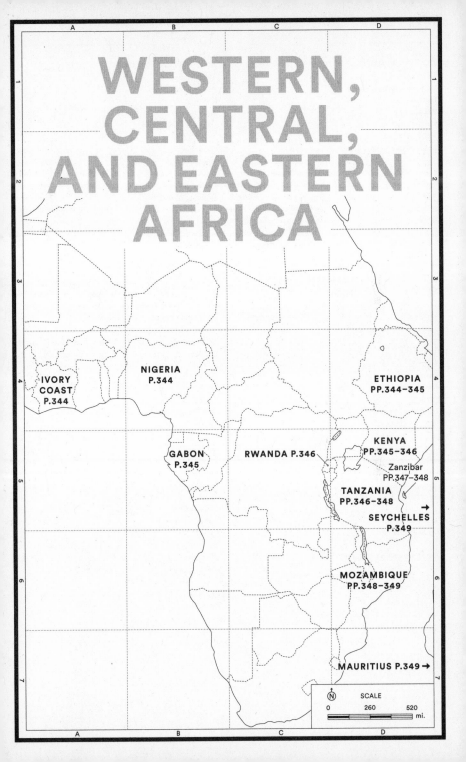

WESTERN, CENTRAL, AND EASTERN AFRICA

IVORY
COAST
P.344

NIGERIA
P.344

ETHIOPIA
PP.344–345

GABON
P.345

RWANDA P.346

KENYA
PP.345–346

Zanzibar
PP.347–348

TANZANIA
PP.346–348

SEYCHELLES
P.349 →

MOZAMBIQUE
PP.348–349

MAURITIUS P.349 →

SCALE

0   260   520
mi.

SOFITEL ABIDJAN HOTEL IVOIRE
Boulevard Hassan II
08 Boîte Postale 01
Cocody
Abidjan 8
Ivory Coast
+225 22482626
accorhotels.com

CREDIT CARDS.....................................Accepted but not Amex
PRICE...Mid-range
TYPE..Hotel
ACCOMMODATION.................................423 Rooms and Suites
FACILITIES.........................5 Bars, Gym, Outdoor swimming
pool, 4 Restaurants, Spa
GOOD TO KNOW...Babysitting
RECOMMENDED FOR...Urban

"A beautiful Modernist ensemble in the Cocody neighborhood."—Driss Kettani

Recommended by: Driss Kettani, Driss Kettani Architecte

THE GEORGE
30 Lugard Avenue
Ikoyi
Lagos 101233
Nigeria
+234 014663664
thegeorgelagos.com

CREDIT CARDS.....................................Accepted but not Amex
PRICE...Mid-range
TYPE..Hotel
ACCOMMODATION......................................61 Rooms and Suites
FACILITIES....................Bar, Gym, Outdoor swimming pool,
Restaurant
GOOD TO KNOW...Free parking
RECOMMENDED FOR...Where I live

Recommended by: Olajumoke Adenowo, AD Consulting

SHERATON ADDIS
Taitu Street
Addis Ababa
Ethiopia
+251 115171717
sheratonaddis.com

CREDIT CARDS...Accepted
PRICE...Mid-range
TYPE..Hotel
ACCOMMODATION....................295 Rooms, Suites, and Villas
FACILITIES...6 Bars, Gym,
Outdoor swimming pools,
3 Restaurants, Spa
GOOD TO KNOW...Babysitting
RECOMMENDED FOR..............................All-time favorite

A 295-key luxury hotel sited on a hill overlooking the city, the Sheraton Addis provides an oasis of calm in bustling urban surroundings. Facilities include a selection of bars and restaurants that serve a range of international cuisines, and an opulently designed spa.

Recommended by: Mphethi Morojele, MMA Design Studio

TUKUL VILLAGE HOTEL
Lalibela
Ethiopia
+251 333360564
tukulvillage.com

CREDIT CARDS...Accepted
PRICE...Low-cost
TYPE..Village hotel
ACCOMMODATION..24 Rooms
FACILITIES...Bar
GOOD TO KNOW..Child friendly
RECOMMENDED FOR...Worth the travel

"This place is more than worth the journey; discover ancient churches in Lalibela and enjoy fascinating views of the town and its surroundings."—Satyendra Pakhalé

Recommended by: Satyendra Pakhalé, Satyendra Pakhalé Associates

LIMALIMO LODGE
Simien Mountains National Park
North Gondar
Ethiopia
+251 931688062
limalimolodge.com

CREDIT CARDS..Not accepted
PRICE.................................Low-cost (all-inclusive)
TYPE...Lodge
ACCOMMODATION..12 Rooms
FACILITIES...Bar, Restaurant
GOOD TO KNOW.......................Birdwatching, Child friendly,
No internet, Trekking
RECOMMENDED FOR..Mountain

A boutique lodge comprising twelve en suite rooms spread across the twenty-five-acre (ten-hectare) site, Limalino Lodge has breathtaking views of the surrounding Simien Mountains National Park. It was founded by two mountain guides who were keen to open up the benefits of tourism to local people and communities, while offering visitors to the UNESCO World Heritage area a taste of Ethiopia's famously warm hospitality. The lodge is also a member of Pack for a Purpose, an initiative that allows visitors to provide the local community with supplies.

Recommended by: Hugo Sauzay, Festen Architecture

RÉSIDENCE HÔTELIÈRE DU PHARE
La Sablière BP 7972
Libreville
Gabon
+241 04120000
residencehotelhiereduphare.com

CREDIT CARDS.....................................Accepted but not Amex
PRICE...Mid-range
TYPE..Hotel
ACCOMMODATION.........................16 Rooms and Suites
FACILITIES..Bar, Restaurant
GOOD TO KNOW..............................Fishing, Hiking, Trekking
RECOMMENDED FOR..Beach

"While there are many great beach hotels on isolated coastlines around the world, the Du Phare is perhaps the best in a major city, despite not being recommended for swimming. It is well known for its restaurant, which is probably the best in Libreville, and is a great place to meet diplomats, artists, travelers, and dealmakers, and enjoy a cold Régab beer and roasted peanuts under the canvas umbrellas."—Dan Wood

Recommended by: Dan Wood, WORKac

ARIJIJU
Laikipia County
Nanyuki
Borana Conservancy, Kenya
arijiju.com

CREDIT CARDS...Accepted
PRICE..Blow-out (all-inclusive)
TYPE...Safari lodge
ACCOMMODATION..5 Suites
FACILITIES...Gym, Hammam,
Outdoor swimming pool,
Spa, Squash, Tennis, Yoga
GOOD TO KNOW.........................Rent exclusively, Fly-fishing,
Helicopter safaris,
Horse riding, Malaria-free
RECOMMENDED FOR.................................Best-kept Secret

"A beautiful luxury retreat, perfect for escaping into the African highlands."—Alex Michaelis

Arijiju, in the Borana Lewa Conservancy, is where to experience the big five. The elegant family home and retreat is designed to blend in with the natural surroundings yet there are luxury facilities which include a spa and hammam, a gym, clay tennis, and squash courts and pool. There is also horse riding and hiking on Mount Kenya.

Recommended by: Alex Michaelis, Michaelis Boyd

CAMPI YA KANZI
Mtito Andei
Chyulu Hills National Park, Kenya
+254 720461300
maasai.com

CREDIT CARDS...Accepted
PRICE..Blow-out
TYPE...Safari lodge
ACCOMMODATION.............10 Cottages and Tented cottages
and suites, and Villa
FACILITIES...Yoga
GOOD TO KNOW............................Child friendly, Horse riding
RECOMMENDED FOR................................Eco-conscious

"Sophisticated simplicity."—Emre Arolat

Campi Ya Kanzi is a boutique eco-lodge in the Chyulu Hills of southern Kenya that works in partnership with the Maasai Wilderness Conservation Trust, and is the only luxury safari lodge on a Maasai-owned reserve. Accommodation includes luxury safari tents and also Kanzi House and Pool Cottage, which can be booked for larger groups.

Recommended by: Emre Arolat, EAA

WARANDALE COTTAGES DIANI BEACH

Kijiji Cottages Road
Diani Beach
Ukunda
Kwale County 80400
Kenya
+254 724923585
warandale.com

CREDIT CARDS	Not accepted
PRICE	Low-cost
TYPE	Serviced house rental
ACCOMMODATION	5 Cottages
FACILITIES	Outdoor swimming pool
GOOD TO KNOW	Cook and housekeeper, Deep-sea fishing, Water sports
RECOMMENDED FOR	Beach

"This was designed in the late 1970s by the Danish architect Leif Damgaard as his own private summerhouse. Later he moved there permanently and designed a series of cottages, as well as his own architect's practice, in a cluster of buildings named Warandale. The cottages are built entirely of local materials—coral blocks, mangrove construction, and palm leaf roofs—though have a distinct Scandinavian touch in the design and interiors."—Ene Cordt Andersen

Recommended by: Ene Cordt Andersen, Andersen & Sigurdsson Architects

KILAGUNI SERENA SAFARI LODGE

Tsavo National Park
Taita-Taveta
Kenya
+254 734699698
serenahotels.com

CREDIT CARDS	Accepted
PRICE	Mid-range
TYPE	Safari lodge
ACCOMMODATION	56 Rooms and Suites
FACILITIES	Restaurant
GOOD TO KNOW	Child friendly, Near a watering hole
RECOMMENDED FOR	Countryside

"A remote location in the middle of nature."—Urko Sanchez

Recommended by: Urko Sanchez, Urko Sanchez Architects

AKAGERA CAMPSITES

Akagera National Park
Kayonza
Rwanda
+250 786182871
akagerarwandanationalpark.com

CREDIT CARDS	Not accepted
PRICE	Low-cost
TYPE	Campsite
ACCOMMODATION	3 Campsites
FACILITIES	Washrooms
GOOD TO KNOW	Boat trips, Birdwatching, Self-catering, Tents for hire
RECOMMENDED FOR	Countryside, Worth the travel

"You can sleep with elephants and lions nearby!"
—Sébastien Dachy

Recommended by: Sébastien Dachy, MAMOUT architectes

&BEYOND LAKE MANYARA TREE LODGE

Lake Manyara National Park
Arusha Region
Tanzania
+27 118094300
andbeyond.com

CREDIT CARDS	Accepted
PRICE	High-end (all-inclusive)
TYPE	Lodge
ACCOMMODATION	1 Treehouse, 9 Suites
FACILITIES	Outdoor swimming pool, Restaurant
GOOD TO KNOW	Babysitting, Tree-climbing
RECOMMENDED FOR	Eco-conscious

"Luxury and excellent architectural standards."
—Rafael de La-Hoz Castanys

Recommended by: Rafael de La-Hoz Castanys, Rafael de La-Hoz Arquitectos

&BEYOND NGORONGORO CRATER LODGE

Ngorongoro
Arusha Region
Tanzania
+27 118094300
andbeyond.com

CREDIT CARDS..Accepted
PRICE..Blow-out (all-inclusive)
TYPE...Lodge
ACCOMMODATION...30 Stilted suites
FACILITIES...Boutique, Restaurant
GOOD TO KNOW...Babysitting,
Day trips to Olduvai Gorge
RECOMMENDED FOR...Mountains

Recommended by: Fernando Sordo Madaleno,
Sordo Madaleno

KIRAWIRA SERENA CAMP

Western Serengeti National Park
Arusha Region
Tanzania
+255 282621518
serenahotels.com

CREDIT CARDS..Accepted
PRICE...Mid-range
TYPE...Lodge
ACCOMMODATION...25 Tents
FACILITIES...............................Bar, Outdoor swimming pool,
Restaurant, Yoga
GOOD TO KNOW..........................Birdwatching, Child friendly,
Lake cruises
RECOMMENDED FOR...All-time favorite

"A very special place, totally unique in the world."
—Victor Legorreta Hernández

Recommended by: Victor Legorreta Hernández, Legorreta

&BEYOND KLEIN'S CAMP

Kuka Hills
Serengeti National Park
Mara Region
Tanzania
+27 118094300
andbeyond.com

CREDIT CARDS..Accepted
PRICE..High-end (all-inclusive)
TYPE...Lodge
ACCOMMODATION...10 Cottages
FACILITIES.....................Boutique, Outdoor swimming pool,
Restaurant
GOOD TO KNOW.................................Babysitting, Bush walks,
Maasai community visits
RECOMMENDED FOR...Worth the travel

Recommended by: Louis Hedgecock, HOK Architects

DHOW INN ZANZIBAR

Paje Beach
East Coast Zanzibar
Zanzibar
Tanzania
+255 777525828
dhowinn.com

CREDIT CARDS...................................Accepted but not Amex
PRICE...Low-cost
TYPE...Hotel
ACCOMMODATION...28 Rooms
FACILITIES...............................Bar, Outdoor swimming pool,
2 Restaurants
GOOD TO KNOW.................Child friendly, Dolphin watching,
Scuba diving, Spice tours
RECOMMENDED FOR...Beach

Located on the island's quieter east side, Dhow Inn is
situated on the beautiful Paje Beach. Rooms are bright and
spacious, each with an outdoor terrace. There are also three
separate dining options, ranging from the casual bar and
lounge area to the elegant restaurant on the first floor, only
open to hotel guests.

Recommended by: Mphethi Morojele, MMA Design Studio

EMERSON SPICE

4044 Tharia Street
Stone Town
Zanzibar
Tanzania
+255 774483483
emersonspice.com

CREDIT CARDS	Accepted
PRICE	Mid-range
TYPE	Hotel
ACCOMMODATION	11 Rooms
FACILITIES	2 Restaurants
GOOD TO KNOW	Restored merchant's house
RECOMMENDED FOR	All-time favorite

"This is the most beautiful hotel in the heart of ancient Stone Town; a palace reimagined. Every room is a theater of dreams, evoking a magical and timeless experience of Africa. From each balcony the sounds, scents, and sights of the old city unfold in constant poetry. Within the rooms, deep colors sooth the soul; a place of respite for even the weariest traveler."—Paul Brislin

Recommended by: Paul Brislin, Arup

ZANZIBAR SERENA HOTEL

Shangani Street
Stone Town
Zanzibar
Tanzania
+255 242233567
serenahotels.com

CREDIT CARDS	Accepted
PRICE	Mid-range
TYPE	Hotel
ACCOMMODATION	51 Rooms and Suites
FACILITIES	Bar, Outdoor swimming pool, 2 Restaurants
GOOD TO KNOW	Babysitting, Dolphin watching, Spice tours
RECOMMENDED FOR	Worth the travel

"Island waterfront town setting, with fantastic views and historical context."—Anthony Mallows

Recommended by: Anthony Mallows, WATG

&BEYOND BENGUERRA ISLAND

Benguerra Island
Bazaruto Archipelago
Mozambique
+27 118094300
andbeyond.com

CREDIT CARDS	Accepted but not Amex
PRICE	Blow-out (all-inclusive)
TYPE	Lodge
ACCOMMODATION	15 Cabanas, Casinhas, and Villas
FACILITIES	Bar, Outdoor swimming pool, Restaurant, Spa
GOOD TO KNOW	Child friendly, Horse riding, Scuba diving, Snorkelling, Sea kayaking
RECOMMENDED FOR	Eco-conscious, Worth the travel

"Absolute luxury."—Alex Michaelis

[This property was designed by Michaelis Boyd.]

Recommended by: Alex Michaelis, Michaelis Boyd; Matteo Thun, Matteo Thun & Partners

BARRA BEACH RESORT

Praia de Barra
Inhambane
Mozambique
+27 129919600
barrabeachresort.com

CREDIT CARDS	Not accepted
PRICE	Low-cost
TYPE	Cabin
ACCOMMODATION	19 Cabins
FACILITIES	Kitchenettes
GOOD TO KNOW	Child friendly, Free parking, Scuba diving, Self-catering
RECOMMENDED FOR	Worth the travel

A collection of modest yet charming, self-catering, thatched cabins that overlook the palm tree-fringed beaches of Inhambane, Barra Beach Resort is the ideal spot for scuba divers. The resort is also a stone's throw from the area's numerous restaurants and markets.

Recommended by: Mphethi Morojele, MMA Design Studio

JARDIM DOS ALOÉS
Rua Presidente Kaunda
Ilha de Moçambique
Nampula
Mozambique
+258 871765517
jardim-dos-aloes.com

CREDIT CARDS.................................Accepted but not Amex
PRICE...Low-cost
TYPE...Bed and Breakfast
ACCOMMODATION...3 Rooms and Suites
FACILITIES...Restaurant
GOOD TO KNOW....................Boat trips, Ice-cream making
RECOMMENDED FOR...................................Countryside

"The Ilha de Moçambique must be one of the world's
most special places—it is in the center of a bay connected
to the mainland by a more than a mile-long (two-kilometer)
bridge. It is a UNESCO World Heritage Site, but unlike
a lot of other places it remains unspoiled, largely because
it isn't particularly accessible. It's run by a wonderful couple
whose hospitality knows no bounds."—Jo Noero

Recommended by: Jo Noero, Noero Architects

NORTH ISLAND
North Island
Seychelles
+27 610890462
north-island.com

CREDIT CARDS..Accepted
PRICE....................................Blow-out (all-inclusive)
TYPE...Resort
ACCOMMODATION..11 Villas
FACILITIES.....................Bar, Gym, Outdoor swimming pool,
Restaurant, Spa, Yoga
GOOD TO KNOW.......................Bicycle rentals, Child friendly,
Fishing, Scuba diving, Snorkelling
RECOMMENDED FOR..Island

Featuring only eleven villas, North Island is one of the
world's most exclusive private island resorts. Sustainability
is a key foundation of North Island's guiding philosophy
and it prides itself on its 'ocean-to-table' dining and its 'Noah's
Ark' conservation projects.

Recommended by: Stefan Antoni, SAOTA

THE RESIDENCE MAURITIUS
Coastal Road
Belle Mare
Mauritius
+230 4018888
cenizaro.com

CREDIT CARDS.................................Accepted but not Amex
PRICE...Mid-range
TYPE...Resort
ACCOMMODATION.........................163 Rooms and Suites
FACILITIES...................Bar, Gym, Outdoor swimming pool,
3 Restaurants, Sauna, Spa
GOOD TO KNOW....................Tennis lessons, Undersea walk,
Water sports
RECOMMENDED FOR..............................Family friendly

"Visit for an easy family holiday with great food and lots
of activities for children. The resort includes tennis, water
sports, a pool, and gym, as well as a personal butler to
look after all your needs."—Achille Salvagni

Recommended by: Achille Salvagni, Salvagni Architetti

LUX* GRANDE GAUBE
Grand Gaube
Rivière du Rempart
Mauritius
+230 204 9191
luxresorts.com

CREDIT CARDS..Accepted
PRICE...High-end
TYPE...Resort
ACCOMMODATION..................186 Rooms, Suites, and Villas
FACILITIES..7 Bars, Gym,
2 Outdoor swimming pools,
6 Restaurants, Spa, Tennis
GOOD TO KNOW..............................Babysitting, Water sports
RECOMMENDED FOR..Beach

A beachside resort with plenty of personality. The elegant,
positive energy of LUX* Grande Gaube's rooms continues
throughout the resort, from the dining spaces to the luxury
wellness spa, topped off by remarkably warm hospitality.

[This hotel was designed by Kelly Hoppen Interiors.]

Recommended by: Kelly Hoppen, Kelly Hoppen Interiors

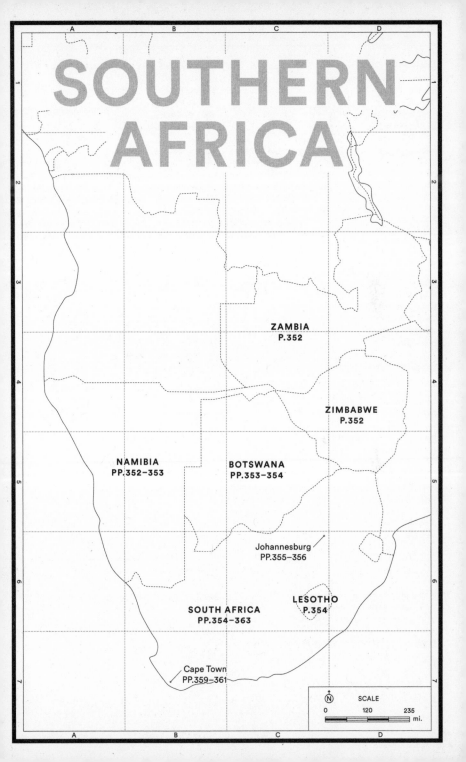

MFUWE LODGE
South Luangwa National Park
Mfuwe
Zambia
+260 216246041
bushcampcompany.com

CREDIT CARDS....................................Accepted but not Amex
PRICE...Mid-range
TYPE..Lodge
ACCOMMODATION..................18 Chalets, Rooms, and Suites
FACILITIES..................................Bar, Gym, 2 Lagoons,
Outdoor swimming pool,
Restaurant, Spa
GOOD TO KNOW..................Walking safaris available
RECOMMENDED FOR.................................Eco-conscious

"For a sustainable hotel, I found the Bushcamp Company's
Mfuwe Lodge in Zambia's South Luangwa National Park
to be a good example of what can be done when a local
tourist organization takes community engagement seriously.
The fact that guests are also encouraged to participate by
supporting the local school is even more admirable."
—Ian Ritchie

Recommended by: Ian Ritchie, Ian Ritchie Architects

SINDABEZI ISLAND
Zambezi River
Victoria Falls
Zambia
+260 213327468
tongabezi.com

CREDIT CARDS....................................Accepted but not Amex
PRICE.......................................High-end (all-inclusive)
TYPE..Lodge
ACCOMMODATION..5 Chalets
FACILITIES....................Bar, Gym, Outdoor swimming pool,
Restaurant
GOOD TO KNOW................................Fishing, No wifi
RECOMMENDED FOR.................................Eco-conscious

"A most extraordinary location above the Victoria Falls.
We ate crocodile stew by moonlight and were taught how
to listen for approaching elephants."—Anthony Hudson

Recommended by: Anthony Hudson, Hudson Architects

ELEPHANT HILLS RESORT
300 Parkway
Victoria Falls
Zimbabwe
+263 1344793
elephanthillsresort.com

CREDIT CARDS....................................Accepted but not Amex
PRICE...Mid-range
TYPE...Resort
ACCOMMODATION................................276 Rooms and Suites
FACILITIES....................Bar, Gym, Outdoor swimming pool,
3 Restaurants, Spa
GOOD TO KNOW..........................Canoeing, Bungee jumping
RECOMMENDED FOR...Mountains

"Go for the view over verdant landscapes and encounters
with tame wildlife—monkeys are common visitors."
—Olajumoke Adenowo

Recommended by: Olajumoke Adenowo, AD Consulting

HILTON WINDHOEK
Rev Michael Scott Street
Windhoek
Khomas
Namibia
+264 612962929
hilton.com

CREDIT CARDS...Accepted
PRICE...Mid-range
TYPE..Hotel
ACCOMMODATION................................150 Rooms and Suites
FACILITIES..........................2 Bars, Outdoor swimming pool,
3 Restaurants,
Rooftop terrace bar, Spa
GOOD TO KNOW......................................Child friendly
RECOMMENDED FOR...Urban

"This place gives new urban vitality to the center of the
Namibian capital."—Martin Kruger

Recommended by: Martin Kruger, Martin Kruger Architects

PENDUKA VILLAGE

Goreangab Reservoir
(via Green Mountain Dam Road)
Windhoek
Khomas
Namibia
+264 61257210
penduka.com

CREDIT CARDS..Accepted but not Amex
PRICE..Low-cost
TYPE..Village
ACCOMMODATION.................10 Bungalows, Chalets, Dorms,
Rondavels, and Rooms
FACILITIES..Restaurant
GOOD TO KNOW............................Child friendly, Self-catering
RECOMMENDED FOR..Wish I'd designed

"Penduka is a living village where you can take part in different activities organized by Harmonature [a sustainability program]. Traditional architecture is combined with refreshing new design elements. The environment means you can engage with people from the townships around Namibia."—Satyendra Pakhalé

Penduka Village is the headquarters of NGO Penduka, an organization which works with women in Namibia to provide them with professional skills and empowerment. Situated on the shoreline of the Goreangab Reservoir in north-western Windhoek, the Village has a range of accommodation options from dorms and a campsite to a six-person villa. It also features a restaurant with a floating terrace, conference facilities, and an artisan's shop. All facilities are run by the women of Penduka, and guests are able to partake in craft workshops during their stay.

Recommended by: Satyendra Pakhalé, Satyendra Pakhalé Associates

WOLWEDANS DUNES LODGE

Namib Rand Nature Reserve
Namib Desert
Namibia
+264 61230616
wolwedans.com

CREDIT CARDS..Accepted but not Amex
PRICE..Blow-out (all-inclusive)
TYPE...Lodge
ACCOMMODATION...9 Chalets
FACILITIES...................................Outdoor swimming pool,
Restaurant
GOOD TO KNOW..............................Child friendly (6 and over),
Hot-air ballooning, Solar power
RECOMMENDED FOR..Worth the travel

"The Wolwedans (Afrikaans for Dances of Wolves) Dunes Lodge is located on the serenely beautiful edge of the Namib Desert. It is far from Windhoek, so you have to rent a four-wheel drive, but it is well worth the effort. The location is unlike anywhere else; the soft light is always changing the environment. It is secluded, serene, and surreal, and you feel intimately part of nature. The experience is unique, African, and quite magical."—Martin Kruger

Recommended by: Martin Kruger, Martin Kruger Architects

&BEYOND SANDIBE OKAVANGO SAFARI LODGE

Okavango Delta
Moremi Game Reserve
Botswana
+27 118094300
sandibe.com

CREDIT CARDS..Accepted
PRICE..Blow-out (all-inclusive)
TYPE...Safari lodge
ACCOMMODATION..12 Suites
FACILITIES......................................Bar, Gym, Spa, Restaurant
GOOD TO KNOW..............................Bush walks, Child friendly,
Helicopter flights
RECOMMENDED FOR...Eco-conscious

"This is one of the most beautiful places on earth."
—Alex Michaelis

Recommended by: Alex Michaelis, Michaelis Boyd

DUBA PLAINS CAMP
Okavango Delta
Moremi Game Reserve
Botswana
+278 73546591
greatplainsconservation.com

CREDIT CARDS	Not Accepted
PRICE	Blow-out (all-inclusive)
TYPE	Tented camp
ACCOMMODATION	5 Tents
FACILITIES	Outdoor swimming pool, Restaurant
GOOD TO KNOW	Birdwatching, Canoeing, Child friendly (8 and over)
RECOMMENDED FOR	Desert

"This conservation-based safari in a tented camp treats its surroundings and wildlife with exceptional sensitivity."
—Todd-Avery Lenahan

Duba Plains is in the heart of the Okavango Delta under the shade of giant ebony trees, and its luxurious interiors have been designed to evoke the classic 1920s safari experience. A maximum of ten guests are housed in five tents, each with private verandas and plunge pools.

Recommended by: Todd-Avery Lenahan, TAL Studio

OLD BRIDGE BACKPACKERS
Maun
Ngamiland East
Botswana
+267 6862406
maun-backpackers.com

CREDIT CARDS	Accepted but not Amex
PRICE	Low-cost
TYPE	Hostel
ACCOMMODATION	Campsites and 10 Fixed tents
FACILITIES	Bar, Kitchen, Outdoor swimming pool, Restaurant
GOOD TO KNOW	Basket weaving workshops, Canoeing, Gateway to the Okavango Delta
RECOMMENDED FOR	Countryside

"Very 'back to nature'."—Mphethi Morojele

Recommended by: Mphethi Morojele, MMA Design Studio

MALIBA LODGE
Tsehlanyane National Park
Butha Buthe
Maluti Mountains
Lesotho
+27 317028791
maliba-lodge.com

CREDIT CARDS	Accepted but not Amex
PRICE	Mid-range
TYPE	Villa
ACCOMMODATION	13 Chalets, Huts, and Lodges
FACILITIES	Bar, Restaurants
GOOD TO KNOW	Archery, Dinosaur footprint tour, Self-catering available, Trail running
RECOMMENDED FOR	Mountains

Situated among the mountains of Tsehlanyane National Park, Maliba Lodge is a collection of private villas with an on-site restaurant and bistro. A range of local activities is available, including examining dinosaur footprints and tours to nearby villages. If desired, the concierge can arrange visits to a local shaman.

Recommended by: Mphethi Morojele, MMA Design Studio

DROSTDY HOTEL
30 Church Street
Graaff-Reinet
Eastern Cape 6280
South Africa
+27 498922161
newmarkhotels.com

CREDIT CARDS	Accepted
PRICE	Mid-range
TYPE	Hotel
ACCOMMODATION	48 Rooms
FACILITIES	Bar, Gym, Outdoor swimming pool, 2 Restaurants, Spa
GOOD TO KNOW	Babysitting, Near Camdeboo National Park
RECOMMENDED FOR	Desert

Recommended by: Ludovico Centis, The Empire

SAMARA KAROO LODGE

Petersburg Road (via R63 to Pearston)
Samara Private Game Reserve
Graaff-Reinet
Eastern Cape 6280
South Africa
+27 312620324
samara.co.za

CREDIT CARDS	Accepted but not Amex
PRICE	High-end (all-inclusive)
TYPE	Safari lodge
ACCOMMODATION	9 Suites
FACILITIES	Bar, Outdoor swimming pool, Restaurant
GOOD TO KNOW	Book exclusively, Cheetah tracking, Wilderness picnics
RECOMMENDED FOR	Spa

"Situated in the Karoo, in the Valley of Desolation. The spa is a welcome treat after a day of safari on this large game reserve."—Martin Kruger

Recommended by: Martin Kruger, Martin Kruger Architects

BULUNGULA LODGE

Nqileni Village
Elliotdale District
Nqileni
Eastern Cape 5070
South Africa
+27 475778900
bulungula.com

CREDIT CARDS	Accepted
PRICE	Low-cost
TYPE	Lodge
ACCOMMODATION	10 Huts
FACILITIES	Bar, Outdoor hot forest shower, Restaurant
GOOD TO KNOW	Bonfire, Local Xhosa community enterprise, Solar power, Water sports
RECOMMENDED FOR	Budget

"Deeply rural region far from the main highway."
—Artem Vakhrin

Recommended by: Artem Vakhrin, AKZ Architectura

FOUR SEASONS HOTEL
THE WESTCLIFF, JOHANNESBURG

67 Jan Smuts Avenue
Westcliff
Johannesburg
Gauteng 2132
South Africa
+27 114816000
fourseasons.com

CREDIT CARDS	Accepted
PRICE	High-end
TYPE	Hotel
ACCOMMODATION	117 Rooms and Suites
FACILITIES	Bar, Gym, Outdoor swimming pool, 5 Restaurants, Spa
GOOD TO KNOW	Child friendly
RECOMMENDED FOR	Spa

"Excellent service."— Sarah de Villiers

Recommended by: Sarah de Villiers, Counterspace

PROTEA HOTEL FIRE & ICE!
JOHANNESBURG MELROSE ARCH

22 Whiteley Road
Melrose Arch Precinct
Johannesburg
Gauteng 2076
South Africa
+27 112184000
marriott.com

CREDIT CARDS	Accepted
PRICE	Mid-range
TYPE	Hotel
ACCOMMODATION	197 Rooms and Suites
FACILITIES	Gym, Outdoor swimming pool, Restaurant, Spa
GOOD TO KNOW	Biking, Fly-fishing
RECOMMENDED FOR	Where I live

"Good design, nice ambience."—Mphethi Morojele

Recommended by: Mphethi Morojele, MMA Design Studio

SAXON HOTEL, VILLAS & SPA
36 Saxon Road
Sandhurst
Johannesburg
Gauteng 2196
South Africa
+27 112926000
saxon.co.za

CREDIT CARDS..Accepted
PRICE..High-end
TYPE...Hotel
ACCOMMODATION......................53 Suites and Villas
FACILITIES....................Bar, Gym, Outdoor swimming pool,
3 Restaurants, Spa
GOOD TO KNOW............................Babysitting, Bicycle rentals
RECOMMENDED FOR....................................Where I live

"Quiet, good spa, and excellent food."—Sarah de Villiers

Recommended by: Sarah de Villiers, Counterspace

FORUM HOMINI
Letamo Game Estate, Kromdraai, R540
Mogale City
Krugersdorp
Gauteng 1732
South Africa
+27 116687000
forumhomini.com

CREDIT CARDS..Accepted
PRICE..Mid-range
TYPE...Hotel
ACCOMMODATION..14 Suites
FACILITIES..................................Bar, Outdoor swimming pool,
Restaurant, Spa, Yoga
GOOD TO KNOW............Cooking classes, In-room massages,
Monthly wine tastings
RECOMMENDED FOR..............................Eco-conscious

Designed to blend in harmoniously with its location in the
stunning Cradle of Humankind, Forum Homini is a boutique
hotel with a difference. Fourteen cave-style suites have been
cut into the earth, and the hotel's award-winning restaurant,
Roots, offers guests a superlative fine-dining experience.

Recommended by: Mphethi Morojele, MMA Design Studio

DE HOEK COUNTRY HOTEL
R98
Magaliesburg
Gauteng 1791
South Africa
+27 145779600
dehoek.com

CREDIT CARDS..Accepted
PRICE..Mid-range
TYPE...Hotel
ACCOMMODATION..28 Suites
FACILITIES..................................Bar, Outdoor swimming pool,
Restaurant, Spa
GOOD TO KNOW............................Child friendly (12 and over)
Helicopter flights,
Hot-air ballooning, Walking trails
RECOMMENDED FOR...Spa

Located in the Magaliesburg Mountains, five-star De Hoek
Country Hotel is an ideal retreat from the nearby city
life of Johannesburg and Pretoria. Although the original
sandstone building was built in 1991, many of its features
have been repurposed, including wooden door lintels from
Durban station, giving the hotel a sense of history and
South African heritage.

Recommended by: Mphethi Morojele, MMA Design Studio

PROTEA HOTEL DURBAN EDWARD
149 OR Tambo Parade
South Beach
Durban
KwaZulu-Natal 4001
South Africa
+27 313373681
marriott.com

CREDIT CARDS..Accepted
PRICE..Low-cost
TYPE...Hotel
ACCOMMODATION..........................131 Rooms and Suites
FACILITIES...Bar,
Indoor and outdoor swimming pools,
2 Restaurants, Spa
GOOD TO KNOW................................Babysitting, Free parking
RECOMMENDED FOR.............................Best-kept secret

A beachfront hotel in the heart of Durban, Protea has a
range of rooms to suit every budget, the majority benefiting
from pristine sea views. Located on the city's so-called
Golden Mile, it's also an ideal base for exploring attractions
such as the Botanic Gardens.

Recommended by: Mphethi Morojele, MMA Design Studio

KOSI FOREST LODGE

Kosi Bay Nature Reserve
iSimangaliso Wetland Park
Manguzi
KwaZulu-Natal 3815
South Africa
+27 354741473
kosiforestlodge.co.za

CREDIT CARDS......................................Accepted but not Amex
PRICE...Mid-range
TYPE..Lodge
ACCOMMODATION...8 Cabins
FACILITIES..............................Bar, Outdoor bathrooms and
swimming pool, Restaurant
GOOD TO KNOW................................4x4 transfers, Boat trips,
Candlelight (limited electricity),
Snorkelling
RECOMMENDED FOR..Beach

"I canoed on a river with hippos and saw sea turtles laying their eggs in the sand at night. A unique African experience, with amazing local food and hospitality."—Martin Kruger

Recommended by: Martin Kruger, Martin Kruger Architects

THE OYSTER BOX HOTEL

2 Lighthouse Road
Umhlanga Rocks
Umhlanga
KwaZulu-Natal 4319
South Africa
+27 315145000
oysterboxhotel.com

CREDIT CARDS..Accepted
PRICE...High-end
TYPE..Hotel
ACCOMMODATION.................................86 Rooms and Suites
FACILITIES...........................3 Bars, Outdoor swimming pool,
3 Restaurants, Spa
GOOD TO KNOW...Babysitting
RECOMMENDED FOR..................................All-time favorite

A multi-award-winning beachfront hotel overlooking the iconic Umhlanga Lighthouse, The Oyster Box, with its striking decor, offers hospitality with plenty of personality, warmth, and charm.

Recommended by: Sarah de Villiers, Counterspace

CHAMPAGNE CASTLE HOTEL

R600 Champagne Valley
Central Drakensberg
Winterton
KwaZulu-Natal 3340
South Africa
+27 364681063
champagnecastle.co.za

CREDIT CARDS..Accepted
PRICE...Mid-range
TYPE..Hotel
ACCOMMODATION....................71 Chalets, Rooms, and Suites
FACILITIES......................Bar, Gym, Outdoor swimming pool,
Restaurant, Spa
GOOD TO KNOW..........................Child friendly, Horse riding,
On-site animal farm, Trout fishing
RECOMMENDED FOR..Countryside

"Incredible mountainous landscape and quality of light."
—Sarah de Villiers

Recommended by: Sarah de Villiers, Counterspace

ROYAL MALEWANE

Avoca Road, Off Orpen Gate Road
Hoedspruit
Limpopo 1380
South Africa
+27 157930150
theroyalportfolio.com

CREDIT CARDS......................................Accepted but not Amex
PRICE...High-end
TYPE...Safari lodge
ACCOMMODATION...2 Houses, 11 Suites
FACILITIES......................Bar, Gym, Outdoor swimming pool,
Restaurant, Spa
GOOD TO KNOW...................Horse riding, Hot-air ballooning
RECOMMENDED FOR..................................All-time favorite

Royal Malewane is renowned for offering high-end safari experiences. Situated in the Greater Kruger National Park, guests can embark on a Big Five safari by helicopter, hot-air balloon, horseback, cruise, or open-top, four-wheel drive. The lodge also benefits from an award-winning spa and an exceptional dining experience.

Recommended by: Kelly Hoppen, Kelly Hoppen Interiors

MADI A THAVHA MOUNTAIN LODGE
Off R522 Makhado, Vivo Road
Louis Trichardt
Limpopo 920
South Africa
+27 833424162
madiathavha.com

CREDIT CARDS	Accepted but not Amex
PRICE	Mid-range
TYPE	Lodge
ACCOMMODATION	9 Rooms and Suites
FACILITIES	Boutique, Outdoor swimming pool, Restaurant
GOOD TO KNOW	Bicycle rentals, Child friendly On-site textile studio
RECOMMENDED FOR	Countryside

"Besides providing comfortable, tasteful accommodation in a beautiful setting, they also do great community work supporting local Venda arts and culture projects, and they've assisted us with many aspects of our own school project."—Steve Kinsler

Recommended by: Steve Kinsler, East Coast Architects

GARONGA SAFARI CAMP
Selati Portion 12 KT 143
Greater Makalali Private Game Reserve
Phalaborwa
Limpopo 1390
South Africa
+27 878062080
garonga.com

CREDIT CARDS	Accepted but not Amex
PRICE	High-end
TYPE	Tented camp
ACCOMMODATION	6 Tented rooms
FACILITIES	Bar, Outdoor swimming pool, Restaurant, Spa, Yoga
GOOD TO KNOW	Game drives, Walking safaris
RECOMMENDED FOR	Eco-conscious

Recommended by: Guy Geier, FXCollaborative

WALKERSONS HOTEL & SPA & COTTAGES
Walkersons Private Estate
Dullstroom
Mpumalanga 1110
South Africa
+27 132537000
walkersons.co.za

CREDIT CARDS	Accepted
PRICE	Mid-range
TYPE	Hotel
ACCOMMODATION	27 Cottages and Rooms
FACILITIES	Bar, Gym, Outdoor swimming pool, 2 Restaurants, Spa
GOOD TO KNOW	Fly-fishing, Hiking trails, Mountain biking, Self-catering available
RECOMMENDED FOR	Eco-conscious, Mountains

"The cottages have roaring fires and overlook the river, where you can go trout fishing."—Luis Ferreira-da-Silva

Recommended by: Luis Ferreira-da-Silva, Luis Ferreira-da-Silva Architects

SINGITA LEBOMBO LODGE
N'wanetsi River
Kruger National Park
Mpumalanga 1350
South Africa
+27 216833424
singita.com

CREDIT CARDS	Accepted
PRICE	Blow-out (all-inclusive)
TYPE	Lodge
ACCOMMODATION	16 Suites, 1 Villa
FACILITIES	Gym, Outdoor swimming pool, Restaurant, Spa
GOOD TO KNOW	Child friendly (10 and over)
RECOMMENDED FOR	Countryside, Luxury, Worth the travel

"The edge of the lodge hovers above the river, with hippos and elephants below. The game tours are great, and the rooms are very cool, very minimal—this is one I wish I had designed."—Antoine Predock

Recommended by: Stefan Antoni, SAOTA; Antoine Predock, Antoine Predock Architect; Michel Rojkind, Rojkind Arquitectos

SINGITA SWENI LODGE

Sweni River
Kruger National Park
Mpumalanga 1350
South Africa
+27 137355500
singita.com

CREDIT CARDS	Accepted
PRICE	Blow-out (all-inclusive)
TYPE	Lodge
ACCOMMODATION	7 Suites
FACILITIES	Gym, Outdoor swimming pool, Restaurant, Spa
GOOD TO KNOW	Child friendly, Cooking classes, Stargazing
RECOMMENDED FOR	Countryside

"The Singita Sweni Lodge is one of the most incredible hotels that I've ever visited. Located on the grounds of Kruger National Park at the edge of the Sweni River, it's fascinating to watch animals gravitate toward the river to drink or wallow in the water."—David Rockwell

"The spectacle and the quality of light in the South African wilderness is exceptionally special."—Sumayya Vally

Recommended by: David Rockwell, Rockwell Group; Sumayya Vally, Counterspace

NKOMAZI PRIVATE GAME RESERVE

Tjakastad Road
Between Badplaas and Lochiel
Manzana
Mpumalanga 1190
South Africa
+27 178441922
newmarkhotels.com

CREDIT CARDS	Accepted
PRICE	High-end
TYPE	Lodge
ACCOMMODATION	10 Tents
FACILITIES	Bar, Outdoor swimming pool, Restaurant, Spa
GOOD TO KNOW	Bicycle rentals, Birding safari, Fly-fishing
RECOMMENDED FOR	Worth the travel

"Stunning landscape."—Much Untertrifaller

Recommended by: Much Untertrifaller, Dietrich Untertrifaller Architects

STAYEASY RUSTENBERG

Corner of N4 and R24
Waterval East
Rustenburg
North West 300
South Africa
+27 114619744
tsogosun.com

CREDIT CARDS	Accepted
PRICE	Mid-range
TYPE	Hotel
ACCOMMODATION	125 Rooms
FACILITIES	Outdoor swimming pool, Restaurant
GOOD TO KNOW	Free parking
RECOMMENDED FOR	Budget

With its comfortable and contemporary, budget-friendly rooms, StayEasy Rustenberg is conveniently located for exploring nearby attractions, such as the region's vineyards and Kgaswane Mountain Reserve.

Recommended by: Mphethi Morojele, MMA Design Studio

DADDY LONG LEGS ART HOTEL

134 Long Street
Centre
Cape Town
Western Cape 8001
South Africa
+27 214223074
daddylonglegs.co.za

CREDIT CARDS	Accepted but not Amex
PRICE	Low-cost
TYPE	Hotel
ACCOMMODATION	138 Rooms and Suites
FACILITIES	Bar
GOOD TO KNOW	Breakfast included, Self-catering available
RECOMMENDED FOR	Budget

"Each room is designed by a different artist."
—Cristian Santandreu

Recommended by: Cristian Santandreu, A2arquitectos

THE TOWNHOUSE HOTEL

60 Corporation Street
Centre
Cape Town
Western Cape 8001
South Africa
+27 214657050
townhouse.co.za

CREDIT CARDS	Accepted
PRICE	Low-cost
TYPE	Townhouse hotel
ACCOMMODATION	106 Rooms and Suites
FACILITIES	Bar, 2 Restaurants
GOOD TO KNOW	Undercover parking
RECOMMENDED FOR	Best-kept secret

"Near Parliament and in central Cape Town, this hotel is well located and good value for money. It is a real old-fashioned Cape Town hotel with great service, friendly staff, and a fantastic breakfast."—Martin Kruger

Recommended by: Martin Kruger, Martin Kruger Architects

BELMOND MOUNT NELSON HOTEL

76 Orange Street
Gardens
Cape Town
Western Cape 8001
South Africa
+27 214831000
belmond.com

CREDIT CARDS	Accepted
PRICE	High-end
TYPE	Hotel
ACCOMMODATION	198 Rooms and Suites
FACILITIES	Bar, Gym, 2 Restaurants, Outdoor swimming pool, Spa, Yoga
GOOD TO KNOW	Child friendly
RECOMMENDED FOR	Where I live

"An institution beloved by most Capetonians."
—Luis Ferreira-da-Silva

Recommended by: Luis Ferreira-da-Silva, Luis Ferreira-da-Silva Architects

MANNABAY

8 Bridle Road
Oranjezicht
Cape Town
Western Cape 8001
South Africa
+27 214611094
mannabay.com

CREDIT CARDS	Accepted
PRICE	Mid-range
TYPE	Hotel
ACCOMMODATION	8 Rooms and Suites
FACILITIES	Bar, Gym, Outdoor swimming pool, Restaurant, Spa
GOOD TO KNOW	In-room spa treatments
RECOMMENDED FOR	Beach

"Interesting personal touches and a beautiful location."
—Sumayya Vally

Recommended by: Sumayya Vally, Counterspace

WINCHESTER MANSIONS

221 Beach Road
Sea Point
Cape Town
Western Cape 8060
South Africa
+27 214342351
winchester.co.za

CREDIT CARDS	Accepted
PRICE	Mid-range
TYPE	Hotel
ACCOMMODATION	76 Rooms and Suites
FACILITIES	Bar, Outdoor swimming pool, Restaurant
GOOD TO KNOW	Babysitting, Child friendly
RECOMMENDED FOR	Where I live

"It is a small hotel with a veranda that overlooks the sea, and very friendly staff."—Martin Kruger

Recommended by: Martin Kruger, Martin Kruger Architects

CAPE GRACE
West Quay Road
V&A Waterfront
Cape Town
Western Cape 8002
South Africa
+27 214107100
capegrace.com

CREDIT CARDS...Accepted
PRICE...High-end
TYPE..Hotel
ACCOMMODATION........................120 Rooms and Suites
FACILITIES.....................Bar, Gym, Outdoor swimming pool,
Restaurant, Spa
GOOD TO KNOW.......................................Child friendly
RECOMMENDED FOR..Luxury

"Terrific location on a private quay and great service."
—Anthony Mallows

Recommended by: Anthony Mallows, WATG

RADISSON RED CAPE TOWN
Silo Square
V&A Waterfront
Cape Town
Western Cape 8001
South Africa
+27 870861578
radissonred.com

CREDIT CARDS...Accepted
PRICE..Mid-range
TYPE..Hotel
ACCOMMODATION.......................252 Rooms and Suites
FACILITIES...........................Gym, Outdoor swimming pool
Rooftop terrace bar, Spa
GOOD TO KNOW..Pet friendly
RECOMMENDED FOR........................Wish I'd designed

Recommended by: Martin Kruger, Martin Kruger Architects

THE SILO HOTEL
Silo Square
V&A Waterfront
Cape Town
Western Cape 8801
South Africa
+27 216700500
theroyalportfolio.com

CREDIT CARDS...Accepted
PRICE...Blow-out
TYPE..Hotel
ACCOMMODATION..........................28 Rooms and Suites
FACILITIES.....................Bar, Gym, Outdoor swimming pool,
Restaurant, Spa
GOOD TO KNOW...............................Underground parking
RECOMMENDED FOR..Luxury

"The refurbishment of this old industrial structure [by
Thomas Heatherwick] has been done in a very
contemporary and audacious way."—Stéphane Rasselet

The Silo Hotel itself is designed by Liz Biden.

Recommended by: Stéphane Rasselet, Naturehumaine

BUSHMANS KLOOF WILDERNESS RESERVE AND WELLNESS RETREAT
Agert Pakhuis Pass
Cederberg Mountains
Clanwilliam
Western Cape 8000
South Africa
+27 214379278
bushmanskloof.co.za

CREDIT CARDS...Accepted
PRICE...High-end
TYPE..Safari lodge
ACCOMMODATION....................19 Rooms, Suites, and Villas
FACILITIES...........................Gym, Outdoor swimming pool,
Restaurant, Spa
GOOD TO KNOW.................Canoeing, Hiking, Wine tastings
RECOMMENDED FOR.....................................Mountains

"This is an authentic retreat and safari lodge. A South
African Natural Heritage Site, it has more than 130
documented Bushman rock art locations and is home to
the internationally renowned Rooibos tea. It is truly a
once-in-a-lifetime experience in Africa."—Martin Kruger

Recommended by: Martin Kruger, Martin Kruger Architects

BABYLONSTOREN

Klapmuts Simondium Road
Simondium
Drakenstein Valley
Western Cape 7670
South Africa
+27 218633852
babylonstoren.com

CREDIT CARDS..................................Accepted but not Amex
PRICE..Mid-range
TYPE..Hotel
ACCOMMODATION..............................22 Cottages and Rooms
FACILITIES...Gym,
Indoor and outdoor swimming pools,
2 Restaurants, Spa
GOOD TO KNOW.......................Bicycle rentals, Child friendly,
Rowing, Wine tastings
RECOMMENDED FOR...Eco-conscious

"Farm-fresh, organic food with a stunning view of the surrounding hills. The farm animals give such a quaint touch."—Olajumoke Adenowo

"We stayed in cottages converted from old workers' homes. Babylonstoren has stunning views from the farm. But the best thing is its collection of very valuable cycads which is amazing."—John Pawson

Recommended by: Olajumoke Adenowo, AD Consulting; John Pawson

BLUE HORIZON

56 Boundary Road
Gordon Heights
Gordon's Bay
Western Cape 7140
South Africa
+27 218565324
bhorizon.co.za

CREDIT CARDS..................................Accepted but not Amex
PRICE..Low-cost
TYPE..Bed and Breakfast
ACCOMMODATION...7 Rooms
FACILITIES..............................Outdoor swimming pool
GOOD TO KNOW...Free parking
RECOMMENDED FOR.................................Family friendly

"Very comfortable."—Sarah de Villiers

Recommended by: Sarah de Villiers, Counterspace

LORD MILNER HOTEL

1 Logan Street, Matjiesfontein
Central Karoo District
Matjiesfontein
Western Cape 6901
South Africa
+27 235613011
matjiesfontein.com

CREDIT CARDS...Accepted
PRICE..Mid-range
TYPE..Hotel
ACCOMMODATION..15 Rooms
FACILITIES............................Bar, Outdoor swimming pool,
Restaurant
GOOD TO KNOW...Free parking
RECOMMENDED FOR...Desert

"Beautiful hotel set in a sensitively restored nineteenth-century spa settlement in the semi-desert."
—Jack Diamond

Recommended by: Jack Diamond, Diamond Schmitt

FOUR OAKS GUEST HOUSE

46 Long Street
Montagu
Western Cape 6720
South Africa
+27 236143483
four-oaks.co.za

CREDIT CARDS..................................Accepted but not Amex
PRICE..Low-cost
TYPE...Guesthouse
ACCOMMODATION...4 Rooms
FACILITIES...Bar, Restaurant
GOOD TO KNOW...Near hot springs
RECOMMENDED FOR..Budget

"The setting is stunning; look out for the ibis birds in town."
—Ludovico Centis

Recommended by: Ludovico Centis, The Empire

OUDEBOSCH ECO CABINS

Kogelberg Nature Reserve
Oudebosch
Western Cape 7690
South Africa
+27 214830160
capenature.co.za

CREDIT CARDS	Accepted
PRICE	Low-cost
TYPE	Cabin
ACCOMMODATION	5 Cabins
FACILITIES	Outdoor swimming pool
GOOD TO KNOW	Mountain biking, Rock climbing, Self-catering, Whale watching
RECOMMENDED FOR	Eco-conscious

A collection of five self-catering properties with stunning views of the UNESCO World Heritage Site of Kogelberg Nature Reserve. An ideal base from which to try out a range of outdoor activities, including white water kayaking, wildlife watching, and mountain biking.

Recommended by: Stefan Antoni, SAOTA

RESTIO RIVER HOUSE

577 Anne Road
Kogelberg Nature Reserve
Pringle Bay
Western Cape 7196
South Africa
+27 735577009
restioriverhouse.co.za

CREDIT CARDS	Not accepted
PRICE	High-end
TYPE	House rental
ACCOMMODATION	5 Bedrooms
FACILITIES	Pool table, Sonos music system, Table tennis
GOOD TO KNOW	Horse riding, Self-catering, Water sports
RECOMMENDED FOR	Luxury

With a sleek, contemporary style, Restio River House is a self-catering property with space for up to ten guests. Set in the village of Pringle Bay, on the edge of the Buffels River, the house has numerous mountain views, and is only moments from the beach.

Recommended by: Stefan Antoni, SAOTA

SILVER BAY VILLA

7 18th Street
Shelley Point
Western Cape 7390
South Africa
+27 823316758
silverbay.co.za

CREDIT CARDS	Not accepted
PRICE	High-end
TYPE	House rental
ACCOMMODATION	4 Rooms
FACILITIES	Outdoor swimming pool
GOOD TO KNOW	Self-catering
RECOMMENDED FOR	Best-kept secret

An elegant and modern self-catering, beachfront villa that sleeps up to eight people, Silver Bay Villa enjoys stunning views of St. Helena and Stompneus Bay.

Recommended by: Stefan Antoni, SAOTA

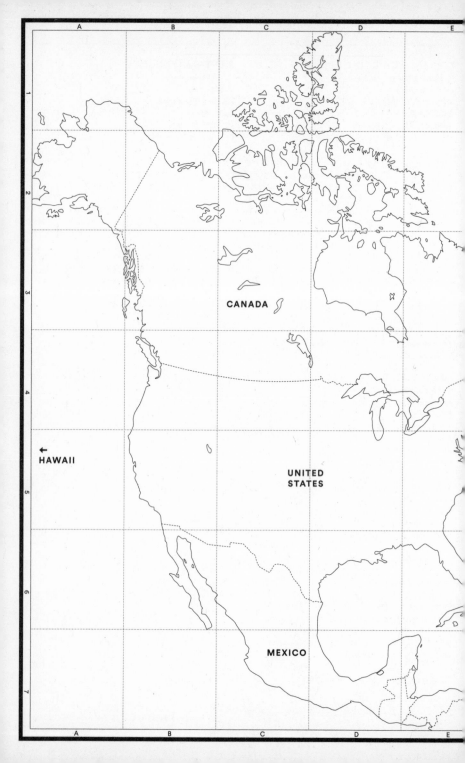

NORTH
AMERICA

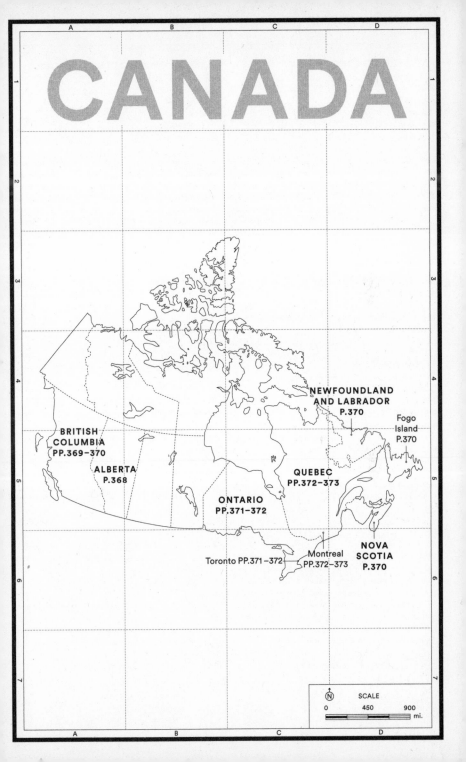

CANADA

SCALE

0   450   900
mi.

FAIRMONT BANFF SPRINGS
405 Spray Avenue
Banff
Alberta T1L 1J4
Canada
+1 4037622211
fairmont.com

CREDIT CARDS..Accepted
PRICE..High-end
TYPE..Hotel
ACCOMMODATION........................757 Rooms and Suites
FACILITIES...................................3 Bars, Gym, Golf,
Indoor swimming pool,
9 Restaurants, Spa, Tennis, Yoga
GOOD TO KNOW...........................Child friendly, Valet parking
RECOMMENDED FOR...Mountains

"One of the great nineteenth-century railway hotels."
—Jack Diamond

Recommended by: Jack Diamond, Diamond Schmitt; Bruce
Kuwabara, KPMB Architects

FIELD HOUSE
Exact address released at time of booking
Calgary
Alberta
Canada
airbnb.ca/rooms/20385199

CREDIT CARDS..Accepted
PRICE...Low-cost
TYPE..Home rental
ACCOMMODATION...1 Bedroom
FACILITIES...Fire pit, Sauna,
Wood-burning fireplace
GOOD TO KNOW..Free parking
RECOMMENDED FOR...............................Eco-conscious, Urban

"Field House is a renovated mid-century home overlooking
Calgary from the inner-city community of Albert Park.
A solarium has been added to the south side of the house
as an all-seasons greenhouse, providing a gathering space
that features herbs, vegetables, and a full-sized fig tree.
Field House's garden was designed in collaboration with
permaculturalists and includes a fire pit. Only ten minutes
from the airport and downtown."—Matthew Kennedy

Recommended by: Matthew Kennedy, Studio North

BASECAMP RESORTS CANMORE
1102 Bow Valley Trail
Canmore
Alberta T1W 1N6
Canada
+1 8552194707
basecampresorts.com

CREDIT CARDS..Accepted
PRICE..High-end
TYPE..Resort
ACCOMMODATION...16 Lodges
FACILITIES...BBQs, Hot tubs
GOOD TO KNOW............................Pet friendly, Self-catering
RECOMMENDED FOR....................Family friendly, Mountains,
Where I live

"Basecamp is a refuge for intrepid travelers exploring the
charms of downtown and the splendors of the surrounding
Rocky Mountains. The hotel is an interpretation of the
traditional mountain cabin—both an architectural homage
to the bygone days of the former mining community and
a forward-thinking development for the future of the town
as an outdoor adventure hub."—Matthew Kennedy

Recommended by: Matthew Kennedy, Studio North

FAIRMONT CHATEAU LAKE LOUISE
111 Lake Louise Drive
Lake Louise
Alberta T0L 1E0
Canada
+1 4035223511
fairmont.com

CREDIT CARDS..Accepted
PRICE..Blow-out
TYPE..Hotel
ACCOMMODATION........................539 Rooms and Suites
FACILITIES......................Bar, Gym, Indoor swimming pool,
6 Restaurants, Spa, Steam room, Yoga
GOOD TO KNOW...Babysitting
RECOMMENDED FOR...Mountains

"The views and surroundings of mountains and Lake Louise
are breathtaking in all seasons. The hotel and location offer
a variety of activities for any season—walking and canoeing
in summer, ice skating in winter."—Tim Black

Recommended by: Tim Black, BKK Architects

SILVERTIP LODGE
Cariboo Mountains
British Columbia
Canada
+1 7782087044
silvertipheliskiing.com

CREDIT CARDS	Accepted
PRICE	Blow-out
TYPE	Lodge
ACCOMMODATION	10 Rooms
FACILITIES	Bar, Restaurant, Sauna, Spa, Steam room
GOOD TO KNOW	Travel and food included
RECOMMENDED FOR	Mountains

"The location, the peace and quiet. Without people, without children, without music…"—Rafael de La-Hoz Castanys

Recommended by: Rafael de La-Hoz Castanys, Rafael de La-Hoz Arquitectos

EXPLORERS SOCIETY
111 First Street West
Revelstoke
British Columbia V0E 2S0
Canada
+1 8558142565
explorers-society.com

CREDIT CARDS	Accepted
PRICE	Mid-range
TYPE	Hotel
ACCOMMODATION	9 Rooms and Suites
FACILITIES	Bar, Restaurant, Rooftop terrace bar, Wood-burning fireplace
GOOD TO KNOW	Free parking
RECOMMENDED FOR	Best-kept secret

"Beautifully restored hotel in Revelstoke's town center. The town is a gem with great food, skiing, stunning landscapes, and it's not busy."—Matthew Kennedy

Recommended by: Matthew Kennedy, Studio North

SOOKE HARBOUR HOUSE HOTEL & RESORT
1528 Whiffen Spit Road
Sooke
British Columbia V9Z 0T4
Canada
+1 2506423421
sookeharbourhouse.com

CREDIT CARDS	Accepted
PRICE	Mid-range
TYPE	Hotel
ACCOMMODATION	28 Rooms and Suites
FACILITIES	Bar, Restaurant, Spa, Wood-burning fireplace, Yoga
GOOD TO KNOW	Creative workshops, Pet friendly
RECOMMENDED FOR	Worth the travel

"Seasonality is an integral part of the Sooke Harbour House experience. Located on the southern coast of Vancouver Island, with stunning views of the Olympic Mountain Range, the character of the place changes with the light, weather, and seasons. The restaurant's local, seasonal, and often foraged dishes alone are also worth the trip."—Nicolas Koff

Recommended by: Nicolas Koff, Office Ou

THE SYLVIA HOTEL
1154 Gilford Street on English Bay
West End
Vancouver
British Columbia V6G 2P6
Canada
+1 6046819321
sylviahotel.com

CREDIT CARDS	Accepted
PRICE	Mid-range
TYPE	Hotel
ACCOMMODATION	120 Rooms and Suites
FACILITIES	Bar, Restaurant
GOOD TO KNOW	Babysitting
RECOMMENDED FOR	Urban

Recommended by: Tom Kundig, Olson Kundig

FAIRMONT CHATEAU WHISTLER
4599 Chateau Boulevard
Whistler
British Columbia V8E 0Z5
Canada
+1 6049388000
fairmont.com

CREDIT CARDS	Accepted
PRICE	Mid-range
TYPE	Hotel
ACCOMMODATION	528 Rooms and Suites
FACILITIES	Bar, Golf, Indoor and outdoor swimming pools, 5 Restaurants, Sauna, Spa, Steam room, Tennis, Wood-burning fireplace, Yoga
GOOD TO KNOW	Babysitting, Pet friendly
RECOMMENDED FOR	Mountains

Recommended by: Marianne Kwok, Kohn Pedersen Fox

BIRD HUT
Exact address released at time of enquiry
Windermere
British Columbia
Canada

CREDIT CARDS	Not accepted
PRICE	Free
TYPE	Treehouse
ACCOMMODATION	1 Cabin
FACILITIES	Birdhouses
GOOD TO KNOW	No booking
RECOMMENDED FOR	Countryside

The Bird Hut is a treetop perch that sits on wooden stilts on a forested hillside. Immersed in the tree canopy, the hut accommodates two people, and whatever inquisitive critters come by to visit. In addition to being an inviting place for people to nest, the facade has twelve birdhouses, each designed for various local birds that live in the mountains of the Columbia Valley.

[This property was designed by Studio North.]

Recommended by: Matthew Kennedy, Studio North

FOGO ISLAND INN
210 Main Road
Joe Batt's Arm
Fogo Island
Newfoundland and Labrador A0G 2X0
Canada
+1 7096583444
fogoislandinn.ca

CREDIT CARDS	Accepted
PRICE	High-end (all-inclusive)
TYPE	Inn
ACCOMMODATION	29 Rooms and Suites
FACILITIES	Bar, Cinema, Gym, Library, Sauna, Restaurant, Wood-burning fireplace
GOOD TO KNOW	Bicycle rentals, Child friendly
RECOMMENDED FOR	Beach, Eco-conscious, Island, Wish I'd designed, Worth the travel

"It's a faraway place where nature, art, food, economy, silence, and travel have found a new balance."
—Jürgen Mayer H.

Recommended by: Jack Diamond, Diamond Schmitt; Craig Dykers, Snøhetta; Bruce Kuwabara, KPMB Architects; Jürgen Mayer H., J. Mayer H. und Partner, Architekten; Stéphane Rasselet, Naturehumaine

SHOBAC COTTAGES
386–440 Net Yard Lane
Upper Kingsburg
Nova Scotia B0J 2W0
Canada
+1 9024412672

CREDIT CARDS	Accepted
PRICE	Mid-range
TYPE	Home rental
ACCOMMODATION	4 Cottages
FACILITIES	Jacuzzi
GOOD TO KNOW	Horse riding
RECOMMENDED FOR	Family friendly

"Our entire clan each got their own private little cottage with fireplaces and ocean views, coming together to cook meals every day in the large studio. Quiet, serene, and absolutely beautiful, this is a place where you can go off-road driving, beach combing, horseback riding, and stargazing while drinking local white wine with fresh Atlantic mussels. The resident dogs add a homely warmth to the whole compound."—Grace Cheung

Recommended by: Grace Cheung, XRANGE Architecture + Design

LANGDON HALL COUNTRY HOUSE HOTEL & SPA
1 Langdon Drive
Cambridge
Ontario N3H 4R8, Canada
+1 8002681898
langdonhall.ca

CREDIT CARDS...Accepted
PRICE...High-end
TYPE..Country house hotel
ACCOMMODATION....................................60 Rooms and Suites
FACILITIES...Bar, Gym,
Indoor and outdoor swimming pools,
Restaurant, Sauna, Spa, Tennis
GOOD TO KNOW....................................Child and pet friendly,
Valet parking
RECOMMENDED FOR...Spa

"Originally an Astor summer villa, it's now an intimate country inn, with exquisite attention to detail and attentive spa personnel. Near Stratford, Ontario, the location is perfect for the summer Shakespeare Festival."
—Jack Diamond

Recommended by: Jack Diamond, Diamond Schmitt; Bruce Kuwabara, KPMB Architects

STE. ANNE'S SPA
1009 Massey Road
Grafton
Ontario K0K 2G0, Canada
+1 8883466772
steannes.com

CREDIT CARDS...Accepted
PRICE..................................High-end (all-inclusive)
TYPE..Hotel
ACCOMMODATION...............35 Cottages, Rooms, and Suites
FACILITIES...Bakery, Gym,
Outdoor swimming pool,
Restaurant, Spa,
Steam room, Yoga
GOOD TO KNOW...Horse riding
RECOMMENDED FOR.................................Countryside

"Just an hour and a half outside of Toronto; a rustic, serene, and all-inclusive resort with the best spa services in the region. They take care of you from head to toe. The food is incredible. Spend the day walking the gardens and trails, relaxing in the large heated outdoor pool and spa, or horse riding. A local favorite!"—Jodi Batay-Csorba

Recommended by: Jodi Batay-Csorba, Batay-Csorba Architects

THE DRAKE HOTEL
1150 Queen Street West
Toronto
Ontario M6J 1J3
Canada
+1 4165315042
thedrake.ca

CREDIT CARDS...Accepted
PRICE...Mid-range
TYPE..Hotel
ACCOMMODATION....................................19 Rooms and Suites
FACILITIES...Bar, Restaurant,
Rooftop Terrace Bar, Yoga
GOOD TO KNOW.......................................Child friendly
RECOMMENDED FOR.................................Where I live

"Very historic Toronto. A hip, energetic, vibrant, and creative atmosphere in the center of the city. Each boutique hotel room is original with a mix of vintage and modern styles. Awesome artwork."—Jodi Batay-Csorba

Recommended by: Jodi Batay-Csorba, Batay-Csorba Architects

SHANGRI-LA HOTEL, TORONTO
188 University Avenue
Entertainment District
Toronto
Ontario M5H 0A3
Canada
+1 6477888888
shangri-la.com

CREDIT CARDS...Accepted
PRICE...High-end
TYPE..Hotel
ACCOMMODATION................................202 Rooms and Suites
FACILITIES........................Bar, Gym, Indoor swimming pool,
Restaurant, Sauna, Spa
GOOD TO KNOW..................Babysitting, Pet friendly
RECOMMENDED FOR.................................Where I live

Recommended by: Randa Tukan, HOK Architects

THE HAZELTON
118 Yorkville Avenue
Yorkville
Toronto
Ontario ON M5R 1C2
Canada
+1 4169636300
thehazeltonhotel.com

CREDIT CARDS..Accepted
PRICE..High-end
TYPE...Hotel
ACCOMMODATION.......................................77 Rooms and Suites
FACILITIES..........................Bar, Gym, Indoor swimming pool,
Restaurant, Spa
GOOD TO KNOW...................................Babysitting, Pet friendly
RECOMMENDED FOR...Where I live

Recommended by: Jack Diamond, Diamond Schmitt;
George Yabu and Glenn Pushelberg, Yabu Pushelberg

DRAKE DEVONSHIRE
24 Wharf Street
Wellington
Ontario K0K 3L0
Canada
+1 6133993338
thedrake.ca

CREDIT CARDS..Accepted
PRICE..Mid-range
TYPE...Hotel
ACCOMMODATION.......................................13 Rooms and Suites
FACILITIES..Bar, Restaurant,
Wood-burning fireplace, Yoga
GOOD TO KNOW.........................Bicycle rentals, Child friendly
RECOMMENDED FOR..Worth the travel

"This is a really great hotel, it sits on the coastline of Lake
Ontario. The hotel has a fantastic restaurant and the
grounds have these marvelous pathways with curated art
installations that rotate year after year."—Matthew Kennedy

Recommended by: Matthew Kennedy, Studio North

HÔTEL & SPA LE GERMAIN CHARLEVOIX
50 Rue de la Ferme
Baie-Saint-Paul
Quebec G3Z 0G2
Canada
+1 8442404700
legermainhotels.com

CREDIT CARDS..Accepted
PRICE..Mid-range
TYPE...Hotel
ACCOMMODATION.....................................145 Rooms and Suites
FACILITIES.....................Bar, Gym, Outdoor swimming pool,
Patisserie, 2 Restaurants, Sauna,
Spa, Steam room
GOOD TO KNOW.......................................Child and pet friendly
RECOMMENDED FOR...Countryside

"Le Germain Charlevoix is a study in exhilarating contrasts.
It is an enormous hotel arranged as a compound of five
contemporary buildings that take visual cues from rural
typologies—like huge barns—grouped around a working
farm near the banks of the Saint Lawrence river. It has
a fantastic spa and restaurants and is good for families.
The result is a stay in elegantly modern accommodation
where children play with goats and geese while other guests
walk around in terrycloth robes. It is a satisfyingly surreal
place to spend a week."—Dan Wood

Recommended by: Dan Wood, WORKac

HOTEL GAULT
449 Sainte-Hélène Street
Old Montreal
Montreal
Quebec H2Y 2K9
Canada
+1 5149041616
hotelgault.com

CREDIT CARDS..Accepted
PRICE..Mid-range
TYPE...Apartment hotel
ACCOMMODATION..............30 Apartments, Lofts, and Suites
FACILITIES..Bar, Gym, Restaurant
GOOD TO KNOW.......................................Child and pet friendly
RECOMMENDED FOR...Where I live

"Chic and classic Montreal style with a contemporary touch
given by YH2 architects."—Stéphane Rasselet

Recommended by: Stéphane Rasselet, Naturehumaine

LOEWS HÔTEL VOGUE

1425 rue de la Mountain
Golden Square Mile
Montreal
Quebec H3G 1Z3
Canada
+1 8443352284
loewshotels.com

CREDIT CARDS	Accepted
PRICE	Mid-range
TYPE	Hotel
ACCOMMODATION	142 Rooms and Suites
FACILITIES	Bar, Gym, Restaurant
GOOD TO KNOW	Babysitting, Pet friendly
RECOMMENDED FOR	Urban

"The staff are very friendly and helpful, and the rooms are excellent. The size is perfect and their bathrooms are spacious."—Adil Kerai

Recommended by: Adil Kerai, Habib Fida Ali Architects

HÔTEL DE GLACE

1860 Boulevard Valcartier
Saint-Gabriel-de-Valcartier
Quebec G0A 4S0
Canada
+1 8883845524
hoteldeglace-canada.com

CREDIT CARDS	Accepted but not Amex
PRICE	Mid-range
TYPE	Ice hotel
ACCOMMODATION	42 Rooms and Suites
FACILITIES	Bar, Outdoor swimming pool, 3 Restaurants, Sauna, Spa
GOOD TO KNOW	Child friendly
RECOMMENDED FOR	Family friendly

Recommended by: Stéphane Rasselet, Naturehumaine

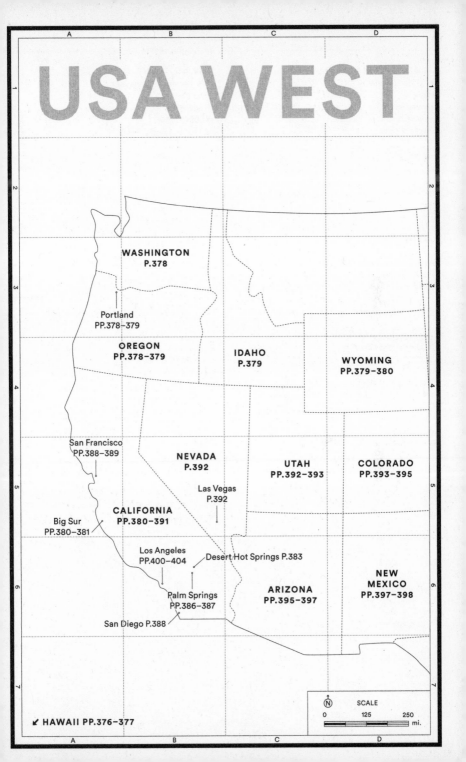

TRAVAASA HANA, MAUI
5031 Hana Highway
Hana
Hawaii 96713
+1 8888201043
travaasa.com

CREDIT CARDS...Accepted
PRICE...Mid-range
TYPE...Resort hotel
ACCOMMODATION...........................71 Bungalows and Rooms
FACILITIES....................................Bar, Outdoor restaurant and
swimming pool, Spa
GOOD TO KNOW...........................Bicycle rentals, Free parking
RECOMMENDED FOR...Beach

An enchanting, family friendly resort hotel on the eastern tip
of Maui, Travaasa Hana has been designed with bright, light,
airy space and tranquility in mind. Rooms and bungalows
are laid-back but elegant—a vibe that flows through to the
low-key, open-air restaurant overlooking the ocean.

Recommended by: Bernardo and Paulo Jacobsen,
Jacobsen Arquitetura

THE LAYLOW
2299 Kūhiō Avenue
Honolulu
Hawaii 96815
+1 8089226600
laylowwaikiki.com

CREDIT CARDS...Accepted
PRICE...Mid-range
TYPE...Hotel
ACCOMMODATION................251 Cabanas, Rooms, and Suites
FACILITIES..................................Bar, Outdoor swimming pool,
Restaurant
GOOD TO KNOW..................................Babysitting, Pet friendly,
Valet parking
RECOMMENDED FOR...Beach

"Cool design that captures a playful, retro Hawaiian
experience."—Alex Mok

Recommended by: Alex Mok, Linehouse

THE MODERN HONOLULU
1775 Ala Moana Boulevard
Honolulu
Hawaii 96815
+1 8084503396
themodernhonolulu.com

CREDIT CARDS...Accepted
PRICE...Mid-range
TYPE...Hotel
ACCOMMODATION...................................353 Rooms and Suites
FACILITIES.....................Bar, Gym, Outdoor swimming pool,
Restaurant, Spa, Yoga
GOOD TO KNOW...Child friendly
RECOMMENDED FOR...Luxury

Recommended by: Daniel Sundlin, Bjarke Ingels Group

THE ROYAL HAWAIIAN, A LUXURY COLLECTION RESORT, WAIKIKI
2259 Kalakaua Avenue
Honolulu
Hawaii 96815
+1 8089237311
royal-hawaiian.com

CREDIT CARDS...Accepted
PRICE...Mid-range
TYPE...Hotel
ACCOMMODATION...................................528 Rooms and Suites
FACILITIES..................................Bar, Outdoor swimming pool,
Restaurant, Spa, Yoga
GOOD TO KNOW...Valet parking
RECOMMENDED FOR...........................All-time favorite, Beach

Recommended by: Alex Mok, Linehouse; Isabelle Toland,
Aileen Sage Architects

FOUR SEASONS RESORT O'AHU AT KO OLINA

92–1001 Olani Street
Kapolei
Hawaii 96707
+1 8443870308
fourseasons.com

CREDIT CARDS..Accepted
PRICE..High-end
TYPE...Resort hotel
ACCOMMODATION....................................371 Rooms and Suites
FACILITIES....................Bar, Gym, Outdoor swimming pool,
4 Restaurants, Spa, Tennis
GOOD TO KNOW..Babysitting
RECOMMENDED FOR...Spa

"A magical place that offers an incredibly relaxing experience surrounded by birdsong at sunset."
—Claire Bétaille and Bruno Moinard

Recommended by: Claire Bétaille and Bruno Moinard, 4BI & Associés

MAUNA KEA BEACH HOTEL

62–100 Mauna Kea Beach Drive
Kohala Coast
Hawaii 96743
+1 8088827222
maunakeabeachhotel.com

CREDIT CARDS..Accepted
PRICE..High-end
TYPE..Hotel
ACCOMMODATION....................................252 Rooms and Suites
FACILITIES....................Bar, Gym, Outdoor swimming pool,
2 Restaurants, Spa, Tennis
GOOD TO KNOW..........................Babysitting, Bicycle rentals,
Valet parking
RECOMMENDED FOR....................................Beach, Where I live

"Classic 1960s Modern architecture that is timeless in its design—and beside the best beach in Hawaii."
—Mark de Reus

Recommended by: Marianne Kwok, Kohn Pedersen Fox; Michael Meredith and Hilary Sample, MOS; Mark de Reus, de Reus Architects

FOUR SEASONS RESORT LANAI

1 Manele Bay Road
Lanai City
Hawaii 96763
+1 8085652000
fourseasons.com

CREDIT CARDS..Accepted
PRICE..Blow-out
TYPE...Resort hotel
ACCOMMODATION....................................213 Rooms and Suites
FACILITIES....................Bar, Gym, Outdoor swimming pool,
4 Restaurants, Spa, Tennis, Yoga
GOOD TO KNOW..............................Babysitting, Child friendly
RECOMMENDED FOR................................Family friendly

"Situated atop Hulopoe Bay, there are few places in the world where you can swim among dolphins and whales in their natural habitat of the Pacific Ocean. Seemingly endless coral reefs for snorkeling, precipitous cliffs for hiking, verdant mountain peaks for climbing and seven-star caliber accommodation. This is Hawaii at its best."
—Todd-Avery Lenahan

Recommended by: Todd-Avery Lenahan, TAL Studio

HILTON WAIKOLOA VILLAGE

69–425 Waikoloa Beach Drive
Waikoloa Village
Hawaii 96738
+1 8882259664
hilton.com

CREDIT CARDS..Accepted
PRICE..Mid-range
TYPE..Hotel
ACCOMMODATION....................................113 Rooms and Suites
FACILITIES....................................Bar, Gym, Hot tub,
Outdoor swimming pool,
Restaurant, Spa
GOOD TO KNOW........................Bicycle rentals, Valet parking
RECOMMENDED FOR................................Family friendly

"Disneyland squared."—Florian Idenburg

Recommended by: Florian Idenburg, SO–IL

INN AT LANGLEY

400 1st Street
Langley
Washington 98260
+1 3602213033
innatlangley.com

CREDIT CARDS...Accepted
PRICE..High-end
TYPE..Inn
ACCOMMODATION.................28 Cottages, Rooms, and Suites
FACILITIES.......................Bar, Restaurant, Steam room, Yoga
GOOD TO KNOW...Restaurant open for
dinner from Friday to Sunday
RECOMMENDED FOR...Where I live

"Comfortable island lifestyle."—David Miller

Recommended by: David Miller, Miller Hull Partnership

ROLLING HUTS

18381 Highway 20
Winthrop
Washington 98862
+1 8772231137
rollinghuts.com

CREDIT CARDS...Accepted
PRICE...Mid-range
TYPE...Campsite
ACCOMMODATION...6 Huts
FACILITIES..Bar, Restaurant
GOOD TO KNOW...Pet friendly
RECOMMENDED FOR...Mountains

"A small step above camping for a real mountain experience."
—Tom Kundig

Recommended by: Tom Kundig, Olson Kundig

WHALE COVE INN

2345 Highway 101
Depoe Bay
Oregon 97341
+1 8006283409
whalecoveinn.com

CREDIT CARDS...Accepted
PRICE..High-end
TYPE..Hotel
ACCOMMODATION..8 Suites
FACILITIES..Bar, Restaurant
GOOD TO KNOW...Free parking
RECOMMENDED FOR.............................Beach, Best-kept secret

"Nothing like it in that part of Oregon. Romantic getaway, amazing views, and only eight rooms—all suites, very private, and an amazing restaurant. Great for couples."
—Brent Kendle

Recommended by: Brent Kendle, Kendle Design Collaborative

THE ALLISON INN & SPA

2525 Allison Lane
Newberg
Oregon 97132
+1 8772942525
theallison.com

CREDIT CARDS...Accepted
PRICE...Mid-range
TYPE..Hotel
ACCOMMODATION.......................................85 Rooms and Suites
FACILITIES.........................Bar, Gym, Indoor swimming pool,
Restaurant, Sauna, Spa, Steam room
GOOD TO KNOW...Babysitting
RECOMMENDED FOR.....................Countryside, Eco-conscious

"Luxurious, contemporary rooms and public areas, and a focus on wine, food, and casual elegance. Located in the heart of wine country, The Allison is also a LEED Platinum certified hotel."—Brent Kendle

Recommended by: Brent Kendle, Kendle Design Collaborative

ACE HOTEL PORTLAND

1022 South West Harvey Milk Street
Portland
Oregon 97205
+1 5032282277
acehotel.com

CREDIT CARDS...Accepted
PRICE...Mid-range
TYPE..Hotel
ACCOMMODATION..78 Rooms
FACILITIES..Bar, Restaurant
GOOD TO KNOW.......................................Bicycle rentals
RECOMMENDED FOR...Wish I'd designed

"I love the aesthetic here, it is apparent that not a lot of money was spent on the finishes and fixtures but the feel of the place is hip. The person who designed this hotel and developed the look of the Ace brand is a genius!"
—Matthew Kennedy

Recommended by: Matthew Kennedy, Studio North

THE HOTEL ZAGS (FORMERLY HOTEL MODERA)
515 South West Clay Street
Portland
Oregon 97201
+1 5034841084
hotelmodera.com

CREDIT CARDS	Accepted
PRICE	Mid-range
TYPE	Hotel
ACCOMMODATION	174 Rooms
FACILITIES	Restaurant
GOOD TO KNOW	Pet friendly, Bicycle rentals, Valet parking
RECOMMENDED FOR	Where I live

"Bold colors and vibrant design surround an exterior courtyard filled with a living wall and gorgeous plants. I love this little gem in the heart of Portland. Though I live here, my wife and I will sometimes visit for a little 'staycation' and it's where I put up friends visiting Portland."—Eric Corey Freed

Recommended by: Eric Corey Freed, OrganicArchitect

KIMPTON HOTEL VINTAGE PORTLAND
422 South West Broadway
Portland
Oregon 97205
+1 5032281212
hotelvintage-portland.com

CREDIT CARDS	Accepted
PRICE	Mid-range
TYPE	Hotel
ACCOMMODATION	117 Rooms and Suites
FACILITIES	Bar, Restaurant
GOOD TO KNOW	Bicycles available, Valet parking
RECOMMENDED FOR	Urban

Kimpton Hotel Vintage Portland is a wine-inspired design hotel with as much character as the wines themselves. Each floor is dedicated to a different Willamette Valley region, and each room to a local winery. The hotel's ethos also reflects its Portland identity, offering complimentary bike use and yoga mats in every room. It also has green credentials; those guests who decline housekeeping are given credit for use at the hotel restaurant, Il Solito.

Recommended by: Chris McDonough, The Gettys Group

SUN VALLEY LODGE
1 Sun Valley Road
Sun Valley
Idaho 83353
+1 8007868259
sunvalley.com

CREDIT CARDS	Accepted
PRICE	High-end
TYPE	Hotel
ACCOMMODATION	108 Rooms and Suites
FACILITIES	Bar, Golf, Gym, Hot tub, Outdoor swimming pool, 3 Restaurants, Sauna, Spa, Steam room, Yoga
GOOD TO KNOW	Child friendly
RECOMMENDED FOR	Spa

"First-class spa, outdoor hot tub, and great view of the mountains."—Mark de Reus

Recommended by: Mark de Reus, de Reus Architects

AMANGANI
1535 North East Butte Road
Jackson
Wyoming 83001
+1 3077347333
aman.com

CREDIT CARDS	Accepted
PRICE	Blow-out
TYPE	Hotel
ACCOMMODATION	40 Suites
FACILITIES	Bar, Gym, Outdoor swimming pool, 3 Restaurants, Spa, Steam room, Yoga
GOOD TO KNOW	Child friendly
RECOMMENDED FOR	Mountains

"Clean design with luxuriously scaled rooms. The open, uncomplicated architecture allows for a successful integration of the extraordinary exterior landscape with a luxury hospitality experience. The overall effect is elegant but calm and uncomplicated."—Hayes and James Slade

Recommended by: Hayes and James Slade, Slade Architecture

FOUR SEASONS RESORT JACKSON HOLE
7680 Granite Loop Road
Teton Village
Wyoming 83025
+1 3077325000
fourseasons.com

CREDIT CARDS..Accepted
PRICE..Blow-out
TYPE...Resort hotel
ACCOMMODATION..........158 Residences, Rooms, and Suites
FACILITIES......................Bar, Gym, Outdoor swimming pool,
3 Restaurants, Spa, Yoga
GOOD TO KNOW.............................Babysitting, Bicycle rentals
RECOMMENDED FOR...Family friendly

"Ski in, ski out; great concierge service with ski lessons, equipment, great food, and a fantastic location."
—Mark de Reus

Recommended by: Mark de Reus, de Reus Architects

HOTEL TERRA JACKSON HOLE
3335 West Village Drive
Teton Village
Wyoming 83025
+1 8553188707
hotelterrajacksonhole.com

CREDIT CARDS..Accepted
PRICE...High-end
TYPE..Hotel
ACCOMMODATION...................................132 Rooms and Suites
FACILITIES..Bar, Gym, Hot tub,
Outdoor swimming pool,
Restaurant, Spa, Steam room
GOOD TO KNOW...Free parking
RECOMMENDED FOR..Mountains

"One of the greenest hotels in the country sits in the heart of Teton Village, in Jackson Hole. This cozy hotel is beautifully designed and located among a collection of shops and restaurants that offers respite after a day of skiing, hiking, or exploring the adorable town."
—Eric Corey Freed

Recommended by: Eric Corey Freed, OrganicArchitect

OLD FAITHFUL INN
3200 Old Faithful Inn Road
Yellowstone National Park
Wyoming 82190
+1 3073447311
yellowstonenationalparklodges.com

CREDIT CARDS..Accepted
PRICE...High-end
TYPE..Lodge
ACCOMMODATION...................................327 Rooms and Suites
FACILITIES..Bar, Restaurant,
Wood-burning fireplace
GOOD TO KNOW......................Ski lessons, Snow shoe rentals
RECOMMENDED FOR..Family friendly

"The National Parks are amazing and the experience of nature for urban kids is transformative. The inn is a classic old lodge with a soaring wood interior. It is next to the geyser walk, which is pretty empty early in the morning before the crowds come."—Marianne Kwok

Recommended by: Marianne Kwok, Kohn Pedersen Fox

DEETJEN'S BIG SUR INN
48865 California 1
Big Sur
California 93920
+1 8316672377
deetjens.com

CREDIT CARDS..Accepted
PRICE...Mid-range
TYPE..Hotel
ACCOMMODATION........20 Apartments, Cabins, and Rooms
FACILITIES...Bar, Restaurant
GOOD TO KNOW...Free parking
RECOMMENDED FOR........................Beach, Best-kept secret

"A delightful compound of rustic cabins from the 1940s, Deetjen's is located along a stream at the base of the Big Sur mountains. Redwoods, gardens, a canyon waterfall, and the crashing surf provide an abundance of beauty and wonder. This relaxed retreat feels untouched by modernity. It is on the National Register of Historic Places."—Buzz Yudell

Recommended by: Sam Chermayeff, Meyer-Grohbrügge & Chermayeff; Buzz Yudell, Moore Ruble Yudell

ESALEN INSTITUTE

55000 California 1
Big Sur
California 93920
+1 7033420500
esalen.org

CREDIT CARDS	Accepted
PRICE	High-end (all-inclusive)
TYPE	Lodge
ACCOMMODATION	Bunkbeds, Rooms, Sleeping bag space, and Suites
FACILITIES	Bar, Hot-spring and open-air baths, Restaurant, Yoga
GOOD TO KNOW	Workshops
RECOMMENDED FOR	Eco-conscious

This famous non-profit retreat center is situated between the mountains and ocean of Big Sur, with a purpose of providing humanistic alternative education. Rooms are basic and meals are inclusive, as the emphasis is on guests' spiritual journeys. The Esalen Institute hosts a variety of workshops from art courses to talks on meditation, relationships, wellbeing, and sustainability.

Recommended by: Bernardo and Paulo Jacobsen, Jacobsen Arquitetura

LUCIA LODGE

62400 California 1
Big Sur
California 93920
+1 8664244787
lucialodge.com

CREDIT CARDS	Accepted
PRICE	Mid-range
TYPE	Lodge
ACCOMMODATION	10 Cabins and Rooms
FACILITIES	Bar, Restaurant
GOOD TO KNOW	No pets
RECOMMENDED FOR	Beach

"Nice place on the fantastic Big Sur road; a highly recommended detour en route from Los Angeles to San Francisco."—Alfredo Payá Benedito

Recommended by: Alfredo Payá Benedito, Noname29

POST RANCH INN

47900 Highway 1
Big Sur
California 93920
+1 8005272200
postranchinn.com

CREDIT CARDS	Accepted
PRICE	Blow-out
TYPE	Hotel
ACCOMMODATION	39 Rooms
FACILITIES	Bar, Gym, Outdoor swimming pool, Restaurant, Spa, Yoga
GOOD TO KNOW	No pets, Valet parking
RECOMMENDED FOR	Beach, Countryside, Luxury, Spa, Worth the travel

"Designed by C. K. Muenning, a protégé of Bruce Goff, the hotel is nestled into the most spectacular coastal landscape. It's breathtaking."—Deborah Berke

Recommended by: Forth Bagley, Kohn Pedersen Fox; Deborah Berke, Deborah Berke Partners; Sam Chermayeff, Meyer-Grohbrügge & Chermayeff; Eric Corey Freed, OrganicArchitect; Tom Kundig, Olson Kundig; Much Untertrifaller, Dietrich Untertrifaller Architects; Alexander Wong, Alexander Wong Architects

TREEBONES RESORT, THE AUTONOMOUS TENT

71895 Highway 1
Big Sur
California 93920
+1 8774244787
treebonesresort.com

CREDIT CARDS	Accepted but not Amex
PRICE	High-end
TYPE	Tented camp
ACCOMMODATION	1 Tent
FACILITIES	Outdoor swimming pool, Restaurant, Wood-burning fireplace, Yoga
GOOD TO KNOW	Massage available, Seasonal whale watching
RECOMMENDED FOR	Eco-conscious

"Big Sur is one of the most beautiful places, and experiencing it as close to nature as possible is truly special. The shape of the cocoon tent ['The Autonomous Tent' is one form of lodging within the Treebones Resort] is also really great."
—Marianne Kwok

Recommended by: Marianne Kwok, Kohn Pedersen Fox

CALISTOGA RANCH, AN AUBERGE RESORT

580 Lommel Road
Calistoga
California 94515
+1 8559424220
calistogaranch.aubergeresorts.com

CREDIT CARDS...Accepted
PRICE...High-end
TYPE..Resort
ACCOMMODATION...50 Lodges
FACILITIES.................................Bar, Outdoor swimming pool,
Restaurant, Spa,
Wood-burning fireplace, Yoga
GOOD TO KNOW..............................Bicycle rental, Pet friendly
RECOMMENDED FOR.......................................Countryside

"Each room is a magical retreat in the forest.
You're surrounded by nature in a glorious escape."
—Eric Corey Freed

Recommended by: Eric Corey Freed, OrganicArchitect

INDIAN SPRINGS CALISTOGA

1712 Lincoln Avenue
Calistoga
California 94515
+1 7077098139
indianspringscalistoga.com

CREDIT CARDS...Accepted
PRICE...High-end
TYPE..Resort
ACCOMMODATION..........................115 Bungalows, Cottages,
Houses, and Rooms
FACILITIES......................................Bar, Hot-spring bath,
Outdoor swimming pool,
Restaurant, Spa, Steam room
GOOD TO KNOW..Free parking
RECOMMENDED FOR.........................All-time favorite, Urban

"Historic resort with unique architecture and rare,
beautiful natural resources."—Hans Baldauf

Recommended by: Hans Baldauf, BCV Architecture
+ Interiors

THE NORMANDY INN

Ocean Avenue
Carmel-by-the-Sea
California 93923
+1 8316243825
normandyinncarmel.com

CREDIT CARDS...Accepted
PRICE..Mid-range
TYPE...Hotel
ACCOMMODATION..............48 Cottages, Rooms, and Suites
FACILITIES...Outdoor swimming pool
GOOD TO KNOW...Free parking
RECOMMENDED FOR.................................Best-kept secret

Recommended by: Erin and Ian Besler, Besler & Sons

HOTEL DEL CORONADO

1500 Orange Avenue
Coronado
California 92118
+1 800 4683533
hoteldel.com

CREDIT CARDS...Accepted
PRICE...High-end
TYPE...Hotel
ACCOMMODATION.................................757 Cottages, Rooms,
Suites, and Villas
FACILITIES..................................Bar, Outdoor swimming pool,
7 Restaurants, Spa, Yoga
GOOD TO KNOW.....................................Child and pet friendly
RECOMMENDED FOR..Beach

Recommended by: Luca Gazzaniga, Luca Gazzaniga
Architects; Guy Geier, FXCollaborative

THE OASIS AT DEATH VALLEY

California 190
Death Valley
California 92328
+1 8002367916
oasisatdeathvalley.com

CREDIT CARDS...Accepted
PRICE..Mid-range
TYPE...Hotel
ACCOMMODATION............Campsite, 312 Casitas and Rooms
FACILITIES................................Bar, Outdoor swimming pool,
5 Restaurants, Spa
GOOD TO KNOW..No pets
RECOMMENDED FOR..Desert

Recommended by: Simon Mitchell, Sybarite

HOPE SPRINGS RESORT
68075 Club Circle Drive
Desert Hot Springs
California 92240
+1 7603294003
hopespringsresort.com

CREDIT CARDS..Accepted
PRICE...Mid-range
TYPE..Hotel
ACCOMMODATION.......................................10 Rooms
FACILITIES...Hot-spring bath,
Outdoor swimming pool, Spa, Yoga
GOOD TO KNOW.......................Near Coachella Valley Music
and Arts Festival, Joshua Tree
Music Festival, and Palm Springs
RECOMMENDED FOR...Desert

"Architecture by Albert Frey, with simple rooms and
three pools with the best [spring] mineral water at three
different temperatures."—Beppe Caturegli and
Giovannella Formica

Recommended by: Beppe Caturegli and Giovannella
Formica, Caturegli Formica Architetti Associati; Johanna
Grawunder, Johanna Grawunder

THE LAUTNER
67710 San Antonio Street
Desert Hot Springs
California 92240
+1 7608325288
thelautner.com

CREDIT CARDS....................................Accepted but not Amex
PRICE...Mid-range
TYPE...Home rental
ACCOMMODATION....................................4 Residences
FACILITIES.................................Wood-burning fireplace
GOOD TO KNOW............................Free parking, Self-catering
RECOMMENDED FOR............................Best-kept secret, Desert

"John Lautner designed this jewel box of four suites in the
desert in 1947. It was recently renovated to full glory and
is the most amazing place. If you're in Palm Springs for the
Coachella Music Festival, you can escape to this gorgeous
geometric masterpiece."—Eric Corey Freed

"The only Lautner residence open to public bookings."
—Uwe Schmidt-Hess

Recommended by: Eric Corey Freed, OrganicArchitect;
Uwe Schmidt-Hess, Patalab Architecture

MIRACLE MANOR
12589 Reposo Way
Desert Hot Springs
California 92240
+1 7603296641
miraclemanor.com

CREDIT CARDS..Accepted
PRICE...Mid-range
TYPE...Bed and Breakfast
ACCOMMODATION...8 Rooms
FACILITIES...Hot-spring bath,
Outdoor swimming pool, Spa
GOOD TO KNOW...Adults only
RECOMMENDED FOR...................................Countryside

"Stay here for the size (it's small), its remote location
(it's out there), and its pool (it's full of minerals)."—Kelly Bair

Recommended by: Kelly Bair, Central Standard Office of
Design

TWO BUNCH PALMS
67425 Two Bunch Palms Trail
Desert Hot Springs
California 92240
+1 8004724334
twobunchpalms.com

CREDIT CARDS..Accepted
PRICE...Mid-range
TYPE..Hotel
ACCOMMODATION.................................68 Rooms and Suites
FACILITIES....................Bar, Hot-spring and open-air baths,
Restaurant, Spa
GOOD TO KNOW.......................................Valet parking
RECOMMENDED FOR...Spa

"Regress into a world virtually without thought. Total
physical and mental relaxation."—Louis Hedgecock

Recommended by: Louis Hedgecock, HOK Architects

L&M MOTEL

70 Healdsburg Avenue
Healdsburg
California 95448
+1 7074336528
landmmotel.com

CREDIT CARDS...Accepted
PRICE...Mid-range
TYPE..Motel
ACCOMMODATION...17 Rooms
FACILITIES...Outdoor swimming pool
GOOD TO KNOW...Pet friendly
RECOMMENDED FOR.......................................Countryside

"Quaint, family owned, friendly, and inexpensive motel
in the heart of wine country. Great for an easy walk into
town."—Johanna Grawunder

Recommended by: Johanna Grawunder, Johanna Grawunder

RENAISSANCE INDIAN WELLS RESORT & SPA

44400 Indian Wells Lane
Indian Wells
California 92210
+1 7607734444
marriott.com

CREDIT CARDS...Accepted
PRICE...Mid-range
TYPE..Resort
ACCOMMODATION...................................560 Rooms and Suites
FACILITIES.....................Bar, Gym, Outdoor swimming pool,
3 Restaurants, Spa,
Steam room, Tennis, Yoga
GOOD TO KNOW...Bicycle rentals
RECOMMENDED FOR.........................Countryside, Desert, Spa

Recommended by: Erin and Ian Besler, Besler & Sons

MANKA'S INVERNESS LODGE

30 Callendar Way
Inverness
California 94937
+1 4156691034

CREDIT CARDS...Accepted
PRICE...High-end
TYPE..Lodge
ACCOMMODATION.............9 Boathouses, Cabins, and Suites
FACILITIES..Bar, Restaurant,
Wood-burning fireplace
GOOD TO KNOW.......................................In-room dining,
Sir and Star restaurant at The Olema
RECOMMENDED FOR.................Best-kept secret, Where I live

Recommended by: Hans Baldauf, BCV Architecture
+ Interiors

LA JOLLA COVE HOTEL & SUITES

1155 Coast Boulevard
La Jolla
California 92037
+1 8584592621
lajollacove.com

CREDIT CARDS...Accepted
PRICE...Mid-range
TYPE..Hotel
ACCOMMODATION....................................117 Rooms and Suites
FACILITIES...Bar, Gym,
Outdoor swimming pool, Yoga
GOOD TO KNOW.......................................Child friendly
RECOMMENDED FOR..Beach

"Affordable accommodation in the middle of a very
unaffordable area."—Johanna Grawunder

Recommended by: Johanna Grawunder, Johanna Grawunder

THE RITZ-CARLTON, LAGUNA NIGUEL
One Ritz Carlton Drive
Laguna Niguel
California 92629
+1 9492402000
ritzcarlton.com

CREDIT CARDS..Accepted
PRICE..High-end
TYPE...Hotel
ACCOMMODATION.................................396 Rooms and Suites
FACILITIES.....................Bar, Gym, Outdoor swimming pool,
2 Restaurants, Spa, Steam room, Yoga
GOOD TO KNOW..............................Pet friendly, Valet parking
RECOMMENDED FOR...Luxury

"Gorgeous."—Kiyoshi Sey Takeyama

Recommended by: Kiyoshi Sey Takeyama, Amorphe
Takeyama & Associates

LOS ANGELES: SEE PAGES 400–404

THE M MALIBU
22541 Pacific Coast Highway
Malibu
California 90265
+1 3104566169
themmalibu.com

CREDIT CARDS..Accepted
PRICE...Mid-range
TYPE...Hotel
ACCOMMODATION...18 Rooms
FACILITIES.....................................Outdoor swimming pool
GOOD TO KNOW...Free parking
RECOMMENDED FOR...Beach

"The best located hotel I've ever stayed in, where I can step
onto the beach and into the surf."—Simon Mitchell

Recommended by: Simon Mitchell, Sybarite

NOBU RYOKAN MALIBU
22752 Pacific Coast Highway
Malibu
California 90265
noburyokanmalibu.com

CREDIT CARDS..Accepted
PRICE..Blow-out
TYPE...Hotel
ACCOMMODATION...16 Rooms
FACILITIES.............................Open-air soaking tubs,
Restaurant,
Wood-burning fireplace
GOOD TO KNOW...................Access to Malibu Racquet Club
RECOMMENDED FOR...Beach

"Probably the best hotel in the world."—Simon Mitchell

Recommended by: Simon Mitchell, Sybarite

MENDOCINO GROVE
9601 California 1
Mendocino
California 95460
+1 7078807710
mendocinogrove.com

CREDIT CARDS..Accepted
PRICE...Mid-range
TYPE..Tented camp
ACCOMMODATION...60 Tents
FACILITIES..............................Wood-burning fireplace, Yoga
GOOD TO KNOW...Free parking
RECOMMENDED FOR..Countryside

"Glamping site in a stunningly beautiful location,
which promotes connectivity to, and exploration of,
the surrounding natural environment."—Hans Baldauf

Recommended by: Hans Baldauf, BCV Architecture
+ Interiors

MONTEREY MARRIOTT

350 Calle Principal
Monterey
California 93940
+1 8316494234
marriott.com

CREDIT CARDS	Accepted
PRICE	Mid-range
TYPE	Hotel
ACCOMMODATION	341 Rooms and Suites
FACILITIES	Bar, Gym, Outdoor swimming pool, Restaurant
GOOD TO KNOW	Bicycle rentals, Valet parking
RECOMMENDED FOR	Beach

"Within walking distance of Cannery Row; don't forget to check out the seals at Hopkins Marine Station."
—Erin and Ian Besler

Recommended by: Erin and Ian Besler, Besler & Sons

LIDO HOUSE, AUTOGRAPH COLLECTION

3300 Newport Boulevard
Newport Beach
California 92663
+1 9495248500
marriott.com

CREDIT CARDS	Accepted
PRICE	High-end
TYPE	Hotel
ACCOMMODATION	130 Cottages, Rooms, and Suites
FACILITIES	Bar, Gym, Outdoor swimming pool, Restaurant, Rooftop terrace bar, Spa
GOOD TO KNOW	Valet parking
RECOMMENDED FOR	Where I live

"A unique, boutique, beach-house-style hotel with Newport Beach's only rooftop bar, alongside a street-front restaurant that adds life to the town."—Anthony Mallows

Recommended by: Anthony Mallows, WATG

OJAI VALLEY INN

905 Country Club Road
Ojai
California 93023
+1 8556978780
ojaivalleyinn.com

CREDIT CARDS	Accepted
PRICE	High-end
TYPE	Hotel
ACCOMMODATION	Penthouse, 308 Rooms and Suites
FACILITIES	Bar, Golf, Gym, Outdoor swimming pool, Spa, Tennis, Wood-burning fireplace, Yoga
GOOD TO KNOW	Bicycle rentals, Child and pet friendly
RECOMMENDED FOR	Spa

"The spa is top notch, and the fireplace is a feature I remember fondly."—Salvador Reyes Ríos

Recommended by: David Miller, Miller Hull Partnership; Salvador Reyes Ríos, Reyes Ríos + Larraín Arquitectos

ACE HOTEL & SWIM CLUB

701 East Palm Canyon Drive
Palm Springs
California 92264
+1 7603259900
acehotel.com

CREDIT CARDS	Accepted
PRICE	Mid-range
TYPE	Hotel
ACCOMMODATION	182 Rooms and Suites
FACILITIES	Bar, Gym, Outdoor swimming pool, Restaurant, Spa
GOOD TO KNOW	Pet friendly
RECOMMENDED FOR	Desert, Eco-conscious

"Stylish and lively with a distinctly 'Palm Springs' vibe."
—Stephen Barrett

"A retro, hipster paradise in the heart of Palm Springs, whose main restaurant—a remodeled Howard Johnson's—is the place to be. I love the details, from the towels to the artifacts in the rooms."—Eric Corey Freed

Recommended by: Kelly Bair, Central Standard Office of Design; Stephen Barrett, Rogers Stirk Harbour + Partners; Eric Corey Freed, OrganicArchitect; Matthew Kennedy, Studio North

THE HIDEAWAY

370 West Arenas Road
Palm Springs
California 92262
+1 7606737100
thehideawayps.com

CREDIT CARDS..Accepted
PRICE..Mid-range
TYPE..Hotel
ACCOMMODATION............................10 Rooms and Suites
FACILITIES.. Outdoor swimming pool
GOOD TO KNOW..........................Bicycle rentals, Self-catering
RECOMMENDED FOR..Desert

"On a road trip through the western U.S. enjoy this property
and be delighted by its authentic vintage style, quirky
charm, and intentional modesty, all while knowing that
you're among fellow guests who have sought out this
road-stop for the same reasons as you."
—Todd-Avery Lenahan

Recommended by: Todd-Avery Lenahan, TAL Studio

KORAKIA PENSIONE

257 South Patencio Road
Palm Springs
California 92262
+1 7608646411
korakia.com

CREDIT CARDS..Accepted
PRICE..Mid-range
TYPE..Villa
ACCOMMODATION............28 Bungalows, Rooms, and Suites
FACILITIES................................Outdoor swimming pool, Yoga
GOOD TO KNOW..........................Bicycle rentals, Free parking
RECOMMENDED FOR....................................Best-kept secret

"This collection of early twentieth-century casitas in
downtown Palm Springs is a unique oasis from busy lives.
One can truly get away as the suites, while distinctively
furnished with antiques, have no TVs. It doesn't get more
authentic than a disconnected stay at this getaway."
—Daniel Welborn

Recommended by: Daniel Welborn, The Gettys Group

PARKER PALM SPRINGS

4200 East Palm Canyon Drive
Palm Springs
California 92264
+1 7607705000
parkerpalmsprings.com

CREDIT CARDS..Accepted
PRICE..High-end
TYPE..Hotel
ACCOMMODATION..1 Private residence;
141 Rooms, Suites, and Villas
FACILITIES....................Bar, Gym, Outdoor swimming pool,
Restaurant, Spa, Tennis, Yoga
GOOD TO KNOW..Bicycle rentals
RECOMMENDED FOR....................Desert, Spa, Family friendly

"It's a cool marriage of stuffy and contemporary chic,
which seems highly appropriate and fun for the setting.
The pool garden area is spectacular. Uniquely perfect
for the area."—Hayes and James Slade

Recommended by: Jodi Batay-Csorba, Batay-Csorba
Architects; Bernard Dubois, Bernard Dubois Architects;
Hayes and James Slade, Slade Architecture

DINAH'S GARDEN HOTEL

4261 El Camino Real
Palo Alto
California 94306
+1 8002278220
dinahshotel.com

CREDIT CARDS..Accepted
PRICE..High-end
TYPE..Hotel
ACCOMMODATION..................................129 Rooms and Suites
FACILITIES....................Bar, Gym, Outdoor swimming pool,
Restaurant
GOOD TO KNOW................................Free parking, Pet friendly
RECOMMENDED FOR..Family friendly

Recommended by: Charles Renfro, Diller Scofidio + Renfro

PIONEERTOWN MOTEL
5240 Curtis Road
Pioneertown
California 92268
+1 7603657001
pioneertown-motel.com

CREDIT CARDS	Accepted
PRICE	Mid-range
TYPE	Motel
ACCOMMODATION	19 Rooms
FACILITIES	24-hour bar
GOOD TO KNOW	Free parking, Pet friendly
RECOMMENDED FOR	Desert

Recommended by: Urko Sanchez, Urko Sanchez Architects

BLUE SEA BEACH HOTEL
707 Pacific Beach Drive
San Diego
California 92109
+1 8584884700
blueseabeachhotel.com

CREDIT CARDS	Accepted
PRICE	High-end
TYPE	Hotel
ACCOMMODATION	126 Rooms and Suites
FACILITIES	Bar, Outdoor swimming pool, Spa
GOOD TO KNOW	Bicycle rentals
RECOMMENDED FOR	Beach

Recommended by: Luca Gazzaniga, Luca Gazzaniga Architects

OMNI SAN DIEGO HOTEL
675 L Street
San Diego
California 92101
+1 6192316664
omnihotels.com

CREDIT CARDS	Accepted
PRICE	Mid-range
TYPE	Hotel
ACCOMMODATION	511 Rooms and Suites
FACILITIES	Bar, Gym, Outdoor swimming pool, Restaurant, Rooftop terrace bar, Spa, Wood-burning fireplace
GOOD TO KNOW	Valet parking
RECOMMENDED FOR	Family friendly

"San Diego is a popular vacation spot for families and the Omni goes the extra distance for kids. Every child receives a backpack full of games and coloring books that are San Diego-specific, and they bring milk and cookies to your room at night. The pool is great and the hotel is near to the New Children's Museum, which takes its art and art-making play very seriously."—Dan Wood

Recommended by: Dan Wood, WORKac

THE PEARL HOTEL
1410 Rosecrans Street
San Diego
California 92106
+1 6192266100
thepearlsd.com

CREDIT CARDS	Accepted
PRICE	Mid-range
TYPE	Hotel
ACCOMMODATION	23 Rooms
FACILITIES	Bar, Outdoor swimming pool, Restaurant
GOOD TO KNOW	Mid-century Modern building
RECOMMENDED FOR	Family friendly

Recommended by: Paolo Brambilla, Calvi Brambilla

HOTEL NIKKO SAN FRANCISCO
222 Mason Street
San Francisco
California 94102
+1 4153941111
hotelnikkosf.com

CREDIT CARDS	Accepted
PRICE	Mid-range
TYPE	Hotel
ACCOMMODATION	532 Rooms and Suites
FACILITIES	Bar, Gym, Indoor swimming pool, Restaurant, Sauna, Spa, Steam room
GOOD TO KNOW	Pet friendly, Valet parking
RECOMMENDED FOR	Urban

Recommended by: Fumihiko Maki, Maki and Associates

HOTEL VITALE
8 Mission Street
San Francisco
California 94105
+1 4152783700
jdvhotels.com

CREDIT CARDS	Accepted
PRICE	Mid-range
TYPE	Hotel
ACCOMMODATION	199 Rooms and Suites
FACILITIES	Bar, Gym, Open-air bath, Restaurant, Spa, Yoga
GOOD TO KNOW	Pet friendly, Valet parking
RECOMMENDED FOR	Where I live

"Great location, nice rooms, and reasonably priced."
—Johanna Grawunder

Recommended by: Johanna Grawunder, Johanna Grawunder

MADONNA INN
100 Madonna Road
San Luis Obispo
California 93405
+1 8055433000
madonnainn.com

CREDIT CARDS	Accepted
PRICE	Mid-range
TYPE	Hotel
ACCOMMODATION	110 Rooms and Suites
FACILITIES	Bar, Gym, Outdoor swimming pool, Restaurant, Spa, Tennis
GOOD TO KNOW	Bicycle rentals
RECOMMENDED FOR	Spa

"Visit for the weirdness of this place."—Sam Chermayeff

Recommended by: Sam Chermayeff, Meyer-Grohbrügge & Chermayeff

THE MONTECITO INN
1295 Coast Village Road
Santa Barbara
California 93108
+1 8008432017
montecitoinn.com

CREDIT CARDS	Accepted
PRICE	Mid-range
TYPE	Hotel
ACCOMMODATION	60 Rooms and Suites
FACILITIES	Bar, Gym, Restaurant, Spa
GOOD TO KNOW	Bicycle rentals
RECOMMENDED FOR	Best-kept secret

"In a great location in the heart of Montecito, this 1920s building was created by the American actor Charlie Chaplin. It has a wonderful little bar and restaurant, polite staff, is clean and tidy, and right out of the early film era of California."
—Simon Jacobsen

Recommended by: Simon Jacobsen, Jacobsen Architecture

SHUTTERS ON THE BEACH
1 Pico Boulevard
Santa Monica
California 90405
+1 3104580030
shuttersonthebeach.com

CREDIT CARDS	Accepted
PRICE	High-end
TYPE	Hotel
ACCOMMODATION	198 Rooms and Suites
FACILITIES	Bar, Gym, 2 Restaurants, Spa, Steam room
GOOD TO KNOW	Child friendly
RECOMMENDED FOR	Where I live

"This hotel is comfortable like a favorite old sweater. Located at the edge of a broad white beach, it provides the calming effects of ocean and sand, complimented by the liveliness of skateboards, bicycles, and scooters sliding by on the beach promenade. A great place to have breakfast or lunch in the ocean breeze."—Buzz Yudell

Recommended by: Buzz Yudell, Moore Ruble Yudell

CAVALLO POINT LODGE
601 Murray Circle
Sausalito
California 94965
+1 8557306984
cavallopoint.com

CREDIT CARDS	Accepted
PRICE	High-end
TYPE	Hotel
ACCOMMODATION	142 Rooms and Suites
FACILITIES	Bar, Cooking school, Gym, Restaurant, Spa, Steam room
GOOD TO KNOW	Babysitting, Pet friendly, Valet parking
RECOMMENDED FOR	Family friendly

"Beautifully restored buildings and plenty of outdoor space—great sweeping lawn, a local children's museum, the Marin Headlands—for families to enjoy."—Hans Baldauf

Recommended by: Hans Baldauf, BCV Architecture + Interiors

SEA RANCH LODGE
60 Sea Walk Drive
Sea Ranch
California 95497
+1 7077852371
searanchlodge.com

CREDIT CARDS	Accepted
PRICE	Mid-range
TYPE	Hotel
ACCOMMODATION	19 Rooms
FACILITIES	Bar, Restaurant, Spa
GOOD TO KNOW	Hiking trails
RECOMMENDED FOR	Worth the travel

"Deep Pacific refreshment in no-man's-land, by legendary architect Charles Moore."—Charlotte von Moos

Recommended by: Charlotte von Moos, Sauter von Moos

ALISAL GUEST RANCH & RESORT
1054 Alisal Road
Solvang
California 93463
+1 8056934208
alisal.com

CREDIT CARDS	Accepted
PRICE	High-end
TYPE	Ranch
ACCOMMODATION	73 Rooms and Suites
FACILITIES	Bar, Gym, 2 Restaurants, Spa, Tennis, Yoga
GOOD TO KNOW	Bicycle rentals, Child friendly
RECOMMENDED FOR	Family friendly

"There is a wide range of family activities, and the staff have personality."—Maria Warner Wong

Recommended by: Maria Warner Wong, WOW Architects | Warner Wong Design

CAMP RICHARDSON
1900 Jameson Beach Road
South Lake Tahoe
California 96150
+1 8005441801
camprichardson.com

CREDIT CARDS	Accepted
PRICE	Mid-range
TYPE	Resort
ACCOMMODATION	72 Cabins, Rooms, and Tents
FACILITIES	Bar, Restaurant
GOOD TO KNOW	Bicycle rentals
RECOMMENDED FOR	Mountains

"Basically like camping with a roof and clean sheets. Amazing location and great swimming and hiking just outside the door."—Johanna Grawunder

Recommended by: Johanna Grawunder, Johanna Grawunder

LAS ALCOBAS, A LUXURY COLLECTION HOTEL, NAPA VALLEY

1915 Main Street
St Helena
California 94574
+1 7079637000
marriott.com

CREDIT CARDS	Accepted
PRICE	Blow-out
TYPE	Hotel
ACCOMMODATION	68 Rooms and Suites
FACILITIES	Bar, Gym, Outdoor swimming pool, Spa
GOOD TO KNOW	Bicycle rentals, Valet parking
RECOMMENDED FOR	Urban

"This Napa Valley hotel fits comfortably in its environment and encapsulates all things a hotel should be."
—George Yabu and Glenn Pushelberg

Recommended by: George Yabu and Glenn Pushelberg, Yabu Pushelberg

THE LODGE AT SUGAR BOWL

629 Sugar Bowl Road
Truckee
California 96161
+1 5304266742
sugarbowl.com

CREDIT CARDS	Accepted
PRICE	High-end
TYPE	Resort lodge
ACCOMMODATION	27 Rooms
FACILITIES	Bar, Gym, Outdoor swimming pool, Restaurant, Sauna, Spa, Steam room, Yoga
GOOD TO KNOW	Winter season only
RECOMMENDED FOR	Mountains

"Bavarian-style lodge designed by William Wurster within a unique Californian ski village."—Hans Baldauf

Recommended by: Hans Baldauf, BCV Architecture + Interiors

THE MAJESTIC YOSEMITE HOTEL

1 Ahwahnee Drive
Yosemite National Park
California 95389
+1 8884138869
travelyosemite.com

CREDIT CARDS	Accepted
PRICE	Mid-range
TYPE	Hotel
ACCOMMODATION	123 Rooms, Suites, and Cottages
FACILITIES	Bar, Outdoor swimming pool, Restaurant, Tennis
GOOD TO KNOW	Bicycle rentals, Valet parking
RECOMMENDED FOR	Family friendly, Mountains

"This spectacular hotel is one of the great examples of 1920s rustic regionalism. Its spirited and ingenious use of timber, stone, concrete, and glass creates memorable architecture and creatively crafted interiors. Harmonious in its natural setting, it is also expressive in itself."—Buzz Yudell

Dating back to 1927, the Majestic Yosemite Hotel combines grand public spaces with cozy and comfortable guest rooms, suites, and cottages. Facilities include a store of local artisan objects and a heated outdoor pool. Guests also have additional benefits, such as discounts on ski lifts.

Recommended by: Mark de Reus, de Reus Architects; Buzz Yudell, Moore Ruble Yudell

HOTEL YOUNTVILLE

6462 Washington Street
Yountville
California 94599
+1 7079677900
hotelyountville.com

CREDIT CARDS	Accepted
PRICE	High-end
TYPE	Hotel
ACCOMMODATION	80 Rooms and Suites
FACILITIES	Bar, Outdoor swimming pool, Restaurant, Spa
GOOD TO KNOW	Bicycle rentals, Free parking
RECOMMENDED FOR	Countryside

Recommended by: Waro Kishi, K.ASSOCIATES/Architects

THE VENETIAN
3355 South Las Vegas Boulevard
Las Vegas
Nevada 89109
+1 8666599643
venetian.com

CREDIT CARDS	Accepted
PRICE	Mid-range
TYPE	Hotel
ACCOMMODATION	7,000 Suites
FACILITIES	Bar, Gym, Outdoor swimming pool, 30 Restaurants, Sauna, Spa, Steam room
GOOD TO KNOW	Valet parking
RECOMMENDED FOR	Desert

Recommended by: Waro Kishi, K.ASSOCIATES/Architects

WYNN LAS VEGAS
3131 South Las Vegas Boulevard
Las Vegas
Nevada 89109
+1 8773219966
wynnlasvegas.com

CREDIT CARDS	Accepted
PRICE	High-end
TYPE	Hotel
ACCOMMODATION	2,611 Rooms and Suites
FACILITIES	Bar, Gym, Outdoor swimming pool, Restaurant, Sauna, Spa, Steam room
GOOD TO KNOW	Valet parking
RECOMMENDED FOR	Where I live

"Arguably THE most over-the-top (yet brilliant) hotel in the world, not just Las Vegas. As the only integrated destination resort in the world with four Forbes Five-Star components on the same premises, the service and facilities here are exceptional in every way. Drop your guard when it comes to 'restraint' and conservative taste, and allow yourself to smile."—Todd-Avery Lenahan

Recommended by: Todd-Avery Lenahan, TAL Studio

AMANGIRI
1 Kayenta Road
Canyon Point
Utah 84741
+1 4356753999
aman.com

CREDIT CARDS	Accepted
PRICE	Blow-out
TYPE	Hotel
ACCOMMODATION	34 Suites
FACILITIES	Bar, Gym, Outdoor swimming pool, Restaurant, Sauna, Spa, Wood-burning fireplace, Yoga
GOOD TO KNOW	Airport transfer
RECOMMENDED FOR	All-time favorite, Best-kept secret, Countryside, Desert, Luxury, Spa, Wish I'd designed, Worth the travel

"Designed by the great desert Modernist Wendell Burnette with Rick Joy, the architecture frames and heightens the experience of the landscape."—Deborah Berke

Amangiri is a remote luxury retreat, surrounded by the dramatic desert, lakes, cliffs, and mountains of Southern Utah. It is a minimalist's dream, a symphony of clean lines and natural materials that blend serenely into the wilderness beyond. Each suite has an outdoor lounge and fireplace, and some also have a private pool. Activities on offer include early morning hot-air balloon rides, horse-riding adventures, and candlelit yoga.

Recommended by: Michel Abboud, SOMA; Emre Arolat, EAA; Deborah Berke, Deborah Berke Partners; Boris Bernaskoni, Bernaskoni; Hasan Çalışlar, Erginoğlu & Çalışlar; Manuel Cervantes, CC Arquitectos; Farid Chacon, NMD NOMADAS; Marco Costanzi, Marco Costanzi Architects; Vincenzo De Cotiis, Vincenzo De Cotiis Architects and Gallery; Bernard Dubois, Bernard Dubois Architects; Craig Dykers, Snøhetta; Karl Fournier and Olivier Marty, Studio KO; Sean Godsell, Sean Godsell Architects; Johanna Grawunder, Johanna Grawunder; Bernardo and Paulo Jacobsen, Jacobsen Arquitetura; Brent Kendle, Kendle Design Collaborative; Driss Kettani, Driss Kettani Architecte; Robert Konieczny, KWK Promes; Anastasios Kotsiopoulos, AM Kotsiopoulos & Partners Architects; Margot Krasojevic, Margot Krasojevic Architecture; Tom Kundig, Olson Kundig; Bruce Kuwabara, KPMB Architects; Victor Legorreta Hernández, Legorreta; Todd-Avery Lenahan, TAL Studio; Daniel Libeskind, Studio Libeskind; Piero Lissoni, Lissoni Associati; Fernando Sordo Madaleno, Sordo Madaleno; Alex Mok, Linehouse; Grace Mortlock, Other Architects; Enrique Norten, TEN Arquitectos; Dennis Pieprz, Sasaki; Ron Radziner, Marmol Radziner; Alireza Razavi, Studio Razavi

Architecture; Andres Remy, Andres Remy Architects; Mark de Reus, de Reus Architects; Salvador Reyes Ríos, Reyes Ríos + Larraín Arquitectos; Pedro Rica and Marta Urtasun, Mecanismo; José Juan Rivera Rio, JJRR/Arquitectura; Michel Rojkind, Rojkind Arquitectos; Fernando Romero, FR—EE/Fernando Romero Enterprise; Lauren Rottet, Rottet Studio; Fran Silvestre, Fran Silvestre Arquitectos; Dorin Stefan, Dorin Stefan Birou de Arhitectura; Randa Tukan, HOK Architects; Much Untertrifaller, Dietrich Untertrifaller Architects; Dieter Vander Velpen, Dieter Vander Velpen Architects; David Welsh and Chris Major, Welsh + Major; Artem Vakhrin, AKZ Architectura; Kateryna Zuieva, AKZ Architectura

THE ST. REGIS DEER VALLEY

2300 Deer Valley Drive East
Park City
Utah 84060
+1 4359405700
marriott.com

CREDIT CARDS...Accepted
PRICE...High-end
TYPE..Hotel
ACCOMMODATION....................................173 Rooms and Suites
FACILITIES....................Bar, Gym, Outdoor swimming pool,
Restaurant, Sauna, Spa
GOOD TO KNOW.............................Bicycle rentals, Pet friendly,
Valet parking
RECOMMENDED FOR...Mountains

Recommended by: Randa Tukan, HOK Architects

STEIN ERIKSEN LODGE DEER VALLEY

7700 Stein Way
Park City
Utah 84060
+1 8004531302
steinlodge.com

CREDIT CARDS...Accepted
PRICE...Mid-range
TYPE..Hotel
ACCOMMODATION....................................180 Rooms and Suites
FACILITIES................................Bar, Outdoor swimming pool,
Restaurant, Sauna, Spa, Steam room
GOOD TO KNOW.............................Babysitting, Bicycle rentals
RECOMMENDED FOR...Mountains

"Makes skiing completely perfect in every way."
—Hani Rashid

Recommended by: Hani Rashid, Asymptote Architecture

THE HOTEL JEROME

330 East Main Street
Aspen
Colorado 81611
+1 9709201000
aubergeresorts.com

CREDIT CARDS...Accepted
PRICE...Mid-range
TYPE..Hotel
ACCOMMODATION....................................93 Rooms and Suites
FACILITIES....................Bar, Gym, Outdoor swimming pool,
Restaurant, Spa, Yoga
GOOD TO KNOW...Pet friendly
RECOMMENDED FOR.............................Best-kept secret

"If I told you, it would no longer be a secret. The hidden gems of this legendary historic hotel must be self-discovered and never extolled. Therein lies its enduring mystery and intrigue. More than a jewel, it is an extraordinary treasure chest."—Todd-Avery Lenahan

Recommended by: Todd-Avery Lenahan, TAL Studio

THE ST. REGIS ASPEN RESORT

315 East Dean Street
Aspen
Colorado 81611
+1 9709203300
marriott.co.uk

CREDIT CARDS...Accepted
PRICE...High-end
TYPE..Hotel
ACCOMMODATION....................................154 Rooms and Suites
FACILITIES....................Bar, Gym, Outdoor swimming pool,
3 Restaurants, Spa,
Steam room, Yoga
GOOD TO KNOW............................Babysitting, Bicycle rentals,
Pet friendly
RECOMMENDED FOR...Mountains

Recommended by: Simon Jacobsen, Jacobsen Architecture

THE RITZ-CARLTON, BACHELOR GULCH
0130 Daybreak Ridge Road
Avon
Colorado 81620
+1 9707486200
ritzcarlton.com

CREDIT CARDS	Accepted
PRICE	High-end
TYPE	Hotel
ACCOMMODATION	180 Rooms and Suites
FACILITIES	Bar, Gym, Outdoor swimming pool, 3 Restaurants, Spa, Tennis, Wood-burning fireplace
GOOD TO KNOW	Valet parking
RECOMMENDED FOR	Mountains

Recommended by: Antoine Predock, Antoine Predock Architect

EMBASSY SUITES BY HILTON BOULDER
2601 Canyon Boulevard
Boulder
Colorado 80302
+1 3034432600
embassysuites3.hilton.com

CREDIT CARDS	Accepted
PRICE	Mid-range
TYPE	Hotel
ACCOMMODATION	204 Rooms and Suites
FACILITIES	Bar, Gym, Outdoor swimming pool, Restaurant, Yoga
GOOD TO KNOW	Child friendly, Pet friendly, Valet parking
RECOMMENDED FOR	Best-kept secret, Budget

"The Embassy Suites in Boulder are certainly affordable, and while you may already have an idea of what you think it will be, think again. There are three different kinds of kombucha in the gift shop; there is local art everywhere that is refreshingly edgy and different; the location is great; and the rooms are generous. It is standard and different all at once."—Dan Wood

Recommended by: Dan Wood, WORKac

THE BROADMOOR
1 Lake Avenue
Colorado Springs
Colorado 80906
+1 8007555011
broadmoor.com

CREDIT CARDS	Accepted
PRICE	High-end
TYPE	Resort
ACCOMMODATION	784 Cottages, Residences, Rooms, and Suites
FACILITIES	Bar, Golf, Gym, Indoor and outdoor swimming pools, 10 Restaurants, Sauna, Spa, Steam room, Tennis, Yoga
GOOD TO KNOW	15 minutes from Colorado Springs Airport
RECOMMENDED FOR	Family friendly, Mountains

"Activities for every age, including no activity for those who prefer it. Good food, very well-managed, and no worries for those with children."—Louis Hedgecock

Recommended by: Guy Geier, FXCollaborative; Louis Hedgecock, HOK Architects

KIMPTON HOTEL BORN
1600 Wewatta Street
Denver
Colorado 80202
+1 3033230024
hotelborndenver.com

CREDIT CARDS	Accepted
PRICE	Mid-range
TYPE	Hotel
ACCOMMODATION	200 Rooms and Suites
FACILITIES	Bar, Gym, Restaurant
GOOD TO KNOW	Pet friendly, Valet parking
RECOMMENDED FOR	Budget

Recommended by: Bruce Kuwabara, KPMB Architects

DUNTON HOT SPRINGS

52068 Road 38
Dolores
Colorado 81323
+1 8772889922
duntonhotsprings.com

CREDIT CARDS	Accepted
PRICE	High-end (all-inclusive)
TYPE	Spa resort
ACCOMMODATION	12 Cabins
FACILITIES	Bar, Hot-springs, Restaurant, Spa, Wood-burning fireplace, Yoga
GOOD TO KNOW	Child friendly
RECOMMENDED FOR	Countryside, Mountains

Dunton Hot Springs is a restored 1800s ghost town, which has been lovingly transformed into a small and exclusive resort situated deep in the Colorado Rockies. Each hand-built cabin has its own distinct character, and rates include all meals. After a day of seasonal activities, unwind beneath the stars in the hot springs or in the sheltered Bathhouse.

Recommended by: Rick Joy, Studio Rick Joy; Annabelle Selldorf, Selldorf Architects

FAR VIEW LODGE

Mile Marker 15
Mesa Verde National Park
Colorado 81330
+1 8004492288
visitmesaverde.com

CREDIT CARDS	Accepted
PRICE	Mid-range
TYPE	Hotel
ACCOMMODATION	150 Rooms
FACILITIES	Bar, Restaurant
GOOD TO KNOW	Free parking
RECOMMENDED FOR	Mountains

"Spartan rooms, magnetic landscape."—Ludovico Centis

Recommended by: Ludovico Centis, The Empire

FOUR SEASONS RESORT AND RESIDENCES VAIL

One Vail Road
Vail
Colorado 81657
+1 9704778600
fourseasons.com

CREDIT CARDS	Accepted
PRICE	High-end
TYPE	Resort hotel
ACCOMMODATION	140 Rooms, Suites, and Residences
FACILITIES	Bar, Gym, Outdoor swimming pool, Restaurant, Sauna, Spa, Steam room, Yoga
GOOD TO KNOW	Child friendly
RECOMMENDED FOR	Mountains

A luxury ski resort in the Colorado Rockies at the foot of Vail Mountain. It has an excellent spa for a truly relaxing après-ski experience.

Recommended by: José Juan Rivera Rio, JJRR/Arquitectura

LITTLE AMERICA HOTEL FLAGSTAFF

2515 East Butler Avenue
Flagstaff
Arizona 86004
+1 9287797900
littleamerica.com

CREDIT CARDS	Accepted
PRICE	Mid-range
TYPE	Hotel
ACCOMMODATION	247 Rooms and Suites
FACILITIES	Bar, Gym, Outdoor swimming pool, Restaurant
GOOD TO KNOW	Near the Grand Canyon
RECOMMENDED FOR	Countryside

"Big rooms, outdoor facilities, and Route 66 history."
—Brent Kendle

Recommended by: Brent Kendle, Kendle Design Collaborative

ARCOSANTI

13555 S Cross L Road
Mayer
Arizona 86333
+1 9286327135
arcosanti.org

CREDIT CARDS	Accepted
PRICE	Low-cost
TYPE	Hotel
ACCOMMODATION	Apartment; 13 Rooms and Suites
FACILITIES	Outdoor swimming pool
GOOD TO KNOW	Call, email, or fax to book
RECOMMENDED FOR	Desert

"Arcosanti is Paolo Soleri's built prototype for his vision of the city of the future. Masterplanned as an eventual community of 5,000 people, it has housed acolytes who came to learn Soleri's construction techniques and help manufacture cast bells, which were sold to finance the project. It is a magical environment, 'hippie modernism' at its best with domes and carvings and different plazas and rooftops that look out on to the majestic Sonoran Desert just north of Phoenix."—Dan Wood

Recommended by: Florian Idenburg, SO–IL; Dan Wood, WORKac

SANCTUARY CAMELBACK MOUNTAIN RESORT

5700 East McDonald Drive
Paradise Valley
Arizona 85253
+1 8552452051
sanctuaryoncamelback.com

CREDIT CARDS	Accepted
PRICE	High-end
TYPE	Resort
ACCOMMODATION	109 Casitas and Suites
FACILITIES	Bar, Golf, Gym, 2 Outdoor Swimming Pools, 2 Restaurants, Tennis, Spa, Yoga
GOOD TO KNOW	Pet friendly
RECOMMENDED FOR	Spa

Recommended by: Grace Keeley, GKMP Architects

ARIZONA BILTMORE, A WALDORF ASTORIA RESORT

2400 East Missouri Avenue
Phoenix
Arizona 85016
+1 6029556600
arizonabiltmore.com

CREDIT CARDS	Accepted
PRICE	Mid-range
TYPE	Hotel
ACCOMMODATION	740 Rooms and Suites
FACILITIES	Bar, Gym, Outdoor swimming pool, 2 Restaurants, Sauna, Spa, Steam room, Tennis, Yoga
GOOD TO KNOW	Bicycle rentals, Child and pet friendly
RECOMMENDED FOR	Desert, Family friendly

"A Frank Lloyd Wright-designed complex with beautiful details in a setting of courtyards, gardens, and elegant landscapes."—Dennis Pieprz

Recommended by: Peter Eisenman, Eisenman Architects; Guy Geier, FXCollaborative; Dennis Pieprz, Sasaki; Daniel Welborn, The Gettys Group

ENCHANTMENT RESORT

525 Boynton Canyon Road
Sedona
Arizona 86336
+1 9282822900
enchantmentresort.com

CREDIT CARDS	Accepted
PRICE	Mid-range
TYPE	Resort
ACCOMMODATION	218 Rooms and Suites
FACILITIES	Bar, Golf, Gym, Outdoor swimming pool, 5 Restaurants, Sauna, Spa, Steam room, Tennis, Wood-burning fireplace
GOOD TO KNOW	Bicycle rentals
RECOMMENDED FOR	Family friendly

"It has great suites that can be grouped together, as well as remarkable views, hiking, and nature. It's for families, couples, nature lovers, and new-agers seeking the meaning of life."—Brent Kendle

Recommended by: Brent Kendle, Kendle Design Collaborative

KIMPTON AMARA RESORT & SPA
100 Amara Lane
Sedona
Arizona 86336
+1 9282824828
amararesort.com

CREDIT CARDS...Accepted
PRICE..Mid-range
TYPE..Resort
ACCOMMODATION.................................100 Rooms and Suites
FACILITIES.....................Bar, Gym, Outdoor swimming pool,
Restaurant, Spa, Steam room
GOOD TO KNOW..Valet parking
RECOMMENDED FOR..............................Best-kept secret

"Beautiful setting—it feels like you discovered it all by
yourself. It's better to go off-season when it's empty."
—Simon Mitchell

Recommended by: Simon Mitchell, Sybarite

ARIZONA INN
2200 East Elm Street
Tucson
Arizona 85719
+1 5203251541
arizonainn.com

CREDIT CARDS...Accepted
PRICE..Mid-range
TYPE...Hotel
ACCOMMODATION............92 Residences, Rooms, and Suites
FACILITIES...Bar, Gym,
Outdoor swimming pool,
Restaurant, Sauna, Tennis
GOOD TO KNOW.........................Bicycle rentals, Valet parking
RECOMMENDED FOR....................................Where I live

"It's a historic and lovingly maintained hotel—an oasis in the
middle of Tucson. The grounds are lush, and there are clay
tennis courts and a large swimming pool for sporty leisure."
—Rick Joy

Recommended by: Rick Joy, Studio Rick Joy

LOEWS VENTANA CANYON RESORT
7000 North Resort Drive
Tucson
Arizona 85750
+1 5202992020
loewshotels.com

CREDIT CARDS...Accepted
PRICE..Mid-range
TYPE..Resort
ACCOMMODATION................................398 Rooms and Suites
FACILITIES.................................Bar, Outdoor swimming pool,
Restaurant, Sauna, Spa, Steam room
GOOD TO KNOW..........................Child friendly, Free parking
RECOMMENDED FOR...Desert

"I stay here when visiting family, and I like the way the
property is situated to capture its surroundings. The
architecture integrates the beauty of the desert well."
—Josh Chaiken

Recommended by: Josh Chaiken, Kohn Pedersen Fox

TEN THOUSAND WAVES
21 Ten Thousand Waves Way
Santa Fe
New Mexico 87501
+1 5059829304
tenthousandwaves.com

CREDIT CARDS...Accepted
PRICE..Mid-range
TYPE..Spa resort
ACCOMMODATION..14 Rooms
FACILITIES.......................................Hot tub, Open-air bath,
Outdoor swimming pool,
Restaurant, Sauna, Spa
GOOD TO KNOW...............................Free parking, Pet friendly
RECOMMENDED FOR..Countryside, Spa

"Memorable for natural hotsprings, the women's bathhouse,
and going to the sushi restaurant in your massage robe."
—V. Mitch McEwen

Recommended by: V. Mitch McEwen, A(n) Office

MABEL DODGE LUHAN HOUSE
240 Morada Lane
Taos
New Mexico 87571
+1 8008462235
mabeldodgeluhan.com

CREDIT CARDS	Accepted
PRICE	Mid-range
TYPE	Inn
ACCOMMODATION	21 Rooms
FACILITIES	Restaurant, Wood-burning fireplace
GOOD TO KNOW	Free parking
RECOMMENDED FOR	Family friendly

"We came here annually for fifteen years to ski when my kids were growing up. They could play outside, right on the edge of Taos Pueblo lands."—Rick Joy

Recommended by: Rick Joy, Studio Rick Joy

HOTEL ST. BERNARD & CONDOMINIUMS
112 Sutton Place
Taos
New Mexico 87525
+1 5757762251
stbernardtaos.com

CREDIT CARDS	Accepted
PRICE	High-end (all-inclusive)
TYPE	Hotel
ACCOMMODATION	10 Residences and Rooms
FACILITIES	Bar, Hot tub, Restaurant, Yoga
GOOD TO KNOW	Child friendly, Valet parking
RECOMMENDED FOR	Family friendly

"It's a skier's dream. You're looked after by Jean Mayer, a master skier and hotel owner. It's not a luxe hotel at all, but it's comfy and cozy. The rooms aren't anything special, although the views are. It's all about Jean, his aura, and his brilliant hospitality. Summer's great here, too."
—Antoine Predock

Recommended by: Antoine Predock, Antoine Predock Architect

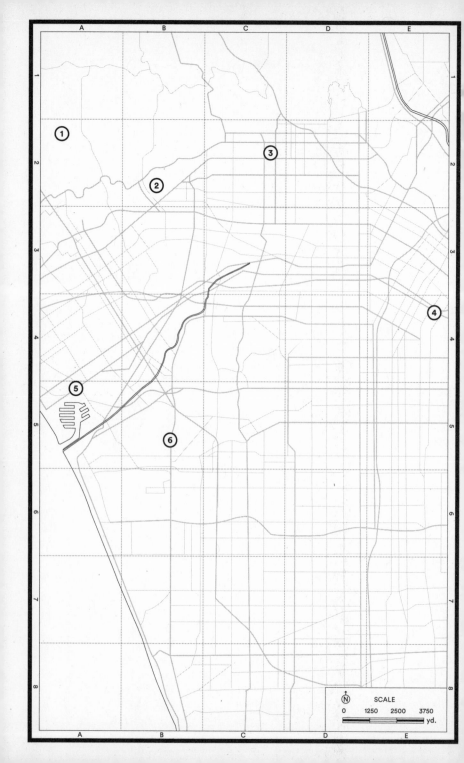

LOS ANGELES

THE BEL AIR HOTEL
701 Stone Canyon Road
Bel Air
Los Angeles
California 90077
+1 3104721211
dorchestercollection.com

CREDIT CARDS	Accepted
PRICE	Blow-out
TYPE	Hotel
ACCOMMODATION	103 Bungalows
FACILITIES	Bar, Gym, Outdoor swimming pool, Restaurant, Spa, Steam room, Yoga
GOOD TO KNOW	Pet friendly
RECOMMENDED FOR	Luxury

"Excellent rooms with private pools, lush gardens, and great service; an out-of-the-way oasis away from LA. It has a 1930s-era swimming pool, and bungalows instead of a big block hotel design."—Simon Jacobsen

Recommended by: Simon Jacobsen, Jacobsen Architecture; Buzz Yudell, Moore Ruble Yudell

THE BEVERLY HILLS HOTEL
9641 Sunset Boulevard
Beverly Hills
Los Angeles
California 90210
+1 3102762251
dorchestercollection.com

CREDIT CARDS	Accepted
PRICE	Blow-out
TYPE	Hotel
ACCOMMODATION	210 Bungalows, Rooms, and Suites
FACILITIES	Bar, Gym, Outdoor swimming pool, Restaurant, Sauna, Spa, Steam room, Yoga
GOOD TO KNOW	Babysitting
RECOMMENDED FOR	Luxury, Spa, Wish I'd designed

"If we had just designed its glitzy sign, we would be more than happy."—Charlotte von Moos

Recommended by: Doriana and Massimiliano Fuksas, Studio Fuksas; Simon Jacobsen, Jacobsen Architecture; Charlotte von Moos, Sauter von Moos

BEVERLY WILSHIRE, A FOUR SEASONS HOTEL
9500 Wilshire Boulevard
Beverly Hills
Los Angeles
California 90212
+1 3102755200
fourseasons.com

CREDIT CARDS	Accepted
PRICE	High-end
TYPE	Hotel
ACCOMMODATION	395 Rooms and Suites
FACILITIES	Bar, Gym, Outdoor swimming pool, 2 Restaurants, Spa, Steam room
GOOD TO KNOW	Child friendly
RECOMMENDED FOR	Urban

A Los Angeles landmark located at the intersection of Wilshire Boulevard and Rodeo Drive, Beverly Wilshire is every bit as glamorous and exclusive as its famous neighbors. And, as if the hotel's A-list credentials weren't already enough, the pool is modeled on the design found in Sophia Loren's villa.

Recommended by: Doriana and Massimiliano Fuksas, Studio Fuksas

CHATEAU MARMONT
West Hollywood
Los Angeles
California 90046
+1 3236561010
chateaumarmont.com

CREDIT CARDS	Accepted
PRICE	High-end
TYPE	Hotel
ACCOMMODATION	63 Bungalows, Rooms, and Suites
FACILITIES	Bar, Gym, Outdoor swimming pool, Restaurant
GOOD TO KNOW	Valet parking
RECOMMENDED FOR	All-time favorite, Luxury, Urban

"Privacy and peace. The history of the Chateau is filled with amazing stories, guests, and incidences. The bungalows, low-lit corridors, and polished tile floors, not to mention the service, pool, and private bar: this place is like a film setting itself. A lift takes you from the garage straight to your room floor, bypassing reception, lobbies, and public areas. This place was built for secrets."—Margot Krasojevic

Recommended by: Karl Fournier and Olivier Marty, Studio KO; Margot Krasojevic, Margot Krasojevic Architecture; Michel Rojkind, Rojkind Arquitectos; Fernando Romero, FR–EE/Fernando Romero Enterprise; Isabelle Toland, Aileen Sage Architects

MONDRIAN LOS ANGELES
8440 Sunset Boulevard
West Hollywood
Los Angeles
California 90069
+1 8006066090
morganshotelgroup.com

CREDIT CARDS	Accepted
PRICE	Mid-range
TYPE	Hotel
ACCOMMODATION	237 Rooms and Suites
FACILITIES	Bar, Gym, Outdoor swimming pool, Rooftop terrace bar
GOOD TO KNOW	Pet friendly
RECOMMENDED FOR	Wish I'd designed

"Great location and an exclusive rooftop bar."—Ken Yeang

Recommended by: Ken Yeang, Hamzah & Yeang

SUNSET TOWER HOTEL
8358 Sunset Boulevard
West Hollywood
Los Angeles
California 90069
+1 3236547100
sunsettowerhotel.com

CREDIT CARDS	Accepted
PRICE	High-end
TYPE	Hotel
ACCOMMODATION	81 Rooms and Suites
FACILITIES	Bar, Gym, Outdoor swimming pool, Restaurant, Spa
GOOD TO KNOW	Pet friendly
RECOMMENDED FOR	Urban

Recommended by: Bernard Dubois, Bernard Dubois Architects; Tom Kundig, Olson Kundig

ACE HOTEL DOWNTOWN LOS ANGELES
929 South Broadway
Downtown
Los Angeles
California 90015
+1 2136233233
acehotel.com

CREDIT CARDS	Accepted
PRICE	Mid-range
TYPE	Hotel
ACCOMMODATION	182 Rooms and Suites
FACILITIES	Bar, Gym, Outdoor swimming pool, Restaurant, Rooftop terrace bar
GOOD TO KNOW	Valet parking
RECOMMENDED FOR	Budget

"It has the Los Angeles Downtown vibe and concerts just next door."—Michel Rojkind

Recommended by: Michel Rojkind, Rojkind Arquitectos

JW MARRIOTT LOS ANGELES LA LIVE
900 West Olympic Boulevard
Downtown
Los Angeles
California 90015
+1 2137658600
marriott.com

CREDIT CARDS	Accepted
PRICE	High-end
TYPE	Hotel
ACCOMMODATION	878 Rooms and Suites
FACILITIES	Gym, Outdoor swimming pool, 4 Restaurants, Rooftop terrace bar, Spa, Steam room
GOOD TO KNOW	Bicycle rentals, Valet parking
RECOMMENDED FOR	Urban

Recommended by: Erin and Ian Besler, Besler & Sons

THE WESTIN BONAVENTURE HOTEL & SUITES
404 South Figueroa Street
Downtown
Los Angeles
California 90071
+1 2136241000
marriott.com

CREDIT CARDS	Accepted
PRICE	Mid-range
TYPE	Hotel
ACCOMMODATION	1,358 Rooms and Suites
FACILITIES	Bar, Gym, Outdoor swimming pool, Restaurant
GOOD TO KNOW	Pet friendly
RECOMMENDED FOR	Where I live

"Always a pleasant diversion to go and wander around inside of Portman's bizarre, post-urban, creepily hygienic utopian fantasy space."—Erin and Ian Besler

Recommended by: Erin and Ian Besler, Besler & Sons

THE ROSE HOTEL VENICE
15 Rose Avenue
Venice
Los Angeles
California 90291
+1 3104503474
therosehotelvenice.com

CREDIT CARDS	Accepted
PRICE	Mid-range
TYPE	Hotel
ACCOMMODATION	15 Rooms and Suites
FACILITIES	Cafe
GOOD TO KNOW	Bicycle rentals, Massage, Water sports
RECOMMENDED FOR	Best-kept secret

Recommended by: Stephen Barrett, Rogers Stirk Harbour + Partners

LOS ANGELES AIRPORT MARRIOTT
5855 West Century Boulevard
Westchester
Los Angeles
California 90045
+1 3106415700
marriott.com

CREDIT CARDS	Accepted
PRICE	Mid-range
TYPE	Hotel
ACCOMMODATION	1,004 Rooms
FACILITIES	Bar, Gym, Outdoor swimming pool, Restaurant
GOOD TO KNOW	Valet parking
RECOMMENDED FOR	Worth the travel

"Always worth the trip to LAX."—Erin and Ian Besler

Recommended by: Erin and Ian Besler, Besler & Sons

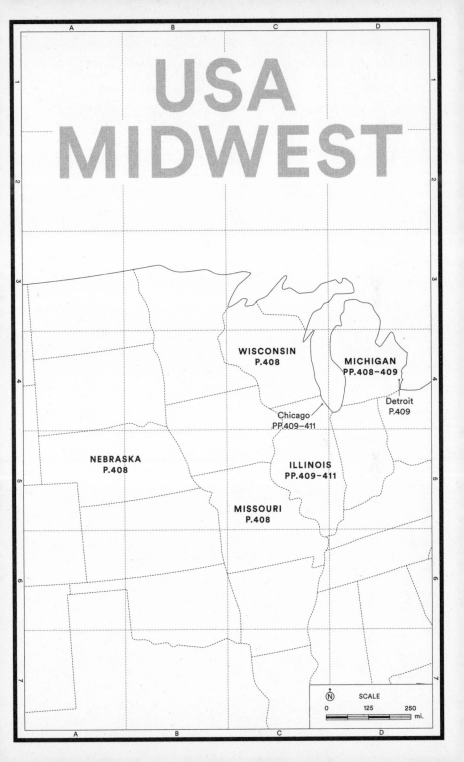

GRADUATE LINCOLN
141 North 9th Street
Lincoln
Nebraska 68508
+1 4024754011
graduatehotels.com

CREDIT CARDS..Accepted
PRICE...Mid-range
TYPE..Hotel
ACCOMMODATION....................................231 Rooms and Suites
FACILITIES.....................................Bar, Indoor swimming pool,
2 Restaurants
GOOD TO KNOW...Child friendly
RECOMMENDED FOR....................................Where I live

"Funky cowboy, corn huskers' decoration in the rooms
and arcade games in the lobby."—Nathalie Frankowski
and Cruz Garcia

Recommended by: Nathalie Frankowski and Cruz Garcia,
WAI Architecture Think Tank

MILWAUKEE MARRIOTT DOWNTOWN
323 East Wisconsin Avenue
Milwaukee
Wisconsin 53202
+1 4142785999
marriott.com

CREDIT CARDS..Accepted
PRICE...Mid-range
TYPE..Hotel
ACCOMMODATION....................................205 Rooms and Suites
FACILITIES..Bar, Gym,
Indoor swimming pool, Restaurant
GOOD TO KNOW.......................Bicycle rentals, Valet parking
RECOMMENDED FOR...Family friendly

"Large rooms and great views of the river and downtown
sites."—Kelly Bair

Recommended by: Kelly Bair, Central Standard Office
of Design

MOONRISE HOTEL
6177 Delmar in The Loop
St. Louis
Missouri 63112
+1 3147211111
moonrisehotel.com

CREDIT CARDS..Accepted
PRICE...Mid-range
TYPE..Hotel
ACCOMMODATION....................................125 Rooms and Suites
FACILITIES...Bar, Gym, Restaurant,
Rooftop terrace bar
GOOD TO KNOW.............................Pet friendly, Valet parking
RECOMMENDED FOR...Budget

"This boutique hotel is furnished based on the owner's
fascination with astronomy and space travel. It has a 1960s
vibe and is located close to good restaurants, music venues,
and Washington University in St. Louis. Easy access to
great museums, botanical gardens, parks, and downtown."
—Buzz Yudell

Recommended by: Buzz Yudell, Moore Ruble Yudell

FRANK LLOYD WRIGHT PALMER HOUSE
227 Orchard Hills Drive
Ann Arbor
Michigan 48104
+1 7345551212
flwpalmerhouse.com

CREDIT CARDS..Accepted
PRICE...High-end
TYPE..House rental
ACCOMMODATION...............................1 House (3 Bedrooms)
FACILITIES..Wood-burning fireplace
GOOD TO KNOW.................................Free parking, No pets
RECOMMENDED FOR...Countryside

"The Palmer House is a late period Frank Lloyd Wright house
set in a woodland landscape."—Ania Jaworska

Recommended by: Ania Jaworska, Ania Jaworska
& Associates

THE INN AT 97 WINDER

97 Winder Street
Detroit
Michigan 48201
+1 8009251538
theinnat97winder.com

CREDIT CARDS	Accepted
PRICE	Mid-range
TYPE	Hotel
ACCOMMODATION	10 Rooms and Suites
FACILITIES	Spa
GOOD TO KNOW	No pets
RECOMMENDED FOR	Urban

"Classic Detroit."—V. Mitch McEwen

Recommended by: V. Mitch McEwen, A(n) Office

TRUMBULL AND PORTER HOTEL

1331 Trumbull Avenue
Detroit
Michigan 48216
+1 3134961400
trumbullandporterhotel.com

CREDIT CARDS	Accepted
PRICE	Mid-range
TYPE	Hotel
ACCOMMODATION	144 Rooms
FACILITIES	Bar, Gym, Restaurant
GOOD TO KNOW	Bicycle rentals, Pet friendly
RECOMMENDED FOR	Urban

Recommended by: V. Mitch McEwen, A(n) Office

THE DUNES RESORT

333 Blue Star Highway
Douglas
Michigan 49406
+1 2698571401
dunesresort.com

CREDIT CARDS	Accepted
PRICE	Mid-range
TYPE	LGBTQ resort
ACCOMMODATION	146 Cottages, Rooms, and Suites
FACILITIES	Bar, Restaurant, Swimming pool
GOOD TO KNOW	Pet friendly
RECOMMENDED FOR	Beach

Recommended by: V. Mitch McEwen, A(n) Office

LONGMAN & EAGLE

2657 North Kedzie Avenue
Logan Square
Chicago
Illinois 60647
+1 7732767110
longmanandeagle.com

CREDIT CARDS	Accepted
PRICE	Low-cost
TYPE	Hotel
ACCOMMODATION	6 Rooms
FACILITIES	Bar, Restaurant
GOOD TO KNOW	Free parking
RECOMMENDED FOR	Urban

Recommended by: Kelly Bair, Central Standard Office
of Design

CHICAGO MARRIOTT DOWNTOWN MAGNIFICENT MILE

540 North Michigan Avenue
Near North
Chicago
Illinois 60611
+1 3128360100
marriott.com

CREDIT CARDS	Accepted
PRICE	Mid-range
TYPE	Hotel
ACCOMMODATION	1,165 Rooms and Suites
FACILITIES	Bar, Gym, 2 Restaurants, Yoga
GOOD TO KNOW	Babysitting, Valet parking
RECOMMENDED FOR	Luxury, Urban

"Excellent location and very comfortable."
—Sarah de Villiers

Recommended by: Erin and Ian Besler, Besler & Sons;
Sarah de Villiers, Counterspace

INTERCONTINENTAL CHICAGO MAGNIFICENT MILE

505 North Michigan Avenue
Near North
Chicago, Illinois 60611
+1 3129444100
icchicagohotel.com

CREDIT CARDS	Accepted
PRICE	Mid-range
TYPE	Hotel
ACCOMMODATION	792 Rooms and Suites
FACILITIES	Bar, Gym, Indoor swimming pool, Restaurant, Sauna
GOOD TO KNOW	Child friendly
RECOMMENDED FOR	Worth the travel

Recommended by: Felino Palafox, Jr., Palafox Associates

SOFITEL CHICAGO MAGNIFICENT MILE

20 East Chestnut Street
Near North
Chicago, Illinois 60611
+1 3123244000
sofitel-chicago.com

CREDIT CARDS	Accepted
PRICE	Mid-range
TYPE	Hotel
ACCOMMODATION	415 Rooms and Suites
FACILITIES	Bar, Gym, Restaurant
GOOD TO KNOW	Child and pet friendly
RECOMMENDED FOR	Urban

[Jean-Paul Viguier et Associés designed Sofitel Water Building.]

Recommended by: Jean-Paul Viguier, Jean-Paul Viguier et Associés

FREEHAND CHICAGO

19 East Ohio Street
River North
Chicago, Illinois 60611
+1 3129403699
freehandhotels.com

CREDIT CARDS	Accepted
PRICE	Mid-range
TYPE	Hotel
ACCOMMODATION	217 Dorms, Rooms, and Suites
FACILITIES	Bar, Gym, Restaurant
GOOD TO KNOW	Child friendly
RECOMMENDED FOR	Urban

Freehand Chicago is the second outpost from the hip hotel chain and situated in Chicago's vibrant River North neighbourhood. Rooms are bright and thoughtfully designed, there is an on-site coffee shop which serves breakfast and lunch, and cocktails are served at the Broken Shaker bar. As well as DJ residencies, the hotel also hosts a constantly evolving range of activities, from sunset yoga in the park, to palm readings, and storytelling.

Recommended by: Sarah de Villiers, Counterspace

THE LANGHAM

330 North Wabash Avenue
River North
Chicago
Illinois 60611
+1 3129239988
langhamhotels.com

CREDIT CARDS	Accepted
PRICE	High-end
TYPE	Hotel
ACCOMMODATION	318 Rooms and Suites
FACILITIES	Bar, Gym, Indoor swimming pool, Restaurant, Sauna, Spa, Steam room
GOOD TO KNOW	Pet friendly, Valet parking
RECOMMENDED FOR	Luxury, Wish I'd designed

"I love the Infinity Suite, which has a grand piano in the living room. I can practice playing in front of the city's incredible skyline."—David Rockwell

Recommended by: Chris McDonough, The Gettys Group; David Rockwell, Rockwell Group; Claudia Urdaneta, NMD NOMADAS

THE BLACKSTONE

636 South Michigan Avenue
South Loop
Chicago
Illinois 60605
+1 3124470955
theblackstonehotel.com

CREDIT CARDS	Accepted
PRICE	Mid-range
TYPE	Hotel
ACCOMMODATION	335 Rooms and Suites
FACILITIES	Bar, Gym, Restaurant
GOOD TO KNOW	Valet parking
RECOMMENDED FOR	Where I live

"This *grande dame* has played a part in Chicago's often-turbulent political scene for more than a hundred years. As a landmark building, this unique history is preserved and the latest renovation enhances the story with a modern elegance. Recommended for politically minded urban enthusiasts."—Daniel Welborn

Recommended by: Daniel Welborn, The Gettys Group

HOTEL BLAKE
500 South Dearborn Street
South Loop
Chicago
Illinois 60605
+1 3129861234
hotelblake.com

CREDIT CARDS	Accepted
PRICE	Mid-range
TYPE	Hotel
ACCOMMODATION	162 Rooms and Suites
FACILITIES	Bar, Gym, Restaurant
GOOD TO KNOW	Valet parking
RECOMMENDED FOR	Urban

"The northern rooms offer views to the Monadnock Building."
—Job Floris

Recommended by: Job Floris, Monadnock

THE ALISE CHICAGO
1 West Washington Street
The Loop
Chicago
Illinois 60602
+1 3129407997
staypineapple.com

CREDIT CARDS	Accepted
PRICE	Mid-range
TYPE	Hotel
ACCOMMODATION	122 Rooms and Suites
FACILITIES	Bar, Gym, Restaurant
GOOD TO KNOW	Bicycle rentals, Dog friendly, Valet parking
RECOMMENDED FOR	Urban

"Beautifully restored Burnham, Root and Atwood building that's also very well located."—Grace Keeley

Recommended by: Grace Keeley, GKMP Architects

CHICAGO ATHLETIC ASSOCIATION
12 South Michigan Avenue
The Loop
Chicago
Illinois 60603
+1 3127923581
chicagoathletichotel.com

CREDIT CARDS	Accepted
PRICE	Mid-range
TYPE	Hotel
ACCOMMODATION	241 Rooms and Suites
FACILITIES	13 Bars, Gym, 7 Restaurants
GOOD TO KNOW	Bicycle rentals, Pet friendly, Valet parking
RECOMMENDED FOR	Urban

"Great location, historic buildings, and a fantastic lounge."
—Ania Jaworska

Chicago Athletic Association is a chic hotel set in an 1890s Gothic building which was once home to an exclusive sportsmen's club. Rooms are spacious and designed by Roman & Williams, with a design that alludes to the building's past. There are plenty of bars and restaurants—including rooftop Cindy's. Experiences include rooftop yoga and complimentary bike hire for guests' trips to Green City farmers' market.

Recommended by: Ania Jaworska, Ania Jaworska & Associates

DOUBLETREE HOTEL SKOKIE
9599 Skokie Boulevard
Skokie
Illinois 60077
+1 8476797000
doubletree.hilton.com

CREDIT CARDS	Accepted
PRICE	Mid-range
TYPE	Hotel
ACCOMMODATION	369 Rooms and Suites
FACILITIES	Bar, Gym, Outdoor swimming pool, Restaurant
GOOD TO KNOW	Child friendly, Free parking
RECOMMENDED FOR	All-time favorite

Recommended by: Erin and Ian Besler, Besler & Sons

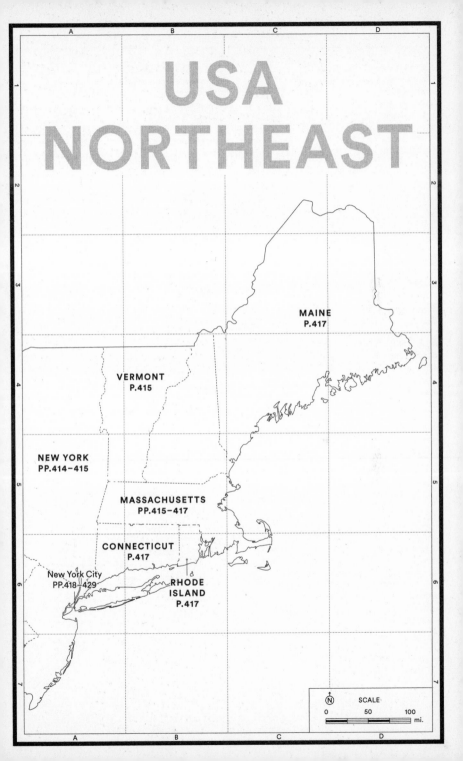

USA
NORTHEAST

MAINE
P.417

VERMONT
P.415

NEW YORK
PP.414–415

MASSACHUSETTS
PP.415–417

CONNECTICUT
P.417

New York City
PP.418–429

**RHODE
ISLAND**
P.417

N

SCALE

0   50   100
                              mi.

THE SAGAMORE RESORT
110 Sagamore Road
Bolton Landing
New York 12814
+1 8663841944
thesagamore.com

CREDIT CARDS	Accepted
PRICE	Blow-out
TYPE	Resort
ACCOMMODATION	184 Rooms and Suites
FACILITIES	3 Bars, Gym, Outdoor swimming pool, 5 Restaurants, Spa, Tennis, Yoga
GOOD TO KNOW	Child friendly
RECOMMENDED FOR	Mountains

"In the Adirondack State Park, it has a history of creative and artistic legacy."—Michael Meredith and Hilary Sample

Recommended by: Michael Meredith and Hilary Sample, MOS

GLENMERE MANSION
634 Pine Hill Road
Chester
New York 10918
+1 8454691900
glenmeremansion.com

CREDIT CARDS	Accepted
PRICE	High-end
TYPE	Hotel
ACCOMMODATION	18 Rooms and Suites
FACILITIES	Bar, Gym, Outdoor swimming pool, Restaurant, Spa, Wood-burning fireplace
GOOD TO KNOW	Adult only
RECOMMENDED FOR	Best-kept secret, Countryside

"A surprising hotel in the midst of the Hudson Valley, and a romantic getaway just forty-five minutes from New York City. It is known by very few people, despite being one of the most beautiful and comfortable retreats I have ever experienced—not to mention the beautiful spa."
—Michel Abboud

Recommended by: Michel Abboud, SOMA

THE DUTCHESS
Exact location released at time of booking
Hudson Valley
New York
thedutchess.com

CREDIT CARDS	Accepted
PRICE	Mid-range
TYPE	Farmhouse hotel
ACCOMMODATION	14 Cottages, Rooms, and Suites
FACILITIES	Bar, Restaurant, Spa, Yoga
GOOD TO KNOW	Babysitting
RECOMMENDED FOR	Best-kept secret

Recommended by: Daniel Sundlin, Bjarke Ingels Group

MOHONK MOUNTAIN HOUSE
1000 Mountain Rest Road
New Paltz
New York 12561
+1 8457653286
mohonk.com

CREDIT CARDS	Accepted
PRICE	High-end
TYPE	Hotel
ACCOMMODATION	259 Cottages, Rooms, and Suites
FACILITIES	Bar, Golf, Gym, Indoor swimming pool, Restaurant, Spa, Tennis, Wood-burning fireplace, Yoga
GOOD TO KNOW	Bicycle rentals, Child friendly, Horse riding, Water sports
RECOMMENDED FOR	Countryside

"Located in the Shawangunk Mountains, Mohonk Mountain House has an amazing range of family activities, from hiking and mountain biking, to horseback riding."—David Rockwell

Recommended by: David Rockwell, Rockwell Group

NEW YORK: SEE PAGES 418–429

SUNSET BEACH HOTEL
35 Shore Road
Shelter Island Heights, New York 11965
+1 6317492001
sunsetbeachli.com

CREDIT CARDS	Accepted
PRICE	High-end
TYPE	Hotel
ACCOMMODATION	20 Rooms
FACILITIES	Bar, Outdoor restaurant, Yoga
GOOD TO KNOW	Bicycle rentals
RECOMMENDED FOR	Beach

Recommended by: Hani Rashid, Asymptote Architecture

WOODSTOCK INN & RESORT
14 The Green
Woodstock, Vermont 05091
+1 8883382745
woodstockinn.com

CREDIT CARDS	Accepted
PRICE	High-end
TYPE	Resort
ACCOMMODATION	143 Rooms and Suites
FACILITIES	Bar, Golf, Gym, Outdoor swimming pool, 4 Restaurants, Sauna, Spa, Steam room, Tennis, Yoga
GOOD TO KNOW	Bicycle rentals, Family friendly
RECOMMENDED FOR	Countryside

"Timelessly elegant and set in the heart of one of the most beautiful villages in the United States."—Anthony Mallows

Recommended by: Anthony Mallows, WATG; Hayes and James Slade, Slade Architecture

HOTEL UMASS
1 Campus Center Way
Amherst, Massachusetts 01003
+1 8778222110
hotelumass.com

CREDIT CARDS	Accepted
PRICE	Mid-range
TYPE	Hotel
ACCOMMODATION	116 Rooms
FACILITIES	Bar, Gym, Indoor swimming pool, Restaurant
GOOD TO KNOW	Free parking
RECOMMENDED FOR	Wish I'd designed

"Marcel Breuer was a master of concrete, light, and shadow. The Hotel UMass in the center of a university campus is like a miniature version of Le Corbusier's Unité d'Habitation, but with even more patterns and presence. It is not well-loved by locals, but even now it remains a transformative experience, the best of Modernism in the most unlikely of settings."—Dan Wood

Recommended by: Dan Wood, WORKac

THE RITZ-CARLTON, BOSTON
10 Avery Street
Boston
Massachusetts 02111
+1 6175747100
ritzcarlton.com

CREDIT CARDS	Accepted
PRICE	High-end
TYPE	Hotel
ACCOMMODATION	193 Rooms and Suites
FACILITIES	Bar, Gym, Indoor swimming pool, Restaurant, Sauna, Spa, Steam room
GOOD TO KNOW	Babysitting, Pet friendly
RECOMMENDED FOR	Luxury

Recommended by: Felino Palafox, Jr., Palafox Associates

THE CHARLES HOTEL
1 Bennett Street
Cambridge
Massachusetts 02138
+1 6178641200
charleshotel.com

CREDIT CARDS	Accepted
PRICE	High-end
TYPE	Hotel
ACCOMMODATION	295 Rooms and Suites
FACILITIES	Bar, Gym, Indoor swimming pool, 2 Restaurants, Spa, Steam room, Yoga
GOOD TO KNOW	Valet parking
RECOMMENDED FOR	Where I live

"A great hotel in the prime location of Harvard Square."
—Dennis Pieprz

The Charles Hotel is an upmarket destination on bustling Harvard Square. Rooms are spacious and designed in classic New England-style. The hotel has a spa, fitness centre, and pool, as well as an extensive art collection which includes drawings, photographs, and quilts.

Recommended by: Dennis Pieprz, Sasaki

WEQUASSETT RESORT AND GOLF CLUB
2173 Route 28
Harwich
Massachusetts 02645
+1 5083793388
wequassett.com

CREDIT CARDS	Accepted
PRICE	High-end
TYPE	Hotel
ACCOMMODATION	120 Cottages, Rooms, and Suites
FACILITIES	2 Bars, Golf, 3 Restaurants, 2 Outdoor swimming pools, Tennis
GOOD TO KNOW	Water sports
RECOMMENDED FOR	Family friendly

"Let the kids go… and then find them for dinner! A vast hotel on the water, with boat rentals and killer outdoor dining—the kind you find in a private club."—Simon Jacobsen

Recommended by: Simon Jacobsen, Jacobsen Architecture

CANYON RANCH
165 Kemble Street
Lenox
Massachusetts 01240
+1 8007429000
canyonranch.com

CREDIT CARDS	Accepted
PRICE	Blow out (all-inclusive)
TYPE	Wellness resort
ACCOMMODATION	126 Rooms and Suites
FACILITIES	Gym, Restaurant, Sauna, Spa, Yoga
GOOD TO KNOW	Child friendly (14 and over)
RECOMMENDED FOR	Spa

Recommended by: Guy Geier, FXCollaborative

THE WAUWINET
120 Wauwinet Road
Nantucket
Massachusetts 02584
+1 8004268718
wauwinet.com

CREDIT CARDS	Accepted
PRICE	High-end
TYPE	Hotel
ACCOMMODATION	1 House, 32 Rooms and Suites
FACILITIES	Bar, Restaurant, Spa, Tennis
GOOD TO KNOW	Bicycle rentals, Child friendly
RECOMMENDED FOR	Wish I'd designed

The Wauwinet is a luxury boutique hotel on the island of Nantucket with access to two private beaches. Interiors are plush and cozy, and the private Anchorage House is also available for larger groups. The hotel restaurant serves locally sourced produce and seafood. Guests have access to the spa facilities at the sister hotel, White Elephant, although in-room massages are available.

Recommended by: Simon Jacobsen, Jacobsen Architecture

HARBORSIDE HOTEL, WHITE ELEPHANT
50 Easton Street
Nantucket
Massachusetts 02554
+1 5082282500
whiteelephanthotel.com

CREDIT CARDS	Accepted
PRICE	High-end
TYPE	Resort
ACCOMMODATION	66 Rooms
FACILITIES	Bar, Gym, Restaurant, Spa
GOOD TO KNOW	Bicycle rentals, Child friendly
RECOMMENDED FOR	Beach

"Off-center from town with elegant views of the harbor; rooms are 'Cottage Cool.'"—Simon Jacobsen

Recommended by: Simon Jacobsen, Jacobsen Architecture

OLD INN ON THE GREEN
134 Hartsville-New Marlborough Road
New Marlborough
Massachusetts 01230
+1 4132297924
oldinn.com

CREDIT CARDS	Accepted
PRICE	Mid-range
TYPE	Hotel
ACCOMMODATION	5 Rooms
FACILITIES	Bar, Jacuzzi, Restaurant, Wood-burning fireplace
GOOD TO KNOW	Pet friendly
RECOMMENDED FOR	Countryside

"Pared-back rooms and amazing food."—Forth Bagley

Recommended by: Forth Bagley, Kohn Pedersen Fox

THE COLONY OF WELLFLEET
640 Chequessett Neck Road
Wellfleet
Massachusetts 02667
+1 5083493761
colonyofwellfleet.com

CREDIT CARDS	Not accepted
PRICE	Mid-range
TYPE	Cottage (rentals)
ACCOMMODATION	10 Cottages
FACILITIES	Gardens, Self-catering kitchens
GOOD TO KNOW	Bauhaus style, No pets
RECOMMENDED FOR	Eco-conscious

Recommended by: Sam Chermayeff, Meyer-Grohbrügge & Chermayeff

THE STUDY AT YALE
1157 Chapel Street
New Haven
Connecticut 06511
+1 2035033900
thestudyatyale.com

CREDIT CARDS	Accepted
PRICE	Mid-range
TYPE	Hotel
ACCOMMODATION	124 Rooms and Suites
FACILITIES	Bar, Gym, Restaurant
GOOD TO KNOW	Pet friendly
RECOMMENDED FOR	Budget

"Not a budget hotel at all, but extremely economical with clean, modern rooms and a vibrant but cozy lobby-restaurant-bar. I always love staying here, whatever mood I'm in."—Forth Bagley

Recommended by: Forth Bagley, Kohn Pedersen Fox

THE DEAN HOTEL
122 Fountain Street
Providence
Rhode Island 02903
+1 4014553326
thedeanhotel.com

CREDIT CARDS	Accepted
PRICE	Mid-range
TYPE	Hotel
ACCOMMODATION	52 Rooms and Suites
FACILITIES	Bar, Restaurant
GOOD TO KNOW	Bicycle rentals, Valet parking
RECOMMENDED FOR	Urban

"Once a brothel, now a hip hotel with the best coffee in eastern USA."—Hani Rashid

Recommended by: Hani Rashid, Asymptote Architecture

OCEAN HOUSE
1 Bluff Avenue
Watch Hill
Rhode Island 02891
+1 8556780364
oceanhouseri.com

CREDIT CARDS	Accepted
PRICE	High-end
TYPE	Hotel
ACCOMMODATION	60 Rooms and Suites
FACILITIES	Bar, Gym, Indoor swimming pool, 3 Restaurants, Spa, Tennis, Yoga
GOOD TO KNOW	Bicycle rentals, Pet and child friendly, Valet parking
RECOMMENDED FOR	Worth the travel

"The perfect setting; an amazing renovation and wonderful food."—Adam Meshberg

Recommended by: Adam Meshberg, Meshberg Group

WHITE BARN INN
37 Beach Avenue
Kennebunk
Maine 04043
+1 8332428847
aubergeresorts.com

CREDIT CARDS	Accepted
PRICE	High-end
TYPE	Hotel
ACCOMMODATION	27 Cottages, Rooms, and Suites
FACILITIES	Bar, Outdoor swimming pool, 2 Restaurants, Spa, Wood-burning fireplace, Yoga
GOOD TO KNOW	Bicycle rentals, Pet and child friendly
RECOMMENDED FOR	Countryside

A local institution, the White Barn Inn is a quaint yet elegant retreat housed in a 150-year-old restored barn. Accommodation spans a collection of rooms, suites, and cottages, and local activities include picnicking on the nearby beach and visits to a local farm.

Recommended by: Peter Eisenman, Eisenman Architects

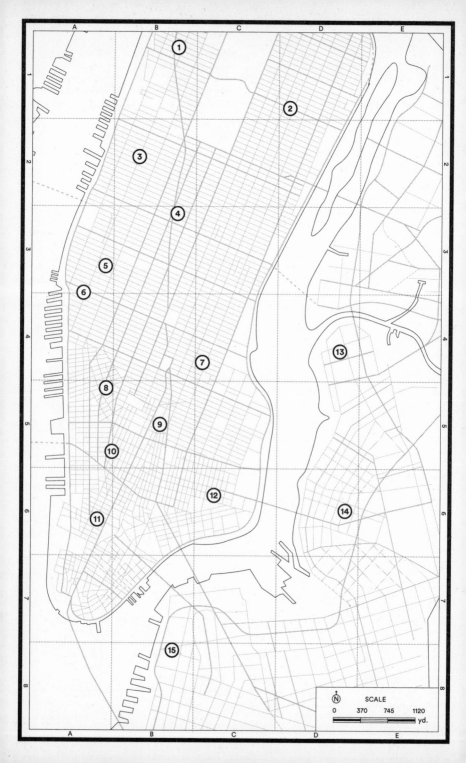

SCALE

0   370   745   1120

yd.

NEW YORK CITY

MANDARIN ORIENTAL, NEW YORK
80 Columbus Circle
Upper West Side
Manhattan
New York City 10023
+1 2128058800
mandarinoriental.com

CREDIT CARDS	Accepted
PRICE	High-end
TYPE	Hotel
ACCOMMODATION	244 Rooms and Suites
FACILITIES	2 Bars, Indoor swimming pool, Restaurant, Spa, Steam room, Yoga
GOOD TO KNOW	Pet friendly
RECOMMENDED FOR	Luxury, Spa

"The most beautifully designed spa with the best view of Central Park in New York City. The service is superb. It is an amazing experience to observe the hustle and bustle of the city from huge windows on the thirty-fifth floor while enjoying relaxing music, aromatherapy, and sipping exotic teas in luxurious bathrobes."—Francesca Bucci

"The bird's eye view over Central Park is amazing, and you can walk to the Museum of Arts and Design and Lincoln Center in five minutes."—Belén Moneo and Jeffrey Brock

Recommended by: Francesca Bucci, BG Studio International; Belén Moneo and Jeffrey Brock, Moneo Brock

THE CARLYLE, A ROSEWOOD HOTEL
35 East 76th Street
Upper East Side
Manhattan
New York City 10021
+1 2127441600
rosewoodhotels.com

CREDIT CARDS	Accepted
PRICE	High-end
TYPE	Hotel
ACCOMMODATION	190 Rooms and Suites
FACILITIES	Bar, Gym, Restaurant, Spa, Yoga
GOOD TO KNOW	Pet friendly, Valet parking
RECOMMENDED FOR	Where I live

"Stay here for the bar and the rabbits on the wall."
—Sam Chermayeff

Recommended by: Sam Chermayeff, Meyer-Grohbrügge & Chermayeff; Charles Renfro, Diller Scofidio + Renfro

THE LOWELL
28 East 63rd Street
Upper East Side
Manhattan
New York City 10065
+1 2128381400
lowellhotel.com

CREDIT CARDS	Accepted
PRICE	High-end
TYPE	Hotel
ACCOMMODATION	74 Rooms and Suites
FACILITIES	Bar, Restaurant, Wood-burning fireplace
GOOD TO KNOW	Pet friendly
RECOMMENDED FOR	Where I live

Recommended by: Craig Dykers, Snøhetta

THE MARK
25 East 77th Street
Upper East Side
Manhattan
New York City 10075
+1 2127444300
themarkhotel.com

CREDIT CARDS	Accepted
PRICE	High-end
TYPE	Hotel
ACCOMMODATION	152 Rooms, Penthouses, and Suites
FACILITIES	Bar, Gym, Restaurant
GOOD TO KNOW	Bicycle rentals, Child and pet friendly
RECOMMENDED FOR	Luxury, Urban, Wish I'd designed

"It's the perfect oasis away from the hustle of New York City life."—Achille Salvagni

"In the heart of Manhattan. All of New York is at your fingertips. A luxury hotel comme il faut."
—Murat Tabanlıoğlu

Recommended by: Achille Salvagni, Salvagni Architetti; Daniel Suduca and Thierry Mérillou, Suduca & Mérillou; Murat Tabanlıoğlu, Tabanlıoğlu Architects

THE SHERRY-NETHERLAND
781 5th Avenue
Upper East Side
Manhattan
New York City 10022
+1 2123552800
sherrynetherland.com

CREDIT CARDS	Accepted
PRICE	High-end
TYPE	Hotel
ACCOMMODATION	50 Rooms and Suites
FACILITIES	Bar, Gym, Restaurant
GOOD TO KNOW	Pet friendly, Valet parking
RECOMMENDED FOR	Spa

This charmingly opulent, five-star hotel evokes a bygone era of glamour throughout its public and private spaces. The restaurant—Harry Cipriani—is a near duplicate of the famous Harry's Bar in Venice, and the little extras, including Louis Sherry chocolates and daily fresh flowers, are a nice touch.

Recommended by: Mattheo Thun, Matteo Thun & Partners

THE SURREY
20 East 76th Street
Upper East Side
Manhattan
New York City 10021
+1 2122883700
thesurrey.com

CREDIT CARDS	Accepted
PRICE	High-end
TYPE	Hotel
ACCOMMODATION	189 Rooms and Suites
FACILITIES	Bar, Gym, Restaurant, Rooftop terrace bar, Spa
GOOD TO KNOW	Pet friendly, Valet parking
RECOMMENDED FOR	Where I live

"Great Upper East Side location with perfect service, and it has one of the city's best restaurants downstairs."
—Louis Hedgecock

Recommended by: Louis Hedgecock, HOK Architects

HUDSON HOTEL
358 West 58th Street
Hell's Kitchen
Manhattan
New York City 10019
+1 2125546000
morganshotelgroup.com

CREDIT CARDS	Accepted
PRICE	Mid-range
TYPE	Hotel
ACCOMMODATION	876 Rooms and Suites
FACILITIES	Bar, Gym, Rooftop terrace bar
GOOD TO KNOW	Valet parking
RECOMMENDED FOR	All-time favorite, Luxury

Hudson New York is a boutique hotel designed by Philippe Starck, situated just a short walk from The Museum of Arts and Design and the Time Warner Center. Rooms are inspired by the romance of transatlantic travel and have wood-paneling as one of Starck's design touches.

Recommended by: Hiéronyme Lacroix and Simon Chessex, Lacroix Chessex; Andrea Maffei, Andrea Maffei Architects

YOTEL NEW YORK
570 10th Avenue
Hell's Kitchen
Manhattan
New York City 10036
+1 6464497700
yotel.com

CREDIT CARDS	Accepted
PRICE	Mid-range
TYPE	Hotel
ACCOMMODATION	713 Rooms and Suites
FACILITIES	Cabaret bar, Gym, 2 Restaurants, Rooftop terrace bar
GOOD TO KNOW	Bicycle rentals
RECOMMENDED FOR	Budget

YOTEL New York, situated in the heart of Midtown—just three blocks from Times Square—offers convenience, innovative design, and all the perks of a conventional hotel at a reasonable price. "Cabins" are compact yet well-designed, and there are several bar and dining options including the Terrace, which is one of the largest in New York.

Recommended by: Craig Dykers, Snøhetta

1 HOTEL CENTRAL PARK
1414 Avenue of the Americas
Midtown
Manhattan
New York City 10019
+1 2127032001
1hotels.com

CREDIT CARDS	Accepted
PRICE	High-end
TYPE	Hotel
ACCOMMODATION	229 Rooms and Suites
FACILITIES	Bar, Gym, Restaurant
GOOD TO KNOW	Valet parking
RECOMMENDED FOR	Eco-conscious

"This is a luxurious eco hotel very close to Central Park. The interior is adorned with 24,000 plants in a wildly imaginative 'enchanted forest' design. You'll be surrounded by natural and reclaimed materials that effectively bring the outside in."—Belén Moneo and Jeffrey Brock

Recommended by: Belén Moneo and Jeffrey Brock, Moneo Brock

THE ALGONQUIN HOTEL
59 West 44th Street
Midtown
Manhattan
New York City 10036
+1 2128406800
algonquinhotel.com

CREDIT CARDS	Accepted
PRICE	Mid-range
TYPE	Hotel
ACCOMMODATION	181 Rooms and Suites
FACILITIES	Bar, Gym, Restaurant
GOOD TO KNOW	Pet friendly
RECOMMENDED FOR	Luxury

An elegant, delightfully old-fashioned hotel with historic charm, where poet Dorothy Parker held her famous round tables. It is situated just moments from the Rockefeller Center and Times Square.

Recommended by: Alberto Lievore, Lievore Altherr

CHAMBERS HOTEL
15 West 56th Street
Midtown
Manhattan
New York City 10019
+1 2129745656
chambershotel.com

CREDIT CARDS	Accepted
PRICE	Mid-range
TYPE	Hotel
ACCOMMODATION	77 Rooms and Suites
FACILITIES	Gym
GOOD TO KNOW	Pet friendly
RECOMMENDED FOR	All-time favorite

"Great location in New York's Midtown, close to Central Park."
—Ken Yeang

Recommended by: Ken Yeang, Hamzah & Yeang

CITIZENM NEW YORK TIMES SQUARE HOTEL
218 West 50th Street
Midtown
Manhattan
New York City 10019
+1 2124613638
citizenm.com

CREDIT CARDS	Accepted
PRICE	Mid-range
TYPE	Hotel
ACCOMMODATION	230 Rooms
FACILITIES	Cafe, Gym, Rooftop bar and terrace
GOOD TO KNOW	Triple glazing
RECOMMENDED FOR	Urban, Where I live

"This hotel has a great lobby and public spaces for visitors, which is where I spend most my time."—Tim Black

Recommended by: Tim Black, BKK Architects; V. Mitch McEwen, A(n) Office

DREAM DOWNTOWN
355 West 16th Street
Midtown
Manhattan
New York City 10011
+1 2122292559
dreamhotels.com

CREDIT CARDS...Accepted
PRICE..High-end
TYPE...Hotel
ACCOMMODATION.......................314 Rooms and Suites
FACILITIES..Cafe, Gym,
Outdoor swimming pool, Restaurant,
Rooftop terrace bar, Salon
GOOD TO KNOW.......................................Pet friendly
RECOMMENDED FOR...........................All-time favorite

A lively and luxurious design hotel located just moments from the High Line, Dream Downtown is vibrant and thoughtfully curated. Amenities include forty-inch (one meter) Samsung LED TVs with media hubs in every room and recessed audio speakers in the bathrooms. There is direct access to the beach club—the only sand beach in Manhattan—and pool from the deluxe rooms, the latter being fifty foot (fifteen meters) long and glass-bottomed.

Recommended by: Boris Bernaskoni, Bernaskoni

EXECUTIVE HOTEL LE SOLEIL NEW YORK
38 West 36th Street
Midtown
Manhattan
New York City 10018
+1 2126950003
hotellesoleil.com

CREDIT CARDS...Accepted
PRICE..Low-cost
TYPE...Hotel
ACCOMMODATION.......................161 Rooms and Suites
FACILITIES...............................Bar, Cafe, Gym, Restaurant
GOOD TO KNOW........................Pet friendly, Valet parking
RECOMMENDED FOR..Budget

"Best budget rooms in New York City."—Randa Tukan

Recommended by: Randa Tukan, HOK

THE KITANO HOTEL NEW YORK
66 Park Avenue
Midtown
Manhattan
New York City 10016
+1 2128857000
kitano.com

CREDIT CARDS...Accepted
PRICE..Mid-range
TYPE...Hotel
ACCOMMODATION.......................150 Rooms and Suites
FACILITIES....................................Bar, Gym, 2 Restaurants
GOOD TO KNOW.....................................Valet parking
RECOMMENDED FOR...Urban

Recommended by: Fumihiko Maki, Maki and Associates

MOXY NYC TIMES SQUARE
485 7th Avenue
Midtown
Manhattan
New York City 10018
+1 2129676699
marriott.com

CREDIT CARDS...Accepted
PRICE..Mid-range
TYPE...Hotel
ACCOMMODATION.......................612 Rooms and Suites
FACILITIES.........................Bar, Cafe, Gym, Restaurant,
Rooftop terrace bar
GOOD TO KNOW.......................................Pet friendly
RECOMMENDED FOR...Budget

"A hotel that brings whimsical design to a low budget construction that truly delights."—Andre Fu

Recommended by: André Fu, AFSO; George Yabu and Glenn Pushelberg, Yabu Pushelberg

NEW YORK MARRIOTT MARQUIS

1535 Broadway
Midtown
Manhattan
New York City 10036
+1 2123981900
marriott.com

CREDIT CARDS	Accepted
PRICE	High-end
TYPE	Hotel
ACCOMMODATION	1,966 Rooms and Suites
FACILITIES	3 Bars, Gym, Restaurant
GOOD TO KNOW	Valet parking
RECOMMENDED FOR	Family friendly, Wish I'd designed

Recommended by: Felino Palafox, Jr., Palafox Associates;
Rui Veloso, Adapteye

THE NEW YORKER, A WYNDHAM HOTEL

Corner 481 8th Avenue and 34th Street
Midtown
Manhattan
New York City 10001
+1 2129710101
newyorkerhotel.com

CREDIT CARDS	Accepted
PRICE	Mid-range
TYPE	Hotel
ACCOMMODATION	1,122 Rooms and Suites
FACILITIES	Bar, Gym, 3 Restaurants
GOOD TO KNOW	Pet friendly, Valet parking
RECOMMENDED FOR	Wish I'd designed

A stylish Art Deco hotel that dates from New York's exciting
Jazz Age, The New Yorker has classically furnished rooms and
three themed restaurants: a retro diner, an Italian trattoria,
and a bank-themed steakhouse in the vaults, all of which draw
upon the building's rich history.

Recommended by: Fosbury Architecture

THE NOMAD HOTEL

Corner 1170 Broadway and 28th Street
Midtown
Manhattan
New York City 10001
+1 2127961500
thenomadhotel.com

CREDIT CARDS	Accepted
PRICE	Mid-range
TYPE	Hotel
ACCOMMODATION	168 Rooms and Suites
FACILITIES	Bar, Gym, Restaurant
GOOD TO KNOW	Valet parking, Pet friendly
RECOMMENDED FOR	Where I live

"It feels like traveling to another era. Outstanding kitchen
and unique design."—Michel Abboud

Recommended by: Michel Abboud, SOMA; Guy Geier,
FXCollaborative

THE PENINSULA NEW YORK

Corner 700 Fifth Avenue and 55th Street
Midtown
Manhattan
New York City 10019
+1 2129562888
peninsula.com

CREDIT CARDS	Accepted
PRICE	Blow-out
TYPE	Hotel
ACCOMMODATION	239 Rooms and Suites
FACILITIES	2 Bars, Gym, Indoor swimming pool, Restaurant, Rooftop terrace bar, Sauna, Spa, Steam room
GOOD TO KNOW	Pet friendly
RECOMMENDED FOR	Where I live

"It represents quintessential Beaux-Arts glamour, with
bespoke finishes and grand ambience. Also, it still has the
best rooftop terrace in the city!"—Francesca Bucci

Recommended by: Francesca Bucci, BG Studio International

THE PLAZA NEW YORK
Corner 5th Avenue and Central Park South
Midtown
Manhattan
New York City 10019
+1 2127593000
theplazany.com

CREDIT CARDS	Accepted
PRICE	Blow-out
TYPE	Hotel
ACCOMMODATION	282 Rooms and Suites
FACILITIES	2 Bars, Gym, 3 Restaurants, Sauna, Spa
GOOD TO KNOW	Babysitting, Pet friendly
RECOMMENDED FOR	Where I live

Situated on the corner of Fifth Avenue and Central Park South, the Plaza Hotel has been an iconic New York City landmark since it first opened in 1907. Each of the guest rooms and suites is luxurious in the traditional hotel sense. For dining, the Palm Court has long been regarded as serving the finest afternoon tea in the city; the Todd English Food Hall has nine stations of international cuisine, and the Plaza Food Hall showcases high-end brands such as Ladurée and Épicerie Boulud.

Recommended by: Peter Eisenman, Eisenman Architects

POD51 HOTEL
230 East 51st Street
Midtown
Manhattan
New York City 10022
+1 8447637666
thepodhotel.com

CREDIT CARDS	Accepted
PRICE	Low-cost
TYPE	Hotel
ACCOMMODATION	348 Pods
FACILITIES	Cafe, Rooftop terrace
GOOD TO KNOW	Some pods have shared bathrooms
RECOMMENDED FOR	Budget

"A playful and modestly priced hotel with a great location in Manhattan."—Dennis Pieprz

Recommended by: Dennis Pieprz, Sasaki

THE RIVER CLUB OF NEW YORK
447 East 52nd Street
Midtown East
Manhattan
New York City 10022
+1 2127510100
riverclubnyc.com

CREDIT CARDS	Accepted
PRICE	Mid-range
TYPE	Hotel
ACCOMMODATION	11 Rooms
FACILITIES	Bar, Gym, Golf simulator, Indoor swimming pool, Restaurant, Tennis
GOOD TO KNOW	Child friendly
RECOMMENDED FOR	Best-kept secret

A private, family friendly sporting club that has been in operation since 1931. Rooms are designed to be a comfortable "home-from-home," and extra facilities—including car services—are also available.

Recommended by: Dominique Perrault, Dominique Perrault Architecture

THE ST. REGIS NEW YORK
Corner Two East 55th Street and 5th Avenue
Midtown
Manhattan
New York City 10022
+1 2127534500
marriott.com

CREDIT CARDS	Accepted
PRICE	Blow-out
TYPE	Hotel
ACCOMMODATION	230 Rooms and Suites
FACILITIES	Bar, Gym, Restaurant
GOOD TO KNOW	No pets, Valet parking
RECOMMENDED FOR	Luxury

"Every floor of this hotel has its own butler. Enough said."
—Dan Wood

Recommended by: Dan Wood, WORKac

MARITIME HOTEL
363 West 16th Street
Chelsea
Manhattan
New York City 10011
+1 2122424300
themaritimehotel.com

CREDIT CARDS...Accepted
PRICE..Mid-range
TYPE...Hotel
ACCOMMODATION.............................122 Rooms and Suites
FACILITIES...Bar, Gym, Restaurant
GOOD TO KNOW..Bicycle rentals
RECOMMENDED FOR..Wish I'd designed

"There is something so joyously optimistic about this
portholed building. I really like the well-equipped,
super-functional rooms in terms of design."
—Thomas Bartlett

Recommended by: Thomas Bartlett, Waldo Works

THE STANDARD HIGH LINE, NYC
848 Washington Street
Meatpacking District
Manhattan
New York City 10014
+1 2126454646
standardhotels.com

CREDIT CARDS...Accepted
PRICE..High-end
TYPE...Hotel
ACCOMMODATION.....................................338 Rooms
FACILITIES...4 Bars, Cafe, Gym,
Restaurant, Rooftop bar
GOOD TO KNOW.....................On-site nightclub, Pet friendly
RECOMMENDED FOR............................All-time favorite,
Urban, Where I live,
Wish I'd designed

Recommended by: Aljoša Dekleva and Tina Gregorič,
Dekleva Gregorič Architects; Juan Manuel Peláez Freidel
JUMP/Juan Manuel Peláez Arquitectos; Stéphane
Rasselet, Naturehumaine; Patrick Reymond, Atelier Oï;
Robert Sakula, Ash Sakula Architects; Hayes and James
Slade, Slade Architecture; Leonid Slonimskiy, KOSMOS
Architects; Dieter Vander Velpen, Dieter Vander Velpen
Architects; Ken Yeang, Hamzah & Yeang; Kateryna Zuieva,
AKZ Architectura

GRAMERCY PARK HOTEL
2 Lexington Avenue
Gramercy Park
Manhattan
New York City 10010
+1 2129203300
gramercyparkhotel.com

CREDIT CARDS...Accepted
PRICE..High-end
TYPE...Hotel
ACCOMMODATION.............................186 Rooms and Suites
FACILITIES...Bar, Restaurant
GOOD TO KNOW...................Child friendly, Valet parking
RECOMMENDED FOR..........................Best-kept secret,
Urban, Where I live

"It's in a nice part of New York City, and has wonderful
interiors and a great art collection. The staff offer
exceptional service. I have been coming to this hotel for
years, and they also know my favorite room. It has stunning
suites where you can work comfortably."—Ben van Berkel

Recommended by: Alfredo Payá Benedito, Noname29;
Ben van Berkel, UNStudio; Vincenzo De Cotiis, Vincenzo
De Cotiis Architects and Gallery; Florian Idenburg, SO–IL

THE JANE HOTEL
113 Jane Street
Greenwich Village
Manhattan
New York City 10014
+1 2129246700
thejanenyc.com

CREDIT CARDS...Accepted
PRICE..Mid-range
TYPE...Hotel
ACCOMMODATION.....................................170 Rooms
FACILITIES...Bar, Restaurant
GOOD TO KNOW..Bicycle rentals
RECOMMENDED FOR..Luxury, Urban

"Doesn't get any more luxurious than The Jane!"
—Erin and Ian Besler

Recommended by: Erin and Ian Besler, Besler & Sons;
Kateryna Zuieva, AKZ Architectura

THE BOWERY HOTEL

335 Bowery
Bowery
Manhattan
New York City 10003
+1 2125059100
theboweryhotel.com

CREDIT CARDS...Accepted
PRICE...Mid-range
TYPE...Hotel
ACCOMMODATION......................................135 Rooms and Suites
FACILITIES.................................Bar, Gym, Restaurant
GOOD TO KNOW............................Babysitting, Bicycle rentals,
Valet parking
RECOMMENDED FOR..Best-kept secret

"This place is in the heart of the Bowery has all the best amenities. The interior is finished with carpets, velvet-upholstered furniture, and glazed tiles —a historic recreation done well."—Rick Joy

Recommended by: Rick Joy, Studio Rick Joy

CROSBY STREET HOTEL

79 Crosby Street
SoHo
Manhattan
New York City 10012
+1 2122266400
firmdalehotels.com

CREDIT CARDS...Accepted
PRICE...High-end
TYPE...Hotel
ACCOMMODATION......................................86 Rooms and Suites
FACILITIES.................................Bar, Gym, Restaurant,
Screening room
GOOD TO KNOW................................Pet friendly, Valet parking
RECOMMENDED FOR...Urban

With interiors designed by Kit Kemp, Crosby Street Hotel is a seriously stylish boutique hotel with plenty of personality. Kemp's passion for art is reflected in the personal collection on display throughout the hotel—Crosby Street also organizes regular guided art walks, which start with a tour of the hotel itself and also take in some of Chelsea and Tribeca's leading commercial galleries. Other memorable features include a rooftop kitchen garden, which supplies the restaurant with fresh, seasonal produce and eggs from the hotel's Araucana chickens.

Recommended by: Kelly Hoppen, Kelly Hoppen Interiors

THE JAMES NEW YORK SOHO

27 Grand Street
SoHo
Manhattan
New York City 10013
+1 2124652000
jameshotels.com

CREDIT CARDS...Accepted
PRICE...Mid-range
TYPE...Hotel
ACCOMMODATION......................................114 Rooms and Suites
FACILITIES....................Bar, Gym, Outdoor swimming pool,
Restaurant, Rooftop terrace bar
GOOD TO KNOW............................Child friendly, Valet parking
RECOMMENDED FOR...Urban

"Great location in SoHo with a rooftop bar, lounge, pool, and great service."—Jodi Batay-Csorba

Recommended by: Jodi Batay-Csorba, Batay-Csorba Architects

THE MERCER

147 Mercer Street
SoHo
Manhattan
New York City 10012
+1 2129666060
mercerhotel.com

CREDIT CARDS...Accepted
PRICE...High-end
TYPE...Hotel
ACCOMMODATION......................................74 Lofts and Suites
FACILITIES.................................Bar, Restaurant, Yoga
GOOD TO KNOW................................Pet friendly, Valet parking
RECOMMENDED FOR................................Family friendly, Urban

"It is elegant and understated at the same time. It looks like it has always been there."—Piero Lissoni

Recommended by: Piero Lissoni, Lissoni Associati; Christian de Portzamparc, 2Portzamparc; Fernando Romero, FR–EE/ Fernando Romero Enterprise

SOHO GRAND NEW YORK
310 West Broadway
SoHo
Manhattan
New York City 10013
+1 2129653000
sohogrand.com

CREDIT CARDS...Accepted
PRICE..High-end
TYPE..Hotel
ACCOMMODATION..353 Lofts and Suites
FACILITIES................................Bar, Gym, Outdoor Restaurant
GOOD TO KNOW...............................Pet friendly, Valet parking
RECOMMENDED FOR..Urban

"It has great food, coziness, service, and location, and they always remember our names. The staircase is uber-cool." —Mark Landini

SoHo Grand Hotel is a stylish seventeen-story hotel located within easy access of all that Manhattan has to offer. Nespresso coffee machines, acoustic guitars and MacBook laptops are available in-room on request and there are three drinking and dining options, including outdoor space Gilligan's. It is a pet-friendly hotel, and complimentary bikes are available to hire.

Recommended by: Mark Landini, Landini Associates

FOUR SEASONS HOTEL NEW YORK DOWNTOWN
27 Barclay Street
Tribeca
Manhattan
New York City 10007
+1 6468801999
fourseasons.com

CREDIT CARDS...Accepted
PRICE..High-end
TYPE..Hotel
ACCOMMODATION................................189 Rooms and Suites
FACILITIES........................Bar, Gym, Indoor swimming pool,
Restaurant, Spa
GOOD TO KNOW....................................Child and pet friendly,
Valet parking
RECOMMENDED FOR...............Where I live, Wish I'd designed

Recommended by: Emre Arolat, EAA; Daniel Libeskind, Studio Libeskind

THE GREENWICH HOTEL
377 Greenwich Street
Tribeca
Manhattan
New York City 10013
+1 2129418900
thegreenwichhotel.com

CREDIT CARDS...Accepted
PRICE..High-end
TYPE..Hotel
ACCOMMODATION............................88 Penthouses and Suites
FACILITIES................................Gym, Indoor swimming pool,
Restaurant, Spa, Yoga
GOOD TO KNOW..Pet friendly
RECOMMENDED FOR....................................Where I live

"As a New Yorker, it's a hotel that feels like New York. Fantastic food and a tailored, comfortable lobby lounge, the place feels like home."—Forth Bagley

"The hotel's courtyard is a quiet, private retreat for guests only, where you can get a cocktail, relax, and gaze up at the sky."—David Rockwell

Recommended by: Forth Bagley, Kohn Pedersen Fox; David Rockwell, Rockwell Group

PUBLIC HOTEL
215 Chrystie Street
Lower East Side
Manhattan
New York City 10002
+1 2127356000
publichotels.com

CREDIT CARDS...Accepted
PRICE..Mid-range
TYPE..Hotel
ACCOMMODATION...........367 Lofts, Penthouses, and Rooms
FACILITIES............................2 Bars, Cafe, Gym, Restaurant,
GOOD TO KNOW..Pet friendly
RECOMMENDED FOR...All-time favorite,
Luxury, Urban, Where I live,
Wish I'd designed

"Excellent in all aspects. The attention to detail, from the room and its layout to the public areas and garden, to the furniture and arrival sequence, are all fantastic." —Anthony Mallows

Recommended by: Emre Arolat, EAA; Boris Bernaskoni, Bernaskoni; Ben Duckworth, Hassell; Matthias Hollwich, Hollwich Kushner; Marianne Kwok, Kohn Pedersen Fox; Anthony Mallows, WATG; Michael Meredith and Hilary Sample, MOS; Much Untertrifaller, Dietrich Untertrifaller Architects

THE WILLIAM VALE

111 North 12th Street
Greenpoint
Brooklyn
New York City 11249
+1 7186318400
thewilliamvale.com

CREDIT CARDS..Accepted
PRICE..High-end
TYPE..Hotel
ACCOMMODATION....................................183 Rooms and Suites
FACILITIES................................Bar, Outdoor swimming pool,
Restaurant, Rooftop terrace bar
GOOD TO KNOW...............................Pet friendly, Valet parking
RECOMMENDED FOR..Where I live

"Great rooms with views of Manhattan, and a mind-blowing rooftop bar and restaurant."—Adam Meshberg

Recommended by: Adam Meshberg, Meshberg Group

THE WILLIAMSBURG HOTEL

96 Wythe Avenue
Williamsburg
Brooklyn
New York City 11249
+1 7183628100
thewilliamsburghotel.com

CREDIT CARDS..Accepted
PRICE..High-end
TYPE..Hotel
ACCOMMODATION....................................147 Rooms and Suites
FACILITIES................................Bar, Outdoor swimming pool,
Restaurant, Rooftop terrace bar
GOOD TO KNOW...Pet friendly
RECOMMENDED FOR..Urban

"Amazing new-build industrial hotel full of character and charm."—Alex Michaelis

Recommended by: Alex Michaelis, Michaelis Boyd

WYTHE HOTEL

80 Wythe Avenue
Williamsburg
Brooklyn
New York City 11249
+1 7184608000
wythehotel.com

CREDIT CARDS..Accepted
PRICE..Mid-range
TYPE..Hotel
ACCOMMODATION..70 Lofts and Rooms
FACILITIES..Bar, Restaurant
GOOD TO KNOW..Pet friendly
RECOMMENDED FOR..All-time favorite,
Where I live, Wish I'd designed

"Discreet and hip. It also has the best burgers in Williamsburg."—Hani Rashid

Recommended by: Hiéronyme Lacroix and Simon Chessex, Lacroix Chessex; Adam Meshberg, Meshberg Group; Hani Rashid, Asymptote Architecture; Daniel Sundlin, Bjarke Ingels Group

1 HOTEL BROOKLYN BRIDGE

60 Furman Street
Brooklyn Heights
Brooklyn
New York City 11201
+1 3476962500
1hotels.com

CREDIT CARDS..Accepted
PRICE..High-end
TYPE..Hotel
ACCOMMODATION....................................195 Rooms and Suites
FACILITIES....................Bar, Cafe, Outdoor swimming pool
Restaurant, Spa
GOOD TO KNOW..Child and pet friendly
RECOMMENDED FOR..Where I live

"Best view of the city."—Thomas Leeser

The Brooklyn outpost of the stylish, environmentally conscious 1 Hotels has been designed with an emphasis on bringing nature inside. Rooms are bright and spacious, with accents of greenery and reclaimed materials, and dining focuses on seasonal, farm-to-fork eating supplied by local purveyors. Harriet's Rooftop & Lounge (complete with plunge pool), is where to head for panoramic views of the Manhattan skyline. The spa is in partnership with Bamford.

Recommended by: Thomas Leeser, Leeser Architecture

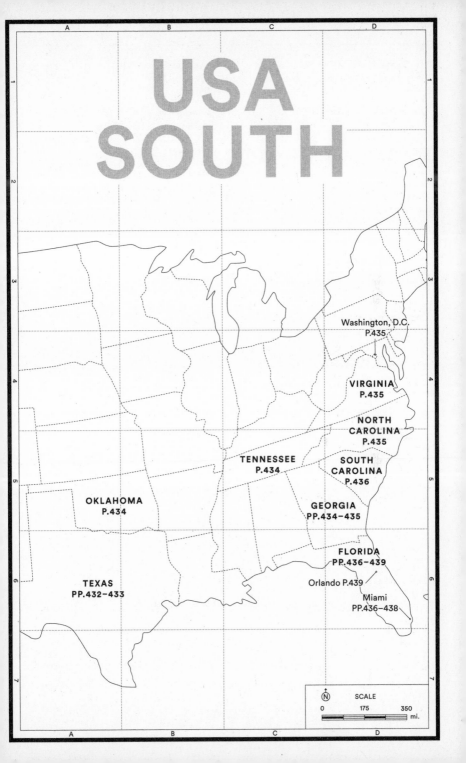

USA
SOUTH

Washington, D.C.
P.435

VIRGINIA
P.435

NORTH
CAROLINA
P.435

TENNESSEE
P.434

SOUTH
CAROLINA
P.436

OKLAHOMA
P.434

GEORGIA
PP.434–435

FLORIDA
PP.436–439

Orlando P.439

TEXAS
PP.432–433

Miami
PP.436–438

SCALE

0   175   350 mi.

HOTEL SAN JOSÉ

1316 South Congress Avenue
Austin
Texas 78704
+1 5128522350
sanjosehotel.com

CREDIT CARDS	Accepted
PRICE	Mid-range
TYPE	Hotel
ACCOMMODATION	40 Rooms and Suites
FACILITIES	Bar, Outdoor swimming pool
GOOD TO KNOW	Bicycle rentals, Pet friendly
RECOMMENDED FOR	All-time favorite, Eco-conscious

"The transformation of this run down motel into one of Austin's essential hotels is legendary. The imaginative integration of existing buildings with new buildings shows the true value of sustainability."—Carlos Jiménez

"The perfect interpretation of what a contemporary hotel should be like. Simple, yet emotionally generous."
—Ola Rune

Recommended by: Carlos Jiménez, Carlos Jiménez Studio; Ola Rune, Claesson Koivisto Rune Architects

CAVALRY COURT

200 Century Court
College Station
Texas 77840
+1 9794855586
calvarycourt.com

CREDIT CARDS	Accepted
PRICE	Mid-range
TYPE	Hotel
ACCOMMODATION	141 Rooms and Suites
FACILITIES	Bar, Outdoor swimming pool, Restaurant
GOOD TO KNOW	Bicycle rentals, Pet friendly
RECOMMENDED FOR	Budget

"Its courtyard has fire pits and a lawn, giving it a fun communal feel."—Lauren Rottet

[This hotel was designed by Rottet Studio.]

Recommended by: Lauren Rottet, Rottet Studio

HOTEL ALESSANDRA

1070 Dallas Street
Houston
Texas 77002
+1 7132428555
hotelalessandra-HOUSTON.com

CREDIT CARDS	Accepted
PRICE	Mid-range
TYPE	Hotel
ACCOMMODATION	223 Rooms and Suites
FACILITIES	Bar, Gym, Outdoor swimming pool, Restaurant, Spa
GOOD TO KNOW	Bicycle rentals, Valet parking
RECOMMENDED FOR	Where I live

"Wonderful location in downtown Houston, comfortable and convenient, with a quiet elegance and spartan luxury."
—Carlos Jiménez

"Blends Houston and old-world Spanish styles."
—Lauren Rottet

[This hotel was designed by Rottet Studio.]

Recommended by: Carlos Jiménez, Carlos Jiménez Studio; Lauren Rottet, Rottet Studio

HOTEL ZAZA HOUSTON MUSEUM DISTRICT

5701 Main Street
Houston
Texas 77005
+1 8888803244
hotelzaza.com

CREDIT CARDS	Accepted
PRICE	Mid-range
TYPE	Hotel
ACCOMMODATION	315 Rooms and Suites
FACILITIES	Bar, Outdoor swimming pool, Restaurant, Rooftop terrace bar, Sauna, Spa
GOOD TO KNOW	Pet friendly
RECOMMENDED FOR	Where I live

"Excellent location, exciting design, and exquisite gastronomic offering."—Farid Chacon

Recommended by: Farid Chacon, NMD NOMADAS

THE GAGE HOTEL
102 NW First Street Highway 90W
Marathon
Texas 79842
+1 4323864205
gagehotel.com

CREDIT CARDS...Accepted
PRICE...Mid-range
TYPE...Hotel
ACCOMMODATION....................47 Casitas, Rooms, and Suites
FACILITIES.....................Bar, Gym, Outdoor swimming pool,
Restaurant, Spa
GOOD TO KNOW...Pet friendly
RECOMMENDED FOR..Desert

"A true Texan hotel at the edge of Big Bend National Park.
Rustic, colorful, and charming rooms in the wilderness.
The White Buffalo Bar and the hotel's restaurant add to a
memorable stay."—Carlos Jiménez

Recommended by: Carlos Jiménez, Carlos Jiménez Studio

CIBOLO CREEK RANCH
67 County Road
Marfa
Texas 79843
+1 4322293737
cibolocreekranch.com

CREDIT CARDS...Accepted
PRICE...Mid-range
TYPE...Hotel
ACCOMMODATION.......70 Cottages, Haciendas, and Rooms
FACILITIES..Bar, Restaurant,
Wood-burning fireplace
GOOD TO KNOW..........................Bicycle rentals, Horse riding
RECOMMENDED FOR..................................Countryside, Desert

"Historic mission converted into a small hotel around a
lake, and offers amazing horseback riding through the
natural terrrain. It's also near Marfa, for Donald Judd's
Chinati Foundation."—Lauren Rottet

Recommended by: Roger Duffy, Skidmore, Owings & Merrill;
Lauren Rottet, Rottet Studio

EL COSMICO
802 South Highland Avenue
Marfa
Texas 79843
+1 4327291950
elcosmico.com

CREDIT CARDS...Accepted
PRICE..Low-cost
TYPE...Hotel
ACCOMMODATION........................1 Apartment and Campsite,
48 Trailers, Safari tents, and Yurts
FACILITIES..Yoga
GOOD TO KNOW..........................Bicycle rentals, Free parking
RECOMMENDED FOR....................................Eco-conscious

"There is something quite strange about staying in a
metal box in the desert next to Donald Judd's metal boxes
in the desert. These trailers are lined with ply and super
comfortable, with brilliant bedding and added-on terraces,
from which you can try to spot the 'Marfa lights' at night.
I love this town and this hotel."—Thomas Bartlett

Recommended by: Thomas Bartlett, Waldo Works

THUNDERBIRD HOTEL
601 West San Antonio Street
Marfa
Texas 79843
+1 4327291984
thunderbirdmarfa.com

CREDIT CARDS...Accepted
PRICE...Mid-range
TYPE...Hotel
ACCOMMODATION..24 Rooms
FACILITIES..............................Outdoor swimming pool
GOOD TO KNOW..........................Bicycle rentals, Free parking
RECOMMENDED FOR..................................Countryside, Desert

"From its famous 'Marfa Lights' to the Minimalist appeal
of Donald Judd's house and studio, Marfa is all about
the atmosphere. It appears mirage-like on the roadside,
after a day-long drive from Houston or San Antonio. The
Thunderbird Hotel looks like your standard Americana
motel, but has just enough sophisticated touches to make
your stay comfortable and chic. For a one-horse town,
there are an improbably large number of great bars and
restaurants within walking distance."—Grace Mortlock

Recommended by: Sam Chermayeff, Meyer-Grohbrügge
& Chermayeff; Mårten Claesson, Claesson Koivisto
Rune Architects; Johanna Meyer-Grohbrügge, Meyer-
Grohbrügge; Adrian Moreno and Maria Samaniego,
Arquitectura X; Grace Mortlock, Other Architects

INN AT PRICE TOWER

510 South Dewey Avenue
Bartlesville
Oklahoma 74003
+1 9183361000
pricetower.org

CREDIT CARDS..Accepted
PRICE...Mid-range
TYPE...Hotel
ACCOMMODATION.......................................19 Rooms and Suites
FACILITIES...Bar, Restaurant
GOOD TO KNOW..Pet friendly
RECOMMENDED FOR...Family friendly

"An intact, important Frank Lloyd Wright design with
inexpensive duplex suites. An amazing experience for
the price."—Louis Hedgecock

Recommended by: Louis Hedgecock, HOK Architects

21C MUSEUM HOTEL
OKLAHOMA CITY

900 West Main Street
Oklahoma City
Oklahoma 73106
+1 8449826900
21cmuseumhotels.com

CREDIT CARDS..Accepted
PRICE...Mid-range
TYPE...Hotel
ACCOMMODATION.......................................135 Rooms and Suites
FACILITIES.........................Bar, Gym, Restaurant, Sauna, Spa
GOOD TO KNOW..Valet parking
RECOMMENDED FOR...Urban

"The original building was designed by Albert Kahn as a
Ford factory. It's a really wonderful early Modernist building,
with a special and unique hospitality experience."
—Deborah Berke

[This hotel was designed by Deborah Berke Partners.]

Recommended by: Deborah Berke, Deborah Berke Partners

BLACKBERRY FARM

1471 West Millers Cove Road
Walland
Tennessee 37886
+1 8659848166
blackberryfarm.com

CREDIT CARDS..Accepted
PRICE...High-end (all-inclusive)
TYPE...Hotel
ACCOMMODATION....................................62 Cottages, Houses,
Rooms, and Suites
FACILITIES....................Bar, Gym, Outdoor swimming pool,
Restaurant, Spa, Yoga
GOOD TO KNOW........................Bicycle rentals, Child friendly
RECOMMENDED FOR..Countryside

"An idyllic and vast pastoral farm in the shadow of
America's Great Smoky Mountains; a few days at Blackberry
Farm make time stand still and are restorative beyond
explanation. A combination of exquisite refinement and
authentic country rusticity envelop the guests (of which
there are no more than 150) in a manner that is both
cinematic and poetic—what more could one ask for as the
quintessential country experience?"—Todd-Avery Lenahan

Recommended by: Todd-Avery Lenahan, TAL Studio

ATLANTA MARRIOTT MARQUIS

265 Peachtree Center Avenue
Atlanta
Georgia 30303
+1 4045210000
marriott.com

CREDIT CARDS..Accepted
PRICE...Mid-range
TYPE...Hotel
ACCOMMODATION................................1,569 Rooms and Suites
FACILITIES...Bar, Gym,
Indoor and outdoor swimming pools,
Spa
GOOD TO KNOW..Valet parking
RECOMMENDED FOR...Wish I'd designed

"Amazing spatial experience."—Daniel Sundlin

Recommended by: Daniel Sundlin, Bjarke Ingels Group

GREYFIELD INN
4 North Second Street
Cumberland Island
Georgia 32034
+1 9042616408
greyfieldinn.com

CREDIT CARDS..Accepted
PRICE...High-end (all-inclusive)
TYPE..Hotel
ACCOMMODATION.......................................16 Rooms and Suites
FACILITIES..Bar, Restaurant,
Wood-burning fireplace
GOOD TO KNOW...........................Bicycle rentals, Free parking
RECOMMENDED FOR...Island

Recommended by: Robert Sakula, Ash Sakula Architects

FOUR SEASONS HOTEL WASHINGTON, D.C.
2800 Pennsylvania Avenue North West
Washington
District of Columbia, 20007
+1 2023420444
fourseasons.com

CREDIT CARDS..Accepted
PRICE...High-end
TYPE..Hotel
ACCOMMODATION..................................222 Rooms and Suites
FACILITIES.......................Bar, Gym, Indoor swimming pool,
2 Restaurants,
Sauna, Spa, Steam room
GOOD TO KNOW.................................Babysitting, Pet friendly,
Valet parking
RECOMMENDED FOR...Where I live

"The saying goes, 'A gentleman never has knowledge of
any hotel in his own town,' but this place is always jumping
with politicians, actors, heads of state, and news types.
Great food and drinks, spa, services, valets who remember
your name (sort of), and elegant architecture."
—Simon Jacobsen

Recommended by: Simon Jacobsen, Jacobsen Architecture

THE INN AT LITTLE WASHINGTON
309 Middle Street
Washington
Virginia 22747
+1 5406753800
theinnatlittlewashington.com

CREDIT CARDS..Accepted
PRICE...High-end
TYPE..Inn
ACCOMMODATION..................23 Houses, Rooms, and Suites
FACILITIES...Restaurant
GOOD TO KNOW..................Bicycle rentals, Valet parking
RECOMMENDED FOR...Best-kept secret

"Just outside the capital of Washington, D.C., we discovered
this inn on a bike ride with friends, which covered the
battlefields of the American Civil War. I remember it for its
rare combination of good rooms, great atmosphere, and a
truly outstanding restaurant."—Norman Foster

Recommended by: Norman Foster, Foster + Partners

PROXIMITY HOTEL
704 Green Valley Road
Greensboro
North Carolina 27408
+1 8003798200
proximityhotel.com

CREDIT CARDS..Accepted
PRICE...Mid-range
TYPE..Hotel
ACCOMMODATION..................................147 Rooms and Suites
FACILITIES.....................Bar, Gym, Outdoor swimming pool,
Restaurant, Spa
GOOD TO KNOW..................Bicycle rentals, Valet parking
RECOMMENDED FOR...Eco-conscious

"This was the first LEED Platinum certified hotel in the
world, and offers a surprising and delightful bit of design
and culture in the South. The reception area offers a
bold cantilevered front desk, surrounded by a sunlight-filled
courtyard. I like to enjoy southern home cooking while
sitting in one of the large, comfy chairs."—Eric Corey Freed

Recommended by: Eric Corey Freed, OrganicArchitect

THE INN AT MIDDLETON PLACE

4290 Ashley River Road
Charleston
South Carolina 29414
+1 8435560500
theinnatmiddletonplace.com

CREDIT CARDS	Accepted
PRICE	Mid-range
TYPE	Hotel
ACCOMMODATION	24 Rooms and Suites
FACILITIES	Outdoor swimming pool, Restaurant
GOOD TO KNOW	Bicycle rentals, Child and pet friendly, Valet parking
RECOMMENDED FOR	Family friendly

"A family hotel where you can spend a week in the American countryside, riding horses, cycling, walking, and more. Close to the amazing Middleton Gardens Place, one of the most important American landscape heritage sites."
—Alfredo Payá Benedito

Recommended by: Alfredo Payá Benedito, Noname29

HAWKS CAY RESORT

61 Hawks Cay Boulevard
Duck Key
Florida 33050
+1 3057437000
hawkscay.com

CREDIT CARDS	Accepted
PRICE	Mid-range
TYPE	Hotel
ACCOMMODATION	177 Rooms and Villas
FACILITIES	Bar, Gym, Outdoor swimming pool, 4 Restaurants, Spa, Tennis
GOOD TO KNOW	Bicycle rentals, Water sports
RECOMMENDED FOR	Family friendly

Hawks Cay Resort is a laid-back resort on the secluded island of Duck Key. It has a range of experiences and activities to suit every guest, from water sports, scuba diving, and swimming with dolphins to its award-winning spa.

Recommended by: Randa Tukan, HOK

THE SAINT HOTEL KEY WEST, AUTOGRAPH COLLECTION

417 Eaton Street
Key West
Florida 33040
+1 3052943200
thesainthotelkeywest.com

CREDIT CARDS	Accepted
PRICE	Mid-range
TYPE	Hotel
ACCOMMODATION	36 Rooms
FACILITIES	Outdoor swimming pool, Restaurant
GOOD TO KNOW	Bicycle rentals, Valet parking
RECOMMENDED FOR	Beach

The Saint Hotel Key West is situated in the heart of Key West's "Old Town," just a short walk from the Ernest Hemingway House and Duval Street. Each of the rooms is bold in design and is equipped with flat-screen TVs and iPod docking stations. The hotel also has a pool; and a bar and restaurant serving French Creole cuisine.

Recommended by: Kelly Bair, Central Standard Office of Design

FOUR SEASONS HOTEL MIAMI

1435 Brickell Avenue
Downtown
Miami
Florida 33131
+1 3053583535
fourseasons.com

CREDIT CARDS	Accepted
PRICE	Mid-range
TYPE	Hotel
ACCOMMODATION	221 Residences, Rooms, and Suites
FACILITIES	Bar, Gym, Outdoor swimming pool, 2 Restaurants, Spa, Steam room
GOOD TO KNOW	Babysitting, Valet parking
RECOMMENDED FOR	Urban

"I stay here consistently for work; the rooms are always clean and well appointed, the facilities are great. I always enjoy talking with the staff and they take care of everything."—Adam Meshberg

Recommended by: Adam Meshberg, Meshberg Group

1 HOTEL SOUTH BEACH

2341 Collins Avenue
Miami Beach
Miami
Florida 33139
+1 8336253111
1hotels.com

CREDIT CARDS..Accepted
PRICE...High-end
TYPE...Hotel
ACCOMMODATION...................426 Rooms and Suites
FACILITIES....................Bar, Gym, Outdoor swimming pool,
4 Restaurants, Rooftop terrace bar,
Spa, Yoga
GOOD TO KNOW.....................................Child and pet friendly
RECOMMENDED FOR..Eco-conscious

An eco-conscious, family friendly hotel on the Miami
beachfront; rooms and communal spaces are furnished
using reclaimed materials. A wide range of dining options
is also available, including an organic poolside cafe.

Recommended by: Kelly Hoppen, Kelly Hoppen Interiors

COMO METROPOLITAN MIAMI BEACH

2445 Collins Avenue
Miami Beach
Miami
Florida 33140
+1 3056953600
comohotels.com

CREDIT CARDS..Accepted
PRICE..Mid-range
TYPE...Hotel
ACCOMMODATION.......................74 Rooms and Suites
FACILITIES..Bar, Gym,
Outdoor swimming pool,
Restaurant, Spa, Steam room
GOOD TO KNOW.........................Babysitting, Bicycle rentals
RECOMMENDED FOR..Spa

An elegant Art Deco hotel located on Miami's famous
beachfront, COMO Metropolitan Miami Beach is renowned
for its spa facilities. COMO Shambhala Urban Escape
is on the eighth floor, and includes a steam room, four
treatment rooms, and a stunning rooftop pool. There
are also complimentary yoga sessions available for guests.

Recommended by: Peter Eisenman, Eisenman Architects

FONTAINEBLEAU MIAMI BEACH

4441 Collins Avenue
Miami Beach
Miami
Florida 33140
+1 8005488886
fontainebleau.com

CREDIT CARDS..Accepted
PRICE...High-end
TYPE...Hotel
ACCOMMODATION................1,504 Rooms and Suites
FACILITIES...Bar, Gym,
Indoor and outdoor swimming pools,
9 Restaurants,
Spa, Steam room, Yoga
GOOD TO KNOW.......................................Pet friendly (small)
RECOMMENDED FOR..........Family friendly, Wish I'd designed

"This hotel, designed by legendary architect Morris
Lapidus, combines architectural history with lots and
lots of swimming pools, some made especially shallow
for younger kids."—Dieter Vander Velpen

Recommended by: David Rockwell, Rockwell Group;
Dieter Vander Velpen, Dieter Vander Velpen Architects

THE MIAMI BEACH EDITION

2901 Collins Avenue
Miami Beach
Miami
Florida 33140
+1 7862574500
editionhotels.com

CREDIT CARDS..Accepted
PRICE...High-end
TYPE...Hotel
ACCOMMODATION...................270 Rooms and Suites
FACILITIES....................Bar, Gym, Outdoor swimming pool,
Restaurant, Spa, Steam room
GOOD TO KNOW.......................................Bicycle rentals
RECOMMENDED FOR..Family friendly

Recommended by: George Yabu and Glenn Pushelberg,
Yabu Pushelberg

DELANO SOUTH BEACH
1685 Collins Avenue
South Beach
Miami
Florida 33139
+1 8005555001
morganshotelgroup.com

CREDIT CARDS	Accepted
PRICE	Mid-range
TYPE	Hotel
ACCOMMODATION	1 Apartment, 194 Bungalows, Rooms, and Suites
FACILITIES	Bar, Gym, Outdoor swimming pool, 2 Restaurants, Spa, Yoga
GOOD TO KNOW	Beach access
RECOMMENDED FOR	Best-kept secret, Luxury, Wish I'd designed

"Miami beach life with an outdoor bar."—V. Mitch McEwen

Recommended by: Piero Lissoni, Lissoni Associati;
V. Mitch McEwen, A(n) Office

THE STANDARD MIAMI
40 Island Avenue
South Beach
Miami
Florida 33139
+1 3056731717
standardhotels.com

CREDIT CARDS	Accepted
PRICE	Mid-range
TYPE	Hotel
ACCOMMODATION	100 Rooms and Suites
FACILITIES	Bar, Gym, Hammam, Outdoor swimming pool, Restaurant, Sauna, Spa, Steam room, Yoga
GOOD TO KNOW	Pet friendly, Valet parking
RECOMMENDED FOR	Spa

"Best pool and Turkish hammam in the western world;
I love going to Miami just to stay here."—Marcio Kogan

Recommended by: Marcio Kogan, Studio MK27

IBEROSTAR BERKELEY SHORE HOTEL
1610 Collins Avenue
South Beach
Miami
Florida 33139
+1 7866050810
iberostarberkeley.com

CREDIT CARDS	Accepted
PRICE	Mid-range
TYPE	Hotel
ACCOMMODATION	96 Rooms
FACILITIES	Bar, Gym, Outdoor swimming pool, Restaurant
GOOD TO KNOW	Valet parking
RECOMMENDED FOR	Best-kept secret

"Historic Art Deco building in an excellent South Beach
location with great dining, friendly staff, comfortable rooms,
and a fantastic terrace."—Claudia Urdaneta

Recommended by: Claudia Urdaneta, NMD NOMADAS

W SOUTH BEACH
2201 Collins Avenue
South Beach
Miami
Florida 33139
+1 3059383000
marriott.com

CREDIT CARDS	Accepted
PRICE	High-end
TYPE	Hotel
ACCOMMODATION	408 Rooms and Suites
FACILITIES	Bar, Gym, Outdoor swimming pool, Restaurant, Spa
GOOD TO KNOW	Bicycle rentals, Pet friendly
RECOMMENDED FOR	Urban

"I like to sit on the terrace and just watch the sun rising and
setting over the sea. The apartments allow for independent
living—a home away from home."—Olajumoke Adenowo

Recommended by: Olajumoke Adenowo, AD Consulting

FOUR SEASONS RESORT ORLANDO AT WALT DISNEY WORLD® RESORT

10100 Dream Tree Boulevard
Lake Buena Vista
Orlando
Florida 32836
+1 4073137777
fourseasons.com

CREDIT CARDS	Accepted
PRICE	High-end
TYPE	Resort
ACCOMMODATION	443 Rooms and Suites
FACILITIES	Bar, Gym, Outdoor swimming pool, 4 Restaurants, Spa, Tennis
GOOD TO KNOW	Babysitting, Valet parking
RECOMMENDED FOR	Family friendly

A luxury, secluded lakeside resort deep within the park, Four Seasons Resort Orlando at Walt Disney World® Resort is a relaxing holiday destination with plenty of facilities to keep younger and older guests alike entertained. The rooftop steakhouse, Capa, is an ideal spot from which to watch the nightly fireworks display.

Recommended by: Fernando Sordo Madaleno, Sordo Madaleno

SHERATON VISTANA RESORT VILLAS, LAKE BUENA VISTA/ORLANDO

8800 Vistana Centre Drive
Orlando
Florida 32821
+1 4072393100
marriott.com

CREDIT CARDS	Accepted
PRICE	Mid-range
TYPE	Resort
ACCOMMODATION	1,682 Villas
FACILITIES	Bar, Gym, Outdoor swimming pool, 3 Restaurants, Tennis
GOOD TO KNOW	Bicycle rentals
RECOMMENDED FOR	Family friendly

"All the services and facilities for great family vacations." —Gaston Atelman

Recommended by: Gaston Atelman, AFT Arquitectos

FOUR SEASONS HOTEL AT THE SURF CLUB

9011 Collins Avenue
Surfside
Florida 33154
+1 3053813333
fourseasons.com

CREDIT CARDS	Accepted
PRICE	High-end
TYPE	Hotel
ACCOMMODATION	77 Cabanas, Rooms, and Suites
FACILITIES	Bar, Gym, Outdoor swimming pool, 4 Restaurants, Sauna, Spa, Steam room, Yoga
GOOD TO KNOW	Bicycle rentals, Valet parking
RECOMMENDED FOR	Beach, Where I live

Recommended by: Vincenzo De Cotiis, Vincenzo De Cotiis Architects and Gallery; Bernardo Fort-Brescia, Arquitectonica; Richard Meier, Richard Meier & Partners Architects

COSTA D'ESTE BEACH RESORT & SPA

3244 Ocean Drive
Vero Beach
Florida 32963
+1 7725629919
costadeste.com

CREDIT CARDS	Accepted
PRICE	Mid-range
TYPE	Hotel
ACCOMMODATION	94 Rooms and Suites
FACILITIES	Bar, Gym, Outdoor swimming pool, Restaurant, Spa, Steam room, Yoga
GOOD TO KNOW	Bicycle rentals, Pet friendly, Valet parking
RECOMMENDED FOR	Best-kept secret

"This is Gloria Estefan's hotel, and it is just perfect. It is a converted five-story beach condo from the 1970s, located right on the beach, and the pool is almost on it too. Beach umbrellas, towels, and services are available surfside. Hotels like this can be picky and finicky, but not this one. The ocean sounds always prevail."—Simon Jacobsen

Recommended by: Simon Jacobsen, Jacobsen Architecture

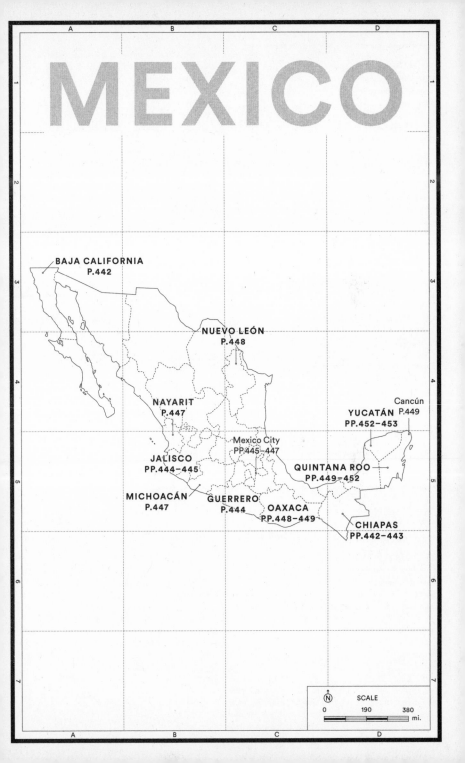

BRUMA
22760 Valle de Guadalupe
Valle de Guadalupe
Ensenada
Baja California 22760, Mexico
+52 16461168031
bruma.mx

CREDIT CARDS	Accepted
PRICE	Mid-range
TYPE	Resort
ACCOMMODATION	8 Rooms
FACILITIES	Outdoor swimming pool, Restaurant
GOOD TO KNOW	On-site vineyard
RECOMMENDED FOR	Countryside

"Amazing food at the hotel's restaurant."—Michel Rojkind

Recommended by: Michel Rojkind, Rojkind Arquitectos

CUATROCUATROS
El Tigre, Carretera libre Tijuana-Ensenada km89
El Sauzal de Rodriguez
Ensenada
Baja California 22760, Mexico
+52 6461746789
cabanascuatrocuatros.com.mx

CREDIT CARDS	Accepted
PRICE	Mid-range
TYPE	Hotel
ACCOMMODATION	14 Tents
FACILITIES	Bar, Restaurant
GOOD TO KNOW	On-site vineyard
RECOMMENDED FOR	Beach

Recommended by: Juan Manuel Peláez Freidel, JUMP/Juan Manuel Peláez Arquitectos

ENCUENTRO GUADALUPE
Carretera Tecate-Ensenada km75
Valle de Guadalupe
Ensenada
Baja California 22750, Mexico
+52 6461552935
grupoencuentro.com.mx

CREDIT CARDS	Accepted
PRICE	Mid-range
TYPE	Hotel
ACCOMMODATION	1 House, 22 Rooms and Suites
FACILITIES	Outdoor swimming pool
GOOD TO KNOW	Free parking, Pet friendly
RECOMMENDED FOR	Desert, Eco-conscious

"A campsite-feel but with modern details, situated in Mexico's leading wine-producing region."
—Salvador Reyes Ríos

Recommended by: Boris Bernaskoni, Bernaskoni; Salvador Reyes Ríos, Reyes Ríos + Larraín Arquitectos

HACIENDA UAYAMÓN
Carretera Uayamon-China-Edzna km20
Uayamón
Campeche 24530
Mexico
+52 9818130530
marriott.com

CREDIT CARDS	Accepted
PRICE	Mid-range
TYPE	Hacienda
ACCOMMODATION	12 Rooms and Suites
FACILITIES	Indoor swimming pool, Outdoor restaurant, Spa
GOOD TO KNOW	Child friendly, Free parking
RECOMMENDED FOR	All-time favorite

Recommended by: Salvador Reyes Ríos, Reyes Ríos + Larraín Arquitectos

CASA NA BOLOM
Avenida Vicente Guerrero 33
Barrio del Cerrillo
San Cristóbal de las Casas
Chiapas 29220
Mexico
+52 9676781418
nabolom.org

CREDIT CARDS	Accepted
PRICE	Low-cost
TYPE	Hotel
ACCOMMODATION	16 Rooms and Suites
FACILITIES	Restaurant
GOOD TO KNOW	Former home of archaeologist Frans Blom and his wife, Gertrude
RECOMMENDED FOR	Mountains

"It has a no-frills, laid-back feel, and its social and enviromental programs seek to help the local community thrive."—Salvador Reyes Ríos

Recommended by: Salvador Reyes Ríos, Reyes Ríos + Larraín Arquitectos

HOTEL BO

5 de Mayo 38
Barrio de Mexicanos
San Cristóbal de la Casas
Chiapas 29240
Mexico
+52 9676781516
hotelbo.mx

CREDIT CARDS	Accepted
PRICE	Mid-range
TYPE	Hotel
ACCOMMODATION	22 Rooms and Suites
FACILITIES	Restaurant, Spa
GOOD TO KNOW	Child friendly
RECOMMENDED FOR	Worth the travel

"This is a beautiful hotel in a magical city."
—Victor Legorreta Hernández

Recommended by: Victor Legorreta Hernández, Legorreta

HACIENDA DE SAN ANTONIO

Domicilio Conocido S/N
San Antonio
Comala
Colima 28463
Mexico
+52 3123160300
haciendadesanantonio.com

CREDIT CARDS	Accepted
PRICE	High-end
TYPE	Hacienda
ACCOMMODATION	25 Suites
FACILITIES	Bar, Gym, Outdoor swimming pool, Private airstrip, Restaurant, Tennis, Wood-burning fireplace, Yoga
GOOD TO KNOW	No pets
RECOMMENDED FOR	All-time favorite, Mountains

"A wonderful location and excellent renovation of a historic site."—Enrique Norten

Recommended by: Enrique Norten, TEN Arquitectos

LA CASA RODAVENTO

De Las Ratas 18
Centro Histórico
Valle de Bravo
Estado de México 51200
Mexico
+52 7266885546
lacasarodavento.com

CREDIT CARDS	Accepted
PRICE	Mid-range
TYPE	Hotel
ACCOMMODATION	7 Suites
FACILITIES	Jacuzzi, Outdoor swimming pool, Restaurant, Rooftop bar
GOOD TO KNOW	No pets
RECOMMENDED FOR	Eco-conscious, Mountains

"In the middle of the charming mountain town of Valle de Bravo, this is great architecture in a great place."
—Victor Legorreta Hernández

Recommended by: Victor Legorreta Hernández, Legorreta

DOS CASAS

Quebrada 101
Centro
San Miguel de Allende
Guanajuato 37700
Mexico
+52 4151544073
doscasas.com

CREDIT CARDS	Accepted
PRICE	Mid-range
TYPE	Hotel
ACCOMMODATION	1 Townhouse, 12 Rooms and Suites
FACILITIES	Gym, Hammam, Restaurant, Rooftop terrace bar, Sauna
GOOD TO KNOW	Award-winning restaurant
RECOMMENDED FOR	Best-kept secret

"A beautiful little hotel in San Miguel de Allende."
—Victor Legorreta Hernández

Recommended by: Victor Legorreta Hernández, Legorreta

BOCA CHICA
Caletilla 68B
Las Playas
Acapulco de Juárez
Guerrero 39390
Mexico
+52 7444827879
hotel-bocachica.com

CREDIT CARDS	Accepted
PRICE	Low-cost
TYPE	Hotel
ACCOMMODATION	36 Rooms and Suites
FACILITIES	Bar, Outdoor swimming pool, Restaurant, Sauna
GOOD TO KNOW	On-site disco
RECOMMENDED FOR	Beach

"Great service and ambience."—Fernando Romero

Recommended by: Fernando Romero, FR–EE/Fernando Romero Enterprise

LAS BRISAS IXTAPA
Playa Vista Hermosa
Alsace
Ixtapa
Guerrero 40880
Mexico
+52 7555532121
lasbrisashotels.com.mx

CREDIT CARDS	Accepted
PRICE	Low-cost
TYPE	Resort
ACCOMMODATION	416 Rooms and Suites
FACILITIES	Bar, Gym, Outdoor swimming pool, Private plunge pools, 6 Restaurants, Spa, Tennis
GOOD TO KNOW	Child friendly, No pets
RECOMMENDED FOR	Beach

"This hotel, designed by the great Mexican architect Ricardo Legorreta, is a bold, modern form that fits into the slope of the cliff."—Buzz Yudell

Recommended by: Buzz Yudell, Moore Ruble Yudell

AMULETO HOTEL
Calle Escenica 9
Playa la Ropa
Zihuatanejo
Guerrero 40880
Mexico
+1 2132801037
amuleto.net

CREDIT CARDS	Accepted
PRICE	Mid-range
TYPE	Hotel
ACCOMMODATION	5 Suites
FACILITIES	Bar, Gym, Outdoor restaurant and swimming pool, Yoga
GOOD TO KNOW	Free parking
RECOMMENDED FOR	Family friendly

"It's a luxury beach resort that is small and graciously accommodating."—David Miller

Recommended by: David Miller, Miller Hull Partnership

CASA HABITA (FORMERLY CASA LA FAYETTE)
Calle Miguel Lerdo de Tejada 2308
Lafayette
Guadalajara
Jalisco 44160
Mexico
+52 3336792000
casafayette.com

CREDIT CARDS	Accepted
PRICE	Low-cost
TYPE	Hotel
ACCOMMODATION	37 Rooms and Suites
FACILITIES	Bar, Barber shop, Outdoor swimming pool, Restaurant, Spa, Steam room
GOOD TO KNOW	Bicycle rentals, Valet parking
RECOMMENDED FOR	Budget

"The interior design style of Dimore Studio transported to a Mexican location and culture."—Salvador Reyes Ríos

Recommended by: Salvador Reyes Ríos, Reyes Ríos + Larraín Arquitectos

VERANA

Calle Zaragoza 404
Yelapa
Jalisco 48304
Mexico
+52 5553510984
verana.com

CREDIT CARDS	Accepted
PRICE	Mid-range
TYPE	Hotel
ACCOMMODATION	10 Houses
FACILITIES	Bar, Outdoor swimming pool, Restaurant, Spa, Yoga
GOOD TO KNOW	Access only by boat
RECOMMENDED FOR	Beach

Recommended by: Much Untertrifaller, Dietrich
Untertrifaller Architects

HOTEL CARLOTA

Río Amazonas 73
Cuauhtémoc
Mexico City 06500
Mexico
+52 5555116300
hotelcarlota.com

CREDIT CARDS	Accepted
PRICE	Mid-range
TYPE	Hotel
ACCOMMODATION	35 Rooms and Suites
FACILITIES	Outdoor swimming pool, Pool bar, Restaurant
GOOD TO KNOW	Valet parking
RECOMMENDED FOR	Where I live

Hotel Carlota was designed by a collective including
architecture firm Javier Sanchez and Cadena + Asoc.
Concept Design. It is a chic urban oasis which blends
original structural elements with modern sensibilities.
Rooms are chic and spacious, and the restaurant is a casual
affair focusing on healthy, sustainable produce.

Recommended by: Fernando Sordo Madaleno,
Sordo Madaleno

CONDESA DF

Avenia Veracruz 102
Condesa
Mexico City 6700
Mexico
+52 5552412600
condesadf.com

CREDIT CARDS	Accepted
PRICE	Mid-range
TYPE	Hotel
ACCOMMODATION	40 Rooms and Suites
FACILITIES	Gym, Restaurant, Rooftop terrace bar, Sauna
GOOD TO KNOW	Access only by boat
RECOMMENDED FOR	All-time favorite, Urban, Where I live, Worth the travel

"Elegant and peaceful adaptive architecture in the middle
of a megacity."—David Miller

"A casual, modern, and well-designed hotel with a locally
rooted vibe, unique room layouts, and a great rooftop bar."
—Daniel Sundlin

Recommended by: Diego Arraigada, Diego Arraigada
Arquitectos; Manuel Cervantes, CC Arquitectos; David
Miller, Miller Hull Partnership; Daniel Sundlin, Bjarke
Ingels Group

CONDESA HAUS

Cuernavaca 142
Condesa
Mexico City 6700
Mexico
+52 5552562494
condesahaus.com

CREDIT CARDS	Accepted
PRICE	Low-cost
TYPE	Bed and Breakfast
ACCOMMODATION	9 Rooms and Suites
FACILITIES	Rooftop terrace bar
GOOD TO KNOW	No pets
RECOMMENDED FOR	Best-kept secret

"Located in the tree-lined Condesa area of Mexico City,
the hotel and its owners are full of conviviality and charm."
—Isabelle Toland

Recommended by: Isabelle Toland, Aileen Sage Architects

STELLA

Amsterdam 141
Condesa
Mexico City 6100
Mexico
+52 5584355572
stellabb.com

CREDIT CARDS	Accepted
PRICE	Low-cost
TYPE	Bed and Breakfast
ACCOMMODATION	7 Rooms
FACILITIES	Terrace
GOOD TO KNOW	Bicycle rentals, Pet friendly
RECOMMENDED FOR	Budget

The house was originally built by Francisco Serrano in 1930 and is now a charming, budget-friendly, and eco-conscious bed and breakfast that has been restored in an Art Deco style that pays homage to Stella's past.

Recommended by: Juan Manuel Peláez Freidel, JUMP/Juan Manuel Peláez Arquitectos

DOWNTOWN MEXICO

Isabel la Catolica 30
El Centro
Mexico City 06002
Mexico
+52 5552822199
downtownmexico.com

CREDIT CARDS	Accepted
PRICE	Mid-range
TYPE	Hotel
ACCOMMODATION	17 Rooms and Suites
FACILITIES	Rooftop swimming pool
GOOD TO KNOW	Pet friendly
RECOMMENDED FOR	Urban

"The hotel is located in the midst of Mexico City's historic center; each room is a different take on modest urban luxury, with beautiful light and distinct ceiling heights and profiles. It is a radical transformation of a historical building."—Carlos Jiménez

Recommended by: Carlos Jiménez, Carlos Jiménez Studio

CAMINO REAL POLANCO

Calzada General Mariano Escobedo 700
Polanco
Mexico City 11590
Mexico
+52 5552638888
caminoreal.com

CREDIT CARDS	Accepted
PRICE	Mid-range
TYPE	Hotel
ACCOMMODATION	712 Rooms and Suites
FACILITIES	Gym, 3 Outdoor swimming poos, 10 Restaurants
GOOD TO KNOW	Babysitting, Valet parking
RECOMMENDED FOR	All-time favorite, Family friendly, Urban, Where I live, Wish I'd designed, Worth the travel

"Legorreta's bold colors and dramatic forms appeal to all ages."—Deborah Berke

"One of the most successful architectural hotels by the late Ricardo Legorreta, influenced by the great Mexican architect Luis Barragán."—Richard England

"Although a prime business hotel, it is also a great family friendly place filled with space and light. Like a small city, it is crossed by color-infused streets that look into gardens, fountains, trees, and pools. It never disappoints."
—Carlos Jiménez

"It is a shining example of South American Modernism with lots of bright color."—Chris Wilkinson

Camino Real Polanco was originally designed as a museum by Ricardo Legorreta, and today is an iconic hotel situated just a short distance from the Museum of Modern Art, Chapultepec Castle, and the Museum of Anthropology. Rooms are in six adjoining properties, and facilities include three pools and ten restaurants serving a range of cuisines.

Recommended by: Deborah Berke, Deborah Berke Partners; Sam Chermayeff, Meyer-Grohbrügge & Chermayeff; Richard England, Richard England Architects; Carlos Ferrater, OAB; Luis Ferreira-da-Silva, Luis Ferreira-da-Silva Architects; Angela García de Paredes, Paredes Pedrosa Arquitectos; Carlos Jiménez, Carlos Jiménez Studio; Rafael de La-Hoz Castanys, Rafael de La-Hoz Arquitectos; Victor Legorreta Hernández, Legorreta; Michel Rojkind, Rojkind Arquitectos; Chris Wilkinson, Wilkinson Eyre Architects

HABITA HOTEL

Avenida Presidente 201
Polanco
Mexico City 11580
Mexico
+52 5552823100
hotelhabita.com

CREDIT CARDS..Accepted
PRICE..Mid-range
TYPE..Hotel
ACCOMMODATION........................32 Rooms and Suites
FACILITIES..................................Gym, Jacuzzi, Restaurant,
Rooftop terrace bar and pool
GOOD TO KNOW...............................Pet friendly, Valet parking
RECOMMENDED FOR...Urban

Habita Hotel is a chic design hotel in the heart of the
fashionable Polanco district and has a range of minimalist-chic
rooms—some with private terraces. There's an open-air
terrace and bar on the sixth floor, and a pool deck on the fifth
floor. Amenities include access to the BMW house car,
curated in-house music channels, and toiletries by New York
brand Malin + Goetz.

Recommended by: Enrique Norten, TEN Arquitectos

CASA GRANDE HOTEL BOUTIQUE

Portal Matamoros 98
Centro Histórico
Morelia
Michoacán 58000
Mexico
+1 8000874200
casagrandemorelia.com.mx

CREDIT CARDS..Accepted
PRICE..Mid-range
TYPE..Hotel
ACCOMMODATION...12 Suites
FACILITIES........................Bar, Restaurant, Rooftop terrace
GOOD TO KNOW...Babysitting
RECOMMENDED FOR...Urban

"A colonial house restored to become a modern boutique
hotel in downtown Morelia."—Salvador Reyes Ríos

Recommended by: Salvador Reyes Ríos, Reyes Ríos +
Larraín Arquitectos

FOUR SEASONS RESORT
PUNTA MITA

Ramal Carretera Federal 200 km19
Punta Mita
Bahía de Banderas
Nayarit 63734
Mexico
+52 3292916000
fourseasons.com

CREDIT CARDS..Accepted
PRICE..High-end
TYPE...Resort
ACCOMMODATION....................177 Rooms, Suites, and Villas
FACILITIES.......................Gym, 4 Outdoor swimming pools,
4 Restaurants, Yoga
GOOD TO KNOW.........................Beach access, Child friendly
RECOMMENDED FOR...Luxury

"Excellent service in a beautiful place."
—Victor Legorreta Hernández

Recommended by: Victor Legorreta Hernández, Legorreta

HARAMARA RETREAT

Playa Escondida
Sayulita
Nayarit 63734
Mexico
+52 3292913038
haramararetreat.com

CREDIT CARDS..Accepted
PRICE..Mid-range
TYPE...Resort
ACCOMMODATION....................................18 Casitas and Dorms
FACILITIES.............................Outdoor swimming pool,
Private beach, Restaurant,
Spa, Yoga
GOOD TO KNOW..No pets
RECOMMENDED FOR...Eco-conscious

"Simple, cliffside rooms without walls in the middle of acres
of private tropical jungle, with a pristine, isolated beach.
There are also great yoga facilities."—Craig Dykers

"Completely off-grid, self-sustaining, and quiet—heaven!"
—Louis Hedgecock

Recommended by: Craig Dykers, Snøhetta;
Louis Hedgecock, HOK Architects

HABITA MTY

Avenida José Vasconcelos 150 Ote
San Pedro Garza García
Monterrey
Nuevo León 66220
Mexico
+52 8183355900
hotelhabitamty.com

CREDIT CARDS..Accepted
PRICE...Mid-range
TYPE...Hotel
ACCOMMODATION.........................39 Rooms and Suites
FACILITIES......................................Gym, Restaurant,
Rooftop pool and bar
GOOD TO KNOW...Pet friendly
RECOMMENDED FOR.............................Worth the travel

Recommended by: Belén Moneo and Jeffrey Brock,
Moneo Brock

CASA OAXACA

García Vigil 407
Centro Histórico
Oaxaca 68000
Mexico
+52 9515144173
casaoaxaca.com.mx

CREDIT CARDS..Accepted
PRICE...Mid-range
TYPE...Hotel
ACCOMMODATION.............................7 Rooms and Suites
FACILITIES..................Outdoor swimming pool, Restaurant,
Roofrop terrace, Steam room
GOOD TO KNOW...Free parking
RECOMMENDED FOR...................................Countryside

"In the middle of the beautiful colonial city of Oaxaca.
Great food."—Victor Legorreta Hernández

Recommended by: Victor Legorreta Hernández, Legorreta

LA CASONA DE TITA

Calle Manuel Garcia Vigil 805
Centro Histórico
Oaxaca 68000
Mexico
+52 9515161400
lacasonadetitaoaxaca.com

CREDIT CARDS..Accepted
PRICE...Mid-range
TYPE...Hotel
ACCOMMODATION..6 Rooms
FACILITIES....................................Bar, Restaurant
GOOD TO KNOW...No pets
RECOMMENDED FOR...........................Best-kept secret

La Casona de Tita is a quaint, well-appointed hotel housed in
a nineteenth-century building in the center of Oaxaca. Each of
the six rooms is spacious and individually decorated with
antique and contemporary furniture and Oaxacan textiles.
All of the artwork on show in the hotel is part of a temporary
exhibition, and available to purchase from the reception.
Food focuses on Oaxacan cuisine, incorporating old family
recipes. A nearby private apartment is also available to book.

Recommended by: Enrique Norten, TEN Arquitectos

BAHÍA DE LA LUNA

Playa la Boquilla
Pochutla
Oaxaca 70900
Mexico
+52 9585895020
bahiadelaluna.com

CREDIT CARDS....................Accepted but not Amex
PRICE...Mid-range
TYPE...Resort
ACCOMMODATION..................12 Cabanas and Rooms
FACILITIES.......................................Bar, Restaurant
GOOD TO KNOW...............Beach access, Pet friendly
RECOMMENDED FOR...............................Eco-conscious

"Blissful is the word that comes to mind. Atop high cliffs,
overlooking the Pacific and facing west. No hot running
water, no windows, pool, or amenities. Just the endless
sound of giant waves crashing against rocks. Earthly delight.
This is, by far, the most minimized human footprint in
dwelling I have experienced in my life."—Alireza Razavi

Recommended by: Alireza Razavi, Studio Razavi
Architecture

HOTEL ESCONDIDO
Carretera Federal km113
Puerto Escondido
Oaxaca 71983
Mexico
+52 9545822224
hotelescondido.com

CREDIT CARDS..Accepted
PRICE..Mid-range
TYPE..Hotel
ACCOMMODATION...16 Palapas
FACILITIES.....................................Outdoor swimming pool,
Private beach, Plunge pools,
Restaurant, Spa
GOOD TO KNOW................................Children not allowed
RECOMMENDED FOR.....................................Beach, Countryside

Hotel Escondido is a charming hotel located on a tranquil
beach, just a short distance from the surfing hub of
Puerto Escondido. Each of the sixteen palapas (traditional
thatched-roof cottages) has been tastefully finished and
has its own private pools and terraces, where massages
can be arranged.

**Recommended by: Bernard Dubois, Bernard Dubois
Architects; Enrique Norten, TEN Arquitectos**

LE BLANC SPA RESORT
Boulevard Kukulcan km10
Cancún
Quintana Roo 77500
Mexico
+1 8887020913
leblancsparesort.com

CREDIT CARDS..Accepted
PRICE..High-end (all-inclusive)
TYPE...Resort
ACCOMMODATION..................................260 Rooms and Suites
FACILITIES..5 Bars, Gym,
3 Outdoor swimming pools,
5 Restaurants, Sauna, Spa
GOOD TO KNOW..Free parking
RECOMMENDED FOR...All-time favorite

Le Blanc Spa Resort is an all-inclusive, adults-only beachside
resort. Rooms are bright and spacious and include double
whirlpool baths, pillow menus, and in-room aromatherapy.
Personal butler service is also available. The resort offers
a range of dining options, from fine dining to Japanese and
Mexican-inspired cuisine.

Recommended by: Guy Geier, FXCollaborative

NIZUC
Boulevard Kukulcan Mz 59 Lote 1-03 km 21.26
Punta Nizuc
Cancún
Quintana Roo 77500
Mexico
+52 9988915700
nizuc.com

CREDIT CARDS..Accepted
PRICE...High-end
TYPE..Hotel
ACCOMMODATION...274 Rooms and Suites
FACILITIES...Gym,
Outdoor and private swimming pools,
Restaurant, Spa
GOOD TO KNOW...........Beach access, Child and pet friendly,
Free parking
RECOMMENDED FOR...Beach

Nizuc is a stunning luxury resort inspired by Mayan
architecture that combines beautiful design, excellent
cuisine, and world-class wellness facilities with practicality
and a desire to create the ultimate guest experience.
The separate accommodations have even been divided
into adult-only and family only areas.

Recommended by: Chris McDonough, The Gettys Group

COQUI COQUI COBA PAPHOLCHAC
RESIDENCE & SPA
Lado Sur Laguna
Coba
Quintana Roo 87780
Mexico
+52 19841681600
coquicoqui.com

CREDIT CARDS..Accepted
PRICE..Mid-range
TYPE..Hotel
ACCOMMODATION...5 Suites and Villa
FACILITIES.........................Bar, 2 Outdoor swimming pools,
Restaurant, Spa
GOOD TO KNOW..On-site perfumery
RECOMMENDED FOR..Best-kept secret,
Worth the travel

"A very relaxed ambience."—Manuel Cervantes

"A luxury resort hidden in the jungle that celebrates the
local culture, traditions, and landscape."—Isabelle Toland

**Recommended by: Manuel Cervantes, CC Arquitectos;
Isabelle Toland, Aileen Sage Architects**

POSADA MAWIMBI

Igualdad Manzana 1 Lote 1
Playa de Holbox
Holbox Island
Quintana Roo 77310
Mexico
+52 9848752003
mawimbi.com

CREDIT CARDS..Accepted
PRICE...Mid-range
TYPE..Hotel
ACCOMMODATION..........................11 Bungalows and Rooms
FACILITIES................................Bar, Private beach, Restaurant
GOOD TO KNOW..Child friendly
RECOMMENDED FOR..Best-kept secret

"The simple and straightforward design of the buildings allows the guest to sleep to the sound of the wind and the sea. Breakfast and lunch are served in a restaurant where the floor is the white sand of the beach itself. The bedrooms are located in front of one of the most beautiful and unspoiled beaches in Mexico, with pristine waters and idyllic weather most of the year. The island is in the Yum-Balam Biosphere Reserve, which is home to pink flamingos, dolphins, and whale sharks."—Daniel Mangabeira

Recommended by: Daniel Mangabeira, BLOCO Arquitetos

BANYAN TREE MAYAKOBA

Carretera Federal Chetumal-Puerto Juárez km298
Riviera Maya
Playa del Carmen
Quintana Roo 77710
Mexico
+1 8552890202
banyantree.com

CREDIT CARDS..Accepted
PRICE...High-end
TYPE...Resort
ACCOMMODATION..............................117 Residences and Villas
FACILITIES.......................................Outdoor swimming pool,
Poolside bar, 4 Restaurants,
Spa, Tennis
GOOD TO KNOW..Pet friendly
RECOMMENDED FOR..Worth the travel

Recommended by: Claudio Lucchesi, Urban Future Organization

ROSEWOOD MAYAKOBA

Carretera Federal Cancún-Playa del Carmen km298
Solidaridad
Playa del Carmen
Quintana Roo 77710
Mexico
+52 9848758000
rosewoodhotels.com

CREDIT CARDS..Accepted
PRICE...High-end
TYPE...Resort
ACCOMMODATION..................................129 Rooms and Suites
FACILITIES.......................................Golf, Gym, Private beach,
Private plunge pools, 5 Restaurants,
Sauna, Spa, Steam room
GOOD TO KNOW..Child friendly
RECOMMENDED FOR..Family friendly

"Great design, beaches, and food."—Bruce Kuwabara

Recommended by: Bruce Kuwabara, KPMB Architects

THE EXPLOREAN KOHUNLICH

Desviacion Ruinas de Kohunlich km6.5
Chetumal
Ruinas Kohunlích
Quintana Roo 43110
Mexico
+52 5552018350
explorean.com

CREDIT CARDS..Accepted
PRICE...Mid-range (all-inclusive)
TYPE..Hotel
ACCOMMODATION........................40 Bungalows and Cabanas
FACILITIES....................Bar, Gym, Outdoor swimming pool,
Sauna, Spa
GOOD TO KNOW..No pets
RECOMMENDED FOR..Family friendly

"Beautiful hotel hidden in the middle of the Mayan jungle."
—Victor Legorreta Hernández

Recommended by: Victor Legorreta Hernández, Legorreta

SCUBA CLUB COZUMEL

Avenida Rafael E Melgar km1.5
Colonos Cuzamil
San Miguel de Cozumel
Quintana Roo 77600
Mexico
+52 9878720663
scubaclubcozumel.com

CREDIT CARDS	Accepted
PRICE	Low-cost (all-inclusive)
TYPE	Hotel
ACCOMMODATION	61 Rooms
FACILITIES	Bar, Dive center, Gym, Outdoor swimming pool, Restaurant
GOOD TO KNOW	Beach access
RECOMMENDED FOR	Budget

"This is where hardcore divers hang out and tell their war stories by the Caribbean. It's cheap, very minimal—it has hammocks—and it's all about the diving."—Antoine Predock

Recommended by: Antoine Predock, Antoine Predock Architect

VENTANAS AL MAR

Carretera Costera Oriente km43.5
Playa Chen Rio
San Miguel de Cozumel
Quintana Roo 77600
Mexico
+52 9842672237
ventanasalmarcozumel.com

CREDIT CARDS	Accepted but not Amex
PRICE	Mid-range
TYPE	Hotel
ACCOMMODATION	16 Rooms
FACILITIES	Bar, Outdoor swimming pool, Restaurant
GOOD TO KNOW	Beach access, Child friendly
RECOMMENDED FOR	Eco-conscious

"Probably the most ecologically minded place I have ever stayed. Turtles lay their eggs on the beach, and later, everyone helps the newborns into the sea."
—Simon Mitchell

Recommended by: Simon Mitchell, Sybarite

AZULIK

Carretera Tulum Ruinas km5
Tulum
Quintana Roo 77780, Mexico
+52 9849800640
azulik.com

CREDIT CARDS	Accepted
PRICE	Mid-range
TYPE	Resort
ACCOMMODATION	48 Villas
FACILITIES	Beach bar, Spa
GOOD TO KNOW	No electric lights or television
RECOMMENDED FOR	Beach, Best-kept secret, Eco-conscious

An eco-conscious collection of beautifully designed villas, designed to blend effortlessly with the surrounding jungle. There is no electric light or television in the villas, allowing guests (adults only) to truly switch off from the outside world. Dining options include Mexican-Japanese fusion and Mayan-Mexican avant-garde cuisine, and the spa has a range of wellness therapies inspired by Mayan traditions.

Recommended by: Hasan Çalışlar, Erginoğlu & Çalışlar; Andres Remy, Remy Architects; Hugo Sauzay, Festen Architecture

BE TULUM

Carretera Tulum-Boca Paila km10
Zona Hotelera
Tulum
Quintana Roo 77780, Mexico
+52 9848032243
betulum.com

CREDIT CARDS	Accepted
PRICE	High-end
TYPE	Hotel
ACCOMMODATION	64 Suites
FACILITIES	Beach bar, Outdoor swimming pool, 3 Restaurants, Sauna, Spa, Yoga
GOOD TO KNOW	Cash free
RECOMMENDED FOR	Beach, Eco-conscious

Be Tulum is a lifestyle hotel which epitomizes the barefoot luxury experience. Its suites have been designed to capture the serene nature of its location between the jungle, white sand beaches, and the sea. There is a wellness center for daily yoga classes as well as traditional temazcal ceremonies.

Recommended by: Florian Idenburg, SO–IL; Fernando Romero, FR–EE/Fernando Romero Enterprise

HOTEL TIKI TIKI TULUM
Calle 6 Bis Sur S/N Tulum
Quintana Roo 77780, Mexico
+52 9846885005
hoteltikitikitulum.com

CREDIT CARDS	Accepted
PRICE	Mid-range
TYPE	Hotel
ACCOMMODATION	15 Suites
FACILITIES	Outdoor swimming pool, Restaurant
GOOD TO KNOW	Child friendly
RECOMMENDED FOR	Beach

"This hotel is 1950s Miami meets a tropical, boho vibe. The striped pool is Instagram gold."—Dieter Vander Velpen

Recommended by: Dieter Vander Velpen, Dieter Vander Velpen Architects

MAYA TULUM RESORT
Carretera Tulum-Boca Payla Lote 10 km7
Tulum
Quintana Roo 77780, Mexico
+52 19841164495
mayatulum.com

CREDIT CARDS	Accepted
PRICE	High-end
TYPE	Resort
ACCOMMODATION	49 Bungalows, Cabanas, and Suites
FACILITIES	Beach access, Restaurant, Yoga
GOOD TO KNOW	Child friendly
RECOMMENDED FOR	Beach, Eco-conscious

Recommended by: Thomas Leeser, Leeser Architecture

NÔMADE
Carretera Cancún–Tulum km10
Tulum
Quintana Roo 77880, Mexico
+52 9848032243
nomadetulum.com

CREDIT CARDS	Accepted
PRICE	Mid-range
TYPE	Hotel
ACCOMMODATION	51 Rooms, Suites, Tents, and Villas
FACILITIES	Outdoor swimming pool, 2 Restaurants, Yoga
GOOD TO KNOW	Beach access, Cash-free
RECOMMENDED FOR	Beach

"Great for local cultural activities and events."
—Michel Rojkind

"Jungle hotel with a Bedouin-inspired design close to the beach. It's a transcendental experience."—Daniel Sundlin

Recommended by: Michel Rojkind, Rojkind Arquitectos; Daniel Sundlin, Bjarke Ingels Group

HACIENDA SAC CHICH
Casa de Maquinas Calle 16
Acanceh
Yucatán 97380
Mexico
+52 9993519400
haciendasacchich.com

CREDIT CARDS	Accepted
PRICE	Blow-out
TYPE	Hacienda
ACCOMMODATION	9 Rooms
FACILITIES	Outdoor swimming pool, Rooftop lounge
GOOD TO KNOW	Child friendly
RECOMMENDED FOR	Best-kept secret

Recommended by: Salvador Reyes Ríos, Reyes Ríos + Larraín Arquitectos

CHABLÉ RESORT & SPA
Tablaje 642
Chocholá
Yucatán 97816
Mexico
+52 5541614262
chableresort.com

CREDIT CARDS	Accepted
PRICE	Blow-out
TYPE	Resort
ACCOMMODATION	40 Casitas and Villas
FACILITIES	Gym, Outdoor and private swimming pools, 3 Restaurants, Spa
GOOD TO KNOW	Pet friendly
RECOMMENDED FOR	All-time favorite, Countryside, Spa

Recommended by: Fernando Sordo Madaleno, Sordo Madaleno; Rui Veloso, Adapteye

HACIENDA ITZINCAB CÁMARA

Calle 35, 60 and 63
Colonia Buenavista
Mérida
Yucatán 97125
Mexico
+52 9999234777
privatehaciendas.com

CREDIT CARDS..Accepted
PRICE.................................High-end (all-inclusive)
TYPE..Hacienda
ACCOMMODATION...................................14 Rooms
FACILITIES............................3 Outdoor swimming pools
GOOD TO KNOW......................................Child friendly
RECOMMENDED FOR................................Family friendly

A stunning restored private hacienda built on an ancient
Mayan site (and complete with an ancient Mayan pyramid).
It has a total of fourteen bedrooms in the main house
and outbuildings, three swimming pools, a massage space,
hammocks, and bicycles. All meals are included. It is the
ideal base for a large family reunion or group holiday.

Recommended by: José Juan Rivera Rio, JJRR/Arquitectura

ROSAS & XOCOLATE

Paseo Montejo 480
Centro
Mérida
Yucatán 97000
Mexico
+52 9999242992
rosasandxocolate.com

CREDIT CARDS..Accepted
PRICE...Mid-range
TYPE..Hotel
ACCOMMODATION........................17 Rooms and Suites
FACILITIES.............................Bar, Outdoor swimming pool,
Restaurant, Spa
GOOD TO KNOW.........................Award-winning restaurant
RECOMMENDED FOR...................................Where I live

"A great location on Montejo Avenue; the interpretation
of Mexican culture is fresh and contemporary."
—Salvador Reyes Ríos

Recommended by: Salvador Reyes Ríos, Reyes Ríos +
Larraín Arquitectos

HACIENDA PETAC

Domicilio Conocido S/N
Petac
Yucatán 97315
Mexico
+52 9991617265
haciendapetac.com

CREDIT CARDS..Accepted
PRICE.................................High-end (all-inclusive)
TYPE..Hacienda
ACCOMMODATION...7 Rooms
FACILITIES....................Gym, Outdoor swimming pool, Spa
GOOD TO KNOW......................................Child friendly
RECOMMENDED FOR................................Countryside

"Lush surroundings and top service; the atmosphere is made
all the better by the colonial hacienda."
—Salvador Reyes Ríos

Recommended by: Salvador Reyes Ríos, Reyes Ríos +
Larraín Arquitectos

HACIENDA TEMOZON

Carretera Merida-Uxmal km182
Temozon Sur
Yucatán 97825
Mexico
+52 9999238089
thehaciendas.com

CREDIT CARDS..Accepted
PRICE...Mid-range
TYPE..Hacienda
ACCOMMODATION........................27 Rooms and Suites
FACILITIES..Bar, Heliport,
Outdoor swimming pool,
Restaurant, Spa, Tennis
GOOD TO KNOW......................................Child friendly
RECOMMENDED FOR................................Countryside

"This is a great, adaptive reuse of an old hacienda with a
luxurious and charming atmosphere. The stables have been
converted into beautiful rooms."—Hasan Çalışlar

Recommended by: Hasan Çalışlar, Erginoğlu & Çalışlar;
José Juan Rivera Rio, JJRR/Arquitectura

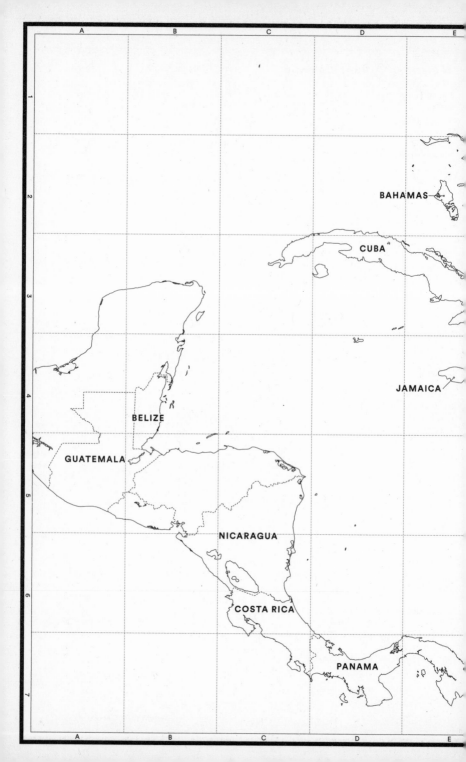

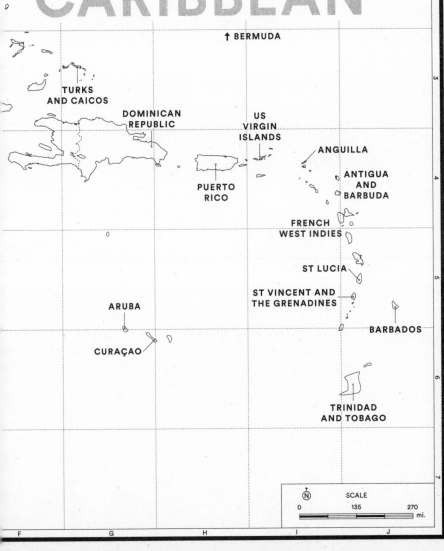

CENTRAL
AMERICA AND
CARIBBEAN

↑ BERMUDA

TURKS
AND CAICOS

DOMINICAN
REPUBLIC

US
VIRGIN
ISLANDS

ANGUILLA

ANTIGUA
AND
BARBUDA

PUERTO
RICO

FRENCH
WEST INDIES

ST LUCIA

ST VINCENT AND
THE GRENADINES

ARUBA

BARBADOS

CURAÇAO

TRINIDAD
AND TOBAGO

↑ N   SCALE

0   135   270
                   mi.

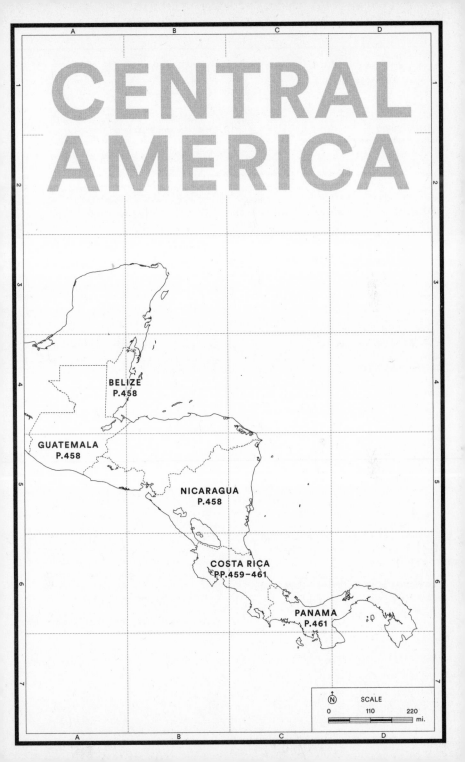

CENTRAL AMERICA

BELIZE
P.458

GUATEMALA
P.458

NICARAGUA
P.458

COSTA RICA
PP.459-461

PANAMA
P.461

N

SCALE

0   110   220
mi.

LAS LAGUNAS

Carretera San Miguel km1.5
Flores
Petén 17001
Guatemala
+502 77900300
laslagunashotel.com

CREDIT CARDS	Accepted
PRICE	Mid-range
TYPE	Hotel
ACCOMMODATION	19 Suites
FACILITIES	Nature reserve, Restaurant, Spa
GOOD TO KNOW	Bicycle rentals, Child friendly
RECOMMENDED FOR	Beach, Worth the travel

"A wonderful experience surrounded by nature in the middle of a forest."—Andrea Maffei

Recommended by: Andrea Maffei, Andrea Maffei Architects

HOTEL QUINTA DE LAS FLORES

Calle del Hermano Pedro 6
Antigua
Sacatepéquez 03001
Guatemala
+502 77937900
quintadelasflores.com

CREDIT CARDS	Accepted
PRICE	Low-cost
TYPE	Hotel
ACCOMMODATION	19 Casitas and Rooms
FACILITIES	Bar, Outdoor swimming pool, Restaurant
GOOD TO KNOW	Free parking
RECOMMENDED FOR	Family friendly

"A former seventeenth-century bath house, this offers great views of the landscape and a historical context." —Salvador Reyes Ríos

Recommended by: Salvador Reyes Ríos, Reyes Rios + Larraín Arquitectos

TURTLE INN

Placencia
Stann Creek District
Belize
+1 8663565881
thefamilycoppolahideaways.com

CREDIT CARDS	Accepted
PRICE	High-end
TYPE	Resort
ACCOMMODATION	25 Cottages and Villas
FACILITIES	Beach bar, Outdoor restaurant and swimming pool, 3 Restaurants, Spa
GOOD TO KNOW	Child friendly
RECOMMENDED FOR	Eco-conscious

This was the first luxury resort that filmmaker Francis Ford Coppola opened in the 1990s. Turtle Inn is an idyllic retreat with seventeen thatched cottages, eight villas—a private island for a truly secluded holiday—and a range of dining options. It is also a stone's throw from the artisan shops of Placencia, a nearby fishing village with bags of charm.

Recommended by: Chris McDonough, The Gettys Group

DEREK'S PLACE

Little Corn Island 54214
Nicaragua
+505 84421398
dereksplacelittlecorn.com

CREDIT CARDS	Accepted
PRICE	Low-cost
TYPE	Hotel
ACCOMMODATION	5 Cabanas
FACILITIES	Beach access, Restaurant
GOOD TO KNOW	On-site dive center
RECOMMENDED FOR	Island

A simple yet charming collection of five beachfront cabanas made of natural, recycled materials. All verandas face east so guests can enjoy watching sunrise from their rooms. Derek's Place also has an on-site dive center, and optional home-cooked meals are served family style.

Recommended by: Charles Renfro, Diller Scofidio + Renfro

FOUR SEASONS RESORT COSTA RICA AT PENINSULA PAPAGAYO

Liberia Guanaste km26 al Norte del Doit
Peninsula Papagayo
Carrillo
Guanacaste 05000, Costa Rica
+506 26960000
fourseasons.com

CREDIT CARDS..Accepted
PRICE..High-end
TYPE..Resort
ACCOMMODATION....:.....182 Residences, Rooms, and Suites
FACILITIES..Golf, Gym,
3 Outdoor swimming pools,
5 Restaurants, Sauna, Spa
GOOD TO KNOW..Free parking
RECOMMENDED FOR...............................Eco-conscious

"Supports the local economy by buying produce only from local farmers that are committed to environmentally sensitive growing techniques. All the fish and seafood is caught locally."—Michel Abboud

Recommended by: Michel Abboud, SOMA

HOTEL PUNTA ISLITA

160 Punta Islita Beach
Playa Islita
Bejuco
Guanacaste 50201, Costa Rica
+506 26563500
marriott.com

CREDIT CARDS..Accepted
PRICE..Mid-range
TYPE..Resort
ACCOMMODATION.....................57 Rooms, Suites, and Villas
FACILITIES............................Beach access, Beach bar, Gym,
Outdoor swimming pool,
2 Restaurants, Spa
GOOD TO KNOW..............................Babysitting, Child friendly
RECOMMENDED FOR...............................Eco-conscious

Hotel Punta Islita is a stylish, family friendly, eco-luxury resort on a lush hilltop overlooking the stunning Costa Rican coastline. Sustainability—for both the environment and local communities—is a strong focus for the hotel, which is involved in a number of initiatives including with NGOs. The resort also has a range of complimentary activities, including cookery classes, zip-lining, art classes, and horse riding.

Recommended by: Fernando Sordo Madaleno, Sordo Madaleno

POAS VOLCANO LODGE

Vara Blanca
Heredia 31698
Costa Rica
+506 24822194
poasvolcanolodge.com

CREDIT CARDS..Accepted
PRICE..Mid-range
TYPE..Lodge
ACCOMMODATION................................1 House and 11 Rooms
FACILITIES...Restaurant,
Wood-burning fireplace, Yoga
GOOD TO KNOW..No pets
RECOMMENDED FOR....................................Mountains

"The hotel brings the spirit of Costa Rica's mountains alive through the expression of its site-sourced materials."
—Rodrigo Carazo

Recommended by: Rodrigo Carazo, Carazo Architecture

HOTEL BANANA AZUL

Playa Negra Limón
Puerto Viejo de Talamanca
Limón 70401
Costa Rica
+506 27502035
bananaazul.com

CREDIT CARDS..Accepted
PRICE..Low-cost
TYPE..Hotel
ACCOMMODATION...................................22 Cabins, Rooms,
Suites, and Villas
FACILITIES......................................Bar, Beach access,
Outdoor swimming pool,
Restaurant
GOOD TO KNOW...Child friendly
RECOMMENDED FOR..Budget

"Impressive location, surrounded by tropical gardens, a beautiful pool, and an ocean view."—Michel Abboud

Recommended by: Michel Abboud, SOMA

PACUARE LODGE

Pacuare River Turrialba
Siquirres
Limón 1000
Costa Rica
+506 40330060
pacuarelodge.com

CREDIT CARDS	Accepted
PRICE	Blow out (all-inclusive)
TYPE	Lodge
ACCOMMODATION	20 Suites and Villas
FACILITIES	Outdoor swimming pool, Pool bar, Restaurant, Spa
GOOD TO KNOW	Arrivals by white-wafter rafting
RECOMMENDED FOR	Eco-conscious

With its stylish, Cabécar-inspired architecture, locally sourced cuisine, and unrivalled jungle location—accessed by four-wheel drive, raft, or helicopter—Pacuare Lodge is an ideal base from which to explore the Costa Rican landscape in style. Its suites are spacious and luxurious, and built using lumber from a reforestation project run by small farmers. A range of cultural, culinary, and adventure experiences are available, as well as a selection of luxurious spa treatments.

Recommended by: Urko Sanchez, Urko Sanchez Architects

LAPA RIOS ECOLODGE

Cabo Matapalo
Puerto Jiménez
Puntarenas 00011
Costa Rica
+506 40400418
laparios.com

CREDIT CARDS	Accepted
PRICE	High-end (all-inclusive)
TYPE	Lodge
ACCOMMODATION	17 Bungalows
FACILITIES	Bar, Outdoor swimming pool, Restaurant
GOOD TO KNOW	Child friendly
RECOMMENDED FOR	Eco-conscious

"A place that shows you how delicate the ecosystem is. As a guest, you feel a real relationship to nature rather than a large hotel that pushes back and creates barriers to keep it at bay."—Simon Jacobsen

Recommended by: Simon Jacobsen, Jacobsen Architecture

PLAYA CATIVO LODGE

Playa Cativo
Golfo Dulce
Puntarenas 60701
Costa Rica
+506 27756262
playacativo.com

CREDIT CARDS	Accepted
PRICE	Blow-out
TYPE	Hotel
ACCOMMODATION	18 Rooms
FACILITIES	Bar, Outdoor swimming pool, Spa
GOOD TO KNOW	Access only by boat
RECOMMENDED FOR	Eco-conscious

"A unique, off-grid luxury experience on an inaccessible beach, surrounded by jungle, and with seven-star service." —Rodrigo Carazo

Recommended by: Rodrigo Carazo, Carazo Architecture

PRANAMAR VILLAS

Playa Hermosa
Santa Teresa
Cobano
Puntarenas 60111
Costa Rica
+506 26400852
pranamarvillas.com

CREDIT CARDS	Accepted
PRICE	Mid-range
TYPE	Hotel
ACCOMMODATION	10 Bungalows and Villas
FACILITIES	Bar, Beach access, Outdoor swimming pool, Restaurant, Spa, Yoga
GOOD TO KNOW	Child friendly
RECOMMENDED FOR	Family friendly

"With individual villas set next to the ocean, it also has a great pool surrounded by nature."—Rodrigo Carazo

Recommended by: Rodrigo Carazo, Carazo Architecture

HOTEL GRANO DE ORO

Calle 30, Avenida 2 and 4
San José 10107
Costa Rica
+506 22553322
hotelgranodeoro.com

CREDIT CARDS	Accepted
PRICE	Mid-range
TYPE	Hotel
ACCOMMODATION	40 Rooms and Suites
FACILITIES	Bar, Restaurant, Sauna
GOOD TO KNOW	Child friendly
RECOMMENDED FOR	Where I live

"The hotel brings back the glory of early twentieth-century
San José through its architecture and a great attention
to detail."—Rodrigo Carazo

Recommended by: Rodrigo Carazo, Carazo Architecture

PUNTA CARACOL ACQUA LODGE

Punta Caracol
Bocas del Toro Island
Panama
+507 7579410
puntacaracol.com.pa

CREDIT CARDS	Accepted
PRICE	Mid-range
TYPE	Lodge
ACCOMMODATION	9 Suites
FACILITIES	Private beach, Restaurant
GOOD TO KNOW	Pet friendly, Snorkeling
RECOMMENDED FOR	Eco-conscious

Recommended by: Dan Wood, WORKac

VILLA CAMILLA

Playa Los Destiladeros
Pedasí
Los Santos
Panama
+ 507 9943100
pedasioceanproperties.com

CREDIT CARDS	Accepted
PRICE	Mid-range
TYPE	Hotel
ACCOMMODATION	7 Rooms and Suites
FACILITIES	Bar, Beach access, Gym, Outdoor restaurant and swimming pool
GOOD TO KNOW	Free parking
RECOMMENDED FOR	Where I live

"Great architecture and building craftsmanship. Unusual in
the level of detail for both buildings and furniture, it's an
eclectic combination of historic and vernacular styles, but
very well done."—Nilson Ariel Espino

Recommended by: Nilson Ariel Espino, Suma Arquitectos

WALDORF ASTORIA PANAMA

Corner 47th and Uruguay Streets
Panama City
Panama
+507 2948000
waldorfastoria.hilton.com

CREDIT CARDS	Accepted
PRICE	Mid-range
TYPE	Hotel
ACCOMMODATION	130 Rooms and Suites
FACILITIES	Gym, Outdoor swimming pool, Poolside bar, Restaurant
GOOD TO KNOW	No pets
RECOMMENDED FOR	Best-kept secret

Recommended by: Ludovico Centis, The Empire

THE BUENAVENTURA GOLF & BEACH RESORT PANAMA, AUTOGRAPH COLLECTION

340 Calle 3ra Buenaventura
Rio Hato
Coclé
Panama
+507 9083333
thebuenaventurahotel.com

CREDIT CARDS	Accepted
PRICE	Mid-range
TYPE	Resort
ACCOMMODATION	114 Rooms, Suites, and Villas
FACILITIES	Golf, 12 Outdoor pools, 2 Poolside bars, Private beach, 8 Restaurants, Tennis
GOOD TO KNOW	Babysitting, Pet friendly
RECOMMENDED FOR	Family friendly

"Extraordinary surroundings: Spanish colonial architecture
with beautiful landscaping, beach, and pool facilities."
—Claudia Urdaneta

Recommended by: Claudia Urdaneta, NMD NOMADAS

CUBA AND CARIBBEAN

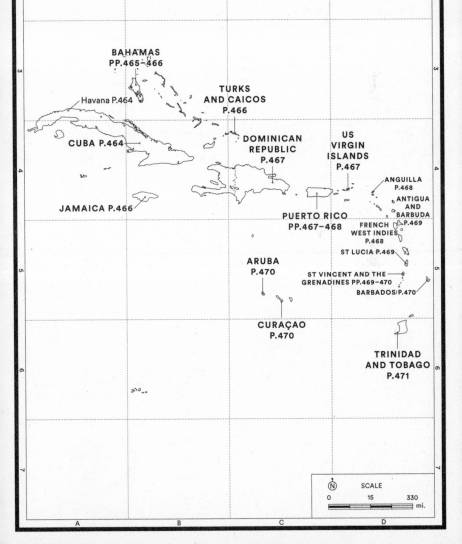

↑ BERMUDA
PP.464–465

BAHAMAS
PP.465–466

Havana P.464

TURKS
AND CAICOS
P.466

CUBA P.464

DOMINICAN
REPUBLIC
P.467

US
VIRGIN
ISLANDS
P.467

ANGUILLA
P.468

ANTIGUA
AND
BARBUDA
P.469

JAMAICA P.466

PUERTO RICO
PP.467–468

FRENCH
WEST INDIES
P.468

ST LUCIA P.469

ARUBA
P.470

ST VINCENT AND THE
GRENADINES PP.469–470

BARBADOS P.470

CURAÇAO
P.470

TRINIDAD
AND TOBAGO
P.471

Ⓝ   SCALE
0   15   330
                    mi.

HOTEL CLUB AMIGO FARO LUNA
Carretera Pasacaballo km18
Cienfuegos 55100
Cuba
+53 43548012

CREDIT CARDS	Accepted
PRICE	Low-cost
TYPE	Hotel
ACCOMMODATION	41 Rooms
FACILITIES	Bar, Outdoor swimming pool, Restaurant
GOOD TO KNOW	Child friendly, Free parking
RECOMMENDED FOR	Budget

"The family learned to scuba dive in the nearby coral reefs. This place recalled a time when every hotel looked like a Hilton, albeit here a small Communist slab of concrete."
—Simon Henley

Recommended by: Simon Henley, Henley Halebrown

ROC PRESIDENTE HOTEL
Corner Calle Calzada Numero 110 and Esquina
Avenida de los Presidentes
Vedado
Havana 10400
Cuba
+53 78381801
hotelrocpresidente.com

CREDIT CARDS	Accepted but not Amex
PRICE	Low-cost
TYPE	Hotel
ACCOMMODATION	158 Rooms and Suites
FACILITIES	Bar, Outdoor swimming pool, 3 Restaurants
GOOD TO KNOW	Wifi not included
RECOMMENDED FOR	Budget

Recommended by: Alberto Lievore, Lievore Altherr

TRYP HABANA LIBRE
Calle M
Vedado
Havana 10400
Cuba
+53 78346100
hotelhabanalibre.com

CREDIT CARDS	Accepted
PRICE	Mid-range
TYPE	Hotel
ACCOMMODATION	569 Rooms
FACILITIES	2 Bars, Outdoor swimming pool, 4 Restaurants, Salon
GOOD TO KNOW	Child friendly, On-site nightclub
RECOMMENDED FOR	Worth the travel

"You'll find yourself in a time capsule when you enter this hotel, with its 1950s lobby interior still completely intact. Definitely have dinner at the restaurant El Polinesio at the base of the hotel—Tiki style done right!"
—Dieter Vander Velpen

Recommended by: Dieter Vander Velpen, Dieter Vander Velpen Architects

COCO REEF
South Shore Road
Mt Pleasant
Paget Parish PG04
Bermuda
+1 4412365416
cocoreefbermuda.com

CREDIT CARDS	Accepted
PRICE	Mid-range
TYPE	Resort
ACCOMMODATION	128 Rooms and Suites
FACILITIES	Bar, Outdoor swimming pool, Private beach, Tennis
GOOD TO KNOW	No pets
RECOMMENDED FOR	Best-kept secret

"One of the least expensive hotels on one of the most beautiful pink beaches in Bermuda."—Francesca Bucci

Recommended by: Francesca Bucci, BG Studio International

CORAL BEACH & TENNIS CLUB

34 South Road
Mt Pleasant
Paget Parish PG04
Bermuda
+1 4412362233
coralbeachclub.com

CREDIT CARDS	Accepted
PRICE	High-end
TYPE	Hotel
ACCOMMODATION	40 Cottages, Rooms, and Suites
FACILITIES	Bar, Gym, Outdoor swimming pool, Private beach, 3 Restaurants
GOOD TO KNOW	Child friendly
RECOMMENDED FOR	Best-kept secret

"Its worn-in, slightly nostalgic look makes the beach sparkle and the cocktail bar feels like a time machine."
—Forth Bagley

Recommended by: Forth Bagley, Kohn Pedersen Fox

ELBOW BEACH

60 South Shore Road
Elbow Beach
Paget Parish PG04
Bermuda
+1 4412363535
elbowbeachbermuda.com

CREDIT CARDS	Accepted
PRICE	Mid-range
TYPE	Resort
ACCOMMODATION	98 Cottages, Rooms, and Suites
FACILITIES	Beach access, Gym, 4 Restaurants, Spa
GOOD TO KNOW	Babysitting
RECOMMENDED FOR	Beach

"The hotel dates back to 1903 and it was considered the prime resort for celebrities in the 1950s and 1960s. The main building is quite traditional and elegant, but you really want to stay in the secluded, luxurious, and very modern cottages in the garden by the pink beach. And, as Mark Twain said, 'You go to heaven if you want to, I'd rather stay right here in Bermuda.'"—Francesca Bucci

Recommended by: Francesca Bucci, BG Studio International

FAIRMONT SOUTHAMPTON

101 South Shore Road
Southampton SN02
Bermuda
+1 4412388000
fairmont.com

CREDIT CARDS	Accepted
PRICE	Mid-range
TYPE	Resort
ACCOMMODATION	593 Rooms and Suites
FACILITIES	Indoor and Outdoor swimming pools, Private beach, 10 Restaurants, Sauna, Spa
GOOD TO KNOW	Child friendly, No pets
RECOMMENDED FOR	Family friendly

"It is the closest hotel to Horseshoe Bay, with an extraordinary view of the island. The hotel has an extensive children's club with all-day organized activities and island excursions for both parents and children."
—Francesca Bucci

Recommended by: Francesca Bucci, BG Studio International

THE LANDING

Bay Street
Dunmore Town
Harbour Island
Bahamas
+1 2423332707
harbourislandlanding.com

CREDIT CARDS	Accepted
PRICE	Mid-range
TYPE	Hotel
ACCOMMODATION	13 Cottages and Rooms
FACILITIES	Bar, Outdoor swimming pool, Restaurant, Tennis
GOOD TO KNOW	Pink sand beaches
RECOMMENDED FOR	Beach

"Nothing can distract you from the beach."
—Marco Costanzi

Recommended by: Marco Costanzi, Marco Costanzi Architects

PINK SANDS
Chapel Street
Dunmore Town
Harbour Island
Bahamas
+1 2423332030
pinksandsresort.com

CREDIT CARDS..Accepted
PRICE...Blow-out
TYPE..Resort
ACCOMMODATION....................................29 Cottages and Villas
FACILITIES............................2 Bars, Outdoor swimming pool,
Private beach, 2 Restaurants, Tennis
GOOD TO KNOW..............................Babysitting, Child friendly
RECOMMENDED FOR..Family friendly

Recommended by: Bernardo Fort-Brescia, Arquitectonica

THE CLIFF HOTEL
West End Road
Negril
Jamaica
+1 8766320919
thecliffjamaica.com

CREDIT CARDS..Accepted
PRICE..Mid-range
TYPE...Hotel
ACCOMMODATION...33 Suites and Villas
FACILITIES...Bar, Beach access,
Outdoor swimming pool,
Restaurant, Spa
GOOD TO KNOW...Free parking
RECOMMENDED FOR..Family friendly

"Staff are lovely and the kids and parents are all well
looked after."—Simon Mitchell

Recommended by: Simon Mitchell, Sybarite

AMANYARA
Northwest Point
Providenciales
Turks and Caicos
+1 6499418133
aman.com

CREDIT CARDS..Accepted
PRICE...Blow-out
TYPE..Resort
ACCOMMODATION.................................54 Pavilions and Villas
FACILITIES...Bar, Gym,
Outdoor swimming pool,
Private beach, 2 Restaurants,
Snorkelling, Spa, Tennis, Yoga
GOOD TO KNOW...................Babysitting, On-site dive center,
Pet friendly
RECOMMENDED FOR..Island, Luxury

"No air conditioning and only strictly necessary electricity;
the hotel has a strong connection to the water—from the
seaview to the pools."—Piero Lissoni

Recommended by: Michel Abboud, SOMA;
Manuel Cervantes, CC Arquitectos; Bruce Kuwabara,
KPMB Architects; Piero Lissoni, Lissoni Associati

COMO PARROT CAY
Parrot Cay
Turks and Caicos
+1 6499467788
comohotels.com

CREDIT CARDS..Accepted
PRICE...Blow-out
TYPE..Resort
ACCOMMODATION.........................61 Rooms, Suites, and Villas
FACILITIES..............................Gym, Outdoor swimming pool,
Private beach,
3 Restaurants, Spa, Tennis, Yoga
GOOD TO KNOW...Babysitting,
On-site coconut and
banana plantations
RECOMMENDED FOR...All-time favorite,
Luxury, Spa

"Great villas with total privacy and every conceivable luxury."
—Joana Leandro Vasconcelos

Recommended by: Antoine Predock, Antoine Predock
Architect; Joana Leandro Vasconcelos, Atelier In.vitro

SECRET HARBOUR BEACH RESORT

6280 Estate Nazareth
Nazareth Bay
Saint Thomas 00802
US Virgin Islands
+1 3407756550
secretharbourvi.com

CREDIT CARDS...Accepted
PRICE...Mid-range
TYPE...Condominium resort
ACCOMMODATION.........................48 Apartments and Rooms
FACILITIES...Beach bar, Gym,
Outdoor swimming pool,
3 Restaurants, Tennis
GOOD TO KNOW...........................Child friendly, Water sports
RECOMMENDED FOR...............................Beach, Family friendly,
Best-kept secret, Worth the travel

"This hotel is perfect for a simple, tropical vacation with intimate, safe beaches and a good restaurant. The staff are attentive but don't hover, and the atmosphere allows parents to relax while kids can safely amuse themselves." —Hayes and James Slade

Recommended by: Hayes and James Slade, Slade Architecture

LUXURY BAHIA PRINCIPE ESMERALDA

Arena Gorda Macao
Punta Cana
La Alracia 23000
Dominican Republic
+1 8095521444
bahia-principe.com

CREDIT CARDS...Accepted
PRICE.......................................Blow-out (all-inclusive)
TYPE...Resort
ACCOMMODATION....................570 Rooms and Suites
FACILITIES...3 Bars, Gym,
2 Outdoor swimming pools,
6 Restaurants, Spa
GOOD TO KNOW...........................Child friendly, On-site disco
RECOMMENDED FOR...............................Family friendly

"The sheer size of the interconnected properties offer so much for every family member; there are water sports of every type. The hotel hosts spontaneous activities, plus it's right on the beach."—Olajumoke Adenowo

Recommended by: Olajumoke Adenowo, AD Consulting

EDEN ROC AT CAP CANA

Cap Cana
Punta Cana
La Alracia 23002
Dominican Republic
+1 8094697469
edenroccapcana.com

CREDIT CARDS...Accepted
PRICE...High-end
TYPE...Resort
ACCOMMODATION............60 Bungalows, Rooms, and Suites
FACILITIES.......................Gym, 2 Outdoor swimming pools,
Private beach, 3 Restaurants, Spa
GOOD TO KNOW..Child friendly
RECOMMENDED FOR..............................Family friendly

"The kids' club and the staff make this one of the best family resorts. They offer tons of activities for kids, so there is plenty for the whole family to do."—Adam Meshberg

Recommended by: Adam Meshberg, Meshberg Group

EL SAN JUAN HOTEL

6063 Isla Verde Avenue
Carolina 979
Puerto Rico
+1 7877911000
elsanjuanhotel.com

CREDIT CARDS...Accepted
PRICE...Mid-range
TYPE..Hotel
ACCOMMODATION...................388 Rooms, Suites, and Villas
FACILITIES.....................Bar, Gym, Outdoor swimming pool,
5 Restaurants, Sauna, Spa, Yoga
GOOD TO KNOW.....................................Child friendly, No pets
RECOMMENDED FOR..Wish I'd designed

San Juan hotel has been beloved by locals and visitors alike since its opening in 1958. It was designed by the legendary Morris Lapidus, the architect behind Miami Beach, and is renowned for its blend of tropical and old-world elegance. Over the years it has hosted a range of headliners on its entertainment stage, including Frank Sinatra and Nat King Cole.

Recommended by: Cruz Garcia and Nathalie Frankowski, WAI Architecture Think Tank

HIX ISLAND HOUSE
Route 995 km1.5
Vieques 765
Puerto Rico
+1 7874354590
hixislandhouse.com

CREDIT CARDS	Accepted
PRICE	Mid-range
TYPE	Hotel
ACCOMMODATION	19 Adobes, Lofts, and Studios
FACILITIES	Outdoor swimming pool, Spa, Yoga
GOOD TO KNOW	Child friendly
RECOMMENDED FOR	Eco-conscious

"Off-grid, passive design."—Bruce Kuwabara

Recommended by: Bruce Kuwabara, KPMB Architects

BELMOND CAP JULUCA
Maundays Bay
West End Village 2640
Anguilla
+1 2644976666
belmond.com

CREDIT CARDS	Accepted
PRICE	High-end
TYPE	Hotel
ACCOMMODATION	108 Rooms, Suites, and Villas
FACILITIES	Bar, Cocktail lounge, Gym, Outdoor swimming pool, 2 Restaurants, Spa, Tennis
GOOD TO KNOW	Snorkeling, Valet parking
RECOMMENDED FOR	Beach

"Located in a cove in the Caribbean, and with very good service. A perfect spot for paddleboarding."
—Lauren Rottet

Recommended by: Lauren Rottet, Rottet Studio

CHEVAL BLANC ST-BARTH ISLE DE FRANCE
Baie des Flamands
Place de Saint Jean
Saint Barthélemy 97133
French West Indies
+59 0590276181
chevalblanc.com

CREDIT CARDS	Accepted
PRICE	Blow-out
TYPE	Resort
ACCOMMODATION	61 Bungalows, Rooms, Suites, and Villas
FACILITIES	Bar, Gym, Outdoor swimming pool, 2 Restaurants, Spa
GOOD TO KNOW	Babysitting
RECOMMENDED FOR	Worth the travel

"Lovely beachfront location. Great restaurant. Relaxed style with perfect service."—Lauren Rottet

Recommended by: Lauren Rottet, Rottet Studio

EDEN ROCK ST BARTHS
Baie de Saint Jean
Saint Barthélemy 97133
French West Indies
+59 0590297999
oetkercollection.com

CREDIT CARDS	Accepted
PRICE	Blow-out
TYPE	Hotel
ACCOMMODATION	37 Rooms, Suites, and Villas
FACILITIES	Beach access, Gym, 2 Restaurants, Spa
GOOD TO KNOW	Child friendly
RECOMMENDED FOR	Family friendly

"Though it is not technically a 'family' hotel, it works for those with well-behaved children who love the beach and great lunches with family. Set on an inlet in St. Barths where the water is calm, the hotel offers beach activities that are perfect for all ages."—Lauren Rottet

Recommended by: Lauren Rottet, Rottet Studio

CARLISLE BAY
Old Road
Saint Mary Parish
Antigua Island
Antigua and Barbuda
+1 2684840000
carlisle-bay.com

CREDIT CARDS	Accepted
PRICE	Mid-range
TYPE	Hotel
ACCOMMODATION	87 Suites
FACILITIES	Gym, Outdoor swimming pool, 7 Restaurants
GOOD TO KNOW	Babysitting, Valet parking
RECOMMENDED FOR	Beach

Recommended by: Michael Stiff, Stiff + Trevillion

SUGAR BEACH, A VICEROY RESORT
Val des Pitons
La Baie de Silence
Soufrière
Saint Lucia
+1 7584568000
viceroyhotelsandresorts.com

CREDIT CARDS	Accepted
PRICE	High-end
TYPE	Resort
ACCOMMODATION	96 Bungalows, Residences, Rooms, and Villas
FACILITIES	3 Bars, Gym, Private beach and plunge pools, 3 Restaurants, Spa, Tennis, Watersports
GOOD TO KNOW	Child friendly
RECOMMENDED FOR	Island

"Beautiful and understated luxury—a perfect escape."
—Alex Michaelis

Recommended by: Alex Michaelis, Michaelis Boyd

ANSE CHASTANET
Old French Road
Mamin
Soufrière
Saint Lucia
+1 8002231108
ansechastanet.com

CREDIT CARDS	Accepted
PRICE	High-end
TYPE	Resort
ACCOMMODATION	49 Rooms and Suites
FACILITIES	Bar, Gym, Outdoor swimming pool, Private beaches, 5 Restaurants, Spa, Yoga
GOOD TO KNOW	Bicycle rentals, No pets
RECOMMENDED FOR	Wish I'd designed

"Wonderful beach resort with the perfect combination of value and friendly service."—Louis Hedgecock

Recommended by: Louis Hedgecock, HOK Architects

COTTON HOUSE RESORT MUSTIQUE
Mustique Island
Saint Vincent and the Grenadines
+1 7844564777
cottonhouse.net

CREDIT CARDS	Accepted
PRICE	High-end
TYPE	Hotel
ACCOMMODATION	17 Cottages, Residences, Rooms, and Suites
FACILITIES	Bar, Beach access, Restaurant, Spa, Tennis
GOOD TO KNOW	Child friendly
RECOMMENDED FOR	Island

"A good example of quiet and silent architecture, the resort is spread out over tropical terrain facing the ocean."
—Rafael de La-Hoz Castanys

Recommended by: Rafael de La-Hoz Castanys, Rafael de La-Hoz Arquitectos

PETIT ST VINCENT

Petit Saint Vincent Island
Saint Vincent and the Grenadines
+1 8006549326
petitstvincent.com

CREDIT CARDS	Accepted
PRICE	Blow-out (all-inclusive)
TYPE	Resort
ACCOMMODATION	22 Cottages and Villas
FACILITIES	Bar, Gym, Private beach, 2 Restaurants, Spa, Tennis, Yoga
GOOD TO KNOW	Rent entire island
RECOMMENDED FOR	Island

"Visit for its laid-back private island vibe and semi-retro beach villas. No TVs, phones, or internet (except at the bar); wicker, red-tiled floors, and buzzing ceiling fans. The most relaxing week-long beach vacation of my life."
—Forth Bagley

Recommended by: Forth Bagley, Kohn Pedersen Fox

THE CRANE RESORT

Saint Philip
Barbados
+1 2464236220
thecrane.com

CREDIT CARDS	Accepted
PRICE	Mid-range
TYPE	Resort
ACCOMMODATION	252 Suites
FACILITIES	Bar, Gym, 5 Outdoor swimming pools, 5 Restaurants, Spa, Tennis
GOOD TO KNOW	Child friendly
RECOMMENDED FOR	Worth the travel

"It takes a while to get to, but one of the best beaches in the world resides at the foot of this majestic, service-oriented hotel. Great rooms, some with private pools, and restaurants overlooking the sea."—Simon Jacobsen

Recommended by: Simon Jacobsen, Jacobsen Architecture

HYATT REGENCY ARUBA RESORT SPA AND CASINO

JE Irausquin Boulevard 85
Eagle Beach
Aruba
+297 5861234
hyatt.com

CREDIT CARDS	Accepted
PRICE	Mid-range
TYPE	Hotel
ACCOMMODATION	359 Rooms and Suites
FACILITIES	Bar, Beach access, Gym, Outdoor swimming pool, Restaurant, Spa
GOOD TO KNOW	Free parking
RECOMMENDED FOR	Worth the travel

"Exuberant landscapes and ocean views, with amazing food and luxurious accommodation."—Claudia Urdaneta

Recommended by: Claudia Urdaneta, NMD NOMADAS

HOTEL KURA HULANDA VILLAGE AND SPA, GHL HOTEL

Langestraat 8
Willemstad 33328
Curaçao
+599 94347700
kurahulanda.com

CREDIT CARDS	Accepted
PRICE	Mid-range
TYPE	Resort
ACCOMMODATION	82 Rooms and Suites
FACILITIES	Bar, Gym, 2 Outdoor swimming pools, 2 Restaurants, Spa
GOOD TO KNOW	Child friendly
RECOMMENDED FOR	Best-kept secret

The Kura Hulanda Village and Spa, GHL Hotel is a beachfront retreat that is laid back yet elegant. The luxury resort is situated in Curaçao's tranquil West End and comprises meticulously restored eighteenth- and nineteenth-century Dutch Colonial Caribbean buildings which are spread around several quaint courtyards. It also has multiple pools, restaurants, a spa, and fitness center.

Recommended by: Farid Chacon, NMD NOMADAS

STARFISH TOBAGO
1 Courland Bay
Scarborough
Trinidad and Tobago
+1 8779574051
starfishresorts.com

CREDIT CARDS	Accepted
PRICE	Mid-range (all-inclusive)
TYPE	Resort
ACCOMMODATION	125 Suites
FACILITIES	Outdoor swimming pool, Poolside bar, Restaurant, Scuba diving, Tennis
GOOD TO KNOW	Child friendly, Free parking
RECOMMENDED FOR	Island

"I don't often go to the beach, but the Starfish Tobago is probably my favorite island destination, and a very family friendly hotel."—Ian Ritchie

Recommended by: Ian Ritchie, Ian Ritchie Architects

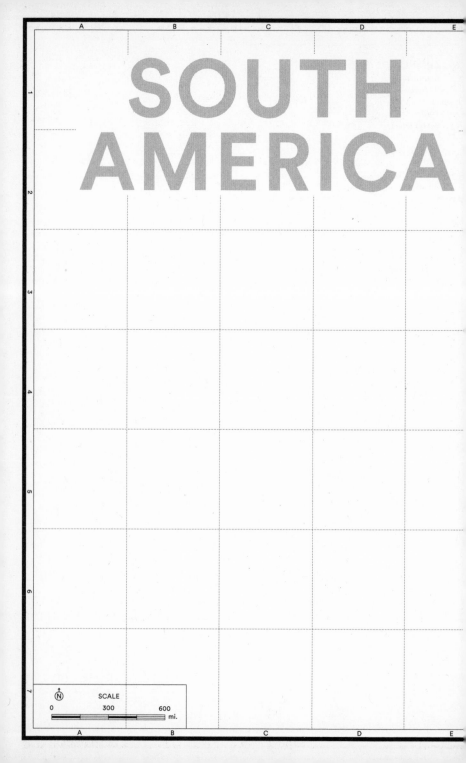

SOUTH AMERICA

SCALE

0   300   600 mi.

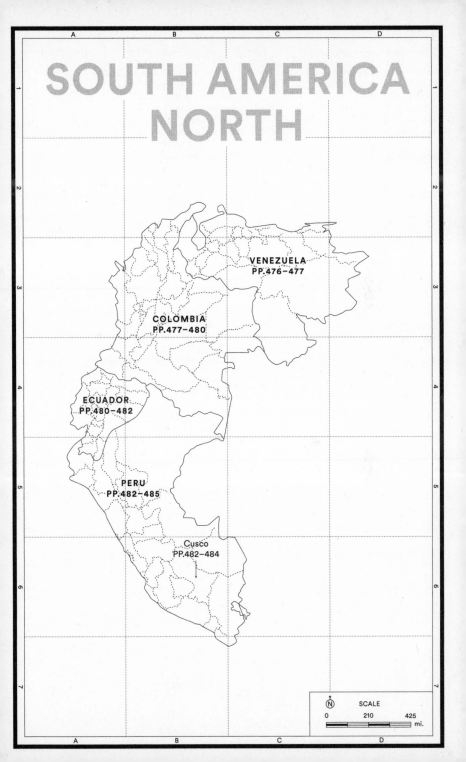

CACAONI LODGE

Calle Principal Choroní S/N
Choroní
Girardot 2110
Aragua
Venezuela
+58 4126934460
cacaonilodge.com

CREDIT CARDS...Accepted
PRICE...Mid-range
TYPE..Hotel
ACCOMMODATION...12 Suites
FACILITIES.................................Bar, Outdoor swimming pool,
Restaurant
GOOD TO KNOW...Call or email to book
RECOMMENDED FOR...Worth the travel

"Incredible design; a truly unique experience."
—Farid Chacon

Recommended by: Farid Chacon, NMD NOMADAS

WAKU LODGE

Parque Nacional Canaima
Canaima 8011
Bolívar
Venezuela
+58 2869620559
wakulodge.com

CREDIT CARDS...Accepted
PRICE...High-end (all-inclusive)
TYPE..Lodge
ACCOMMODATION.......................................19 Rooms and Suites
FACILITIES...Outdoor restaurant
GOOD TO KNOW..Call or email to book
RECOMMENDED FOR...Family friendly

"Incredible! This is a lost paradise of the world."
—Farid Chacon

Recommended by: Farid Chacon, NMD NOMADAS

POSADA LA ARDILEÑA

Parque Nacional Morrocoy
Agua Salobre
Silva 2055
Falcón
Venezuela
+58 2598122971
ardilena.com

CREDIT CARDS...Not accepted
PRICE...Low-cost
TYPE..Hotel
ACCOMMODATION...12 Rooms
FACILITIES.......................................Outdoor restaurant, Spa
GOOD TO KNOW...Child friendly
RECOMMENDED FOR...............................Beach, Eco-conscious

"The location is a dream. Morrocoy National Park is paradise
and the food and service are incredible."—Farid Chacon

"Fine dining and hospitality in a natural and privileged
location. The hotel is proactive in its social and ecological
responsibilities."—Claudia Urdaneta

Recommended by: Farid Chacon and Claudia Urdaneta,
NMD NOMADAS

XINIA Y PETER

La Mucuy Baja, Qta Xinia 5116
Tabay
Libertador 5101
Mérida
Venezuela
+58 2122610469
xiniaypeter.com

CREDIT CARDS...Accepted
PRICE...Mid-range
TYPE..Hotel
ACCOMMODATION...21 Rooms
FACILITIES...Restaurant
GOOD TO KNOW...Call or email to book
RECOMMENDED FOR..Mountains

"There's an incredible energy to this place; a lovely
experience in the mountains."—Farid Chacon

"A gastronomic jewel of the area."—Claudia Urdaneta

Recommended by: Farid Chacon and Claudia Urdaneta,
NMD NOMADAS

HOTEL BOUTIQUE ISABEL LA CATÓLICA

Casco Histórico de Pampatar
Pampatar
Isla de Margarita 6316
Nueva Esparta
Venezuela
+58 2959350152
hotelisabellacatolica.com

CREDIT CARDS	Accepted
PRICE	Mid-range
TYPE	Hotel
ACCOMMODATION	14 Rooms and Suites
FACILITIES	Outdoor swimming pool, Restaurant
GOOD TO KNOW	Call or email to book
RECOMMENDED FOR	Countryside

Recommended by: Joana Leandro Vasconcelos, Atelier In.vitro

IKIN MARGARITA HOTEL & SPA

Calle El Melonal
El Cardón
Isla de Margarita 6317
Nueva Esparta
Venezuela
+58 2955004555
ikinmargarita.com

CREDIT CARDS	Accepted
PRICE	Mid-range
TYPE	Hotel
ACCOMMODATION	55 Rooms and Suites
FACILITIES	Bar, Outdoor swimming pool, Restaurant, Spa
GOOD TO KNOW	Child friendly
RECOMMENDED FOR	All-time favorite, Beach, Countryside

"Amazing location overlooking the Caribbean Sea; delightful atmosphere and incredible service."—Farid Chacon

"The best luxury hospitality and accommodation in natural surroundings where the beautiful architecture evokes local craftsmanship."—Claudia Urdaneta

Recommended by: Farid Chacon and Claudia Urdaneta, NMD NOMADAS

HOTEL BOTERO MEDELLÍN

Carretera 50a, 53–45
Medellín
Valle de Aburrá
Antioquia
Colombia
+57 3182826223
hotelboteromedellin.com.co

CREDIT CARDS	Accepted
PRICE	Low-cost
TYPE	Hotel
ACCOMMODATION	84 Rooms
FACILITIES	Restaurant, Rooftop terrace bar, Sauna
GOOD TO KNOW	Call or email to book
RECOMMENDED FOR	Best-kept secret

Featuring simple yet comfortable rooms, Hotel Botero Medellín is ideally positioned for proximity to local sites, including Medellín Cathedral and the art museum Museo de Antioquia.

Recommended by: Giancarlo Mazzanti, El Equipo Mazzanti

PATIO DEL MUNDO

Calle 5G, 32–49 El Poblado
Medellín
Valle de Aburrá 050022
Antioquia
Colombia
+57 43112064
patiodelmundo.com

CREDIT CARDS.....................................Accepted but not Amex
PRICE...Low-cost
TYPE...Villa
ACCOMMODATION...7 Rooms
FACILITIES...Hot tub, Yoga
GOOD TO KNOW......................................No pets, Valet parking
RECOMMENDED FOR..Where I live

Patio del Mundo is a lovingly restored, family owned villa located in the heart of Medellín. Rooms are stylish, and the lush garden is the perfect place to escape the city. Breakfast is served on the terrace, and a path lined with avocado and orange trees leads to a sundeck complete with a Jacuzzi.

Recommended by: Juan Manuel Peláez Freidel, JUMP/Juan Manuel Peláez Arquitectos

CORALINA ISLAND HÔTEL ISLAS DEL ROSARIO

Isla de Marina
Cartagena de Indias
Bolívar
Colombia
+57 3132459244
coralinaisland.com

CREDIT CARDS...Accepted
PRICE..Mid-range
TYPE...Hotel
ACCOMMODATION.............................8 Bungalows and Rooms
FACILITIES..Restaurant
GOOD TO KNOW....................................Call or email to book
RECOMMENDED FOR..Beach

"The Islas del Rosario have all the natural beauty of the Caribbean just off the coast of Cartagena, one of the most stunning, historic cities in South America. The weather and water temperature are perfect for scuba diving or just enjoying the white sand coves."—Adrian Moreno and Maria Samaniego

Recommended by: Adrian Moreno and Maria Samaniego, Arquitectura X

BLUE SUITES HOTEL

Calle 93, 17–48
Chapinero
Bogotá
Colombia
+57 17452222
bluesuiteshotel.com

CREDIT CARDS...Accepted
PRICE...Low-cost
TYPE...Hotel
ACCOMMODATION.................................40 Rooms and Suites
FACILITIES...Bar, Gym, Restaurant,
Spa, Steam room
GOOD TO KNOW................................Babysitting, Free parking
RECOMMENDED FOR...Budget

"Very well located, easily accessible, and close to Bogotá's Zona Rosa area. Simple and spacious design, comfortable rooms and bathrooms, and a good breakfast."
—Adrian Moreno and Maria Samaniego

Recommended by: Adrian Moreno and Maria Samaniego, Arquitectura X

HOTEL DE LA OPERA

Calle 10, Street Coliseo 5–72
La Candelaria
Bogotá
Colombia
+57 13362066
hotelopera.com.co

CREDIT CARDS...Accepted
PRICE...Low-cost
TYPE..Townhouse hotel
ACCOMMODATION.................................42 Rooms and Suites
FACILITIES...Indoor swimming pool,
2 Restaurants, Sauna, Spa
GOOD TO KNOW...Child friendly
RECOMMENDED FOR..Where I live

Located in Bogotá's historic quarter, Hotel de la Opera is a beautiful colonial townhouse hotel with varied architecture that spans three centuries of history. This eclectic legacy is reflected in the room design, from colonial to Art Deco. It also has a spa and two restaurants.

Recommended by: Giancarlo Mazzanti, El Equipo Mazzanti

ESTELAR PAIPA HOTEL

Orillas del Lago Sochagota S/N
Paipa
Tundama
Boyacá
Colombia
+57 87625252
estelarpaipa.com

CREDIT CARDS...Accepted
PRICE...Low-cost
TYPE..Hotel
ACCOMMODATION.....................105 Rooms and Suites
FACILITIES...Bar, Restaurant,
Sauna, Spa, Steam room
GOOD TO KNOW....................Child and pet friendly,
Horse riding, Kayaking
RECOMMENDED FOR..............................Family friendly

A spa and convention center next to Lake Sochagota,
suitable for both business travelers and family retreats.
For holidaymakers, the hotel organizes activities include
horse riding, spa treatments, and kayaking.

Recommended by: Giancarlo Mazzanti, El Equipo Mazzanti

MORROMICO

Gulf of Tribugá
Nuquí
Chocó
Colombia
+57 3127956321
morromico.com

CREDIT CARDS...Accepted
PRICE...Low-cost
TYPE...Lodge
ACCOMMODATION.....................5 Bungalows and Rooms
FACILITIES...Restaurant
GOOD TO KNOW..............................Accessible only by boat,
Call or email to book,
No internet access
RECOMMENDED FOR.............All-time favorite, Eco-conscious

A family run eco-resort on a stunning private beach,
surrounded by jungle, and framed by two waterfalls.
Excursions, boat trips, and treks to local indigenous
communities can also be arranged.

Recommended by: Giancarlo Mazzanti, El Equipo Mazzanti

RANCHERÍA UTTA

Cabo de la Vela vía Al Faro S/N
Uribia
La Guajira
Colombia
+57 3138178076
rancheriautta.com

CREDIT CARDS...Accepted
PRICE...Mid-range
TYPE..Hotel
ACCOMMODATION...11 Rooms
FACILITIES...Restaurant
GOOD TO KNOW...............................No internet access
RECOMMENDED FOR..Desert

A family owned beachfront hotel with plenty of charm,
Ranchería Utta has simple rooms, a break-out space filled
with colorful hammocks, and a restaurant serving breakfast,
lunch, and dinner.

Recommended by: Giancarlo Mazzanti, El Equipo Mazzanti

RESERVA ONE LOVE

Vía La Sierra km2
Palomino
Dibulla
La Guajira
Colombia
+57 3176820722
reservaone.love

CREDIT CARDS...Not accepted
PRICE...Low-cost
TYPE..Hotel
ACCOMMODATION..5 Bungalows
FACILITIES...Restaurant
GOOD TO KNOW..................................Child friendly
RECOMMENDED FOR..............................Family friendly

A family friendly hotel located within a private reserve in
the lush Sierra Nevada, Reserva One Love combines luxury
facilities and amenities with an immersive jungle experience.
Rooms are pared-back but chic, and a variety of cultural
and adventure experiences are on offer.

Recommended by: Juan Manuel Peláez Freidel, JUMP/Juan
Manuel Peláez Arquitectos

ECOHABS TAYRONA SANTA MARTA
Parque Nacional Tayrona
Playa de Cañaveral
Santa Marta
Magdalena
Colombia
+57 3116001614
ecohabsantamarta.com

CREDIT CARDS	Accepted
PRICE	Mid-range
TYPE	Lodge
ACCOMMODATION	14 Bungalows
FACILITIES	Restaurant, Spa
GOOD TO KNOW	No wifi
RECOMMENDED FOR	Eco-conscious

"Incredible location, amazing rooms, and spectacular views."
—Farid Chacon

Recommended by: Farid Chacon, NMD NOMADAS

SIERRA ALTA FINCA BOUTIQUE
Parque Nacional Sierra Nevada de Santa Marta
Minca
Magdalena
Colombia
+57 3126208475

CREDIT CARDS	Accepted
PRICE	Low-cost
TYPE	Finca
ACCOMMODATION	4 Rooms
FACILITIES	Jacuzzi, Outdoor restaurant, Sun terrace
GOOD TO KNOW	Badminton equipment, Hiking
RECOMMENDED FOR	Family friendly, Mountains

A charming boutique hotel with an on-site restaurant
and a friendly team who can arrange a variety of excursions,
including coffee plantation tours and birdwatching.

Recommended by: Juan Manuel Peláez Freidel, JUMP/Juan
Manuel Peláez Arquitectos

GLAMPING HUB
Parque Nacional Galápagos
Isla Santa Cruz
Galápagos
Ecuador
+1 7202120854
glampinghub.com

CREDIT CARDS	Accepted
PRICE	High-end
TYPE	Tented camp
ACCOMMODATION	9 tents
FACILITIES	Bar, Outdoor swimming pool, Restaurant
GOOD TO KNOW	Bicycle rentals, Child friendly
RECOMMENDED FOR	Eco-conscious

A collection of nine stylish, safari-style tents on stilts spread
out among the greenery of Santa Cruz island. Each has a
large balcony with hammocks and chairs, perfect for taking
in the stunning vistas.

Recommended by: Juan Manuel Pelaez Freidel, JUMP/Juan
Manuel Peláez Arquitectos

TERMAS DE PAPALLACTA
Kilómetros 65 vía Quito-Baeza
Papallacta
Quijos
Napo
Ecuador
+593 62895060
termaspapallacta.com

CREDIT CARDS	Accepted but not Amex
PRICE	Mid-range
TYPE	Spa resort
ACCOMMODATION	39 Bungalows, Rooms, and Suites
FACILITIES	Bar, Hot-spring bath, Outdoor swimming pool, Restaurant, Spa
GOOD TO KNOW	Child friendly, No pets
RECOMMENDED FOR	Spa

"Papallacta is a natural volcanic hot spring region, and this
spa is the best in town. The rooms have both outdoor pools
and private pools attached."—Adrian Moreno and
Maria Samaniego

Recommended by: Adrian Moreno and Maria Samaniego,
Arquitectura X

CASA GANGOTENA

Bolivar Oe6–41 y Cuenca
San Roque
Quito 170401
Ecuador
+593 997146787
casagangotena.com

CREDIT CARDS	Accepted
PRICE	High-end
TYPE	Hotel
ACCOMMODATION	31 Rooms and Suites
FACILITIES	Bar, Restaurant, Rooftop terrace bar
GOOD TO KNOW	Child friendly, Call or email to book
RECOMMENDED FOR	Luxury

"This former republican period house, with two courtyards and a garden, is located in one of the most beautiful squares in Latin America, the San Francisco Plaza. The building has been carefully updated for its new use with rooms that enjoy privileged views over Quito's city center."
—Adrian Moreno and Maria Samaniego

Recommended by: Adrian Moreno and Maria Samaniego, Arquitectura X

HOTEL CARLOTA

Benalcázar N6-26 y Mejía
Centro Histórico
Quito 170401
Ecuador
+593 2801410
carlota.ec

CREDIT CARDS	Accepted
PRICE	Mid-range
TYPE	Hotel
ACCOMMODATION	12 Lofts, Rooms, and Suites
FACILITIES	Bar, Restaurant, Rooftop terrace bar
GOOD TO KNOW	Laptops and tablets available on request
RECOMMENDED FOR	Best-kept secret

"The owner tried to keep the spirit of his grandmother's house while adding contemporary design touches. The result is very welcoming, with cozy rooms and a fantastic sequence of common areas that start in the courtyards and culminate on the roof terrace overlooking the city."—Adrian Moreno and Maria Samaniego

Recommended by: Adrian Moreno and Maria Samaniego, Arquitectura X

HILTON COLÓN QUITO

Amazonas N 1914 y Patria Avenida
Mariscal Sucre
Quito 170143
Ecuador
+593 23828300
hiltonhotels.com

CREDIT CARDS	Accepted
PRICE	Mid-range
TYPE	Hotel
ACCOMMODATION	255 Rooms and Suites
FACILITIES	Bar, Gym, Outdoor swimming pool, 2 Restaurants
GOOD TO KNOW	Babysitting, Pet friendly
RECOMMENDED FOR	Where I live

"Not only one of the best hotels in Quito, but one of the best buildings in the city, designed in the 1970s by architect Ovidio Wappenstein. It has been carefully updated and keeps the original spirit, both at street level and in the rooms. The restaurants, cafes, and lobby are classic meeting places in town."—Adrian Moreno and Maria Samaniego

Recommended by: Adrian Moreno and Maria Samaniego, Arquitectura X

MASHPI LODGE

Reserva Privada Mashpi
Mashpi
Quito 150150
Ecuador
+593 24004100
mashpilodge.com

CREDIT CARDS	Accepted
PRICE	Blow-out
TYPE	Hotel
ACCOMMODATION	23 Rooms and Suites
FACILITIES	Bar, Restaurant, Spa, Yoga
GOOD TO KNOW	Call or email to book
RECOMMENDED FOR	Eco-conscious

"Located in the rainforest reserve northwest of Quito, the lodge is immersed in one of the most biodiverse forests of the world, providing great comfort and direct contact with nature due to its architecture. Wonderful food prepared with local produce."—Adrian Moreno and Maria Samaniego

Recommended by: Adrian Moreno and Maria Samaniego, Arquitectura X

ARASHA RESORT
Km121 (via Quito -Calacalí-La Independencia)
Pedro Vicente Maldonado
Pichincha
Ecuador
+593 3900008
arasharesort.com

CREDIT CARDS	Accepted
PRICE	Mid-range
TYPE	Resort
ACCOMMODATION	61 Bungalows, Cabins, and Suites
FACILITIES	Outdoor swimming pool, Restaurant, Spa
GOOD TO KNOW	Call or email to book
RECOMMENDED FOR	Eco-conscious

"The resort is located in one of the most biodiverse areas, with endemic species, in the world. All the available activities, from night walks in the jungle to eco-workshops, put you in direct contact with the exuberant natural surroundings. The facilities are eco-friendly, and most importantly, the resort is in charge of the conservation of the surrounding rainforest."—Adrian Moreno and Maria Samaniego

Recommended by: Adrian Moreno and Maria Samaniego, Arquitectura X

TAMBOPAXI COTOPAXI LODGE
Area Nacional de Recreacion El Boliche
Mejía
Pichincha
Ecuador
+593 26000365
tambopaxi.com

CREDIT CARDS	Accepted
PRICE	Low-cost
TYPE	Lodge
ACCOMMODATION	14 Dorms and 6 Rooms
FACILITIES	Restaurant
GOOD TO KNOW	Email or call to book, Horse riding
RECOMMENDED FOR	Mountains

"Located at the foot of one of the most beautiful active volcanoes in the world, the comfortable rooms have amazing views. There are also lots of great outdoor activities provided."—Adrian Moreno and Maria Samaniego

Recommended by: Adrian Moreno and Maria Samaniego, Arquitectura X

PACHAMAMA
San Pedro S/N
Cabanaconde
Caylloma
Arequipa 04124
Peru
+51 959316322
pachamamahome.com

CREDIT CARDS	Accepted
PRICE	Low-cost
TYPE	Hostel
ACCOMMODATION	16 Dorms and Rooms
FACILITIES	Bar, Restaurant, Rooftop terrace
GOOD TO KNOW	Call or email to book
RECOMMENDED FOR	Countryside

"Eat their woodfired pizza after a trek down to one of the deepest canyons in the world."—Laurent Gravier

Recommended by: Laurent Gravier, FRES Architectes

BELMOND HOTEL MONASTERIO
Calle Plazoleta Nazarenas 337
Centro Histórico
Cusco 08002
Peru
+51 84604000
belmond.com

CREDIT CARDS	Accepted
PRICE	Mid-range
TYPE	Hotel
ACCOMMODATION	122 Rooms and Suites
FACILITIES	Bar, Indoor swimming pool, 2 Restaurants, Spa
GOOD TO KNOW	Child friendly
RECOMMENDED FOR	All-time favorite, Luxury, Mountains, Worth the travel

"Historic building with a stunning art collection."
—Roger Duffy

"Oxygen is pumped into the rooms at night to help you acclimatize to the great height before you ascend to Machu Picchu."—Ken Yeang

Recommended by: Roger Duffy, Skidmore, Owings & Merrill; Valerio Olgiati, Valerio Olgiati; Ken Yeang, Hamzah & Yeang

INKATERRA LA CASONA CUSCO

Plaza Las Nazarenas 211
Centro Histórico
Cusco 08002
Peru
+51 84236748
inkaterra.com

CREDIT CARDS...Accepted
PRICE...Blow-out
TYPE...Manor house hotel
ACCOMMODATION...11 Suites
FACILITIES...Bar, Restaurant, Spa
GOOD TO KNOW...Babysitting
RECOMMENDED FOR...All-time favorite

Inkaterra La Casona Cusco is a beautiful sixteenth-century manor house situated in the historic Plaza Las Nazarenas. It has been sensitively restored, with a picturesque inner courtyard, suites that all feature heated floors, bespoke design touches, stone fireplaces, and large bath tubs. The hotel is a model of warm hospitality, and there are many thoughtful extras including oxygen for acclimatization, high tea, and cocktail hour.

Recommended by: Alex Michaelis, Michaelis Boyd

INKATERRA HACIENDA URUBAMBA

Cusco-Urubamba-Pisac-Calca (via km63)
Sacred Valley
Urubamba
Cusco 08670
Peru
+51 84600700
inkaterra.com

CREDIT CARDS...Accepted
PRICE..High-end
TYPE...Hacienda
ACCOMMODATION..................36 Casitas, Suites, and Rooms
FACILITIES...Bar, Restaurant, Spa
GOOD TO KNOW..Child friendly
RECOMMENDED FOR............................Luxury, Worth the travel

"An extraordinary location in the Sacred Valley of the Incas where the surrounding natural treasures are beyond words. Great views, food, and wine, it is perfect for couples."
—Brent Kendle

Recommended by: Brent Kendle, Kendle Design Collaborative

JW MARRIOTT EL CONVENTO CUSCO

Esquina de la Calle Ruinas 432 y San Agustin
Centro Histórico
Cusco 08001
Peru
+51 84582200
marriott.com

CREDIT CARDS...Accepted
PRICE...Mid-range
TYPE..Hotel
ACCOMMODATION...............................153 Rooms and Suites
FACILITIES.......................................Bar, Indoor swimming pool,
Restaurant, Spa, Steam room
GOOD TO KNOW...No pets
RECOMMENDED FOR...Luxury

"A competent recycling of a Spanish colonial convent as a luxury hotel in the middle of Cusco. The spaces are tasteful and incorporate a lot of artwork. Great food too."
—Nilson Ariel Espino

Recommended by: Nilson Ariel Espino, Suma Arquitectos

PALACIO MANCO CAPAC BY ANANAY HOTELS

Avenida Don Bosco S/N
Centro Histórico
Cusco 08002
Peru
+51 84255770
ananay-hotels.com

CREDIT CARDS...Accepted
PRICE...Mid-range
TYPE..Hotel
ACCOMMODATION...5 Rooms and Suites
FACILITIES...Bar, Restaurant
GOOD TO KNOW..Airport transfers
RECOMMENDED FOR..Urban

"A fifteenth-century Italian villa built on the foundation of an original Incan emperor's palace."—Brent Kendle

Recommended by: Brent Kendle, Kendle Design Collaborative

PANORAMA B&B

Avenida Hermanos Ayar 305
Aguas Calientes (Machu Picchu)
Urubamba
Cusco 08681
Peru
+51 84211192
mapipanorama.com

CREDIT CARDS	Accepted
PRICE	Low-cost
TYPE	Bed and Breakfast
ACCOMMODATION	8 Rooms
FACILITIES	Snack bar
GOOD TO KNOW	Child friendly
RECOMMENDED FOR	Mountains

"Small, simple, and very friendly with a fantastic location looking out on to Machu Picchu."—Matthias Sauerbruch and Louisa Hutton

Recommended by: Matthias Sauerbruch and Louisa Hutton, Sauerbruch Hutton

SKYLODGE ADVENTURE SUITES

Pista 224km, Urubamba-Ollantaytambo
Sacred Valley
Urubamba
Cusco
Peru
+51 84201253
naturavive.com

CREDIT CARDS	Accepted
PRICE	High-end (all-inclusive)
TYPE	House rental
ACCOMMODATION	3 Suites
FACILITIES	Zip lines
GOOD TO KNOW	Airbnb or email to book
RECOMMENDED FOR	Worth the travel

"Can you imagine hanging from a cliff more than 330 feet (100 meters) high, sleeping in a transparent capsule?"
—Felipe Assadi

Recommended by: Felipe Assadi, Felipe Assadi Architects

TAMBO DEL INKA

Avenida Ferrocarril S/N
Sacred Valley
Urubamba
Cusco 08660
Peru
+51 84581777
marriott.com

CREDIT CARDS	Accepted
PRICE	High-end
TYPE	Hotel
ACCOMMODATION	128 Rooms and Suites
FACILITIES	Bar, Gym, Indoor swimming pool, Restaurant, Sauna, Spa
GOOD TO KNOW	Bicycle rentals, No pets
RECOMMENDED FOR	Mountains

"Serenity amidst antiquity."—Bernardo Fort-Brescia

Recommended by: Bernardo Fort-Brescia, Arquitectonica

HOTEL PARACAS, A LUXURY COLLECTION RESORT

Avenida Paracas S/N
Pisco
Ica 11550
Peru
+51 56581333
marriott.com

CREDIT CARDS	Accepted
PRICE	Mid-range
TYPE	Resort
ACCOMMODATION	120 Rooms and Suites
FACILITIES	Bar, Gym, Outdoor swimming pool, 3 Restaurants, Sauna, Spa, Steam room
GOOD TO KNOW	Valet parking
RECOMMENDED FOR	Desert

A sleek, modern resort facing the Paracas National Reserve—one of the most diverse oceanfront sanctuaries in the world—Hotel Paracas is a tranquil retreat ideally placed for exploring the desert and the sea. Excursions include a luxury yacht experience and the opportunity to fly over the Nazca Lines.

Recommended by: Bernardo Fort-Brescia, Arquitectonica

INKATERRA HACIENDA CONCEPCIÓN

Rio Madre de Dios km7
Puerto Maldonado
Tambopata
Madre de Dios 17000
Peru
+51 82573534
inkaterra.com

CREDIT CARDS..Accepted
PRICE...High-end
TYPE..Hacienda
ACCOMMODATION................................30 Cabanas and Rooms
FACILITIES...Bar, Restaurant
GOOD TO KNOW...Child friendly
RECOMMENDED FOR..Eco-conscious

"Amazing jungle tours and an incredible place to experience Amazon river life."—Roger Duffy

Recommended by: Roger Duffy, Skidmore, Owings & Merrill

INKATERRA RESERVA AMAZÓNICA

Rio Madre De Dios km15
Puerto Maldonado
Tambopata
Madre de Dios 17000
Peru
+51 82573534
inkaterra.com

CREDIT CARDS..Accepted
PRICE...High-end
TYPE..Lodge
ACCOMMODATION.................................35 Cabanas and Suites
FACILITIES..Bar, Restaurant, Spa
GOOD TO KNOW...Child friendly
RECOMMENDED FOR..Luxury

Inkaterra Reserva Amazónica is a luxury eco-lodge that overlooks the Madre de Dios River. It has beautifully designed cabanas and a spa, and offers a range of excursions with the assistance of expert guides—including low-impact, child friendly routes—and will organize entrance fees to Lake Sandoval.

Recommended by: Juan Manuel Peláez Freidel, JUMP/Juan Manuel Peláez Arquitectos

TITILAKA

Lake Titicaca
Puno
Peru
+51 17005105
titilaka.pe

CREDIT CARDS..Accepted
PRICE...High-end
TYPE...Hotel
ACCOMMODATION...18 Rooms
FACILITIES...Bar, Restaurant
GOOD TO KNOW...Babysitting
RECOMMENDED FOR..Countryside

"Perched on the legendary Lake Titicaca, this hotel is incredibly comfortable and stuffed with local objects you want to keep. It's rare to find a piece of tourist architecture that works so well with the culture and heritage of a place. They even supply oxygen if you start to fail at the high altitude!"—Thomas Bartlett

Recommended by: Thomas Bartlett, Waldo Works

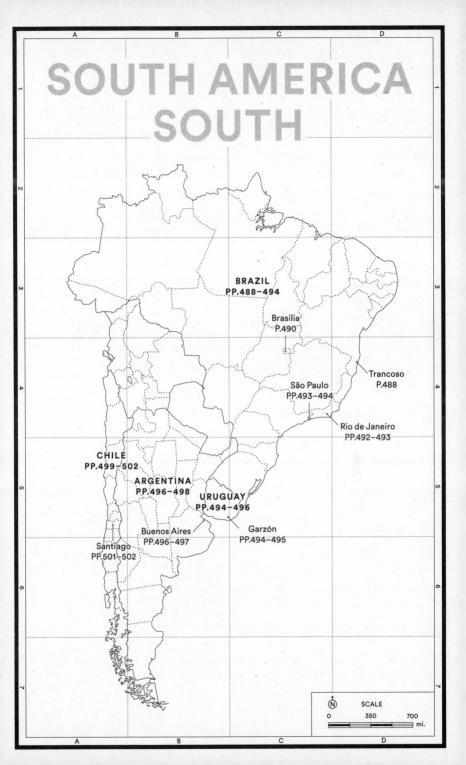

SOUTH AMERICA SOUTH

BRAZIL
PP.488-494

Brasilia
P.490

Trancoso
P.488

São Paulo
PP.493-494

Rio de Janeiro
PP.492-493

CHILE
PP.499-502

ARGENTINA
PP.496-498

URUGUAY
PP.494-496

Buenos Aires
PP.496-497

Garzón
PP.494-495

Santiago
PP.501-502

SCALE

0   350   700
mi.

KENOA RESORT

Rua Escritor Jorge de Lima 58
Barra Mar
Maceió
Alagoas 57180-000
Brazil
+55 82988121000
kenoaresort.com

CREDIT CARDS	Accepted
PRICE	Blow-out
TYPE	Resort
ACCOMMODATION	23 Suites and Villas
FACILITIES	Bar, Gym, Outdoor swimming pool, Restaurant, Sauna
GOOD TO KNOW	Boat rides, Horse riding
RECOMMENDED FOR	Luxury

"The hotel has an amazing location right in front of some of Brazil's finest beaches. Its buildings and interiors were designed by the architect Osvaldo Tenório, and they display an interesting mix of modern architecture and vernacular construction techniques."—Daniel Mangabeira

Recommended by: Daniel Mangabeira, BLOCO Arquitetos

ANAVILHANAS JUNGLE LODGE

Parque Nacional de Anavilhanas
Novo Airão
Rio Negro
Amazonas
Brazil
+55 9236228996
anavilhanaslodge.com

CREDIT CARDS	Accepted
PRICE	High-end
TYPE	Lodge
ACCOMMODATION	22 Bungalows and Cottages
FACILITIES	Bar, Outdoor swimming pool, Restaurant
GOOD TO KNOW	Email to book
RECOMMENDED FOR	Eco-conscious

"A hotel that justifies a trip to the Amazon. Better visit before it's all gone."—Marcio Kogan

"Located in a conservation area in the center of the Brazilian Amazon."—Marcelo Morettin

Recommended by: Marcio Kogan, Studio MK27; Marcelo Morettin, Andrade Morettin Arquitetos

TERRAVISTA VILAS TRANCOSO

Estrada Municipal de Trancoso km18 S/N
Trancoso
Porto Seguro
Bahia 45810-000
Brazil
+55 7336682355
terravistavilas.com.br

CREDIT CARDS	Accepted
PRICE	High-end
TYPE	Hotel
ACCOMMODATION	15 Villas
FACILITIES	Bar, Restaurant, Spa
GOOD TO KNOW	Beach access, Child friendly
RECOMMENDED FOR	All-time favorite, Beach

Recommended by: François Valentiny, Valentiny HVP Architects

UXUA CASA HOTEL & SPA

Praça São João Batista S/N
Trancoso
Porto Seguro
Bahia 45810-000
Brazil
+55 7336682277
uxua.com

CREDIT CARDS	Accepted
PRICE	High-end
TYPE	Hotel
ACCOMMODATION	12 Casas
FACILITIES	Bar, Gym, Outdoor swimming pool, Restaurant, Spa, Yoga
GOOD TO KNOW	Email to book
RECOMMENDED FOR	Beach, Countryside

"Best experience at the most beautiful village on the Brazilian coast. The place is sensational, rustic, and extremely tasteful. This alone is worth a trip to Brazil."
—Marcio Kogan

"Glamping at its tropical best—you'll never miss your glass window. Just don't be surprised if a monkey is sleeping with you."—Charles Renfro

Recommended by: Marcio Kogan, Studio MK27; David Miller, Miller Hull Partnership; Charles Renfro, Diller Scofidio + Renfro

HOTEL FAZENDA CALÁ & DIVINO

Estrada de Trancoso km22
Porto Seguro
Bahia 45818-000
Brazil
+55 73991726964
divinoespelho.com.br

CREDIT CARDS	Accepted
PRICE	Mid-range
TYPE	Hotel
ACCOMMODATION	8 Bungalows
FACILITIES	Bar, Restaurant
GOOD TO KNOW	Child friendly
RECOMMENDED FOR	Worth the travel

Recommended by: Paolo Brambilla, Calvi Brambilla

PESTANA CONVENTO DO CARMO

Rua do Carmo 1
Santo Antônio Além do Carmo
Salvador
Bahia 40301-330
Brazil
+55 7133278400
pestana.com

CREDIT CARDS	Accepted but not Amex
PRICE	Low-cost
TYPE	Hotel
ACCOMMODATION	67 Rooms and Suites
FACILITIES	Library, Outdoor swimming pool, Restaurant, Sauna, Steam room
GOOD TO KNOW	Child and pet friendly
RECOMMENDED FOR	Budget

"Located in a sixteenth-century convent in the center of Salvador, the hotel is a unique experience in a historic building."—Marcelo Morettin

Recommended by: Marcelo Morettin, Andrade Morettin Arquitetos

ALIZÉES MORERÉ

Praia da Moreré S/N
Ilha da Boipeba
Cairu
Bahia 45426-000
Brazil
+55 7536538917
hotelalizeesmorere.com

CREDIT CARDS	Accepted
PRICE	Low-cost
TYPE	Hotel
ACCOMMODATION	17 Bungalows
FACILITIES	Restaurant, Spa
GOOD TO KNOW	Email to book, No pets
RECOMMENDED FOR	Beach

"This small, engagingly difficult-to-reach hotel is run by a friendly French family. A handful of glass-fronted bungalows are spread across a hillside of lush tropical vegetation that overlooks a turquoise bay. At low tide, people play football on the beach."—Matthias Sauerbruch and Louisa Hutton

Recommended by: Matthias Sauerbruch and Louisa Hutton, Sauerbruch Hutton

KA BRU BEACH BOUTIQUE HOTEL & VILLA

Ponta Da Ingazeira 9995
Maraú
Bahia 45520-000
Brazil
+55 7399866 4424
kabrubrazil.com

CREDIT CARDS	Accepted but not Amex
PRICE	Mid-range
TYPE	Hotel
ACCOMMODATION	9 Suites and Villas
FACILITIES	Bar, Outdoor swimming pool, Restaurant, Yoga
GOOD TO KNOW	Bicycle rentals, No pets, Private beach
RECOMMENDED FOR	Wish I'd designed

This boutique hotel and collection of three beautifully designed villas are situated close to tranquil Barra Grande and trendy Itacaré, set on the Bahian coast. Guests can choose from luxury jungle, river, and beach villa experiences—all provide excellent service and a plethora of activities, including adventure trips and cookery classes.

Recommended by: Juan Manuel Peláez Freidel, JUMP/Juan Manuel Peláez Arquitectos

RANCHO DO PEIXE
Rua da Praia S/N
Cruz
Ceará 62595-000
Brazil
+55 8836603118
ranchodopeixe.com.br

CREDIT CARDS..Accepted
PRICE..Mid-range
TYPE...Resort
ACCOMMODATION...26 Bungalows
FACILITIES...............................Bar, Outdoor swimming pool,
Restaurant, Spa
GOOD TO KNOW..............................Babysitting, Child friendly
RECOMMENDED FOR...Best-kept secret

Located on the tranquil Praia do Preá, this is a relaxed resort
with stylish bungalows. A truly idyllic holiday spot,
it combines beautiful architecture, inspired by the simplicity
of a fishing village, with high-quality service. The resort
offers pilates classes and spa treatments and, in addition to
the bar, there are plenty of relaxing communal areas
throughout.

Recommended by: Marcelo Morettin, Andrade Morettin
Arquitetos

BRASÍLIA PALACE HOTEL
SHTN Trecho 01 Conjunto 01
Brasília
Distrito Federal 70800-200
Brazil
+55 6133069000
brasiliapalace.com.br

CREDIT CARDS..Accepted
PRICE...Low-cost
TYPE...Palace hotel
ACCOMMODATION..................................158 Rooms and Suites
FACILITIES...................Outdoor swimming pool, Restaurant
GOOD TO KNOW...Free parking
RECOMMENDED FOR...Where I live

"One of the first hotels to be built in Brasília, but recently
renovated. It was designed by Oscar Niemeyer and displays
beautiful murals designed by his artist friend and longtime
collaborator Athos Bulcão. Its location is beautiful: it faces
the artificial Paranoá Lake and it is close to the Alvorada
Palace, the official home of the Brazilian presidents and
another one of Niemeyer's masterpieces."
—Daniel Mangabeira

Recommended by: Daniel Mangabeira, BLOCO Arquitetos

POUSADA MUNDO DHA LUA
Rua 12 S/N
São Jorge
Chapada dos Veadeiros
Goiás 73770-000
Brazil
+55 6199838577
pousadamundodhalua.com.br

CREDIT CARDS..Accepted
PRICE...Low-cost
TYPE..Pousada
ACCOMMODATION..11 Rooms
FACILITIES..Bar, Garden
GOOD TO KNOW...No pets
RECOMMENDED FOR..Countryside

"Incredibly beautiful natural surroundings, charming,
and comfortable. Hiking to Vale da Lua—Moon Valley—
makes this basic hotel a unique experience. Having freshly
baked pão de queijo (Brazilian cheese bread) for breakfast
is a memory I cherish from this place."—Satyendra Pakhalé

Recommended by: Satyendra Pakhalé, Satyendra Pakhalé
Associates

GRANDE HOTEL OURO PRETO
Rua Senador Rocha Lagoa 164
Centro
Ouro Preto
Minas Gerais 35400-000
Brazil
+55 3135511488
grandehotelouropreto.com.br

CREDIT CARDS..Accepted
PRICE...Low-cost
TYPE...Hotel
ACCOMMODATION................................35 Rooms and Suites
FACILITIES....................Outdoor swimming pool, Restaurant
GOOD TO KNOW...Free parking
RECOMMENDED FOR..Countryside

"The hotel was designed by Oscar Niemeyer around 1940
as part of the central government effort to improve tourism
in Brazilian colonial towns, which have their origins in the
Portuguese exploration of gold and diamonds. The hotel
has beautiful views to the city of Ouro Preto, and although
it is not really well-kept, it is an architectural delight."
—Daniel Mangabeira

Recommended by: Daniel Mangabeira, BLOCO Arquitetos

HOTEL SOLAR DO ENGENHO

BR 040 km479 S/N
Sete Lagoas
Minas Gerais 35702-184
Brazil
+55 31987339012
solardoengenho.com.br

CREDIT CARDS..Accepted
PRICE..Mid-range
TYPE..Hotel
ACCOMMODATION..27 Suites
FACILITIES..................................Outdoor swimming pool,
Restaurant, Steam room
GOOD TO KNOW..Email or call to book
RECOMMENDED FOR..Countryside

"Natural, vernacular, with horses and green spaces."
—Dorin Stefan

Recommended by: Dorin Stefan, Dorin Stefan Birou
de Arhitectura

HOTEL TIJUCO

Rua Macau de Baixo 211
Diamantina
Minas Gerais 39100-000
Brazil
+55 3835311022
hoteltijuco.com.br

CREDIT CARDS..Accepted
PRICE..Low-cost
TYPE..Hotel
ACCOMMODATION..25 Rooms
FACILITIES..Near Diamond Museum,
No pets
GOOD TO KNOW..Free parking
RECOMMENDED FOR..Urban

"One of the classics of Brazilian Modernist architecture,
designed by the architect Oscar Niemeyer and located in
the historic city of Minas Gerais."—Marcelo Morettin

Recommended by: Marcelo Morettin, Andrade Morettin
Arquitetos

TAMBAÚ HOTEL

Avenida Almirante Tamandaré 229
Tambaú
João Pessoa
Paraíba 58039-010
Brazil
+55 8321071900
tambauhotel.com.br

CREDIT CARDS..Accepted
PRICE..Low-cost
TYPE..Hotel
ACCOMMODATION..................................173 Rooms and Suites
FACILITIES..............................Bar, Outdoor swimming pool,
Restaurant, Sauna, Steam room
GOOD TO KNOW............................Child friendly, Free parking
RECOMMENDED FOR..Beach

"Designed by Brazilian Modernist master Sérgio Bernardes,
the hotel's circular building forms an artificial peninsula
that juts out into the sea on one side, placing it in direct
contact with the waves, depending on the tide. The city of
João Pessoa has some of the most amazing beaches in Brazil,
with good weather and warm waters all year long."
—Daniel Mangabeira

Recommended by: Daniel Mangabeira, BLOCO Arquitetos

POUSADA MARAVILHA

BR-363 S/N
Fernando de Noronha
Recife
Pernambuco 53990-000
Brazil
+55 8126261227
pousadamaravilha.com.br

CREDIT CARDS..Accepted
PRICE..Mid-range
TYPE..Pousada
ACCOMMODATION............................9 Bungalows and Rooms
FACILITIES......................................Outdoor swimming pool,
Restaurant, Sauna, Spa
GOOD TO KNOW....................................Child friendly, No pets
RECOMMENDED FOR..Best-kept secret

Recommended by: Bernardo and Paulo Jacobsen,
Jacobsen Arquitetura

BELMOND COPACABANA PALACE

Avenida Atlântica 1702
Copacabana
Rio de Janeiro 22021-001
Brazil
+55 2125487070
belmond.com

CREDIT CARDS..Accepted
PRICE..High-end
TYPE..Palace hotel
ACCOMMODATION...................................239 Rooms and Suites
FACILITIES...................Bar, Gym, Outdoor swimming pool,
2 Restaurants, Sauna, Spa,
Steam room
GOOD TO KNOW...Pet friendly
RECOMMENDED FOR...All-time favorite,
Luxury, Where I live

"Classic and elegant in a wonderful location. The brunch
is fantastic."—Farid Chacon

"Iconic Art Deco building overlooking Copacabana beach."
—Luis Ferreira-da-Silva

Recommended by: Ludovico Centis, The Empire;
Farid Chacon, NMD NOMADAS; Luis Ferreira-da-Silva,
Luis Ferreira-da-Silva Architects; Bernardo and Paulo
Jacobsen, Jacobsen Arquitetura

FASANO RIO DE JANEIRO

Avenida Viera Souto 80
Ipanema
Rio de Janeiro 22420-002
Brazil
+55 2132024000
fasano.com.br

CREDIT CARDS..Accepted
PRICE..High-end
TYPE...Hotel
ACCOMMODATION.....................................79 Rooms and Suites
FACILITIES.....................Bar, Gym, Outdoor swimming pool,
Restaurant, Rooftop terrace bar,
Sauna, Spa, Steam room
GOOD TO KNOW...Pet friendly
RECOMMENDED FOR...Wish I'd designed

A chic and sleek hotel across the road from the Ipanema
beachfront. Designed by Philippe Starck, the hotel's
architecture and interiors pay homage to mid-century
Brazilian, Bossa Nova-era design. The hotel's infinity pool
extends out over the beach.

Recommended by: Carlo Ratti, Carlo Ratti Associati

SHERATON GRAND RIO HOTEL & RESORT

Avenida Niemeyer 121
Leblon
Rio de Janeiro 22450-220
Brazil
+55 2122741122
marriott.com

CREDIT CARDS..Accepted
PRICE...Mid-range
TYPE...Hotel
ACCOMMODATION...................................543 Rooms and Suites
FACILITIES.....................Bar, Gym, Outdoor restaurant and
swimming pool, 3 Restaurants, Spa
GOOD TO KNOW............................Bicycle rentals, Pet friendly
RECOMMENDED FOR....................................Family friendly

"I love Rio, and when I stay with my children, this hotel
offers a lot of activities, being next to the beach—a private
one near Leblon—and it has a lot of restaurants and
swimming pools."—Felipe Assadi

Recommended by: Felipe Assadi, Felipe Assadi Architects

CASA COLONIAL PARATY

Rua Dona Geralda 200
Centro Histórico
Paraty
Rio de Janeiro 23970-000
Brazil
+55 2433712244
casacolonialparaty.com

CREDIT CARDS..Accepted
PRICE...Mid-range
TYPE..Townhouse hotel
ACCOMMODATION...8 Rooms
FACILITIES..Contact property
GOOD TO KNOW..............................Call or email to book,
Free parking
RECOMMENDED FOR...Urban

"Beautiful, contemporary interiors in a sensitively restored
historic house in the center of the historic town of Paraty.
There is a beautiful courtyard garden, a plunge pool,
and luscious greenery. Very relaxing, rejuvenating, and
harmonizing."—Alex Warnock-Smith

Recommended by: Alex Warnock-Smith, Urban
Projects Bureau

POUSADA LITERÁRIA DE PARATY
Rua do Comercio 362
Centro Histórico
Paraty
Rio de Janeiro 28950-000
Brazil
+55 2433711568
pousadaliteraria.com.br

CREDIT CARDS..Accepted
PRICE...Mid-range
TYPE...Pousada
ACCOMMODATION.............26 Apartments, Suites, and Villas
FACILITIES.......................................Outdoor swimming pool,
Restaurant, Spa
GOOD TO KNOW...Child friendly
RECOMMENDED FOR...Urban

"The hotel is located in the center of Paraty, Brazil's historic seafront city, allowing you to enjoy the city and the beaches nearby."—Marcelo Morettin

Recommended by: Marcelo Morettin, Andrade Morettin Arquitetos

MAKSOUD PLAZA
Rua São Carlos do Pinhal 424
Bela Vista
São Paulo 01333-000
Brazil
+55 1131458000
maksoud.com.br

CREDIT CARDS..Accepted
PRICE...Mid-range
TYPE...Hotel
ACCOMMODATION.........................416 Apartments and Suites
FACILITIES.......................Bar, Gym, Indoor swimming pool,
Restaurant, Sauna, Spa, Steam room
GOOD TO KNOW...Valet parking
RECOMMENDED FOR...Where I live

"A classic of São Paulo located in the heart of the city."
—Marcelo Morettin

Recommended by: Marcelo Morettin, Andrade Morettin Arquitetos

FAZENDA DONA CAROLINA
Estrada Municipal Manoel Stefani km39.5
Bragança Paulista
São Paulo 13252-670
Brazil
+55 1145349100
hotelfazendadonacarolina.com.br

CREDIT CARDS..Accepted
PRICE...Mid-range
TYPE...Fazenda
ACCOMMODATION....................................95 Rooms and Suites
FACILITIES..............................Bar, Outdoor swimming pool,
2 Restaurants, Spa
GOOD TO KNOW..........................Child friendly, Horse riding
RECOMMENDED FOR..Countryside

"Located in an old, late nineteenth-century coffee farm in the interior of São Paulo state, the hotel is home to the restored main house and coffee drying *terreiros* that have been preserved and are still in use. The gardens and woods within the grounds are impressive and accessible by numerous trails."—Marcelo Morettin

Recommended by: Marcelo Morettin, Andrade Morettin Arquitetos

FASANO SÃO PAULO
Rua Vittorio Fasano 88
Cerqueira César
Jardim América
São Paulo 01414-020
Brazil
+55 1138964000
fasano.com.br

CREDIT CARDS..Accepted
PRICE...High-end
TYPE...Hotel
ACCOMMODATION...........................50 Apartments and Suites
FACILITIES....................................Bar, Indoor swimming pool,
2 Restaurants, Sauna, Spa
GOOD TO KNOW...Pet friendly
RECOMMENDED FOR...Urban

"Great design and food in an equally great city."
—Victor Legorreta Hernández

Recommended by: Manuel Cervantes, CC Arquitectos; Victor Legorreta Hernández, Legorreta

HOTEL UNIQUE

Avenida Brigadeiro Luís Antônio 4700
Jardim Paulista
São Paulo 01402-002
Brazil
+55 1130554700
hotelunique.com.br

CREDIT CARDS	Accepted
PRICE	High-end
TYPE	Hotel
ACCOMMODATION	94 Rooms and Suites
FACILITIES	Outdoor swimming pool, Restaurant, Rooftop terrace bar, Spa
GOOD TO KNOW	Pet friendly
RECOMMENDED FOR	Urban

"An unusual building with well-designed interiors and a rooftop bar with wonderful views of the city. Its location is also very central, close to the Ibirapuera Park, designed by Oscar Niemeyer. Ruy Ohtake, the hotel's architect, worked with Niemeyer when he was young, and shortly after that he designed some of the finest examples of exposed concrete architecture in São Paulo. However, later in his career he adopted an unconventional approach that has made him one of the most polemic figures in contemporary Brazilian architecture."—Daniel Mangabeira

Recommended by: Daniel Mangabeira, BLOCO Arquitetos

FAZENDA CATUÇABA

Bairro do Pinga S/N
Catuçaba
Sao Luiz do Paraitinga
São Paulo 12240-000
Brazil
+55 1124951586
catucaba.com

CREDIT CARDS	Accepted but not Amex
PRICE	High-end
TYPE	Fazenda
ACCOMMODATION	10 Rooms and Suites
FACILITIES	Restaurant
GOOD TO KNOW	Babysitting, Email, call, or fax to book
RECOMMENDED FOR	Family friendly

"Charming and authentic take on the Brazillian colonial farms."—Marcio Kogan

Recommended by: Marcio Kogan, Studio MK27

POUSADA PICINGUABA

Rua G. Picinguaba 130
Picinguaba
Ubatuba
São Paulo 11680-000
Brazil
+33 642383782
picinguaba.com

CREDIT CARDS	Accepted
PRICE	Mid-range
TYPE	Pousada
ACCOMMODATION	10 Rooms and Suites
FACILITIES	Outdoor swimming pool, Restaurant, Sauna, Spa, Yoga
GOOD TO KNOW	Some activities must be booked in advance
RECOMMENDED FOR	Beach

"Visit for the pristine beaches and national park setting."
—Germán del Sol

Recommended by: Germán del Sol, Germán del Sol, Architects

HOTEL GARZÓN

Costa Jose Ignacio
Garzón
Maldonado 20401
Uruguay
+598 44102809
restaurantegarzon.com

CREDIT CARDS	Accepted
PRICE	High-end
TYPE	Hotel
ACCOMMODATION	5 Rooms
FACILITIES	Bar, Outdoor swimming pool, Restaurant
GOOD TO KNOW	Bicycle rentals, Pet friendly
RECOMMENDED FOR	Countryside

"A timeless classic and a great food experience."
—Marco Costanzi

Recommended by: Marco Costanzi, Marco Costanzi Architects

POSADA DEL FARO

Calle de la Bahia esq Timonel
Faro José Ignacio
Garzón
Maldonado 20402
Uruguay
+598 44862110
posadadelfaro.com

CREDIT CARDS	Accepted
PRICE	Mid-range
TYPE	Hotel
ACCOMMODATION	15 Rooms
FACILITIES	Bar, Outdoor swimming pool, Restaurant
GOOD TO KNOW	Bicycle rentals, Horse riding
RECOMMENDED FOR	Best-kept secret, Wish I'd designed

Posada del Faro is a laid-back hotel with a charming beach restaurant, bright and modern rooms, and opportunities to fish, ride horses, and visit local art galleries.

Recommended by: Gaston Atelman, AFT Arquitectos

ARGENTINO HOTEL CASINO & RESORT

Rambla de los Argentinos
Piriápolis
Maldonado 20200
Uruguay
+598 44322791
argentinohotel.com

CREDIT CARDS	Accepted
PRICE	Low-cost
TYPE	Hotel
ACCOMMODATION	300 Rooms and Suites
FACILITIES	Bar, Gym, Indoor and outdoor swimming pools, 5 Restaurants, Spa
GOOD TO KNOW	Babysitting, Free parking
RECOMMENDED FOR	All-time favorite

"The South American 'Grand Budapest Hotel.' Huge, retro-chic, beautiful, and slightly absurd in its scale."
—Leonid Slonimskiy

Recommended by: Leonid Slonimskiy, KOSMOS Architects

LA SOLANA HOTEL

Ruta Interbalnearia km118
Solanas Beach
Punta del Este
Maldonado 20003
Uruguay
+598 42578044
lasolana.com.uy

CREDIT CARDS	Accepted
PRICE	High-end
TYPE	Hotel
ACCOMMODATION	1 Apartment, 6 Rooms and Suites
FACILITIES	Gym, Restaurant
GOOD TO KNOW	Email, call, or fax to book
RECOMMENDED FOR	Beach

"Designed in 1945 by architect Antonio Bonet, this hotel is a masterful blend of modern architecture, Surrealism, vernacular traditions, and beautiful landscape."
—Diego Arraigada

Recommended by: Diego Arraigada, Diego Arraigada Arquitectos

FASANO LAS PIEDRAS

Camino Cerro Egusquiza y Paso del Barranco
La Barra
San Carlos
Maldonado 20400
Uruguay
+598 42670000
laspiedrasfasano.com

CREDIT CARDS	Accepted
PRICE	High-end
TYPE	Hotel
ACCOMMODATION	30 Bungalows, Rooms, and Suites
FACILITIES	Bar, Golf, Gym, Outdoor swimming pool, Private beach, Restaurant, Spa
GOOD TO KNOW	Child friendly, Email, call, or fax to book
RECOMMENDED FOR	Wish I'd designed

"Las Piedras has integrated itself among the sprawling vistas of the Uruguay countryside and coastline. The design has magnified the beauty of the surrounding landscape, with which there is an undeniable connection."
—George Yabu and Glenn Pushelberg

Recommended by: George Yabu and Glenn Pushelberg, Yabu Pushelberg

ESPLENDOR CERVANTES

Soriano 868
Centro
Montevideo 11100
Uruguay
+598 29001900
wyndhamhotels.com

CREDIT CARDS...Accepted
PRICE...Low-cost
TYPE...Hotel
ACCOMMODATION....................................84 Rooms and Suites
FACILITIES.................................Gym, Indoor swimming pool,
Restaurant, Rooftop terrace bar,
Sauna, Spa
GOOD TO KNOW.......................................Bicycle rentals,
Child and pet friendly
RECOMMENDED FOR...Urban

"A historic building; Julio Cortázar's famous short story *La Puerta Condenada* takes place here."—Diego Arraigada

Recommended by: Diego Arraigada, Diego Arraigada Arquitectos

HOTEL FAENA BUENOS AIRES

Martha Salotti 445
Puerto Madero
Buenos Aires C1107CMB
Argentina
+54 1140109070
faena.com

CREDIT CARDS...Accepted
PRICE...High-end
TYPE...Hotel
ACCOMMODATION.......................87 Lofts, Rooms, and Suites
FACILITIES.................................Bar, Outdoor swimming pool,
2 Restaurants, Sauna, Spa,
Steam room
GOOD TO KNOW.......................................Bicycle rentals
RECOMMENDED FOR...Luxury

"The pool terrace has a fantastic ambience."—Ola Rune

Recommended by: Ola Rune, Claesson Koivisto Rune Architects

ALVEAR PALACE HOTEL

Avenida Alvear 1891
Recoleta
Buenos Aires C1129AAA
Argentina
+54 1148082100
alvearpalace.com

CREDIT CARDS...Accepted
PRICE...High-end
TYPE...Hotel
ACCOMMODATION....................................207 Rooms and Suites
FACILITIES.................................Indoor swimming pool,
2 Restaurants, Rooftop terrace bar, Spa
GOOD TO KNOW.......................................Child friendly, No pets
RECOMMENDED FOR...All-time favorite

"It encompasses everything a classic hotel should be; it makes you feel as though you are in a novel or film. It's an integral part of Buenos Aires and Recoleta, with that unique mix of European and South American character that makes it one of our favorite cities in the world."
—Adrian Moreno and Maria Samaniego

Recommended by: Adrian Moreno and Maria Samaniego, Arquitectura X

PALACIO DUHAU

Avenida Alvear 1661
Recoleta
Buenos Aires C1014AAD
Argentina
+54 1151711234
hyatt.com

CREDIT CARDS...Accepted
PRICE...High-end
TYPE...Palace hotel
ACCOMMODATION....................................165 Rooms and Suites
FACILITIES.................................Bar, Gym, Indoor swimming pool,
2 Restaurants, Sauna, Spa
GOOD TO KNOW.......................................Babysitting, Pet friendly,
Valet parking
RECOMMENDED FOR...Worth the travel

"A former palace, but now a contemporary hotel in a global city, it still feels as if it were from another time altogether."
—Carlos Jiménez

Recommended by: Carlos Jiménez, Carlos Jiménez Studio

L'HÔTEL PALERMO

Thames 1562
Palermo
Buenos Aires B1838AHR
Argentina
+54 1148317198
lhotelpalermo.com

CREDIT CARDS..Accepted
PRICE..Low-cost
TYPE...Hotel
ACCOMMODATION...23 Rooms
FACILITIES...Outdoor swimming pool,
Rooftop terrace bar
GOOD TO KNOW...Child friendly
RECOMMENDED FOR...Best-kept secret

"Very charming and hidden in the center of a city block, this hotel is unnoticeable from the outside."—Diego Arraigada

Recommended by: Diego Arraigada, Diego Arraigada Arquitectos

HOTEL SOFITEL LA RESERVA CARDALES

Ruta Panamericana No. 9 km61
Campana
Buenos Aires B2804
Argentina
+54 3489435555
accorhotels.com

CREDIT CARDS..Accepted
PRICE...Mid-range
TYPE...Hotel
ACCOMMODATION....................................159 Rooms and Suites
FACILITIES..Bar, Gym,
Indoor and outdoor swimming pools,
2 Restaurants, Sauna
GOOD TO KNOW.............................Babysitting, Valet parking
RECOMMENDED FOR...Spa, Where I live

"Very comfortable with excellent services and amenities, including a spa."—Gaston Atelman

Recommended by: Gaston Atelman, AFT Arquitectos

ALPASIÓN

Ruta Provincial 94
Los Sauces
Tunuyán
Mendoza
Argentina
+54 92613202999
alpasion.com

CREDIT CARDS..Accepted
PRICE...Mid-range
TYPE...Lodge
ACCOMMODATION..6 Rooms
FACILITIES.................Outdoor swimming pool, Restaurant,
Rooftop terrace bar
GOOD TO KNOW...On-site vineyard
RECOMMENDED FOR..Eco-conscious

Alpasión is a winery, lodge, and restaurant created by a group of like-minded oenophiles in the stunning Uco Valley. The lodge is luxurious, in a rustic-chic style, with six unique rooms, each of which has a private terrace with views of either the Andes Mountains or the vineyards. Facilities include a wine cellar, of course, featuring myriad wines from the region, a library with a fireplace, a roof terrace with outside fireplace, pool, and Jacuzzi.

Recommended by: Matthias Hollwich, Hollwich Kushner

ENTRE CIELOS LUXURY WINE HOTEL & SPA

Guardia Vieja 1998
Vistalba
Luján de Cuyo
Mendoza 5509
Argentina
+54 2614983377
entrecielos.com

CREDIT CARDS..Accepted
PRICE...Mid-range
TYPE...Wine hotel
ACCOMMODATION....................................24 Rooms and Suites
FACILITIES..............................Bar, Outdoor swimming pool,
Restaurant, Spa, Steam room, Yoga
GOOD TO KNOW...On-site vineyard
RECOMMENDED FOR...Where I live

Recommended by: Andres Remy, Remy Architects

LA ESCONDIDA
Avenida Arrayanes 7014
Puerto Manzano
Los Lagos
Neuquén 8407
Argentina
+54 2944475313
laescondida.house

CREDIT CARDS..Accepted
PRICE...Mid-range
TYPE..Guesthouse
ACCOMMODATION..................................15 Rooms and Suites
FACILITIES......................Bar, Gym, Outdoor swimming pool,
Sauna, Spa, Yoga
GOOD TO KNOW...Child friendly
RECOMMENDED FOR..All-time favorite

Situated on the shores of Nahuel Huapi Lake, La Escondida
is a beautiful, intimate boutique hotel that prides itself
on its warm hospitality and relaxed atmosphere. Each room
enjoys a view of the water, and there is a focus on locally
sourced produce. In summer, enjoy picnics on the isolated
lakeside beaches, and in winter, ski at nearby Cerro Bayo.

Recommended by: Derek Dellekamp, Dellekamp
Arquitectos

HOTEL TUNQUELÉN
Avenida Ezequiel Bustillo km24.5
Villa Llao Llao
San Carlos de Bariloche
Bariloche
Río Negro 8409
Argentina
+54 1143949605
tunquelen.com

CREDIT CARDS..Accepted
PRICE...Mid-range
TYPE..Hotel
ACCOMMODATION..................................40 Rooms and Suites
FACILITIES........................Bar, Gym, Indoor swimming pool,
Restaurant, Sauna, Spa
GOOD TO KNOW..................................Babysitting, Free parking
RECOMMENDED FOR...Mountains

"Historical building designed by Ernesto de Estrada in
the 1930s, who was in charge of the architecture of the
Argentine national parks in Patagonia."—Diego Arraigada

Recommended by: Diego Arraigada, Diego Arraigada
Arquitectos

ESPLENDOR SAVOY ROSARIO
Calle San Lorenzo 1022
Distrito Centro
Rosario
Santa Fe 02000
Argentina
+54 3414296000
esplendorhoteles.com

CREDIT CARDS..Accepted
PRICE..Low-cost
TYPE..Hotel
ACCOMMODATION..................................75 Rooms and Suites
FACILITIES...Bar, Gym,
Indoor and outdoor swimming pools,
Restaurant, Sauna, Spa
GOOD TO KNOW.......................................No pets, Valet parking
RECOMMENDED FOR..Where I live

"A historic building that's been very well restored."
—Diego Arraigada

Recommended by: Diego Arraigada, Diego Arraigada
Arquitectos

INTI WATANA CASA DE CAMPO
Madre Teresa de Calcuta S/N
El Churqui
Tafí del Valle
Tucumán 4137
Argentina
+54 3867420178
posadaintiwatana.com

CREDIT CARDS..Accepted
PRICE..Low-cost
TYPE..Posada
ACCOMMODATION....................................4 Rooms and Suites
FACILITIES.................................Wood-burning fireplace
GOOD TO KNOW.............................Pet friendly, Valet parking
RECOMMENDED FOR.......................................Eco-conscious

A charming, family run and family friendly eco-country
house. Rooms are simple but cosy, some featuring
panoramic views of the mountains and the large organic
gardens surrounding the property.

Recommended by: Gaston Atelman, AFT Arquitectos

EXPLORA ATACAMA
Domingo Atienza S/N
San Pedro de Atacama
El Loa
Antofagasta
Chile
+56 232442000
explora.com

CREDIT CARDS..Accepted
PRICE...............................Blow out (all-inclusive)
TYPE...Hotel
ACCOMMODATION....................................50 Rooms and Suites
FACILITIES.................................Bar, Outdoor swimming pool,
Restaurant, Sauna, Spa, Steam room
GOOD TO KNOW..Child friendly
RECOMMENDED FOR............................All-time favorite, Desert

"A true desert hotel surrounded by rugged sand mountains. An unforgettable pool and bar."—Forth Bagley

[This hotel was designed by Germán del Sol Architects.]

Recommended by: Forth Bagley, Kohn Pedersen Fox; Carlos Ferrater, OAB; Louis Hedgecock, HOK Architects; Germán del Sol, Germán del Sol Architects

HOTEL CUMBRES SAN PEDRO DE ATACAMA
Avenida Las Chilcas S/N Lote 10 Parcela 2
San Pedro de Atacama
El Loa
Antofagasta
Chile
+56 552852136
cumbressanpedro.com

CREDIT CARDS..Accepted
PRICE..Mid-range
TYPE...Hotel
ACCOMMODATION....................................60 Rooms and Suites
FACILITIES.....................Bar, Gym, Outdoor swimming pool,
Restaurant, Sauna, Spa
GOOD TO KNOW..Child friendly
RECOMMENDED FOR...Worth the travel

A luxury retreat deep within the Atacama desert, the hotel's design was inspired by the ancient Atacameño villages. The result is an elegant hotel with a pool, spa, and expert guides ready to take you on excursions, including volcano climbing, desert yoga, and trips to the salt flats.

Recommended by: Giancarlo Mazzanti, El Equipo Mazzanti

TIERRA ATACAMA HOTEL & SPA
Domingo Atienza S/N
San Pedro de Atacama
El Loa
Antofagasta
Chile
+56 552555975
tierrahotels.com

CREDIT CARDS..Accepted
PRICE................................High-end (all-inclusive)
TYPE...Hotel
ACCOMMODATION....................................32 Rooms
FACILITIES.................................Bar, Outdoor swimming pool,
Restaurant, Spa, Steam room, Yoga
GOOD TO KNOW..Child friendly
RECOMMENDED FOR............................All-time favorite, Desert

"Among the many hotels in the Atacama desert, this one has a different approach to the landscape. When you are in the desert, you want to experience it, and Tierra Atacama offers fantastic views of the Andes mountain range and its volcanoes."—Felipe Assadi

Recommended by: Felipe Assadi, Felipe Assadi Architects; Gaston Atelman, AFT Arquitectos; Juan Manuel Peláez Freidel, JUMP/Juan Manuel Peláez Arquitectos; Matthias Sauerbruch and Louisa Hutton, Sauerbruch Hutton; Gert Wingårdh, Wingårdhs

HOTEL ANTUMALAL
Camino Pucón a Villarrica km2
Cautín
Araucanía
Chile
+56 452441011
antumalal.com

CREDIT CARDS..Accepted
PRICE..Mid-range
TYPE...Hotel
ACCOMMODATION......20 Chalets, Rooms, Suites, and Villas
FACILITIES..................Indoor and outdoor swimming pools,
Restaurant, Sauna, Spa
GOOD TO KNOW..Free parking
RECOMMENDED FOR..................Spa, Urban, Worth the travel

"One of the most beautiful Modernist hotels in the south of Chile, with wonderful spaces, furniture, and great views over the Villarrica lake."—Felipe Assadi

Recommended by: Felipe Assadi, Felipe Assadi Architects; Grace Mortlock, Other Architects; Germán del Sol, Germán del Sol Architects

PUYUHUAPI LODGE & SPA
Bahía Dorita S/N
Puyuhuapi
Aysén
Chile
+56 222256489
puyuhuapilodge.com

CREDIT CARDS	Accepted
PRICE	Mid-range
TYPE	Lodge
ACCOMMODATION	30 Rooms
FACILITIES	Bar, Gym, Indoor and outdoor swimming pools, Restaurant, Spa
GOOD TO KNOW	Babysitting, Bicycle rentals, No pets
RECOMMENDED FOR	Spa

"Some of the most amazing views of the mountains and the lakes beneath them. To access the hotel, guests have to take a boat and cross some of the most beautiful fjords and lakes in the region. The natural hot springs inside and around the hotel allow visitors to bathe while looking to the eternal ice of the Andes."—Daniel Mangabeira

Recommended by: Daniel Mangabeira, BLOCO Arquitetos

TIERRA CHILOÉ HOTEL & SPA
Sector San José
Castro
Chiloé
Los Lagos
Chile
+56 652772080
tierrahotels.com

CREDIT CARDS	Accepted
PRICE	Blow out (all-inclusive)
TYPE	Hotel
ACCOMMODATION	24 Rooms
FACILITIES	Bar, Indoor and outdoor swimming pools, Restaurant, Sauna, Spa, Steam room
GOOD TO KNOW	Child friendly, Free parking
RECOMMENDED FOR	Countryside, Spa

"The most perfect setting in the hills, near the water. Lots of activities and amazing local food."—Adam Meshberg

"A cozy and beautiful hotel where you can enjoy the great spa and incredible landscape."—Marcelo Morettin

Recommended by: Adam Meshberg, Meshberg Group; Marcelo Morettin, Andrade Morettin Arquitetos

AWASI PATAGONIA
Torres del Paine National Park
Última Esperanza
Magallanes
Chile
+56 222339641
awasipatagonia.com

CREDIT CARDS	Accepted
PRICE	Blow out (all-inclusive)
TYPE	Lodge
ACCOMMODATION	14 Villas
FACILITIES	Hot tub, Restaurant
GOOD TO KNOW	Private guide and car
RECOMMENDED FOR	Countryside, Mountains, Worth the travel

"One of the most amazing places I've ever been to. The lodge has a view of the Torres del Paine, where you can experience the extreme south of Chile."—Felipe Assadi

Recommended by: Felipe Assadi, Felipe Assadi Architects; Adam Meshberg, Meshberg Group; Michel Rojkind, Rojkind Arquitectos; Matteo Thun, Matteo Thun & Partners

EXPLORA PATAGONIA HOTEL SALTO CHICO
Torres del Paine National Park
Última Esperanza
Magallanes
Chile
+56 223952580
explora.com

CREDIT CARDS	Accepted
PRICE	High-end (all-inclusive)
TYPE	Hotel
ACCOMMODATION	49 Rooms and Suites
FACILITIES	Bar, Indoor swimming pool, Restaurant, Sauna, Spa
GOOD TO KNOW	Child friendly, Horse riding
RECOMMENDED FOR	Mountains, Worth the travel

"The view alone is worth the trip. The food, horseback rides, and chic design are the icing on the cake."—Forth Bagley

"An architectural tour de force designed by two of the most talented contemporary Chilean architects, José Cruz Ortiz and Germán del Sol. Torres del Paine National Park is one of the most beautiful places on earth."—Daniel Mangabeira

Recommended by: Forth Bagley, Kohn Pedersen Fox; Daniel Mangabeira, BLOCO Arquitetos

REMOTA

Route 9 North km1.5
Puerto Natales
Última Esperanza
Magallanes
Chile
+56 612414040
remotahotel.com

CREDIT CARDS..Accepted
PRICE...Mid-range
TYPE...Hotel
ACCOMMODATION...72 Rooms
FACILITIES....................................Bar, Indoor swimming pool,
Restaurant, Sauna, Spa
GOOD TO KNOW..................................Bicycle rentals, No pets
RECOMMENDED FOR.....................Family friendly, Mountains,
Wish I'd designed,
Worth the travel

"Located in a preserved natural setting, the hotel is beautiful and offers family adventures of a lifetime."—Germán del Sol

[This hotel was designed by Germán del Sol Architects.]

Recommended by: Bernardo and Paulo Jacobsen, Jacobsen Arquitetura; Germán del Sol, Germán del Sol Architects

TIERRA PATAGONIA

Torres del Paine National Park
Últimga Esperanza
Magallanes
Chile
+56 223705301
tierrahotels.com

CREDIT CARDS..Accepted
PRICE...Blow out (all-inclusive)
TYPE...Hotel
ACCOMMODATION.......................................40 Rooms and Suites
FACILITIES....................................Bar, Indoor swimming pool,
Restaurant, Spa, Steam room, Yoga
GOOD TO KNOW..Child friendly
RECOMMENDED FOR..Eco-conscious

"A complete getaway: great spa and amazing landscape."
—Achille Salvagni

Recommended by: Achille Salvagni, Salvagni Architetti

TUMUÑAN LODGE

Camino a Sierra de Bellavista
El Llano
Colchagua
O'Higgins
Chile
+56 996301152
tumunanlodge.com

CREDIT CARDS..Accepted
PRICE...Low-cost
TYPE...Lodge
ACCOMMODATION...................................6 Rooms and Suites
FACILITIES.............................Bar, Outdoor swimming pool,
Restaurant, Yoga
GOOD TO KNOW..........................Child friendly, Horse riding,
No pets, Wine tastings
RECOMMENDED FOR..Countryside

"The owners will take you on tours in the surrounding Andes Mountains, winetasting in their own vineyards, on horseback tours to bathe under secluded waterfalls, plus trekking, flyfishing, and camping."—Ene Cordt Andersen

Recommended by: Ene Cordt Andersen, Andersen & Sigurdsson Architects

THE AUBREY

Constitución 317
Providencia
Santiago
Chile
+56 229402800
theaubrey.com

CREDIT CARDS..Accepted
PRICE...Mid-range
TYPE...Hotel
ACCOMMODATION...15 Rooms
FACILITIES.............................Bar, Outdoor swimming pool,
Restaurant
GOOD TO KNOW..........................Child friendly, Free parking
RECOMMENDED FOR...Where I live

Recommended by: Felipe Assadi, Felipe Assadi Architects

W SANTIAGO
Isidora Goyenechea 3000
Las Condes
Santiago
Chile
+56 227700000
marriott.com

CREDIT CARDS	Accepted
PRICE	Mid-range
TYPE	Hotel
ACCOMMODATION	196 Rooms and Suites
FACILITIES	Bar, Gym, Outdoor restaurant, 2 Restaurants
GOOD TO KNOW	Pet friendly
RECOMMENDED FOR	Urban, Where I live

"Awesome rooftop views and excellent location."
—Gaston Atelman

Recommended by: Gaston Atelman, AFT Arquitectos; Germán del Sol, Germán del Sol Architects

HOTEL PALACIO ASTORECA
Calle Montealegre 149
Cerro Alegre
Valparaíso
Chile
+56 232844200
hotelpalacioastoreca.com

CREDIT CARDS	Accepted
PRICE	Mid-range
TYPE	Hotel
ACCOMMODATION	23 Rooms and Suites
FACILITIES	Bar, Indoor swimming pool, Restaurant, Sauna, Steam room
GOOD TO KNOW	No pets, Valet parking
RECOMMENDED FOR	Urban

"Set within the dynamic and dense hillside of Valparaíso, this hotel is a work of art. The striking, bold, red-and-white facade immediately suggests it as a place of adventure and spirit. Beautifully designed rooms and public spaces make it a wonderful experience for a long weekend exploring the city."—Dennis Pieprz

Recommended by: Dennis Pieprz, Sasaki

SKI PORTILLO
Ruta 60 420, the Andes
San Esteban
Valparaíso
Chile
+56 223617000
skiportillo.com

CREDIT CARDS	Accepted but not Amex
PRICE	High-end
TYPE	Hotel
ACCOMMODATION	123 Apartments, Rooms, and Suites
FACILITIES	Bar, Gym, Outdoor swimming pool, Restaurant, Sauna, Spa, Yoga
GOOD TO KNOW	Babysitting, No pets
RECOMMENDED FOR	Mountains

"Best ski conditions and a refined yet relaxed atmosphere."
—Germán del Sol

Recommended by: Germán del Sol, Germán del Sol Architects

INDEX BY COUNTRY

506

INDEX BY TYPE

INDEX BY HOTEL

About the author

Sarah Miller runs Sarah Miller and Partners, an independent agency that creates brand strategies and content for a range of luxury and lifestyle brands. She was the founding Editor-in-Chief of *Condé Nast Traveller UK*, which she launched in 1997 and ran for fifteen years before launching *Condé Nast Traveller* in India and China, after which she was appointed European Editor of *Travel + Leisure*. Prior to this she had a career in journalism which spans being Associate Editor and Arts Editor of the *Daily Telegraph*, Assistant Editor of *The Sunday Times* (launching *Style* magazine), editing arts and design for *Elle* magazine and helping to found *Blueprint*, the leading architecture and design magazine. She was also content editor of *London Uprising: Fifty Fashion Designers, One City* (Phaidon, 2017) and *Fashion in LA* (Phaidon, 2019). She has won Editor of the Year seven times. Sarah sits on the International Advisory Board of École hôtelière de Lausanne, the world's leading hospitality institution. She is also a trustee of the Whitechapel Gallery and is an Honorary Fellow of the Royal College of Art, both in London, where she was a governor for fifteen years.

Author acknowledgments

I would like to thank everyone, worldwide, who helped in the making of this book: chiefly the architects and designers who took the time to fill in the questionnaires and share their invaluable suggestions. My brilliant team at Sarah Miller and Partners—Beatrice Guazzi, Annabel Colterjohn, and particularly my Junior Content Editor Rachel Spratley—who not only contacted all the contributors but then painstakingly collated and fact-checked the data. I'd also like to thank my father John and step-mother Su who instilled a love of architecture in me from an early age; and my husband Deyan, who thankfully likes hotels as much as I do—preferably with good architecture and a view. Last but not least the wonderful team at Phaidon, especially Belle Place whose patience is formidable and Emilia Terragni whose brilliant idea commissioning this book was in the first place.

Phaidon Press Limited
Regent's Wharf
All Saints Street
London N1 9PA

Phaidon Press Inc.
65 Bleecker Street
New York, NY 10012

phaidon.com

First published 2020
© 2020 Phaidon Press Limited

ISBN 978 0 7148 7926 0

As some hotels close for extended
periods at different times of the year, it
is always advisable to check before
booking your travel. Please check with
the hotel at the time of booking as to
the availability of pet-friendly rooms. All
information is correct at the time of
going to print, but is subject to change.

Commissioning Editor: Emilia Terragni
Project Editor: Belle Place
Production Controller: Sarah Kramer
Design: Hans Stofregen

Printed in Italy

The publisher would like to thank all
the participating contributors for
their generosity, time, and insightful
recommendations. The publisher
would also like to thank Caitlin Arnell
Argles, Emma Barton, Rebecca Barton,
George Beleznay, Vanessa Bird, Clive
Burroughs, Laura Button, Lesley Malkin,
Anthony Naughton, Emily Paul,
Rosie Pickles, Rebecca Roke, Ellie Rowe,
Natalie Testa, Emily Wigoder, and
Alexandra Zirinis for their contributions
to the making of this book.